HUMAN LEARNING

SECOND EDITION

Jeanne Ellis Ormrod
University of Northern Colorado

Merrill,
an imprint of Prentice Hall
Englewood Cliffs, New Jersey   Columbus, Ohio

Library of Congress Cataloging-in-Publication Data

Ormrod, Jeanne Ellis.
Human learning / Jeanne Ellis Ormrod.—2nd ed.
p. cm.
Includes bibliographical references and index.
ISBN 0-02-389482-2
1. Learning, Psychology of. 2. Behaviorism (Psychology)
I. Title.
BF318.076   1995
153.1'5—dc20   94-12863
                                                                                          CIP

Cover art: Nicholas Hill
Editor: Kevin M. Davis
Production Editor: Sheryl Glicker Langner
Text Designer: Ed Horcharik
Cover Designer: Proof Positive
Production Buyer: Pamela D. Bennett
Electronic Text Management: Marilyn Wilson Phelps, Matthew Williams, Jane Lopez, Karen
    L. Bretz

This book was set in Garamond by Prentice Hall

© 1995 by Prentice-Hall, Inc.
A Simon & Schuster Company
Englewood Cliffs, New Jersey 07632

Earlier edition, entitled *Human Learning: Theories, Principles, and Educational Applications,* © 1990 by Merrill, an imprint of Macmillan Publishing Company.

Printed in the United States of America

10 9 8 7 6 5 4

ISBN: 0-02-389482-2

Prentice-Hall International (UK) Limited, *London*
Prentice-Hall of Australia Pty. Limited, *Sydney*
Prentice-Hall of Canada, Inc., *Toronto*
Prentice-Hall Hispanoamericana, S. A., *Mexico*
Prentice-Hall of India Private Limited, *New Delhi*
Prentice-Hall of Japan, Inc., *Tokyo*
Simon & Schuster Asia Pte. Ltd., *Singapore*
Editora Prentice-Hall do Brasil, Ltda., *Rio de Janeiro*

Dedication

To my father and mother, James and Nancy Ellis

Preface

Human learning is a complex and fascinating process. I have been excited about how much psychologists have learned about learning since the turn of the century. Yet I have been discouraged about how little their knowledge of the learning process has been used to help people learn more efficiently and effectively. For many years I searched for a textbook that explains principles and theories of human learning in a readable and down-to-earth fashion and that also applies those theories and principles to educational practice. I continued to hope someone would write such a book, but finally realized that the "someone" would have to be me.

I have written this book with particular students in mind: students who would like to learn about learning, but often do not have much background in psychology. Such students may benefit from studying the historical roots of learning theories but prefer to focus their energies on studying contemporary perspectives and ideas. These students might find learning theories fascinating but lose patience when they cannot see the relevance of those theories to everyday practice. These students are capable of reading a dry, terse textbook but probably learn more effectively from a book that shows how different concepts relate to one another, provides numerous examples, and, especially, emphasizes meaningful learning—true *understanding*—of the material it presents.

This second edition of the book is noticeably longer than the first one, in large part because the study of human learning has been growing by leaps and bounds. I have added three new chapters—one on metacognition and study strategies, and two on human motivation. I have added sections on such topics as self-efficacy, parallel distributed processing, and conceptual change, and have expanded my treatment of such topics as self-regulation, expository instruction, and meaningful problem solving. I have included more educational applications; for example, I now describe how teacher questioning, wait time, and classroom testing practices influence student learning. And I have gone through the rest of the book with a fine-toothed comb, updating theories and principles as well as the research on which both are tested.

Although I am listed as the sole author, I have certainly not written this book alone. Many people have helped me along the way:

- Frank Di Vesta, my advisor and mentor at Penn State, who taught me a great deal about learning and who absolutely refused to let me graduate until I also learned a great deal about writing.
- Dave Faherty and Kevin Davis, administrative editors for the first and second editions, respectively, who provided me with guidance when I needed it but trusted my instincts about how best to present the field of human learning to my readers.
- My colleagues across the nation who read earlier drafts most thoroughly and conscientiously and whose suggestions have greatly improved the final product: Livingston Alexander, Western Kentucky University; Sarah Huyvaert, Eastern Michigan University; Janina Jolley, Clarion University of Pennsylvania; Joseph Kersting, Western Illinois University; Gerald Larson, Kent State University; Mark Lewis, University of Texas at Tyler; John Newell, University of Florida at Gainesville; Jim O'Connor, California State University at Bakersfield; Karen Zabrucky, Georgia State University; Jean C. Faieta, Edinboro University of Pennsylvania; Ralph F. Darr, Jr., The University of Akron; Michael S. Meloth, University of Colorado; and Margaret W. Cohen, University of Missouri—St. Louis.
- My colleague at the University of Northern Colorado, Steven Pulos, who read much of the second edition's final draft and helped me polish the rough edges.
- My husband, Richard, and my children, Christina, Alex, and Jeffrey, who have been eternally supportive of my writing endeavors, and who have provided me with numerous examples of human learning in action.
- My parents, James and Nancy Ellis, who long ago taught me the value of higher education.
- My students, who urged me to write the book in the first place and continue to give me feedback about how I can make it better.

Jeanne Ellis Ormrod

Contents

CHAPTER 3

Classical Conditioning   29

CHAPTER 4

Operant Conditioning   45

CHAPTER 5

Applications of Operant Conditioning   77

PART FOUR

COGNITIVE VIEWS OF LEARNING   161

CHAPTER 8

Antecedents and Assumptions of Cognitivism   163

CHAPTER 9

Perception and Attention   193

CHAPTER 16

Transfer and Problem Solving   371

PART SIX

MOTIVATION   409

CHAPTER 17

Motivation and Affect   411

CHAPTER 18

Cognitive Factors in Motivation   437

PART ONE

INTRODUCTION TO HUMAN LEARNING

CHAPTER 1

Definitions and Perspectives of Learning

When my son Alex was in kindergarten, his teacher asked me please to do something about his shoes. Alex had been leaving the house every morning with his shoes carefully and lovingly tied by his mother, but by the time he arrived at school the laces were untied and flopping every which way, a state to which they returned within 10 minutes of anyone else's retying them. I had repeatedly suggested to Alex that we double-knot his laces, but Alex had rejected that method as too babyish. As an alternative, I had purchased numerous pairs of shoes with Velcro instead of laces, but the Velcro always seemed to separate from the shoes within a month. I had, of course, also tried a series of shoe-tying lessons with Alex, but they had never been successful. The teacher was justifiably irritated that she had to tie Alex's shoes so many times in one day and asked that Alex learn to tie them himself. Her request reflected such exasperated desperation that I guiltily sat down with him one more time and demonstrated how to put two laces together into a presentable bow. This time, however, I accompanied my explanation with a magical statement: "Alex, when you learn to tie your shoes, I will give you a quarter." Alex had shoe-tying perfected in five minutes, and we haven't had a complaint from school since—at least not about his shoes.

When my daughter Tina was in fourth grade, she experienced considerable difficulty with a series of homework assignments in subtraction. She had never learned basic subtraction facts, despite my continual nagging to do so, with the result being that she could not solve two- and three-digit subtraction problems successfully. One night, after her typical half-hour tantrum about "these stupid problems," my husband explained to Tina that subtraction was nothing more than reversed addition and that her knowledge of addition facts could help her with subtraction. Something must have clicked in Tina's head, because we weren't subjected to any more tantrums about subtraction. Multiplication, yes, but not subtraction.

Human learning takes many forms, some of them easily seen and some not. Some instances of learning are readily observable, such as when a child learns to tie shoes. But other instances of learning are more subtle, such as when a child gains a new understanding of mathematical principles. And people learn for many different reasons. Some learn for the rewards their achievements bring—for example, good grades, recognition, or money (consider my capitalistic son). But others learn for less obvious reasons—perhaps for a sense of accomplishment, or perhaps simply to make life easier.

In this book, I will describe human learning from the various perspectives that have evolved in psychological theory throughout the twentieth century. As you will soon discover, learning is a complicated process, and psychologists disagree even about such basic issues as what learning is, how it occurs, and which factors are necessary for it to occur at all.

THE IMPORTANCE OF LEARNING

Many species have things easy compared to humans, or at least so it would seem. Birds, for example, are born with a wealth of knowledge that we humans must learn. Birds instinctively know how to build their houses; we either have to be taught somehow about framing, roofing, and drywalling, or else we have to hire someone to do it for us. Birds know, without being told, exactly when to fly south and how to get there; we have to look at our calendars and road maps. Birds instinctively know how to care for their young; we have to go to prenatal classes, read child-care books, and learn how to change diapers.

On the other hand, it is the humans, not the birds, who are getting ahead in this world. Over the years, humans have learned to make increasingly stronger and more comfortable homes for themselves, while birds are still making the same flimsy, drafty nests they have been building for thousands of years. Humans have developed fast, dependable modes of transportation for themselves and their goods, while birds are still winging it. And humans are learning how better to feed themselves and care for themselves and their young, so that each generation grows taller, stronger, and healthier than the one before. Birds, meanwhile, are still eating worms.

The learning process allows the human race a greater degree of flexibility and adaptability than is true for any other species on the planet. Because so little of our behavior is instinctive and so much is learned, we are able to benefit from our experiences. We know which behaviors are likely to lead to successful outcomes and which are not, and we modify our behaviors accordingly. And as adults pass on to children the wisdom gleaned from their ancestors and from their own experiences, each generation is just that much more capable of behaving intelligently. Let's face it: We can get from New York to Miami in two hours, but how long does it take the birds?

DEFINING LEARNING

My son Alex's learning to tie his shoes and my daughter Tina's learning how subtraction relates to addition are both examples of learning. Consider these instances of learning as well:

- The mother of a five-year-old boy insists that her son assume some household chores, for which he earns a small weekly allowance. The allowance, when saved for two or three weeks, enables the boy to purchase small toys of his own choosing. As a result, he develops an appreciation for the value of money.
- A college freshman from a small town is exposed, for the first time, to political viewpoints different from her own. After engaging in heated political debates with her classmates, she evaluates and modifies her own political philosophy.
- A toddler is overly affectionate with a neighborhood dog, and the dog responds by biting the boy's hand. After that, the child cries and runs quickly to his mother every time he sees a dog.

Learning is the means through which we acquire not only skills and knowledge, but values, attitudes, and emotions as well.

Just what do we mean by the term **learning**? Different psychologists conceptualize and define learning differently. Here are two definitions that reflect common yet quite different conceptions of what learning is:

1. Learning is a relatively permanent change in behavior due to experience.
2. Learning is a relatively permanent change in mental associations due to experience.

What do these definitions have in common? Both speak of learning as involving a "relatively permanent" *change*; in other words, the change will last for some time, although not necessarily forever. And both definitions attribute that change to *experience*; in other words, learning takes place as a result of one or more events in the learner's life. Other changes, such as those due to maturational changes in the body, organic damage, and temporary body states (e.g., fatigue, drugs), are not attributable to experience, and so do not reflect learning.

How do the definitions differ? The first refers to a change in *behavior*—an external change that we can observe. The second focuses on a change in *mental associations*—an internal change that we cannot observe. Herein lies the most fundamental difference in perspective in the theories of learning that we examine in this book.

The first definition reflects the perspective of a group of theories collectively known as **behaviorism**. These theories focus on the learning of tangible, observable *behaviors*, or *responses*, such as tying shoes, solving a subtraction problem, or complaining about a stomachache to avoid going to school.

The second definition reflects the perspective of a group of theories collectively known as **cognitivism**. These theories focus not on behavioral outcomes, but on the *thought processes* (sometimes called *mental events*) involved in human learning. Examples of such processes include the way a child interrelates addition and subtraction facts, the memory gimmick a student uses to remember French vocabulary words, and the idiosyncratic meanings a student has attached to her understanding of basic physics principles.

In this book, I will describe both of these perspectives in considerable detail; I will also include perspectives that lie somewhere between the two extremes. Most psychologists tend to align themselves with one perspective or the other, and I, whose graduate training and research program have been rooted firmly in cognitivist traditions, am no exception. I firmly believe, however, that both the behaviorist and cognitive perspectives have something important to say about human learning and that both provide useful suggestions for education.

THE NATURE OF PRINCIPLES AND THEORIES

The systematic study of human behavior, including human and animal learning processes, has emerged only within the last century, making psychology a relative newcomer to scientific inquiry. But in a century's time, thousands of experiments have investigated how people and animals learn, and patterns in the results of these experiments have led psychologists to generalize about the learning process through the formulation of both principles and theories of learning.

Principles of learning identify specific factors that consistently influence learning and describe the particular effects that these factors have. For example, consider this learning principle:

> *A behavior that is followed by a satisfying state of affairs (a reward) is more likely to be learned than a behavior not followed by such a reward.*

In this principle, a particular factor (a reward consequent to a behavior) is identi-fied as having a particular effect on learning (an increase in the frequency of behavior). The principle is apparent in many different situations, including these:

- A pigeon is given a small pellet of food every time it turns its body in a complete circle. It begins turning more and more frequently.
- Dolphins who are given fish for "speaking" in Dolphinese quickly become quite chatty.
- A boy who completes a perfect spelling paper and is praised for it by a favorite teacher works diligently for future success in spelling assign-ments.
- A high school girl who receives compliments on her new hairstyle contin-ues to style her hair that way.

Principles are most useful when they can be applied to a wide variety of situa-tions. The "reward" principle is an example of such broad applicability: It applies to both animals and humans, and it holds true for different types of learning and different rewards. When a principle such as this one is observed over and over again—when it stands the test of time—it is sometimes called a **law**.

Theories of learning provide explanations about the underlying mechanisms involved in the learning process. Whereas principles tell us *what* factors are important for learning, theories tell us *why* these factors are important. For example, consider one aspect of social learning theory (described in Chapter 7):

People learn what they pay attention to. Reward increases learning because it makes people pay attention.

Here we have an explanation of why a reward affects learning. Attention is identified as the underlying process responsible for the observed effect of reward on learning.

Advantages of Theories

Theories have several advantages over principles. First, theories allow us to sum-marize the results of many research studies and integrate numerous principles of learning. In that sense, theories are very concise (psychologists use the term **par-simonious**). Second, theories provide starting points for conducting new research; they suggest research questions worthy of study. For example, the the-ory that attention is more important than reward leads to the following predic-tion: *When an individual's attention can be drawn to the information to be learned, learning can occur in the absence of reward.* In fact, this prediction has been supported by research (e.g., Faust & Anderson, 1967).

Research conducted outside the context of a particular theoretical perspec-tive will frequently yield results that are trivial and nongeneralizable. Interpreted from a theoretical perspective, however, those same results become significant. For example, consider an experiment by Seligman and Maier (1967). In this classic study, dogs were placed in individual cages and given a number of painful and unpredictable shocks. Some dogs were able to escape the shocks by pressing a panel in the cage, while others were unable to escape. The following day, the dogs were placed in different cages, and again shocks were administered. This time, however, each shock was preceded by a signal (a tone) that the shock was coming, and the dogs could escape the shocks by jumping over a barrier as soon as the tone occurred. The dogs that had been able to escape the shocks on the preceding day learned to escape in this new situation, but the dogs that had been unable to escape previously did *not* learn to escape the shocks now that they could do so.

On the surface, this experiment, while interesting, might not seem especially relevant to human learning. However, Seligman and his colleagues used this and other experiments to develop their theory of *learned helplessness*: Individuals who learn that they have no control over unpleasant or painful events in one situation are unlikely, in later situations, to attempt to escape or avoid those aversive events even when it is possible for them to do so. As you will learn in Chapters 6 and 18, studies such as Seligman and Maier's research with dogs, because they have led to the development of theories of learned helplessness, have implications for classroom practice.

A third advantage of theories over principles is that theories explain learning, whereas principles only describe it. An understanding of the mechanisms underlying learning processes will ultimately help psychologists and educators design learning environments that facilitate human learning to the greatest possible degree. For example, consider the teacher who is familiar with the theory that attention is a key factor in learning. That teacher may decide to employ a variety of techniques, including rewards, that increase student attention to learning materials. In contrast, consider the teacher who is familiar only with the principle that rewarded behaviors are learned. That teacher may use rewards, such as small toys, that are counterproductive because they distract students' attention away from their academic tasks.

Disadvantages of Theories

Despite their advantages, theories also have at least two disadvantages. First, no theory explains all we know about learning. Current theories of learning tend to focus on specific aspects of learning. Behaviorist theories, for example, limit themselves to situations in which learning involves a behavior change. Cognitive theories tend to focus instead on how information is organized or remembered. Observed phenomena that do not fit comfortably within a particular theoretical perspective are excluded from that perspective.

Second, theories affect what new information is published, therefore biasing the knowledge that we have about learning. For example, imagine that a team of researchers proposes a particular theory of learning and conducts a research study to support their idea. However, the results of their research are exactly opposite to what they expected, therefore casting doubt on their theory. If these researchers are fully committed to demonstrating that their theory is correct, they are unlikely to publish results that will indicate otherwise! In this way, theories may sometimes impede progress toward a truly accurate understanding of the learning process.

A Perspective on Theories and Principles

You should probably think of the theories I describe in this book as dynamic, changing models of the learning process. Each theory is based on several decades of research results, and each has some validity. However, as research continues in the decades ahead, theories of learning will undoubtedly be revised to account for new evidence that emerges. In this sense, no single theory can be considered "fact."

At the same time, you might think of learning principles as relatively enduring conclusions about cause-effect relationships in the learning process. Principles generally maintain their validity longer than theories do. The "reward" principle was introduced by Edward Thorndike in 1898 and has remained with us in one form or another ever since. Thorndike's theory of *why* reward affects learning, however, has been largely replaced by other explanations.

Both principles and theories provide a means to predict the conditions under which learning is likely to occur. To the extent that principles and theories are useful in this way, we are better off with them—imperfect and temporary as they may be—than without them.

APPLYING PRINCIPLES AND THEORIES TO CLASSROOM SITUATIONS

A great deal of learning takes place in schools. For example, most students learn such basic skills as reading and subtraction. Unfortunately, students may also learn things their teachers never intended for them to learn. For example, while they have learned to read, they may also have learned that studying means memorizing, word for word, what they read. And while they have learned their subtraction facts, they may also have learned that mathematics is frustrating or incomprehensible.

The learning that takes place in schools should not be left to chance. The better we understand the factors that influence learning (principles) and the processes that underlie it (theories), the better we can train teachers and design instructional materials to maximize learning that will benefit students and minimize learning that will interfere with their later achievement.

The theories I have included in this book portray human learning from different perspectives and at times even contradict one another. Yet I hope you will take an eclectic perspective, resisting the temptation to choose one theory over others as the "right" one. Different theories are applicable in different situations, depending on the environmental factors under consideration, the specific content being learned, and the objectives of instruction. At the same time, each theory provides unique insights into how and why humans learn (e.g., see Catania, 1985, and Epstein, 1991) and how schools might be designed to enhance student learning. It is probably more helpful to think of theories in terms of their usefulness rather than in terms of their correctness.

As theories of learning are revised over the years, educational practices will also change. In the meantime, educators can use current theories to help students learn more effectively and less painfully than they seem to learn now. The time has come to make schools places of success and pleasure rather than places of failure and pain.

OVERVIEW OF THE BOOK

In Part Two of the book, we will explore principles and theories of learning from the behaviorist perspective, beginning with an introduction and historical overview of behaviorism in Chapter 2. We will then examine in depth the two most commonly used models of learning within the behaviorist perspective: classical conditioning (Chapter 3) and operant conditioning (Chapters 4 and 5). We will also look at the role of unpleasant events, such as punishment, in the learning process (Chapter 6).

In Part Three (Chapter 7), we will make the transition from behaviorism to cognitivism as we examine social learning theory, an approach to learning that has evolved over the years from its behaviorist roots into a cognitive model of how people learn through observation of their fellow human beings.

In Part Four, we will turn to cognitive perspectives of learning, beginning with an introduction and overview of cognitivism in Chapter 8. We will then examine in depth the internal mental processes involved in learning, including perception and attention processes (Chapter 9) and the various components of the human memory system (Chapters 10 through 12). We will consider several specific educational applications of cognitivism in Chapter 13.

In Part Five, we will look at some of the more complex aspects of human learning: concept learning in Chapter 14, self-regulation of thought processes (*metacognition*) in Chapter 15, and transfer and problem solving in Chapter 16.

Finally, in Part Six, we will consider the role that motivation plays in human learning. In Chapter 17, we will look at the effects of motivation on learning and behavior and examine several theoretical explanations of those effects. In Chapter 18, we will discover that cognition and motivation are closely interrelated phenomena.

As we proceed, we will identify numerous applications for teaching and instruction. I believe that psychology has much to say about how learning and instruction can be improved. I hope, once you have finished the final chapter, that you will agree with me.

SUMMARY

Learning allows human beings a greater degree of flexibility and adaptability than is true for any other species. Currently, two major theoretical perspectives help us understand how people learn. The behaviorist perspective emphasizes relationships among observable stimuli and responses. The cognitive perspective emphasizes the role of internal mental processes involved in learning. Principles (descriptions of what factors affect learning) and theories (explanations of why those factors have the effects they do) from both behaviorism and cognitivism help educators optimize learning environments and facilitate student achievement.

BEHAVIORIST VIEWS OF LEARNING

CHAPTER 2

Overview of Behaviorism

Behaviorism, the first psychological perspective to have a significant impact on our understanding of how human beings learn, is the topic of Chapters 2 through 6. This chapter will present an overview of the major assumptions of the behaviorist approach to learning, provide an historical overview of some of the key theorists who have contributed to the behaviorist movement, give you a brief glimpse of how behaviorism has changed in recent years, and discuss some general applications of behaviorist theories to educational practice. The chapters that follow will cover more specific aspects of behaviorism, including classical conditioning (Chapter 3), operant conditioning and its educational applications (Chapters 4 and 5), and the effects of aversive stimuli (Chapter 6).

ASSUMPTIONS OF BEHAVIORISM

Before the advent of behaviorism around the turn of the century, the two dominant perspectives in psychology were **structuralism** (e.g., Wilhelm Wundt's work) and **functionalism** (e.g., John Dewey's writings). Although these two perspectives differed considerably in their underlying assumptions and topics of study, they shared a common characteristic: they lacked a precise, carefully defined research methodology. The primary means of investigating learning and other psychological phenomena, especially for the structuralists, was a method called **introspection**: People were simply asked to "look" inside their minds and describe what they were "thinking."

Beginning with the works of the Russian physiologist Ivan Pavlov and the American psychologist Edward Thorndike, however, a more objective approach to the study of learning—one that focused on measuring observable phenomena rather than on nonobservable mental events—was introduced. With the advent of methodologies that emphasized stimuli and responses in learning, the behaviorist movement was born.

As will become clear later in the chapter, behaviorists have not always agreed on the specific processes that account for learning. However, most of them have historically shared certain basic assumptions about learning:

1. Underlying most behaviorist theories is the assumption of **equipotentiality**; that is, principles of learning apply equally to different behaviors and to different species of animals, including human beings. Behaviorists often use the term **organism** to refer to both humans and other animals.

2. Due to this equipotentiality across species, principles of learning developed from research with one species should apply to other species as well. Thus, behaviorist principles derived primarily from research with such animals as rats and pigeons are often applied to human learning situations.

3. Organisms enter the world as "blank slates" (the assumption of **tabula rasa**). Aside from certain species-specific instincts, people and animals are not born predisposed to behave in particular ways.

4. The study of learning is a science similar to the physical sciences. As such, it must focus on events that can be observed and measured. Only two kinds of events fit the criteria of observation and measurement: **stimuli** (S) within the environment and **responses** (R) by an organism.

5. Many behaviorists believe that we cannot directly observe and measure internal processes (thoughts, motives, emotions, etc.); therefore, we should not consider these processes in the scientific study of learning. These behaviorists consider an organism a "black box": things that

impinge on the box (stimuli) and things that emerge from it (responses) can be studied, but the processes that occur within it cannot.

6. Principles of learning reflect relationships between stimuli and responses; hence, behaviorism is sometimes called **S-R psychology**.

7. Rather than using the term *learning*, behaviorists often speak of **conditioning**: an organism's behavior is conditioned by environmental events. The things we learn—the results of our past and present experiences—are often beyond our control.

8. We can only assume learning has occurred when we observe a change in behavior. Some behaviorists propose that if no behavior change occurs, learning has not taken place.

9. We should explain the learning of all behaviors, from the most simple to the most complex, by as few learning principles as possible, an assumption reflecting a preference for **parsimony** (conciseness)in explaining learning and behavior.

Not all behaviorists would agree with all nine of these assumptions. For instance, many theorists disagree with the "black box" assumption, believing that internal factors—those within the organism (O)—are also important in understanding learning. Such **neo-behaviorist** theorists are sometimes called S-O-R (stimulus-organism-response) theorists rather than S-R theorists.

EARLY THEORISTS IN THE BEHAVIORIST TRADITION

Numerous theorists contributed to the rise of behaviorism during the early decades of the twentieth century. The contributions of six of them—Pavlov, Thorndike, Watson, Guthrie, Hull, and Skinner—will be briefly described in this chapter. Two of these six, Ivan Pavlov and B. F. Skinner, have had such a significant impact that their theories will be described again in more detail in Chapters 3 and 4.

Ivan Pavlov

The Russian physiologist Ivan Pavlov, while investigating salivation reflexes in dogs, discovered that a dog would salivate not only because of food, but also because of other environmental events that it associated with food—for example, the laboratory assistant who often brought the dog its meals. Through a systematic study of how dogs learn to salivate to different stimuli, Pavlov developed a theory of learning most commonly known as *classical conditioning* (Pavlov, 1927).

Pavlov's theory of learning begins with a stimulus-response connection, in which a particular stimulus (e.g., meat) leads to a particular response (e.g., salivation). When that stimulus is repeatedly presented in association with one or more other stimuli (e.g., the lab assistant or the sound of his footsteps in the hall), those other stimuli begin to elicit a similar response. This process of classical conditioning, which I will describe in greater detail in Chapter 3, appeared in the work of other early psychologists (e.g., John Watson and B. F. Skinner) as well. We now acknowledge classical conditioning as a powerful force in learning, especially in the learning of emotional responses.

Edward L. Thorndike

In 1898, Edward Thorndike introduced a theory of learning that emphasized the role of experience in the strengthening and weakening of stimulus-response connections; this perspective is now known as connectionism (Thorndike, 1898, 1911, 1913). In Thorndike's classic first experiment (his doctoral dissertation), he placed a cat in a "puzzle box" with a door that opened when some device (for example, a wire loop) was appropriately manipulated. Thorndike observed the cat initiating numerous, apparently random movements in its attempts to get out of the box; eventually, by chance, the cat triggered the mechanism that opened the door and allowed escape. When returned to the box a second time, the cat again engaged in trial-and-error movements but managed to escape in less time than it had previously. With successive trials in the box, the cat, although continuing to demonstrate trial-and-error behavior, managed to escape within shorter and shorter time periods.

From his observations of cats in the puzzle box, Thorndike concluded that the learning of a behavior is affected by the consequence of that behavior (e.g., escape from a confining situation). We can sum up Thorndike's *law of effect* as follows:

> *Responses to a situation that are followed by satisfaction will be strengthened; responses that are followed by discomfort will be weakened.*

According to Thorndike, learning consists of trial-and-error behavior and a gradual "stamping in" of some behaviors (those leading to satisfaction) and "stamping out" of other behaviors (those leading to discomfort). In other words, rewarded responses increase, and punished responses diminish and disappear.

In addition to his law of effect, Thorndike proposed that practice influences S-R connections as well. His *law of exercise* is as follows:

> *Stimulus-response connections that are repeated are strengthened; stimulus-response connections that are not used are weakened.*

In other words, practice facilitates the learning of responses. Responses that are not practiced eventually disappear.

Thorndike later revised his law of effect and discarded his law of exercise (Thorndike, 1935). The original law of effect implied that reward and punishment have opposite but equal effects on behavior: One strengthens and the other weakens. Thorndike's later research (1932a, 1932b) indicated that punishment may not be effective in weakening responses, however. For example, in one experiment (Thorndike, 1932a), human subjects completed a multiple-choice Spanish vocabulary test in which they were to choose the English translation for each of a long list of Spanish words. Every time subjects chose the correct English word out of five alternatives, the experimenter said "Right!" (i.e., rewarding the response); every time subjects chose an incorrect alternative, the experimenter said "Wrong!" (i.e., punishing the response). In responding to the same multiple-choice questions over a series of trials, subjects increased the responses for which they had been rewarded but did not necessarily decrease those for which they had been punished. In his *revised law of effect* (e.g., Thorndike, 1935), Thorndike continued to maintain that rewards strengthen the behaviors they follow, but he deemphasized the role of punishment. Instead, he proposed that punishment has an *indirect* effect on learning: As a result of an annoying state of affairs, an organism may engage in certain other behaviors (for example, crying or running away) that interfere with performance of the punished response.

Thorndike also conducted research (described by Trowbridge & Cason, 1932) that cast doubt on the effect of practice alone on learning. For example, in one experiment, human subjects were blindfolded and asked to draw a series of four-inch lines. Subjects could not see the results of their efforts, and they received no information from the experimenter about the correctness of their drawings. Without feedback, subjects did not improve in accuracy despite their practice, a result that led Thorndike to repudiate his law of exercise.

Despite the weaknesses of Thorndike's early ideas, his work provided a significant contribution to the study of learning. The idea that the consequences of responses influence learning continues to be a major component of behaviorism today.

John B. Watson

Although Pavlov and Thorndike are considered among the earliest contributors to the behaviorist tradition, it was actually John Watson (1913) who introduced the term *behaviorism* and served as the most vocal advocate for the behaviorist perspective in the early part of the century.

In his major writings (Watson, 1914, 1919, 1925), Watson adamantly called for the introduction of scientific objectivity and experimentation into the study of psychological phenomena. He emphasized the need for focusing scientific inquiry on observable behaviors rather than on such nonobservable phenomena as "thinking." Not only did Watson oppose the study of internal mental events, he denied any existence of the mind at all! Thought, he proposed, was nothing more than tiny movements of the tongue and larynx and thus was a behavior just like any other.

Greatly influenced by the work of both Pavlov and another Russian, Vladimir Bechterev (Bechterev, 1913), Watson adopted the classically conditioned S-R habit as the basic unit of learning and extended it to human learning (Watson, 1916; Watson & Rayner, 1920). Watson proposed two laws that described how such habits developed. First, his *law of frequency* (similar to Thorndike's law of exercise) stressed the importance of repetition:

> *The more frequently a stimulus and response occur in association with each other, the stronger that S-R habit will become.*

Second, Watson's *law of recency* was as follows:

> *The response that has most recently occurred after a particular stimulus is the response most likely to be associated with that stimulus.*

In other words, the last response to a stimulus is the one that will occur the next time the stimulus is presented. Through his law of recency, Watson rejected Thorndike's law of effect. According to Watson, reward has only an indirect effect on learning in that the most *recent* response is the one rewarded. For example, when a cat is in a puzzle box, the last response is the one that leads to escape and so is most likely to be connected to that stimulus situation.

Watson asserted that past experience accounts for virtually all behavior. His extreme environmentalism, which denied any effect on behavior by hereditary factors, was reflected in the following infamous quote:

> Give me a dozen healthy infants, well-formed, and my own specified world to bring them up in and I'll guarantee to take any one at random and train him to become any type of specialist I might select—doctor, lawyer, artist, merchant-chief, and yes, even beggar-man and thief, regardless of his talents, penchants, tendencies, abilities, vocations and race of his ancestors. (Watson, 1925, p. 82)

Watson's influence continued to be felt long after he retired from academia in 1920. His strong advocacy of psychology as an objective and precise science and his insistence that environment plays a key role in human behavior led to a behaviorist tradition that dominated the first half of the century.

Edwin R. Guthrie

Edwin Guthrie's **contiguity theory** (Guthrie, 1935, 1942) was similar to John Watson's ideas in that it emphasized S-R connections and rejected the role of reward in developing these connections. Guthrie's basic principle of learning was as follows:

> *A stimulus that is followed by a particular response will, upon its recurrence, tend to be followed by the same response again. This S-R connection gains its full strength on one trial.*

In other words, if an individual responds to a particular stimulus in a particular way at one time, that individual will make the same response the next time the same stimulus is encountered; thus, a habit has been formed. Guthrie contended that the critical factor in learning is the **contiguity** of stimulus and response.

Guthrie also shared John Watson's belief that *recency* is critical in learning: an organism will respond to a stimulus in the way it last responded to that stimulus. A reward facilitates learning only to the extent that it removes the organism from the stimulus, thus preventing subsequent responses from being associated with that stimulus.

Guthrie's notion of **one-trial learning**—that an S-R connection is fully formed on one pairing—was quite different from Thorndike's idea that responses are gradually "stamped in." Guthrie explained the gradual learning of complex behavior by proposing that complex behavior is actually composed of many tiny S-R connections; with each practice trial, more and more appropriate S-R connections are formed, thus leading to the gradual changes observed in overall behavior.

The parsimony of Guthrie's theory—his proposal that the contiguity of stimuli and responses is the basis of all learning—is definitely appealing. Guthrie conducted little research to support his views, however, and later research has cast doubt on the notion that learning is as simple as Guthrie described it (Bower & Hilgard, 1981). Nevertheless, three techniques for breaking S-R habits that Guthrie derived from his theory continue to be used in educational and therapeutic practice. We will discuss each of these techniques later in the chapter.

Clark L. Hull

It was primarily the work of Clark Hull (Hull, 1943, 1951, 1952) that introduced "organismic" characteristics—those unique to different organisms—into behaviorist learning theory. Like many of his predecessors, Hull maintained that learned S-R habits form the basis of behavior. Furthermore, he agreed with Thorndike about the importance of rewards in the learning process. However, he believed that the presence of a particular stimulus and one's past experiences with that stimulus are not the only determinants of whether a particular response will occur or how strongly it will be made. Hull proposed that a number of other factors (**intervening variables**) unique to each organism and each occasion must be considered to predict the likelihood and strength of a response's occurrence. Hull's theory was therefore the first major theory of the S-O-R genre.

According to Hull, one intervening variable influencing the occurrence of a response is **habit strength**, the degree to which a particular stimulus and a particular response are associated. The more often a response has previously been rewarded in the presence of the stimulus, the greater is the habit strength, and the more likely the response is to occur.

A second intervening variable critical for a response to occur is the organism's **drive**, an internal state of arousal that motivates its behavior. Hull suggested that some drives (e.g., hunger and thirst) have direct impact on an organism's survival. Others (called *acquired drives*) serve no apparent biological purpose; they are instead the result of previous associations of neutral stimuli with drive-reducing stimuli such as food. To illustrate, one might become "driven" by a need for approval if approval had previously been associated with a candy bar. Rewards increase the strength of an S-R habit by reducing the organism's drive; for example, food reduces hunger.

Hull proposed that intervening variables such as habit strength, drive, stimulus intensity (an intense stimulus is more likely than a weak stimulus to bring about a strong response), and incentive (based on the amount and immediacy of reward) all work together to increase the likelihood and relative strength of a particular response. At the same time, **inhibitory factors** (e.g., fatigue) decrease the likelihood and strength of the response.

Hull argued that an organism might learn several different responses to the same stimulus, each with a different degree of habit strength. The combination of the various S-R habits for a given stimulus, with their respective habit strengths, is known as a **habit-family hierarchy**. When presented with a stimulus, an organism will, if possible, make the response for which the habit strength is the strongest. However, if that response is for some reason blocked, the organism will make the second response, or, if again foiled, the third response, and so on down the hierarchy.

As an illustration of this concept of habit-family hierarchy, consider Stan, who faces a homework assignment involving multiplication of fractions. Stan may first try to complete the assignment using the technique his teacher taught him for multiplying fractions. When he finds he cannot remember the technique, Stan may instead ask his friend Angela if he may copy her answers. If Angela refuses the request, Stan may resort to a third response in his hierarchy: telling his teacher that the family dog ate his homework.

Hull developed a series of mathematical formulas that could predict the occurrence and strength of responses once the various intervening variables were measured and their values entered. The precision of Hull's formulas permitted a careful testing of his theory through research, which found many specifics of the theory to be incorrect (Bower & Hilgard, 1981; Klein, 1987). For example, learning apparently can take place in the absence of drive; you will see some examples of such learning in Chapters 7 and 8. In addition, Hull proposed that a reward is a stimulus that reduces drive, yet some rewards actually appear to increase drive (e.g., Olds & Milner, 1954).

Hull's theory was a predominant force in behaviorism throughout the 1940s and 1950s. Although many details of the theory did not hold up under empirical scrutiny, Hull's emphasis on intervening variables made such notions as *motivation* and *incentive* prominent concepts in learning research. And his many productive students—among them, Kenneth Spence, Neil Miller, John Dollard, and O. H. Mowrer—have continued to advance and modify Hullian ideas.

Burrhus Frederic Skinner

B. F. Skinner (e.g., Skinner, 1938, 1953, 1958, 1966b, 1971, 1989; Skinner & Epstein, 1982) is unquestionably the best known psychologist in the behaviorist tradition. Originally a fiction writer, Skinner was lured into psychology by the ideas of Pavlov and Watson (Skinner, 1967). His principles of *operant conditioning*, first proposed in 1938, underwent little change in the five decades prior to his death in 1990. Operant conditioning principles have served as the basis for thousands of research studies and have been applied extensively in both educational and therapeutic settings. I will present an overview of Skinner's ideas here and then describe operant conditioning again in more detail in Chapter 4.

Skinner, like Thorndike and Hull, proposed that we learn behaviors when they precede certain consequences. Unlike his predecessors, however, Skinner spoke only about the strengthening of responses, not the strengthening of S-R habits. Skinner's use of the term *reinforcer* instead of *reward* reflects his concern that psychologists remain objective in their examination of behavior and not try to guess what subjects find pleasing (rewarding) or why the reinforcer has the effect on behavior that it does.

To study the effects of reinforcers using precise measurement of responses in a carefully controlled environment, Skinner developed a piece of equipment, now known as the Skinner box, that has gained widespread popularity in animal learning research. As shown in Figure 2-1, the Skinner box used in studying rat behavior includes a metal bar that, when pushed down, causes a food tray to swing into reach long enough for the rat to grab a food pellet. In the pigeon version of the box, instead of a metal bar, a lighted plastic disk ("key") is located on one wall; when the pigeon pecks the key, the food tray swings into reach for a short time. Through observation of rats and pigeons in their respective Skinner boxes under varying conditions of reinforcement, Skinner developed a set of principles of learning that focuses on a description of behavior rather than an explanation of it (hence, some psychologists view Skinner's model as a "nontheory").

Skinner's most fundamental principle of operant conditioning, his *law of conditioning*, is paraphrased as follows:

> *A response that is followed by a reinforcing stimulus is strengthened and therefore more likely to occur again.*

A corollary to this principle, Skinner's *law of extinction*, is:

> *A response that is not followed by a reinforcing stimulus is weakened and therefore less likely to occur again.*

Figure 2–1
A prototypic Skinner box:
The food tray swings into
reach for reinforcement.

Metal Bar

Unlike Watson, Skinner acknowledged the existence of thought, particularly as it is reflected in verbal behavior (e.g., Skinner, 1963, 1989). However, he contended that the *causes* of mental events (including thoughts) lie in the environment; therefore, a stimulus-response approach to the study of learning, which emphasizes the impact of environment on behavior, is still defensible.

Despite the fact that his research focused almost exclusively on the simple responses of animals, Skinner nonetheless extended his conditioning principles to complex human behavior in general (e.g., Skinner, 1948b, 1957, 1971) and to educational practice in particular (e.g., Skinner, 1954, 1958, 1968, 1973). The numerous educational applications of operant conditioning (e.g., behavioral objectives, programmed instruction, and behavior modification) will be described in Chapter 5.

CONTEMPORARY BEHAVIORISM

Although much of the work in human learning has shifted toward a cognitive perspective in recent years, the behaviorist movement is still very much alive and well. Pavlov's classical conditioning and Skinner's operant conditioning remain as major theoretical perspectives that are continually refined by ongoing research (still conducted primarily with animals) and are applied successfully to educational and clinical settings.

Several trends characterize the gradual evolution of early behaviorist theories into contemporary behaviorism. One trend is an increased focus on motivation as a major factor affecting learning and performance (e.g., Herrnstein, 1977). A second change subsequent to early theories is increased attention to the role of negative consequences (punishment) in learning. Early theorists such as Thorndike, Guthrie, and Skinner maintained that punishment had little or no effect on behavior; however, a growing body of research (some of which I will present in Chapter 6) indicates that negative consequences *do* influence behavior (e.g., Rachlin, 1991). Still a third trend is an increasing recognition that learning and performance must be considered as separate, albeit related, entities. A number of psychologists (e.g., Brown & Herrnstein, 1975; Estes, 1969a; Herrnstein, 1977; Schwartz & Reisberg, 1991) have proposed that many behaviorist laws are more appropriately applied to an understanding of what influences the *performance* of learned behaviors rather than what influences learning itself. But perhaps the most dramatic (and certainly the most surprising) change in recent years is the growing belief among traditionally "behaviorist" psychologists that they can more effectively understand both human and animal behavior when they consider *cognitive factors* as well as environmental events (Church, 1993; Hulse, 1993; Rachlin, 1991; Rescorla, 1988; Schwartz & Reisberg, 1991; Wasserman, 1993). We will get the flavor of some of these cognitive factors as we examine contemporary perspectives on classical and operant conditioning in Chapters 3 and 4.

GENERAL EDUCATIONAL APPLICATIONS OF BEHAVIORISM

Behaviorist theories have numerous implications for teaching. Some educational practices suggested by behaviorist ideas are an emphasis on behavior, drill and practice, methods for breaking habits, and rewards (reinforcement) for desirable behavior.

Emphasis on Behavior

Behaviorists define learning as a change in behavior due to experience. This emphasis on behavior has at least two implications for education. First, students should be *active respondents* throughout the learning process rather than just passive recipients of whatever information is being taught. For example, students should not just listen (a nonobservable response); they should also talk, write, and do (observable behaviors).

A second implication of a behavioral emphasis relates to the *assessment* of student learning. Regardless of how effective teachers think a certain lecture or a particular set of curriculum materials might be, they should never assume that learning is occurring; rather, they should observe whether student behaviors actually change as a result of instruction. Only behavior changes—for example, improved test scores or better study habits—can confirm that learning has taken place. This emphasis on behavior as the only means for assessing learning points to the importance of frequently observing and measuring student responses in some way.

Drill and Practice

Many behaviorists have stressed the principle that repetition of stimulus-response habits strengthens those habits. To learn responses to particular stimuli thoroughly, *practice* is essential. For example, students will learn basic addition and subtraction facts better and recall them more quickly if they repeat those facts numerous times (e.g., through the use of flashcards). In a similar way, many reading teachers advocate that the best way for students to improve their reading level is simply to read, read, read.

Breaking Habits

Guthrie's notion of recency—that an organism will respond to a stimulus in the same way that it responded on the most recent previous encounter with that stimulus—implies that habits, once formed, are difficult to break. The trick in breaking a habit, from the point of view of the recency principle, is to lead an individual, somehow or other, to make a new response to the same old stimulus.

As an example, Guthrie (1935) described a girl who, upon entering the house after school each day, had the nasty habit of throwing her hat and coat on the floor rather than hanging up her garments. Despite repeated entreaties by the child's mother to change the sloppy behavior, the habit continued. One day, however, rather than admonishing the girl, the mother insisted that her daughter put her hat and coat back on, go outside, reenter the house, and hang up her clothes. The hanging-up response, being the one most recently exhibited, now became a new habit for the girl, and the throwing-on-the-floor response disappeared.

Guthrie proposed three ingenious techniques specifically designed to break habits: the exhaustion method, the threshold method, and the incompatible stimulus method.

Exhaustion Method

One way to break a stimulus-response habit is to continue to present the stimulus until the individual is too tired to respond in the habitual way. At that point, a new response will occur and a new S-R habit will form. For example, in breaking a bucking bronco, the persistent rider (the stimulus) stays on the horse's back until the horse is too exhausted to continue bucking; a new response (behavior reflecting acceptance of the rider, such as standing still) then becomes associated with the "rider" stimulus. Similarly, a teacher might eliminate a child's spitball-throwing behavior by having that child stay after school to make and throw spitballs until the child is too tired to continue.

Threshold Method

Another way of breaking a habit is to begin by presenting the stimulus so faintly that the individual does not respond to it in the habitual manner. The intensity of the stimulus is then increased so gradually that the individual continues *not* to respond to it. For example, when a student has test anxiety (when a test stimulus leads to an anxiety response), a teacher might eliminate that child's anxiety by first presenting tasks that are enjoyable to the child and only remotely resemble a test; over time, the teacher can present a series of tasks that increasingly (but gradually) begin to take on test-like qualities.

Incompatible Stimulus Method

A third method for breaking an S-R connection is to present the stimulus when the habitual response cannot occur and when an opposite, or *incompatible*, response will occur. For example, Guthrie recommended tying a dead chicken around a dog's neck to teach the dog not to catch and eat chickens. The dog will struggle to get rid of the annoying chicken, a response that is incompatible with catching and eating the chicken. Similarly, imagine a classroom of highly achievement-motivated students who are overly competitive with one another. To reduce the competition among students, the teacher might divide the class into small groups and assign each group an academic task that requires cooperation rather than competition (e.g., developing an argument for one side of an issue in a class debate). Assigning grades on the basis of group performance rather than individual performance should enhance the likelihood that students will cooperate. Hence, cooperative behavior will replace competitive behavior in that classroom environment.

Rewards (Reinforcement) for Desirable Behavior

Many behaviorists, among them Thorndike and Skinner, have emphasized the importance of rewards or reinforcement for learning. Students are most likely to learn and exhibit behaviors that lead to positive results. The kinds of reinforcers that are effective, and the many ways in which reinforcement principles can be incorporated into classroom practice, will be addressed in greater detail in Chapters 4 and 5.

SUMMARY

Behaviorism encompasses a group of theories that share several common assumptions, including the generalizability of learning principles across species, the "blank slate" nature of organisms, and the need to focus on external, observable events (i.e., stimuli and responses). Early learning theorists—Pavlov, Thorndike, Watson, Guthrie, Hull, and Skinner—all viewed learning somewhat differently, but each made a unique contribution to our understanding of how human beings learn. For example, Pavlov outlined the basic components of classical conditioning, Watson and Guthrie described the importance of contiguity between a stimulus and a response, and Thorndike, Skinner, and Hull documented how the consequences that follow responses bring about behavior change. All of them made us aware that past and present events influence the behaviors we exhibit.

Contemporary behaviorist perspectives reject some traditional behaviorist assumptions; for example, we find a distinction being made between learning and performance and an increasing interest in the cognitive factors that underlie behavior. The influence of behaviorism on contemporary educational practice can be seen in an emphasis on observable behavior, the use of drill and practice, methods for breaking habits, and attention to the consequences of student behaviors.

CHAPTER 3

Classical Conditioning

I have a "thing" about bees. Whenever a bee flies near me, I scream, wave my arms frantically, and run around like a wild woman. Yes, yes, I know, I will be better off if I remain perfectly still, but somehow I just can't control myself. My overreaction to bees is probably due to the several painful bee stings I received as a small child.

The learning of an involuntary response to a particular stimulus, such as my fearful reaction to bees, can be explained by a theory of learning known as **classical conditioning**. This paradigm originated with the work of Ivan Pavlov, so we will begin this chapter by reviewing his classic research. We will then explore how to apply Pavlov's learning paradigm to an understanding of human behavior. We will survey several phenomena associated with classical conditioning: extinction, spontaneous recovery, stimulus generalization and discrimination, higher-order conditioning, and sensory preconditioning. We will also see how the behaviorist perspective on classical conditioning has changed in recent years. Finally, we will look at ways of eliminating undesirable responses using the classical conditioning model and at some specific implications of the model for educational settings.

PAVLOV'S EXPERIMENT

Pavlov, a Russian physiologist whose work on digestion earned him a Nobel Prize in 1904, was conducting a series of experiments related to salivation in dogs. To study a dog's salivation responses, he would make a surgical incision in the dog's mouth, thus allowing the dog's saliva to be collected and measured, and strap the dog into an immobile position. He would then give powdered meat to the dog and observe its resulting salivation. However, Pavlov noticed that the dog soon began to salivate before it saw or smelled the meat—in fact, it salivated as soon as the lab assistant entered the room with the meat. Apparently, the dog had learned that the lab assistant meant food was on the way and responded accordingly. Pavlov devoted a good part of his later years to a systematic study of this learning process that he had so inadvertently discovered, and he eventually summarized his research in his book *Conditioned Reflexes* (Pavlov, 1927).

Pavlov's original studies of classical conditioning went something like this:

1. He first observed whether the dog salivated in response to a particular stimulus—perhaps to a flash of light, the sound of a tuning fork, or the ringing of a bell. For simplicity's sake, we'll continue with our discussion using a bell as the stimulus in question. As you might imagine, the dog did not find a bell especially appetizing and so did not salivate.
2. Pavlov then rang the bell again, and this time it was immediately followed by the presentation of some powdered meat. The dog of course salivated. He rang the bell several more times. always presenting meat immediately afterwards. The dog salivated on each occasion.
3. Pavlov then rang the bell again *without* presenting any meat. Nevertheless, the dog salivated. The bell, to which the dog had previously been unresponsive (step one), now led to a salivation response. There had been *a change in behavior due to experience;* in the behaviorist definition of the term, *learning* had taken place.

Let's analyze the three steps in Pavlov's experiment in much the same way that Pavlov did:

Figure 3–1
A classical conditioning
analysis of Pavlov's dog

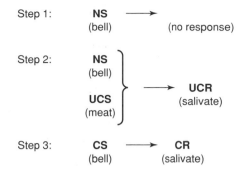

1. A **neutral stimulus** (**NS**) is a stimulus to which the organism does not respond. In the case of Pavlov's dog, the bell was originally a neutral stimulus that did not elicit a salivation response.
2. The neutral stimulus is presented just before another stimulus, one that *does* lead to a response. This second stimulus is called an **unconditioned stimulus** (**UCS**), and the response to it is called an **unconditioned response** (**UCR**), because the organism responds to the stimulus unconditionally, without having learned to do so. (Pavlov's original term was actually uncondition*al*, but the mistranslation to condition*ed* remains in most classical conditioning literature.) For Pavlov's dog, meat powder was an unconditioned stimulus to which it responded with the unconditioned response of salivation.
3. After being paired with an unconditioned stimulus, the previously neutral stimulus now elicits a response, so it is no longer "neutral." The NS has become a **conditioned stimulus** (**CS**) to which the organism has learned a **conditioned response** (**CR**). In Pavlov's experiment, the bell, after being paired with the meat (the unconditioned stimulus) became a conditioned stimulus that led to the conditioned response of salivation. The diagram in Figure 3–1 shows graphically what happened from a classical conditioning perspective.

Pavlov's studies of classical conditioning continued long after this initial experiment, and many of his findings have been replicated with other responses and in other species, including humans. Let's take a closer look at the process of classical conditioning and some examples of its occurrence in human learning.

THE CLASSICAL CONDITIONING MODEL

Classical conditioning has been demonstrated in many species, not only in dogs and laboratory rats, but also in newborn human infants (Lipsitt & Kaye, 1964;

Reese & Lipsitt, 1970), unborn human fetuses (Macfarlane, 1978), and even organisms as simple as a flatworm (Thompson & McConnell, 1955). The applicability of classical conditioning clearly extends widely across the animal kingdom.

As Pavlov's experiments showed, classical conditioning occurs when two stimuli occur at approximately the same time. One of these stimuli is an unconditioned stimulus: It has previously been shown to elicit an unconditioned response. The second stimulus, through its association with the unconditioned stimulus, begins to elicit a response as well: It becomes a conditioned stimulus that brings about a conditioned response.

Classical conditioning is most likely to occur when the conditioned stimulus is presented just *before* (perhaps by half a second) the unconditioned stimulus. For this reason, some psychologists describe classical conditioning as a form of **signal learning**. By being presented first, the conditioned stimulus serves as a signal that the unconditioned stimulus is coming, much as Pavlov's dog might have learned that the sound of a bell indicated that yummy meat powder was on its way.

Classical conditioning usually involves the learning of *involuntary* responses, responses over which one has no control. When we say that a stimulus **elicits** a response, we mean that the stimulus brings about a response automatically, without the individual having much control over the occurrence of that response. In most cases, the conditioned response is similar to the unconditioned response (see Klein, 1987, or Hergenhahn, 1988, for exceptions), with the two responses differing primarily in terms of which stimulus elicits the response and sometimes in terms of the strength of the response.

The conditioned stimulus may serve as a signal that the unconditioned stimulus is coming.

CLASSICAL CONDITIONING IN HUMAN LEARNING

We frequently use classical conditioning theory to help us understand how people learn a variety of involuntary responses. For example, many people develop aversions to particular foods as a result of associating those foods with an upset stomach (Garb & Stunkard, 1974; Logue, 1979). To illustrate, after associating the taste of creamy cucumber salad dressing (CS) with the nausea I experienced during pregnancy (UCS), I developed an aversion (CR) to cucumber dressing that lasted for several years.

For many people, darkness is a conditioned stimulus for going to sleep, perhaps because it has frequently been associated with fatigue. I once became uncomfortably aware of how conditioned I was when I attended my daughter's "astronomy night" at school. We parents were ushered into a classroom and asked to sit down. Then the lights were turned off, and we watched a half-hour filmstrip describing a NASA space museum. Although I am usually quite alert during early evening hours, I found myself growing increasingly drowsy, and probably only my upright position in an uncomfortable metal chair kept me from losing consciousness altogether. In that situation, the darkness elicited a go-to-sleep response, and no stimuli (certainly not the filmstrip) were eliciting a stay-awake response.

Classical conditioning is also a useful model for explaining some of the fears and phobias that people develop. For example, my bee phobia can probably be explained by the fact that bees (CS) were previously associated with a sting (UCS), such that I became increasingly fearful (CR) of the nasty insects. In a similar way, people who are bitten by a particular breed of dog sometimes become afraid of that breed, or even of all dogs.

Probably the best known example of a classically conditioned fear of an animal is the case of "Little Albert," an infant who learned to fear white rats through procedures used by John Watson and Rosalie Rayner (1920). Albert was an even-tempered, 11-month-old child who rarely cried or displayed fearful reactions. One day, Albert was shown a white rat. As he reached out and touched the rat, a large steel bar behind him was struck, producing a loud, unpleasant noise. Albert jumped, obviously very upset by the startling noise. Nevertheless, he reached forward to touch the rat with his other hand, but the steel bar was struck once again. After five more pairings of the rat (CS) and the loud noise (UCS), Albert was truly rat-phobic: Whenever he saw the rat he cried hysterically and crawled away as quickly as his hands and knees would allow. Watson and Rayner reported that Albert responded in a similarly fearful manner to a rabbit, a dog, a sealskin coat, cotton wool, and a Santa Claus mask with a fuzzy beard, although none of these had ever been paired with the startling noise. (Watson and Rayner never "undid" their conditioning of poor Albert. Fortunately, the ethical standards of the American Psychological Association would now prohibit such negligence.)

When I was growing up, my mother had an effective means of keeping my behavior within reasonable limits. Whenever I began to step out of bounds, she simply gave me "The Look," a scowl accompanied by a wrinkled brow and sinister, piercing eyes. I suspect that this facial expression must have been paired with physical punishment sometime in my early childhood years, because The Look alone was eventually sufficient to send me to my bedroom in quick retreat. A threat of punishment such as The Look can be anxiety-arousing enough to control a child's behavior without one's actually having to resort to the punishment threatened. However, a threat can only become a conditioned stimulus if it has in fact been associated with punishment at one time or another, with that punishment following the threat in close proximity (Klein, 1987).

The use of punishment itself is a controversial procedure because stimuli frequently associated with it—the home or school environment, or a child's parent or teacher—can become a conditioned stimulus also leading to fear and anxiety responses. We will examine punishment in more detail in Chapter 6 and will then look at guidelines for reducing the chances that this classically conditioned side effect will develop.

Fear of failure is still another example of a response that may be classically conditioned. In some cases, people who are unusually afraid of failing may have previously associated failure with unpleasant circumstances, perhaps painful punishment from an angry parent or ridicule by insensitive classmates. Yet occasional failure is a natural consequence of attempting new tasks, whether in school, at home, or elsewhere. Teachers and parents must be careful that failure does not become such a strong conditioned stimulus for children that they resist engaging in new activities and attempting challenging but possibly risky problems.

These examples of classical conditioning at work will, I hope, help you recognize a classically conditioned response when you see one. We will now turn to several phenomena associated with classical conditioning.

BASIC CONCEPTS IN CLASSICAL CONDITIONING

Pavlov described a number of phenomena characteristic of classical conditioning. Here we will examine several of them: extinction, spontaneous recovery, stimulus generalization, stimulus discrimination, higher-order conditioning, and sensory preconditioning.

Extinction

Let's return for a moment to Pavlov's dog. Remember that the dog learned to salivate at the sound of a bell alone after that bell had rung on several occasions in conjunction with meat powder. But what would happen if the bell continued to ring over and over without the meat powder's ever again being presented along with it? Pavlov discovered that repeated presentations of the conditioned stimulus alone led to successively weaker and weaker conditioned responses. Eventually, the dog no longer salivated at the sound of the bell; in other words, the conditioned response disappeared.

The disappearance of a conditioned response when a conditioned stimulus is repeatedly presented without the unconditioned stimulus is a phenomenon

Pavlov called **extinction**. For example, The Look from my mother no longer has the effect it used to: Whatever punishment was once associated with it has long since disappeared (besides, now I'm bigger than she is).

Sometimes conditioned responses will disappear, and sometimes they will not. The unpredictability of extinction is a source of frustration to anyone working with people who have acquired inappropriate, yet involuntary, conditioned responses. Later in the chapter, we will discuss an alternative procedure for situations in which inappropriate responses *don't* become extinct.

Spontaneous Recovery

Even though Pavlov quickly extinguished his dog's conditioned salivation response by repeatedly presenting the bell in the absence of meat powder, when he entered his laboratory the following day he discovered that the bell once again elicited salivation in the dog, almost as if extinction had never taken place. This reappearance of the salivation response after it had previously been extinguished is something Pavlov called **spontaneous recovery**.

In more general terms, spontaneous recovery is a recurrence of a conditioned response when a period of extinction is followed by a rest period. For example, if I am near lots of bees for a period of time, I eventually settle down and regain my composure. However, my first response on a later encounter with a bee is to fly off the handle once again.

Pavlov found that a conditioned response appearing in spontaneous recovery is typically weaker than the original conditioned response and disappears more quickly. In situations in which a CR spontaneously recovers several times, each time after a period of rest has elapsed, each response is weaker than the one before it and diminishes more rapidly.

Stimulus Generalization

You may recall that Little Albert, after being conditioned to fear a white rat, also became afraid of a rabbit, a dog, a fur coat, cotton wool, and a fuzzy-bearded Santa Claus mask. When individuals respond to other stimuli in the same way that they respond to conditioned stimuli, **stimulus generalization** is occurring. The more similar a stimulus is to the conditioned stimulus, the greater the probability of stimulus generalization. Albert exhibited fear of all objects that were white and fuzzy like the rat, but he was not afraid of his nonwhite, nonfuzzy toy blocks. In a similar way, a child who fears an abusive father may generalize that fear to other men, but not to women.

In some cases, generalization of conditioned fear responses may actually increase over time—that is, as time goes on, an individual becomes fearful of an increasing number of objects (McAllister & McAllister, 1965). Thus, conditioned responses that do not quickly decrease may actually become more frequent because they are being elicited by a greater number of stimuli.

Stimulus Discrimination

Pavlov observed that when he conditioned a dog to salivate in response to a high-pitched tone, the dog would generalize that conditioned response to a low-pitched tone. To teach the dog the difference between the two tones, Pavlov repeatedly presented the high tone in conjunction with meat powder and presented the low tone without meat. After several such presentations of the two tones, the dog eventually learned to salivate only to the high tone. In Pavlov's terminology, *differentiation* between the two tones had taken place. Psychologists today more frequently use the term **stimulus discrimination** for this phenomenon.

Stimulus discrimination occurs when one stimulus (the CS+) is presented in conjunction with an unconditioned stimulus, and another stimulus (the CS-) is presented without that UCS. The individual learns a conditioned response to the CS+ but does not generalize the response to the CS-. For example, if a child who is abused by her father simultaneously has positive interactions with other adult men, she is not as likely to generalize her fear of her father to those other individuals.

Higher-Order Conditioning

Pavlov also discovered a phenomenon known as **second-order conditioning**, or more generally as **higher-order conditioning.** When a dog had been conditioned to salivate at the sound of a bell, and the bell was later presented in conjunction with a neutral stimulus such as a flash of light, that neutral stimulus would also elicit a salivation response, even though it had never been directly associated with meat. In other words, the light flash became a conditioned stimulus through its pairing, not with the unconditioned stimulus, but with another conditioned stimulus.

Higher-order conditioning works like this. First, a neutral stimulus (NS_1) becomes a conditioned stimulus (CS_1) by being paired with an unconditioned stimulus (UCS) and therefore elicits a conditioned response (CR). Next, a second neutral stimulus (NS_2) is paired with CS_1, and then independently elicits a similar conditioned response—that second stimulus has also become a conditioned stimulus (CS_2).

A diagram of higher-order conditioning appears in Figure 3–2. Steps one and two depict the original conditioning; steps three and four depict higher-order conditioning, in which a second neutral stimulus becomes a CS_2 by virtue of its being paired with the CS_1.

Higher-order conditioning is a possible explanation for some of the fears that students exhibit in the classroom (e.g., Klein, 1987). Let's say, first of all, that failure has previously been associated with painful physical punishment. Then another situation—perhaps a test, an oral presentation in front of classmates, or even school itself—becomes associated with failure. The painful punishment is the UCS. Failure, originally a NS_1, becomes a CS_1 after its association with the

Figure 3–2
An example of higher-
order conditioning

Step 1: NS$_1$ (bell)
         UCS (meat) } ⟶ UCR (salivate)

Step 2: CS$_1$ (bell) ⟶ CR (salivate)

Step 3: NS$_2$ (light)
         CS$_1$ (bell) } ⟶ CR (salivate)

Step 4: CS$_2$ (light) ⟶ CR (salivate)

UCS. Some other aspect of school (e.g., a test), while first a NS$_2$, becomes an additional conditioned stimulus (CS$_2$) through its association with CS$_1$. In this way, a student may develop test anxiety, fear of public speaking, or even school phobia—fear of school itself.

Sensory Preconditioning

Higher-order conditioning is one way an individual can develop a conditioned response to a stimulus that has never been directly paired with an unconditioned stimulus. **Sensory preconditioning** is very similar to higher-order conditioning, except that the steps occur in a different order. Let me first illustrate the process by once again conditioning Pavlov's poor, overworked dog. Suppose that we first present the sound of a bell and a flash of light simultaneously. Then we pair the bell with meat powder. Not only does the dog salivate at the sound of a bell, we discover that it also salivates at the flash of light!

In more general terms, sensory preconditioning occurs like this. First, two neutral stimuli (NS$_1$ and NS$_2$) are presented simultaneously. Then one of these neutral stimuli (NS$_1$) is associated with an unconditioned stimulus (UCS), thus becoming a conditioned stimulus (CS$_1$) and eliciting a conditioned response (CR). In cases of sensory preconditioning, the second neutral stimulus (NS$_2$) *also* elicits the conditioned response (i.e., NS$_2$ has become CS$_2$) by virtue of its prior association with CS$_1$.

Klein (1987) has suggested that sensory preconditioning may be an alternative explanation for some cases of test anxiety. School (NS$_1$) is first associated with tests (NS$_2$). If school is later associated with some traumatic event (UCS), then not only will school become a conditioned stimulus (CS$_1$) eliciting anxiety

Figure 3–3
An example of sensory preconditioning

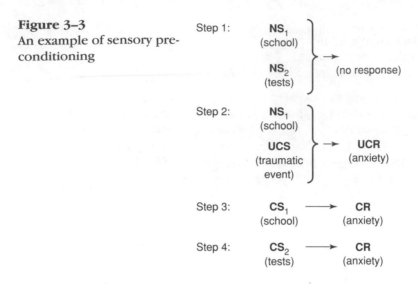

(CR), but tests may become a conditioned stimulus (CS₂) as well. A diagram of how test anxiety might develop through sensory preconditioning is presented in Figure 3–3.

CONTEMPORARY PERSPECTIVES ON CLASSICAL CONDITIONING

Numerous psychologists have followed up on Pavlov's original studies. Their research has led to several refinements in our understanding of when and how classical conditioning occurs.

• *Contingency between the conditioned and unconditioned stimuli is probably more important than their contiguity.* Pavlov proposed that classical conditioning occurs when the unconditioned stimulus and the would-be conditioned stimulus are presented at approximately the same time; in other words, there must be *contiguity* between the two stimuli. In fact, as we noted earlier, classical conditioning is most likely to occur when the conditioned stimulus is presented just before the unconditioned stimulus. Conditioning is less likely to occur when the CS and UCS are presented at *exactly* the same time, and it rarely occurs when the CS is presented *after* the UCS (e.g., Miller & Barnet, 1993). Furthermore, people sometimes develop an aversion to certain foods (remember my aversion to creamy cucumber dressing!) when the delay between the conditioned stimulus (food) and the unconditioned stimulus (nausea) is as much as 24 hours (Logue, 1979). As you can see, contiguity between the two stimuli is an overly simplistic explanation of how a conditioned response is acquired.

More recent theorists (e.g., Granger & Schlimmer, 1986; Rachlin, 1991; Rescorla, 1967, 1988) have proposed that *contingency* is the essential condition:

The potential conditioned stimulus must occur *only* when the unconditioned stimulus is about to follow. When two stimuli that are usually presented separately occur together a few times by coincidence, classical conditioning is unlikely to occur.

•*Characteristics of the would-be conditioned stimulus affect the degree to which conditioning occurs.* The more noticeable (*salient*) a neutral stimulus is—in other words, the extent to which it is bright, loud, or otherwise intense—the more likely it is to become a conditioned stimulus when it is presented in conjunction with an unconditioned stimulus (Rachlin, 1991; Schwartz & Reisberg, 1991). Furthermore, some stimuli are especially likely to become associated with certain unconditioned stimuli; for example, food is more likely to become a conditioned stimulus associated with nausea (a UCS) than, say, a light or the sound of a tuning fork. In other words, associations between certain stimuli are more likely to be made than are associations between others—a phenomenon known as **associative bias** (e.g., Garcia & Koelling, 1966; Schwartz & Reisberg, 1991).

•*Classical conditioning involves cognition as well as responding.* Some contemporary theorists now believe that classical conditioning involves the formation of associations, not between two stimuli, but between internal *mental representations* of those stimuli (Furedy & Riley, 1987; Miller & Barnet, 1993; Rachlin, 1991; Rescorla, 1988; Schwartz & Reisberg, 1991; Wagner, 1976, 1978, 1979, 1981). Furthermore, the conditioned stimulus may enable an organism to *predict* (in a decidedly mental fashion) that the unconditioned stimulus is coming (Martin & Levey, 1987; Rescorla, 1967, 1988; Rescorla & Wagner, 1972; Schwartz & Reisberg, 1991; Wagner & Rescorla, 1972). As you can see, then, some behaviorists are now beginning to talk about the thinking processes that they so deliberately steered clear of in earlier years.

CHANGING INAPPROPRIATE CONDITIONED RESPONSES

Conditioned responses are often not easily eliminated because they are involuntary: People have little or no control over them. Yet some classically conditioned responses (e.g., some irrational fears) may be detrimental to an individual's functioning. How can we get rid of counterproductive conditioned responses? Extinction and counterconditioning are two possible methods.

Extinction

One obvious way to eliminate a conditioned response might be through the process of extinction. If the conditioned stimulus is presented in the absence of the unconditioned stimulus frequently enough, the conditioned response should disappear. Often this is exactly what happens.

Unfortunately, though, extinction is notoriously unpredictable as a means of eliminating conditioned responses: It simply doesn't always work. There are at least three reasons why:

1. The speed at which extinction occurs is unpredictable. If, during the conditioning process, the conditioned stimulus was sometimes presented in conjunction with the unconditioned stimulus but sometimes alone (i.e., the stimulus pairings were inconsistent), extinction is likely to be particularly slow (Humphreys, 1939).

2. People tend to avoid a stimulus they have learned to fear, thus reducing the chances of encountering the conditioned stimulus in the absence of the unconditioned stimulus. For example, a student who has learned to fear mathematics after a history of failing the subject typically avoids math as much as possible, thus minimizing any chance of associating math with success.

3. Even when a response has been extinguished, it may reappear through spontaneous recovery. You can never be totally sure when a response will spontaneously recover and when it will not.

Counterconditioning

In an alternative procedure to extinction, called **counterconditioning**, one conditioned response is replaced with a new, more appropriate conditioned response. Counterconditioning tends to be more effective than extinction in eliminating undesirable conditioned responses; it also minimizes the chances that those responses will recur through spontaneous recovery.

Mary Cover Jones' classic work with "Little Peter" (Jones, 1924) provides an excellent example of counterconditioning. Peter was a two-year old boy who had somehow learned to be afraid of rabbits. To rid him of his fear, Jones placed Peter in a high chair and gave him some candy. As he ate, she brought the rabbit into the far side of the same room. Under different circumstances the rabbit might have elicited anxiety; however, the pleasure Peter felt as he ate the candy was a stronger response and essentially overpowered any anxiety Peter might have felt about the rabbit's presence. Jones repeated the same procedure every day over a two-month period, each time sitting Peter in a high chair with candy and bringing the rabbit slightly closer than she had the time before, and Peter's anxiety about rabbits eventually disappeared.

In general, counterconditioning involves these components:

1. A new response is chosen that is **incompatible** with the existing conditioned response. Two responses are incompatible with each other when they cannot be performed at the same time. Because classically conditioned responses are often emotional in nature, an incompatible response is often some sort of opposite emotional reaction. For example,

CHAPTER 3 Classical Conditioning

in the case of Little Peter, happiness was used as an incompatible response for fear. Since fear and anxiety create bodily tension, any response involving relaxation would be incompatible.

2. A stimulus that elicits the incompatible response must be identified; for example, candy elicited a "happy" response for Peter. If we are seeking to develop a happy response in a student for a stimulus that has previously elicited displeasure, we need to find a stimulus that already elicits pleasure—perhaps a friend, a party, or a favorite food. If we want someone to learn a relaxation response, we might ask that person to imagine lying in a cool, fragrant meadow or on a lawn chair by a pool.

3. The stimulus that elicits the new response is presented to the individual, and the conditioned stimulus eliciting the undesirable conditioned response is *gradually* introduced into the situation. In treating Peter's fear of rabbits, Jones initially presented the rabbit at some distance from Peter, only gradually bringing it closer and closer in successive sessions. The trick in counterconditioning is to ensure that the stimulus eliciting the positive response is always *stronger* than the stimulus eliciting the negative response; otherwise, the negative response might prevail.

Counterconditioning provides a means for decreasing or eliminating many conditioned anxiety responses. For example, **systematic desensitization** (e.g., Wolpe, 1958, 1969), a therapeutic technique designed to replace anxiety with a relaxation response, is now widely used as a means of treating such difficulties as test anxiety and fear of public speaking (e.g., Morris, Kratochwill, & Aldridge, 1988; Silverman & Kearney, 1991). I should point out, however, that treating test anxiety alone, without remediating possible academic sources of a student's poor test performance as well, may reduce test anxiety without any concurrent improvement in test scores (Tryon, 1980).

A technique I recommend to many graduate students who dread their required statistics course because of mathematics anxiety is that they find a math textbook that begins well below their own skill level—at the level of basic number facts, if necessary—so that the problems are not anxiety-arousing. As they work through the text, the students begin to associate mathematics with success rather than failure. Programmed instruction (described in Chapter 5) is another technique that can be useful in reducing anxiety about a given subject matter, because it allows a student to progress through the material in small, easy steps.

GENERAL EDUCATIONAL IMPLICATIONS OF CLASSICAL CONDITIONING

The durability and generalizability of some classically conditioned responses point to the need for a positive classroom climate for our students. When school-work, a teacher, or even the school environment itself is associated with punishment, humiliation, failure, or frustration, school and its curriculum can become sources of excessive anxiety.

Some classroom activities—for example, tests, oral presentations, and difficult subject matter—are particularly likely to be associated with unpleasant circumstances such as failure or embarrassment, and many students may soon become anxious when involved in them. Teachers should therefore take special precautions when asking students to engage in any such "risky" activities. For example, I suspect that many students have early unpleasant experiences in public speaking because they receive little if any instruction about how to prepare and deliver an effective oral presentation. Students who are asked to speak in front of a group should be given specific suggestions regarding what material to present and how to present it in such a way that classmates will react positively rather than derisively.

Mathematics is a difficult, anxiety-arousing subject for many students. I firmly believe that mathematics anxiety is so prevalent because most schools teach too much, too fast, and too soon, so that students quickly begin to associate mathematics with frustration and failure. Part of the problem may lie in the tendency to teach mathematical concepts before children are cognitively ready to deal with them. According to the developmentalist Jean Piaget, children do not acquire certain capabilities for mathematical reasoning until age 11 or 12 at the earliest (see Chapter 8 for more details). One of these late acquisitions is the ability to understand the idea of *proportion*, the concept underlying fractions and decimals. Yet schools typically introduce fractions and decimals sometime around fourth grade, when students are only 9 or 10 years of age.

Educators have often argued that school should be a place where a student encounters more success than failure, and classical conditioning provides a justification for their argument. This is not to say that students should never encounter failure; people need feedback about what they are doing wrong as well as what they are doing right. However, when students experience failure too frequently, either in their schoolwork or in their social relationships, school may quickly become a conditioned stimulus that leads to counterproductive conditioned responses such as fear and anxiety. These responses, once conditioned, may be very resistant to extinction and may interfere with a student's ability to learn effectively for years to come.

SUMMARY

Through a systematic study of salivation responses in dogs, Ivan Pavlov developed his theory of classical conditioning, an explanation of how certain involuntary responses develop. Classical conditioning occurs when two stimuli are presented at approximately the same time. One is an unconditioned stimulus that has previously elicited an unconditioned response. The second stimulus, through its association with the unconditioned stimulus, begins to elicit a response as well: It becomes a conditioned stimulus that brings about a conditioned response. However, when the conditioned stimulus is presented numerous times in the absence of the unconditioned stimulus, the conditioned response decreases and may eventually disappear (extinction), although it may reappear after a period of rest (spontaneous recovery).

Once an organism has learned to make a conditioned response in the presence of a particular conditioned stimulus, it may respond in the same way to a similar stimulus (stimulus generalization) unless that stimulus has repeatedly been experienced in the absence of the unconditioned stimulus (stimulus discrimination). Classically conditioned associations can build on one another through the processes of higher-order conditioning and sensory preconditioning; in both cases, a stimulus may become a conditioned stimulus (eliciting a conditioned response), not directly by its association with the unconditioned stimulus, but indirectly by its association with a stimulus that either has been or will be experienced in conjunction with that UCS.

Contemporary psychologists propose that a contingent relationship between conditioned and unconditioned stimuli is more critical than a contiguous one. Many of them speculate that the classical conditioning phenomenon involves the formation of associations between internal, mental representations of stimuli rather than associations between the stimuli themselves.

The classical conditioning paradigm is frequently used to explain human fears such as test anxiety, fear of failure, and school phobia. Undesirable conditioned responses can sometimes be eliminated by either extinction or counterconditioning.

CHAPTER 4

Operant Conditioning

D ifferent individuals work for different rewards. When my son Alex needs money to buy something he wants desperately, he will engage in behaviors he never does otherwise—for example, scrubbing the bathtub or sweeping up rotten crabapples that have fallen on the driveway. My daughter Tina can rarely be enticed into doing household chores with financial incentives, but she will make her bed and put away her clothes willingly if doing so enables her to have a friend spend the night.

The idea of rewarding behavior (learning theorists more frequently use the term *reinforcement*) provides the foundation for B. F. Skinner's principles of **operant conditioning** (sometimes called **instrumental conditioning**). In this chapter, we will study operant conditioning in depth, contrasting it with classical conditioning and then examining the concepts of free operant level, terminal behavior, extinction, superstitious behavior, and shaping. We will look at the many forms that reinforcement can take and also at the effects of reinforcing responses on either a continuous or intermittent basis. Reinforcers are stimuli that follow responses, but, as we consider stimulus control, we will find that stimuli that come *before* responses can influence behavior as well. Toward the end of the chapter, we will discover several ways in which contemporary views of operant conditioning differ somewhat from Skinner's original notions. Finally, we will apply operant conditioning to an educational setting as we identify several ways of reducing undesirable behaviors and learn what Skinner had to say about operant conditioning in the classroom.

THE OPERANT CONDITIONING MODEL

We can paraphrase Skinner's basic principle of operant conditioning (Skinner, 1938) as follows: *A response that is followed by a reinforcer is strengthened and is therefore more likely to occur again.* In other words, responses that are reinforced tend to increase in frequency. Because a response increase is a change in behavior, then, from a behaviorist viewpoint, reinforcement brings about learning. For example, Skinner found that rats will learn to press metal bars, and pigeons will peck at round plastic disks, to get pellets of food. Likewise, my daughter Tina will increase her housekeeping behavior if it allows her to see a friend, and my son Alex will do just about anything if the price is right.

Defining Reinforcers and Reinforcement

Skinner intentionally used the term *reinforcer* instead of *reward* to describe a consequence that increases the frequency of a behavior. The word *reward* implies that the stimulus following a behavior is somehow both pleasant and desirable, an implication Skinner tried to avoid for two reasons. First of all, some individuals will work for what others see as unpleasant consequences; for example, my daughter occasionally does something she knows will irritate me because she enjoys watching me blow my stack. Secondly, "pleasantness" and "desirability" are subjective judgments, and behaviorists such as Skinner prefer that psychological principles be restricted to the domain of objectively observable events. A reinforcer can be defined without any allusion to either pleasantness or desirability, in this way:

> A ***reinforcer*** *is a stimulus that increases the frequency of a response it follows. (The act of following a response with a reinforcer is called **reinforcement**.)*

Notice how I have just defined a reinforcer totally in terms of observable phenomena, without reliance on any subjective judgment.

Now that I have given you definitions of both operant conditioning and a reinforcer, I need to point out a major problem with my definitions: Taken together, they constitute circular reasoning. I have said that operant conditioning is an increase in a behavior when it is followed by a reinforcer, but I cannot seem to define a reinforcer in any other way except to say that it increases behavior. I am therefore using reinforcement to explain a behavior increase, and a behavior increase to explain reinforcement! Fortunately, a paper by Meehl (1950) has enabled learning theorists to get out of this circular mess by pointing out the **transituational generality** of a reinforcer: The same reinforcer will increase many different behaviors in many different situations.

Three Important Conditions for Operant Conditioning

Three important conditions are necessary for operant conditioning to take place.

•*The reinforcer must follow the response.* "Reinforcers" that precede a response rarely have an effect on that response. For example, about 10 years ago, a couple of instructors at my university were concerned that grades, because they were "threatening," interfered with student learning; therefore they announced on the first day of class that everyone would receive an A for the course. Many students never attended class after that first day, so there was little learning for any grade to interfere with. Reinforcers must always, always *follow* the desired behavior.

• *The reinforcer must follow immediately*. A reinforcer tends to reinforce the response that has occurred just before it. Thus, reinforcement is less effective when its presentation is delayed: In the meantime, an organism may have made one or more responses that are reinforced instead. Once, when I was teaching a pigeon named Ethel to peck a lighted plastic disk, I made a serious mistake: I waited too long after she had pecked the disk before reinforcing her, and in the meantime she had begun to turn around. After eating her food pellet, Ethel began to spin frantically in counterclockwise circles, and it was several minutes before I was able to get her back to the pecking response I had in mind for her.

Our schools are notorious for delayed reinforcement. How many times have you completed an exam or turned in a written assignment, only to receive your grade days or even weeks later? Immediate reinforcers are typically more effective than delayed reinforcers in classroom situations (Kulik & Kulik, 1988). Furthermore, immediate reinforcers are probably the *only* effective reinforcers for animals and young children.

• *The reinforcer must be contingent on the response*. A reinforcer should never be presented unless the desired response has occurred. For example, teachers often specify certain conditions that children must meet before going on a field trip: They must bring their permission slips, they must complete their assignments, and so on. When these teachers feel badly for children who have not met the stated conditions and allow them to go on the field trip anyway, the reinforcement is not contingent on the response, and the children are not learning acceptable behavior. If anything, they are learning they can break rules!

What Behaviors Can Be Reinforced?

Virtually any behavior—academic, social, psychomotor—can be learned or modified through operant conditioning. As a teacher, I keep reminding myself of what student behaviors I want to increase and try to follow those behaviors with positive consequences. For example, when typically quiet students raise their hands to answer a question or make a comment, I call on them and give them whatever positive feedback I can. I also try to make my classes lively, interesting, and humorous, as well as informative, to reinforce students' attendance in the first place.

Unfortunately, undesirable behaviors can be reinforced just as easily as desirable ones. Aggression and criminal activity often lead to successful outcomes: Crime usually *does* pay. Disruptive behavior in class may get the teacher's attention in a way that no other behavior can. Getting "sick" allows the school-phobic child to stay home from school. Students sometimes appear at my office at the end of the semester pleading for a higher grade than their class performance has warranted, or else for the chance of completing an extra-credit project. I almost invariably turn them down, for a simple reason: I want good grades to be contingent on good study habits throughout the semester, not on begging behavior at my office door. Teachers must be extremely careful about what they reinforce and what they do not.

OPERANT CONDITIONING AND CLASSICAL CONDITIONING CONTRASTED

Skinner suggested that there are really two different kinds of learning: classical conditioning (he used the term *respondent conditioning*) and operant conditioning. The two forms of conditioning are different in several major respects; these differences are summarized in Figure 4–1.

Classical conditioning results from the pairing of two stimuli, the UCS and the CS. The learned response is a direct and immediate reaction to the stimulus that precedes it; that is, the conditioned stimulus brings about, or **elicits**, the conditioned response. The conditioned response is automatic and involuntary, such that the organism has virtually no control over what it is doing. Skinner's term *respondent* reflects the fact that the organism's behavior is an involuntary *response* to a stimulus.

Operant conditioning, on the other hand, results when a response is followed by a reinforcing stimulus. The response is a voluntary one **emitted** by the organism, with the organism having complete control over whether the response occurs. Skinner's term **operant** reflects the fact that the organism voluntarily *operates* on, and thereby has some effect on, the environment. Because operant conditioning reflects an R→S_{Rf} model, where S_{Rf} symbolizes a reinforcing stimulus, Skinner was not really an S-R psychologist at all—he was actually an R-S psychologist.

Some theorists have questioned whether classical and operant conditioning really reflect different learning processes at all (e.g., see Bower & Hilgard, 1981). In most situations, however, the traditional classical and operant conditioning models will help us understand many instances of learning, so I will continue to treat them as two distinct forms of learning.

Figure 4–1
Differences between classical and operant conditioning

	Classical Conditioning	Operant Conditioning
Occurs when:	Two stimuli (UCS and CS) are paired	Response (R) is followed by a reinforcing stimulus (S_{Rf})
Nature of response:	Involuntary: elicited by a stimulus	Voluntary: emitted by the organism
Model:	CS → CR	R → S_{Rf}

BASIC CONCEPTS IN OPERANT CONDITIONING

A number of concepts are related to operant conditioning, including free operant level, terminal behavior, extinction, superstitious behavior, and shaping. Let's look at each of these.

Free Operant Level

An **operant** is a voluntary response that has a particular effect on the environment. The **free operant level** is the frequency of an operant in the absence of reinforcement—in other words, the prereinforcement, or **baseline**, frequency of the response. Students will vary in their free operant levels for different responses. For some students, getting-out-of-seat behavior will be quite frequent, while for others it will be rare. Similarly, some students will read frequently without being asked to do so, while others will seldom read on their own initiative.

Terminal Behavior

The **terminal behavior** is the form and frequency of the desired response at the end of a reinforcement program. Let's say, for example, that a second-grade boy rarely stays in his seat for more than five minutes at a time, and when he does sit down, he slouches so low in the chair that his head is barely level with the desk. A teacher who plans to alter this child's classroom behavior through reinforcement may specify the terminal behavior as sitting up straight for a 10-minute period.

When using reinforcement to change behavior, it is essential that we describe the terminal behavior ahead of time in concrete terms. Specifying the exact form of the desired behavior (e.g., sitting up straight) and the frequency or duration of the behavior (e.g., 10 minutes at a stretch) enables us to determine objectively whether our reinforcement program has been effective.

Extinction

In classical conditioning, when the CS is repeatedly presented in the absence of the UCS, the CR decreases and eventually disappears—that is, the response extinguishes. In operant conditioning, **extinction** occurs when a response is no longer followed by a reinforcer. A nonreinforced response will decrease—although sometimes a brief increase in the behavior will first be observed—and eventually return to its baseline rate. For example, a class clown who finds that no one laughs at her jokes anymore is likely to decrease her joke telling. A student who is never called on when he raises his hand may stop trying to participate in class discussions. A student who continues to fail exams despite hours of studying for them may eventually stop studying.

Although we want to extinguish undesirable behaviors such as disruptive joke telling, we need to take precautions that *desirable* behaviors are reinforced frequently enough that they *don't* extinguish. For example, a student whose studying produces no reinforcement at exam time needs assistance of some kind. If many other students find the same exams too difficult to pass, something may be wrong with those exams or with classroom instruction. If only one student is failing, perhaps that student needs help in developing more appropriate study techniques, more individualized instruction, or placement in a class better matched to his or her current ability level.

Superstitious Behavior

What happens when reinforcement is random and not contingent on any particular behavior? Skinner once left eight pigeons in their cages overnight with the food tray mechanism adjusted to present reinforcement at regular intervals, regardless of what responses were occurring at the time. By morning, six of the pigeons were acting bizarrely: For example, one repeatedly thrust its head into an upper corner of the cage, and two others were swinging their heads and bodies in rhythmic pendulum movements (Skinner, 1948a).

Reinforcement administered randomly will tend to reinforce whatever response occurred immediately beforehand, and an organism will increase that response, thus displaying what Skinner called **superstitious behavior**. A nonbehaviorist way of describing the learning of a superstitious behavior is that the organism thinks that the response and reinforcement are related when in fact they are not. For example, a student may have a "lucky sweater" to wear on exam days, or a football player may, before every game, perform a ritual totally unrelated to successful football.

Superstitious behavior in the classroom can occur either when reinforcement is not contingent on behavior or when students do not accurately see which of their many responses are responsible for bringing about reinforcement. It behooves teachers to ensure that classroom reinforcers such as praise, attention, and grades *are* contingent on desired behaviors, and that response-reinforcement contingencies are clearly specified.

Shaping

For the frequency of a response to be increased, that response must be reinforced. And for it to be reinforced, it must be emitted. But sometimes the free operant level of a response is so low that it rarely, if ever, occurs. What do we do then?

To handle such a situation, Skinner introduced a method called **shaping**, a technique also known as **successive approximations**. Shaping is a means of teaching a behavior when the free operant level for that behavior is very low or when the desired terminal behavior is different in form from any responses the organism exhibits.

To shape a particular behavior, we begin by reinforcing the first response that in any way approximates the desired behavior and continue reinforcing that response until the organism is emitting it fairly frequently. At that point we reinforce only those responses that more closely resemble the desired behavior, then those that resemble it more closely still, until eventually only the desired behavior itself is being reinforced. In other words, shaping is a process of reinforcing successively closer and closer approximations to the terminal behavior until the terminal behavior is exhibited.

To illustrate, when I taught my pigeon Ethel to peck a lighted disk in her Skinner box, I began by reinforcing her every time she faced the wall on which the disk was located. Once this response was occurring frequently, I began to reinforce her only when her beak was near the wall, then only when her beak touched the wall, then only when she pecked within a two-inch radius of the disk, and so on. Within an hour, I had Ethel happily pecking the lighted disk and eating the food pellets that followed each correct peck.

Legend has it that a group of students once shaped a professor of mine a few days after he had given a lecture on shaping. Every time the professor stood on the side of the classroom near the door, the students all appeared interested in what he was saying, sitting forward in their seats and taking notes feverishly. Every time he walked away from the door, they acted bored, slouching back in their seats and looking anxiously at their watches. As the class went on, they reinforced him only as he moved closer and closer to the door until, by the end of class, he was lecturing from the hallway!

In much the same way, we gradually shape such behaviors as handwriting, sedentary behavior, and mathematical problem solving. For example, kindergarten students are taught to print their letters on wide-lined paper, with the bottoms of the letters resting on one line and the tops touching the line above. As children progress through the primary grades, the spaces between the lines become smaller, and teachers are more particular about how well the letters are written. Gradually children begin to write consistently sized and carefully shaped letters with the benefit of only a lower line, and eventually with no line at all. Teachers also shape the sedentary behavior of their students: As students grow older, teachers expect them to sit quietly in their seats for longer and longer periods. We can think of mathematics as a shaped behavior, too: Teachers introduce complex problem solving only after students have mastered the more basic skills such as counting, number recognition, and addition.

Teachers may inadvertently shape undesirable behaviors as well, thereby intensifying them. For example, let's say that Molly frequently exhibits such disruptive behaviors as talking out of turn and physically annoying other students. Molly's teacher decides to eliminate these disruptive behaviors by ignoring (i.e., extinguishing) them. Although the teacher is able to ignore minor infractions, he finds himself unable to ignore Molly's more extreme disruptions and reprimands her for them. If Molly finds the teacher's negative attention reinforcing, as many students do, she may engage in more and more extreme disruptive behavior to get that attention. In other words, the teacher's strategy is counterproductive: Because he ignores minor disruptions and reinforces major ones, he is unintentionally shaping Molly into an increasingly more disruptive student.

THE NATURE OF REINFORCERS

I have talked at length about how reinforcers can change behavior. It is time now to talk more about reinforcers themselves. I will first make distinctions between primary and secondary reinforcers and between positive and negative reinforcement (which I will also contrast with punishment). I will then describe the different kinds of reinforcers that teachers can effectively use to change student behavior.

Primary and Secondary Reinforcers

A **primary reinforcer** is one that satisfies a biological need. Food, water, oxygen, and warmth are examples of possible primary reinforcers. Physical affection and cuddling may also address biological needs (Harlow & Zimmerman, 1959), thus serving as primary reinforcers. Different individuals may have different primary reinforcers: For example, sex will be reinforcing to some individuals but not to

Primary versus secondary reinforcers

others, and a certain drug will be a primary reinforcer for a drug addict but not for a nonaddicted individual.

A **secondary reinforcer**, also known as a **conditioned reinforcer**, is a previously neutral stimulus that has become reinforcing to an organism through repeated association with another reinforcer (e.g., Wolfe, 1936). Examples of secondary reinforcers, which do not satisfy any obvious biological necessities, are praise, grades, money, and feelings of success.

Why do secondary reinforcers become reinforcing? An early explanation was that we learn secondary reinforcers through classical conditioning. A neutral stimulus is paired with an existing reinforcer (UCS) that elicits some form of biological satisfaction (UCR). That neutral stimulus becomes a CS (i.e., it becomes a secondary reinforcer) that elicits the same satisfaction (CR). For example, my daughter learned very early that she could use money (CS) to buy candy (UCS) to satisfy her sweet tooth. The more often a secondary reinforcer has been associated with another reinforcer and the stronger that other reinforcer is, the more powerful the secondary reinforcer will be (Bersh, 1951; D'Amato, 1955).

More recently, some theorists have proposed that secondary reinforcers are effective to the extent that they give an organism information that a primary reinforcer is coming (Bower, McLean, & Meachem, 1966; Green & Rachlin, 1977; Mazur, 1993; Perone & Baron, 1980). This explanation has a decidedly cognitive flavor to it: An organism is *seeking information* about the environment rather than just responding to that environment in a "thoughtless" manner.

The relative influences of primary and secondary reinforcers on our lives probably depend a great deal on economic circumstances. When such biological necessities as food and warmth are scarce, these primary reinforcers, and the secondary reinforcers closely associated with them (e.g., money), may be major factors in reinforcing behavior. On the other hand, in times of economic well-being, when cupboards are full and houses are warm, such secondary reinforcers as praise, grades, and feelings of success are more likely to play a major role in the learning process.

Positive Reinforcement, Negative Reinforcement, and Punishment

In addition to distinguishing between primary and secondary reinforcers, we can also distinguish between positive and negative reinforcement. Let's examine these two forms of reinforcement and look at how they are different from punishment.

Positive Reinforcement

Up to this point, the reinforcers I have mentioned have all been positive reinforcers. **Positive reinforcement** involves the *presentation* of a stimulus after the response. Food, praise, a smile, and success are all positive reinforcers.

Negative Reinforcement

In contrast to positive reinforcement, **negative reinforcement** increases a response through the *removal* of a stimulus, usually an aversive or unpleasant one. For example, rats will learn to press a bar to terminate an electric shock; removal of the aversive shock is a negative reinforcer. As another example, many newer cars sound a loud buzzer if the keys are still in the ignition when the driver's door is opened; removal of the keys from the ignition gets negatively reinforced because the buzzer stops.

The removal of anxiety or guilt can be an extremely powerful negative reinforcer. A child may confess to a crime committed days or even weeks earlier because she has been feeling guilty about the transgression all that time and needs to get it off her chest. Anxiety may drive one student to complete a term paper early, thereby removing an item from his "things to do" list. Another student confronted with the same term paper might procrastinate until the last minute, thereby removing anxiety—although only temporarily—about the more difficult aspects of researching and writing that paper.

Teachers may develop methods of classroom discipline that are effective over the short run but not over the long run because those teachers get negative reinforcement for using such discipline methods. For example, if Ms. Jones yells at Marvin for talking too much, Marvin may temporarily stop talking, which negatively reinforces Ms. Jones's yelling behavior. If Marvin likes getting Ms. Jones' attention (a positive reinforcer), however, he will be chattering again before very long.

Punishment

Both positive reinforcement and negative reinforcement increase the responses they follow. **Punishment**, on the other hand, is likely to *decrease* those responses. I will describe the effects of punishment in more detail in Chapter 6, but will define punishment here so you can see how it differs from negative reinforcement.

Punishment takes one of two forms, frequently referred to as Punishment I and Punishment II. **Punishment I** involves the *presentation* of a stimulus, usually an aversive one. Scolding and spanking are examples of this form of punishment. **Punishment II** involves the *removal* of a stimulus, usually a pleasant one. Examples include fines for misbehaviors (because money is being taken away) and loss of privileges. Figure 4–2 illustrates the differences among positive reinforcement, negative reinforcement, Punishment I, and Punishment II.

A particular source of confusion for many people is the difference between negative reinforcement and Punishment I. Although both involve an aversive stimulus, they differ in their time line. With negative reinforcement, the aversive stimulus *stops* when the response is emitted. With Punishment I, on the other hand, the aversive stimulus *begins* when the response is emitted. Figure 4-3 illustrates this difference graphically. The termination of an aversive stimulus nega-

Figure 4–2
Positive reinforcement, negative reinforcement, and punishment

Stimulus is:	Nature of Stimulus	
	Pleasant	Aversive
Presented after the response	Positive Reinforcement (response increases)	Punishment I (response decreases)
Removed after the response	Punishment II (response decreases)	Negative Reinforcement (response increases)

tively reinforces a response; the initiation of an aversive stimulus punishes a response.

Different Kinds of Reinforcing Stimuli

When using reinforcement in the classroom, teachers often unnecessarily limit themselves to just a handful of reinforcers. In fact, a wide variety of events can be reinforcing to students. Let's look at several possibilities.

Material Reinforcers
A **material**, or tangible, **reinforcer** is an actual object; food and toys are examples. For many people, the word *reinforcer* brings to mind such tangible consequences for good behavior. However, most psychologists recommend using a material reinforcer only as a last resort, when absolutely no other reinforcer works.

Social Reinforcers
A **social reinforcer** is a gesture or sign from one person to another that communicates positive regard. Praise, a smile, a pat on the back, and a hug are all social reinforcers. Social reinforcement is a common occurrence in the classroom and can be quite effective. Teacher attention, approval, and praise are powerful classroom reinforcers (Becker, Madsen, Arnold, & Thomas, 1967; Drabman, 1976; Madsen, Becker, & Thomas, 1968; Schepis, Reid, & Fitzgerald, 1987; Ward & Baker, 1968). The approval of peers can be effective as well (Evans & Oswalt, 1968; Lovitt, Guppy, & Blattner, 1969).

Figure 4–3
The difference between negative reinforcement and punishment is primarily one of time.

Activity Reinforcers

Speaking nonbehavioristically, an **activity reinforcer** is an opportunity to engage in a favorite activity. (A quick quiz: Which word is the nonbehaviorist part of my definition, and why?) David Premack (1959, 1963) discovered that people will often perform one activity if doing so enables them to perform another. His **Premack principle** for activity reinforcers is as follows:

> A *normally high-frequency response, when it follows a normally low-frequency response, will increase the frequency of the low-frequency response.*

A high-frequency response is, in essence, a response that an organism enjoys doing, while a low-frequency response is one that the organism does not enjoy. Another way of stating the Premack principle, then, is that organisms will perform less preferred tasks so that they can subsequently engage in more preferred tasks.

To illustrate, my own free operant level for housework is extremely low. I have found that I am more likely to do household chores if I make a higher-frequency behavior, such as reading a mystery novel or having a party, contingent on doing the housework. In a similar way, appropriate classroom behavior can be improved through the Premack principle. Young children can quickly be taught to sit quietly and pay attention if they are allowed to engage in higher-frequency "active" behaviors (e.g., talking and running around the room) only after they have been quiet and attentive for a certain period (Homme, deBaca, Devine, Steinhorst, & Rickert, 1963).

Although psychologists agree that the Premack principle works, they disagree as to *why* it works. If you are interested in exploring the theoretical underpinnings of the Premack principle, see the discussions by Bower and Hilgard (1981) and Timberlake and Allison (1974).

Intrinsic Reinforcers

In many situations, individuals will engage in certain responses not because of any external reinforcers but because of the internal good feelings—the **intrinsic reinforcers**—that such responses bring. Feeling successful after solving a difficult puzzle, feeling proud after returning a valuable item to its rightful owner, and feeling relieved after completing a difficult assignment are all examples of intrinsic reinforcers. People who continue to engage in responses for a long time without external reinforcers are probably working for intrinsic sources of satisfaction.

Positive Feedback

Material and social reinforcers may improve classroom behavior and lead to better learning of academic skills because they provide **feedback** to students about which responses are desirable and which are not (e.g., Gagné & Driscoll, 1988). For many students, the true reinforcers for learning are probably the internal reinforcers—feelings of success, competence, mastery, and pride—that scholastic accomplishments bring. For such students, external reinforcers, both material and social, are more helpful if they provide feedback that academic tasks have been performed well. Grades are probably also reinforcing for the same reason: Good grades reflect high achievement, a reason to feel proud.

I once spent a half hour each day for several weeks working with Michael, a 9-year-old learning-disabled boy who was having difficulty learning his cursive letters. Over the first three weeks, neither Michael nor I could see any improvement, and we were becoming increasingly frustrated. To give ourselves more concrete feedback on the results of our sessions together, I decided to start graphing Michael's daily performance. I explained to Michael how we would chart his progress on a piece of graph paper by marking off the number of cursive letters he could remember each day. I also told him that as soon as he had reached a certain dotted line (indicating 26 correct letters) three days in a row, he could have a special treat: His choice was a purple felt-tip pen.

At the beginning of each session, I tested Michael on his cursive letters, and together we counted the number he had right. We entered his performance on the chart in the form of a bar of the appropriate height, and then Michael practiced the letters he had missed. Michael's daily performance began to improve dramatically. Not only was he making noticeable progress, but he also looked forward to charting his performance and seeing a higher bar each day. Within two weeks, Michael had successfully met the criterion for his felt-tip pen: he had written all 26 cursive letters three days in succession. As it turns out, the pen was probably not the key ingredient for our success: Michael lost it within 24 hours of receiving it. Instead, I suspect that the concrete positive feedback about his own improvement reinforced Michael's learning.

Positive feedback and the intrinsic reinforcement that such feedback brings are, from a teacher's perspective, probably the most desirable forms of classroom reinforcement. Keep in mind, however, that consistent positive feedback and resulting feelings of success and mastery can occur only when instruction has been carefully tailored to individual skill levels and abilities, and only when students have learned to value academic achievement. When, for whatever reasons, children are not motivated to achieve academic success, then other reinforcers, such as social and activity reinforcers, can be useful.

Always remember that what is reinforcing for one individual may not be reinforcing for another. Reinforcement, like beauty, is in the eyes of the beholder. And even for the same individual, a reinforcer on one occasion may not be a reinforcer on another. Several other factors influence the effectiveness of reinforcers, as we shall see now.

FACTORS AFFECTING THE EFFECTIVENESS OF REINFORCEMENT

At least three factors influence the effectiveness of reinforcement in operant conditioning: timing, magnitude and appeal, and consistency.

Timing

Earlier in this chapter, I stressed the importance of *immediate* reinforcement for operant conditioning. In most cases, greater delays in reinforcement lead to slower acquisition of responses (e.g., Hockman & Lipsitt, 1961; Lett, 1973, 1975; Terrell & Ware, 1961). Fortunately, in situations when immediate reinforcement is impossible, the presence of other environmental cues indicating that reinforcement will come eventually may help to minimize the negative effect of a delay (Perin, 1943; Fowler & Baer, 1981). For example, a teacher who wants to reinforce her students' persistence through a difficult lesson might say, "Because we have all worked so hard this morning, we will spend this afternoon practicing the class play you all seem to be enjoying so much."

Magnitude and Appeal

The larger and more appealing the reinforcer, the faster a response will be learned and the more frequently it will be exhibited (e.g., Atkinson, 1958; Siegel & Andrews, 1962). For example, in a study by Siegel and Andrews (1962), 3- to 5-year-old boys learned more quickly when reinforced with such treats as candy, coins, balloons, and small toys than when the reinforcers were unexciting buttons.

But interestingly enough, it is not always the absolute magnitude of reinforcement that affects behavior as much as it is the *relative* magnitude compared with prior experience. For example, in a classic study by Crespi (1942), rats ran a runway to reach a food reinforcer at the far end. When rats accustomed to a small quantity of food were suddenly reinforced with a greater amount, they ran faster than rats who had always received that same large amount. Similarly, rats used to a large amount of reinforcement who then began receiving less food ran more slowly than rats who had always had that smaller amount. Crespi's results have been replicated in other rat studies (e.g., McHale, Brooks, & Wolach, 1982), although the results of analogous studies with infants have been inconsistent (e.g., Fagen & Rovee, 1976; Lipsitt & Kaye, 1965).

The changes in behavior observed when quantities of reinforcement increase or decrease are commonly known as **contrast effects**. One contrast effect—the **elation effect**—occurs when the amount of reinforcement is increased: The response rate becomes *faster* than it would be if the reinforcement had always been at that higher level. The opposite of the contrast effect—the **depression effect**—occurs when the amount of reinforcement is decreased: The result is that the response rate becomes *slower* than what it would be if reinforcement had always been that low. The depression effect may be at least partly due to negative emotions associated with a reduction in reinforcement (Flaherty, 1985).

Consistency

One of the most critical factors affecting both the rate at which responses are learned and the rate at which they can be extinguished is the consistency of reinforcement (e.g., Staddon & Higa, 1991). To illustrate how consistency plays a role, consider this fantasy I have for the handful of students in my classes each semester who don't read their textbook:

> *The student is locked in a small room. The assigned textbook lies on a nearby table. Every time the student opens the book to one of the assigned pages and looks at the page, a small piece of delicious junk food falls from a hole in the ceiling.*

Essentially, I would like to put unmotivated students into my own version of a Skinner Box—the Ormrod Box!

Now imagine 20 students in 20 Ormrod Boxes. Ten of these students, randomly selected, are in Group A: They receive a piece of junk food every time they open the textbook and look at it. The other 10 are in Group B: They get junk food for some of their book-reading responses (perhaps one response out of every four), but receive nothing for their efforts the rest of the time. Group A is receiving **continuous reinforcement**: Every response is reinforced. Group B is receiving **intermittent reinforcement**: Some of the responses are reinforced and some are not. Which group is going to increase its textbook-reading behavior faster? The answer, of course, is Group A, the group with continuous reinforcement. Continuously reinforced responses are acquired faster than intermittently reinforced responses.

Now suppose that, after a few hours in their respective Ormrod Boxes, all 20 students have begun to show a high frequency of textbook-reading responses, so I turn off the junk-food-dropping mechanisms. Which students are first going to notice that they are no longer being reinforced? The answer is again Group A. Those students who have been reinforced for every single response will notice rather quickly that reinforcement has stopped, and their textbook-reading should extinguish rapidly (unless, of course, they find such behavior intrinsically reinforcing). Group B students, on the other hand, have been receiving reinforcement for only 25 percent of their responses, so they are accustomed to nonreinforcement; these students will probably continue to read their textbooks for some time before they realize that reinforcement has ceased. Intermittently reinforced responses are extinguished more slowly than continuously reinforced responses.

Psychologists usually recommend reinforcing a response continuously until the terminal behavior is reached and then maintaining the behavior through intermittent reinforcement so that it does not diminish. Intermittent reinforcement can follow a variety of **reinforcement schedules**, each of them having a different effect, both on resistance to extinction and on the frequency and pattern of the response being reinforced. Let's take a look at these different schedules and the behavior patterns that result from each one.

SCHEDULES OF REINFORCEMENT

In this section I will describe three different groups of intermittent reinforcement schedules: ratio schedules (those in which reinforcement occurs after a certain number of responses), interval schedules (those in which reinforcement occurs for the first response after a certain time interval has elapsed), and differential schedules (those in which reinforcement is contingent on a certain rate of responding).

Ratio Schedules: Reinforcing a Certain Number of Responses

A **ratio schedule** is one in which reinforcement occurs following a certain number of responses. That certain number can either be constant (a fixed-ratio schedule) or vary from one reinforcement to the next (a variable-ratio schedule).

Fixed Ratio (FR)

A **fixed-ratio** reinforcement schedule presents a reinforcer after a certain constant number of responses have occurred. For example, reinforcement might occur after every third response (a 1:3 ratio schedule) or after every 50th response (a 1:50 schedule). Such a reinforcement schedule can lead to a high and consistent response rate over an indefinite period; for example, pigeons whose pecking is maintained on a high ratio schedule will peck as often as 10 times per second (Ferster & Skinner, 1957).

Whitlock (1966) has described the use of a series of ratio schedules with a 6-year-old boy who had been unable to acquire basic reading skills. At first, the boy was asked to read words presented to him on flash cards. Every time he read a word correctly, he received a plastic poker chip as a reinforcer, reflecting a continuous reinforcement schedule. He could then trade filled jars of 36 poker chips for a variety of activities; for example, with two jars he could play a game and with seven jars he could watch a cartoon. Once the boy was able to read from beginning reader storybooks, he was reinforced on a 1:2 fixed-ratio schedule; that is, he received one chip for every two words he read correctly. Eventually he was reinforced for every four words (a 1:4 schedule), then every page (one reinforcer for every 10 to 25 words), then every story (one reinforcer for every 50 to 70 words), and finally every four stories. After 15 sessions of such individualized instruction, reinforcement was phased out altogether, and the boy was placed in his class' regular reading program; three months later he was still reading at grade level. (One thing has always struck me about this study: Because so many poker chips were required to make a "purchase," the boy must have actually bought very few activities. I suspect that his increasing success in reading was the true reinforcer in this case.)

Ratio schedules even as high as 1:1,000, when introduced through a series of successively higher ratios (as in the Whitlock study), have been found to maintain a response (Ferster & Skinner, 1957). In fact, high ratios typically lead to higher rates of responding than low ratios (Collier, Hirsh, & Hamlin, 1972; Stephens, Pear, Wray, & Jackson, 1975), although organisms under high ratio schedules tend to exhibit a **postreinforcement pause** (a temporary decrease in responding) after each reinforced response (Ferster & Skinner, 1957).

Variable Ratio (VR)

A **variable-ratio** reinforcement schedule is one in which reinforcement is presented after a certain variable number of responses have been emitted and is described by the average number of responses needed to obtain reinforcement. For example, in a 1:5 VR schedule, reinforcement might take place after four responses, then after seven more, then after three, and so on. As you can see, the occurrence of reinforcement in a VR schedule is somewhat unpredictable.

Playing a Las Vegas slot machine is an example of a response that is reinforced on a variable-ratio schedule. The more times you put a quarter into the machine, the more times you will be reinforced by having quarters come back out again, but those quarters do not come out after any predictable number of quarters have gone in. In a similar way, telephone solicitation is also reinforced on a VR schedule. The greater the number of calls made, the greater the number of sales, but the soliciting caller never knows just which call will lead to reinforcement.

Margaret, one of my daughter's friends, has always been very persistent when she wants something; she seldom takes no for an answer. The source of her persistence became clear to me one evening when my daughter and I had dinner at a restaurant with Margaret and her mother. The girls gobbled their

Telephone solicitation is reinforced on a variable-ratio schedule.

food quickly and went off to explore the restaurant while we ladies nursed our coffee. Margaret quickly returned to the table to make a request of her mother:

> "Mom, can I have a quarter for a video game?"
> "No."
> "Please, mom?"
> "I said no, Margaret."
> "But Tina has one." (I look absentmindedly into space.)
> "No."
> "I'll pay you back as soon as we get home."
> "*No*, Margaret."
> "*Pretty please*?!" (Margaret puts on a desperate face.)
> "Oh, all right, here's a quarter."

Margaret's asking behaviors were clearly on a variable-ratio reinforcement schedule: She had learned that persistence eventually paid off.

Variable-ratio schedules result in higher response rates than fixed-ratio schedules. Furthermore, responses reinforced on a VR schedule are highly resistant to extinction. In fact, pigeons working on very high VR schedules may expend more energy responding than they gain in food reinforcement, thus eventually working themselves to death (Swenson, 1980).

Interval Schedules: Reinforcing the First Response After a Time Period

An **interval schedule** is one in which reinforcement is contingent on the first response emitted after a certain time interval has elapsed. The time interval can either be constant (a fixed interval schedule) or vary from one reinforcement to the next (a variable interval schedule).

Fixed Interval (FI)

With a **fixed-interval** reinforcement schedule, reinforcement is contingent on the first response emitted after a certain fixed time interval has elapsed. For example, the organism may be reinforced for the first response emitted after five minutes have elapsed, regardless of how many responses may or may not have been made during those five minutes. Following reinforcement, another five-minute interval must elapse before a response is again reinforced.

A fixed-interval schedule produces a unique response pattern: Following reinforcement, the response rate tapers way off in a postreinforcement pause until the end of the time interval approaches, at which point responding picks up again (e.g., Ferster & Skinner, 1957; Shimoff, Catania, & Matthews, 1981). To illustrate, when my daughter was in fifth grade, she had a spelling test every Friday. She got the week's list of spelling words each Monday, so had four evenings in which to study the list. Occasionally she began on Wednesday, but she more often waited until Thursday night to study her spelling. If we were to graph

Tina's studying behavior, it might look something like the graph in Figure 4–4. This "scallop" pattern is typical of behaviors reinforced on a fixed interval schedule. We do not see the high rate of responding with an FI schedule that is observed for fixed and variable-ratio schedules, nor do we see as much resistance to extinction.

Variable Interval (VI)

In a **variable-interval** reinforcement schedule, reinforcement is contingent upon the first response emitted after a certain variable time interval has elapsed. For example, the organism may be reinforced for the first response after five minutes, then the first response after eight minutes, then the first response after two minutes, and so on, with the VI schedule being identified by the average time interval.

You may have a friend who really enjoys talking on the telephone, so that when you try to call this individual, you often hear a busy signal. If you have an urgent need to get in touch with your friend, you may continue to dial the phone number once every few minutes until eventually your call goes through. In a similar way, students who have been told that there is always the possibility of an unannounced ("pop") quiz in class are likely to study a little bit every night. They never know on exactly which day their studying will pay off. Your pattern of dialing your gabby friend and students' pattern of studying for pop quizzes are typical of the response pattern observed for variable-interval schedules: a slow, steady rate of responding. The longer the average time interval until reinforcement, the slower the response rate will be (e.g., Catania & Reynolds, 1968). (We should note here that, for other reasons, pop quizzes are generally not recommended; see Sax, 1989, or Ormrod, 1995, for their "down" side.)

For both ratio and interval schedules, then, variable schedules lead to steadier response rates than fixed schedules, probably because of the unpredictability of reinforcement after a correct response. A variable schedule always allows the possibility that the next correct response will pay off. Variable schedules also appear to inhibit extinction, again possibly because of their unpredictable nature.

When using ratio or interval schedules of reinforcement to prevent the extinction of a previously acquired response, the best schedule to use depends

Figure 4–4
Responses reinforced on a fixed-interval schedule follow a "scallop" pattern.

on the rate of response desired. In most cases, a variable ratio is recommended for a high rate of responding, with a variable interval schedule being better for a slow but steady rate. Ideally, when intermittent reinforcement first replaces continuous reinforcement, the ratio should be small (e.g., 1:2 or 1:3) or the time interval short. The ratio or interval can then gradually be extended until the response continues with very little reinforcement at all.

Differential Schedules: Reinforcing Rates of Responding

When a particular rate of responding is required, a **differential schedule of reinforcement** is appropriate: A specific number of responses occurring within a specific length of time leads to reinforcement. There are at least three such schedules:

- reinforcement of a differential rate of high responding
- reinforcement of a differential rate of low responding
- reinforcement of the *non*occurrence of the response (differential reinforcement of other behaviors)

Differential Rate of High Responding (DRH)

A **DRH schedule** provides reinforcement only when a specific, large number of responses (or even more responses) have occurred within a particular period of time. For example, consider Tina's friend Margaret, the girl who persistently asked her mother for money to play a video game. Margaret may actually have been on a DRH schedule rather than a variable-ratio schedule, in that she had to ask for a quarter several times *all at once* to get reinforcement. With a ratio schedule, the time it takes to emit the necessary number of responses is irrelevant, but with a DRH schedule, this time period is critical. Because a DRH schedule requires many responses in a short amount of time, a high response rate is typical.

Theoretically, studying for regularly scheduled exams is really on a DRH schedule: The more studying that occurs, the greater the probability of reinforcement at exam time. However, as Klein (1987) has pointed out, too many students instead treat exams as fixed interval schedules, thus showing the "goof off now, cram later" study pattern.

Differential Rate of Low Responding (DRL)

A **DRL schedule** reinforces the first response after a certain time interval has elapsed in which the organism has not made the response at all. This might sound like a fixed interval schedule, but remember that in an FI schedule, responses during the time interval, although not reinforced, are otherwise acceptable. One example of a response on a DRL schedule is trying to start a car with a flooded engine. Repeated attempts at starting it will fail; you must wait for a few minutes, then try again, before you are likely to succeed.

Students' requests for their teacher's assistance are an example of responses that might be most appropriately reinforced on a DRL schedule. Reinforcing students continuously when they ask for the teacher's help might lead to a high rate of such requests and a resulting overdependence on the teacher. On the other hand, reinforcing students who ask for help only after they have been working independently for a period of time will teach them that independence with occasional questions is more acceptable.

We should note here that learning the appropriate response pattern for a DRL schedule often takes time, because it requires one *not* to perform a behavior that has previously been reinforced (Reynolds, 1975).

Differential Reinforcement of Other Behaviors (DRO)

A **DRO schedule** provides reinforcement when a particular response does not occur during a certain time interval. In other words, the organism is reinforced for doing anything else *except* that response for a certain length of time. As an example, consider the teacher who says, "I am going to write on the chalkboard the name of every student who speaks out of turn today. If your name is not on the board by three o'clock, you may have a half hour of free time." That teacher is using a DRO schedule, because she is reinforcing children for *not* talking without permission.

Continuous reinforcement is clearly the most effective way of teaching a response. However, once the terminal behavior has been reached, the various intermittent-reinforcement schedules—ratio, interval, and differential—can help both in preventing extinction (the DRO schedule excepted) and in controlling the frequency and pattern of that response.

STIMULUS CONTROL

Earlier in the chapter, I described Skinner's operant conditioning as an R→S$_{Rf}$ model (where S$_{Rf}$ is reinforcement) rather than the S→R model more typical of other early behaviorists. Actually, a stimulus that precedes a response *can* influence the likelihood that the response will occur again, although the role of this **antecedent stimulus** in operant conditioning is different from the role it plays in other behaviorist models such as classical conditioning.

To illustrate, here is a typical scenario in a high school class: The teacher begins to describe the evening's homework assignment to a class of quiet and attentive students but is interrupted by a bell marking the end of the class period. Immediately the students, no longer interested in hearing their assignment, slam their notebooks shut and begin to push and shove their way toward the classroom door. These students are under **stimulus control**: They have learned that a particular response (leaving class) is acceptable under certain stimulus conditions (when the bell rings). A wise teacher would stand in front of the door while giving the homework assignment and not let the students leave their seats, bell or no bell. In that way, students would learn that leaving class is permissible only after a different stimulus—the teacher's movement away from the door—has occurred.

In operant conditioning, the antecedent stimulus does not directly elicit the response, as it does in classical conditioning. Instead, the stimulus *sets the occasion* for a response to be reinforced. When an antecedent stimulus influences the likelihood that a response will occur, we call that stimulus a **discriminative stimulus**, often symbolized as S+ (Skinner used the symbol S^D), and say that the response is under stimulus control. Responses to stimuli in operant conditioning reflect the phenomena of stimulus generalization and stimulus discrimination similar to the generalization and discrimination observed in classical conditioning.

Stimulus Generalization

When an organism has learned to respond in a certain way in the presence of one stimulus (the S+), it is likely to respond in the same way in the presence of similar stimuli; this operant conditioning phenomenon is known as **stimulus generalization**. Just as in classical conditioning, stimulus generalization is more likely to occur to stimuli that are similar to the discriminative stimulus. For example, kindergarten students may learn such appropriate classroom behaviors as raising their hands and waiting to be called on before speaking. Such behaviors are more likely to generalize to a similar situation (such as first grade) than to a dissimilar situation (such as the family dinner table). This tendency of organisms to generalize more as stimuli become more similar to the discriminative stimulus is known as a **generalization gradient**.

Stimulus Discrimination

In classical conditioning, **stimulus discrimination** occurs when one stimulus (the CS+) is presented in conjunction with an unconditioned stimulus, and another stimulus (the CS –) is presented in the absence of the UCS. Similarly, in operant conditioning organisms can learn that a certain response may be reinforced in the presence of one stimulus (S+) but not in the presence of another stimulus, symbolized as S – (Skinner used the symbol S^Δ):

$$(S+) \quad R \longrightarrow S$$

$$(S-) \quad R \longrightarrow \quad \text{(nothing)}$$

Learning under what circumstances a response will and will not be reinforced is operant conditioning's form of stimulus discrimination. Stimulus discrimination is essentially a process of learning that a conditioned response made in the presence of S+ should not be generalized to S –.

Consider the preschooler who has learned to say "bee" whenever she sees this symbol:

b

She then sees a similar stimulus:

d

and responds "bee" once again—that is, she generalizes. (Anyone who has worked with young children who are learning their alphabet has probably observed that, consistent with the generalization gradient, children are much more likely to generalize the "bee" response to the letter *d* than to less similar letters such as *j* or *s*.) If the teacher does not reinforce her for the "bee" response to the symbol *d*, the child will eventually learn to discriminate between the letters *b* and *d*.

Stimulus Control in the Classroom

Reinforcement plays a crucial role in helping children to discover the situations in which particular responses are desirable and to generalize and discriminate among situations appropriately. Initially, teachers themselves can provide discriminative stimuli that serve as cues for letting students know how to behave. These stimuli may be either very explicit **direct cues** or more subtle **indirect cues** (Krumboltz & Krumboltz, 1972). For example, an elementary teacher whose students are preparing to walk to the lunchroom might provide a direct cue for appropriate behavior by reminding them to "go quietly and in single file." The teacher then reinforces the desired behavior by allowing students to proceed only when they behave as they have been instructed. A teacher who wishes to be more subtle in reminding students about the necessity for accomplishing a task quickly might use an indirect cue such as this one: "After you have all finished pages 14 and 15 in your workbooks, I will hand out next week's lunch menus." With a gradual shift from direct to indirect cues, teachers can help students become increasingly independent of reminders for good behavior. Eventually students should learn to identify for themselves the discriminative stimuli that signal the appropriateness of various behaviors.

CONTEMPORARY PERSPECTIVES ON OPERANT CONDITIONING

As we noted in Chapter 2, B. F. Skinner's ideas about operant conditioning underwent little change from 1938 until his death in 1990. The views of other behaviorists have evolved considerably over the past 50 years, however. Here are some examples of how contemporary perspectives of operant conditioning differ from Skinner's original notions.

•*Behavior is better understood by looking at a larger context and longer time frame than has traditionally been the case.* Early behaviorists tended to think in terms of specific S-R relationships within a relatively short time period—for example, a researcher might look at the immediate consequence of a particular response. In contrast, many behaviorists are now looking at larger and longer environment-behavior relationships (e.g., see Herrnstein, 1990; Rachlin, 1990, 1991). For example, rather than looking at specific stimuli, they may look at the relatively complex environmental conditions—**setting events**—under which certain behaviors are most likely to occur (Brown, Bryson-Brockmann, & Fox, 1986; Brown, Fox, & Brady, 1987; Kantor, 1959; Martin, Brady, & Williams, 1991; Morris, 1982; Wahler & Fox, 1981). They may also examine the conditions under which certain behaviors are likely to persist despite *changes* in environmental stimuli—a phenomenon sometimes known as **behavioral momentum** (Mace et al., 1988; Nevin, Mandell, & Atak, 1983). And they look at the choices that organisms make in situations where several different behaviors–each leading to a different reinforcer—are possible (de Villiers, 1977; Rachlin, 1991).

•*Operant conditioning involves cognition as well as responding.* Many theorists now propose that operant conditioning can best be understood when we consider nonobservable mental processes as well as observable stimuli and responses (Colwill, 1993; Rachlin, 1991; Schwartz & Reisberg, 1991; Vaughan, 1988; Wasserman, 1993). For example, they talk about an organism forming *expectations* as to what reinforcer is likely to follow a particular response (Colwill, 1993; Rachlin, 1991; Schwartz & Reisberg, 1991). They find that humans and nonhumans alike develop *categories* of stimuli they learn to respond to; to illustrate, we can train pigeons to discriminate (by making different responses) between members of different categories, including cats versus flowers, cars versus trucks, pictures of Charlie Brown versus those of other Peanuts characters, and even different lengths of time (Killeen, 1991; Rachlin, 1991; Vaughan, 1988; Wasserman, 1993). And they are beginning to use such phrases as *paying attention* to discriminative stimuli, mentally *encoding* response-reinforcement relationships, and *seeking information* about the environment–phrases with definite cognitive overtones (e.g., Colwill, 1993; Colwill & Rescorla, 1986; Rachlin, 1991; Rescorla, 1987; Schwartz & Reisberg, 1991).

•*Operant and classical conditioning, taken together, do not completely determine the behaviors an organism will exhibit on any given occasion.* B. F. Skinner was a **determinist**: He proposed that if we were to have complete knowledge of an organism's past reinforcement history and present environmental circumstances, as well as knowledge of any genetic predispositions that the organism might have to behave in certain ways, we would be able to predict the organism's next response with total accuracy. The views of some contemporary behaviorists are not so deterministic in nature: They propose that any organism's behavior reflects a certain degree of variability that S-R relationships cannot explain (Epstein, 1991; Rachlin, 1991). For example, if you think about it, shaping behavior—refining it through successively "fussier" reinforcement contingencies—would not be possible unless an organism varied its responses somewhat from one occasion to another. Ultimately, it is only by making changes in responses (however small those changes may be) and experiencing their consequences that new and perhaps more adaptive behaviors can emerge over time (Epstein, 1991).

• *Just as reinforcement increases the frequency of a response, punishment can be an effective means of decreasing a response.* Early research by Thorndike (1932a, 1932b) and Skinner (1938) indicated that punishment was unlikely to reduce the behavior it followed. But later research studies have shown that punishment *can* be effective in many situations. As a result, some theorists have revived the "punishment" part of Thorndike's original law of effect, asserting that responses that precede discomfort are in fact weakened (e.g., Aronfreed, 1968; Aronfreed & Reber, 1965; Lentz, 1988; Parke, 1972, 1977; Rachlin, 1991). We should note that when behaviorists describe the effects of both reinforcement and punishment in learning and behavior, they typically use the term *instrumental conditioning* rather than Skinner's *operant conditioning*.

We will discuss punishment, including its effects and guidelines for its use, in Chapter 6. In the meantime, three methods are available for eliminating undesirable behavior within the traditional, reinforcement-based operant conditioning paradigm. We turn to those now.

ELIMINATING UNDESIRABLE BEHAVIORS

I have talked at length about how new responses are learned, modified, and maintained through operant conditioning. But sometimes we may instead want to stop a behavior that has previously been acquired through reinforcement. Three methods of reducing and eliminating misbehavior derived from Skinner's model of operant conditioning are extinction, differential reinforcement of other behaviors, and reinforcement of incompatible behaviors.

Extinction

A psychologist was once consulted about Jimmy, a child who had been hospitalized for an extended period. Nurses in the children's ward were very concerned because Jimmy kept banging his head on the side of his crib; whenever they heard him doing so, they would rush to his room and stop the behavior, thereby inadvertently reinforcing and maintaining the head-banging response. The psychologist successfully eliminated Jimmy's head-banging through a process of extinction: A protective helmet was strapped on Jimmy's head to prevent injury, and the nurses were instructed to ignore Jimmy during his head-banging episodes. At the same time, because Jimmy clearly craved attention, the nurses *did* attend to him on occasions when he was behaving appropriately.

Extinction—the withdrawal of reinforcement—can often be an effective method for eliminating inappropriate responses. Students who engage in disruptive behavior may stop if such behavior no longer results in the teacher attention they seek (i.e., if the teacher ignores them). Similarly, cheating on classroom tests may soon end if students do not receive credit for the scores they obtain on those exams.

Unfortunately, however, extinction is typically not the most reliable method of eliminating unwanted behavior, for several reasons. First, it is not always possible to remove *all* reinforcers of a behavior; for example, although a teacher may be able to ignore the comments of a class clown, other students in the class may continue to reinforce those comments. Second, extinguished behaviors will sometimes show spontaneous recovery: A response that disappears one day may pop up again at a later date. And third, some responses, because of the way they were originally reinforced, may be particularly resistant to extinction. As I stated earlier in the chapter, a response that has previously been reinforced on an intermittent schedule will resist extinction more than one that has been continuously reinforced. When responses cannot be extinguished for any of these reasons, other methods will be more effective in reducing them.

Differential Reinforcement of Other Behaviors

As noted earlier, the differential reinforcement of other behaviors—a DRO reinforcement schedule—is a procedure whereby an organism is reinforced for *not* exhibiting a particular behavior during a specified time interval. For example, when a teacher praises a student who manages to get through an entire recess without fighting with any of his classmates, that teacher is using a DRO schedule. The differential reinforcement of other behaviors tends to work better and longer than extinction (Uhl, 1973; Uhl & Garcia, 1969; Zeiler, 1971) and has been shown effective in reducing inappropriate classroom behavior (Parrish, Cataldo, Kolko, Neef, & Egel, 1986; Repp & Deitz, 1974).

Reinforcement of Incompatible Behaviors

We have previously encountered the use of incompatible responses in Chapter 2's discussion of breaking habits and Chapter 3's discussion of counterconditioning. Within the operant conditioning model, the notion of incompatibility is equally useful. The first step is to identify a response that is incompatible with the undesirable response—a response that cannot be performed at the same time as the undesirable response. That incompatible behavior is then reinforced. For example, a child's inappropriate out-of-seat behavior may be reduced by reinforcing the child whenever she is sitting down. Similarly, an aggressive student can be reinforced whenever he is interacting in a prosocial manner with his class-mates. Krumboltz and Krumboltz (1972) described how reinforcing an incompat-ible behavior was effective in handling the chronic litterbug at a junior high school: The student was put in charge of his school's antilitter campaign and given considerable recognition and praise for his efforts.

The reinforcement of incompatible behaviors sounds similar to the DRO schedule, but a subtle difference exists between the two methods. The DRO schedule involves the reinforcement of *nonoccurrence* of a particular response. Reinforcing incompatible behaviors involves reinforcing a *specific, opposite* response. Like a DRO schedule, it is typically more effective than extinction in eliminating undesirable behaviors (e.g., Lentz, 1988).

When none of the above techniques—extinction, differential reinforcement of other behaviors, or reinforcement of incompatible behaviors—proves effec-tive, punishment may be a viable alternative for eliminating an inappropriate behavior, as you will discover in Chapter 6.

WHEN REINFORCEMENT DOESN'T WORK

The basic principle of operant conditioning—that a reinforced response will increase in frequency—has been used successfully in many different situations to change a wide variety of behaviors. When reinforcement doesn't work, the source of difficulty can often be traced to one of four circumstances: (1) the "reinforcer" is not reinforcing; (2) reinforcement is not consistent; (3) the indi-vidual loses too much, or gains too little, by changing a behavior; or (4) too much is expected too soon.

"Reinforcer" Doesn't Reinforce

A first-grade teacher once consulted me about one of her students, a boy so dis-ruptive that he was only able to spend a half day in the classroom. In an effort to modify the disruptive behavior, the teacher had attached to the boy's desk a large sheet of heavy cardboard cut and painted to look like a clown, with a small red light bulb for a nose. When the boy exhibited appropriate classroom behaviors, such as sitting quietly or attending to his workbook, the teacher would light up the red nose. "I don't understand why his behavior isn't changing," she told me. "Maybe this clown isn't reinforcing to the boy," I suggested. "Nonsense!" exclaimed the teacher. "The clown has always worked with *other* children!"

One of the most common mistakes teachers make in using operant condition-ing techniques is to assume that certain consequences will be reinforcing to all stu-dents. Not all students will work for the same reinforcers; a consequence that increases the positive behavior of one child may not increase the behavior of another. For example, although most students find their teacher's praise reinforcing, some students do not (e.g., Pfiffner, Rosén, & O'Leary, 1985). A bright girl may view too much teacher praise as an indication to her classmates that she is teacher's pet; a teenage boy may value the friendship of peers who shun high achievers.

How can we determine what events will be reinforcing for different students? One way is to watch the students to see what kinds of consequences seem to affect their behavior. Another approach is to ask the students' parents, or even the students themselves. The one thing *not* to do is guess.

Reinforcement Is Inconsistent

Sometimes it is inconvenient to reinforce a behavior every time it occurs. But remember, continuous reinforcement brings about more rapid behavior change than intermittent reinforcement. If a student's behavior has been particularly disruptive and time-consuming, a little extra time devoted *now* to the continuous reinforcement of appropriate behaviors, inconvenient as that may occasionally be, will probably save time over the long run.

Change Isn't Worthwhile

An individual may lose too much, or gain too little, by changing a behavior. Consider the college student who estimates that she will have to study at least 20

The "reinforcer" must be reinforcing.

hours a week to get an A in her physics class. Although the A may be an effective reinforcer, it may not be worth the amount of time the student will have to spend to earn it. And consider the teenage boy who shies away from teacher praise because his peer group does not approve of academic achievement. It may be that teacher praise *is* a reinforcer to this boy, but he risks losing his status in the group if he is praised too frequently or profusely. Praise given privately, out of the earshot of peers, will probably be much more reinforcing in this case than public praise.

Consciously or otherwise, people may sometimes engage in a cost-benefit analysis when looking at the consequences of different behaviors (e.g., Eccles & Wigfield, 1985; Feather, 1982). Although they may have learned that a certain response will be reinforced, they will nevertheless not respond in that way if they have too much to lose, or too little to gain, by doing so. For people to respond positively to reinforcement, it must be worth their while.

Shaping Proceeds Too Rapidly

Reinforcement is ineffective when too much is expected too soon. In many situations, establishing a desirable behavior requires a process of *shaping* that behavior. Remember that shaping involves the reinforcement of a series of responses that more and more closely approximate the terminal behavior. Each response should be well learned before reinforcement proceeds to a closer approximation. If an attempt at shaping moves too quickly, such that each response is not well established before a more complicated one is expected, the reinforcement program will be ineffective in bringing about behavior change.

To illustrate, let's say that a teacher wants to reinforce a hyperactive boy for sitting quietly in his seat; her goal (the terminal behavior) is for him to sit quietly for 20 minutes. On the first morning of the intervention program, the boy sits quietly for one minute, and so the teacher reinforces him. She probably does *not* want to move on to a two-minute criterion just because he has met the one-minute criterion once. Instead, she should continue reinforcing the boy for one-minute "sits" until it is clear, from the frequency of his sitting behavior, that she can begin to expect that behavior for a longer period of time.

SKINNER ON EDUCATION

B. F. Skinner wrote prolifically on the weaknesses of our schools from an operant conditioning perspective (e.g., Skinner, 1953, 1954, 1958, 1968, 1973). He contended that reinforcement in the classroom usually occurs inconsistently and too long after a desired response has occurred. Although "natural" reinforcers (e.g., the control of nature, or the intrinsically rewarding value of the subject matter) can and should be used to increase appropriate academic behaviors, in fact most classroom reinforcers are artificially imposed. A problem inherent in our educational system is that teachers must teach behaviors that will be useful to students in the *future* rather than in the present, so these behaviors are not likely to lead to the naturally positive consequences now that they might later. For example, although a student might find algebra useful several years from now as a practicing engineer, she does not find it particularly useful in her current life. As a result, teachers resort to artificial reinforcers such as teacher approval, grades, stickers, or free time to foster academic achievement. These reinforcers are often ineffective, however, partly because the relationship between them and specific responses is not well specified.

In desperation, teachers often find themselves punishing *mis*behaviors, through such aversive consequences as displeasure, ridicule, and failing grades, rather than reinforcing appropriate responses; as Skinner puts it, teachers "induce students to learn by threatening them for not learning" (Skinner, 1968, p. 57). Not only is such aversive control of behavior ineffective, but students will engage in behaviors that enable them to escape or avoid school tasks altogether.

Skinner urged educators to focus on reinforcing student successes rather than on punishing student failures. He proposed a "technology of teaching" whereby instruction is individualized, complex verbal behaviors are gradually shaped, reinforcement for appropriate responses is consistent and immediate, and learned behaviors are maintained through intermittent reinforcement schedules. Skinner's suggestions for how operant conditioning might be successfully applied to classroom situations, and the suggestions of other psychologists and educators as well, are the subject of the next chapter.

SUMMARY

The basic principle of operant conditioning is that responses that are followed by reinforcement increase in frequency. For operant conditioning to occur, a reinforcer must follow immediately after a response and also be contingent on that response. Operant conditioning is different from classical conditioning in at least three ways: (1) it occurs as a result of a response being followed by a reinforcing stimulus rather than as a result of two stimuli being paired, (2) it involves voluntary rather than involuntary responses, and (3) it is better described as an R→S relationship than an S→R relationship.

The free operant level, or baseline, of a response is its frequency in the absence of reinforcement; the terminal behavior is the form and frequency of the desired response at the end of a reinforcement program. Even when a response-reinforcer sequence occurs by coincidence rather than by design, an increase in the frequency of that response is observed (superstitious behavior). A response that has previously been reinforced, but is being reinforced no longer, tends to decrease in frequency to its baseline rate (extinction). Complex behaviors can be taught through a process of reinforcing successive approximations to the desired terminal behavior (shaping).

Reinforcement takes a variety of forms. A primary reinforcer is one that satisfies a biological need; a secondary (conditioned) reinforcer is one that becomes reinforcing through repeated association with another reinforcer. Whereas positive reinforcement involves the presentation of a (presumably pleasant) stimulus, negative reinforcement involves the removal of a (presumably aversive) stimulus; since negative reinforcement increases behavior just as positive reinforcement does, it is *not* a form of punishment. A reinforcer is not always a material object; for instance, it can also be a social event, a favorite activity, an intrinsic feeling of satisfaction, or positive feedback.

Timing, magnitude, and consistency of reinforcement affect the rate at which new behaviors are learned. Different schedules of reinforcement influence the frequency of a response as well as its rates of acquisition and extinction. Antecedent stimuli also affect the occurrence of a response. For example, when an organism has learned to respond in a certain way in the presence of one stimulus, it is likely to respond in the same way in the presence of similar stimuli (stimulus generalization). However, if a particular response has been reinforced in the presence of one stimulus but not in the presence of another, the organism will exhibit the response only when the former stimulus is presented (stimulus discrimination).

Contemporary perspectives of operant conditioning differ somewhat from Skinner's original notions. For example, some theorists propose that behavior is better understood by looking beyond specific S-R relationships to a larger context and longer time frame. In addition, some current explanations of why operant conditioning takes place include a discussion of the cognitive factors that underlie conditioning. And many theorists now believe that behavior may never be totally predictable—that human and nonhuman behavior is somewhat variable even when reinforcement histories and stimulus conditions remain the same.

In addition to punishment (which, according to many contemporary behaviorists, *does* lead to a response decrease), three techniques based on a traditional, reinforcement-based model of operant conditioning—extinction, the differential reinforcement of other behaviors, and the reinforcement of incompatible behaviors—serve as viable means of eliminating undesirable behaviors. B. F. Skinner contended that, in classroom situations, appropriate behaviors are usually reinforced inconsistently and undesirable behaviors are often unintentionally reinforced.

CHAPTER 5

Applications of Operant Conditioning

Within the past 40 years, operant conditioning has perhaps had more impact on educational practice than any other single model of human learning. At least five educational innovations depend either directly or indirectly on operant conditioning principles: (1) instructional objectives, (2) programmed instruction and its offspring, computer-assisted instruction, (3) mastery learning, (4) contingency contracting, and (5) behavior modification. In this chapter I will describe the basic components of these innovations, present empirical evidence concerning their effectiveness, and then address common concerns regarding the use of reinforcement in classroom situations.

INSTRUCTIONAL OBJECTIVES

In its 1947 report, the President's Commission on Higher Education described the primary goal of the United States educational system as "the full, rounded, and continuing development of the person" (cited in Dyer, 1967, p. 14). At first glance, this might seem to be a worthwhile and appropriate goal for education, but on closer inspection the statement provides very little *specific* information regarding what an educated person should be like. Dyer (1967) has presented the President's Commission report as an example of "word magic": It sounds nice, but we realize we don't have a clue as to what the words really mean. When we don't know exactly what our educational objectives are, we don't know what or how to teach, nor do we know whether our instruction is accomplishing its goals.

A standard practice in using operant conditioning is to specify the terminal behavior in precise, observable terms before conditioning begins, thereby allowing us to develop appropriate methods of shaping the desired behavior and of determining when that behavior has been acquired. This principle of *a priori* specification of the terminal behavior in observable, measurable terms has been applied to classroom instruction in the form of instructional objectives, and, more specifically, behavioral objectives.

Behavioral Objectives

Ideally, a behavioral objective has three components (e.g., Mager, 1962, 1984). First, the outcome is stated in terms of an observable and measurable behavior. Consider this objective:

The student will be aware of current events.

A student's "awareness" is not easily observable. The same objective can be stated in terms of one or more specific behaviors that a student should exhibit; consider this one as an example:

The student will recite the major cause of political unrest in South Africa.

Some verbs do not specify observable behaviors—for example, *understand*, *appreciate*, *know*, *be aware of*, and *remember*—whereas other verbs do communicate observable responses—for example, *write*, *compute*, *list*, *recite*, and *select* (e.g., Sax, 1989). You can probably conceptualize almost any objective in behavioral terms when you consider what specific things people would have to do to convince someone that they had met the objective (Mager, 1972).

Second, a behavioral objective specifies the conditions under which the behavior should be exhibited. Sometimes we expect desired behaviors to occur in specific situations (stimulus conditions). For example, one of my objectives for my graduate course in educational testing is

The student will correctly compute test-retest reliability.

I do not expect students to memorize the formula for calculating test-retest reliability, however. Hence, there is a condition under which I expect the behavior to occur, as follows:

Given the formula for a correlation coefficient, the student will correctly compute test-retest reliability.

Finally, the objective includes a criterion for judging the acceptable performance of the behavior. Many behaviors are not strictly right or wrong, but vary on a continuum of relative "rightness" and "wrongness." In cases where right and wrong behaviors are not obvious, a behavioral objective should specify the criterion for acceptable performance, perhaps in terms of a certain percentage of correct answers, a certain time limit, or the degree of acceptable deviation from the correct response (Mager, 1962, 1984). Here are some examples to illustrate this point:

On weekly written spelling tests, the student will correctly spell at least 85% of the year's 500 spelling words.

Given a sheet of 100 addition problems involving the addition of two single-digit numbers, including all possible combinations of the digits 0 through 9, the student will correctly write the answers to these problems within five minutes.

Given the formula for a correlation coefficient, the student will correctly compute test-retest reliability, with differences from a computer-calculated coefficient being attributable to rounding-off errors.

The Current Perspective on Instructional Objectives

Behavioral objectives have frequently been criticized for focusing on concrete, picayune details rather than on more central, but probably more abstract, educational goals. For example, many lists of behavioral objectives emphasize behaviors that depend on rote memorization of facts rather than on behaviors that reflect more complex and sophisticated learning (Trachtenberg, 1974); in other words, they focus on **lower-level skills** rather than **higher-level skills**. Such lower-level objectives may be prevalent simply because they are the easiest ones to conceptualize and write.

School personnel have many goals in mind for each classroom in any given year; these goals will typically encompass both lower-level and higher-level skills. Writing behavioral objectives that cover each and every goal can sometimes become a burdensome, if not impossible, task. As a result, many educators have more recently proposed a smaller number of general, nonbehavioral objectives as an acceptable alternative (Dressel, 1977; Gage & Berliner, 1984; Gronlund, 1978; Popham, 1988; Posner & Rudnitsky, 1986; Sax, 1989; Zahorik, 1976). But in such situations, it is nevertheless helpful to list examples of behaviors that reflect each abstract objective. To illustrate, if one goal of instruction is for students to read using critical thinking (a higher-level skill), we might list such behavioral manifestations of critical reading as these:

1. Distinguishing between facts and opinions
2. Distinguishing between facts and inferences
3. Identifying cause-effect relations
4. Identifying errors in reasoning
5. Distinguishing between relevant and irrelevant arguments
6. Distinguishing between warranted and unwarranted conclusions
7. Formulating valid conclusions from written material
8. Specifying assumptions needed to make conclusions true (adapted from Gronlund, 1978, p. 14).

This is hardly an exhaustive list of what critical reading entails, but it does give us an idea of the terminal behaviors we want to see.

Formulating Different Levels of Objectives

Sometimes objectives reflecting basic knowledge and skills are appropriate. But in many circumstances, objectives reflecting relatively sophisticated levels of learning are desired, especially as students get older (e.g., see Cole, 1990). In such situations, **taxonomies** of objectives—the various behaviors we might want to see students demonstrate, listed in order of increasing complexity—are helpful (e.g., Bloom, Englehart, Furst, Hill, & Krathwohl, 1956; Harrow, 1972; Krathwohl, Bloom, & Masia, 1964). As an example, Bloom's Taxonomy of Educational Objectives (Bloom et al., 1956) describes six general levels of knowing and using information—that is, six possible objectives in the **cognitive domain**. An overview of this taxonomy is presented in Figure 5–1.

Bloom and his colleagues originally presented the six levels as a hierarchy, with each one depending on those preceding it in the list. Although the hierarchical nature of Bloom's cognitive domain is in doubt (Furst, 1981; Seddon,

Figure 5-1
Bloom's Taxonomy of Educational Objectives

---

1. **Knowledge:** rote memorizing of information in a basically word-for-word fashion; for example, reciting definitions of terms or remembering lists of items.

2. **Comprehension:** translating information into one's own words; for example, rewording a definition or paraphrasing a rule.

3. **Application:** using information in a new situation; for example, applying mathematical principles to the solution of word problems or applying psychological theories of learning to educational practice.

4. **Analysis:** breaking information down into its constituent parts; for example, discovering the assumptions underlying a philosophical essay or identifying fallacies in a logical argument.

5. **Synthesis:** constructing something new by integrating several pieces of information; for example, developing a theory or presenting a logical defense of a particular viewpoint within a debate.

6. **Evaluation:** placing a value judgment on data; for example, critiquing a theory or determining the appropriateness of conclusions drawn from a research study.

Source: From *Taxonomy of educational objectives. The classification of educational goals. Handbook I: Cognitive domain* by B. S. Bloom, M. B. Englehart, E. J. Furst, W. H. Hill, & D. R. Krathwohl, 1956, New York: Longmans Green.

1978), the taxonomy nevertheless provides a useful reminder that behavioral objectives should encompass higher-level cognitive skills as well as the knowledge of simple, discrete facts (Gronlund, 1978; Hastings, 1977; Popham, 1988).

The Usefulness and Effectiveness of Objectives

From a teacher's perspective, objectives serve several useful functions (Gronlund, 1978; Mager, 1962, 1984). First, specification of a lesson's objectives in behavioral terms helps a teacher choose the most effective method of teaching that lesson. For example, when teaching a unit on basic addition, a teacher might use flashcards if the objective is *knowledge* of number facts, but should probably use word problems if the objective is the *application* of those number facts. A second advantage is that behavioral objectives are easily communicated from one teacher to another. For example, although teachers may differ in their conception of what "application of addition principles" means, they will be likely to interpret "correct solution of addition word problems" similarly. Finally, behavioral objectives facilitate the evaluation of both the student and the instructional program: When an objective is described in behavioral terms, both student accomplishment and program effectiveness can be evaluated on the basis of whether those specific behaviors are observed. From a student's perspective, behavioral objectives have an additional advantage: Students who are told what behaviors they should be able to demonstrate at the conclusion of an instructional unit have tangible goals to strive for and are better able to judge correctly their own completion of those behaviors (McAshan, 1979).

Because behavioral objectives specify the outcomes of instruction so explicitly, students typically view them favorably. However, research studies investigating the effectiveness of objectives for improving academic performance have yielded mixed results (Melton, 1978). Objectives tend to focus teachers' and students' attention toward certain information (what is included in the objectives) and away from other information (what has been omitted from the objectives) (e.g., Slavin, 1990). If the stated objectives encompass *all* important information, the use of objectives in the classroom will enhance learning. However, if the objectives include only a portion of the information the teacher deems important while excluding other, equally important, material, some critical information is not as likely to be learned as it might otherwise be.

PROGRAMMED INSTRUCTION AND COMPUTER-ASSISTED INSTRUCTION

According to the operant conditioning model of learning, reinforcement must occur immediately after a response to have a significant impact on that behavior. However, many reinforcers of classroom learning are delayed by hours, days, or, in the case of a high school diploma or college degree, even years. To provide a means by which responses can be reinforced immediately, Skinner (1954) developed a technique most frequently known as **programmed instruction**, or **PI**.

In its earliest form, programmed instruction involved an adaptation of Pressey's (1926, 1927) **teaching machine**. This "machine" was a box enclosing a long roll of printed material that a student could advance past a display window, thereby viewing small portions of information successively and systematically. Since the teaching machine, programmed instruction has evolved into programmed textbooks and, more recently, computer-assisted instruction.

Regardless of the form it takes, programmed instruction consists of several standard features. First, the material to be learned is presented through a series of discrete segments, or **frames**. The first frame presents a small piece of information and poses a question about it. The student responds to the question, then turns to the next frame; that frame provides the correct answer to the question of the previous frame, presents more information, and asks another question. The student continues through the frames, encountering new information, responding to questions, and checking answers against those provided by the program.

To illustrate the PI process, I have developed some possible frames for a unit on writing behavioral objectives, as follows:

FRAME 1

An *objective* is a goal for an instructional unit. **(information)**

> Another name for the goal of an instructional unit is an
> _____ . **(question)**

FRAME 2

objective **(answer to previous question)**

A behavioral *objective* is an objective that specifies the goals of an instructional unit in terms of the *behaviors* that the student should be able to demonstrate at the completion of that unit.

> An objective that specifies instructional goals in terms of
> behaviors that the student can demonstrate is called a
> _____ objective.

FRAME 3

behavioral

A behavioral objective should describe the desired behavior in such a way that the behavior is both *observable* and *measurable*.

> A behavioral objective is an instructional goal in which an
> observable and _____ behavior is described.

FRAME 4

measurable

The student will write the correct answer to the problem "2 + 2 = ?" In this objective, the word *write* describes an observable behavior.

> Which one of the following verbs is an example of an observable behavior: *think, appreciate, write,* or *learn*?
>
> _____

Intrinsic to programmed instruction are a number of concepts and principles based on operant conditioning, including the following:

1. *Terminal behavior*. The goal of instruction is specified before the instructional program is developed, in terms of the terminal behavior (behavioral objective) to be demonstrated upon completion of instruction.

2. *Active responding*. The student is required to make a response in each frame.

3. *Shaping*. Instruction begins with information that the student already knows. The new information to be learned is broken into tiny pieces, and instruction proceeds through a gradual presentation of increasingly more difficult pieces. As the successive pieces are presented and questions of increasing difficulty are answered, the terminal behavior is gradually shaped.

4. *Immediate reinforcement*. Because instruction involves a gradual shaping process, the probability is quite high that a student will provide correct answers to the questions asked. Each correct answer is reinforced immediately in the form of feedback that it is correct.

5. *Individual differences in learning rate*. Programmed instruction is self-paced, allowing students to progress at their own rates of speed through an instructional unit.

The earliest form of programmed instruction was the **linear program**, in which all students proceeded through exactly the same sequence of frames in exactly the same order. A more recent trend is to use a **branching program**, a technique introduced by Norman Crowder (e.g., Crowder & Martin, 1961). Branching programs typically progress in larger steps than linear programs (i.e., each frame presents more information), so error rates in responding are somewhat higher. A student who responds incorrectly is directed to one or more "remedial" frames for further practice on that part of the lesson before being allowed to continue with new information. To illustrate, let's resume our lesson on behavioral objectives (beginning where we left off, with Frame 4), but now using a branching format:

FRAME 4

measurable

The student will write the correct answer to the problem "2 + 2 = ?" In this objective, the word *write* describes an observable behavior.
Which one of the following verbs is an example of an observable behavior: *think*, *appreciate*, *write*, or *learn*?

FRAME 5

If you answered *think*, *appreciate*, or *learn*, go to Frame 6.
If you answered *write*, go to Frame 7.

FRAME 6

The verbs *think*, *appreciate*, and *learn* all describe internal mental events; they are not observable behaviors. Only the verb *write* describes an observable behavior. Return to Frame 4 and try again.

FRAME 7

Yes, the verb *write* is the only one of the four that describes an observable behavior. The other verbs—*think*, *appreciate*, and *learn*—cannot be directly observed.

The student will learn the alphabet. This is not a behavioral objective because the verb *learn* does not describe an observable behavior.

The above objective could be changed into a behavioral objective by replacing the verb *learn* with which one of the following: *remember*, *memorize*, or *recite*? _____

FRAME 8

If you answered *remember* or *memorize*, go to Frame 9.

If you answered *recite*, go to Frame 13.

FRAME 9

The verbs *remember* and *memorize* do not reflect observable behaviors. Only *recite* is a directly observable response.

The student will _____ the Pledge of Allegiance. One of these verbs would make this objective a behavioral objective: *know*, *say*, *memorize*, or *learn*.

Which one of the four verbs can be used to make the statement a behavioral objective? _____

FRAME 10

If you answered *know*, *memorize*, or *learn*, go to Frame 11.
If you answered *learn*, go to Frame 12.

FRAME 11

No. *Knowing*, *memorizing*, and *learning* cannot be directly observed. Only *saying* is an observable behavior. Return to Frame 7 and review this section again.

FRAME 12

Yes. Only the verb *say* describes an observable behavior.

[The lesson continues with new information.]

The major advantage of a branching program is that it provides remedial instructional frames only for students who have difficulty with a particular concept; other students can move on to new information without having to spend time on practice they don't need. Unfortunately, however, a branching program can be cumbersome, at least in its textbook form. Students are referred to different frames, and often to different pages, for each response they make, so progression through the program is rarely smooth. Fortunately, this drawback of the branching program has been virtually eliminated by the advent of computer-assisted instruction.

Computer-assisted instruction, or **CAI**, is programmed instruction presented by means of a computer. It has a number of advantages not characteristic of other forms of programmed instruction. First, branching programs can be used without having to instruct students to proceed to one frame or another; the computer automatically presents the appropriate frame for any response the student has given. Second, because of the graphics capabilities of computers (e.g., they can present complex moving visual displays), CAI can present information in a way that traditional programmed instruction cannot. A good example is the use of simulation programs, programs that give students practice in performing skilled operations, such as flying an airplane, without the risk or expense that would be associated with performing those operations in real-life situations. Third, the computer can record and maintain ongoing data for each student, including such information as how far a student has progressed in the program, how often he or she is right and wrong, how quickly he or she responds, and so on. With such data, a teacher can monitor each student's progress through the program and can identify students who are having particular difficulty with the material. And, finally, a computer can be used to provide instruction when flesh-and-blood teachers are not available; for example, CAI is often used to deliver college instruction in rural areas far removed from university settings. (We should note here that, as cognitivism increasingly dominates theories of human learning, computer instruction is no longer restricted to the traditional behaviorism-based CAI approach; hence, you may sometimes see reference to the term *computer-assisted learning* (CAL) rather than CAI.)

The Effectiveness of PI and CAI

Most research indicates that traditional (i.e., noncomputer-based) programmed instruction is no more effective than traditional instructional methods (Feldhusen, 1963; Lange, 1972; Reese & Parnes, 1970; Schramm, 1964). CAI, on the other hand, is frequently shown to be superior to traditional instruction, in terms of both increased academic achievement and improved student attitudes toward schoolwork (Hativa & Shorer, 1989; Kulik, Kulik, & Cohen, 1980; Lepper & Gurtner, 1989).

A cautionary note regarding the use of PI and CAI is in order, however. Some programmed instruction packages may be poorly conceived (Bell-Gredler, 1986; O'Leary & O'Leary, 1972); for example, they may not always adequately incorporate such principles as active responding, immediate reinforcement of responses, or gradual shaping of the terminal behavior. Programmed instruction is less likely to be effective when such principles of operant conditioning are violated.

MASTERY LEARNING

Inherent in behaviorism, and especially in the operant conditioning model, is the belief that, given appropriate environmental conditions (consistent reinforcement of desirable behaviors, gradual shaping of responses over time, etc.), people are capable of acquiring many complex behaviors. As an example of such optimism, you may remember John Watson's famous quote presented in Chapter 2: "Give me a dozen healthy infants, well-formed, and my own specified world to bring them up in and I'll guarantee to take any one at random and train him to become any type of specialist I might select. . . ."

The optimism of behaviorism is reflected in **mastery learning**—an approach to instruction in which students must learn one lesson well (they must *master* the content) before proceeding to the next lesson. This approach assumes that most students *can* learn school subject matter given sufficient time and instruction.

Mastery learning is partially based on the operant conditioning concept of *shaping*: At first, a relatively simple response is reinforced until it is emitted frequently (i.e., until it is mastered), then a slightly more difficult response is reinforced, and so on, until eventually the desired terminal behavior is acquired. Consistent with shaping, mastery learning usually includes the following components:

1. *Small, discrete units.* Course content is broken up into a number of separate units or lessons, with each unit covering a small amount of material.
2. *A logical sequence.* Units are sequenced such that basic concepts and procedures—those that provide the foundation for later units—are learned first. More complex concepts and procedures, including those that build on basic units, are learned later. For example, a unit in which students learn what a fraction *is* would obviously come before a unit in which they learn how to add two fractions together.
3. *Demonstration of mastery at the completion of each unit.* Before "graduating" from one unit to the next, students must show that they have mastered the current unit—for example, by taking a test on the content of that unit.
4. *A concrete, observable criterion for mastery of each unit.* Mastery of a topic is defined in specific, concrete terms. For example, to "pass" a unit on adding fractions with the same denominator, students might have to answer at least 90% of test items correctly.
5. *Additional "remedial" activities for students needing extra help or practice.* Students do not always demonstrate mastery on the first try. Additional support and resources—perhaps alternative approaches to instruction, different materials, workbooks, study groups, and individual tutoring—are provided for students who need them (e.g., Guskey, 1985).

Mastery learning gained prominence during the 1960s; many educators still advocate it (e.g., Block, 1980; Bloom, 1968, 1974, 1976, 1981, 1984a; Carroll, 1963, 1989; Guskey, 1985; Hunter, 1982; Keller, 1968; Lee & Pruitt, 1984). A particular form of mastery learning—Fred Keller's personalized system of instruction—is frequently used at the college level. Let's take a closer look at what this approach entails.

Keller's Personalized System of Instruction (PSI)

As Michael (1974) has pointed out, traditional college instruction suffers from a number of weaknesses, at least when viewed from the perspective of operant conditioning principles. For example, delaying students' grades by days or weeks (a common occurrence) does not immediately reinforce achievement. Furthermore, instructors frequently ask students to proceed to advanced material before they have mastered the more basic information necessary to understand it.

To remedy such weaknesses of college instruction, Fred Keller (1968, 1974) developed the **personalized system of instruction** (also known as **PSI** and the **Keller Plan**) as an alternative approach to teaching college students. In addition to the discrete modules, logical sequence, and frequent measures of mastery characteristic of other mastery learning approaches, PSI encompasses the following features:

1. *Emphasis on individual study.* Most learning occurs through students' independent study of such written materials as textbooks and study guides. One-on-one tutoring provides additional assistance when necessary.
2. *Unit exams.* An examination on each module assesses students' mastery of material. Students receive immediate feedback about how well they have performed on unit exams. (Note that other approaches assess mastery, but not necessarily by exams.)
3. *Self-pacing.* Students report to class to take exams when they are ready to do so; in this sense, learning is self-paced. Some students proceed through the course very quickly, others more slowly. (Note that self-pacing is sometimes, but not always, a component of other mastery approaches as well.)
4. *Supplementary instructional techniques.* Traditional group instructional methods (e.g., lectures, demonstrations, and discussions) are occasionally provided as supplementary presentations of the same information that also appears in the textbook or other assigned readings. These group classes are optional but serve to motivate and stimulate students.
5. *Use of proctors.* Proctors, usually more advanced students, administer and score exams and tutor students on topics with which they are having difficulty.

The teacher of a PSI course plays a different role from that of someone using a more conventional approach to instruction. The PSI teacher is less of a lecturer and more of a curriculum developer, exam writer, proctor coordinator, and recordkeeper. Rather than leading students through course content, the PSI teacher instead provides an elaborate system whereby students, with the assistance of study guides and tutors, find their own way through.

The Effectiveness of Mastery Learning and PSI

Several reviews of research findings (Arlin, 1984; Block & Burns, 1976; Kulik, Kulik, & Bangert-Drowns, 1990; Kulik, Kulik, & Cohen, 1979) indicate that mastery learning (including PSI) facilitates student learning and often leads to higher achievement than more traditional approaches (although note that Slavin [1987, 1990] finds no substantial differences). Furthermore, students in mastery learning programs often retain the things they have learned for longer periods of time (DuNann & Weber, 1976; Kulik, Kulik, & Cohen, 1979); to illustrate, in one study of mastery learning, college students in mastery-based psychology classes remembered 75% to 85% of the material after four months and 70% to 80% after 11 months (Semb, Ellis, & Araujo, 1993). And PSI, at least, facilitates better study habits: Although PSI students don't appear to study more than anyone else, they study regularly rather than procrastinating and cramming the way other students in traditional courses often do (Born & Davis, 1974; Kulik et al., 1979). Lower-ability students in particular seem to benefit from a mastery learning approach (DuNann & Weber, 1976; Kulik et al., 1990).

Mastery learning and PSI are not without their problems, however. For one thing, in many cases those students who learn quickly receive less instruction than other students, raising a concern about possibly inequitable treatment (Arlin, 1984). Furthermore, for logistical reasons, fast-learning students must sometimes wait until their slower classmates have also mastered the material before they can proceed to the next unit; as a result, they learn less than they might otherwise (Arlin, 1984). And some educators argue that teachers in a mastery learning classroom may do more "managing" (distributing materials, grading tests, etc.) than actual teaching (e.g., Prawat, 1992).

Additional weaknesses have been noted for PSI in particular. One difficulty lies in the required mastery of material; some students are unable to meet the criterion for passing exams, despite repeated testings (Sussman, 1981). A second weakness is the lack of interaction among students, interaction that many students see as beneficial to their learning (Gasper, 1980). A third problem is related to the self-paced nature of a PSI course, which is sometimes compromised if university policy requires that students complete a course within one quarter or semester (Sussman, 1981). Poorly motivated students are likely to procrastinate until finally they must withdraw from the course (Sussman, 1981; Swenson, 1980), although withdrawal rates from PSI courses do not seem appreciably higher than withdrawals from traditional courses (Kulik et al., 1979, 1990). Several techniques have been shown to reduce procrastination and withdrawal from PSI, among them setting target dates for the completion of different modules (Reiser & Sullivan, 1977), giving bonus points for early completion of modules (Bufford, 1976), and eliminating the necessity for completing the course within one college term (Sussman, 1981).

Mastery learning is probably most appropriately used when a teacher's main objective is for students to learn specific skills or a specified body of information. In such situations, the immediate feedback and emphasis on mastery of course material may well explain why mastery learning increases student achievement, particularly for low-ability students. However, when the objective is something other than acquiring information or skills—for example, when it is to wrestle with controversial and unresolved issues—a mastery approach may not be the method of choice.

CONTINGENCY CONTRACTS

Programmed instruction and Keller's personalized system of instruction are instances of operant conditioning principles applied to the education of a large number of students. The amount of time needed to prepare materials for both of these techniques makes their use for only one or two students virtually impossible. When the behavior or learning of a single student is of concern, a contingency contract is often more practical.

A **contingency contract** is an agreement between a student and a teacher regarding certain expectations for the student (the terminal behavior) and the consequences of the student's meeting those expectations (the reinforcer). For example, a student and teacher may agree that the student should turn in all homework assignments, on time and with at least 90% accuracy, every day for a week. If the student accomplishes this task, the contract might specify that she will have some time to engage in a favorite activity, or that the teacher and student will spend time after school studying a topic of particular interest to the student. Although a contingency contract can be as simple as a verbal agreement, more often it is an actual written contract. As such, the student and teacher negotiate the conditions of the contract in one or more meetings; both individuals then date and sign the contract.

A contingency contract can be used to reward academic accomplishment; it can also help modify classroom behavior. For example, a teacher might help a student spend more class time attending to assigned work, or engage in more prosocial behaviors on the playground, by contracting with the student that certain desired behaviors will lead to positive consequences. Contingency contracting has been shown effective for addressing such diverse problems as poor study habits (Brooke & Ruthren, 1984), juvenile delinquency (Rueger & Liberman, 1984; Welch, 1985), and drug addiction (Anker & Crowley, 1982; Crowley, 1984; Rueger & Liberman, 1984). It can also be a useful supplement to Keller's personalized system of instruction (Brooke & Ruthren, 1984).

Guidelines for Writing Contingency Contracts

Teachers should keep several guidelines in mind when developing contingency contracts.

   •*The contract should specify the desired behavior of the student and the consequence (reinforcer) that will be contingent on that behavior.* Both the desired behavior and the reinforcer should be specified in clear, precise terminology (Homme, Csanyi, Gonzales, & Rechs, 1970).

•*Early contracts should require small tasks that a student can accomplish within a short time* (Walker & Shea, 1984). Remember the problem with delayed reinforcement: Contracts that provide reinforcement only after the desired behavior has been exhibited for a lengthy period of time simply may not work.

•*Reinforcement should be contingent on accomplishment of the desired behavior* (Homme et al., 1970). Students occasionally tell their teacher that they *tried* to do a task, but for one reason or another could not. Teachers who reinforce students only for successful completion of the task specified in the contract, *not* for their self-described unsuccessful efforts, will give students a clear message that task completion is essential for school success.

•*A criterion for judging the quality of the desired behavior should be specified*. When the task to be accomplished can differ considerably in quality, as is true for an exam or a written composition, a criterion of successful completion of that task should be included in the contract. In the case of an exam, the criterion might be a percentage of correct items. For written work, it is almost inevitable that some subjective judgment will be involved in assessing the work; however, criteria that the evaluation will consider—specific content to be included, organization, clarity, grammar, and so on—should be clearly stated as a part of the contract.

A former colleague of mine once overlooked this critical principle when he used contingency contracts to assign grades in his college classes. For example, some contracts stated that students would take exams on assigned readings without specifying acceptable scores for those exams. Other contracts read something like this: "For an A, the student will write a 10-page paper on the topic of behav-

When used to address individual student needs, contingency contracts should be equivalent in scope.

For an A, ___Mary Lamb___ will read one book somehow related to education.

Signed:

___Mary L.___

___Dr Schmoe___

For an A, ___John Goat___ will write a 500-page treatise on the use of computer-assisted instruction for teaching Chinese calligraphy to dysgraphic children.

Signed:

___John G___

___Dr Schmoe___

ior modification," without describing how well the paper was to be written or what topics should be included. My colleague found himself obligated to award A's for multiple-choice exams with scores of 25% and for papers along the lines of "How I Behavior-Modified My Kid Brother at the Beach Last Summer."

•*When different contingency contracts are used with different students as a way of individualizing requirements for students, all contracts should neverthe-less be equivalent in scope.* Unless there are compelling reasons to do otherwise, contracts should require tasks that are equal in difficulty and reflect equal levels of competence for all students. The need for equivalence across contracts is par-ticularly critical when the reinforcers used are course grades: Assigning grades based on student behaviors differing radically in difficulty level and quality typi-cally renders those grades uninterpretable.

Contingency contracts are often considered a specific form of behavior modi-fication. We turn next to more general behavior modification techniques.

BEHAVIOR MODIFICATION

Behavior modification, sometimes known as **behavior therapy** or **contin-gency management**, is probably the most straightforward application of operant conditioning principles. Based on the assumption that behavior problems are the result of past and present environmental circumstances, behavior modification encompasses a number of procedures that modify an individual's present envi-ronment to promote the reinforcement of acceptable behaviors and the nonrein-forcement of inappropriate ones. Central to behavior modification techniques are such operant conditioning concepts as reinforcement, extinction, shaping, stimulus control, and reinforcement of incompatible behaviors. The concepts of punishment and modeling, while not components of Skinner's model of operant conditioning, are also frequently used in behavior modification programs; these two aspects of behavior modification will be dealt with in Chapters 6 and 7, respectively.

Components of Behavior Modification

Although behavior modification encompasses a number of different techniques, some components are common to all of them.

•*Both the present and the desired behaviors are specified in observable, measurable terms.* Consistent with behaviorist tradition, behavior modifiers focus their attention on specific, concrete responses. The actual behaviors to be increased or decreased are called **target behaviors**. For example, in a program designed to decrease a child's aggressiveness, such target behaviors as screaming, hitting other people, and throwing objects might be identified (Morris, 1985).

•*An effective reinforcer is identified*. We should never assume that particular consequences will be reinforcing to particular students (Pfiffner, Rosén, & O'Leary, 1985). Instead, we can identify one or more reinforcers that are likely to change students' behavior by observing what they will work for or even by asking them outright. When a behavior modification program is instituted in a school setting, social reinforcers, such as praise, or activity reinforcers, such as special privileges, are often effective (e.g., Bates, 1979; Brophy, 1981; Piersel, 1987). In some cases, immediate feedback that a student has done something correctly is all the reinforcement a student needs, particularly when it is not otherwise clear that the student has been successful (Bangert-Drowns, Kulik, Kulik, & Morgan, 1991; Harris & Rosenthal, 1985; Kulik & Kulik, 1988). If material reinforcers are needed (primarily because other reinforcers don't work), having parents provide those reinforcers at home for behaviors exhibited at school often works quite well (Barth, 1979; Kelley & Carper, 1988; Wielkiewicz, 1986).

•*A specific intervention or treatment plan is developed*. Developing a treatment plan involves determining how the target behavior is to be modified. Sometimes a behavior's frequency can be increased simply by reinforcing that behavior every time it occurs. However, when the free operant level (baseline) of a desired response is very low, that response may have to be shaped through the reinforcement of successively closer and closer approximations. An undesirable behavior can be eliminated through such methods as extinction, the differential reinforcement of other behaviors (a DRO schedule), the reinforcement of incompatible behaviors, or stimulus control (i.e., limiting the situations in which the behavior is allowed).

•*Behavior is measured both before and during treatment*. Only through the objective measurement of the target behavior during both baseline and treatment can we determine whether the behavior modification program is effectively changing the target behavior. One way of measuring the target behavior is simply to count the overall *frequency* of a given response; for example, if we have designed a program to modify Johnny's "hitting others" behavior, we would count each instance of hitting. A second method of behavior measurement is to examine the *rate* of responding by counting the number of responses occurring within a specified time interval; for example, we might count the number of times Johnny hits in each hour of the day. Still a third method, called **time-sampling**, involves dividing the time period during which the individual is being observed into equal intervals and then checking whether the target behavior occurred in each interval. For example, we might measure Johnny's hitting behavior by dividing his school day into five-minute intervals and then identifying intervals in which hitting was observed.

Behaviors frequently persist because they are either intentionally or unintentionally reinforced, so it is often helpful to record the consequences of the behavior as well as the behavior itself. In addition, many behaviorists (e.g., Rimm & Masters, 1974; Sulzer-Azaroff, 1981) believe that antecedent events should also be noted to determine whether a behavior is under stimulus control. Figure 5–2 illustrates a time sample of Johnny's hitting responses, with events antecedent and consequent to those responses also recorded.

Figure 5–2
A time sample of target behaviors in conjunction with antecedent and consequent events

		student teased him	none observed		student hit him
Antecedent		student teased him	none observed		student hit him
Target Behavior (hitting)	no	yes	yes	no	yes
Consequence		scolded	scolded		none

| 9:00 | 9:05 | 9:10 | 9:15 | 9:20 |

(Times indicate start of each 5-minute interval.)

Behaviorists urge that target behaviors be observed and recorded as objectively as possible. Ideally, they recommend that one person (e.g., the teacher) administer the program and at least two other individuals trained in observation techniques observe and record occurrences of the target behavior. If the method of behavior measurement is such that the behavior is being objectively and accurately recorded, the agreement between the recordings of the two observers (the **inter-rater reliability**) should be very high.

• *The treatment is monitored for effectiveness as it progresses and is modified if necessary.* When a desired behavior increases in frequency or an unwanted behavior decreases during the treatment program (compared to the baseline rate), the logical conclusion is that the behavior modification program is effective. When little change is observed from baseline to treatment, however, a change in the program is warranted. Perhaps the teacher is trying to shape behavior too quickly. Perhaps the "reinforcer" is not really reinforcing, and a different reinforcer should be substituted. Perhaps an undesired behavior that the teacher is attempting to eliminate through extinction is being maintained by reinforcers outside the teacher's control. An unsuccessful treatment program should be carefully examined for these and other possible explanations for its ineffectiveness and then modified accordingly.

• *Treatment is phased out after the desired behavior is acquired.* Once the terminal behavior has been reached, the behavior modification program should be gradually phased out. In many instances, the newly learned behaviors begin to have their own rewards: For example, the aggressive student who learns more acceptable social behaviors begins to acquire new friends, and the student who has finally learned to read begins to feel successful and enjoy reading. In other situations, maintaining the target behavior may require intermittent reinforcement, such as a series of successively higher variable-ratio reinforcement schedules.

Using Behavior Modification with Groups of Students

The emphasis up until now has been on the use of behavior modification with individual students. But behavior modification can also be used to change the behavior of a group of students, even an entire classroom. Two methods are particularly effective in working with groups: the group contingency and the token economy.

Group Contingency

In a **group contingency**, the entire group must perform a desired behavior for reinforcement to occur. For example, in one study (Lovitt, Guppy, & Blattner, 1969), the performance of a class of 32 fourth-graders on their weekly spelling tests was effectively modified applying a group contingency. In phase one of the study, baseline data indicated that about 12 students (38%) had perfect spelling tests in any given week. In phase two, spelling tests were administered each of four days during the week; any student who obtained a perfect test score one day had free time on any successive days that the same test was repeated. During this individually based contingency period, the average number of perfect spelling tests a week more than doubled to 25.5 (80%). In phase three, the individual contingencies of phase two continued to apply; in addition, when the entire class achieved perfect spelling tests by Friday, the class could listen to the radio for 15 minutes. The group contingency of phase three led to 30 perfect spelling tests (94% of the class) a week!

The "good behavior game" is an example of how a group contingency can reduce classroom misbehaviors. In research conducted by Barrish, Saunders, and Wolf (1969), a class of particularly unruly fourth-graders (seven of the students had repeatedly been referred to the principal for problem behaviors) was divided into two teams whose behaviors were carefully observed during reading and mathematics lessons. Every time a team member committed an out-of-seat or talking-out behavior, that team received a mark on its designated part of the chalkboard. The team that had fewer marks during the lesson would receive special privileges (e.g., first in the lunch line, free time at the end of the day); if both teams had five marks or fewer, both would win privileges.

Figure 5–3 shows the results of Barrish's study. Notice how baseline data were first collected for both math and reading periods. The good behavior game was instituted in the mathematics period on day 23; out-of-seat and talking-out behaviors decreased sharply during mathematics instruction while continuing at a high frequency during reading. On day 45, the game was initiated during reading instruction and stopped during math instruction; notice how the frequencies of misbehaviors changed accordingly. On day 51, the game was reinstated in the math period, and again the misbehavior decreased to a low level in that class. By the way, these techniques of collecting data from two different situations (**multiple baseline data**) and of switching from reinforcement to nonreinforcement and then back again (a technique called **reversal**) are common techniques in behavior modification research for ruling out coincidence as the reason for observed behavior changes.

Figure 5–3
Percentage of one-minute
intervals scored as containing talking-out and out-of-
seat behaviors occurring
during math and reading
periods

From "Good Behavior Game: Effects of Individual Contingencies for Group Consequences on Disruptive
Behavior in a Classroom" by H. H. Barrish, M. Saunders,
& M. M. Wolf, in K. D. O'Leary & S. O'Leary (Eds.), *Classroom Management: The Successful Use of Behavior Modification*, p. 375. Copyright 1972 by Pergamon Press, Ltd.

Numerous other studies support the effectiveness of group contingencies, particularly when they are used within the context of cooperative learning activities (Johnson & Johnson, 1987; Pigott, Fantuzzo, & Clement, 1986; Slavin, 1983a, 1983b). Peer pressure and social reinforcement are clearly among the reasons that group contingencies are effective (O'Leary & O'Leary, 1972; Swenson, 1980). Misbehaving students are encouraged by other students to change their behaviors and frequently get praise when those changes occur (Johnson & Johnson, 1987; Slavin, 1983b). In addition, when increased academic achievement is the desired behavior, high-achieving students often assist their lower-achieving classmates by tutoring and providing extra practice in their academic work (Bronfenbrenner, 1970; Johnson & Johnson, 1987; Pigott, Fantuzzo, & Clement, 1986).

Token Economy

The token economy, undoubtedly the most prevalent behavior modification technique in group settings, is a situation in which individuals who behave appropriately are reinforced with **tokens**, items that can later be traded in for **back-up reinforcers**—objects or privileges of each individual's choice. For example, a teacher using a token economy in the classroom might reward students with one poker chip for each completed assignment. Just before lunch, students can use their poker chips to "buy" small treats, free time in the reading center, or a prime position in the lunch line.

A token economy typically includes the following components:

1. *A set of rules* describing the responses that will be reinforced. The rules should be relatively few in number, so that they can be remembered easily.
2. *Token reinforcers* that can be awarded immediately when appropriate behaviors are exhibited. Such items as poker chips, checkmarks on a grid sheet, play money, and points can be used. Even class grades have been successfully used as tokens (McKenzie, Clark, Wolf, Kothera, & Benson, 1968).
3. *A variety of back-up reinforcers* (objects, activities, and privileges) for which tokens can be exchanged. Examples of back-up reinforcers that have been shown to be effective in classroom token economies are free time (Osborne, 1969), participation in special events (Bushell, Wrobel, & Michaelis, 1968), and parent-awarded allowance (McKenzie et al., 1968).
4. *A "store" at which the back-up reinforcers can be "purchased."* Young children should be allowed at least one purchase opportunity a day; for older children, one or two opportunities a week may be sufficient.

Token reinforcers are advantageous because teachers can use them to reward individual behaviors immediately and conveniently within a group setting. The fact that students can trade tokens for many different back-up reinforcers is another advantage; every individual can probably find at least one desirable item. The tokens themselves often become effective reinforcers (Hundert, 1976); perhaps they become secondary reinforcers through repeated association with other reinforcing objects and events or perhaps they are effective simply because they provide feedback that students are doing something right.

The Effectiveness of Behavior Modification

Behavior modification has been clearly shown to effect behavior change and often works where other techniques fail (e.g., O'Leary & O'Leary, 1972). Numerous studies point to its effectiveness in improving academic performance and study habits (Braukmann, Ramp, & Wolf, 1981; Glover & Gary, 1976; Harris & Sherman, 1973; Iwata, 1987; Lovitt et al., 1969; McLaughlin & Malaby, 1972; McLaughlin & Williams, 1988; McNamara, 1987; Piersel, 1987; Rapport & Bostow, 1976). It is also useful in improving such behaviors as attention (Packard, 1970), social skills (Braukmann et al., 1981; Iwata, 1987; McLaughlin & Williams, 1988), and cleanliness (Taylor & Kratochwill, 1978). Furthermore, it can effectively reduce such undesirable behaviors as hyperactivity, impulsivity, aggression, and violence (Ayllon, Layman, & Kandel, 1975; Braukmann et al., 1981; Mayer & Butterworth, 1979; Plummer, Baer, & LeBlanc, 1977; Shafto & Sulzbacher, 1977; Wulbert & Dries, 1977).

Behavior modification is particularly beneficial in classrooms of students who must be continually motivated to engage in appropriate academic and social behaviors. It is therefore used frequently in the education and therapy of students with special needs, especially those with either learning difficulties or behavioral problems (Braukmann et al., 1981; Haring, Roger, Lee, Breen, & Gaylord-Ross, 1986; Hobbs & Holt, 1976; McLaughlin & Williams, 1988; O'Leary & Becker, 1967; Plummer et al., 1977; Rimm & Masters, 1974; Witt, Elliott, & Gresham, 1988; Wolf, Braukmann, & Ramp, 1987).

Although it is clear that behavior modification works, it is not always clear just *why* it works. One likely factor underlying the effectiveness of behavior modification is the use of clearly specified response-reinforcement contingencies. Because desired behaviors are described in specific, concrete terms, students know exactly what is expected of them. And the immediate feedback that they receive through reinforcement provides them with clear guidance as to when their behaviors are on target and when they are not.

CRITICISMS OF USING REINFORCEMENT IN THE CLASSROOM

Although instructional techniques based on operant conditioning principles are clearly effective, such techniques are not without their critics. Some criticisms are probably ill-founded, while others should be considered more seriously. We will first examine some of the common "bogus" complaints, then turn to more genuine concerns.

Bogus Complaints

Many criticisms directed toward the use of reinforcement in the classroom reflect either a misunderstanding of operant conditioning principles or an ignorance of empirical findings. We will consider some typical examples of such criticisms.

•*Reinforcement is bribery*. The bribery argument is probably the most frequent complaint leveled against the use of reinforcement in the classroom. However, the word *bribery* implies that the behavior being reinforced is somehow illegal or unethical. On the contrary, the appropriate use of reinforcement in the classroom can facilitate attainment of educational objectives, all of which involve academically and socially desirable behaviors.

•*Reinforcement develops dependence on concrete, external rewards for appropriate behavior*. It is often argued that students should learn because of intrinsic rewards—they should learn for learning's sake. This argument can be countered in two ways. First of all, behavior modification does not necessarily involve material reinforcers. Social reinforcers, activities, feedback, and intrinsic

Reinforcement as bribery

reinforcers (e.g., feelings of success or accomplishment) are also effective in changing behavior, and the sensible behavior modifier will use them instead of material reinforcers whenever possible.

Second, even when a teacher must use material reinforcers to change behavior, these reinforcers bring about positive changes in a student—changes that apparently *will not occur any other way*. Reinforcement is often used when more traditional methods of changing behavior have failed, to increase desired academic and social skills and decrease counterproductive behaviors. If the choice comes down to either teaching Johnny to read by reinforcing him for reading or not teaching him to read at all, obviously Johnny must learn to read through whatever means possible. And we must remember, too, that, when material reinforcers are used, social events (e.g., praise) that are paired with them can eventually be used as reinforcers instead.

•*Reinforcing one student for being good teaches other students to be bad.* "Hmmm," Leslie thinks. "Linda has been such a loudmouth the past few weeks that the teacher is now giving her candy so she'll keep quiet. Maybe if I start shooting my mouth off, I'll start getting candy, too." If students are thinking along these lines, then something is clearly wrong with the way reinforcement is being administered in the classroom. All students should be reinforced for their positive behaviors. Praise and positive feedback should not be limited to a handful of chronic misbehavers but should be awarded consistently to all students. If the behavior of a particular student can be modified *only* with material reinforcers such as candy, such reinforcement should be administered discretely and in private.

•*Changing a problem behavior does not change the underlying cause of that behavior; other behavioral manifestations of that underlying cause will appear.* Reflected in this criticism is Sigmund Freud's notion of *symptom substitution*: Problem behaviors are a function of deep-rooted psychological conflicts, so that when a behavior is eliminated without treatment of its underlying cause, another problem behavior will emerge in its place. The best rebuttal to the symptom substitution criticism is an empirical one: When problem behaviors are treated through behavior modification, symptom substitution rarely occurs (Rimm & Masters, 1974).

One likely reason for this finding is that changing an individual's behavior may indirectly address its underlying causes as well. For example, consider the boy who is inappropriately aggressive on the playground. This boy might truly want to interact with his classmates, but aggression is the only way he knows of initiating that interaction. Reinforcing the boy for more appropriate methods of social interaction not only helps him develop friendships, it also deals with the underlying cause for his aggression—his desire for companionship.

•*Reinforced behaviors do not generalize to other situations.* The argument here is that children may learn to engage in appropriate behaviors in the classroom where they are reinforced for doing so, but will not exhibit those behaviors in a setting where no reinforcement occurs. The fact is that reinforced behaviors often *do* generalize to other situations (Rimm & Masters, 1974). When they do not, reinforcement in different situations and the reinforcement of similar behaviors can encourage generalization (Morris, 1985).

Genuine Concerns

The bogus complaints just listed can be easily rebutted. Three major criticisms of operant conditioning techniques should be taken more seriously, however.

•*Attempts at changing behaviors ignore cognitive factors that may be interfering with learning*. When students are capable of learning a new skill but are not motivated to do so, they may only need reinforcement to bring about the desired behavior change. However, when cognitive deficiencies (e.g., specific learning disabilities) exist that interfere with the acquisition of a new skill, reinforcement alone may be insufficient. In the latter situation, we may need to employ teaching techniques based more on cognitive learning theories (which will be explored in later chapters).

•*Reinforcement of particular predetermined behaviors sometimes interferes with maximal learning and performance over the long run*. Reinforcement for accomplishing a certain task focuses students' attention and effort more on getting that task done quickly, perhaps at a minimally acceptable level, than on *learning* from that task (Brophy, 1986; Lepper & Hodell, 1989). When teachers want their students to engage in complex, higher-level thinking—for example, to think flexibly and creatively about the subject matter—then extrinsic reinforcement simply for task accomplishment may sometimes be counterproductive (Brophy, 1986; Deci & Ryan, 1985; Hennessey & Amabile, 1987; Lepper & Hodell, 1989).

•*Extrinsic reinforcement of a behavior already motivated by intrinsic reinforcement may undermine the intrinsically reinforcing value of that behavior*. Individuals often engage in activities because of the internal rewards—for example, pleasure or feelings of success—that those activities bring. A number of research studies indicate that enjoyable activities can be increased by extrinsic reinforcers, but will then *decrease* to a below-baseline frequency once the extrinsic reinforcers are removed (Lepper & Greene, 1978; Lepper & Hodell, 1989). For example, in one study, preschool children who had previously been reinforced for certain drawing activities were actually *less* likely to engage in drawing in a free-play situation than children who had not been reinforced (Lepper, Greene, & Nisbett, 1973). Similar results occurred in a study with college students: Students who received a dollar for each correct solution of a series of block puzzles were less likely to continue to work at such puzzles in the absence of reinforcement than students who had not been paid for their correct solutions (Deci, 1971). It appears, then, that externally reinforcing a behavior that is already occurring because of intrinsic motivation may actually undermine that intrinsic motivation (deCharms, 1968; Deci, 1992; Deci & Porac, 1978; Deci &

Ryan, 1985, 1987; Lepper & Greene, 1978; Lepper & Hodell, 1989; Mayer, 1987; Spaulding, 1992).

WHEN OPERANT CONDITIONING TECHNIQUES ARE MOST APPROPRIATE

Instructional methods based on principles of operant conditioning are probably more appropriate for certain groups of students than for others. Among the students who appear to benefit the most from the structure and clearly specified response-reinforcement contingencies of operant conditioning techniques are students with a history of academic failure, poorly motivated students, anxious students, and students for whom nothing else works.

Experiences that provide frequent opportunities for success and reinforcement, such as programmed instruction, are particularly beneficial to students who have previously had little success in their academic careers. Children officially identified as "developmentally delayed" or "learning disabled" fall into this category, as do many juvenile delinquents and "slow learners" (children with below-normal intelligence whose test scores are not sufficiently low to qualify them for special educational services). Academic success is exactly what such students need to bolster the poor self-concepts that have resulted from a long string of academic failures.

Students with poor motivation for academic tasks can also benefit from operant conditioning techniques. Although some students thrive on the feelings that academic success can bring, others do not value academic achievement. The introduction of extrinsic reinforcers (material, social, or activity reinforcers) contingent on academic accomplishments may help improve the achievement of such students.

Highly anxious students appear to need structure in their curriculum to perform well on academic tasks (Dowaliby & Schumer, 1973; Grimes & Allinsmith, 1961). Such students need a classroom environment that specifies expectations for their behavior and clearly lays out response-reinforcement contingencies. They also seem to require frequent success experiences and positive feedback. Many of the methods derived from operant conditioning principles address the needs of anxious children particularly well: Behavioral objectives spell out desired behaviors in concrete terms, programmed instruction provides success and positive feedback, and behavior modification clearly communicates which behaviors will yield the reinforcers they seek.

Finally, for some students, nothing else works. Techniques based on operant conditioning principles have been shown to change even the most resilient of problem behaviors (Greer, 1983; Rimm & Masters, 1974). Such stubborn problems as childhood autism and juvenile delinquency have been dealt with more successfully by behavior modification than by any other method currently available.

On the other hand, methods based on operant conditioning are probably not suited for everyone. Bright students may find the gradual, inch-by-inch approach of programmed instruction slow and tedious. A token economy in a classroom of highly motivated college-bound students may undermine the intrinsic desire of these students to achieve at a high level. Other learning theories, notably cognitive theories, are probably more appropriate for helping these students learn.

SUMMARY

Instructional objectives—especially behavioral objectives (which express educational goals in terms of precise, observable responses)—are a direct outgrowth of the concept of terminal behavior. Objectives facilitate communication among students and teachers; they also help in selecting appropriate instructional strategies and evaluation techniques. Objectives tend to focus teachers' and students' attention toward the information and skills they identify (an advantage) and away from other information and skills (a possible disadvantage).

Programmed instruction, computer-assisted instruction, and mastery learning incorporate such operant conditioning principles as active responding, shaping, and immediate reinforcement. Although noncomputer-based programmed instruction is probably no more effective than traditional instructional methods, computer-assisted instruction and mastery learning have frequently been shown to facilitate student achievement.

A contingency contract provides a means through which a teacher and student can specify the behavior expected of the student and the consequence (reinforcer) that will follow such behavior. Reinforcement is also a key ingredient of behavior modification, which can be used with students either individually or on a group basis. Contingency contracts and behavior modification have been shown to improve both academic and social behavior.

Use of reinforcement in the classroom has drawn a number of criticisms; some are legitimate, while others indicate a misunderstanding of behavior modification techniques. Operant conditioning techniques are probably best used with certain kinds of students (e.g., those with high anxiety, poor motivation, or a history of academic failure) rather than as a matter of course with all students.

CHAPTER 6

Effects of Aversive Stimuli

The two preceding chapters focused on the influence of positive conse-quences (reinforcers) on learning. This chapter will focus on the impact of *aversive* events on learning and performance, with particular attention to three different situations. We will first examine how people and animals learn to escape and avoid painful events. We will then look at the effects of punish-ment on learning and behavior. Finally, we will examine a phenomenon that occurs when people and animals are exposed to aversive stimuli that they can neither avoid nor escape, a phenomenon known as learned helplessness.

ESCAPE AND AVOIDANCE LEARNING

My university, like most others, abounds in faculty committees. When I first joined the faculty, I eagerly joined committees whenever I could, perceiving them as a means of meeting other faculty members and having input into university decision making. Before long, however, I discovered that most faculty committees spend years chewing on the same old issues without ever arriving at consensus or otherwise accomplishing very much. Frustrated by the amount of time I was wasting, I soon found myself inventing excuses to leave committee meetings early ("I'm *so* sorry, but I have to take my son to the dentist"). Eventually, I stopped volunteering to join committees in the first place, thus avoiding them altogether.

Committee meetings had become an aversive event for me. My learning first to make excuses so I could leave meetings early and then not to volunteer in the first place is typical of what happens when an aversive stimulus is presented: Organisms learn to *escape* and eventually to *avoid* that stimulus if they possibly can.

Escape Learning

Escape learning is the process of learning a response that terminates an aversive stimulus. For example, in Neal Miller's classic study of escape learning (Miller, 1948), rats were placed in one compartment of a two-compartment cage and then given a series of electric shocks. The rats quickly learned to turn a wheel that enabled them to run to the other compartment, thereby escaping the aversive shocks. In an analogous study with humans (Hiroto, 1974), people readily learned to move a knob to turn off an unpleasantly loud noise.

Just as in the laboratory, students learn various ways of escaping unpleasant tasks or situations in the classroom. Making excuses ("My dog ate my math problems!") can be a means of escaping homework assignments. Lying about one's own behaviors ("I didn't do it—*he* did!") is a way of escaping the playground supervisor's evil eye. Chronic truancy and hypochondria are ways of escaping the school environment altogether.

Common escape and avoidance responses

Because escape from an aversive stimulus terminates that stimulus, the escape response is *negatively reinforced*. When rats make a response that stops an electric shock, when children make a response that terminates the evil eye, and when I make an excuse to leave a committee meeting, we are all reinforced by virtue of the fact that an unpleasant event is removed.

The more aversive a stimulus, the more likely people are to learn to escape that stimulus (e.g., Piliavin, Dovidio, Gaertner, & Clark, 1981; Piliavin, Piliavin, & Rodin, 1975). For example, children who have particular difficulty with assignments are more likely to have dogs who eat their homework. And truancy is most likely to occur when school is an unpleasant environment for a student; chronic truants are often those students who have encountered repeated failures both with their academic work and in their relationships with teachers and peers.

Avoidance Learning

Avoidance learning is the process of learning to stay away from an aversive stimulus altogether. For avoidance learning to occur, an organism must have some sort of **pre-aversive stimulus**, a cue signaling the advent of the aversive stimulus. For example, rats who hear a buzzer (the pre-aversive stimulus) before being given an electric shock easily learn to jump a hurdle as soon as the buzzer sounds, thereby avoiding the painful shock (Mowrer, 1938, 1939). Similarly, children quickly learn to pull a brass handle as soon as a light flashes so they can avoid an unpleasantly loud noise (Robinson & Robinson, 1961).

Avoidance learning appears in two forms: active avoidance learning and passive avoidance learning. In **active avoidance learning**, the organism must actively make a particular response to avoid the aversive event. Active avoidance learning explains why many students study as diligently as they do. Unfortunately, most people do not find studying as enjoyable as certain other activities (for example, I would much rather read a mystery novel or watch a television game show). Nevertheless, because studying behavior enables students to avoid an aversive stimulus (a failing grade), they do it fairly frequently. But notice how rarely studying occurs when there is no signal of possible impending doom, such as an assigned research report or an upcoming exam.

In other situations, organisms learn that *not* making a particular response allows them to avoid an aversive event (e.g., Lewis & Maher, 1965; Seligman & Campbell, 1965); this form of learning is called **passive avoidance learning**. For example, people who feel awkward and uncomfortable in social situations tend not to go to parties or other social events. Likewise, students who have difficulty with mathematics rarely sign up for advanced math classes if they can help it.

What learning processes underlie avoidance learning? An early and widely cited theory of avoidance learning is Mowrer's two-factor theory (e.g., Mowrer, 1956; Mowrer & Lamoreaux, 1942). According to Mowrer's theory, avoidance learning is a two-step process that involves both classical conditioning and operant conditioning. In the first step, because the pre-aversive stimulus and the aversive stimulus are presented close together in time, the organism learns to fear the pre-aversive stimulus through a process of classical conditioning, as illustrated in Figure 6–1. In the second step, an avoidance response is reinforced because the response leads to escape from the fear-inducing pre-aversive stimulus, thereby being negatively reinforced.

Logical as Mowrer's proposal may appear, research does not completely support it. For example, rats can learn to avoid an aversive stimulus even when the allegedly fear-inducing pre-aversive stimulus is not escaped (Kamin, 1956), refuting Mowrer's notion that escape from this stimulus negatively reinforces the avoidance response. Furthermore, once an avoidance response has been well learned, organisms may exhibit little if any fear of the pre-aversive stimulus; thus, the avoidance response can no longer be negatively reinforced by a reduction of that fear (e.g., Kamin, Brimer, & Black, 1963).

Since Mowrer's time, numerous other theories of avoidance learning have been advanced as well (e.g., Bolles, 1975; D'Amato, 1970; Herrnstein, 1969; Seligman & Johnston, 1973). For example, some theorists postulate that the actual reinforcer of an avoidance response is a feeling of relief (D'Amato, 1970; Denny & Weisman, 1964). However, because avoidance behavior can occur in the absence of fear, other theorists (e.g., Bolles, 1975; Seligman & Johnston, 1973) have abandoned behaviorism for a cognitive explanation of avoidance learning: Organisms form *expectations* about what situations are aversive and what behaviors enable them to avoid those situations.

Although there is disagreement about the best theoretical explanation of avoidance learning, there is general agreement on one thing: Avoidance responses are difficult to extinguish. When a previously aversive situation loses all sources of aversiveness, organisms nevertheless continue to avoid that situation. For example, dogs will continue to escape from a box that has been previously associated with shock long after the shock has been terminated (Solomon & Wynne, 1954).

One likely reason for the high resistance of avoidance responses to extinction is that, when an organism avoids a formerly aversive situation, it minimizes opportunities to learn that the situation is no longer aversive. Let's examine students' avoidance of mathematics as an example. As I suggested in Chapter 3, mathematics anxiety may be a conditioned response acquired at a time when children are not cognitively ready to learn abstract mathematical concepts. Students with math anxiety may avoid math classes indefinitely, even though they may eventually develop the cognitive maturity necessary for comprehending previously troublesome concepts. If students never again enroll in another math class, they will never learn that they have nothing to fear!

Many psychologists believe that the best way to extinguish an avoidance response is to extinguish the fear that elicits the avoidance in the first place. One way of doing this is through *systematic desensitization*, a technique I described in Chapter 3: Relaxing while imagining a series of increasingly anxiety-arousing scenarios can reduce fear of a situation. Another approach is to prevent the avoidance response, thereby enabling the individual to experience the conditioned stimulus in the absence of a fear-eliciting unconditioned stimulus. For

Figure 6–1

Learning to fear a pre-aversive stimulus through classical conditioning

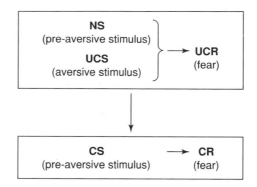

example, if we have a math-anxious student whom we know possesses adequate cognitive skills to succeed in mathematics, we might require that student to enroll in a math class. In some circumstances it is probably true that students don't always know what is best for them!

But, undoubtedly, the best way to deal with both escape and avoidance behaviors in the classroom is to prevent them from being learned in the first place—something we can accomplish only by minimizing aversive classroom stimuli. For example, educational objectives should be established with the cognitive maturity and acquired skills of each group of students clearly in mind so that students can realistically accomplish those objectives. And when students receive adequate instruction, resources, and incentives to achieve success in their classwork (a positive reinforcer), they are more likely to seek out that work than avoid it.

Escape and avoidance learning result when one's responses can terminate or avoid certain stimuli; in these situations, the stimuli (either aversive or pre-aversive) precede the responses. However, when aversive stimuli *follow* responses, we instead have a case of punishment.

PUNISHMENT

Punishment actually takes two forms. **Punishment I** (also called positive punishment) is the more commonly recognized form; it decreases the strength of a response when it is *presented* after that response. Typically, Punishment I involves presenting an aversive stimulus, for example, a spanking or a failing grade. **Punishment II** (sometimes called negative punishment) decreases the strength of a response by virtue of the *removal* of a stimulus, usually a pleasant one. Losing a privilege and being fined (in which case money is lost) are examples of Punishment II. Punishment is a common occurrence in our daily lives; some psychologists believe that even the absence of reinforcement can be punishing (we will explore the latter idea in Chapter 7).

Views on the effectiveness of punishment have changed considerably over the past 60 years. Early research indicated that punishment was a very *in*effective means of changing behavior. For example, Thorndike (1932b) found that, while positive feedback facilitated students' learning of correct responses, negative feedback did not reduce incorrect responses. Similarly, Skinner (1938) found that when rats were punished for a response that had previously been reinforced, the response was temporarily suppressed but soon returned to its pre-punishment frequency. As a result, early behaviorists such as Thorndike, Skinner, and Guthrie discouraged the use of punishment.

Probably because of the negative views on punishment held by prominent learning theorists during the first half of the century, punishment as a means of behavior control was largely ignored until the 1960s. Until that time, concern centered more on disadvantages than on any possible advantages of punishment. More recently, however, research evidence has emerged to indicate that punishment *can* be effective in many situations.

In the following pages we will explore the many-faceted topic of punishment. We will begin by examining punishment's numerous disadvantages. We will then look at evidence supporting the use of punishment as an effective means of behavior control and will also explore various theoretical explanations for its effect on behavior. Finally, we will discuss some guidelines for using punishment in the classroom.

Disadvantages of Punishment

Over the years, psychologists have cited a number of disadvantages associated with the use of punishment.

•*A punished behavior is not eliminated; it is only suppressed*. Punishment *suppresses* a response—it makes the response less likely to occur. However, this suppression effect is often only temporary: the punished behavior may eventually reappear, perhaps when the punishment stops or when the punisher is absent (Appel & Peterson, 1965; Azrin, 1960; Griffore, 1981; Holz & Azrin, 1962; Skinner, 1938).

•*Punishment sometimes leads to an increase in the punished behavior*. In some cases, this effect may be due to the fact that the "punishment" is actually reinforcing. For example, a teacher's reprimands may be reinforcing to the girl who craves her teacher's attention or the boy who wants to look "cool" in front of his classmates. However, even in situations in which the punishment is truly punishing, it may nevertheless lead to an increase in the punished response. More specifically, when a behavior is punished in one situation, it may decrease in that situation but *increase* in a situation in which it has *not* been punished— an effect known as **behavioral contrast** (e.g., Reynolds, 1975; Swenson, 1980). For example, some children who behave badly at school may be described by their parents as being angelic at home. A child who is held to strict behavioral rules on the home front and is punished by a parent for breaking those rules may often engage in the forbidden behaviors at school.

• *The response-punishment contingency may not be recognized.* Punishment, particularly physical punishment, can distract an individual's attention away from the behavior that was punished. Children are often less aware of the response that was punished than they are of the punishment itself (Maurer, 1974). Punishment will clearly be ineffective if children do not know what they are being punished for.

• *Punishment often conditions negative emotional responses and may lead to escape and avoidance behaviors.* When punishment involves a particularly aversive stimulus, the association of that stimulus with other stimuli (e.g., the punisher or the situation in which punishment occurred) can, through classical conditioning, lead to undesirable emotional responses to those other stimuli (Skinner, 1938). For example, when a teacher punishes a student at school, that punishment (the UCS) may be associated with the teacher and the classroom, both of which may then become conditioned stimuli (CSs) that elicit conditioned responses (CRs) such as fear and anxiety.

Furthermore, a fear-eliciting stimulus often leads to escape and avoidance learning (e.g., Redd, Morris, & Martin, 1975). Escape and avoidance behaviors in school take many forms: running away, truancy, avoidance of school tasks, inattention or withdrawal in class, cheating, and lying (e.g., Becker, 1971; Skinner, 1938). Since such undesirable behaviors terminate an aversive stimulus (in this case, the aversive stimulus is the punishment), they are negatively reinforced and so are likely to increase.

• *Punishment may lead to aggression.* When punishment produces pain, it evokes emotional arousal in an individual, arousal that may result in anger and

Physical punishment models aggression.

aggression, especially in characteristically aggressive individuals (Azrin, 1967; Berkowitz & LePage, 1967; Walters & Grusec, 1977). Aggressive behavior in turn appears to reduce the emotional arousal (e.g., Hokanson & Burgess, 1962) and to "feel good" (Bramel, Taub, & Blum, 1968), the result being that aggression is reinforced.

Furthermore, some forms of punishment provide a model of aggression, thus communicating the message that aggression is acceptable. I am reminded of the many hypocritical interactions I have witnessed in the grocery store. A mother yells, "How many times have I told you not to hit your sister?!" and gives her child a solid whack. Children who observe others being aggressive are more likely to be aggressive themselves (Bandura, Ross, & Ross, 1961, 1963; Mischel & Grusec, 1966; Steuer, Applefield, & Smith, 1971). Particularly aggressive children (i.e., juvenile delinquents) are likely to come from homes where severe punishment has been frequent (Welsh, 1976).

•*Punishment does not illustrate the correct behavior.* As Skinner (1938) pointed out, punishment tells an individual what *not* to do, but not what should be done instead. Consider the boy who is consistently aggressive on the playground; perhaps aggression is the only way he knows of interacting with other children. Punishing this child for aggressive behavior without simultaneously teaching him more appropriate social skills does not help him develop friendly relationships with his classmates.

•*Severe punishment may cause physical or psychological harm.* Obviously, severe physical punishment can lead to bodily injury. Severe psychological punishment, such as extreme embarrassment or deflation of one's self-esteem, can be equally harmful. The mother of a college friend of mine constantly degraded my friend with such remarks as "How can you be so stupid!" and "Can't you ever do anything right?" Throughout our four years in college, my friend fought numerous bouts with depression and was in and out of mental institutions. The line between punishment and abuse is often a very fuzzy one.

Despite these many potential disadvantages, punishment *can* be an effective method of behavior control. In the next few pages we'll look at some instances in which punishment *does* work. A bit later in the chapter I'll give you some guidelines for using punishment that will help avert the disadvantages I have just listed.

The Effectiveness of Punishment

Although early research casts doubt on the idea that punishment decreased behavior, more recently researchers have reported evidence that punishment can successfully reduce or eliminate undesirable behaviors (Aronfreed, 1968; Aronfreed & Reber, 1965; Azrin & Holz, 1966; Dinsmoor, 1954, 1955; Rachlin, 1991; Tanner & Zeiler, 1975; Walters & Grusec, 1977). Punishment is often used when methods such as extinction, the differential reinforcement of other behaviors (DRO schedule), or the reinforcement of an incompatible response are ineffective or impractical; furthermore, it appears that punishment may often be more effective than any of these other techniques (Boe & Church, 1967; Corte, Wolf, & Locke, 1971; Pfiffner & O'Leary, 1987; Walters & Grusec, 1977). Punishment is especially advised when a behavior might harm either oneself or another; in such cases, the use of punishment to eliminate such behavior rapidly may actually be the most humane course of action.

In a series of studies, Vance Hall and his colleagues (Hall, Axelrod, Foundopoulos, Shellman, Campbell, & Cranston, 1971) have demonstrated the speed with which punishment can bring about behavior change. For example, in one study, consistent punishment virtually eliminated the aggressive behavior of a 7-year-old deaf girl named Andrea. Initially, this girl pinched and bit both herself and anybody else with whom she came into contact; the frequency of such responses (an average of 72 per school day) was so high that normal academic instruction was impossible. Following a baseline period, punishment for each aggressive act began: Whenever the girl pinched or bit, her teacher pointed at her sternly and shouted "No!" Figure 6–2 shows the changes in Andrea's behavior (the brief *reversal* to nonreinforcement for a few days was used to rule out coincidence as an explanation for the behavior changes). Even though Andrea was deaf, the shouting and pointing virtually eliminated her aggressiveness.

In a second study, Hall and his colleagues modified the whining and complaining behaviors of a boy named Billy. Billy frequently cried, whined, and complained of stomachaches whenever he received a reading or arithmetic assign-

Figure 6–2
Number of bites and pinches by Andrea during the school day

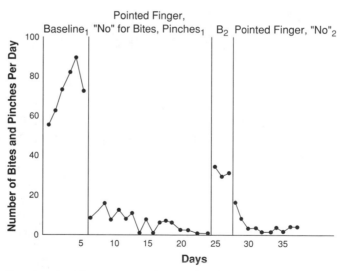

Reprinted with permission from "The Effective Use of Punishment to Modify Behavior in the Classroom" by R. V. Hall, S. Axelrod, M. Foundopoulos, J. Shellman, R. A. Campbell, & S. S. Cranston, 1972, in K. D. O'Leary & S. O'Leary (Eds.), *Classroom Management: The Successful Use of Behavior Modification*, p. 175. Copyright 1972 by Pergamon Press, Ltd.

ment, while apparently being quite healthy the rest of the day. The treatment program consisted of giving Billy five slips of colored paper bearing his name at the beginning of reading and arithmetic periods every day and then removing one slip of paper (Punishment II) each time Billy cried, whined, or complained. Treatment was instituted on day 6 for Billy's reading period and on day 11 for his math period (this *multiple baseline* approach was used to rule out the coincidence factor). Figure 6–3 clearly shows the effectiveness of such obviously mild punishment (note the temporary reversal to nonpunished baseline similar to that shown in Figure 6–2).

In yet another study by Hall and his colleagues, the grades of three tenth-grade students enrolled in a French class were modified using after-school tutoring as the "punishment." These students—Dave, Roy, and Debbie—had been consistently earning D's and F's on daily quizzes. Their teacher informed them that because they were obviously having difficulty with their French, they would have to come in for a half hour of tutoring after school whenever they received a grade lower than C. Quiz grades during baseline and during the time when poor quiz performance would be punished are shown in Figure 6–4 (note the multiple baseline approach once again). As you can see, none of the students ever needed

Figure 6–3
Frequency of Billy's cries (C), whines (W), and complaints (C_1) during reading and arithmetic periods

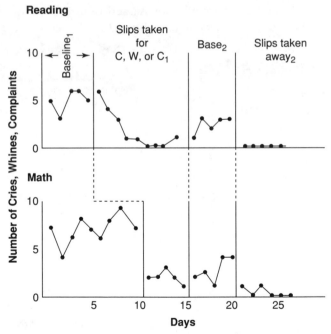

Reprinted with permission from "The Effective Use of Punishment to Modify Behavior in the Classroom" by R. V. Hall, S. Axelrod, M. Foundopoulos, J. Shellman, R. A. Campbell, & S. S. Cranston, 1972, in K. D. O'Leary & S. O'Leary (Eds.), *Classroom Management: The Successful Use of Behavior Modification*, p. 177. Copyright 1972 by Pergamon Press, Ltd.

Figure 6-4
Quiz grades for three high school French class students

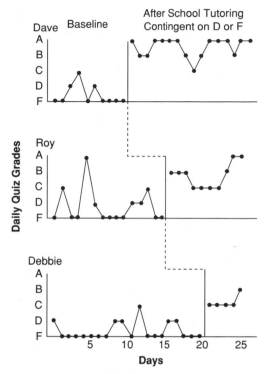

Reprinted with permission from "The Effective Use of Punishment to Modify Behavior in the Classroom" by R. V. Hall, S. Axelrod, M. Foundopoulos, J. Shellman, R. A. Campbell, & S. S. Cranston, 1972, in K. D. O'Leary & S. O'Leary (Eds.), *Classroom Management: The Successful Use of Behavior Modification*, p. 180. Copyright 1972 by Pergamon Press, Ltd.

to report for after-school tutoring! Apparently, the threat of punishment alone was sufficient to bring about desired study behaviors.

What is unique about the studies by Hall and his colleagues is that none of the punishments can be construed as being either physically or psychologically harmful or painful. Yet all of them—pointing and yelling "No," withdrawing colored slips of paper, and requiring after-school tutoring—were clearly effective in bringing about dramatic behavior changes in different students. But just why does punishment work? Let's explore some possible explanations.

Theoretical Perspectives on Punishment

A number of theories have been advanced to explain why punishment decreases the behavior that precedes it. Guthrie (1935) and Skinner (1953) offered two early theories based on the notion of incompatibility: Punishment reduces a response only when it leads to a behavior (such as escape from the situation) that is incompatible with the punished response. Thus, Guthrie and Skinner argued that punishment affects the punished behavior indirectly (by bringing about a new response) rather than directly. An alternative theory (e.g., Estes, 1969b; Walters & Grusec, 1977) is also based on the notion of incompatibility, albeit the incompatibility of motives rather than behaviors. According to this explanation, punishment leads to motives (e.g., fear) incompatible with the motives that originally led to the behavior being punished. For example, when a rat who has learned to press a bar to obtain food is then punished for pressing that bar, the fear induced by the punishment may lower the rat's appetite.

Mowrer (1960) proposed a two-stage theory of punishment similar to his theory of avoidance learning. First, when an organism is punished for a particular behavior, fear of the environment in which punishment occurred is established through a process of classical conditioning. Second, escape from that environment is reinforced because such escape reduces that fear (negative reinforcement). Punishment is effective to the extent that the escape response is incompatible with the punished response. In contrast, Aronfreed (1968; Aronfreed & Reber, 1965) proposed that anxiety is associated, not with stimuli in the environment, but with the initiation of the punished response and perhaps also with the thoughts that precede the response; suppressing the response—*not* emitting it— is negatively reinforced by anxiety reduction.

Still other theorists (e.g., Azrin & Holz, 1966; Fantino, 1973; Rachlin & Herrnstein, 1969) have reverted to Thorndike's original law of effect and view punishment in the same way they view reinforcement—as a consequence that alters the frequency of future behaviors. These researchers advocate an atheoretical approach to punishment; they focus more on the factors influencing the effectiveness of punishment than on the reasons underlying its effectiveness (Walters & Grusec, 1977).

Using Punishment in Classroom Settings

The use of punishment as a means of behavior control is widespread in both child rearing and educational practice (Sears, Maccoby, & Levin, 1957; Wielkiewicz, 1986). One likely reason for the prevalence of punishment as a disciplinary measure is that, because it tends to decrease or eliminate an undesirable behavior fairly quickly, the punisher is actually negatively reinforced for using punishment (i.e., by the termination of the unwanted behavior).

Two particular forms of punishment, time-out and response cost, are frequently used in classroom situations. Both are examples of Punishment II, the withdrawal of a reinforcer. A third type of punishment, the verbal reprimand (an example of Punishment I), is also useful in some instances. Let's examine the empirical evidence for all three.

Time-out

Time-out (e.g., Ullmann & Krasner, 1969; Walters & Grusec, 1977) involves placing the misbehaving individual in an environment with no reinforcers—in other words, in a dull situation. Often, this time-out environment is a separate room, furnished sparsely or not at all, in which the individual cannot interact with others. Other times, it may be a corner of the classroom screened from the rest of the room by partitions or tall furniture. In any event, the time-out environment should be neither reinforcing, as the hall or the principal's office is likely to be, nor frightening, as a dark closet might be (Walker & Shea, 1984; Wielkiewicz, 1986). Foxx and Shapiro (1978) have developed a procedure that easily incorporates time-out into a classroom context without requiring any special facilities. Students wear ribbons that make them eligible to participate in rewarding classroom activities. Students who misbehave remain in the classroom, but their ribbons are removed, making them ineligible to receive the reinforcers available to their classmates.

Time-out effectively reduces a variety of disruptive, aggressive, and dangerous behaviors (Drabman & Spitalnik, 1973; Mace, Page, Ivancic, & O'Brien, 1986; MacPherson, Candee, & Hohman, 1974; Lentz, 1988; Mathews, Friman, Barone, Ross, & Christophersen, 1987; Rolider & Van Houten, 1985; Williams, 1959). It need not be lengthy to be effective, and in fact many psychologists advocate that durations of 10 minutes (even as few as two minutes for preschool children) are sufficient. A key to using time-out effectively is that the inappropriate behavior must *stop* before the child is released from the time-out situation; release from time-out (a negative reinforcer) is therefore contingent on appropriate behavior.

Response Cost

Response cost involves the withdrawal of a previously received reinforcer; a ticket for speeding (resulting in the payment of a fine) and the loss of previously earned privileges are examples. Response cost has been shown to reduce such misbehaviors as aggression, inappropriate speech, disruptiveness, hyperactivity, and tardiness (Iwata & Bailey, 1974; Kazdin, 1972; McLaughlin & Malaby, 1972; Rapport, Murphy, & Bailey, 1982) and appears to be particularly effective when combined with reinforcement of appropriate behavior (Phillips, Phillips, Fixsen, & Wolf, 1971).

Verbal Reprimand

Although some students find teacher attention of any kind reinforcing, most students probably regard a **verbal reprimand**—a scolding or admonishment—as punishment. For example, in a study by O'Leary and his colleagues (O'Leary, Kaufman, Kass, & Drabman, 1970), reprimands were effective in decreasing the disruptive behavior of seven out of nine children. Softly spoken reprimands were noticeably more effective than loud ones, possibly because soft reprimands were less likely to be noticed by other children and thus less likely to draw the (potentially reinforcing) attention of other children to the child being punished. In addition to suppressing undesirable behavior, occasional reprimands also appear to enhance the positive reinforcement value of praise (Pfiffner & O'Leary, 1987).

Punishments such as time-out, response cost, and verbal reprimands appear to have fewer negative side effects than either physical punishment (e.g., spanking) or psychological punishment (e.g., withdrawal of love) (Walters & Grusec, 1977). However, teachers who use the more recommended forms of punishment to reduce inappropriate behavior must nevertheless monitor their effects on the behaviors being punished. For example, some individuals find time-out to be reinforcing rather than punishing (Solnick, Rincover, & Peterson, 1977), and their "punished" behaviors will increase rather than diminish.

In Chapter 4, I discussed the importance of reinforcement as a means of providing feedback about what is appropriate behavior. In much the same way, punishment is probably effective to the extent that it gives feedback about inappropriate behavior. Sometimes students are truly unaware of how frequently they misbehave (e.g., Krumboltz & Krumboltz, 1972), and the occasional punishment of inappropriate responses can provide reminders that keep these students on task. But how do we avoid such negative side effects as aggression, escape responses, and negative emotional reactions? Let's turn to some guidelines for using punishment in the classroom.

Guidelines for Using Punishment Effectively

Psychologists and educators have offered numerous suggestions on how to use punishment effectively, many of which decrease the chances of negative side effects. The guidelines that follow are among the most commonly cited.

Tina is "punished."

•*The "punishment" must be punishing.* Punishment, like reinforcement, is defined by its effect on behavior: True punishment decreases the response it follows. If a given consequence does not decrease the response it is meant to punish, that consequence may not be aversive to the individual being "punished"—in fact, it may even be reinforcing.

Teachers and parents too often make assumptions about what consequences will be punishing for children. For example, a common "punishment" around our house is to be sent to one's room. For my two sons, such a consequence is truly aversive, as they would much rather socialize with the family in the kitchen or living room than be isolated in their rooms for any length of time. On the other hand, when my daughter Tina is banished to her bedroom, she is probably being reinforced: She rearranges her furniture, listens to her radio, or settles under the covers with a good book. And the behaviors for which she has been most often punished in this way—behaviors related in one way or another to annoying and teasing her brothers—seem to be increasing rather than decreasing.

•*The punishment must be strong enough to be effective, but not overly severe.* Punishment that is too short or mild will not be effective (e.g., Parke & Walters, 1967). For example, fines for such behaviors as speeding and drunken driving are obviously insufficient deterrents for some individuals. Similarly, grades in many college classrooms may be too lenient to discourage a student from academically unproductive behaviors. A college teacher may believe that by giving some students a C, she is punishing those students for their lack of class attendance and poor exam performance. Yet a C average is quite acceptable at most institutions, so the students may not be sufficiently "punished" to reduce their frequency of party-going and Frisbee-throwing at times when they should be attending classes or reading their textbooks.

At the same time, punishment must not be overly severe, as it can then lead to such undesirable side effects as resentment, hostility, aggression, or escape behavior. Furthermore, although severe punishment may quickly suppress a response, that response may reappear at its original level once the punisher has left the scene (Appel & Peterson, 1965; Azrin, 1960). The ultimate purpose of administering punishment is to communicate that the limits of acceptable behavior have been exceeded; it should not be so excessive that it undermines the personal relationship between the punisher and the person being punished (Spaulding, 1992).

•*Punishment should be threatened once before it is administered.* (My use of the term *threaten* here means only that people should be warned ahead of time, not that they should be intimidated.) Punishment is most likely to deter behavior when an individual *knows* that the behavior will lead to punishment (e.g., Aronfreed, 1968). Therefore, people should know ahead of time that a particular behavior will be punished and what the punishment will be. I remember an incident, when I was about four years old, in which I was punished without warning. Sitting at lunch one day, apparently considering the old adage "Waste not, want not," I proceeded to lick a large quantity of peanut butter off my butter knife. An adult scolded me sternly for my behavior, and I was devastated. Being the Miss Goody-Two-Shoes that I was at that age, I would never have engaged in knife-licking behavior if I had known it was an unacceptable response.

One common mistake many teachers and parents make is to continue to threaten punishment without ever following through. One threat is advisable, but repeated threats are not. The mother who constantly says to her son, "If you hit your sister again, Tommy, I'll send you to your room for the rest of the week"—but never does send Tommy to his room—is giving her son the message that no response-punishment contingency really exists.

One of the reasons why teachers and parents often fail to follow through with threatened punishment is that they too often *bluff*, proposing punishment that is impractical or unrealistically extreme. Tommy's mother does not punish her son because having Tommy spend "the rest of the week" in his room would be a major inconvenience for both of them. A teacher who threatens that certain behaviors will result in students not going on a promised field trip should do so only if that teacher knows that leaving some students at school that day is logistically possible.

•*The behavior to be punished should be specified in clear, concrete terms.* Students should understand exactly which responses are unacceptable. A student who is told, "If you disrupt the class again this morning, you will have to stay in during recess," may not understand exactly what the teacher means by "disrupt" and so may continue to engage in inappropriate classroom behavior. The teacher should instead take the student aside and say something like this: "Sharon, there are two behaviors that are unacceptable in this classroom. When you talk without permission and when you get out of your seat during seatwork time, you keep other children from getting their work done. This morning I expect you to talk and get out of your seat only when I give you permission to do so. Otherwise, you will have to stay in during recess today and sit quietly at your desk."

•*Punishment should be consistent.* Just as is true for reinforcement, punishment is much more effective when it is a consistent consequence of a particular response (Leff, 1969; Parke & Deur, 1972). When a response is punished only occasionally, with other occurrences of that response being either reinforced or ignored, the response disappears slowly, if at all. Consistent with this principle is the fact that many juvenile delinquents come from home environments in which parental discipline has been administered inconsistently (Glueck & Glueck, 1950; McCord, McCord, & Zola, 1959).

Unfortunately, people can only be punished when they have been caught in the act. Thieves are rarely apprehended, and speeders are ticketed only when the highways they drive on are patrolled. Many undesirable classroom behaviors, such as talking out, getting out of one's seat, being aggressive, and cheating, may be reinforced as frequently as they are punished. To deal with the difficulty of detecting some undesirable student behaviors, the next two guidelines—changing the situation so the misbehavior is less likely to occur and providing a positively reinforceable alternative behavior—are especially critical.

•*Whenever possible, the environment should be modified to make the misbehavior less likely to occur.* In other words, the temptation to engage in a misbehavior should be reduced or, if possible, eliminated. People on diets should not stock their kitchens with junk food. Troublemaking friends should be placed on opposite sides of the classroom or in separate classrooms. Cheating on an exam can be reduced by having students sit apart from one another or by administering two different forms of the exam (perhaps the same test items in two different orders).

•*Desirable alternative behaviors should be taught and reinforced.* Punishment of misbehavior is typically more effective when it is combined with reinforcement of appropriate behavior (Rimm & Masters, 1974; Walters & Grusec, 1977). A misbehavior is more likely to be suppressed permanently when alternative behaviors are reinforced, especially when those behaviors are incompatible with the punished behavior. For example, when punishing aggression on the playground, we should remember also to reinforce appropriate social behavior. We can punish a student for cheating, but we should also reinforce that student for demonstrating good study habits and for working well independently.

•*Whenever possible, punishment should immediately follow the inappropriate behavior.* As is true for reinforcement, the effectiveness of punishment decreases dramatically when it is delayed (Trenholme & Baron, 1975; Walters, 1964; Walters & Grusec, 1977). The more closely punishment follows a misbehavior, the more effective it will be. Punishment is particularly effective when it is administered as soon as the misbehavior *begins* (Aronfreed, 1968; Aronfreed & Reber, 1965). When, for whatever reason, punishment cannot be administered immediately, delayed punishment may be effective provided that the punished behavior is clearly described (Aronfreed & Reber, 1965).

•*An explanation of why the behavior is unacceptable should be given.* Although behaviorists tend to focus their attention on responses and their consequences, a growing body of research indicates that punishment is more effective when *reasons* why certain behaviors cannot be tolerated are given (Baumrind, 1983; Hess & McDevitt, 1984; Parke, 1972, 1974, 1977; Perry & Perry, 1983). For example, notice how Sharon's teacher incorporated reasoning into her description of Sharon's inappropriate behaviors: "When you talk without permission and when you get out of your seat during seatwork time, *you keep other children from getting their work done*."

Providing reasons that behaviors are unacceptable has at least four advantages:

1. When punishment is accompanied by reasoning, it appears to make the immediacy of punishment a less critical factor in its effectiveness (Walters & Grusec, 1977).
2. Reasoning increases the likelihood that when one behavior is punished, similar misbehaviors are also suppressed; that is, the effect of the punishment generalizes to other misbehaviors (Walters & Grusec, 1977).
3. When reasons are given, misbehaviors are likely to be suppressed even when the punisher is absent (Walters & Grusec, 1977).
4. Older children apparently expect to be told why they cannot engage in certain behaviors and are likely to be defiant when reasons are not provided (Cheyne & Walters, 1970).

•*Some punishments are particularly ineffective and should be avoided.* Among the punishments that are generally *not* recommended are physical punishment, psychological punishment, extra classwork, and suspension from school.

Physical punishment may be the only means of keeping very young children from engaging in potentially harmful behaviors. For example, the toddler who takes delight in sticking metal objects into electrical outlets should be quickly discouraged from such behavior, and a slap on the hand may be the only way of doing so. However, the use of physical punishment with older children is likely to provide a model of aggression for those children: Consider as evidence the finding that the great majority of abusive parents have been themselves abused as children (Steele & Pollack, 1968; Steinmetz, 1977; Strauss, Gelles, & Steinmetz, 1980).

Psychological punishment, such as embarrassing or insulting a child, also is not recommended (e.g., Davis & Thomas, 1989; Walker & Shea, 1984). Children who are consistently made to feel inferior or inadequate are likely to develop poor self-concepts that will interfere with their engaging in appropriate and constructive behaviors on future occasions.

Suspension is not an effective punishment.

Extra classwork is appropriate when it is a logical consequence of the misbehavior (for example, when students are failing exams), but in other situations it transmits the message that schoolwork is not fun. When Marcus is punished for his disruptive classroom behaviors by being assigned an additional 100 mathematics problems, he is unlikely to continue to regard mathematics in a positive light.

Finally, suspension from school is typically an ineffective remedy for misbehavior (Doyle, 1990; Moles, 1990). Many chronically misbehaving students are students who have difficulty with their academic work; many high school troublemakers, for example, are students with poor reading skills. Suspending such students from school puts these students at an even greater disadvantage and decreases still further the likelihood of academic success. Additionally, when students find school to be an aversive situation, removal from that environment is negatively reinforcing rather than punishing. (It is also negatively reinforcing to the administrators who have gotten rid of their trouble makers!)

An alternative, more effective punishment for chronic misbehavers is **in-house suspension** (e.g., see anecdotal reports by DiSciullo [1984], Huff [1988], Short & Noblit [1985], Sullivan [1989], and Weiss [1983]). In-house suspension is similar to a time-out in that punished students are placed in a quiet, boring room within the school building. However, in-house suspension typically lasts one or more days rather than just a few minutes, and students suspended in this manner are continually monitored by a member of the school staff. Students bring their schoolwork with them and therefore must keep up with their classroom assignments. In-house suspension tends to be effective because it does not allow students to escape the school environment, yet it prevents the social interactions with peers that most students find reinforcing.

•*Punishment should be used sparingly*. The studies by Hall and his colleagues that I described earlier (Hall et al., 1971) provide several illustrations of how quickly punishment can reduce inappropriate behavior. An effective punishment is one that does not need to be administered very often to be effective. Only when punishment is a frequent occurrence (in which case it is obviously not effective anyway) are the numerous disadvantages of punishment likely to appear.

When used properly, punishment is the fastest way of reducing or eliminating unacceptable behaviors. Remember, behaviorists define punishment as a consequence that decreases the response it follows. A "punishment" that clearly is not suppressing an undesirable behavior very quickly should be replaced by a different consequence.

LEARNED HELPLESSNESS

Imagine that you are a student who is continually failing assignments and exams. You try all kinds of strategies to improve your grade—studying longer hours, memorizing your textbook word for word, having a friend drill you on key points, and even sleeping with your textbook open over your head (hoping that the information will sink in)—and still you get F after F after F. Eventually, you would probably just stop trying to achieve academic success and accept the "fact" that you have no control over the grades you receive.

When aversive stimuli are repeatedly presented—stimuli that cannot be avoided, escaped, or terminated—an organism will eventually give up and passively accept those stimuli. This passive acceptance of uncontrollable aversive events is a phenomenon known as **learned helplessness**.

Let me illustrate the phenomenon by describing research conducted by Seligman and Maier (1967). In the first phase of this classic experiment, dogs received numerous painful and unpredictable shocks. Some dogs were able to escape the shocks by pushing a panel in the cage, whereas other dogs could not escape the shocks regardless of what they did. The following day, each dog was placed in a box that was divided into two compartments by a barrier. While in this box, the dog was presented with a series of tone-shock combinations, with a tone always preceding a shock; the dog could avoid the shock by jumping over the barrier into the other compartment as soon as it heard the tone. Those dogs who had been able to escape the shocks on the previous day quickly learned to escape the shocks on the second day. On the other hand, those dogs who previously had been unable to escape displayed learned helplessness: They made few attempts to escape, instead simply sitting still and whining as the shocks were presented.

People, too, begin to exhibit symptoms of learned helplessness when they cannot control the occurrence of aversive events (e.g., Hiroto, 1974; Hiroto & Seligman, 1975). According to Maier and Seligman (1976), learned helplessness is manifested in three ways. First, there is a *motivational* effect: The individual is slow to exhibit responses that will produce reinforcement or avoid punishment. Second is a *cognitive* effect: The individual has difficulty learning in future situations in which control of consequences *is* possible. Even when the individual's responses do lead to reinforcement or escape from an aversive stimulus, the individual tends not to learn from those experiences. The third effect is an *emotional* one: The individual tends to be passive, withdrawn, fearful, and depressed.

Learned helplessness has been offered as an explanation of clinical depression (Seligman, 1975, 1991): Depressed people typically perceive that they have less control over their lives than nondepressed people. It may also be characteristic of some school children, particular those who frequently experience difficulty completing academic tasks (Dweck, 1986; Eccles & Wigfield, 1985; Fennema, 1987; Stipek & Kowalski, 1989; Wood, Schau, & Fiedler, 1990). Consider the learning-disabled child as an example. Often unidentified as a student with special educational needs, the learning-disabled child may encounter repeated academic failure in academic work despite efforts to achieve and so may eventually stop trying. I have also seen the learned helplessness phenomenon in presumably nondisabled students when I talk with them about certain subject areas. Many students, for example, attribute their mathematics anxiety to the fact that, as elementary school students, they could not comprehend how to solve certain problems no matter what they did or how hard they tried. Others show learned helplessness in the area of spelling: Even when they know they have spelled a word incorrectly, they do not try to correct the spelling, excusing their behavior by such statements as "I'm just a bad speller" or "I never could spell very well" (Ormrod & Wagner, 1987).

Learned helplessness is clearly a situation in which aversive consequences occur unpredictably rather than being contingent on certain behaviors. Ultimately, individuals experiencing such seemingly random consequences may begin to believe, perhaps justifiably, that they have little or no control over the things that happen to them. We will look in more detail at the effects of perceived control (or lack thereof) as we discuss the cognitive side of human motivation in Chapter 18.

In the last three chapters, we have seen how response-reinforcement contingencies increase certain responses and how response-punishment contingencies decrease others. To succeed in the school environment, students must be aware of those contingencies and be able to exhibit the responses that lead to positive outcomes. When students are unable to learn despite clearly specified contingencies and a slow, carefully designed curricular sequence, they may have cognitive problems that teachers cannot deal with from a strictly behaviorist perspective. In such situations, cognitive learning theories, which I will describe in Part IV, may provide a more useful framework.

We will make a gradual transition to the study of cognition in Part III (Chapter 7). There we will look at social learning theory, a theory that originated from the behaviorist perspective (especially operant conditioning) but has more recently begun to use cognitive ideas in its explanation of human behavior.

SUMMARY

Escape learning is the process of learning to terminate an aversive stimulus. Avoidance learning is the process of learning how to avoid an aversive stimulus altogether. Unfortunately, when organisms avoid a particular situation, they never have the opportunity to discover when the situation is no longer aversive; hence, avoidance responses, once learned, are difficult to extinguish.

Views on punishment have changed considerably in the past 50 years: Early researchers found that punishment did little to reduce behaviors and cited numerous disadvantages of its use. More recently, however, some forms of punishment have been found effective in decreasing a variety of inappropriate behaviors. A number of guidelines in the use of punishment promote its effectiveness.

When aversive stimuli are repeatedly presented regardless of how a person behaves, he or she may develop a sense of learned helplessness—a sense of having little control over the environment—with motivational, cognitive, and emotional side effects.

PART THREE

SOCIAL LEARNING THEORY

CHAPTER 7

Social Learning Theory

One summer my sons Alex and Jeff spent quite a bit of time with their Uncle Pete, a large man who could pick them both up at the same time and carry them around on his shoulders. Uncle Pete's feats of strength were quite a contrast to Mom's and Dad's difficulties in lifting either boy alone, or even in opening pickle jars. For several years after that summer, Alex and Jeff spoke often of wanting to be like Uncle Pete, and I found that I could talk them into eating many foods they had previously shunned simply by saying, "This is what helps Uncle Pete get big and strong." The ploy never did work for broccoli, however.

A few years ago, some of my daughter's classmates got in the habit of calling Tina every morning to find out what she would be wearing to school that day. Tina was apparently somewhat of a fashion trend setter at school, and several other girls were mimicking her attire. Given the apparel in which Tina left for school most mornings, I shudder at the thought of what her cronies must have looked like.

Almost daily, we see instances of people watching others and learning from them. Little boys often emulate hero figures like Superman, Batman, and Uncle Pete. Through watching and copying one another, preadolescent girls often begin to behave in similar ways, dressing alike, wearing their hair in faddish styles, and poking fun at the same boys. Children imitate their parents by devel-

My daughter the trendsetter.

oping similar hobbies and interests, by expressing similar political and religious beliefs, and by eventually raising their own children using the same disciplinary techniques used on them. Students in the classroom learn many academic skills, including reading, writing, adding, and subtracting, at least partly through watching and imitating what their teacher and peers do.

Such learning by observation and modeling is the focus of **social learning theory** (e.g., Bandura, 1977b, 1986; Rosenthal & Zimmerman, 1978; Schunk, 1989c). Social learning theory originally evolved from behaviorism but now includes many cognitivist ideas; as a result, it is now often called **social cognitive theory**. In this chapter, we will look at the impact of both environmental and cognitive factors on human learning, particularly as they interact within an individual's social context. We will explore the phenomenon of modeling, examining the mental processes involved, the effects of modeling on behavior, and the characteristics of effective models. We will find that people's beliefs about their own capability to perform behaviors successfully (their self-efficacy) play a role in the responses they choose to make and the effort they exert. And we will discover how the consequences of responses become less influential as people begin to regulate their own behavior. Finally, we will examine a number of implications that social learning theory has for educational practice.

THE SOCIAL LEARNING MODEL

Social learning theory concerns the learning that occurs within a social context. It focuses on how people learn from one another and encompasses such concepts as observational learning, imitation, and modeling. Although nonhuman animals probably can learn by imitation as well (e.g., Hayes & Hayes, 1952; Herbert & Harsh, 1944), social learning theory deals primarily with human learning, and so we will be leaving rat and pigeon studies behind us.

The study of learning through imitation was launched by two of Clark Hull's students, Neal Miller and John Dollard (Miller & Dollard, 1941). It was not until the early 1960s, however, that a theory of imitation and modeling separate from its behaviorist roots began to take shape. Development of this theory, originally called **observational learning**, depended heavily on the research and writings of Albert Bandura of Stanford University (e.g., Bandura, 1969, 1973, 1977b, 1986, 1989; Bandura & Walters, 1963). Bandura's perspective has evolved considerably over the past 30 years and continues to be the driving force in studies of imitation and modeling.

Principles of Social Learning Theory

A number of general principles underlie social learning theory. Let's consider some of the key ideas that have shaped the evolution of the social learning perspective.

•*People can learn by observing the behaviors of others and the outcomes of those behaviors.* Many behaviorists view learning largely as a matter of trial and error: People learn by engaging in different behaviors and then modifying them based on the consequences (i.e., reinforcement and punishment) that those behaviors bring. In contrast, social learning theorists propose that most learning takes place not through trial and error, but instead through watching the behavior of other individuals (**models**).

•*Learning can occur without a change in behavior.* Behaviorists define learning as a relatively permanent change in behavior due to experience; thus, no learning can occur without a behavior change. In contrast, social learning theorists argue that because people can learn through observation alone, their learning will not necessarily be reflected in their performance. In other words, learning may or may not result in a behavior change. Something learned at one time may be reflected in behavior exhibited at the same time, at a later time, or never.

•*Reinforcement plays a role in learning.* The role of reinforcement in social learning theory has evolved as the theory itself has evolved. In Miller and Dollard's (1941) early theoretical analysis of learning new behaviors through imitation, reinforcement of those behaviors was a critical factor. Operant conditioning continued to be a major component of Albert Bandura's early work as well (e.g., Bandura & Walters, 1963). More recently, however, the role of reinforcement has been reconceptualized (e.g., Bandura, 1977b, 1986; Rosenthal & Zimmerman, 1978). Contemporary social learning theorists propose that reinforcement has less critical, *indirect,* effects on learning—effects that we shall examine shortly.

•*Cognitive processes play a role in learning.* Within the past 20 years, social learning theory has become increasingly "cognitive" in its analysis of human learning. For example, contemporary social learning theorists such as Bandura maintain that an individual's *awareness* of response-reinforcement contingencies is an essential component of the learning process. They also assert that *expectations* of future rewards—incentives—can have a major impact on the behaviors that people exhibit. Finally, as you will see, social learning theorists incorporate such cognitive processes as *attention* and *retention* (memory) into their explanations of how learning occurs.

Let's turn now to the ways in which environmental factors—reinforcement and punishment in particular—play a role in learning by observation. We will then look at how cognition is also involved.

ENVIRONMENTAL FACTORS IN SOCIAL LEARNING: REINFORCEMENT AND PUNISHMENT

If we were to explain imitation from an operant conditioning perspective, we might propose that people imitate others because they are reinforced for doing so. In fact, this explanation is exactly what Miller and Dollard proposed back in 1941. According to these theorists, an individual uses another person's behavior as a discriminative stimulus for an imitative response. The observer is then reinforced in some way when imitation is exhibited. For example, let's say that a French teacher carefully enunciates:

Comment allez vous? (Discriminative stimulus)

Students repeat the phrase in more or less the same way:

Comma tally voo? (Response)

The teacher then praises them for their efforts:

Very good! (Reinforcement)

From an operant conditioning perspective, modeling of other people is maintained by an intermittent reinforcement schedule: People are reinforced for imitating the behaviors of others often enough that they continue to do so. Eventually imitation itself becomes a habit, a phenomenon Miller and Dollard called **generalized imitation**.

How the Environment Reinforces Modeling

Clearly, people are often reinforced for modeling the behaviors of others. Bandura has suggested that the environment reinforces modeling in several possible ways.

•*The observer is reinforced by the model.* People often reinforce others who copy what they themselves do. For example, a group of teenage girls is more likely to welcome another girl into the group if she dresses as they do. A gang of delinquent boys will probably accept a new member only if he acts "tough."

In the French lesson I described earlier, the model—the teacher—reinforced students for imitative behavior. Teachers and parents often reinforce children for copying appropriate behaviors. For example, occasionally I hear one of my children use polite, "adult" language on the telephone, perhaps along this line: "I'm sorry, but my mother is busy right now. If you will give me your name and number, I'll have her call you back in a few minutes." Such a statement is similar to what I myself tell callers, and I am likely to praise my child profusely. On the other hand, a statement like this one: "Ma! Telephone! Hurry up and get off the potty!" has *not* been learned through observation of the adults in my house, and I certainly do not reinforce it.

•*The observer is reinforced by a third person.* On some occasions, an individual is reinforced by a third person rather than by the model. For example, children are often reinforced by parents and teachers when they imitate other children. Something I used to tell my youngest child Jeff was this: "Oh, you're such a big boy now! You're getting dressed all by yourself, just like Alex does!"

During the Beatlemania of the 1960s, many teenage boys began sporting "moppet" haircuts like those of the Beatles. Such haircuts were "in," at least in my high school, and none of us girls would have ever been caught dead with a boy who had hair shorter than John Lennon's. My friends and I were, in essence, reinforcing boys who modeled themselves after the Beatles. In earlier days, we would have reinforced anyone who could play the guitar and bat his eyelashes like Ricky Nelson.

•*The imitated behavior itself leads to reinforcing consequences.* Many behaviors that we learn through observing others produce satisfying (reinforcing) results. For example, a French student who pronounces his "Comment allez vous?" correctly will have greater success communicating with a Parisian. An individual who can closely model a tennis instructor's body positions and arm movements is more likely to get the ball over the net.

•*Reinforcement to the model affects the observer's behavior as well.* When people observe a model making a particular response, they may also observe the consequence of that response. If a model is reinforced for a response, chances are greater that the observer will also show an increase in that response, a phenomenon known as **vicarious reinforcement**. For example, if Alan sees Adam gain popularity among the girls because he can play the guitar and bat his eyelashes in a come-hither fashion, Alan may very well buy a guitar and take a few lessons; he may also stand in front of the mirror practicing eyelash batting.

The power of vicarious reinforcement (and of **vicarious punishment** as well) was dramatically illustrated in an early study by Bandura (1965b). Children

Reinforcement of the model affects the observer's behavior as well.

watched a film of a model hitting and kicking an inflated punching doll. One group of children saw the model reinforced for such aggressive behavior, a second group saw the model punished, and a third group saw the model receive no consequences for the aggression. When the children were then placed in a room with the doll, those children who had seen the model being reinforced for aggression displayed the most aggressive behavior toward the doll: They had been vicariously reinforced for aggression. Conversely, those children who had seen the model punished for aggression were the least aggressive of the three groups: They had been vicariously punished for such behavior.

Vicarious punishment indicates to the observer that a particular behavior will not be tolerated; vicarious reinforcement indicates that a behavior is acceptable. Apparently, a *lack* of punishment to the model may also be a form of vicarious reinforcement in that it conveys the message that a behavior will be tolerated (Bandura, 1973, 1977b, 1986; Walters & Parke, 1964; Walters, Parke, & Cane, 1965). For example, in a study by Walters and Parke (1964), children in three different experimental groups watched a film in which a boy (the model) was told by an adult female not to play with a number of toys that lay on the table in front of him but instead to read a book that she had given him. As soon as the woman left the room, however, the boy began to play with the toys. At this point, the film was different for the three experimental groups, as follows:

1. *Reward*. The woman returned, handed the boy some toys, and played with him affectionately.
2. *Punishment*. The woman returned, snatched away the toys the boy was playing with, shook him vigorously, and sat him back down with the book.
3. *No consequence*. The woman did not return to the room.

Children in these three groups, and children in a control group who did not view a film, were then taken to a room full of toys, told not to touch them, given a book to read, and left alone for 15 minutes. Children in the "no consequence" group played with the toys (thus disobeying the experimenter's instructions) just as much as the "reward" group did. Children in the "punishment" group were more obedient, but the most obedient children were those in the control group, who had not watched the disobedient model at all.

When people see others misbehave without negative consequences, they are more likely to misbehave themselves. For example, when my daughter was in elementary school, she came home almost daily with complaints about who had gotten away with what on the playground that day. When playground supervisors ignore transgressions day after day, their inaction not only perpetuates those misbehaviors, but may even increase them. In the same way, I often wonder if individuals who see others quite literally get away with murder aren't more likely to engage in criminal activities themselves.

Thus, imitative behavior can be reinforced by the model, by other people, by consequences intrinsic to the imitative behavior itself, or by vicarious reinforcement. However, we encounter a number of problems when we try to explain modeling strictly from the operant conditioning paradigm. Let's look at some of these problems.

Problems with a Strict Operant Conditioning Analysis of Social Learning

One difficulty we encounter when using operant conditioning to explain imitated behavior is that completely new behaviors can be learned simply by watching others perform them (Bandura, 1977b, 1986; Rosenthal, Alford, & Rasp, 1972). As you should recall, operant conditioning must start with an emitted response, a response that can then be modified through shaping. The learning of entirely novel responses—responses that an individual has seen but never previously emitted in any form—is difficult to explain from a Skinnerian perspective.

A second difficulty in explaining modeling through operant conditioning is the phenomenon of **delayed imitation**: Some behaviors that are learned through observing others do not appear until much later. Remember, the operant conditioning paradigm looks like this:

$$(S+)\ R \to S_{Rf}$$

These three parts of the model—discriminative stimulus (S+), response (R), and reinforcement (S_{Rf})—follow one right after the other, with the response occurring in the presence of the discriminative stimulus. However, as Bandura (1977b) has pointed out, the response and resulting reinforcement do not always appear immediately after the discriminative stimulus, but are instead observed at a later time. For such delayed imitation to be exhibited, learning must actually take place when the discriminative stimulus is presented, despite the absence of reinforcement at that time.

Still a third problem lies in the powerful effect of vicarious reinforcement: Individuals sometimes exhibit behaviors for which they themselves are *never* reinforced.

A Contemporary Social Learning Perspective of Reinforcement

Contemporary social learning theorists (e.g., Bandura, 1977b, 1986; Rosenthal & Zimmerman, 1978) do not view direct reinforcement as essential in human learning. They do believe, however, that reinforcement plays at least two roles in learning and performance.

•*Reinforcement influences the extent to which an individual exhibits a behavior that has been learned.* Social learning theorists believe that, although a person may learn a behavior without any reinforcement present, the person will not demonstrate that behavior unless there is a reason (i.e., reinforcement) for doing so. For example, I learned many years ago that the capital of Alaska is Juneau. Yet I have never had a reason to demonstrate that knowledge, since I have never been tested on the capital of Alaska, nor have I ever been in Alaska desperately seeking a state capital. Now, of course, I do have a reason: I want to impress you with the fact that I know the capital of at least one of the 50 states.

Bandura (1977b, 1986) proposed that an individual forms hypotheses about what responses are most appropriate in different situations. These hypotheses are formed and modified with the feedback that reinforcement and punishment, either of one's own actions or those of others, provide. Although an individual may learn both appropriate and inappropriate behaviors equally well, the appropriate behaviors—those that will lead to reinforcement—are more likely to occur.

•*The expectation of reinforcement influences cognitive processes that promote learning.* As an example of a cognitive process involved in learning, social learning theorists (e.g., Bandura, 1977b, 1986) maintain that *attention* plays a critical role in learning. And attention is influenced by the expectation of reinforcement: People are more likely to pay attention to another's behavior when they believe that they will be reinforced for modeling that behavior.

I have learned the hard way that when I tell my students they will not be held responsible for certain information, I am making a BIG MISTAKE. All I have to do is say something like, "Now I want you to listen carefully to what I have to say for the next five minutes, but *it won't be on your test*," and students put their pens down, settle back in their seats, and start to nod off. People are less likely to pay attention to information when they do not anticipate a payoff for learning it.

As you can see, social learning theorists stress the role of environmental factors in learning, but they acknowledge the importance of cognitive factors as well. Let's now turn our own attention to those cognitive factors.

COGNITIVE FACTORS IN SOCIAL LEARNING

The cognitive side of social learning theory is evident in many aspects of the theory; examples include learning without performance, cognitive processing, expectations, and the awareness of response-reinforcement contingencies.

Learning Without Performance

Bandura makes a distinction between learning through observation (something he calls **vicarious acquisition**) and imitation of what has been learned. As we noted earlier, people can learn by watching others without necessarily imitating the behaviors they have seen (Bandura, 1977b, 1986; Rosenthal & Zimmerman, 1978). At least two sources of evidence indicate that this is so. For one thing, people can verbally describe behavior they have observed without actually performing it (Bandura, 1965a). Secondly, people who observe a model perform a behavior may not demonstrate that behavior until some later time when they have a reason to exhibit the behavior. For example, I previously described a study by Bandura (1965b) in which children watched a film of a model acting aggressively toward an inflated punching doll. As you may recall, the consequences of the aggression to the model (reinforcement, punishment, or no consequence) influenced the extent to which children themselves engaged in aggressive acts toward the doll. Later in the study, however, all the children were promised rewards (stickers and fruit juices) if they could imitate the model's behavior. At that point, differences among the three groups of children disappeared! Clearly they had all *learned* the model's behavior equally well; the consequences to the model apparently affected their earlier performance, but not their learning.

Cognitive Processing

Social learning theory incorporates a number of cognitive processes (i.e., thinking) into its explanation of how people learn. For example, social learning theorists contend that *attention* is a critical factor in learning. Furthermore, people are more likely to remember information when they mentally *rehearse* it and when they develop verbal and visual mental representations (*memory codes*) of this information. I will describe these processes in more detail when I present Bandura's four components of modeling later in the chapter.

Expectations

Social learning theorists believe that, as a result of being reinforced for some behaviors and punished for others, people form expectations about what future behaviors are likely to bring (Bandura, 1977b, 1986, 1989; Rosenthal & Zimmerman, 1978). People often have expectations of what is likely to happen in different situations; for example, they expect certain behaviors will lead to reinforcement and others will lead to punishment. The concept of **incentive**—anticipating that a particular reinforcement will occur if a particular behavior is performed—reflects this idea of expectation. Obviously, when people expect to be rewarded for imitating a behavior, they will be more likely to pay attention to that behavior and try to remember how it is performed. Furthermore, they will be motivated to demonstrate the behavior they have learned. You should notice a critical difference here between the role of reinforcement in operant conditioning and in social learning. In operant conditioning, reinforcement influences learning of the behavior it *follows*. In social learning, on the other hand, an *expectation* of reinforcement influences the learning of a behavior it *precedes* (Bandura, 1977b, 1986).

As we discovered earlier, the absence of expected punishment can be reinforcing. Conversely, the nonoccurrence of expected reinforcement is often a form of punishment (Bandura, 1977b, 1986). Both of these principles describe situations in which expectations are not being met. For example, imagine yourself as a student in a class in which the teacher has clearly described the criteria necessary to earn an A. You work hard, and your performance meets the specified criteria, so you are naturally expecting an A. At the last minute, however, the teacher adds an additional requirement: To earn an A, students must write a 20-page term paper. You are probably angry and frustrated (in a sense, feeling punished), because you had expected reinforcement based on the work you had already completed, and that reinforcement is now being withheld.

Awareness of Response-Reinforcement Contingencies

According to social learning theorists, reinforcement and punishment have little effect on learning and behavior unless people are *aware* of the response-reinforcement and response-punishment contingencies (e.g., Bandura, 1977b, 1986; Spielberger & DeNike, 1966). Reinforcement will increase a response only when an individual realizes which particular response has led to the reinforcement. Similarly, an individual must recognize what particular behavior is being punished before that behavior is likely to decrease. For example, consider a situation in which a student receives an F on a writing assignment with the comments "Poorly written" and "Disorganized." Such feedback will be insufficient to cause an improvement in many students' writing because, among other things, it does not identify the specific parts of the assignment that are poorly written and disorganized.

It should be clear by now that social learning theory incorporates aspects of both behaviorism and cognitive psychology. We have examined some of the environmental and cognitive factors that, from a social learning perspective, are involved in the learning process. We must also consider how environment and cognition *interact* with one another. Let us turn next to that topic, and in particular to Bandura's concept of reciprocal causation.

RECIPROCAL CAUSATION

We have considered how the environment influences behavior and how a person's charactcristics (cognitive processes, expectations, etc.) influence behavior. But Bandura (1989) has proposed that, in a reciprocal fashion, behavior can also influence both the environment and the person. In fact, each of these three variables—environment, person, and behavior—influences the other two, a phenomenon that Bandura now calls **reciprocal causation** (prior to 1989, he called it *reciprocal determinism*). The interaction of environment (E), person (P), and behavior (B) can be depicted like this:

Certainly the environment has an influence on a person's behavior. For example, the occurrence of a desirable or undesirable consequence as a result of a particular response influences the probability that an individual will make that response again. But an individual's perception of the environment (a "person" variable) can be equally influential on behavior. For example, I mentioned earlier that awareness of response-reinforcement contingencies influences the extent to which those contingencies affect behavior. Consider an experiment by Kaufman, Baron, and Kopp (1966) as a case in point. Subjects were all placed on a variable-interval reinforcement schedule, with the average interval being one minute, and told one of three different things about the schedule they were on. Subjects in Group 1 were told that they were on a one-minute variable-interval schedule (i.e., they were told the truth). Group 2 subjects were told that they were on a one-minute *fixed*-interval schedule. Group 3 subjects were told that they were on a variable-ratio (1:150) schedule. The subjects' response patterns corresponded to the reinforcement schedules they *believed* they were on: Group 3 showed the fastest response rate, and Group 2 showed the slowest response rate, consistent with the response patterns actually observed for these different reinforcement schedules. Baron, Kaufman, and Stauber (1969) reported similar results.

Yet behavior affects both the environment individuals encounter and the personal characteristics they develop. The responses people make (the academic courses they choose, the extracurricular activities they pursue, the company they keep, etc.) determine the situations they find themselves in and the consequences they experience (environmental variables). For example, individuals typically behave in ways that increase reinforcement and decrease punishment. Furthermore, the pattern of one's responses over time affects one's self-confidence and expectations for future performance (person variables). For example, a boy who stumbles and falls frequently may begin to think that he is a klutz. By consistently performing well on mathematics assignments, a girl may begin to believe that she is a mathematics whiz.

Finally, person variables and environmental variables affect each other. For example, by directing attention (a person variable) to one stimulus and not another, certain aspects of the environment will be experienced and others will not. And we have already seen how the consequences of past behaviors (an environmental variable) affect the expectations that people have regarding future behaviors (a person variable).

One prime example of the interplay among environment, person, and behavior variables is modeling. We will now look more closely at the modeling process.

MODELING

According to Bandura (1977b, 1986), many of the behaviors that people exhibit have been acquired through observing and modeling others. In this section, we will explore several topics related to the subject of modeling. We will first look at the different types of models we may see and at the kinds of behaviors that can be modeled (focusing in particular on aggression and morality). We will then examine the processes involved in learning through modeling and the ways in which models can affect behavior. Finally, we will identify several characteristics of effective models. Before we proceed, however, I should point out here that social learning theorists sometimes use the term *modeling* to describe what a model does (i.e., demonstrate a behavior) and at other times to describe what the observer does (i.e., copy that behavior). I have tried to write this section in such a way that the term's meaning is, in every case, readily discernible from the context in which it is used.

Types of Models

Bandura identifies three different types of models. When we think of modeling, we most frequently think of a **live model**—an actual person demonstrating a particular behavior. However, we can also learn by observing a **symbolic model**—a person or character portrayed in a film, television show, book, or other medium. For example, many children model their behavior after football players or rock singers, or after such fictional characters as Superman, G.I. Joe, or Nancy Drew. And finally, we can learn from **verbal instructions**—descriptions of how to behave without an actual model being present at all.

Behaviors That Can Be Learned Through Modeling

Many behaviors are learned, at least in part, through modeling. For example, students:

- Are better readers when their parents read frequently at home (Hess & McDevitt, 1989)
- Solve mathematics problems more successfully when they see others demonstrate the appropriate procedure (Schunk & Hanson, 1985)
- Are more likely to resist the enticements of a stranger when a peer has modeled techniques for resisting such enticements (Poche, Yoder, & Miltenberger, 1988)
- Begin to deal with a fear-inducing situation with little or no fear after seeing a model behave fearlessly in that situation (Bandura, Grusec, & Menlove, 1967; Bandura & Menlove, 1968; Silverman & Kearney, 1991).

- Are more likely to show intolerance of racist statements made by others when those around them refuse to tolerate such statements (Blanchard, Lilly, & Vaughn, 1991)
- Are more likely to violate traditional gender stereotypes—that is, to behave without regard to what is "appropriate" behavior for males and females—when they see others behaving in a nonstereotypical manner (Carlson, 1984; Hoffman, 1984; Ruble & Ruble, 1982; Selkow, 1984; Weinraub, Clemens, Sockloff, Ethridge, Gracely, & Myers, 1984).

Considerable research has been conducted concerning the impact of modeling on two kinds of behavior in particular: aggression and morality.

Aggression

Numerous research studies indicate that children become more aggressive when they observe aggressive or violent models (Bandura, 1965b; Bandura, Ross, & Ross, 1961, 1963; Mischel & Grusec, 1966; Steuer, Applefield, & Smith, 1971; Walters & Thomas, 1963; Walters et al., 1962). In the classic study in this area (Bandura, Ross, & Ross, 1961), preschoolers were taken, one at a time, to a playroom containing a variety of toys and seated at a table where they could draw pictures. Some of these children then observed an adult (an aggressive model) enter the room and engage in numerous aggressive behaviors toward an inflatable punching doll, including kicking the doll in the air, straddling it and hitting it over the head with a wooden mallet, and making statements like "Pow!" "Kick him," and "Punch him in the nose." Other children instead observed an adult (a nonaggressive model) come in and play in a constructive way with building blocks. Still other children saw no model while they were in the playroom. The children were then led to another room where they were mildly frustrated: Just as they began to play with some very attractive, entertaining toys, the toys were taken away from them. They were then taken to a third room in which both nonaggressive and aggressive toys (including the inflatable punching doll and wooden mallet) were present; their behaviors were recorded and coded for aggressive content by observers on the other side of a one-way mirror. Children who had seen the aggressive model were clearly the most aggressive of the three groups, and in fact they mimicked many of the same behaviors they had seen the aggressive model display (e.g., straddling the doll and hitting it with the mallet). Children who had seen a nonaggressive model were even less aggressive than the no-model group. In aggression, then, models can have an impact either way: Aggressive models will lead to increased aggression in children, and nonaggressive models will lead to decreased aggression.

Children can also learn aggression from observing it in films or on television (Rushton, 1980). In another study by Bandura and his colleagues (Bandura, Ross, & Ross, 1963), preschool children who had seen a film of either an adult or a cartoon character being aggressive showed just as much aggression toward an inflatable doll as did children who had seen a live adult model; all three of these groups were significantly more aggressive than children who had not observed a model at all. But modeled aggression is not limited to toys: In a study by Steuer,

Applefield, and Smith (1971), children who watched cartoons depicting aggressive and violent behavior were significantly more aggressive toward other children than children who had not seen the cartoons.

The fact that children model aggressive behavior depicted in the media has obvious implications for television and movie violence. Not only do children model aggression, they also tend to model the same *forms* of aggression that they observe (Bandura, Ross, & Ross, 1963; Mischel & Grusec, 1966). Even cartoons that display violent behaviors, including such classics as "Tom and Jerry" and "Roadrunner," may not be as harmless as they appear.

Morality

Many aspects of moral thinking and moral behavior are apparently influenced by observation and modeling. Research has demonstrated the importance of social learning for such behaviors as generosity (Elliott & Vasta, 1970; Radke-Yarrow, Zahn-Waxler, & Chapman, 1983; Rushton, 1975, 1982), self-control (Harter, 1983; Stevenson & Fantuzzo, 1986), and resistance to temptation (Wolf & Cheyne, 1972). Consider this study by Rushton (1975) as an example. Children first observed a model playing a bowling game and reinforcing himself with tokens for high performance. Some children saw the model donate half of the earned tokens to a poor boy named Bobby pictured on a poster in the room; other children observed the model keep all his winnings for himself despite the presence of the poster. The children then had the opportunity to play the game and to reward themselves with tokens. The more tokens they earned, the better prize they could purchase (therefore, donating to Bobby meant that they would have to purchase a lesser prize). Children who had watched generous models were more likely to donate some of their own tokens to Bobby than were children who had watched selfish models. This difference was true not only in the initial session but also in a follow-up session two months later.

Moral judgments regarding right and wrong may also develop, at least in part, through social learning (Bandura & McDonald, 1963; Prentice, 1972; Schliefer & Douglas, 1973). For example, in a study by Bandura and McDonald (1963), experimenters presented children with pairs of stories such as these:

1. John was in his room when his mother called him to dinner. John goes down, and opens the door to the dining room. But behind the door was a chair, and on the chair was a tray with fifteen cups on it. John did not know the cups were behind the door. He opens the door, the door hits the tray, bang go the fifteen cups, and they all get broken.
2. One day when Henry's mother was out, Henry tried to get some cookies out of the cupboard. He climbed up on a chair, but the cookie jar was still too high, and he couldn't reach it. But while he was trying to get the cookie jar, he knocked over a cup. The cup fell and broke. (Bandura & McDonald, 1963, p. 276)

In each pair, stories portrayed one well-intended child (such as John) who caused major damage and another child with malicious intent (such as Henry) who did minor damage. For each pair of stories, the children were asked which child was naughtier. Some children consistently picked the child with the bad intentions as being naughtier; these children were then exposed to a model who used amount of damage as the criterion for naughtiness. Other children had a pattern of judging the well-meaning but more destructive child as being naughtier; they were exposed to a model who used intentions as the criterion for naughtiness. Observing the model had a profound effect on the children's later moral judgments: Children began to make moral decisions similar to those the model had made and opposite to their own previous judgments.

We have already seen that when models on film depict aggressive behavior, that behavior is often imitated. But visual media can model appropriate social responses as well, often quite effectively (Huston, Watkins, & Kunkel, 1989; Rushton, 1980). For example, in a study by Friedrich and Stein (1973), a group of preschool children watched "Mister Rogers' Neighborhood"—a television show that stresses such prosocial behaviors as cooperation, sympathy, and sharing—for 30 minutes each day over a four-week period. These children displayed more socially appropriate behavior and less aggression than children who instead watched shows with aggressive content (e.g., "Batman" and "Superman") during that same period.

What about situations when a model preaches one set of moral values and practices another? A review of research by Bryan (1975) leads to a clear conclusion: When children hear a model say one thing and do something else, they are more likely to imitate what the model *does* than what the model *says*. In other words, to be effective, models must practice what they preach.

Processes Involved in Learning Through Modeling

According to Bandura (1969, 1973, 1977b, 1986), four things are necessary before an individual can successfully model the behavior of someone else: attention, retention, motor reproduction, and motivation.

Attention

To model a behavior, a person must first pay attention to the model, especially to the significant aspects of the modeled behavior. For example, if Martha wishes to learn how to swing a golf club, she should watch how the golf pro stands, how her legs are placed, how her hands hold the club, and so on. Paying attention to the irrelevant parts of the model or her behavior—how she clears her throat or how her socks don't quite match—will of course not be helpful.

I still remember my first French teacher, a woman who came to my fifth-grade class for an hour one day a week. This woman always wore the same dark green wool dress which, unfortunately, turned to a turquoise color in places where she perspired. I remember focusing on those turquoise spots, fascinated that a wool dress could actually change color just because of a little human sweat. Yes, I was paying attention to my model, but no, I did not learn much

French, because I did not pay attention to the important aspect of the model's behavior—her voice.

Retention

The second step in learning from a model is to remember the behavior that has been observed. According to Bandura, people store both verbal representations (such as step-by-step instructions or labels that describe the actions to be performed) and visual images of the behaviors they have seen. These verbal and visual **memory codes** serve as guides when people perform the observed behavior, whether they perform it immediately after the model has illustrated it or at some time in the future. To illustrate such memory codes, my son Jeff's swimming teacher used the words *chicken, airplane,* and *soldier* to describe the three arm movements of the elementary backstroke (see Figure 7–1). The words provided Jeff with verbal codes for these actions; the teacher's demonstration of them facilitated the formation of visual images.

Considerable evidence indicates that learning from a model can be facilitated if learners have help in forming memory codes for the behaviors they observe (Alford & Rosenthal, 1973; Bandura & Jeffery, 1973; Bandura, Jeffery, & Bachicha, 1974; Coates & Hartup, 1969; Cohen, 1989; Gerst, 1971; Rosenthal, Alford, & Rasp, 1972). For example, in a study by Gerst (1971), college students studied a number of words (hand signals) in sign language for the deaf. Three experimental groups received instructions to encode the hand signals either by describing the signals to themselves or by forming mental images of the signals. All three groups were better able to reproduce the signals than a control group given a task that prevented encoding (counting by 7s or 13s from various numbers); the group that learned most successfully was the one instructed to develop verbal

Figure 7–1
Students often remember a model's behaviors more easily when those behaviors have verbal labels.

Arm Movements for the Elementary Back Stroke

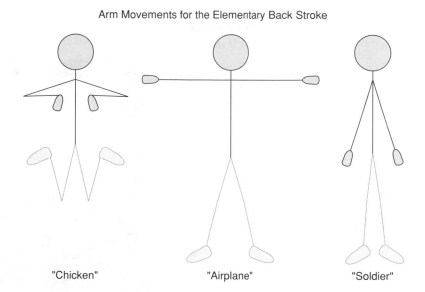

"Chicken"   "Airplane"   "Soldier"

labels descriptive of the hand movements. Teachers, too, can provide codes for learners. For example, in a study by Rosenthal, Alford, and Rasp (1972), second-graders more effectively learned actions modeled by an adult when the adult described each action as well as demonstrating it.

The storage of information in memory and the different forms that such stored information can take have been studied more extensively by information-processing theorists than by social learning theorists. We will therefore return to this topic of memory storage again, and in much greater detail, in Chapter 11.

Motor Reproduction

The third component in modeling is replication of the behavior the model has demonstrated. When an individual cannot reproduce an observed behavior, perhaps because of physical immaturity, lack of strength, or disability, this third step obviously cannot occur. For example, a child with a speech impediment may never be able to pronounce *sassafras* correctly, no matter how many times she has heard the word spoken. And a toddler who watches his teenage brother throw a football does not possess the muscular coordination to mimic that throw.

In my never-ending battle with the bulge, I turn on Jane Fonda's physical workout videocassette tape religiously every night (well, at least twice a month). Jane performs exercises in various pretzel-like contortions that I in my wildest dreams would never be able to do. My body simply is not built to be folded in that many ways. Motor reproduction of everything I watch model Jane do is simply not possible.

Reproduction of an observed behavior at the same time it is observed facilitates learning for at least two reasons. For one thing, it enables learners to

Modeling cannot occur
without physical capability.

encode that behavior, not only in verbal and visual forms, but perhaps in a *motoric* form as well—that is, in terms of the specific actions it encompasses (Cohen, 1989). Furthermore, by modeling a behavior in the presence of the model, learners can get feedback about how to improve their performance (Bandura, 1977b; Schunk, 1981). For example, in teaching division to children having difficulty with mathematics, Schunk (1981) found that instruction that included an opportunity for practice and immediate feedback about the quality of the performance was clearly superior to instruction that provided no opportunity for such specific feedback.

Motivation

The final necessary ingredient for modeling is motivation to exhibit the modeled behavior: People must want to demonstrate what they have learned. For example, most individuals who have grown up in our society have seen numerous models on television point a gun in someone's ribs and say "Reach for the sky" (or at least something to that effect). Fortunately, very few people are motivated to model that behavior, at least with a real gun.

Although parents and teachers are often models for children, children do not model *all* the behaviors they observe their parents and teachers perform. For example, although my children model my ways of speaking to people on the telephone and my cookie-baking techniques, for some reason they don't seem to copy my broccoli-cooking or my floor-scrubbing behaviors. Children model behaviors only when they are motivated to do so.

To review, Bandura's four components of modeling are attention, retention, motor reproduction, and motivation. Because these components vary among individuals, different people will model the same behavior differently. For example, Martha and Mary might pay attention to different aspects of their tennis instructor's tennis swing: Martha may focus on how the instructor is standing while Mary attends more to the way the instructor grips her racket. Or the two girls might store different visual images of the swing, Martha remembering that the instructor was facing the net and Mary remembering her standing with the left shoulder toward the net. Martha may be stronger, but Mary may be more motivated to play tennis well. The end result is that Martha and Mary will model the same tennis swing differently. Not only will the four components lead to individual differences in modeled behaviors, the absence of any one of these components will make modeling unlikely to occur at all.

Effects of Modeling on Behavior

In what ways do models influence behavior? Social learning theorists (e.g., Bandura, 1969, 1973, 1977b, 1986; Bandura & Walters, 1963; Rosenthal & Zimmerman, 1978) believe that modeling has at least three effects.

•*Modeling teaches new behaviors.* Individuals can learn entirely new behaviors by observing others perform those behaviors (e.g., Bandura, Ross, & Ross,

1963). For example, by listening to and imitating the sounds of others, a person learns to speak new words. And by watching how a parent swings a baseball bat and following the parent's verbal instructions ("Keep your eye on the ball!"), a child learns to hit a baseball.

•*Modeling inhibits and disinhibits previously learned behaviors.* People are less likely to perform behaviors for which they have seen others punished; in other words, vicarious punishment has an **inhibition** effect. For instance, a child who observes another child being punished for chewing gum in class is less likely to display the same behavior.

Along a similar vein, people are more likely to perform behaviors when they have seen others reinforced for those behaviors; that is, vicarious reinforcement has a **disinhibition** effect. For example, in studies by Walters and his colleagues (Walters & Thomas, 1963; Walters, Thomas, & Acker, 1962), adults viewed either a film depicting aggression and violence (*Rebel Without a Cause*) or a neutral film (*Picture Making by Teenagers*), then were asked to administer "shocks" to other individuals. (These other individuals were confederates of the experimenter who did not really receive any shocks but behaved as if they did.) Subjects who had watched the violent, aggressive film administered more frequent and more intense "shocks" to the confederates. The film had apparently disinhibited previously learned, aggressive behavior.

•*Modeling elicits similar behaviors.* When a person observes a model performing a particular behavior, that person may display similar rather than identical behavior. For example, a boy who sees his older brother excel at basketball, but who lacks his brother's height advantage, may instead try to become a successful soccer player. As a high school student, I would have liked to become a "cool" cheerleader but did not have the gymnastic skills necessary for cheerleading. Instead, I became a majorette in the marching band, an activity that was almost as cool.

Characteristics of Effective Models

People who are most likely to serve as live or symbolic models for others tend to have one or more characteristic traits.

•*The model is competent.* People demonstrating a particular behavior are more likely to be modeled if they are viewed as being competent, capable individuals (Bandura, 1986). For example, a person trying to learn tennis is more likely to model the techniques of a successful tennis player than those of a friend who cannot even get the ball over the net. And a student trying to learn how to write a better term paper is more likely to look at the work of someone who has consistently received high grades on term papers than at the work of a student who has historically done poorly.

•*The model has prestige and power.* Individuals that have high status, respect, and power, perhaps within a small group or within society as a whole, are more likely to be modeled (Bandura, 1986). A child is more likely to imitate

Models are often competent, respected, and powerful.

the behaviors of a student leader or a famous rock star than the behaviors of a class dunce or a rock-and-roll "has-been." To illustrate, Sasso and Rude (1987) taught a number of nondisabled children (some of whom were popular with their peers and some of whom were not) methods of initiating appropriate social interactions with physically disabled children. Other children who saw their more popular classmates interacting with disabled children were likely to do so as well, but children who saw unpopular students modeling the same behavior were unlikely to follow suit.

•*The model behaves in stereotypical "gender-appropriate" ways.* Males are more likely to model behavior that is consistent with male stereotypes; similarly, females are more likely to model behaviors that follow traditional female patterns. For example, in studies in which children watched adult models of both genders being aggressive (Bandura, Ross, & Ross, 1961, 1963), boys were more likely than girls to imitate the aggressive behaviors, presumably because aggression is a trait more frequently associated with males than with females.

•*The model's behavior is relevant to the observer's situation.* Individuals are more likely to model behaviors that have functional value in their own circumstances (Rosenthal & Bandura, 1978). For example, my daughter models many of my behaviors, but she definitely does not model the way I dress. She has told me, in so many words, that she would be laughed out of school if she dressed the way I do.

Parents and teachers are among the people that children most often model, particularly when those parents and teachers are seen as competent, respected, and powerful. Children also frequently model their behaviors after famous personalities and fictional heroes. And children's peer groups—other children of the same gender and age—can be a source of powerful and influential models as well.

Yet characteristics of the model are not the only variables determining whether modeling takes place. Another important variable is the observer's self-efficacy, a topic to which we turn now.

SELF-EFFICACY

People are more likely to engage in certain behaviors when they believe they are capable of executing those behaviors successfully—that is, when they have high **self-efficacy** (e.g., Bandura, 1977a, 1982, 1986, 1989; Schunk, 1989b). For example, I hope you believe you are capable of understanding and remembering the ideas I present in this book; in other words, I hope you have high self-efficacy for learning about learning. You may or may not believe that, with instruction and practice, you will eventually be able to perform a passable swan dive; in other words, you may have high or low self-efficacy about learning to dive. You are probably quite skeptical that you could ever walk barefoot over hot coals, so my guess is that you have low self-efficacy regarding this activity.

Self-efficacy is a concept similar to *self-esteem*, but with one important difference. One's self-esteem tends to pervade a wide variety of activities; thus, people are described as having generally high or low self-esteem. Self-efficacy is more situation-specific. For example, people may have high self-efficacy about reading a textbook about human learning but not about reading a textbook on neurosurgery. They may have high self-efficacy about learning to perform a swan dive but not about swimming the entire length of a swimming pool underwater. In one recent study, fifth graders had significantly higher self-efficacy about learning social studies than about learning mathematics (Stodolsky, Salk, & Glaessner, 1991).

How Self-Efficacy Affects Behavior

According to social learning theorists (e.g., Bandura, 1977a, 1982, 1986, 1989; Schunk, 1989c), people's feelings of self-efficacy affect several aspects of their behavior, including their choice of activities, their effort and persistence, and ultimately their learning and achievement.

Choice of Activities

People tend to choose tasks and activities at which they believe they can succeed; they also tend to avoid those that they think they will fail. For example, students who believe they can succeed at mathematics are more likely to take math courses than students who believe they are mathematically incompetent. Those who believe they can win a role in the school play are more likely to try out than students with little faith in their acting or singing abilities.

Effort and Persistence

People with a high sense of self-efficacy are more likely to exert effort in attempting to accomplish a task. They are also more likely to persist when they encounter obstacles. Students with low self-efficacy about a particular task will put less effort into it and will give up more quickly in the face of difficulty.

Learning and Achievement

Students with high self-efficacy tend to learn and achieve more than students with low self-efficacy, even when actual ability levels are the same (Bandura, 1986; Collins, 1982; Schunk, 1989a; Spaulding, 1992; Zimmerman, Bandura, & Martinez-Pons, 1992). In other words, when several students have equal ability, those students who *believe* they can do a task are more likely to accomplish it successfully than those who do not believe they are capable of success.

Factors in the Development of Self-Efficacy

Students' feelings of self-efficacy are usually fairly accurate: They typically have a good sense of what they can and cannot do (Bandura, 1986). Sometimes students underestimate their chances of success, however, perhaps because of a few bad experiences. For example, a girl who gets a C in science from a teacher with exceptionally strict grading criteria may erroneously believe that she is "no good" in science. A new boy at school whose attempts at being friendly are rejected by two or three thoughtless classmates may erroneously believe that "no one likes him."

According to social learning theorists (e.g., Bandura, 1986, 1989; Schunk, 1989a; Schunk, Hanson, & Cox, 1987), at least three factors affect the development of self-efficacy: one's own previous successes and failures, persuasion, and the successes and failures of others.

Previous Successes and Failures

Students feel more confident that they can succeed at a task—that is, they have greater self-efficacy—when they have succeeded at that task or similar ones in the past (Bandura, 1986; Klein, 1990; Nicholls, 1984). For example, a student is more likely to believe he can learn to divide fractions if he has successfully mastered the process of multiplying fractions. Similarly, a student will be more confident about her ability to play field hockey if she has already developed skills in soccer.

Once students have developed a high sense of self-efficacy, an occasional failure is unlikely to have much effect on their optimism. In fact, when people encounter small setbacks on the way to achieving success, they learn that sustained effort and perseverance are key ingredients for that success; in other words, they develop what Bandura calls **resilient self-efficacy** (Bandura, 1989). However, when students meet with *consistent* failure in performing a particular task, they will tend to have little confidence in their ability to succeed at that task in the future. Each new failure confirms what they already "know" about the task—they can't do it.

It is not surprising, then, that students with a history of academic success have higher self-efficacy for academic tasks than students with lower school performance. For example, students with learning disabilities—who typically have encountered failure after failure in classroom activities—often have low self-efficacy with regard to the things they study in school (Schunk, 1989c).

Persuasion

To some extent, students' feelings of self-efficacy benefit from assurances that success *is* possible. Statements such as "You can do this problem if you work at it" or "I bet Judy will play with you if you just ask her" do give students a slight boost in self-confidence. However, this boost will be short-lived unless students' efforts at a task ultimately meet with success (Schunk, 1989a).

Successes and Failures of Others

People often acquire information about their own self-efficacy by observing the successes and failures of other individuals, especially those similar to themselves (Schunk, 1983b, 1989c). As an example, students often consider the successes and failures of other students, especially those of similar ability, when appraising their own chances of success on academic tasks. Thus, seeing a classmate model a behavior successfully is often more effective than seeing an adult teacher do it. For example, in one study (Schunk & Hanson, 1985), elementary school children having trouble with subtraction were given 25 subtraction problems to complete. Those who had seen another student successfully complete the problems got an average of 19 correct, whereas those who saw a teacher complete the problems got only 13 correct, and those who saw no model at all only solved 8!

At the same time, students should not depend too much on others as they strive to learn new things. Teachers cannot always be looking over students' shoulders to see what they are doing or goad them into engaging in more appropriate and productive behaviors. Ultimately, students must begin to rely primarily on *themselves* for their own learning. Social learning theorists believe that people can and should ultimately regulate their own behavior. We therefore turn to a topic gaining increasing prominence in psychological and educational literature—the topic of *self-regulation*.

SELF-REGULATION

As social learning theory has evolved over the years, it has increasingly emphasized the role of **self-regulation** of behavior (e.g., Bandura, 1977b, 1982, 1986;
Zimmerman, 1989). Through both direct and vicarious reinforcement and punishment, people gradually learn which behaviors are acceptable and which are
not. Eventually they learn and adopt performance standards that become the
basis for reinforcing themselves. For example, my son Alex's bedroom used to be
a disaster area: getting from the door to the bed was a matter of wading through
several layers of toy trucks, building blocks, and little plastic people. Now, however, Alex keeps his bedroom immaculate even without any parental nagging and
prides himself on his tidiness. (Tina's and Jeff's rooms still resemble the city
landfill, but that's another story.) Similarly, as students mature, they typically
need less prodding to complete assignments and study for tests. Instead, they
begin to talk about feeling good when assignments have been completed or feeling guilty when they are procrastinating.

Aspects of Self-Regulation

Self-regulation entails at least four components: setting standards and goals, self-
observation, self-judgment, and self-reaction (e.g., Bandura, 1986; Schunk,
1989c, 1991).

Setting Standards and Goals
As human beings, we tend to set standards for our own behavior; in other words,
we establish criteria regarding what constitutes acceptable performance. We also
establish certain goals that we value and toward which we direct many of our
behaviors.

The kinds of performance standards that people establish for their own
behavior depend to some degree on the standards they see other people adopt
(Bandura, 1977b, 1986). In a study by Bandura and Kupers (1964), for example,
children watched adult or child models reward themselves with candy and self-
praise for their performance in a bowling game. Some of the children watched
the models reward themselves only after achieving 20 points or more (reflecting
very high performance); these models admonished themselves for lower performance. Other children observed models reward themselves after achieving as few
as 10 points. The children then had the opportunity to play the game themselves
and to help themselves to candy whenever they chose. Bandura and Kupers
found that the children tended to reinforce themselves using performance standards very similar to what they had seen the models use.

People are most apt to adopt the kinds of standards that models similar to
themselves in ability adopt (Bandura, 1977b). They are unlikely to adopt the

standards of models who are much more competent (Bandura & Whalen, 1966) or who apply performance standards inconsistently (Bandura, 1977b).

Self-observation

An important part of self-regulation is observing oneself in action. To make progress toward important goals, individuals must be aware of how well they are doing at present; in other words, they must know what parts of their performance are working well and what parts need improvement.

Self-judgment

People's behaviors are frequently judged by others—for example, by relatives, teachers, classmates, friends, and the general public. Eventually people begin to judge and evaluate their *own* behaviors based on the standards they hold for themselves.

Self-reaction

As students become increasingly self-regulated, they begin to reinforce themselves—perhaps by feeling proud or telling themselves they did a good job—when they accomplish their goals. They also begin to punish themselves—perhaps by feeling sorry, guilty, or ashamed—when they do something that does not meet their own performance standards. Such self-praise and self-criticism can be as influential in altering behavior as the reinforcements and punishments administered by others (Bandura, 1977b, 1986).

To illustrate, consider Jason, a student who perceives himself to have average intelligence; he is likely to form standards for his own academic achievement that match the achievement of other "average" students. Jason is therefore likely to pat himself on the back for "B" work and perhaps maintain a similar level of effort on future tasks. On the other hand, consider Joanna, a student whose close friends are the high achievers of the class. If Joanna believes her ability is similar to that of her friends, she is likely to adopt high standards for herself and to admonish herself for the same B-level achievement of which Jason is so proud. Provided that the B does not appreciably undermine her self-efficacy, Joanna is likely to try harder on the same task the next time around (Bandura, 1989).

Promoting Self-Regulation

Writing a textbook is a major undertaking. As I sit here in my basement tapping at the keys of my word processor day after day, I sometimes wonder why in the world I ever committed myself to such a project when I could instead be upstairs in my warm, comfortable living room reading mystery novels or watching television game shows. Yet each day I drag myself down to the basement to produce a few more pages. How do I do it? I do it by reinforcing myself every time I finish a small section of the book. For example, as soon as I finished the section on self-efficacy that you just read, I gave myself permission to go upstairs to watch my favorite game show. Before I can watch another one, though, I need to finish this section on self-regulation.

A growing body of research provides several techniques for promoting self-regulation (e.g., Mace, Belfiore, & Shea, 1989; Mahoney & Thoresen, 1974; Rimm & Masters, 1974). These techniques (sometimes called *self-control* or *self-management*) include self-instructions, self-monitoring, self-reinforcement, and self-imposed stimulus control.

Self-instructions

One promising technique is to teach learners to give themselves instructions that guide their behavior (Mace et al., 1989; Meichenbaum, 1985; Schunk, 1989c; Shaffer, 1988). As one simple illustration, beginning tennis students improve the accuracy of their returns when they give themselves these four verbal cues:

- "Ball" (to remind them to keep their eye on the ball)
- "Bounce" (to continue tracking the path of the ball)
- "Hit" (to focus on contacting the ball with the racket)
- "Ready" (to get into position for the next ball) (Ziegler, 1987)

Other studies show self-instructions to be effective in promoting independent work habits and decreasing impulsive behavior (Guevremont, Osnes, & Stokes, 1988; Hughes, 1988; Meichenbaum & Goodman, 1971).

Self-monitoring

Another method that can help people control their own behavior is simply to have them observe and measure their own responses, just as someone else might measure those responses in traditional behavior modification (Mace et al., 1989; Mahoney & Thoresen, 1974). The mere recording of responses is often enough to alter the frequency of those responses. For example, my family was once part of a research project in which randomly selected households recorded their own

The author practices self-control.

television-watching habits over a period of several weeks. We were instructed to mark down every instance of television-viewing—including the date, time of day, length of time, and programs watched—on a specially designed record sheet. Every time I thought about turning on the television set, I remembered all the work I would have to go through to record my viewing, and, as often as not, I found something else to do instead. Thus, the simple process of having to record my television-watching behavior altered it.

Self-monitoring can be instituted in a classroom setting as well. For example, in one research study (Harris, 1986), students having difficulty keeping their minds on their spelling seatwork were given tape recorders that emitted a small beep at random intervals about 45 seconds apart. Whenever students heard a beep, they asked themselves, "Was I paying attention?" This simple technique doubled their time on task and tripled their productivity during seatwork sessions. Other studies have obtained similar results in terms of increased on-task behavior and assignment completion (Broden, Hall, & Mitts, 1971; Hallahan, Marshall, & Lloyd, 1981; Mace et al., 1989; Mace & Kratochwill, 1988).

Just as desirable behaviors can be increased, undesirable behaviors can be *de*creased through self-monitoring. For example, self-recording of a target behavior has been found to reduce such disruptive classroom behaviors as talking out of turn, leaving one's seat without permission, and hitting classmates (Bolstad & Johnson, 1972; Broden et al., 1971; Mace et al., 1989; Moletzsky, 1974).

Self-reinforcement

People can often change their own behavior simply by reinforcing themselves when they behave appropriately and withholding reinforcement when they do not (Mace et al., 1989; Mahoney & Thoresen, 1974; O'Leary & O'Leary, 1972; Rimm & Masters, 1974). I am able to maintain my book-writing behavior through use of the Premack principle: I let myself engage in enjoyable activities only after I have completed less enjoyable ones.

When students learn to reinforce themselves for their accomplishments—perhaps by giving themselves some free time, helping themselves to a small treat, or simply praising themselves—their study habits and academic performance improve (Beneke & Harris, 1972; Greiner & Karoly, 1976; Hayes, Rosenfarb, Wulfert, Munt, Korn, & Zettle, 1985; Stevenson & Fantuzzo, 1986). In one research study (Stevenson & Fantuzzo, 1986), students who had been performing poorly in arithmetic were taught to give themselves points when they did well on their assignments; they could later use these points to "buy" a variety of items and privileges. Within a few weeks, these students were doing as well as their classmates on both in-class assignments and homework. In another study (Bandura & Perloff, 1967), self-reinforcement was just as effective in modifying student behaviors as reinforcement administered by a teacher.

Self-imposed Stimulus Control

As you should recall from Chapter 4's discussion of operant conditioning, a response is under stimulus control when it is emitted in the presence of some stimuli but not others. This idea can be translated into an effective means of promoting self-control (Mahoney & Thoresen, 1974); I call it self-imposed stimulus control. To increase a particular desired behavior, an individual might be instructed to seek out an environment where that behavior is most likely to occur. For example, a student who wishes to increase the time actually spent studying each day should sit down at a table in the library rather than on the bed at home. Conversely, to decrease an undesired behavior, an individual should engage in that behavior only in certain situations. For example, I once knew a professor who, in an effort to stop smoking, gradually reduced the number of situations in which he permitted himself to smoke. Eventually, he was able to smoke in only one situation, facing a back corner of his office; at that point, he successfully stopped smoking.

Self-control techniques work only when individuals are themselves motivated to bring about a behavior change, and in such circumstances they work quite well. Two precautions are necessary, however. First, the individuals being trained in self-control must have the capability for exhibiting the desired behaviors; for example, students who wish to modify their study habits will only achieve higher grades if they possess adequate academic skills to ensure success. Second, individuals must be cautioned not to expect too much of themselves too quickly. Many individuals would prefer overnight success, but shaping, either of oneself or of another, is a slow, gradual process. Just as the dieter will not lose 40 pounds in one week, it is equally unlikely that a habitually poor student will achieve honor roll status immediately. For self-control techniques to be effective, one's expectations for oneself must be practical and realistic.

EDUCATIONAL APPLICATIONS OF SOCIAL LEARNING THEORY

Social learning theory has numerous implications for classroom practice. Let's take a look at some of them.

•*Observation alone is sufficient for learning.* Behaviorists such as B. F. Skinner have stressed the necessity of active responding for learning to occur. But in this chapter I have presented examples of how learning can occur through observation alone. Not only can students learn information and academic skills by observing others, they can learn moral values, performance standards, and appropriate and inappropriate modes of conducting themselves as well.

•*Modeling provides an alternative to shaping for teaching new behaviors.* Operant conditioning provides one means—shaping—for teaching a new response. Remember, however, that to shape a particular behavior, one must begin by reinforcing an existing behavior and then gradually modify that behavior through differential reinforcement; for complex behaviors, this process can be time-consuming. Social learning theory offers a faster, more efficient means for teaching new behavior: the modeling process.

•*Teachers and parents should model appropriate behaviors.* Teachers and parents often possess characteristics (e.g., competence, prestige, and power) that make them influential models for children. Adults must therefore be careful that they model appropriate behaviors for the children with whom they interact. I am delighted when I see teachers and other adults show such characteristics as open-mindedness, empathy, and concern for physical fitness; I cringe when I see them express disdain for particular points of view, disregard the needs and concerns of other human beings, or smoke a cigarette.

A child I know once tried out for a role in a Christmas pageant. Lisa went off to school on the morning of pageant tryouts, aware that students could each try out for one part only and thinking that she had a good chance of winning the role of Mrs. Claus. Lisa was convinced that the teacher would award the role of Santa Claus to a girl named Ann; however, because Ann was late that morning and the teacher had announced that latecomers would not be allowed to try out, Lisa instead tried out for Santa himself. When Ann arrived 10 minutes late, the teacher disregarded her rule about latecomers being ineligible, allowed Ann to try out for Santa Claus, and in fact awarded the role to Ann. In doing so, this teacher, one of the school's most visible role models, modeled both hypocrisy and favoritism.

As an educational psychologist who teaches teachers how to teach, my job is a particularly difficult one because I must practice what I preach. If I tell my students that immediate feedback, organization of information, vivid examples, hands-on experiences, and tests that match instructional objectives are all important components of effective teaching, my students' learning will obviously be enhanced if I model all those things as well. To say one thing but do another would not only be hypocritical, it would also be counterproductive.

• *Teachers should expose students to a variety of exemplary models.* Adult models need not be limited to children's teachers and parents. Other adults can be invited to visit classrooms on occasion (Bell-Gredler, 1986); for example, police officers, prominent city officials, business people, and doctors might demonstrate appropriate behaviors and attitudes related to safety, good citizenship, responsibility, and health. Symbolic models can also be effective; for example, studying the lives of such individuals as Helen Keller, Martin Luther King, Jr., and Eleanor Roosevelt is a viable method of illustrating many appropriate behaviors.

• *The four components of modeling—attention, retention, motor reproduction, and motivation—are essential for successful modeling.* Thus, a wise teacher must make sure that all four components are present. First of all, the teacher must make sure that students pay attention to the model and particularly to the relevant aspects of the model's behavior. Second, the teacher can facilitate students' retention of what they observe by helping them form appropriate memory codes for those observations (strategies for doing so will be discussed in Chapter 11). Third, giving students opportunities to practice the behaviors they see and giving them corrective feedback about their attempts will aid their motor reproduction of the responses they are modeling. Finally, remember that students will only display learned behaviors if they have the motivation to do so. Many children will be intrinsically motivated to perform, but others may require external incentives and reinforcers. (We will address additional motivational strategies in Chapters 17 and 18.)

•*Vicarious reinforcement and vicarious punishment may influence student behavior.* Students learn what behaviors are appropriate and what behaviors are inappropriate not only through the consequences of their own behaviors but through the consequences of other people's behaviors as well. Teachers and other school personnel must therefore be consistent in the rewards and punishments they administer, not only from time to time, but also from student to student.

•*Describing the consequences of behaviors can effectively increase appropriate behaviors and decrease inappropriate ones.* As you should recall, social learning theorists propose that the awareness of response-consequence contingencies is an essential component of behavior control. Promises of rewards for good behaviors and threats of punishments for misdeeds can therefore be effective means of improving student behavior. But administering reinforcement or punishment when students do not recognize the relationship between the particular response they have made and its consequence is unlikely to bring about behavior change.

•*Students must believe that they are capable of accomplishing school tasks.* As we have seen, students' self-efficacy affects their learning and academic achievement. To enhance students' self-efficacy, teachers can tell them that similar students have mastered the things they are learning and even have them observe their peers successfully accomplishing those tasks. It may be especially beneficial for students to see a peer struggling with a task or problem at first— something they themselves are likely to do—and then eventually mastering it (Schunk et al., 1987). But teachers best help students develop high self-efficacy when they enable students to be successful themselves—for example, by teaching important basic skills to mastery and providing instructional guidance and support for complex, challenging tasks.

•*Students should have help in setting realistic expectations for their own behavior.* Modeling is a primary means through which students develop standards for their own performance. When a student's standards are unrealistically high, as might be true for a perfectionist, continual disappointment and frustration are likely to result. When a student's standards are too low, underachievement will result. Teachers can facilitate students' academic and social progress by helping them form self-expectations commensurate with their skills and ability.

•*Self-control techniques can be effective methods of modifying student behaviors.* Earlier in the chapter, I described four techniques for promoting self-regulation: self-instructions, self-monitoring, self-reinforcement, and self-imposed stimulus control. When students are intrinsically motivated to change their own behaviors, such techniques can provide a viable alternative to behavioristic approaches.

Clearly, we cannot ignore the social context of the classroom. Students can and do learn from the models—parents, teachers, and peers—that they see every day. And the social learning perspective has shown us that it is important to consider cognitive factors as well as environmental ones in learning. As we move into cognitivism in the next chapter, we will begin to focus on those cognitive factors even more closely.

SUMMARY

Social learning theory focuses on the ways in which individuals learn from observing one another. This perspective reflects a blending of behaviorist concepts (e.g., reinforcement and punishment) with cognitive notions (e.g., expectation and awareness). Environmental and cognitive variables interact with one another and with behavior through a process known as reciprocal causation.

Many behaviors, beliefs, and attitudes are acquired through modeling; aggression and morality are but two examples. Four things are necessary for modeling to occur: attention, retention, motor reproduction, and motivation. Effective models are likely to be competent, prestigious, and powerful, and to exhibit behaviors that are "gender-appropriate" and relevant to the observer's own situation.

Individuals with high self-efficacy—those who believe they can successfully accomplish a particular task—are more likely to choose challenging activities, exert effort and persist at those activities, and show higher learning and achievement over the long run. Self-efficacy can be enhanced through persuasion, the successes of others, and, most importantly, one's *own* successes.

Social learning theorists propose that, although environmental circumstances influence behavior, over time people begin to regulate their own behavior by setting their own standards, observing and judging themselves on the basis of those standards, and reinforcing or punishing themselves (perhaps only mentally and emotionally) for the quality of their performance. Teachers can promote self-control in their students by teaching such techniques as self-instruction, self-monitoring, self-reinforcement, and self-imposed stimulus control.

Social learning theory has numerous implications for education. For example, when teaching new skills, modeling is an effective alternative to operant conditioning techniques. Describing response-reinforcement and response-punishment contingencies makes students aware of what those contingencies are; hence, such descriptions can affect behavior before any consequences have been imposed. And promoting high self-efficacy is one means through which teachers can promote students' school success.

PART FOUR

COGNITIVE VIEWS OF LEARNING

CHAPTER 8

Antecedents and Assumptions of Cognitivism

During the past two decades, cognitive psychology has provided the predominant perspective within which learning research has been conducted and theories of learning have evolved. As we begin to explore this perspective, you will probably notice a change in focus. In contrast to behaviorists, who emphasize the roles of environmental conditions (stimuli) and overt behaviors (responses) in learning, cognitive psychologists look more at how individuals **process** the stimuli they encounter—that is, how individuals perceive, interpret, and mentally "store" the information they receive from the environment. This focus on **information processing** underlies much of cognitive theory.

Early behaviorists chose not to incorporate mental events into their learning theories, arguing that such events were impossible to observe and measure and so could not be studied objectively. During the 1950s and 1960s, however, many psychologists became increasingly dissatisfied with such a "thoughtless" approach to human learning. Major works with a distinctly cognitive flavor began to emerge; publications by Noam Chomsky (1957) in psycholinguistics and by Bruner, Goodnow, and Austin (1956) in concept learning are examples. Ulric Neisser's *Cognitive Psychology*, published in 1967, was a landmark book that helped to legitimize cognitive theory as a major alternative to behaviorism (Calfee, 1981). Increasingly, cognitivism began appearing in educational psychology literature as well, with Jerome Bruner (e.g., 1961a, 1961b, 1966) and David Ausubel (e.g., Ausubel, 1963, 1968; Ausubel & Robinson, 1969) being two well-known early proponents. By the 1970s, the great majority of learning theorists had joined the cognitive bandwagon.

Yet the roots of cognitive psychology preceded the massive discontentment with strict S-R psychology by several decades. Some cognitive learning theories appeared in the 1920s and 1930s, notably those of the Gestalt psychologists of Germany, the American psychologist Edward Tolman, the Swiss developmentalist Jean Piaget, and the Russian developmentalist Lev Vygotsky. These early theories have had considerable influence on contemporary cognitivism, and Piaget's and Vygotsky's theories in particular continue to provide dominant perspectives for developmental research.

Equally important to the cognitive movement was research conducted during the 1930s to 1960s in an area known as **verbal learning**. Verbal learning theorists originally attempted to apply a stimulus-response analysis to human language and verbal behavior, but soon discovered that the complexities of human language-based learning were sometimes difficult to explain from the behaviorist perspective. Increasingly, verbal learning theorists began to incorporate mental processes into their explanations of research results.

In this chapter, I will describe some of the contributions of the Gestaltists, Tolman, Piaget, Vygotsky, and the verbal learning theorists. I will then introduce you to some of the unique assumptions, terminology, and methods of contemporary information processing theory. Finally, I will list some of the more general educational implications of the cognitive perspective.

EARLY COGNITIVE THEORIES

We can trace many ideas and assumptions of cognitivism back to the early decades of the twentieth century, more specifically to the Gestalt psychologists of Germany, Edward Tolman of the United States, Jean Piaget of Switzerland, and Lev Vygotsky of Russia. Let's therefore look at some of the basic premises of these theorists.

Gestalt Psychology

During the early decades of the twentieth century, a perspective emerged in German psychology that was largely independent of behaviorism-dominated American psychology. This perspective, known as **Gestalt psychology**, was advanced by such theorists as Max Wertheimer (1912, 1945, 1959), Wolfgang Köhler (1925, 1929, 1938, 1940, 1947, 1959, 1969), and Kurt Koffka (1935). Gestalt psychologists emphasized the importance of organizational processes in perception, learning, and problem solving and believed that individuals were predisposed to organize information in particular ways. What follow are some of the most basic ideas of Gestalt psychology.

•*Perception may be different from reality.* The origin of Gestalt psychology is usually attributed to Max Wertheimer's (1912) description and analysis of an optical illusion known as the ***phi* phenomenon**. Wertheimer observed that when two lights blink on and off sequentially at a particular rate, they often appear to be only one light moving quickly back and forth. (This effect can be observed in the blinking lights of many roadside signs.) The fact that an individual "sees" motion when observing stationary objects led Wertheimer to conclude that perception of an experience is sometimes different from the experience itself.

•*The whole is more than the sum of its parts.* Gestaltists believed that human experience cannot be successfully understood when various aspects of experience are studied in isolation from one another. For example, the illusion of movement in the *phi* phenomenon is perceived only when two or more lights are present; no motion is perceived in a single light. A combination of elements may show a pattern not evident in any of the elements alone; to use a Gestaltist expression, the whole is more than the sum of its parts.

The importance of the interrelationships among elements in a situation can be seen in Köhler's (1929) **transposition** experiments with chickens. Hens were shown two sheets of gray paper, with one sheet being a darker shade of gray than the other. Grain was placed on both sheets, but the hens were only allowed to feed from the darker one. At a later time, the hens were shown a sheet of paper the same shade as that on which they had previously been fed, along with a sheet of an even darker shade. In this second situation, the hens tended to go not to the shade on which they had been reinforced earlier, but to the darker of the two sheets. The hens had apparently learned something about the relationship between the two sheets of paper; in a sense, they learned that darker is better.

•*The organism structures and organizes experience.* The German word *gestalt*, roughly translated, means "structured whole." Structure is not necessarily inherent in a situation; instead, the organism imposes structure and organization on that situation. For example, the *phi* phenomenon represents a person's synthesis of two flashing lights into the perception of a single moving light.

Figure 8–1 provides another example of how experiences are organized. As you look at this figure, you probably perceive four pairs of lines with individual lines at each end. Now, however, look at Figure 8–2, in which the same lines appear within a particular context. You probably now see the lines differently—as

Figure 8–1

Figure 8–2

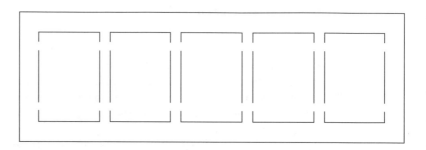

five pairs forming the sides of five rectangles. The lines themselves are identical in both cases, but the way in which you organize them (i.e., which lines you group together) is different. The "structure" of the lines is something that you yourself impose on the figure.

•*The organism is predisposed to organizing experience in particular ways.* Gestaltists believed that organisms are predisposed to structure their experiences in similar, and therefore predictable, ways. For example, when you look at Figure 8–1, the *law of proximity* dictates that you see lines near one another as pairs. However, in Figure 8–2, the *law of closure* takes over: You complete the incomplete rectangles. Gestalt psychologists proposed a number of principles to describe how people organize their experiences, some of which we will explore in Chapter 9.

Gestaltists further proposed that individuals always organize their experience as simply, concisely, symmetrically, and completely as possible, a principle known as the *law of Prägnanz* ("terseness" or "preciseness"; e.g., Koffka, 1935). For example, you are likely to see rectangles in Figure 8–2 because rectangles are simple, symmetric figures. It is unlikely that you would mentally fill in the missing pieces of that figure in a wild and crazy fashion such as that shown in Figure 8–3. People are very simple folks after all!

•*Learning follows the law of Prägnanz.* According to Gestalt psychologists, learning involves the formation of **memory traces**. These memory traces are subject to the law of Prägnanz so that over time they tend to become simpler, more concise, and more complete than the actual input. For example, upon seeing the somewhat irregular objects in Figure 8–4, people are likely later to remember them as being a "circle" and a "square." As another example, consider a study by Tversky (1981), in which people studied maps and then drew them

Figure 8–3

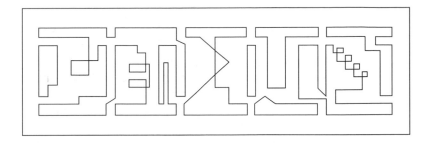

from memory. Distortions in the subjects' reproductions often followed the law of Prägnanz: Curvy, irregular lines were straightened, slanted lines were represented as north–south or east–west lines, and map features were placed in better alignment with one another than they had been in the original maps.

•*Problem solving involves restructuring and insight.* The American psychologist Edward Thorndike had previously described problem solving (such as that exhibited by cats in puzzle boxes) as a process of trial and error (Thorndike, 1898). Gestaltists proposed a very different view of how organisms solve problems. Köhler (1925), for instance, suggested that problem solving involves mentally combining and recombining the various elements of a problem until a structure that solves the problem is achieved. He described numerous observations of chimpanzees solving problems through what he perceived to be the mental manipulation of the problem situation. In one situation, a chimpanzee named Sultan was faced with a dilemma: Some fruit was placed far enough outside his cage that he could not reach it. Sultan had had earlier experiences in which he had successfully used sticks to rake in fruit; however, the only stick inside the cage was too short. A longer stick was outside the cage, but, like the fruit, was beyond Sultan's reach. The following scenario ensued:

> Sultan tries to reach the fruit with the smaller of the two sticks. Not succeeding, he tears at a piece of wire that projects from the netting of his cage, but that, too, in vain. Then he gazes about him (there are always in the course of these tests some long pauses during which the animals scrutinize the whole visible area). He suddenly picks up the little stick, once more goes up to the bars, directly opposite to the long stick, scratches it towards him with the [short stick], seizes it, and goes with it to the point opposite the [fruit], which he secures. From the moment that his eyes fall upon the long stick, his procedure forms one consecutive whole, without hiatus. . . . (Köhler, 1925, p. 180)

Figure 8–4
Irregularly shaped objects
may later be remembered
as "circles" or "squares."

In another situation, Sultan, again confronted with fruit placed outside the cage beyond his reach, had two hollow bamboo rods, one somewhat thinner than the other, and both too short to reach the fruit. After numerous "fruitless" attempts, he seemingly gave up and resorted to playing indifferently with the sticks. At one serendipitous point, Sultan found himself holding the two sticks end to end such that they formed a long, straight line. Immediately he pushed the end of the thinner stick into the end of the thicker one (thus making a single long stick), ran over to the edge of the cage, and successfully obtained the elusive bananas.

In neither of the situations I have just presented did Sultan engage in the random trial-and-error learning that Thorndike had observed for cats. Instead, it appeared to Köhler as if Sultan thought about possible solutions to the problem, arranging the problem elements in various ways, until he arrived at a sudden insight as to a problem solution.

Gestalt psychology continues to have an impact on how cognitive psychologists conceptualize learning and cognition (e.g., Henle, 1985). In Chapter 9, we will examine several Gestaltist laws of perception that have been incorporated into contemporary views of perception and attention. In Chapters 11 and 12, we will look at the very critical role that organization plays in learning and memory and at some of the processes that determine just how individuals organize their experiences. Now, however, let's turn to an early American psychologist who was also influenced by the Gestalt theorists: Edward Tolman.

Edward Tolman's Purposive Behaviorism

Edward Chace Tolman (e.g., 1932, 1938, 1942, 1959) was a prominent learning theorist during the heyday of behaviorism, yet his work had a distinctly cognitive flair. Like his behaviorist contemporaries, Tolman valued the importance of objectivity in conducting research and used nonhuman species (especially rats) as the subjects of his research. Unlike his contemporaries, however, Tolman included internal mental phenomena in his perspective of how learning occurs and adopted a more holistic view of learning than was true of S-R theorists.

Among Tolman's contributions to contemporary cognitive theories of learning were the following ideas.

•*Behavior should be studied at a molar level.* Early theorists in the behaviorist tradition, such as Pavlov, Thorndike, and Watson, attempted to reduce behavior to simple stimulus-response connections. In contrast, Tolman was adamant in his position that more global (molar) behaviors are the appropriate objects of study. Tolman argued that breaking behavior down into isolated S-R reflexes rather than looking at it in its totality obscures the meaning and purpose of that behavior. In this respect, Tolman's view was similar to the "structured whole" view of the Gestaltists.

•*Learning can occur without reinforcement.* Tolman opposed the behaviorist idea that reinforcement is necessary in learning and conducted several experiments to support his contention. As an example, let's look at a study by Tolman and Honzik (1930) in which three groups of rats ran a difficult maze under different reinforcement conditions. Group 1 was reinforced with food for successful completion of the maze. Group 2 received no reinforcement for successful performance. Group 3 was not reinforced during the first 10 days in the maze, but began receiving reinforcement on the 11th day.

Before we examine the results of this experiment, let's predict what should have happened in this situation if reinforcement were a necessary component of the learning process. Because Group 1 rats were continuously reinforced, we would expect their performance to increase. Because Group 2 rats were *not* reinforced, we would expect their performance to stay at a constant low level. And we would expect the rats in Group 3 to show no improvement in performance until after day 11, at which point they should show a pattern of behavior similar to the Group 1 rats' first few days of performance.

The actual results of the Tolman and Honzik experiment appear in Figure 8–5. Notice that the performance of Groups 2 and 3 improved somewhat even when they were not receiving reinforcement. Notice also that once the rats in Group 3 began receiving reinforcement, their performance in the maze equaled (in fact, it surpassed!) Group 1's performance. Apparently, Group 3 rats had learned as much as Group 1 rats despite their lack of reinforcement during the first 10 days.

Figure 8–5
Maze performance of rats receiving food, no food, or food at day 11

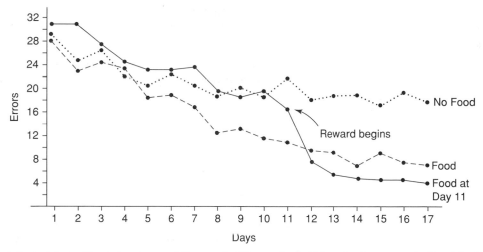

Adapted from "Introduction and Removal of Reward, and Maze Performance in Rats" by E. C. Tolman and C. H. Honzik, 1930, *University of California Publications in Psychology, 4,* p. 267. Copyright 1930 by University of California Press. Adapted with permission.

Results such as these cast doubt on Thorndike's law of effect: Perhaps reinforcement is not as critical a factor in learning as behaviorists have suggested.

•*Learning can occur without a change in behavior.* While behaviorists equated learning with behavior changes, Tolman argued that learning can occur without a concomitant change in performance, using the term **latent learning** for such unobservable learning. The Tolman and Honzik study just described provides an example of latent learning: Group 3 rats must have been learning just as much as Group 1 rats during the first 10 days, even though their behavior did not reflect such learning. (Presumably, Group 2 rats were also learning more than they let on.) Tolman proposed that reinforcement influences *performance* rather than learning—it increases the likelihood that a learned behavior will be exhibited. (As you may recall from the preceding chapter, social learning theorists have since come to a similar conclusion.)

•*Intervening variables must be considered.* As you may recall from Chapter 2, Clark Hull incorporated **intervening variables** into his theory of learning, arguing that variables such as drive, habit strength, and incentive play a critical role. The concept of intervening variables did not originate with Hull, however; as early as 1932, Tolman proposed that variables within the organism (e.g., cognitions and physiological states) affect the behaviors observed. Thus, with Tolman's work, we have an early concern for *individual differences* in the learning process, a concern that continues in contemporary cognitivism.

•*Behavior is purposive.* Tolman believed that learning should be viewed not as the formation of S-R connections but as a process of learning that certain events lead to other events (for example, that running a maze in a particular way leads to reinforcement). He proposed that once an organism has learned that a behavior produces a certain goal, the organism behaves in order to achieve that goal. In other words, behavior has a *purpose*, that of goal attainment. Because of this notion of goal-directed behavior, Tolman's view of learning is often referred to as **purposive behaviorism**.

•*Expectations affect behavior.* According to Tolman, once an organism learns that particular behaviors produce particular results, it begins to form expectations about the outcomes of its behaviors. Rather than reinforcement affecting the response it follows, the organism's *expectation* of reinforcement affects the response it *precedes*. (Once again, we see a similarity with social learning theory.)

When an organism's expectations are not met, its behavior may be adversely affected. For example, in an experiment by Elliott (cited in Tolman, 1932), rats received one of two different reinforcers for running a maze: an experimental group received a favorite rat delicacy—bran mash—while a control group received relatively unenticing sunflower seeds. The experimental group ran the maze faster than the control group, apparently because they were expecting a yummier treat at the end of the maze. On the 10th day, these rats were switched to the sunflower seed reinforcement that the control group rats had been getting all along. After discovering the change in reinforcement, these experimental group rats began to move through the maze more slowly than they had previously, and even more slowly than the control rats. Since both groups were being reinforced identically at this point (i.e., with boring sunflower seeds), the inferior performance of the rats in the experimental group was apparently due to the change in reinforcement, resulting in a depression effect similar to what I described in Chapter 4. As Tolman might put it, the rats' expectation of reinforcement was no longer being confirmed. As you or I might say, the rats were very disappointed with the treat awaiting them.

•*Learning results in an organized body of information.* Through a series of studies, Tolman showed that rats who run a maze learn more than just a set of independent responses. It appears that they also learn how the maze is arranged—the lay of the land, so to speak. For example, in a classic study by Tolman, Ritchie, and Kalish (1946), rats ran numerous times through a maze that looked like Maze 1 of Figure 8–6. They were then put in a situation similar to Maze 2 of Figure 8–6. Since the alley that had previously led to food was now blocked, the rats had to choose among 18 other alleys. Using S-R theory's notion of stimulus generalization, we would expect the rats to make their running response to a stimulus very similar to the blocked alley. We would therefore predict that the rats would choose alleys near the blocked one—particularly Alley 9 or Alley 10. However, few of the rats chose either of these routes. By far the most common choice was Alley 6, the one that presumably would provide a shortcut to the location in which the rats had come to expect food.

Based on such research, Tolman postulated that rats, and other organisms as well, develop **cognitive maps** of their environments: They learn where different parts of the environment are situated in relation to one another. Knowing how things are organized in space enables an organism to get from one place to another, often by the shortest possible route. The concept of a cognitive map (sometimes called a mental map) has continued to be a focus of research for contemporary researchers, psychologists and geographers alike (e.g., Downs & Stea, 1977).

Figure 8–6
Mazes used by Tolman, Ritchie, and Kalish (1946)

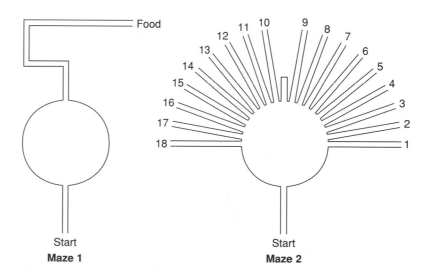

Tolman's notion of a cognitive map reflects his idea that learning is *organized*: Rats integrate their experiences into an organized body of information from which they can then draw inferences (e.g., about shortest routes). We encountered this concept of organization in Gestalt psychology and will see it again in our discussions of Piaget's theory and verbal learning research.

Tolman developed his mentalistic view of learning through some rather ingenious adaptations of traditional behaviorist research methods. At about the same time, a Swiss developmentalist was using research methods radically different from those of American psychologists. It is to this theorist, Jean Piaget, that we turn now.

Jean Piaget's Developmental Theory

Independent of the Gestalt movement in Germany and of Tolman's work in the United States, the Swiss biologist Jean Piaget began a research program during the 1920s that has probably had a greater impact on contemporary theories of cognitive development than that of any other single researcher. Piaget had interests in philosophy as well as biology and was particularly curious about the origins of knowledge, a branch of philosophy known as epistemology. To discover where knowledge comes from and the forms that it takes as it develops, Piaget and his colleagues undertook a series of studies that have provided some unique insights into how children think and learn about the world around them (e.g., Inhelder & Piaget, 1958; Piaget, 1928, 1952, 1959, 1970, 1971, 1972, 1980; Piaget & Inhelder, 1969).

Although Piaget's theory dates from the 1920s, its impact on mainstream psychological thought was not widely felt until the 1960s, probably for several reasons. One likely reason is that Piaget, being Swiss, wrote in French, making his early work less accessible to English-speaking psychologists. Although his writings were eventually translated into English, Piaget's ideas gained widespread prominence and visibility largely through a summary of his early work written by the American psychologist John Flavell (1963).

A second reason that the Geneva research program was largely overlooked for more than three decades was Piaget's unconventional research methodology. Piaget employed what he called the **clinical method**: Human subjects, usually children, were presented with a variety of stimulus situations and asked questions about them. Interviews were tailored to the particular responses that children gave, with follow-up questions varying from one child to the next. Such a procedure was radically different from the standardized, tightly controlled conditions typical of behaviorist animal research and was therefore unacceptable to many of Piaget's contemporaries.

But perhaps the most critical reason that Piaget's theory did not immediately become part of the mainstream of psychological thought was its incompatibility with the behaviorist perspective that dominated the field until the 1960s. Piaget focused on mental events—for example, on logical reasoning processes and the structure of knowledge—at a time when such mentalism was still being rejected by most other learning theorists. The cognitivism that began to emerge in the 1960s was more receptive to Piagetian ideas.

Piaget's work is probably so popular today because it is the single most global theory of intellectual development; it incorporates such diverse topics as language, logical reasoning, moral judgments, and conceptions of time, space, and number. In addition, Piaget's unique studies with children, often involving some clever problem situations, can reveal a great deal about the nature of children's thought. We will now look at some of Piaget's ideas most relevant to our understanding of human learning and cognition.

•*People are active processors of information.* Whereas behaviorists portrayed organisms, including humans, as passive respondents to environmental conditions, Piaget portrayed human beings as being *actively involved* in learning and interpreting events around them. Rather than just responding to stimuli, people act upon those stimuli and observe the effects of their actions. For example, consider Piaget's observation of his son Laurent at 16 months of age:

> Laurent is seated before a table and I place a bread crust in front of him, out of reach. Also, to the right of the child I place a stick about 25 cm. long. At first Laurent tries to grasp the bread without paying attention to the instrument, and then he gives up. I then put the stick between him and the bread. . . . Laurent again looks at the bread, without moving, looks very briefly at the stick, then suddenly grasps it and directs it toward the bread. But he grasped it toward the middle and not at one of its ends so that it is too short to attain the objective. Laurent then puts it down and resumes stretching out his hand toward the bread. Then, without spending much time on this movement, he takes up the stick again, this time at one of its ends . . . and draws the bread to him.
>
> An hour later I place a toy in front of Laurent (out of his reach) and a new stick next to him. He does not even try to catch the objective with his hand; he immediately grasps the stick and draws the toy to him. (Piaget, 1952, p. 335)

In this situation, Laurent is acting on his environment; he is obviously experimenting with the elements of the situation to see what outcomes he can achieve. (You may have noticed a similarity between Laurent's behavior and that of the chimpanzee Sultan that I described earlier in the chapter. Sultan, too, was an active problem solver rather than a passive respondent to environmental events.)

•*Knowledge can be described in terms of structures that change with development.* Piaget proposed the concept of **schema** as the basic structure through which an individual's knowledge is mentally represented. (Piaget used *schemata* as the plural form of *schema*; however, I will use the plural form *schemas*, consistent with most contemporary psychologists.) While Piaget's notion of schema is somewhat abstract, it can be roughly defined as a mental unit that represents a class of similar actions or thoughts. For example, an infant might have a schema for grasping and use it for grabbing everything from bottles to rubber ducks. A teenager may have certain schemas of logic that may be applied to mathematical problems or to opinions about what is wrong with a certain system of government. As children develop, new schemas emerge, and existing schemas are modified and sometimes integrated with one another into **cognitive structures**. A good deal of Piaget's theory focuses on the development of the cognitive structures that govern logical reasoning, structures that Piaget calls **operations**.

• *Cognitive development results from the interactions of individuals with their physical and social environments.* By interacting with the environment, individuals develop and shape schemas. In Piaget's example cited earlier, Laurent actively manipulated his physical environment—the stick and bread—and presumably learned that some objects can be used as tools to obtain other objects. Equally essential to children's development is their interaction with other people. For example, Piaget described young children as being **egocentric**—as having difficulty understanding that others don't share their perspective of the world. Through social interactions, both positive (e.g., conversations) and negative (e.g., conflicts over such issues as sharing and fair play), children begin to realize that they hold a perspective of the world uniquely their own.

• *The processes through which people interact with the environment remain constant.* According to Piaget, people interact with their environment through two unchanging processes (**functions**) known as assimilation and accommodation. In **assimilation**, an individual interacts with an object or event in a way that is consistent with an existing schema. For example, the infant who sees Mama's flashy, dangling earrings may assimilate those earrings to his grasping schema, clutching and pulling at them in much the same way that he grasps bottles. A second grader who has developed a schema for adding two apples and three apples to make five apples may apply this schema to the addition of two dollars and three more dollars. **Accommodation** is a process whereby an individual either modifies an existing schema or forms a new one to account for a new event. For example, an infant who has learned to crawl must adjust her style of crawling somewhat when she meets a flight of stairs. A boy who calls a spider an "insect" must revise his thinking when he learns that insects have six legs but spiders have eight.

Assimilation and accommodation are complementary processes: Assimilation involves modifying one's perception of the environment to fit a schema, and accommodation involves modifying a schema to fit the environment. According to Piaget, these two processes typically go hand in hand, with individuals interpreting new events within the context of their existing knowledge (assimilation) but also modifying their knowledge as a result of those events (accommodation).

Learning results from the conjoint processes of assimilation and accommodation. Learning is especially reflected in the process of accommodation, since it is through accommodation that major cognitive changes occur. An environmental event cannot lead to accommodation of schemas, however, unless that event can be related (assimilated) to those schemas in the first place. For example, consider this sentence:

D. O. Hebb has proposed that learning is a process of developing cell assemblies and phase sequences.

Unless you know who D. O. Hebb is, and unless you are familiar with the concepts of *cell assembly* and *phase sequence,* you can learn very little from the sentence. Assimilation is almost always a necessary condition for accommodation to occur: You must be able to relate a new experience to what you already know before you can learn from it. This necessity for overlap between what you already know and the material to be learned is an important principle not only in Piagetian theory, but in contemporary cognitive theory as well.

•*Cognitive development occurs in distinct stages, with thought processes at each stage being qualitatively different from those at other stages.* A major feature of Piagetian theory is the identification of four distinct stages of cognitive development, each with its own unique patterns of thought. The schemas of each stage are modified and incorporated into the schemas of the following stage, thereby providing a foundation for that next stage. Accordingly, children progress through the four stages in the same, invariant sequence. The characteristics of Piaget's four stages are more completely described in other secondary sources (e.g., Flavell, 1963; Sund, 1976; Wadsworth, 1989), but I will discuss them briefly here.

The first stage, the **sensorimotor stage**, is evident from birth until about two years of age (the exact ages of each stage vary from child to child). This stage is characterized by behavior-based and perception-based schemas rather than by "thought" schemas. According to Piaget, sensorimotor children do not yet possess schemas that enable them to think about objects other than those directly in front of them. For the sensorimotor child, then, "out of sight, out of mind" definitely applies.

The **preoperational stage** emerges when children are about two years old and continues until they are about six or seven. The appearance at this stage of both language and the ability to think about objects and events in their absence involves the development of internal mental schemas representative of external events—from Piaget's perspective, the beginnings of true "thought." However, the preoperational stage is characterized by thinking that is often illogical by adult standards. For example, the child tends to confuse psychological phenomena with physical reality, a confusion manifested by such actions as attributing feelings to inanimate objects and believing that monsters and bogeymen are lurking under the bed.

A commonly used example of the illogical thinking of preoperational children is their reaction to a **conservation of liquid** problem. Imagine three glasses: Glasses A and B are tall, thin, and filled to equal heights with water, while Glass C is short, fat, and empty, as is shown in Figure 8–7. Clearly Glasses A and B contain the same amount of water. But now the contents of Glass B are poured into Glass C, thereby creating the situation shown in Figure 8–8. Do Glass A and Glass C contain the same amount of water, or does one contain more?

Being logical, you would probably conclude that the two glasses hold identical amounts of water (excluding a drop or two that might have been lost in the process of pouring). The preoperational child, however, is likely to say that the glasses hold different amounts of water: Most will say that Glass A has more because it is taller, although a few will say that Glass C has more because it is fatter. The child's thinking depends more on perception than logic during the pre-

Figure 8–7

Figure 8–8

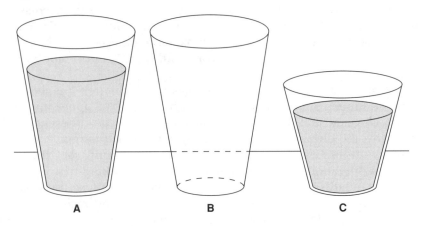

operational stage and is therefore susceptible to outward appearances: The glasses *look* different so must *be* different.

Piaget's third stage of cognitive development, **concrete operations**, appears when children are about six or seven years old and continues until they are at least 11 or 12. Children at this stage begin to think logically about conservation problems and other situations as well. However, concrete operational children are limited in one very important respect: They can apply their logical operations only to concrete, observable objects and events. They have difficulty dealing with abstract information and with hypothetical ideas contrary to their own reality. For example, the concrete operational child should readily agree with the logic that

If all first graders are children,
And if all children are people,
Then all first graders are people.

yet has trouble recognizing the logical validity of a similar problem that includes a contrary-to-fact premise:

> *If all first graders are children,*
> *And if all children are hippopotamuses,*
> *Then all first graders are hippopotamuses.*

Concrete operational children, although generally very logical, cannot readily distinguish between logic and reality, and, after all, first graders are *not* hippopotamuses!

The fourth and final stage, **formal operations**, rarely appears before children are 11 or 12 and continues to evolve for at least several years after that. During formal operations, a child develops the ability to reason with abstract, hypothetical, and contrary-to-fact information. Other abilities essential to mathematical and scientific reasoning emerge as well. For example, proportional thinking develops, through which the child truly begins to understand the concept of *proportion*, as reflected in such mathematical entities as fractions and decimals. The child also begins to separate and control variables: In testing a hypothesis about which factor among many may bring about a particular result, the child tests one variable at a time while holding all others constant. In addition, with the onset of formal operations children are able to consider their own thought processes and evaluate the quality and logic of those thoughts; for example, a child may notice a logical fallacy in something he or she has said.

I should point out here that recent research, while sometimes confirming Piaget's assertions regarding characteristics of the different stages, does not support Piaget's proposed stage characteristics in their entirety (e.g., see Bee, 1985; Case, 1985; Donaldson, 1978; Levin, 1983; Siegler, 1986). For example, it appears that infants and young children are cognitively more sophisticated than Piaget's descriptions of the sensorimotor and preoperational stages would indicate (Carey, 1985; Donaldson, 1978; Siegler, 1986). At the same time, Piaget may have overestimated the capabilities of adolescents and even adults (Siegler, 1986). For instance, many adults (including many college students) show behavior more characteristic of concrete operations than of formal operational thought (Sund, 1976).

A second problem with Piaget's notion of stage-related logical thinking skills is that children often use a given skill in one situation while being unable to use what is presumably the same skill in another situation (Case, 1985). Children's knowledge about topics appears to be critical here (Carey, 1985; Pulos & Linn, 1981). For example, in one study (Pulos & Linn, 1981), seventh graders living in a rural area demonstrated the formal operational ability to separate and control variables on a problem related to fishing, but not on Piaget's traditional laboratory methods for assessing that skill.

•*The rate of cognitive development is controlled to some extent by maturation.* One unique aspect of Piaget's theory is his assertion that children's progression through the four stages is limited by maturation—that is, by genetically controlled physiological changes. Piaget contended that a necessary prerequisite for the transition to each successive stage is the occurrence of certain neurological changes that allow more sophisticated cognitive structures to develop. Because of physiological limitations, it would be virtually impossible for a two-year-old child to think logically like a concrete operations child or for a seven-year-old to deal successfully with abstract ideas. In support of Piaget's proposal, research by Epstein (1978) and Hudspeth (1985) indicates that significant neurological changes do occur at the typical transition ages for progression from one of Piaget's cognitive stages to the next. On the other hand, researchers often find that, with proper training, children become capable of thinking in ways that Piaget suggested were only possible for older individuals; such findings cast doubt on maturation as a limiting factor in cognitive development (Case, 1985; Field, 1987; Mayer, 1992; Murray, 1978; Siegler, 1978).

Many of Piaget's ideas are evident in contemporary cognitivism. The current notion that knowledge is structured and organized can be seen in Piaget's work as well as in that of Tolman and the Gestaltists. Also important in contemporary theories is Piaget's proposal that for learning to occur, an individual must be able to assimilate new information into existing cognitive structures—that is, a new experience and prior knowledge must overlap. Finally, Piaget's proposed stages of cognitive development have provided the impetus for many studies of the development of cognition. Although not all of Piaget's ideas have been validated by research, his theory continues to be a dominant force in both the thinking and methodology of cognitive psychology.

While Piaget was conducting his early, groundbreaking research, another psychologist had ideas of his own about the factors that facilitate cognitive development. We turn to Lev Vygotsky's ideas now.

Lev Vygotsky's Developmental Theory

The Russian psychologist Lev Vygotsky conducted many studies of children's thinking from the 1920s until his premature death from tuberculosis in 1934. Yet the significance and usefulness of Vygotsky's work was not fully appreciated by U.S. psychologists until his writings were translated into English (Vygotsky, 1962, 1978, 1981). Although Vygotsky never had the chance to develop his theory fully, his ideas are clearly evident in our conceptualizations of learning and instruction today.

•*Children's cognitive development is promoted and enhanced through their interactions with more advanced and capable individuals.* Vygotsky distinguished between two aspects of children's development. Their **actual developmental level** is the extent to which they can perform tasks independently, without help from anyone else. Their **level of potential development** is the extent to which they can perform tasks with the assistance of a more competent individual.

Children can typically do more difficult things in collaboration with adults than they can do on their own. For example, children just learning how to use a baseball bat can hit a baseball more successfully when adults are present to guide their swing. Children can play more difficult piano pieces when adults help them locate some of the notes on the keyboard. Students may be able to read more complex prose within a reading group at school than they are likely to read independently at home (reading specialists often distinguish between a student's instructional and independent reading levels; e.g., see Burron & Claybaugh, 1992).

• *Tasks within the zone of proximal development promote maximum cognitive growth.* The range of tasks that children cannot yet perform independently, but *can* perform with the help and guidance of others, is known as the **zone of proximal development** (**ZPD**). A child's zone of proximal development includes learning and problem solving abilities that are just beginning to develop within that child—abilities that are in an immature, "embryonic" form. Vygotsky proposed that children learn very little from performing tasks they can already do independently. Instead, they develop primarily by attempting tasks they can accomplish only in collaboration with a more competent individual—that is, when they attempt tasks within their zone of proximal development.

• *Scaffolding facilitates performance on tasks within the zone of proximal development.* When adults and other more skilled individuals assist children in performing a difficult task, they often provide **scaffolding**—some form of structure that supports children in their efforts. For example, they might make the task simpler than it would otherwise be, give hints about how to proceed, or perhaps model the procedure themselves. As the children become more adept at performing tasks, adult guidance is gradually phased out, and the children are eventually performing those tasks on their own.

• *Thought and language become interdependent at about two years of age.* According to Vygotsky, thought and language are separate functions for infants and young toddlers. In these early years, thinking occurs independently of language, and when language appears, it is first used primarily as a means of communication rather than as a mechanism of thought. But sometime around two years of age, thought and language intertwine: Children begin to express their thoughts when they speak, and they begin to think in terms of words. At this point, we begin to see **self-talk** (whereby children talk to themselves out loud) and eventually **inner speech** (whereby children "talk" to themselves mentally rather than orally). According to Vygotsky, both self-talk and inner speech have a similar purpose: By talking to themselves, children learn to guide and direct their own behaviors through difficult tasks and complex maneuvers in much the same way that adults have previously guided them. In a sense, they begin to provide their *own* scaffolding.

Within the past 10 years, many prominent theorists (including a number of information processing theorists) have shown renewed interest in Vygotsky's work (Brown & Reeve, 1987; Diaz, 1990; Dole, Duffy, Roehler, & Pearson, 1991; Palincsar & Brown, 1989; Pontecorvo, 1993; Rogoff, 1990; Wertsch, 1985; Wood, Bruner, & Ross, 1976; Wozniak, 1987). For example, as we saw in the preceding chapter on social learning theory, self-talk (we called it self-instructions) is useful in promoting self-regulation. Other researchers find that complex thinking processes often develop more readily when children and (presumably more competent) adults talk about what they are doing and thinking, and when adults use some form of scaffolding to facilitate children's development of complex thought. Accordingly, we will encounter Vygotsky's ideas once again when we explore metacognition in Chapter 15.

Piaget's and Vygotsky's ideas had a cognitivist flavor from their inception. Research by certain other theorists of their time, however, emerged from a behaviorist perspective and only gradually began to incorporate cognitivist ideas. Let's turn now to the work of these verbal learning theorists, psychologists who helped pave the way for a wider acceptance of cognitive views of learning.

VERBAL LEARNING RESEARCH: A TRANSITION FROM BEHAVIORISM TO COGNITIVISM

A logical outgrowth of the behaviorist movement was an extension of behaviorist principles to a uniquely human behavior—language. Verbal learning researchers, whose work peaked during the middle of the century (1930s through 1960s), began to study verbal behavior and the learning of verbal materials by applying an S-R approach to these phenomena.

Central to verbal learning research were two learning tasks, serial learning and paired associate learning, that were easily explained from an S-R perspective. **Serial learning** involves learning a sequence of items in their correct order; the alphabet, the days of the week, and the Pledge of Allegiance are all examples. Verbal learning theorists explained serial learning in this way: The first item in the list is a stimulus to which the second item is learned as a response, the second item then serves as a stimulus to which the third item is the learned response, and so.

Paired associate learning involves learning pairs of items. Learning foreign language vocabulary words and their English equivalents (e.g., *le papier* is French for "paper") and learning state capitals (e.g., Juneau is the capital of Alaska) are two examples. Verbal learning theorists described paired associates as being distinct stimulus-response associations: The first item in each pair is the stimulus and the second item is the response.

Increasingly, verbal learning studies yielded results that could not be easily explained in terms of S-R connections, and theorists began to introduce a variety of mental phenomena into their discussions of learning processes. In this section, I will describe some general learning principles that emerged from verbal learning research. Some of the findings are relatively easy to explain from a behaviorist perspective; others are not so easily explained.

•*Serial learning is characterized by a particular pattern.* In a serial learning task, a **serial learning curve** is usually observed: People learn the first few items and last few items more quickly and easily than they learn the middle items (Hall, 1971; McCrary & Hunter, 1953; Roediger & Crowder, 1976). If we were to graph the speed with which the various items in a serial list are learned, we might obtain results similar to what you see in Figure 8–9. An example of the serial

Figure 8–9
A typical serial learning
curve

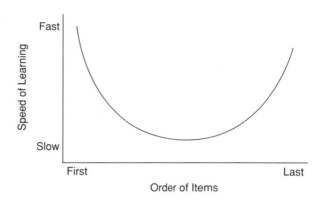

learning curve is the way in which most children learn the alphabet: they learn the first letters (A, B, C, D) and the last letters (X, Y, Z) before they learn the middle letters (e.g., H, I, J, K).

The tendency for the first items in a serial learning curve to be learned quickly is called the **primacy effect**. The tendency for the last items to be learned quickly is called the **recency effect**. Verbal learning theorists explained both effects by proposing that the end points of the list (i.e., the first and last items) served as *anchors* to which the other items would then be attached in a stimulus-response fashion.

•*Overlearned material is more easily recalled at a later time.* What happens when you learn information perfectly and then continue to study it? This process of **overlearning**, in which you learn material to mastery and then practice the material for additional study trials, enables you to remember the information much more accurately at a later time (e.g., Bahrick, Bahrick, Bahrick, & Bahrick, 1993; Krueger, 1929; Underwood, 1954). For example, Krueger (1929) found that overlearning a list of words enhanced recall for up to a month after the learning session. As you may recall from Chapter 2, early behaviorists also emphasized the importance of practice.

•*Distributed practice is usually more effective than massed practice.* Imagine that you have to study for a test. You estimate that you need six hours to master the test material. Would you do better on the test if you studied for six hours all at once or if you broke your study time into smaller chunks of time—say, six one-hour sessions? Research has indicated that **distributed practice**, spreading study time out over several occasions, usually leads to better learning than **massed practice**, in which study time occurs all at once (e.g., Glenberg, 1976; Underwood, 1961; Underwood, Kapelak, & Malmi, 1976). Thus, studying for a test over several short sessions is more likely to be effective than one long cram session. Furthermore, the further apart the study sessions are, the better one's memory for the learned information is likely to be over the long run (Bahrick et al., 1993).

•*Learning in one situation often affects learning and recall in another situation.* Imagine yourself having to learn two sets of paired-associates. The first set looks like this:

Set 1
house—dragon
plant—sled
lamp—music
onion—pillow

The second one looks like this:

Set 2
house—paper
plant—clock
lamp—turkey
onion—chair

After you have first learned Set 1 and then learned Set 2, you are asked to remember the responses to each of the stimulus words in Set 1. Will you have difficulty? You probably will, because you learned different responses to those same words when you learned Set 2. You would have an easier time remembering the correct responses you learned in Set 1 if you had not had to learn the Set 2 responses as well.

Verbal learning theorists observed that when individuals learn two sets of paired associates in succession, their learning of the second set often diminishes their ability to recall the first set (Hall, 1971), a phenomenon known as **retroactive inhibition**. They further observed that individuals in this situation often have difficulty remembering the second set as well as the first (Hall, 1971), a phenomenon known as **proactive inhibition**. The tendency for a set of paired associates learned at one time to interfere with the recall of a set learned either earlier or later is particularly likely to occur when the two sets have the same or similar stimulus words but different response words (Osgood, 1949).

Under different circumstances, learning one set of information may actually improve the recall of information learned at another time, a phenomenon referred to by verbal learning theorists as **retroactive facilitation** or **proactive facilitation**, depending on the order in which the two sets of information are learned (Hall, 1971). Facilitation is most likely to occur when two situations have similar or identical stimuli and similar responses as well (Osgood, 1949). As an example, after learning the stimulus-response pair "house—dragon," you would probably learn "house—monster" rather easily.

Verbal learning theorists (e.g., McGeoch, 1942; Melton & Irwin, 1940; Underwood, 1948) proposed that retroactive and proactive inhibition were major factors in *forgetting* verbal information; they were therefore among the first to propose theories of memory. Although their explanations were based primarily on stimulus-response analyses, many cognitive psychologists believe inhibition still plays a role in memory and forgetting.

•*Characteristics of the material affect the speed with which it can be learned.* Verbal learning researchers discovered a number of characteristics that affect the ease of learning verbal material. Let's look at some of them.

Some items are more
meaningful than others.

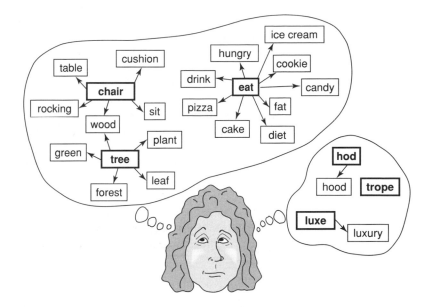

1. Items are more easily learned when they are *meaningful*—that is, when
    they can be easily associated with other ideas (e.g., Cofer, 1971; Paivio,
    1971). This principle was discovered very early by the German psycholo-
    gist Hermann Ebbinghaus (1913). Ebbinghaus, who served as his own
    subject for a number of experiments in serial learning, observed that the
    associations he could make with words helped him learn those words.
    He attempted to eliminate the influence of associations by using presum-
    ably meaningless **nonsense syllables** ("words" like JAD, MON, and ZIV).
    However, even many nonsense syllables have meaningfulness and evoke
    associations, thus making them relatively easy to learn (Hall, 1971). For
    example, the nonsense syllable JAD might make you think of "jade," and
    the syllable MON might remind you of "money."

2. Items are easier to learn when they are *pronounceable* (e.g., Di Vesta &
    Ingersoll, 1969; Underwood & Schulz, 1960). For example, the nonsense
    syllable DNK should be learned faster than BPX because most people can
    pronounce it more easily.

3. *Concrete* items are easier to learn than abstract items (Gorman, 1961;
    Paivio, 1963); for example, items such as these:

    turtle, hammer, sandwich

    are learned faster than items such as these:

    truth, joy, experience

4. One probable reason that the concreteness of items makes them easier
    to learn is that concrete items can be *mentally visualized* more easily.
    The extent to which we form visual images of items appears to influence
    the ease with which we can learn those items (Clark & Paivio, 1991;

Paivio, 1971; Sadoski, Goetz, & Fritz, 1993). For example, it is easier to form a mental image of a turtle than it is to form an image of truth. Notice how, in discussing visual imagery, verbal learning theorists were beginning to talk about mental events. This phenomenon of visual imagery is particularly difficult to explain from an S-R perspective.

•*People often impose meaning when learning new information.* The effect of meaningfulness on learning can be explained from an S-R perspective: When a stimulus word has many other words associated with it, one of those associations may in turn be associated with the response to be learned. What is more troublesome for an S-R approach is the fact that people will go out of their way to *make* information meaningful when they are trying to learn it. For example, when Bugelski (1962) asked subjects to learn paired-associates involving nonsense syllables, subjects invariably reported that they imposed meanings to help them learn the pairs. To illustrate, when given this pair:

DUP—TEZ

one subject used the word "deputize" to help form the connection. Cognitive theories have emerged that probably explain this tendency for human beings to search for meaning better than a behaviorist approach can.

•*People organize what they learn.* When people are allowed to recall items of a serial learning task in any order (a task known as **free recall**), they typically do *not* recall those items in their original presentation order. Instead, the order in which they recall items often reflects an organizational scheme of some kind (e.g., Bousfield, 1953; Buschke, 1977; Jenkins & Russell, 1952). In a classic experiment by Bousfield (1953), college students were given a list of 60 words, 15 from each of four categories: animals, names, vegetables, and professions. Although the words appeared in a random order, subjects tended to recall them in category clusters. For example, a typical recall order might have been something like this:

camel, giraffe, zebra, donkey, Jason, Adam, Howard, pumpkin, cabbage, carrot, lettuce, radish, milkman, baker, dentist

People even try to organize seemingly unorganized material (Tulving, 1962). This tendency people have to insist on organizing the information they learn is difficult to explain from behaviorist principles. As you will see in later chapters, however, it lends itself quite easily to an explanation based on cognitive learning theories.

•*People often use coding strategies to help them learn.* People often change, or *encode,* information in some way to make the information easier to learn (e.g., Bugelski, 1962; Dallett, 1964; Underwood & Erlebacher, 1965). Furthermore, when experimenters specifically tell subjects to use a certain encoding strategy to help them learn information, learning improves (Bugelski, Kidd, &

Segmen, 1968; Hall, 1971). For example, when subjects are instructed in techniques for forming mental visual images, they are able to remember a list of words more accurately than subjects not given such instructions (Bugelski et al., 1968).

•*People are more likely to learn general ideas than to learn words verbatim.* In fact, when people focus on learning ideas rather than on learning information word for word, their learning is faster and their recall more accurate (Briggs & Reed, 1943; English, Welborn, & Killian, 1934; Jones & English, 1926). Verbal learning research focused on the learning of verbatim information. In doing so, it may very well have ignored the way in which human beings actually learn most verbal material.

Clearly, verbal learning research provided us with a number of useful learning principles. It also provided us with two learning tasks, serial and paired associate learning, that continue to be used in learning research. At the same time, in trying to stretch S-R models of learning to explain human verbal behavior, it began to demonstrate some weaknesses of the behaviorist perspective.

In more recent years, the focus of verbal learning research has been on how people learn meaningful verbal material (e.g., prose passages) rather than artificially constructed serial lists or paired associates. In fact, the term *verbal learning* has been largely abandoned (for example, the *Journal of Verbal Learning and Verbal Behavior* became the *Journal of Memory and Language* in 1985) as verbal learning researchers have begun to embrace cognitivist ideas.

INTRODUCTION TO HUMAN INFORMATION PROCESSING THEORY

We have just seen how, even during the heyday of behaviorism, the work of the Gestalt psychologists, Edward Tolman, Jean Piaget, Lev Vygotsky, and verbal learning researchers was laying a foundation for cognitive learning theories. During the 1960s, discontent with the inadequacies of behaviorism became more widespread. The behaviorist perspective could not easily explain why people attempt to organize and make sense of the information they learn or sometimes even alter the form of that information (for example, by remembering general meanings rather than verbatim input). Among learning psychologists grew the realization that mental events—cognition—could no longer be ignored (e.g., see Kendler, 1985).

The predominant approach to the study of human learning at present, as reflected in ongoing research and journal space, is a group of theories known collectively as **human information processing** (HIP). This approach encompasses a dynamic, rapidly changing view of how people acquire, process, and remember information; theories are revised so quickly that describing HIP has often been likened to taking a snapshot of a speeding locomotive. Different aspects of information processing theory will be described in more detail in later chapters, but let me introduce some of its assumptions, terminology, and unique research methods here.

Assumptions of Human Information Processing

The assumptions underlying contemporary information processing theories are radically different from those underlying behaviorism. What follow are some of the central assumptions of HIP.

• *Some learning processes may be unique to human beings.* Because people possess abilities unique to the species (complex language is an example), the processes involved in learning may be different in human beings than in other animals. Accordingly, almost all information processing research involves human subjects, and theories formulated from this research are typically not generalized to other species.

• *Mental events are the focus of study.* Mental events are centrally involved in human learning and must therefore be incorporated into theories of learning processes. To the extent that individuals think about the same situation differently, they will learn different information from that situation.

• *The study of human learning must be objective and scientific.* Like behaviorists, HIP theorists underscore the importance of objective research. Unlike behaviorists, however, HIP theorists believe that mental events can be inferred from carefully designed experiments. Later in the chapter, I will describe some examples of how research involving observable behaviors can lead to inferences about nonobservable mental events.

• *Individuals are actively involved in the learning process.* Rather than being merely passive victims of environmental conditions, people are active participants in the learning process and in fact *control* their own learning. Individuals themselves determine how they mentally process the information they receive, and these cognitive processes in turn determine what, if anything, they will learn in a given situation.

• *Learning involves the formation of mental associations that are not necessarily reflected in overt behavior changes.* This assumption is essentially the same as Tolman's belief in latent learning. According to contemporary cognitive psychologists, learning involves an internal, mental change, but not necessarily the external behavior change that many behaviorists propose. Learning can therefore occur without being reflected in an individual's observed performance. (Of course, others have no way of knowing that learning has taken place until there *is* a behavior change of some sort.)

• *Knowledge is organized.* An individual's knowledge, beliefs, attitudes, and emotions are not isolated from one another, but are instead all associated and interconnected. This emphasis on organization is one that we saw in many early cognitivists—the Gestaltists, Tolman, and Piaget—as well.

• *Learning is a process of relating new information to previously learned information.* Similar to Piaget's assertion that accommodation almost always involves assimilation, information processing theorists believe that learning is most likely to occur when individuals can relate a new experience to the information they have acquired from earlier experiences.

The Terminology of Human Information Processing

Information processing theory is characterized by its own unique terminology. Let's look briefly at some of the terms we will encounter frequently in the chapters that follow.

Cognitive Process

The term **cognitive process** refers to any internal mental event and includes such phenomena as perceiving, paying attention, interpreting, understanding, and remembering. True to its name, the information processing perspective emphasizes the importance of cognitive processes in human learning.

Learning Versus Memory

Up to this point, we have not really separated learning and memory, but information processing theorists do draw a distinction between these two terms. **Learning** is viewed, quite simply, as the acquisition of new information. **Memory**, on the other hand, is related to the ability to recall information that has been previously learned. In some instances, the word *memory* is used to refer to the process of retaining information. In other instances, it is used to refer to the "location" where learned information is placed; for example, we will be talking about working memory and long-term memory. The distinction between learning and memory is an important one; for a number of reasons that you will discover in later chapters, not everything that is learned is necessarily remembered over the long run.

Storage

Storage is the process by which new information is placed in memory. For example, if you can put this fact in your head:

   Jeanne Ormrod's birthday is August 22nd.

then you are storing the information. We will be talking at length about the processes that people use to store information in memory.

Encoding

Encoding, the process by which information is modified as it is stored, often helps people store information more easily. Encoding sometimes involves changing information from one form into another. For example, I once had a combination lock for which the first two numbers of the combination were 22 and 8. I quickly learned these two numbers by encoding them as "the day and month of my birthday." In this case, I encoded numerical information into a verbal form. Encoding may also involve adding new information to the information presented, a process known as **elaboration**. For example, consider this information:

Jeanne Ormrod was born in Providence, Rhode Island.

Upon reading this, you might add some additional information to it, perhaps that I am a native New Englander or that I am a United States citizen, inferences that you might store along with the original information. Yet another encoding process is one of simplifying input, for example, by remembering the overall meaning or gist of a situation rather than the specific details of what happened (you might remember that a certain textbook author talked about her birthday, but not what that date was).

Retrieval

Retrieval is the process by which people "find" the information they have previously stored so that they can use it again. For example, I am hoping that, come mid-August, you will retrieve the date of my birthday and send me a tasteful card. Due to the fact that I get cards from few of my readers (most of whom are on the same campus as I am), we can assume that retrieval is very easy in some cases and very difficult in others. (In still other cases, of course, we may assume that information retrieval is simply not resulting in a behavior change.)

Inference-Drawing in HIP Research

Cognitive psychologists share with behaviorists the beliefs that the study of learning must be objective and that learning theories should be developed from the results of empirical research. However, cognitivists differ from behaviorists in one critical respect: By observing the responses that individuals make to different stimulus conditions, they believe that they can draw inferences about the nature of the internal cognitive processes that produce those responses. In fact, researchers have become increasingly ingenious in designing research studies that enable them to draw conclusions about specific cognitive processes. We will be seeing many instances of such inference-drawing in upcoming chapters, but let me describe a couple of examples here.

A classic experiment by Peterson and Peterson (1959) provides a simple example. In this experiment, adults were given three consonants (e.g., D X P), then immediately asked to count backward by threes from a certain three-digit number. Under these circumstances, subjects had great difficulty remembering the three consonants for more than a few seconds. Apparently, they needed to *process* those consonants in order to remember them, and the counting-backward task inhibited that processing.

Another example of inference-drawing in cognitive research resulted from a study by Bransford and Franks (1971). In this experiment, undergraduate students listened to a set of 24 sentences and answered simple questions about each one. The sentences were variations on four general ideas: a rock rolling down a hill, a man reading a newspaper, a breeze blowing, and ants eating jelly. To illustrate, the six sentences about the ants eating jelly were as follows:

The ants ate the sweet jelly which was on the table.
The ants in the kitchen ate the jelly which was on the table.
The ants in the kitchen ate the jelly.
The ants ate the sweet jelly.
The ants were in the kitchen.
The jelly was on the table.

Subjects then listened to a second set of 28 sentences (variations on the same themes as before) and were asked to indicate whether or not each had been in the first set. Most of the sentences (24 out of 28) were *new* sentences; here are some examples:

The ants in the kitchen ate the sweet jelly which was on the table.
The ants in the kitchen ate the sweet jelly.
The ants ate the jelly which was on the table.
The jelly was sweet.

Subjects erroneously "recognized" most of these new sentences as being "old" ones. Sentences that contained a lot of information were particularly likely to be recognized as having been heard before; for instance, "The ants in the kitchen ate the sweet jelly which was on the table" was more likely to be recognized than "The jelly was sweet." From such results, Bransford and Franks concluded that people abstract ideas from the verbal information they receive (rather than learning it verbatim) and organize similar ideas together in their memories. Sentences in the experiment that included most or all of the information related to a single theme may have more closely resembled subjects' organized memories and therefore have seemed familiar to them.

Obviously, we cannot directly see the mental processing described by Peterson and Peterson, nor can we observe the organizational processes described by Bransford and Franks. Yet inferences about such mental events seem justified in light of subjects' behavior that we *can* see.

GENERAL EDUCATIONAL IMPLICATIONS OF COGNITIVE PSYCHOLOGY

The study of human information processing has numerous specific applications for educational practice, applications that we will consider in more detail in later chapters. However, let's take a brief look at some general educational implications of the cognitive perspective, including those of early cognitive theories.

•*Cognitive processes affect learning.* If learning is a function of how information is mentally processed, then students' cognitive processes should be a major concern to educators. Students' learning difficulties often indicate ineffective or inappropriate cognitive processes; for example, learning disabled children tend to process information less effectively than nondisabled children (e.g., Swanson, 1987). Teachers must become aware not only of *what* students are trying to learn, but also of *how* they are trying to learn it.

•*A student's level of cognitive development affects the kinds of learning and behavior that are possible.* Teachers must consider their students' levels of cognitive development (perhaps in terms of Piaget's stage characteristics) when planning topics and methods of instruction. For example, explanations based on concrete operational logic may be ineffective ways of presenting ideas to kindergartners not yet capable of such logic. Elementary school children often have difficulty understanding abstract ideas that do not tie in with their own experiences and will learn more effectively if the same information is presented through concrete, hands-on examples. Even high school and college students, if they have not completely acquired formal operational characteristics, will need concrete experiences before being presented with abstract material.

•*People organize the information they learn.* Teachers can facilitate students' learning by presenting information in an organized fashion and by helping students see how one thing relates to another. We will identify some strategies for promoting such organization in Chapter 11.

•*New information is most easily acquired when people can associate it with things they have already learned.* Teachers can therefore help students' learning by showing them how new ideas relate to old ones (once again, we will identify more specific strategies in Chapter 11). When students are unable to relate new information to anything with which they are familiar, learning is likely to be slow and ineffective.

•*People control their own learning.* B. F. Skinner (e.g., 1954, 1968) argued from an operant conditioning perspective that students must actively respond if they are to learn. Cognitivists share Skinner's view; however, they emphasize *mental* activity rather than physical activity. If students control their own cognitive processes, it is ultimately the students themselves who determine what information will be learned, and how.

AN OVERVIEW OF UPCOMING CHAPTERS

In the next five chapters, we will explore some of the ideas of cognitive psychology and human information processing in greater detail. In Chapter 9, we will look at the processes of perception and attention, processes that influence what information we receive in the first place. In Chapters 10 through 12, we will examine the human memory system, with a particular focus on the ways in which we store and retrieve information. Throughout these three chapters, we will consider many implications of memory theory for educational practice; however, we will look at some additional applications of cognitive psychology and human information processing in Chapter 13.

SUMMARY

Cognitivism is currently the predominant perspective within which human learning is examined and explained. The roots of cognitive theory began in research and theory dating back to the 1920s and 1930s. Gestalt psychologists emphasized the importance of organizational processes in perception, learning, and problem solving and believed that individuals were predisposed to organize information in particular ways. Conducting laboratory studies similar to those of animal behaviorists, Edward Tolman included internal mental phenomena in his perspective of how learning occurs and adopted a more holistic view of learning than was true of S-R theorists. Jean Piaget and Lev Vygotsky speculated about the thought processes that underlie cognitive development. And midcentury verbal learning theorists, who initially attempted to apply an S-R analysis to the study of human language-based learning, increasingly began to incorporate mental events into their explanations of research results.

Contemporary cognitivism, which most frequently takes the form of human information processing theory, emphasizes thought processes and proposes that many aspects of learning may be unique to the human species. Cognitivists share behaviorists' belief that the study of learning must be objective and that learning theories should be based on empirical research. However, they also believe that by observing the responses people make to different stimulus conditions, they can draw inferences about the cognitive processes that lead to those responses.

CHAPTER 9

Perception and Attention

Imagine, for a minute, that your mind works like a videocassette recorder, such that you record everything you see and hear. Your memory of an event would involve a simple process of finding and replaying the appropriate cassette, and you would be able to remember the event as completely and accurately as if you were reliving it. Studying for an exam would be easy, you might think—no need for reading the textbook more than once or for last-minute cramming or for mindless repetition of meaningless facts over and over again.

Unfortunately, our minds are not accurate recorders of life events. Our *perception* of events alters and distorts the information we learn and remember, so that, in a sense, what we see is not necessarily what we get. Our *attention* or nonattention to information also affects our learning: We are frequently in a position where many things compete for our attention at the same time, and some of those things will not get the attention they deserve.

In this chapter, we will examine the various factors that affect both what events we perceive and how we perceive them. We will look at the processes of perception and attention, with particular emphasis on their constructive nature. We will also explore a variety of implications that perceptual and attentional processes have for educational practice.

PERCEPTION

Let's begin our discussion by distinguishing between sensation and perception. **Sensation** refers to the reaction of our bodies—in particular, our sensory receptors—to environmental stimulation. **Perception**, on the other hand, refers to the meaning (the recognition and interpretation) that we give to that stimulation. For example, when something moves toward you, light waves bounce off it and hit the retinas of your eyes, giving you a certain visual sensation. But, in addition, you may *perceive* that object as a person walking in your direction. On a dark, cloudy afternoon, the sound waves resulting from a lightning bolt reach your ears, causing the sensation of sound that you perceive to be thunder. As you walk past a bakery, certain chemicals drift up your nostrils, and you perceive the aroma of freshly baked bread.

Sensation is a physiological process: The body responds to energy from its surrounding environment. Perception, on the other hand, is a psychological process: The mind interprets and recognizes what the body has sensed. But the process of perception does not always provide an accurate interpretation of the information being received from sensory receptors.

Curiously, perception is both less and more than sensation. Perception is *less* than sensation because people do not attempt to interpret all the sensations that bombard them at any given moment. Right now, as you are looking at this book (and, I hope, perceiving it), light waves are bouncing off the page and hitting the light-sensitive cells at the backs of your eyes. At the same time, you may also be receiving light waves from a table on which your book is resting, the carpet on the floor, and the pictures on the walls. Your ears are probably receiving numerous sound waves, perhaps from a radio, a nearby conversation, an air conditioner, or traffic outside your window. Perhaps a certain smell is drifting through the air, or a certain taste from your last meal lingers in your mouth. It is neither necessary nor possible for you to interpret *all* these sensations, so you will attend to and perceive some of them and ignore the others.

But perception is also much *more* than sensation, because sensation alone provides insufficient information for an adequate interpretation of nearby events. For example, eyes do not continually record visual stimulation; rather, they jump from one focal point to another, taking periodic "snapshots" of the visual field.

People often make assumptions about what they don't see and are often surprised when such assumptions are inaccurate.

These jumps in focus, or **saccades**, occur four or five times a second, with visual sensation occurring primarily during the rest periods between them (e.g., Lima, 1993; Rayner, 1993). If we receive only four or five snapshots of visual information each second, our visual world should appear jerky and erratic, much as an old-time movie does. The fact that we instead see smooth-flowing motion is due in large part to the mental "filling in" that occurs as our minds interpret visual sensations.

Even if human eyes did function 100% of the time, they would typically provide an incomplete picture of the environment, and we would have to fill in mentally the information that we did not sense. For example, imagine walking into a bookstore and seeing the store clerk behind the counter. You probably sense only the clerk's head and upper torso, yet you perceive an entire person. You assume that the clerk has a lower torso and two legs, and in fact you would be quite surprised if the clerk's lower body looked any other way!

Consider, also, the perception of spoken language. You may understand this sentence easily when you hear it:

I read a book

while the identical sentence in Chinese gives you trouble:

Wŏkànshū.

In the first sentence, you probably "hear" four distinct, meaningful words, whereas in the second, you hear just one long nonsense word. To an individual fluent in Mandarin Chinese rather than English, the situation would be reversed; that person would hear this:

Ireadabook.

and this:

Wǒ kàn shū.

In reality, most spoken language comes to us as one continuous stream of sound waves rather than as . . . separate . . . words . . . like . . . this. Only when you are familiar with the particular language spoken can you mentally divide the one long sound into separate words.

Perception as Construction

Certainly perception is based to some extent on the stimuli actually present in the environment. But many information processing theorists believe that perception also involves a process of **construction**: People use the sensations they receive (sensations that typically provide an incomplete scenario of the event they are experiencing) to put together, or *construct*, a perception of that event. For example, let's say that you are in a noisy room and hear someone say:

I -an't -ear a thing in this -lace!

Although you haven't heard everything the person said, you may have enough information to perceive the sentence like so:

I can't hear a thing in this place!

Figure 9–1 shows three pictures first published by C. M. Mooney (1957). Most people perceive the picture on the left as being that of a woman, even though many of her features are missing. Enough features are visible—an eye, parts of the nose, mouth, chin, and hair—that you can construct a meaningful perception from them. Do the other two figures provide enough information for you to construct two more faces? Construction of a face from the figure on the right may take you a while, but it can be done.

Curiously, once you have constructed faces from the figures, they then seem so obvious to you. Furthermore, you tend to perceive the same sensory information in the same way at a future time; a particular construction of sensory input tends to stick. For example, if you were to close this book now and not pick it up again for a week or more, you would see the faces almost immediately, even if you had had difficulty perceiving them originally. (For a more detailed description of constructive processes in perception, see Neisser, 1967, or Ornstein, 1972.)

Figure 9–1
Can you construct a person from each of these pictures?

Reprinted from "Age in the Development of Closure Ability in Children" by C. M. Mooney, 1957, *Canadian Journal of Psychology*, *11*, p. 220. Copyright 1957 by Canadian Psychological Association. Reprinted with permission.

Factors Influencing Perception

Theoretically, people should be able to construct their sensations into an infinite number of different perceptions. Yet most individuals tend to form similar, although not necessarily identical, perceptions of their environments. Several factors influence the ways in which people construct their perceptions, and these things affect everyone in more or less the same manner. Let's take a look at some of them.

Proximity

As you should recall from Chapter 8, Gestalt psychologists proposed that people organize information in certain predictable ways. According to Gestaltists, one of the dominant principles affecting how people organize information is proximity: People tend to perceive as a unit those things that are close together in space. For example, look at the following dots:

● ● ●   ● ● ●   ● ● ●

Not only do you see nine dots, you probably also perceive an arrangement of three groups of three dots each; that is, you see dots that are in closer proximity to one another as somehow belonging together. In the same way, notice how you read this phrase:

One very high way.

and this one:

On every highway.

In both phrases, the same letters appear in exactly the same sequence:

Oneveryhighway.

Yet because of the way the letters are grouped together, you read the phrases differently.

Similarity

Another organizational principle from Gestalt psychology is similarity: People tend to perceive as a unit those things that are similar to one another. For example, look at the dots in Figure 9–2. Can you see the letter Y among them? Perhaps not.

In Figure 9–3 a letter Y is obvious. The arrangement of the dots in both cases is the same, but in the second case those dots forming the Y are all black, and you tend to perceive those similar black dots as a unit. Yet you probably haven't noticed other letters, such as the letter E, that are also formed by some of the dots.

Closure

Still another Gestaltist principle is closure: People tend to fill in missing pieces to form a complete picture. For example, what do you see in Figure 9–4? You should have no difficulty recognizing the letter W, even though parts of it are absent. Can you also recognize the phrase in Figure 9–5? You are probably able to read "Singing in the rain," even though 50% of the print is missing. You simply fill in what isn't there.

Figure 9–2

○ ○ ● ○ ○
○ ● ○ ○ ○
○ ○ ○ ○ ●
● ○ ● ○ ○
○ ○ ● ○ ●

Figure 9–3

● ○ ○ ○ ●
○ ● ○ ● ○
○ ○ ● ○ ○
○ ○ ● ○ ○
○ ○ ● ○ ○

Figure 9–4

Figure 9–5

Context

Figure 9–6 shows something known as Benussi's ring. Both sides of the ring are an equal shade of gray, but many people perceive the right side as being a lighter shade than the left. The context affects the appearance of the two sides of the ring: The right side looks lighter against its black background.

Figure 9–7 shows another example of the effect of context (modeled after an example by Selfridge, 1955). The word, of course, is *Matterhorn*. However, you may have noticed that the second and seventh "letters" are exactly the same figure. Whether you interpret the figure as an A or an H depends on its context within the other letters.

Past Experience

People are prone to perceive objects in ways that they have learned to perceive them in the past (e.g., Deregowski, 1972). For example, consider the picture in Figure 9–8. It is obviously a picture of a boy standing in a room. You probably

Figure 9–6

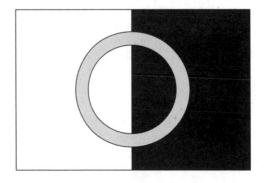

Figure 9–7

MATTERAORN

Figure 9–8

did *not* perceive all the dotted portions of the picture as a unit, despite their proximity and similarity to one another; likewise, you did not perceive the striped parts as belonging together. You have learned from many previous experiences that heads, torsos, arms, and legs—at least when they appear in a certain arrangement—belong together, and in fact all belong to the same person.

When you see someone walking away from you, that person does not appear to shrink, even though the image on your retinas is in fact getting smaller. You have learned from your past experiences that people do not shrink just because they move away from you, and so you make certain mental adjustments regarding people's sizes. What would happen if you had no such prior experience with perceiving people and other things at varying distances? The anthropologist Colin Turnbull (1961) observed exactly this situation while studying the Ba Mbuti pygmies, a tribe living in the thick jungle of the African Congo rain forest. With no open spaces in their environment, the Ba Mbuti never had the opportunity to see objects more than a few feet away from them. Turnbull described one particular incident in which a member of the tribe, a man named Kenge, traveled for the first time to an area of open grasslands. When Kenge spied a herd of buffalo grazing in the far distance, he asked, "What insects are those?" and dismissed as folly Turnbull's reply that they were actually buffalo that were very far away. A short time later, as the men approached the buffalo by car, Kenge grew increasingly frightened as he watched the buffalo "grow" in size, fearful that a magic trick was being played on him.

People are surprisingly adaptable in their ability to learn to perceive in new ways. For example, in a series of experiments described by Kohler (1962), subjects wore special glasses that significantly distorted their vision. Some subjects wore prism glasses that made objects to the left look much thinner than they really were, while objects to the right appeared abnormally wide. After wearing such glasses continuously for several weeks, the wearers no longer perceived any distortions; they actually relearned to perceive the world normally. When they later removed their glasses, the original distortions were reversed: Objects on the left looked fat and objects on the right looked thin. In another experiment, subjects wore glasses that horizontally reversed retinal images (objects actually on the left appeared to be on the right, and vice versa) and quickly adapted to them. Kohler described one individual who, after wearing the glasses for several weeks, could drive his motorcycle through the city streets without difficulty!

Expectation

Read the sentence below:

> *I pledge allegiance to the flag of the United Stetes of American, and to the Repulbic for which it stends, one nation, under God, indivsible, with liberty and justice for all.*

You may have noticed one or two typographical errors in the passage. But did you catch them all? Altogether there were *five* mistakes, as shown below:

> *I pledge allegiance to the flag of the United St<u>e</u>tes of American<u>n</u>, and to the Repul<u>b</u>ic for which it st<u>e</u>nds, one nation, under God, indi<u>v</u>sible, with liberty and justice for all.*

If you didn't notice all the errors—and many people don't—then your expectation of what words *should* have been there influenced your perception of the sentence. If you have seen and heard the United States Pledge of Allegiance as many times as I have, you know that the phrase "I pledge allegiance . . ." is usually followed by a certain sequence of words, and so you may have seen what you expected to see.

Expectations are one reason that people have difficulty with proofreading, especially when they are proofreading something they themselves have written. I have read countless student papers in which I have found obvious misspellings, despite the authors' insistence that they have proofread their work very carefully. The problem with proofreading our own work is that we, as the writers, know very well what *should* be written on the page, and so we may "read" what we expect to be there rather than what actually *is* there.

Expectations are especially likely to influence perception when objects or events are ambiguous. It is to this topic—perceiving ambiguous stimuli—that we turn now.

Expectations and the Perception of Ambiguous Stimuli

Take a close look at the picture in Figure 9–9. Describe to yourself what you see. Notice the shape of the head, the eye, the nose, the mouth, the chin. But just what is it that you *do* see? Is this a picture of a man or of a mouse?

The man-mouse picture in Figure 9–9 is an example of an **ambiguous stimulus**, something that can be constructed into more than one perception. Some people perceive the figure as a bald man with an overbite and a backward tilt to his head. Others instead perceive a mouse or rat with a very short front leg and a long tail curling beneath its body (Bugelski & Alampay, 1961).

Ambiguous stimuli are those most likely to be perceived in accordance with people's expectations (e.g., Eysenck & Keane, 1990). When I show the man-mouse picture to students in my classes, I consistently find that the great majority of students who have been led to expect a mouse—by viewing a picture that is clearly a rodent—*do* in fact see a mouse or rat. Those who are similarly led to expect a man see the baldheaded man. And notice how your expectations concerning how people typically behave influence your initial interpretation of the first statement that follows (from Gleitman, 1985, p. 432):

> *"We're going to have my grandmother for Thanksgiving dinner."*
> *"You are? Well, we're going to have turkey."*

In much the same way, human behaviors are often ambiguous, and individuals tend to interpret the behaviors of others in accordance with their own expectations (Juvonen, 1991; Nisbett & Bellows, 1977; Ritts, Patterson, & Tubbs, 1992; Snyder & Swann, 1978). People expect positive behaviors from a person they like or admire and so are likely to perceive that person's behaviors in a positive light—a phenomenon referred to as the **halo effect**. In much the same way, they expect inappropriate behaviors from a person they dislike, and their perceptions of that person's behaviors are biased accordingly—we could call this the **horns effect**. For example, imagine that Mr. Brighteyes, a fifth-grade teacher, has one

Figure 9–9

Reprinted from "The Role of Frequency in Developing Perceptual Sets" by B. R. Bugelski & D. A. Alampay, 1961, *Canadian Journal of Psychology*, *15*, p. 206. Copyright 1961 by Canadian Psychological Association. Reprinted with permission.

student, Mary, who consistently performs well in classwork, and another, Susan, who more typically turns in sloppy and incomplete work. Let's say that both girls turn in an assignment of marginal quality. Mr. Brighteyes is likely to *over*rate Mary's performance and *under*rate Susan's.

Many things affect people's expectations, and hence their perceptions, of another's behaviors. For example, people often expect higher-quality performance from people who are clean and well groomed than from people who are dirty and disheveled—hence the adage, "Dress for success." Socioeconomic status also appears to make a difference; consider this experiment by Darley and Gross (1983) as an example. Undergraduate students were told that they were participating in a study on teacher evaluation methods and were asked to view a videotape of a fourth-grade girl named Hannah. There were two versions of the videotape designed to give two different impressions about Hannah's socioeconomic status; Hannah's clothing, the kind of playground in which she played, and information about her parents' occupations indirectly conveyed to some students that she was from a low socioeconomic background and to others that she was from a high socioeconomic background. All students then watched Hannah taking an oral achievement test, on which she performed at grade level, and were asked to rate Hannah on a number of characteristics. Students who had been led to believe that Hannah came from wealthy surroundings rated her ability well above grade level, whereas students believing she lived in an impoverished environment evaluated her as being below grade level. The two groups of students also rated Hannah differently in terms of her work habits, motivation, social skills, and general maturity.

Individuals' expectations and perceptions may even be influenced by other people's names. In an experiment by Harari and McDavid (1973), elementary school teachers were asked to grade essays written by 10-year-old children. Teachers who read an essay supposedly written by "Lisa" gave it a better grade than teachers who read the same essay but thought it was written by "Bertha." In the same way, "David" received better grades than "Hubert." Perhaps we should think of student essays as being ambiguous stimuli, since the criteria for perceiving (grading) them are often somewhat subjective. Grading of such ambiguous stimuli may be especially influenced by teachers' past experiences with, and expectations for, their students.

Perception of an ambiguous stimulus is particularly susceptible to biases and expectations because some of the information necessary for an "accurate" perception (if such is possible) is simply not available. However, even when all the necessary information *is* present, people typically attend only to a small part of that information and ignore the rest. The kinds of information that people pay attention to, and the kinds that they ignore, are topics we will explore next.

ATTENTION

Attention is the process by which people select some of the environmental input they receive for further cognitive processing. For example, you are probably attending to only a small part of all the visual input that your eyes sense right now (I hope you are attending to the words on this page!). In the same way, you do not worry about all the sounds you hear at any particular time; you select only certain sounds to pay attention to.

As you will learn in the next chapter, attention plays a central role in learning and memory (e.g., Atkinson & Shiffrin, 1968; Kulhavy, Peterson, & Schwartz, 1986; Piontkowski & Calfee, 1979; Zelniker & Jeffrey, 1979). Because attention is such a critical component of the human information processing system, I would like to address the following pertinent questions in the pages to follow: What kinds of stimuli are likely to capture our attention? What processes allow us to focus our attention on some stimuli and not others? How many different stimuli can we attend to at the same time? Let's explore each of these questions in turn.

Factors Influencing Attention

Certain kinds of stimuli tend to draw attention, while other kinds do not. Let's take a look at some critical factors affecting what people pay attention to.

Size
Which of the following letters first draw your eye?

A B C D E F G

You probably noticed the B and E before the other letters because of their larger size. Attention tends to be drawn to large objects, a fact that newspaper publishers employ when they typeset front-page headlines in large letters, and that advertisers use when they put potentially unenticing information in fine print.

Intensity
More intense stimuli—bright colors and loud noises, for instance—attract attention. Teachers will frequently speak more loudly than usual—**"Be quiet!"**—when they want to get their students' attention. Similarly, toy manufacturers emphasize bright colors in the toys they produce, knowing that children browsing store shelves will be more attracted to vivid reds and yellows than to muted pastels.

Novelty
Stimuli that are novel or unusual in some way tend to draw people's attention. For example, look at the women in Figure 9–10. You probably find yourself attending more to the woman on the right than to the others. A woman with two heads and three legs is not someone you see every day.

Incongruity
Objects that are incongruous—those that don't make sense within their context—tend to capture people's attention. For example, read this sentence:

I took a walk to the rabbit this morning.

Figure 9–10
Novelty draws attention.

Did you spend more time looking at the word *rabbit* than at the other words? If so, it may have been because *rabbit* does not make much sense within the context of the sentence.

Emotion

Stimuli with strong emotional associations attract attention. A nude body flashing through a crowded room will usually draw the attention (and astonished expressions) of just about everyone present. Words such as *blood* and *murder* also are attention-getters because of their emotional overtones.

Personal Significance

Individuals tend to pay attention to stimuli that are important to them at a given point in time (Gibson & Rader, 1979; Voss & Schauble, 1992; Vurpillot & Ball, 1979). When a student sits in front of a television set with an open textbook, the stimulus that the student attends to—the television or the book—depends in large part on which stimulus is more closely related to the student's motives at that particular time. If the textbook is interesting or if an important examination is scheduled for the next day, the student will attend to the book. But if a popular situation comedy or a cliff-hanging soap opera is on, or if the textbook is dry and unenticing, the student may very well forget that the text is even in the same room!

Think, for a moment, about curriculum materials, including textbooks, that you have seen recently. Do they possess characteristics that are likely to catch a student's eye? Do important words and concepts stand out, perhaps because they are larger or **more intense** or *unusual*? Are certain topics likely to grab a student's interest because they are interesting and relevant to the age group? If your answer to these questions is no, then students are likely to have difficulty attending to and learning from those materials.

Processes Underlying Attention

What cognitive processes underlie people's ability to attend to certain aspects of the environment and to ignore others? On the surface, the answer might appear simple: They just focus their eyes directly on what they want to pay attention to. Because more receptors are in the middle of the retinas than at the sides, visual perception is more accurate and more detailed for things in the center of the visual field. Yet you can probably think of many times when you have focused your eyes on an object yet not paid attention to that object at all: Perhaps you were listening intently to a piece of music or were deep in thought about something that wasn't anywhere in sight.

Furthermore, people are able to focus the attention of their other senses without having to orient their receptors in particular directions. Consider the case of auditory attention: you can go to a party at which numerous conversations are going on simultaneously and successfully attend to one conversation over the din of others, regardless of where your ears are "aimed." You may be listening to the person standing directly in front of you, or, if that person has been rambling on for more than an hour about the difficulty he has had cultivating rhubarb in his backyard, you may instead tune in to a more interesting conversation a few feet to your right or left. Even though you may be looking directly at the rhubarb-grower and nodding in mock agreement, your attention is somewhere else altogether!

The ability to attend to one spoken message while ignoring others—aptly called the **cocktail party phenomenon**—has been studied using a technique called **shadowing**: A research subject listens through earphones to two simultaneously spoken messages and tries to repeat the message presented by one of the speakers. By assessing the accuracy of the subject's repetition, researchers have been able to speculate about cognitive processes underlying attention.

In pioneering research by Cherry (1953), subjects who listened simultaneously to two speeches (each consisting of numerous clichés strung together) spoken by the same individual were unable to attend to just one of the speeches: Although the subjects were able to repeat entire clichés accurately, they sampled these clichés equally from the two speeches. On the other hand, when they heard two messages on different topics by different speakers with different voices coming from different directions, repetition of one of the messages was much more accurate.

Subjects who shadow one of two messages notice very little of the other message. They can seldom report any of the words included in that unattended message and typically do not even notice whether the language spoken is their native tongue. Superficial characteristics, such as a change from a man's voice to a woman's voice, are noticed, but the content of the message is not (Cherry, 1953).

Because of Cherry's findings, an early theory of attention (Broadbent, 1958) likened auditory attention to a filter that allowed the selection of one message on the basis of physical characteristics and the screening out of others, much as a television tuner tunes in to one broadcast and shuts out the rest.

However, research subsequent to Broadbent's proposed filter theory has indicated that people do not totally filter out information from a supposedly unattended message. Subjects in shadowing experiments notice particularly meaningful words (such as their own names) in the unattended message (Treisman, 1964). They also hear words from that message if those words fit meaningfully into the attended message (Gray & Wedderburn, 1960; Treisman, 1964). For example, suppose you hear these two sentences simultaneously and are asked to shadow only the first one:

Speaker 1: I bought candy at the plate today.
Speaker 2: Put the rhubarb on my store, please.

You might very well "hear" the first speaker say, "I bought candy at the store today" (borrowing the word *store* from the second speaker) because such a sentence makes more sense than what the speaker really did say.

Rather than thinking of attention as a filter, many psychologists now conceptualize attention as a result of cognitive processing and perhaps as another instance of construction (e.g., Neisser, 1967): Depending on what stimulus they wish to pay attention to, people select certain pieces of information from among those they receive and construct a perception from them. For example, at a cocktail party, they select the sounds that resemble a particular person's voice and that seem to fit into a meaningfully constructed sentence. However, if a word from another speaker seems to fit the meaning, it might very well be incorporated into what is heard.

Attention as a Limited Capacity

Life would be much simpler if people didn't have to choose certain stimuli to pay attention to, but could instead attend to *everything*. Unfortunately, people are incapable of attending to everything at once. For example, Figure 9–11 shows a figure sometimes called the Peter-Paul goblet. At first glance, you probably see a white goblet. But if you look at the black spaces on either side of the goblet, you should also be able to see two silhouettes ("Peter" and "Paul") staring at each other.

Now try this little exercise: See if you can focus on both the goblet and the two silhouettes at *exactly* the same time, so that you can clearly see the details of both. Can you do it? Most people are unable to attend to the goblet and the faces at exactly the same time, although they may be able to shift their focus from the goblet to the faces and back again very quickly.

Figure 9–11
The Peter-Paul goblet

The Peter-Paul goblet illustrates the Gestalt principle of **figure-ground**: An individual can attend to one object (the **figure**) and notice the details of that object. Whatever the individual is not paying attention to (i.e., the background, or **ground**) is not carefully inspected: The individual may notice a few salient characteristics, such as color, but overlook more specific information about unattended objects. Gestalt psychologists proposed that people can pay attention to only one thing at a time, hence the difficulty most folks have in attending to both the goblet and the faces simultaneously. More recently, other theorists (e.g., Broadbent, 1958; Cherry, 1953; Treisman, 1964; Welford, 1977) have proposed something similar: People can only attend to one *complex* source of information at a time. In situations where more than one stimulus requires attention, one's attention must be switched quickly back and forth from one to another.

But now consider a situation in which you are driving your car while also carrying on a conversation with a friend. Are you not attending to two things, the road and the conversation, at once? To account for such a situation, some theorists (e.g., Anderson, 1990; Kahneman, 1973; Norman & Bobrow, 1975; Pashler, 1992) have begun to describe attention as involving a **limited processing capacity**, with the number of stimuli being attended to depending on how much cognitive processing is required for each stimulus. If you are engaging in a difficult task, such as learning to drive a car with a standard transmission, you may very well need to devote your full attention to that task. However, if you are doing something more habitual or automatic, such as driving a standard transmission after years of driving experience, you can easily devote some attention to another activity.

Regardless of how we view attention, one thing is clear: People's ability to attend is limited, which probably prevents them from attending to two *demanding* tasks at the same time. Thus, people must be quite selective about the information they choose to process and must ignore a lot of the information they receive. Since attention plays a critical role in the human memory system, its lim-ited capacity also affects learning and memory. Frustrating as it may seem, people simply cannot attend to, learn, and remember everything they encounter.

PERCEPTION AND ATTENTION IN EDUCATION

Perception and attention both play critical roles in the educational process. In this section, we will focus on several topics related to perception and attention in the classroom: perception and interpretation in learning, attention in the class-room, attentional processes in reading and spelling, and attention in study behavior.

Perception and Interpretation in Learning

Earlier in the chapter, we examined a number of variables affecting how people perceive the world. Two particular influences—past experience and expecta-tions—will of course vary from one individual to the next. As a result, teachers should expect that different students will perceive their classroom experiences differently and will therefore learn different things from those experiences.

Students' perceptions will probably vary most in situations involving ambigu-ous stimuli. Consider this situation as an example. A teacher enters the class-room with a noticeable frown on her face. Sally might perceive her teacher as being sad about a recent event, George might think she is ill, Martha might believe she is angry with the class, and Paul might believe she is showing displea-sure specifically with *his* behavior. Because a frown can reflect a number of dif-ferent emotional and physical states, it is likely to be interpreted in many differ-ent ways.

Teachers must remember that their own perceptions are subject to distortion as well. Students' behaviors can often be ambiguous enough that they suggest a variety of interpretations (as an example, remember the case of Hannah, described earlier in the chapter). Teachers' expectations for students influence their evaluations of those students (Good, 1987; Harari & McDavid, 1973; Ritts et al., 1992). Furthermore, expectations also influence how teachers behave toward students, thus indirectly affecting students' achievement and classroom perfor-mance (Copeland, 1993; Good, 1987). For example, teachers tend to treat low achieving students differently from high achieving students: Low achievers receive less attention, get more criticism for their failures, and receive praise less frequently for their successes (Good, 1987). There does seem to be some truth to Rosenthal and Jacobson's (1968) notion of the **self-fulfilling prophecy**: How teachers expect students to perform to some degree affects how students actually *do* perform.

Attention in the Classroom

Classrooms are usually lively environments, with many stimuli competing for students' attention. Students are almost always attending to *something*, but that something may not be what their teacher wants them to attend to. For example, think of yourself in one of your college classes. Sometimes you pay attention to what the teacher is saying, but at other times your attention drifts to such things as the size of the instructor's nose, the style of another student's clothes, the doodles on your notebook, or the plans you've made for the upcoming weekend. If adults cannot pay attention during every minute of the class day, how can we reasonably expect younger students to do so? But when students' attention wanders away from the topic of instruction, little learning of the kind the teacher desires is likely to occur.

How can teachers keep students' attention on the task at hand? Here are some suggestions.

•*Include variety in topics and presentation styles.* Too many students see their classroom environments as dull and repetitious. For example, when my children come home from school and I ask them what exciting things have happened that day, their responses are usually "Nothing" or "Same old thing." Repetition of the same topics and the same procedures day after day can lead to boredom and reduced attention (Zirin, 1974). Variety and novelty in the subject matter and the mode of presentation will help keep students' attention focused on a lesson (Berlyne, 1960; Good & Brophy, 1984; Keele, 1973; Keller, 1987).

•*Minimize distractions when seatwork is assigned.* As you well know, most students are better able to concentrate on seatwork assignments when the classroom is relatively quiet and subdued. Several "open classroom" schools in my part of the state have recently acquired new walls for this very reason: Too many different activities were occurring in the large, open classroom spaces, and students and teachers alike often found it difficult to focus their attention on any one thing for very long.

•*Monitor students' attention.* Behaviors often provide a clue to whether students are paying attention. For example, students should be directing their eyes at the teacher, workbook, or other appropriate stimulus and should be clearly working on the task at hand (Grabe, 1986; Piontkowski & Calfee, 1979; Samuels & Turnure, 1974).

•*Ask questions.* Questions are an excellent way of maintaining students' attention when it might otherwise wander away from a lesson (Grabe, 1986; Piontkowski & Calfee, 1979; Samuels & Turnure, 1974). By asking questions periodically, occasionally addressing questions to particular students, teachers can help students keep their attention where it should be. (In Chapter 13, we will identify additional benefits of asking questions.)

•*Seat students near the teacher if they have difficulty paying attention.* Research by Schwebel and Cherlin (1972) indicates that students are more likely to pay attention when placed at the front of the room and near the teacher. Front row seats may be particularly appropriate for students with a history of being easily distracted.

Attentional Processes in Reading and Spelling

Attention obviously influences how well students learn academic subjects. Its role is particularly important in reading and spelling, topics to which we turn now.

Reading

Reading is a cognitive process that can be partly understood in terms of the principles of perception and attention we have examined in this chapter. For example, as I showed you earlier, people tend to perceive groups of letters that appear close together as words. They also tend to see what they expect to see on a page; for example, the words *How are* . . . are frequently followed by the word *you*, and so that word may be "perceived" whether it appears on the page or not.

Beginning readers pay close attention to the letters on the page as they read and, as a result, often read slowly and comprehend little. More mature readers tend not to look as carefully at the printed page. Instead, they rely on such things as context, sentence syntax, prior knowledge about a topic, and expectations about what the author is trying to communicate to jump to hasty, although usually accurate, conclusions about what is on the page (e.g., Dole, Duffy, Roehler, & Pearson, 1991; Smith, 1988). It is precisely because mature readers *do* jump to conclusions about what is written, without taking time to look at all the letters, that they can read as quickly and efficiently as they do (Smith, 1988).

At the same time, mature readers run the risk of jumping to the *wrong* conclusions and therefore misinterpreting what they read. For example, my name—Jeanne Ormrod—is frequently misread as "Jeanne Orm*ond*," an error that I find quite annoying. But let's face it: Ormrod is an unusual name, while Ormond is more common. One can almost not blame readers who see *Orm. . .* and just assume that the rest of the word is *. . .ond*; after all, using the first few letters of a word to identify that word is a common strategy in reading (Lima, 1993). (I blame people who read "Ormond" nevertheless.)

The design of reading materials themselves also influences children's attentional processes. For example, an excessive number of pictures in a textbook, while possibly increasing the book's attractiveness, can distract a child's attention away from the more important part of the book—the text (Samuels, 1967). Having questions within a text (for example, questions at the beginning of a chapter) directs students' attention toward information that answers those questions, but sometimes away from information not related to those questions (e.g., Anderson & Biddle, 1975; Andre, 1979).

Spelling

I have long contended that students learn as much about spelling from their reading as they do from specific spelling instruction (e.g., Ormrod, 1986b, 1986c). By the time they reach college, students are expected to spell many words (e.g., *psychology* and *environment*) that were never included in their formal spelling lessons. If students know how to spell such words, it is probably because they have learned the correct spelling through repeated exposures to the words in their reading assignments and recreational reading.

Several research studies (e.g., Frith, 1978, 1980; Ormrod, 1985, 1986a) indicate that spelling ability is probably related to reading style. Although it is quite possible to read without attending closely to the printed page, some students continue to pay close attention to the words they read even as their reading skills mature; these students are often good spellers. Mature readers with good verbal skills who are nevertheless poor spellers tend to rely more on context clues and their own expectations than on the specific letters on the page. Their attention to the page may be sufficient for them to identify words accurately, but insufficient for them to learn how to spell those same words.

Attention in Study Behavior

Even when students are paying attention to the appropriate stimulus, they may be focusing on something very different from what the teacher thinks they are focusing on. The stimulus that the teacher presents to students (sometimes called the **nominal stimulus**) is not necessarily the stimulus that a student is actually attending to (the **effective stimulus**). For example, suppose a teacher teaching a phonics lesson presents a picture of a girl and asks for the first letter of the word it represents. Although the teacher is expecting the answer G, a student who focuses on the girl's dress may instead respond with D.

Once, when I was teaching introductory psychology to college freshmen, a student who had failed my first two examinations came to my office and expressed frustration about her lack of success in my class. When I asked her to describe how she went about completing the assigned readings in the textbook, she told me, "Well, I start looking through the chapter, and when I get to a page that looks important, I read it." With further probing, I discovered that this young woman had been reading approximately one out of every three pages assigned! In this case, the effective stimulus was only one-third of the nominal stimulus.

As another example of how attention can influence students' studying and learning from curriculum materials, let's look at an experiment by Faust and Anderson (1967), in which students studied Russian vocabulary words under one of two conditions. Some students read single statements presenting an English word and its Russian equivalent, then were required to write the Russian word. Below is an example of the materials these students received:

A table is a stohl.
A table is a _____.

Other students were shown short paragraphs, each containing several Russian words and their English equivalents, following which they wrote one of the Russian words. An example follows:

A rag is a tryapka. A bridge is a mohst. A table is a stohl. A college is a vooz. An onion is a look.
A table is a _____.

Faust and Anderson found that students who were shown the paragraphs learned the English meanings of more Russian words than students who were given the single sentences; they reasoned that differences in attention explained the differences in achievement. To understand how attention might differ in the two situations, pretend for a moment that you are a student who wants to complete the Russian vocabulary task with a minimum of time and effort. Now look at the first set of stimulus materials. You don't have to read (attend to) the English word to answer correctly with *stohl*. If you know that the Russian word consistently appears as the last word of the sentence, then you only need to attend to that last word and copy it on the blank line. As a result, you may learn the Russian word but not connect it to its English meaning.

Now look at the second set of stimulus materials. Because several Russian words appear in the paragraph, you must determine which of them is the correct answer. At the very least, you must look at the English word *table* in the incomplete statement at the bottom, then locate that word in the paragraph above. You find "A table is a stohl" and so write *stohl* in the blank. You may or may not have paid attention to other sentences in the paragraph, but at least you have attended to both the English word and its Russian equivalent. Hence you are more likely to learn that *stohl* means "table."

As you have probably concluded, perception and attention can be idiosyncratic processes indeed: Individuals attend to and perceive the world in their own unique ways, and all may arrive at different conclusions about what they have seen and heard. The fact that different students perceive the same educational environment differently may be frustrating for teachers, for it will not be possible to control totally how students perceive instructional materials and events, or even what materials students pay attention to.

There is an old saying, "You can lead a horse to water, but you can't make him drink." Ormrod's corollary is, "The horse can't possibly drink if you don't at least lead him to the water." Drawing students' attention to important information is the first step in helping them learn information: It gets them to the water trough. Helping them drink up that information—that is, helping them store the information in their memory systems—is the next step, one that we will explore in the following chapters.

SUMMARY

Perception is a process of recognizing and interpreting one's sensations of environmental events. People do not perceive everything their bodies have sensed; at the same time, they also perceive things *in addition to* their sensations (for example, by filling in an incomplete picture). Perception is a constructive process that is influenced by proximity, similarity, closure, context, past experience, and expectation.

Attention involves the selection of certain stimuli from among many environmental events for further processing. Like perception, attention is constructive and is influenced by such stimulus characteristics as size, intensity, novelty, incongruity, emotion, and personal significance. Attentional capacity is limited: an individual probably cannot pay attention to more than one demanding task at any given time. Accordingly, people must be selective about what events they attend to.

Our understanding of perception and attention processes has numerous implications for classroom practice. For example, the perceptions of students and teachers alike are subject to distortion, especially when the stimuli involved are ambiguous and therefore consistent with a number of different interpretations. Several strategies promote students' attention in the classroom—providing variety in topics and presentation styles, minimizing distractions, and asking questions are three possibilities. Attention plays a particularly important role in reading, spelling, and study skills.

CHAPTER 10

Theories of Memory

I magine yourself studying for an upcoming exam based on a complicated reading assignment. You understand most of the material and are confident that you will remember it. However, you have trouble learning one section of the assignment because it doesn't make much sense to you. In desperation, you try to memorize this section word for word, but your learning is slow and painful.

Now imagine yourself taking that exam. It was not as difficult as you had anticipated it would be, but you cannot remember the answer to a particularly trivial question: "What was Edward C. Tolman's middle name?" You know you studied the relevant section in the book, but you simply cannot remember the information called for. After considering all the names you can think of that begin with C, you finally give up and turn in your exam paper with the question unanswered.

Immediately afterward, you congregate with your classmates in the hall and rehash the questions. "What was Tolman's middle name?" you ask. Your friend Harry responds smugly, "It was Chace. I can remember that easily because my sister married a guy named Marvin Chace." And then your friend Carol adds, "I learned the name by imagining Tolman *chacing* his rats down their mazes." You grit your teeth, thinking it ridiculous that Harry and Carol would do better than you on a question because of a coincidental brother-in-law or a silly visual image. But let's face it, your classmates remembered and you did not.

Learning a piece of information does not guarantee that the information will be remembered later on. A number of variables determine what information gets into memory in the first place and what information stays there long enough to be remembered when it is needed. In this chapter, we will explore some models of how the human memory system works and how various factors influence its effectiveness.

The study of human cognition follows two major approaches (Calfee, 1981). One approach focuses on the *structures* of the human mind—that is, on its different components and their interrelationships. The second focuses on the mind's *functions*—that is, on how the mind operates to process information. We will begin our examination of theories of memory with a dual-store model, one that focuses primarily on structure. Later in the chapter, we will turn to alternative views of memory that focus more on how memory functions and how information is processed.

A DUAL-STORE MODEL OF MEMORY

In the latter part of the nineteenth century, Harvard psychologist William James (1890) proposed that human memory has three components: an after-image, a primary memory, and a secondary memory. James' model was largely ignored during the behaviorism-dominated early decades of the twentieth century, but the advent of cognitivism in the 1960s brought a renewed interest in human memory, and in 1968, Richard Atkinson and Richard Shiffrin (1968, 1971) proposed a model of memory similar to that of James. This model laid the groundwork for what has become the most prevalent view of human memory today—a **dual-store model** of memory, depicted in simplified form in Figure 10–1.

Like William James, Atkinson and Shiffrin proposed that memory has three components: a sensory register (SR), short-term memory (STM), and long-term memory (LTM). (The model is called *dual*-store in reference to the distinction

Figure 10–1
A simplified dual-store
model of memory

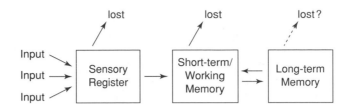

between short-term memory and long-term memory.) Information from the environment—input—first enters the sensory register, where it is held for a very short time (a few seconds at the most). If the information is processed in a particular way, it moves on to short-term memory. Information is held in short-term memory only for a few seconds, however, and must be processed further if it is to move on to long-term memory. Processing information in short-term memory frequently involves the use of information from long-term memory as well (hence the two-way arrows between short-term and long-term memory of Figure 10–1). If a piece of information reaches the sensory register or short-term memory but is not then processed sufficiently for its transference to the next component of the memory system, that information is assumed to be lost from the memory system—in other words, it is forgotten. Whether information can be lost from long-term memory as well (note the dotted arrow and question mark) is still an open question, one that we will address in Chapter 12.

A dual-store model of human memory can be likened to an information selection and storage system similar to what you might use to store important documents at home. You undoubtedly acquire numerous pieces of paper in your home over the course of a few months; among this mass of paper may be such items as newspapers, personal letters, bills, a driver's license, university transcripts, junk mail, and grocery store receipts. You probably discard some items (such as junk mail and grocery receipts) almost as soon as you get them; these things get no further than the "sensory register" of your storage system. Others (such as bills) you need to deal with briefly (e.g., you must *pay* them), then you can more or less forget them; they are processed for a short time in your system's "short-term storage." Still others (such as a driver's license and transcripts) may be important enough that you want to put them in a safe, organized place where you will be able to find them later; they end up in a "long-term storage" compartment such as a wallet, desk drawer, or safe deposit box.

Learning theorists have continued to modify the dual-store model over the years. For example, they have theorized about the forms in which information is stored and the processes through which it is moved from short-term memory to long-term memory. But perhaps the most noticeable change is an increasing reference to short-term memory as a "working" memory that processes information as well as storing it (hence, the term *working* in the second box of Figure 10–1). To be consistent with contemporary theorists, we will use the term *working memory* from this point on.

In this chapter we will examine the three components of the dual-store model; we will also look at the various **control processes** that affect the movement of information from one component to another. As we proceed, however, we must remember that the language we will use in our discussion of human memory is largely metaphorical in nature (e.g., Roediger, 1980). For example, the three components of memory are not necessarily three separate "places" in the brain. Furthermore, when we talk about memory processes, we are not necessarily saying anything about neurological events. Psychologists still have much to learn about how memory processes occur physiologically and how brain structure relates to psychological models of human memory.

THE SENSORY REGISTER

The first component of the dual-store model, the **sensory register** (also called sensory memory, sensory store, iconic memory, or echoic memory) holds incoming information long enough that it can undergo preliminary cognitive processing. All the environmental information that we are capable of sensing probably stays with us in the sensory register for a very brief time. For example, if you have ever waved a flashlight or sparkler in the air on a dark night, you have probably noticed that the light leaves a trail behind it. This trail is not present in the air itself; it is the result of your sensory register holding the light you have seen for a short time after you saw it. As another example, when you sit in a classroom for an hour or more, your attention will almost inevitably wander away from the instructor at some point. You may have noticed that when you tune back in to what the instructor is saying, you can often recall two or three words that the instructor has said *before* your tuning in. Virtually everything the instructor has uttered has probably been recorded in your sensory register despite your mental absence from class, but, alas, only those last two or three words are still there when you decide to be present again.

Characteristics of the Sensory Register

Let's look specifically at three characteristics of the sensory register: capacity, form of storage, and duration.

Capacity
The capacity of the sensory register is, as far as psychologists can tell, unlimited. All the environmental information that human beings are capable of sensing is probably stored briefly in the sensory register.

Form of Storage
Information appears to be stored in the sensory register basically in the form in which it has been sensed: visual input is stored in a visual form, auditory input in

an auditory form, and so on (Coltheart, Lea, & Thompson, 1974; Howard, 1983; Turvey & Kravetz, 1970). At this point, the individual has not yet understood nor interpreted the information. In other words, the sensory register holds information *before* it is processed.

Duration

As I stated earlier, information remains in the sensory register for only a very brief time, although measuring its exact duration is difficult. One problem in studying the characteristics of the sensory register is that once people are asked to process the information stored there, it is automatically moved on to working memory—so it is no longer in the place where we want to study it!

The classic experiment designed to assess the duration of the sensory register was conducted by George Sperling (1960). Using adult subjects, Sperling presented displays of three rows of four letters and digits each, like this:

7	1	V	F
X	L	5	3
B	4	W	7

Each display was presented for a fraction of a second, then subjects were asked to recall either one particular row of symbols or all 12 symbols. When asked to recall a single row, subjects were able to do so with 76% accuracy; because they were not told *which* row they would need to recall until after the display had disappeared, the subjects apparently remembered approximately 76% of the symbols they had seen. Yet when asked to recall all 12 symbols, they could do so with only 36% accuracy! Sperling's explanation of this result was that most of the symbols were stored initially but faded from memory before the subjects had a chance to write them all down. In a follow-up experiment, Sperling (1960) varied the amount of time that elapsed between the display and the signal indicating which row was to be remembered. Subjects could recall little of a display after a delay of more than a quarter second.

From results of research studies like Sperling's, it appears that the duration of visual information in the sensory register is probably less than a second (Loftus & Loftus, 1976; Wingfield & Byrnes, 1981). Auditory information probably lasts longer, with a duration of two to four seconds (Conrad & Hull, 1964; Darwin, Turvey, & Crowder, 1972; Moray, Bates, & Barnett, 1965).

Why does auditory input last longer than visual input? One possible explanation (e.g., Wingfield & Byrnes, 1981) is that a major source of auditory input—human speech—can only be understood within its sequential context. For example, consider this often-heard sentence:

I scream for ice cream.

You can interpret the sounds of the first two words either as *I scream* or *ice cream*. Only when you hear the third word—*for*—can you begin to interpret the first two words accurately. The task of understanding speech, which is often filled with temporarily ambiguous sounds, may be easier if you can hold those sounds in memory in an uninterpreted form until you receive additional, clarifying information.

Two reasons probably account for the rapid disappearance of information from the sensory register. First of all, *interference* may be a factor: New information coming in effectively erases the information already there (e.g., Breitmeyer & Ganz, 1976). Many psychologists also believe that, even without new input, existing information in the sensory register simply fades away, or *decays*, over time (e.g., Loftus & Loftus, 1976; Wingfield & Byrnes, 1981). Regardless of the reasons for the sensory register's short duration, in most instances people don't need to store information there for very long. Important information is probably going to be processed so that it enters working memory. Unimportant information, like junk mail, is probably best dealt with by throwing it away.

The Role of Attention

In Chapter 9, I indicated that attention is critical in human learning and memory. Now I can be more specific with regard to the role it plays. Attention is believed to be the process essential for moving information from the sensory register to working memory. In essence, information that an individual pays attention to advances to working memory, whereas information that is not attended to may be lost from the memory system.

One reason that people don't learn, then, is their lack of attention to information in the first place. If you are sitting in class with your mind a thousand miles away from the professor's lecture, you might say that you forgot what the instructor said, or you might say that you never heard it in the first place. The reality of the situation is somewhere in between: the lecture reached your sensory register but was not sufficiently processed to move on to the next step in your memory system—working memory.

What happens to information that *does* enter working memory? Let's turn to that topic now.

WORKING MEMORY

Atkinson and Shiffrin (1968) used the term **short-term memory** to refer to a storage mechanism that holds information for a brief time while it is mentally processed. As I mentioned earlier, however, most theorists now believe that this component of memory is also where cognitive processing itself takes place, hence their more frequent use of the term **working memory** (e.g., Baddeley, 1978, 1986; Baddeley & Hitch, 1974; Daneman & Carpenter, 1980).

As an example of the storage and processing functions of working memory, try figuring this long division problem in your head, without referring back to the page until you have solved it:

$$37\overline{)4281}$$

Almost impossible, isn't it? You may have found that while you were dividing 37 into 42, you forgot what the last two digits of the dividend were. Although you probably had no trouble holding six numbers in your working memory, you may not have been able to hold all six and still process those numbers at the same time.

Working memory is that component of memory in which the most active processing of information takes place. It selects what information will be attended to in the sensory register and holds that information while it is being processed. In addition, it may also hold information retrieved from long-term memory—information that will help in interpreting newly received environmental input. In a nutshell, working memory is the component in which "thinking" occurs; therefore, you might think of it as the "awareness" or "consciousness" of the memory system (e.g., Bellezza, 1986).

Characteristics of Working Memory

The exact nature of working memory is beyond the scope of this book; for theoretical analyses of its possible structure, I refer you to Baddeley (1986) and to Schneider and Detweiler (1987). Here we will focus on the same three characteristics we examined for the sensory register: capacity, form of storage, and duration.

Capacity

Unlike the sensory register, working memory appears to have a very limited capacity for storing information. After reviewing a number of early studies, George Miller (1956) proposed that the capacity of this component can be characterized as the *magical number seven, plus or minus two*: Individuals can hold from five to nine units of information in working memory at one time, with the average number of memorable units being about seven.

Miller further proposed that although the *number* of information units in working memory cannot be increased beyond about seven, the *amount* of information in each unit can be increased. For example, consider this nine-digit string:

6   3   1   9   8   0   2   5   7

People are more successful in learning long strings of digits if they group the digits into larger numbers, perhaps storing them something like this:

6-3-1   9-8-0   2-5-7

This process of combining pieces of information, called **chunking**, increases the amount of information that can be stored in the limited space of working memory. To use Miller's analogy, if you can only hold seven coins, you're far richer holding seven quarters, or even seven gold pieces, than seven pennies.

Current theorists believe that Miller's original assessment of five to nine units is probably overly simplistic (e.g., Anderson, 1990; Schneider & Detweiler, 1987). It now appears that the number of chunks that can be stored depends on how much information each chunk includes. For example, Simon (1974) found that, while he himself could remember a list of 7 one-syllable or two-syllable words, he could remember only 6 three-syllable words, 4 two-word phrases, and even fewer phrases of more than two words. In other words, the larger the chunks, the fewer of them working memory can hold at any one time. Therefore, as Anderson (1990) has pointed out, it may be difficult to identify the true capacity of working memory, at least in terms of a specific number of discrete items that can be stored there at any given time. Furthermore, there may be a trade-off between how much processing is necessary and how much information working memory can hold: Cognitive processing may take up some of its capacity, leaving less room for information storage. Nonetheless, one thing is clear: Working memory can only hold a small amount of information at any one time.

Form of Storage

Regardless of the form in which information is received, it appears that much of the information stored in working memory is stored in an *auditory* form, particularly when the information is language-based (Baddeley, 1986; Baddeley & Hitch, 1974; Conrad, 1962, 1964, 1971). For example, in a study by Conrad (1964), adults were shown six-letter sequences, with letters presented visually, one at a time, at three-fourths of a second intervals. As soon as the last letter of each sequence had been presented, subjects wrote the letters down, guessing at any letters that they could not easily recall. When subjects recalled letters incorrectly, the letters they said they had seen were more likely to resemble the actual stimuli in terms of how they sounded than how they looked. For example, the letter F was "remembered" as the auditorially similar letter S 131 times, but as the visually similar letter P only 14 times. Similarly, the letter V was remembered as B 56 times, but as X only 5 times.

Working memory probably includes a means of storing information in a visual form as well (Baddeley, 1986; Baddeley & Hitch, 1974). For example, deaf children probably store information in visual form (Conrad, 1972). And young children (e.g., 5-year-olds) are less likely to use an auditory code than older children (e.g., 11-year-olds) (Conrad, 1971). Nevertheless, the auditory encoding of information provides a distinct advantage: It appears to improve the memory of information, at least over the short term (Conrad, 1971).

Duration

Working memory is just what its alternative name, *short-term memory*, implies: It is short. An experiment by Peterson and Peterson (1959), which I previously described in Chapter 8, gives us some idea of how long information in working memory lasts. In this experiment, adults were told three consonant letters (e.g., D X P), then immediately asked to count backward by threes from a three-digit number, which was different in each trial. At a signal that occurred anywhere from 3 to 18 seconds after the three consonants had been presented, the subjects were asked to recall those letters. When their recall was delayed only three seconds, subjects were able to remember the letters with 80% accuracy; after an 18-second interval, however, their accuracy was only about 10%.

Considering research results such as those of Peterson and Peterson, psychologists believe that the duration of working memory is probably somewhere between 5 and 20 seconds. As with the sensory register, both decay and interference have been offered as explanations for this short time span. Some information stored in working memory may simply fade away if it is not processed further (Peterson & Peterson, 1959; Reitman, 1974; Shiffrin & Cook, 1978). Other information may be pushed out by new information (e.g., Keppel & Underwood, 1962; Melton, 1963; Reitman, 1974). For example, with a husband and three children in the house, I find myself frequently interrupted in the middle of tasks. If I have a batch of cookies in the oven, and Jeff asks me to make him a snack and Tina asks me to help her find her homework assignment, my cookies are very likely to be pushed from my working memory until I am confronted with new environmental input: The smell of something burning. My husband calls me absentminded, but I know better. My mind is definitely present, but the working component of it has a limited capacity, and new input interferes with the information already stored there.

Control Processes in Working Memory

Some processes in working memory—storing information in working memory, keeping it there, and retrieving it again so that it can be used—are related only to working memory itself. Still other processes are involved in moving information from working memory into long-term memory. At this point I will describe only the former processes, focusing on three in particular: organization, retrieval, and maintenance rehearsal. The processes that facilitate transference of information into long-term memory will be discussed in the upcoming section on long-term memory.

Organization

Earlier, I described Miller's (1956) proposal that the process of chunking helps increase the amount of information that can be stored in working memory. As they develop, children show an increasing tendency to chunk information, thereby enhancing the capacity of their working memories (Farnham-Diggory, 1972).

Chunking is an organizational process, since it combines two or more pieces of information. Chunking can organize information in a variety of ways. For example, consider again the nine-digit string I presented earlier:

6   3   1   9   8   0   2   5   7

I have already described one way of chunking this string: grouping it into three groups of three digits each. Another frequently observed organizational strategy is to impose a rhythm, or even a melody, to the numbers (Bower & Springston, 1970). Still another way of organizing the digits is to attach some meaning to them—a process that involves retrieving information that has previously been stored in long-term memory. For example, I can store the numbers as three meaningful pieces of information: My son Alex's birthday (the 6th month and 3rd day of *1980*), a quarter (*25* cents), and a week (*7* days).

Retrieval

Retrieval of information from working memory depends largely on how much information is stored there, a point illustrated in a study by Sternberg (1966). In this experiment, college students were presented with a set of from one to six numbers (numbers that presumably were stored in working memory). An additional number was then presented, and the students were asked whether that number had been among the original set. The time it took for subjects to answer the question depended almost entirely on the size of number set already stored in working memory, with each successively larger set yielding a reaction time of about 40 milliseconds longer. Apparently, working memory retrieval is simply a process of scanning all of working memory, successively and exhaustively, until the desired information is found.

Maintenance Rehearsal

You look up a friend's telephone number and store that number in your working memory; its seven digits are about the limit of what your working memory can hold. But then you find that someone else is using the telephone, and so you must wait to place your call. How do you keep your friend's number in working memory? If you are like most people, you probably repeat it to yourself over and over again.

Repeating information to keep it alive in working memory is a process known as **maintenance rehearsal**, which may be a form of subvocal speech (e.g., Landauer, 1962; Sperling, 1967). Maintenance rehearsal provides a means for saving information from the forgetting processes of decay and interference. You may recall that in Peterson and Peterson's (1959) examination of the duration of working memory described earlier, subjects were presented with three consonants, then asked to count backward by threes until the signal for recall. The backward counting kept subjects from rehearsing the three letters; otherwise, they might have kept them in working memory indefinitely simply by repeating them over and over as long as necessary.

Maintenance rehearsal is observed more frequently in older children and adults than in younger children (Conrad, 1971), so it may possibly be a learned skill. I myself used rehearsal frequently in high school and college whenever I had difficulty remembering something I would be tested on—perhaps when I needed to know a complicated formula, a verbatim definition, or a lengthy list of items. I would continue to repeat the information to myself as test papers were distributed, then immediately write it in the margin so it would be there for me if and when I needed it.

Although maintenance rehearsal can be a useful strategy for keeping information in working memory, teachers must remember that information in working memory will disappear once rehearsal stops. Frequent use of maintenance rehearsal may indicate that students are having trouble storing that information in their long-term memories. Yet long-term memory is where important information *should* be stored. Let's turn now to this final component of the dual-store model.

LONG-TERM MEMORY

Long-term memory is the part of the memory system that retains information for a relatively long period of time. It includes both memory for specific events and general knowledge that has been gleaned from those events over the years (e.g., Tulving, 1991, 1993). Some of the things stored in long-term memory may be easily retrievable, while others, even though they may ultimately have an effect on our behavior, may be difficult or even impossible to bring into conscious awareness (e.g., Graf & Schachter, 1985; Jacoby & Hayman, 1987; Jacoby & Witherspoon, 1982; Schachter, 1987).

Long-term memory is clearly the most complicated component of the human memory system. As such, it has been studied more extensively than either the sensory register or working memory, and theories about its characteristics and control processes abound. We will briefly examine the major characteristics of long-term memory here and explore them in more depth in the following two chapters.

Characteristics of Long-Term Memory

As we did for both the sensory register and working memory, we will look at the capacity, form of storage, and duration of long-term memory; we will then turn to control processes.

Capacity
As far as theorists can determine, the capacity of long-term memory is unlimited. In fact, as you will discover in Chapter 11, the more information that is already stored in long-term memory, the easier it is to store additional information there.

Form of Storage
Information is probably stored in long-term memory in a number of different ways. For example, language provides one basis of storing information, and visual imagery may provide another. However, most psychologists agree that the

bulk of information in long-term memory is probably stored *semantically*—in terms of meanings.

Two characteristics of long-term memory storage should be mentioned here. First, information is rarely stored in long-term memory exactly as it was received. Individuals tend to remember the "gist" of what they see and hear rather than word-for-word sentences or precise mental images. Second, information stored in long-term memory is organized, so that related pieces of information tend to be associated together. Ultimately, probably every piece of information is either directly or indirectly connected with every other piece.

Duration

As you will learn in Chapter 12, theorists disagree with regard to the duration of long-term memory. Some theorists believe that information, once stored in long-term memory, remains there permanently. Others, however, believe that information can disappear from long-term memory through a variety of forgetting processes. In fact, although some information may remain in long-term memory for long periods, there is probably no way to show conclusively that *all* information stored there remains permanently. The question about the duration of long-term memory is still an open one, and the best we can say is that long-term memory's duration is indefinitely *long*.

Control Processes in Long-Term Memory

In Chapters 11 and 12, we will examine long-term memory storage and retrieval processes in depth. Nevertheless, let's get a general idea of what these processes entail.

Storage

Storage processes in the first two components of memory are fairly straightforward; anything sensed is stored in the sensory register, and anything attended to is stored in working memory. However, as we shall see in the following chapter, storage of information in long-term memory is not that simple. Although some information may be stored easily (visual images are an example), most information must be consciously and actively processed before it is stored. Information is most likely to be stored in long-term memory when it is understood, organized, and integrated with information already stored there (e.g., Vosniadou & Brewer, 1987).

Remember, the processing necessary for storing information in long-term memory is accomplished in working memory. Remember, too, that working memory has a limited capacity and can only handle so much information at one time. The result is that long-term memory storage occurs slowly, and a great deal is lost from working memory along the way. In essence, working memory is the bottleneck in the memory system: It prevents most information from ever getting into long-term memory.

Retrieval

Retrieval of information from the sensory register and working memory is simple and easy: If the information is still there, it will probably be found. Retrieval of information from long-term memory is more difficult: Long-term memory has much more information than an individual can realistically search through at one time, so the success of retrieval depends largely on whether the individual searches in the right "location." Furthermore, retrieval from long-term memory is closely tied to storage processes: The more completely information has been understood, the better it has been organized, and the more closely it has been integrated with previously stored concepts, the more easily that information can be remembered.

Speaking of retrieval from long-term memory, what was Edward C. Tolman's middle name? Did you perhaps remember your friend Harry's brother-in-law, Marvin *Chace*? Or did you think of Tolman *chacing* his rats down their mazes? The more ways individuals store a piece of information in long-term memory, the more likely it is that the information will be retrieved when it is needed.

ARE WORKING MEMORY AND LONG-TERM MEMORY REALLY DIFFERENT?

Up to this point, we have been talking about working memory and long-term memory as two distinctly different components of memory. Some psychologists have proposed, however, that working and long-term memory are really a single entity. Let's look at the evidence both in favor of and against the working memory/long-term memory distinction.

Evidence Supporting the Distinction

Several research findings have been cited as evidence for the distinction between working and long-term memory. For one thing, the major form of storage in the two memories appears to be different, working memory being primarily acoustic and long-term memory being primarily semantic.

Secondly, you may recall the serial learning curve described in Chapter 8. Given a list of items to remember, individuals more often remember the first few items in the list (the **primacy effect**) and the last few items (the **recency effect**) than the middle items. The serial learning curve has frequently been explained in terms of a dual-store model (e.g., Glanzer & Cunitz, 1966; Norman, 1969). From this perspective, the first few items in the list can be processed sufficiently for their storage in long-term memory, and the last few items are still stored in working memory. The middle items, however, cannot be processed into long-term memory (presumably because the rate of item presentation does not allow adequate time for processing), and they have been pushed out of working memory by later items. In support of the view that early items in the list are stored in long-term memory is the finding that when the presentation rate is slowed down (thus allowing for more processing), the primacy effect is increased (Glanzer & Cunitz, 1966). Conversely, when processing of list items is prevented, the primacy effect disappears; that is, items early in the list are remembered no better than items in the middle of the list (Peterson & Peterson, 1962). On the other hand, the recency effect seems to be more affected by the recall interval: The longer that recall of the list is delayed, the less individuals are able to remember items at the end of the list, a finding consistent with the notion that these items are stored in the short-lived working memory (Glanzer & Cunitz, 1966; Postman & Phillips, 1965).

Third, studies of individuals who have undergone certain brain injuries or neurosurgical procedures sometimes show an impairment of one memory without a corresponding loss of function in the other (Atkinson & Shiffrin, 1968; Eysenck & Keane, 1990; Scoville & Milner, 1957). For example, some individuals can recall events experienced before the brain trauma but are unable to retain new experiences, indicating a possible problem with working memory while long-term memory remains intact. Other individuals can recall new experiences long enough to talk briefly about them but cannot remember them a few minutes later; here are cases where working memory is functioning, but new information seemingly cannot be transferred into long-term memory. Consistent with such findings, some evidence indicates that working memory and long-term memory processes may occur in different parts of the brain (Zola-Morgan & Squire, 1990).

Evidence Against the Distinction

Other research findings indicate that working memory and long-term memory may not be as distinctly different as I have described them. For example, although information is frequently stored acoustically in working memory and semantically in long-term memory, there is also evidence for *semantic* storage in working memory (Shulman, 1971, 1972) and for *acoustic* storage in long-term memory (Nelson & Rothbart, 1972).

Furthermore, some of the evidence used to support the dual-store model can also be explained without resorting to a working/long-term distinction. Wickelgren (1973), for instance, proposed that the serial learning curve can be explained as easily by a single-store model as by a dual-store model. He described forgetting as occurring rapidly at first and then slowly tapering off—a pattern that holds true for many different species and many different tasks (Wixted & Ebbesen, 1991). From this perspective, the recency effect may be due simply to the fact that the last items of a list have not yet undergone that rapid decay.

Alternative explanations also exist for the impairments in memory observed in individuals who have undergone brain traumas (e.g., Glass, Holyoak, & Santa, 1979; Zechmeister & Nyberg, 1982). These impairments may reflect specific difficulties in storage or retrieval processes rather than in working or long-term memory per se.

The debate regarding dual-store and single-store models is by no means resolved; more complete discussions of the issue are presented elsewhere (e.g., Adams, 1980; Ellis & Hunt, 1983; Hintzman 1978; Loftus & Loftus, 1976; Travers, 1982; Wickelgren, 1973). In the meantime, recent memory research has shifted away from a focus on the components of memory to a focus instead on how information is processed. The alternative views I present next are examples of such functional theories.

FUNCTIONAL THEORIES OF HUMAN MEMORY

At least two alternatives to the dual-store model of memory have been proposed: levels of processing and activation. These theories emphasize the cognitive processes involved in human memory rather than its structure. Let's look briefly at each theory.

Levels of Processing

The **levels of processing** model of human memory (Cermak & Craik, 1979; Craik & Lockhart, 1972) was the first major theoretical alternative to the dual-store model. According to this view, incoming information goes through a **central processor** at any one of a number of different levels of complexity. This central processor has a limited capacity, in that it can only hold so much at one time; the information temporarily held there is what we are aware of at any given time.

How long and how well information is remembered after it leaves the central processor depends on how thoroughly it is processed initially. Information that isn't processed at all leaves only a very brief impression (much as it does in the sensory register of the dual-store model). Information that is processed superficially, such that only surface characteristics (appearance, brightness, etc.) are attended to, may last a few seconds (much as it does in the dual-store model's working memory). Only when information undergoes deep processing—that is, when it is interpreted, understood, and related to previously learned information—do we remember it for any length of time.

An experiment by Turnure, Buium, and Thurlow (1976) illustrates how different levels of processing lead to different degrees of retention. Children 4 and 5 years old were given the task of remembering pairs of common objects (for example, remembering that *soap* and *jacket* go together). Children processed the information in one of five different ways, as follows:

1. *Labels*. They repeated the names of the objects.
2. *Sentence generation*. They made up sentences that included both objects in a pair.

3. *Sentence repetition*. They repeated experimenter-generated sentences that stated a relationship between the two objects (e.g., "The soap is hiding in the jacket").
4. *"What" question*. They answered a question about a relationship between the objects (e.g., "What is the soap doing in the jacket?").
5. *"Why" question*. They answered a question concerning why a particular relationship existed between the objects (e.g., "Why is the soap hiding in the jacket?").

In this experiment, children learned most effectively when they were forced to think about (i.e., process) a relationship between the objects: the question-answering conditions (Conditions 4 and 5) led to the greatest recall of the word pairs. Repeating a sentence that expressed such a relationship (Condition 3) led to some recall; presumably repetition promoted some processing of the association between each pair. Least effective for learning were the first two conditions. In the labeling condition (Condition 1), no relationship between objects was processed, and children in the sentence generation condition (Condition 2) often constructed sentences that did not effectively connect the two objects (e.g., "I have some soap and a jacket").

One element that frequently arises as important in learning is **intention to learn**: people who intend to learn something are more likely to learn and remember it than people who do not specifically try to learn that information. Proponents of the levels of processing model have argued that people process information more thoroughly when they are intending to learn it and that the depth of processing, rather than the intention to learn per se, affects the success of learning. In fact, research supports this point: When material is processed deeply, individuals will successfully learn it even when they are not specifically trying to learn that material (Postman, 1964). In other words, nonintentional learning (often called **incidental learning**) is just as effective as intentional learning if the degree of processing is equal in the two situations.

A study by Hyde and Jenkins (1969) provides an example of successful incidental learning due to deep processing. College students were shown a list of 24 words at a rate of one word every two seconds. Some students (a control group) were merely told to learn the words; thus, they would be intentionally learning the words. Different experimental groups received different instructions, as follows:

1. *Pleasantness rating*. Students were told to rate each word for its degree of pleasantness; for example, a word such as *love* might be rated as relatively pleasant, while *hate* might be rated as less pleasant.
2. *Counting letters*. Students were told to count the number of letters in each word.
3. *Counting letter E's*. Students were told to count the number of E's in each word.

At the same time, some of the students receiving each of the different instructions (intentional learning subjects) were told to learn the words as they went along. Other students (incidental learning subjects) were not told to learn the words.

The different tasks used in the Hyde and Jenkins study should lead to different levels of processing. In counting all the letters in a word or the number of E's, an individual needs to look only at the superficial characteristics of the word, not interpret the word's meaning; thus, a counting task should lead to relatively shallow processing. In rating a word's pleasantness, one must examine the word's meaning; hence, deeper, semantic processing of the word should result. Consistent with levels of processing theory, subjects who rated words for their pleasantness remembered more words than subjects who counted letters. More interesting, however, is the fact that incidental learning students who rated the words for their pleasantness generally remembered as many words as any of the intentional learning groups (in fact, they did better than the intentional counting groups). Here was a case where learning was facilitated simply by virtue of the fact that students had to focus on the underlying meaning of the material to be learned. Depth of processing, not intention to learn, was the critical factor affecting the degree of learning.

Despite such convincing evidence, weaknesses of the levels of processing model have begun to surface. Research has mounted to indicate that degree of learning is not always a function of the degree of processing in the way that the model predicts. For example, the more frequently information is repeated, the better it can be remembered *regardless* of the depth of processing it has undergone (Nelson, 1977). Even more damaging, however, is the finding that, in some cases, superficial processing actually leads to *better* recall than deeper processing. In an experiment by Morris, Bransford, and Franks (1977), college students were given a series of words and asked (1) whether each word fit appropriately into a sentence (a task involving "deep" semantic processing) or (2) whether the word rhymed with another word (a task involving "superficial" phonetic processing). Students recalled more words on an unexpected recall test when they had processed them semantically; however, they were more successful at identifying rhymes of the original words when they had processed them phonetically. Stein (1978) has reported similar results.

More recent thinking related to the levels of processing approach is that information processing is most effective not necessarily when it is semantic, but rather when it is *elaborative*—that is, when the learner adds information to the material to be learned in such a way that the new material is encoded more precisely, more meaningfully, and more completely (Craik & Tulving, 1975; Ellis & Hunt, 1983). We will examine the process of elaboration in more detail in the next chapter.

Memory Activation

Some psychologists (e.g., J. Anderson, 1983b, 1984, 1990; Collins & Loftus, 1975) have proposed that working and long-term memory are not separate com-

The author activates part
of her memory.

ponents but instead simply reflect different **activation** states of a single memory. According to this view, all information stored in memory is in either an active or inactive state. Information that is currently active, which may include both incoming information and information previously stored in memory, is the information that individuals are paying attention to and processing—information that I have previously described as being in working memory. As attention shifts, other pieces of information in memory become activated, and the previously activated information gradually becomes inactive. The bulk of the information stored in memory is in an inactive state, so that we are not consciously aware of it—this is information that I have previously described as being in long-term memory. The activation theory of memory is particularly useful in understanding how individuals retrieve information from long-term memory. Accordingly, we will encounter this theory again in Chapter 12.

Clearly, not all theorists agree about exactly how memory is structured or how it functions. However, they do agree about a number of general principles with regard to human memory. Before we conclude this chapter, let's turn our attention to those principles and their educational applications.

GENERAL PRINCIPLES OF MEMORY AND THEIR EDUCATIONAL IMPLICATIONS

Here are four general principles of memory that have particular relevance to educational practice.

•*Attention is essential for learning.* As we have seen, attention is considered to be the process through which information moves from the sensory register into working memory. Although there is no guarantee that attended-to information will be stored in long-term memory (it must be processed further for that to happen), information that is *not* attended to will clearly *not* be learned. Teachers must always keep in mind that students are going to learn information only when they are paying attention to it.

•*Working memory is the bottleneck in the human memory system.* Working memory can hold only so much information and can process it only so fast. Accordingly, getting information into long-term memory will be a slow process. Educators must remember this point in pacing their lectures and choosing their instructional materials. When too much information is presented too fast, students simply cannot store it all in long-term memory.

•*Memory is selective.* Because of the bottleneck nature of working memory, learners must continually make choices about what information to focus on and what information to ignore. The limited capacity of working memory to hold and process information is often forgotten by teachers, who load students up with more details than they can possibly remember (Calfee, 1981). In such situations, students will select the information that they think is probably most important, but, as many teachers well know, students are not always the best judges of what is important and what is not.

Details are often important means of illustrating, clarifying, and elaborating upon the main points of a lecture or textbook. In this sense, they are indispensable. At the same time, students need help sorting through essential and nonessential information so that they don't lose sight of the forest because of the trees.

•*The limited capacity of working memory is not necessarily a bad thing.* The working memory bottleneck forces learners to condense, organize, and synthesize the information they receive (e.g., Gagné & Driscoll, 1988). As you will discover in the following chapter, these processes are beneficial, since they enable students to store information in their long-term memories in an efficient, meaningful way.

SUMMARY

Currently the most prevalent view of human memory—a dual-store model that originated with a classic paper by Atkinson and Shiffrin in 1968—maintains that memory has three distinct components. The first component, the sensory register, holds virtually all the information that has been sensed for a very short period of time (a fraction of a second for visual information, two to four seconds for auditory information). If the information held in the sensory register is not processed in some fashion—at a minimum, by being paid attention to—it apparently disappears from memory.

Information that is attended to moves on to the second component, working memory (originally called short-term memory). This component is the mechanism in which a relatively small amount of information is actively processed;

hence, it is the "thinking" center of the memory system. Information stored in working memory lasts only about 5 to 20 seconds unless it is processed further; at that point, it too disappears.

Information that undergoes further processing (e.g., comprehension, organization, and integration with previously stored information) moves on to the third component—long-term memory. Long-term memory appears to have the capacity to hold a great deal of information for a relatively long period of time.

Theorists disagree as to whether working memory and long-term memory are really distinct entities, and research investigating this issue has yielded mixed results. At least two alternatives to the dual-store model have been proposed: a levels of processing model, in which information processed in depth is retained longer than information processed only superficially; and an activation model, in which the information stored in memory is either in an "active," conscious state or in an "inactive," unconscious state.

CHAPTER 11

Long-Term Memory I: Storage

A t least once a semester, a student will appear at my office door after receiving a low score on one of my exams. "But I studied so *hard*!" the student will whine, displaying a look of frustrated desperation. "I studied twice as long as my roommate did, yet my roommate only missed 1 question while I missed 17!"

Storing information in long-term memory and retrieving it later can be a tricky business. If the two roommates are equally motivated to achieve in my class, the difference between them may be due to their storage and retrieval processes. After more than a decade of talking with students about how they typically study, I have come to the conclusion that most students are sadly uninformed about how best to learn and remember information.

Even when students do store information in their long-term memories, they don't always learn what their teachers *think* they are learning. For example, when my daughter Tina was in fourth grade, she came home one day complaining about a song she was learning in the school choir. "It has bad words in it, Mom," she told me. I was quite surprised to learn that she was talking about "America the Beautiful," but then she recited the guilty line from the second verse:

All *the bastard cities gleam.*

After shuddering about the richness of my daughter's vocabulary, I patiently explained to her that the line in question was actually "Alabaster cities gleam." Two weeks later the rest of the family went to hear Tina's choir performing in concert. As the children began to sing "America the Beautiful," 6-year-old Alex turned to me and whispered, "Why are they singing about spaceship skies?"

Long-term memory provides a mechanism for storing information over a relatively long period of time. It also provides a knowledge base from which to interpret new information. As we shall see, the storage of incoming information in long-term memory is most effectively accomplished when that information can be related to what one already knows—that is, to information already residing in long-term memory. As a result, different individuals will store the same information differently because the information already stored in their respective long-term memories is different. Alex had never heard the word *spacious* before, but *spaceship* was a frequent word in his world of science fiction cartoons. Similarly, Tina was unfamiliar with *alabaster*, but . . . well, never mind.

In this chapter, we will explore the complicated process of storing information in long-term memory. We will begin by focusing on three aspects of storage—the variety of ways in which information may be encoded, the organization of that encoded information, and the specific cognitive processes involved in storage. Later in the chapter, we will find that working memory and current knowledge affect the nature of what is stored and that long-term memory storage is to some extent a constructive process. In the following chapter, we will look at the processes involved in retrieving information from long-term memory and at several possible reasons why some of that information may be forgotten.

ENCODING: HOW INFORMATION IS STORED IN LONG-TERM MEMORY

Take a minute and think about a rose. What things come to mind? Perhaps words like *flower*, *red*, *beautiful*, or *expensive* pop into your head. Perhaps you can picture what a rose looks like or imagine its smell. Perhaps you can even feel a thorn prick your finger as you reach out to clip a rose from its bush.

Information is probably encoded in long-term memory in a number of different ways. For one thing, it may be encoded *verbally*, represented in memory by words; for example, "Roses are red, violets are blue." Sometimes input is stored as an *image* that retains some of its physical characteristics; for example, a rose has a certain look and a particular smell. Input may also be represented as one or more *propositions*, such that its underlying abstract meaning is stored; for example, the fact that "A rose is a flower" may be stored as an abstract idea. Still another way in which information can be stored in long-term memory is *productions*—the procedures involved in performing a particular task. For example, one learns the procedure necessary for clipping a rose from a rose bush. These four forms of information storage—verbal codes, imagery, propositions, and productions—appear frequently in long-term memory theory, and so we will examine each of them in more detail.

Verbal Codes

There is no question that some information is stored in terms of words (e.g., Bower, 1972; Clark & Paivio, 1991; Paivio, 1971, 1986). First of all, people store verbal labels for most of the objects and events in their lives; for example, this thing you are reading is called a *book*. Secondly, people sometimes learn information in a verbatim fashion; Hamlet's soliloquy ("To be or not to be. . . .") and the Preamble to the U.S. Constitution are examples of things that we typically learn word for word (Rubin, 1977). On still other occasions people use language to help them associate things in memory. For example, the French word for "dog" is *chien*; I remember this word by thinking "dog chain." Many of the principles that emerged from verbal learning research (e.g., the serial learning curve) probably apply primarily to information stored in a verbal code.

Imagery

Can you imagine your mother's face? The melody of a favorite song? The smell of a rose? If so, then you are probably using mental imagery. Many psychologists believe that individuals store images in several modalities, including visual, auditory, and olfactory ("smelling"). However, research and theory have emphasized visual imagery, so that is what we will focus on here.

Introspective reports have frequently been cited as support for the existence of visual imagery: People often say that they see "pictures" in their minds. However, given an inherent weakness of introspection—the fact that people cannot always describe their own cognitive processes accurately (Nisbett & Wilson, 1977; Zuriff, 1985)—psychologists have devised other research methods for demonstrating the existence of visual imagery. An example resulted from an ingenious experiment by Shepard and Metzler (1971) involving pictures of three-dimensional block configurations similar to those shown in Figure 11–1. In this experiment, adult subjects compared pairs of these pictures and determined whether they represented the same three-dimensional configuration. For example, *a* and *b* in Figure 11–1 constitute a "match": if *b* were rotated 90 degrees clockwise, it would be identical to *a*. However, *a* and *c* are not a match: if *c* were rotated 90 degrees counterclockwise, it would be apparent that its top branch points in a different direction from that of *a*.

Shepard and Metzler measured subjects' reaction time to each pair of figures, assuming that more extensive cognitive processing would be reflected in longer reaction times. Results were quite dramatic: reaction times were almost totally a function of how much a figure would have to be rotated for it to be lined up with another figure. In other words, subjects were responding as if they were mentally "rotating" mental images: More rotation resulted in a longer reaction time. Similar results were obtained when subjects compared rotated letters (Cooper & Shepard, 1973).

Although at least one theorist has argued against the existence of visual imagery (Pylyshyn, 1973, 1979, 1981, 1984), most psychologists believe it is a distinct form of information storage (e.g., Bower, 1972; Clark & Paivio, 1991; Farah, Hammond, Levine, & Calvanio, 1988; Kosslyn, 1980, 1981, 1983; Paivio, 1971, 1986). The exact nature of visual imagery is still an open question, but one thing is clear: a visual image is probably *not* a mental snapshot. Visual images tend to be imprecise representations of external objects, with many details omitted or altered. Furthermore, individuals can construct mental images of things they have never seen; for example, you can probably visualize a rhinoceros with a pumpkin stuck on its horn even though you have never seen a rhino in that predicament.

Figure 11–1
Figures similar to those used by Shepard and Metzler (1971)

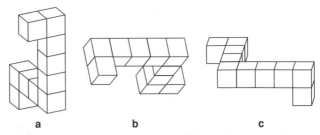

a   b   c

Adapted from "Mental Rotation of Three-dimensional Objects" by R. N. Shepard & J. Metzler, 1971, *Science, 171,* p. 702. Copyright 1971 by the American Association for the Advancement of Science. Adapted with permission.

Figure 11–2
Experimental stimuli and
examples of subjects'
reproductions

Original Stimuli   Examples of Reproductions

Adapted from "An Experimental Study of the Effect of Language on the Reproduction of Visually Perceived Form"
by L. Carmichael, H. P. Hogan, & A. A. Walters, 1932, *Journal of Experimental Psychology*, *15*, pp. 73–86.

Theorists are now beginning to think of imagery as being an *abstract analog* of visual input (e.g., Anderson, 1990; Glass, Holyoak, & Santa, 1979).

Regardless of its exact nature, psychologists have learned a couple of things about visual imagery that have implications for educators. First of all, imagery can be an extremely powerful means of storing information. Numerous studies have shown that people have a remarkably accurate memory for visual information (e.g., Bower, 1972; Mandler & Ritchey, 1977; Shepard, 1967; Standing, 1973; Standing, Conezio, & Haber, 1970). For example, in an experiment by Shepard (1967), college students looked at more than 600 pictures (color photos and illustrations from magazines), with an average inspection time of less than six seconds per picture. Subjects were then given pairs of dissimilar pictures and asked to identify which picture in each pair they had seen; subjects were able to do so with 98% accuracy. (Their accuracy on a similar task using words was only 88%.) Furthermore, images may be relatively enduring: In a study by Mandler and Ritchey (1977), subjects' memory for meaningfully organized pictures declined only slightly over a four-month period.

Another thing that psychologists have learned about visual imagery is that it does not always provide a complete, accurate representation of initial input. Images tend to be fuzzy and less detailed than the original environmental input (Anderson, 1990). They can also be distorted by an individual's general knowl-edge, as an early study by Carmichael, Hogan, and Walters (1932) illustrates. The experimenter asked adults to remember simple pictures like the ones shown on the left side of Figure 11–2. Two different groups of subjects received two differ-ent sets of labels for these pictures. Subjects tended to remember the pictures in ways that more closely fit the labels. For example, as you can see in Figure 11–2, the first picture was reproduced differently depending on whether it had been labeled as eyeglasses or dumbbells. Similarly, recall of the second picture reflected its identification as a kidney bean or a canoe.

Because images tend to be incomplete and inaccurate, they may not be help-ful when precise, detailed information must be stored. For example, many educa-tors have advocated the use of visual imagery in learning to spell (e.g., Harris, 1985; Hillerich, 1976; Radebaugh, 1985; Walker, 1974). Research by Roberts and

Ehri (1983) has provided some support for this practice. Although imagery may help spelling, however, we should remember that one's visual image of a word will not necessarily include *all* of its letters (Ormrod & Jenkins, 1988). To illustrate, my mental image of the word *silhouette*, until I looked it up in the dictionary just now, was something along these lines:

sil⧓⧓ette

I had an image of the word that was sufficient to recognize it when I read it but not sufficiently detailed for spelling it correctly.

Despite this drawback of visual imagery, its increased use in the classroom has been widely recommended. Visual images can be stored quickly and retained over long periods of time. Thus, students tend to learn more and remember it longer when the material they are studying is concrete and easily visualizable (Clark & Paivio, 1991; Mastropieri, Scruggs, McLoone, & Levin, 1985; Sadoski, Goetz, & Fritz, 1993; Thrailkill & Ormrod, 1994). They also benefit when pictures and diagrams are provided to support and supplement the ideas presented verbally (Clark & Paivio, 1991; Denis, 1984; Kulhavy, Lee, & Caterino, 1985; Kulhavy, Schwartz, & Shaha, 1983; Mayer, 1983a, 1989a; Small, Lovett, & Scher, 1993; Waddill, McDaniel, & Einstein, 1988; Wagner, 1989).

Encouraging students to form their own mental images of information can also be an effective instructional technique (Clark & Paivio, 1991). For example, when students are instructed to form visual images connecting object pairs, enhanced memory for those pairs results (e.g., Bower, 1972). Accordingly, imagery provides the foundation for a number of memory strategies called *mnemonics*, strategies that we will consider in Chapter 13.

Meanings and Propositions

People are more likely to remember the meaning of what they see or hear than precise, word-for-word detail. For example, think about the section you just read on imagery. What do you remember about it? You probably do not remember the specific words you read, but you should be able to recall the general ideas of the section. (If you can't, go back and read the section again!)

Many learning theorists (e.g., Anderson, 1976, 1983a, 1990; Ellis & Hunt, 1983; E. Gagné, 1985; Kintsch & van Dijk, 1978; van Dijk & Kintsch, 1983) believe that meanings are stored as **propositions**—that is, as small units of knowledge concerning relationships among objects or events. More specifically, to paraphrase John Anderson's (1990) definition, a proposition is the smallest unit of knowledge that (1) can stand as a separate statement or assertion and (2) can be judged as being either true or false. To illustrate, consider the following sentence:

Mary's uncle, whom she adores, owns a red Ferrari.

This complex sentence can be broken up into four smaller assertions, each containing part of its meaning:

1. Mary has an uncle.
2. Mary adores the uncle.
3. The uncle owns a Ferrari.
4. The Ferrari is red.

Each assertion is either true or false; if any one of them is false, then the entire sentence is false. The four assertions are rough verbal analogs of the abstract propositions that may be stored in memory when the sentence itself is encountered.

Any proposition has two components. First, it includes one or more **arguments**—objects or events that are the topics of the proposition. Second, it involves a single **relation**—a description of an argument or a relationship among two or more arguments. For example, the assertion "Mary has an uncle" contains two arguments ("Mary" and "uncle") and one relation ("has"). Arguments are usually reflected by nouns and pronouns in a sentence, whereas relations are more typically reflected by verbs, adjectives, and adverbs.

Propositions provide a theoretical model of how meanings are stored. It is becoming increasingly clear that a great deal of the information individuals receive is stored primarily in terms of underlying meanings. For example, subjects in research studies can often remember information verbatim if asked to do so immediately after that information has been presented. When recall is delayed, their ability to remember the exact input declines rapidly, yet they continue to remember its *meaning* fairly accurately (Brainerd & Reyna, 1992; Kintsch, 1977; Reder, 1982; Sachs, 1967).

Nonverbal visual information also appears to be stored at least partly in terms of meanings (e.g., Mandler & Johnson, 1976; Mandler & Parker, 1976; Mandler & Ritchey, 1977). An experiment by Mandler and Johnson (1976) illustrates this point well. In the experiment, college students looked at line drawings that included a number of different objects; for instance, one picture was a classroom scene that included a teacher, student, desk, bookshelf, flag, clock, globe, and large map. The students were then shown another set of pictures and asked whether each of the pictures was identical to a previous picture or had been changed in some way. Students were far likelier to notice changes in the pictures that reflected a change in the meaning (e.g., the teacher was talking about a child's drawing instead of a world map) than those that reflected a nonmeaningful change (e.g., the teacher's skirt and hairstyle were different).

According to Anderson (1990), the meaning of the information people receive endures far longer than either verbal or visual information. If this is so, then educators who are concerned that their students remember information over long periods of time should help students focus on the underlying meaning of that information. This idea of *meaningful learning* is one we will explore in considerable detail a little later in the chapter.

Productions

Up to this point, we have been talking about storing information related to "how things are." In other words, we have been talking about ways of storing what psychologists call **declarative knowledge**. But individuals have another kind of knowledge as well: They know "how to do things." For example, you probably know how to ride a bicycle, wrap a gift, and add the numbers 57 and 94. This other kind of knowledge—**procedural knowledge**—may be partly stored in terms of verbal codes, images, and propositions. However, to perform behaviors successfully, you must be able to adapt your behaviors to changing conditions. Codes that allow responsiveness to different situations are known as **productions** (e.g., Anderson, 1976, 1983a, 1987, 1990; E. Gagné, 1985).

Productions can best be described as a set of IF-THEN rules. For example, productions for riding a bicycle would include rules such as these:

1. IF I want to speed up, THEN I pedal at a faster rate.
2. IF I want to slow down, THEN I pedal at a slower rate.
3. IF my route turns to the right, THEN I turn the handlebars in a clockwise direction.
4. IF my route turns to the left, THEN I turn the handlebars in a counter-clockwise direction.
5. IF an object is directly in front of me, THEN I must turn either right or left.
6. IF I want to stop, THEN I squeeze the brakes on the handlebars.

Similarly, productions for adding two two-digit numbers would include these rules:

1. IF the digits in the "ones" column equal nine or less, THEN I write their sum in the "ones" column of the answer space.
2. IF the digits in the "ones" column equal ten or more, THEN I write the digit that appears in the "ones" column of that total in the "ones" column of the answer space and carry the "one" to the "tens" column of the problem.
3. IF the digits in the "tens" column equal nine or less, THEN I write their sum in the "tens" column of the answer space.
4. IF the digits in the "tens" column equal ten or more, THEN I write the digit that appears in the "ones" column of that total in the "tens" column of the answer space and write the "one" in the "hundreds" column of the answer space.

As you can see, the "IF" part of a production specifies the condition under which a particular behavior will occur, and the "THEN" part specifies what that behavior will be. Productions provide a means through which individuals can respond to different conditions in their environment. They are especially relevant to discussions of problem-solving; accordingly, we will encounter them in Chapter 16.

Any one of these four different codes—verbal codes, images, propositions, and productions—may be the form in which new information is encoded. Furthermore, the same information may be encoded simultaneously in two or more different ways. In support of this idea, college students in an experiment by Pezdek (1977) confused information they had seen in pictures with information they had read in sentences. For example, some subjects first saw a picture of a car parked by a tree, then read the sentence, "The car by the tree had ski racks on it." These subjects tended to recognize a picture of a car with ski racks as being one they had seen before, even though the original picture had not included a rack; hence, they were probably storing the same information in both visual and verbal form. Similarly, in the study by Carmichael et al. (1932) that I described earlier, subjects probably stored the stimulus figures both as images (e.g., two balls connected by a line) and as words (e.g., eyeglasses or dumbbells). In fact, the more ways in which information is stored, the likelier it is that the information will be retrieved when it is needed at a later time (Clark & Paivio, 1991; Kulhavy, Lee, & Caterino, 1985; Paivio, 1975).

When the same information is coded in different ways, those different codes are apparently associated in long-term memory. It also appears that different but related pieces of information are frequently stored in connection with one another. It is time now to look more closely at these interconnections—in other words, at the organization of long-term memory.

THE ORGANIZATION OF LONG-TERM MEMORY

Contemporary views of long-term memory are **associationistic**: They propose that pieces of information stored in long-term memory are associated, or connected, with one another. To show you what I mean, get a piece of paper and try this exercise. In just a minute, you will read a common, everyday word. As soon as you read it, write down the first word that comes into your head. Then write down the first word of which *that* word reminds you. Continue writing down the first word that each successive word brings to mind until you have a list of 10 words.

Ready? Here is the word to get your mind rolling:

beach

Once you have completed your list of 10 words, examine it carefully. It should give you an idea of what ideas are associated with what other ideas in your long-term memory.

Here is the list that I constructed using the same procedure and my own long-term memory:

sand
castle

king
queen
Elizabeth
England
London
theater
Hair
nude

Some of my associations might be similar to yours. For example, beach-sand and king-queen are common associates. Others might be unique to me. For instance, the last five items on my list reflect my trip to London many years ago when I attended a different play every night. The most memorable of the plays I saw was the musical *Hair*, in which several actors briefly appeared nude (quite shocking in 1969!).

Psychologists believe that virtually all pieces of information stored in long-term memory are directly or indirectly related to one another. Different individuals relate and organize their long-term memories somewhat idiosyncratically because their past experiences have been different. Nevertheless, the organizational schemes that people use may share some common features. At least three models of long-term memory organization have been proposed: the hierarchy, the propositional network, and parallel distributed processing.

Long-Term Memory as a Hierarchy

An early view of long-term memory organization was that information was stored in a hierarchical arrangement, with more general, superordinate information at the top of the hierarchy, and more specific, subordinate information below it (Ausubel, 1963, 1968; Ausubel & Robinson, 1969; Collins & Quillian, 1969, 1972). An example of such a hierarchy is my own knowledge of the animal kingdom, part of which is depicted in Figure 11–3. Notice how the most general category—animals—is at the top of the hierarchy. Next are two major categories of animals—vertebrates and invertebrates—followed by more and more subordinate categories, until finally specific instances of a category (Rin Tin Tin, Tippy, and Anna are all German Shepherds) are reached. As you can see, part of my hierarchy would resemble that of a biologist (my classes of vertebrates, for instance), but other parts are uniquely my own.

In a classic study, Collins and Quillian (1969) demonstrated how long-term memory might be organized hierarchically. Subjects were given a number of statements (e.g., "A canary can sing") and asked to indicate whether they were true or false; subjects' reaction times to verify or reject the statements were recorded. Here are some examples of true statements and approximate reaction times to them:

Statements About Category Membership	Reaction Times (msec)
A canary is a canary.	1000
A canary is a bird.	1160
A canary is an animal.	1240
Statements About Characteristics	**Reaction Times (msec)**
A canary can sing.	1300
A canary can fly.	1380
A canary has skin.	1470

Notice how the reaction times increased for the three sentences regarding category membership: Subjects most quickly verified that a canary is a canary and least quickly verified that a canary is an animal. Now notice the different reaction times for the three statements concerning a canary's characteristics: Subjects found the statement about singing easiest and that about having skin most difficult. Collins and Quillian argued that the two sets of sentences are actually parallel, because most people associate singing directly with canaries, while they associate flying with birds and having skin with animals.

Collins and Quillian suggested that an individual's knowledge about categories and category characteristics is arranged in a hierarchical fashion similar to what is depicted in Figure 11–4. To verify the statements, subjects had to locate the two components of the statement (e.g., "canary" and "skin") within their

Figure 11–3
The author's hierarchical knowledge of the animal kingdom

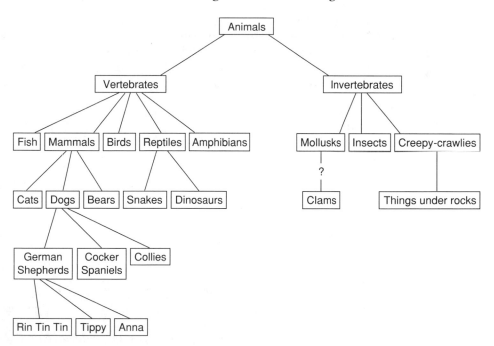

long-term memories and determine if they were associated, either directly or indirectly. The farther apart the two components were in the hierarchy, the longer it would take to verify a statement (hence, the longer the reaction times).

Strictly hierarchical models of long-term memory have been the object of considerable criticism (e.g., Bourne, Dominowski, Loftus, & Healy, 1986; Loftus & Loftus, 1976; Wingfield & Byrnes, 1981). First of all, information is not always hierarchical in nature. Second, predictions consistent with hierarchically arranged information are not always confirmed. For example, just as people verify that a canary is a bird faster than they verify that a canary is an animal, we should expect that people would agree with the statement "A collie is a mammal" faster than the statement "A collie is an animal," because *collie* is closer to *mammal* than it is to *animal* in a logical hierarchy of animals. Yet the opposite holds true: people more quickly agree that a collie is an animal than that it is a mammal (Rips, Shoben, & Smith, 1973).

At this point, it appears that some information in long-term memory may be arranged hierarchically but that most information is probably organized less systematically. An alternative view of long-term memory, the propositional network, may provide a more useful and flexible theoretical model.

Long-Term Memory as a Propositional Network

A **network** model portrays memory as consisting of many pieces of information interconnected through a variety of associations. To illustrate, let's return to my own previous list of successive associations resulting from the word *beach*: sand, castle, king, queen, Elizabeth, England, London, theater, *Hair*, nude. Such a list might have been generated from a long-term memory network such as the one in Figure 11–5. Different individuals should have networks with somewhat different associations and so should generate different lists. Some individuals, depending

Figure 11–4
A simplified version of the Collins and Quillian (1969) knowledge hierarchy

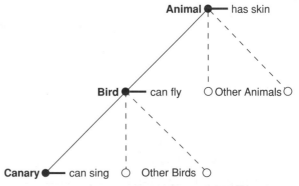

Source: Based on "Retrieval Time from Semantic Memory" by A. M. Collins & M. R. Quillian, 1969, *Journal of Verbal Learning and Verbal Behavior, 8,* 240–247.

Figure 11–5

A hypothetical network of information in long-term memory

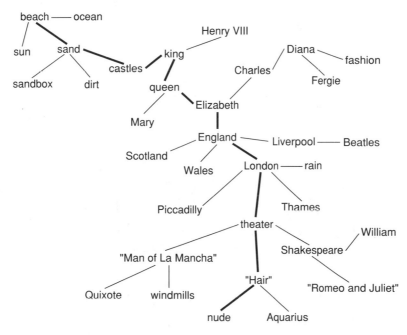

on their past experiences at the beach, might even associate beach and nude directly with each other!

Currently, the most popular model of long-term memory organization is the **propositional network** (e.g., Anderson, 1976, 1983a, 1983b, 1990; Anderson & Bower, 1973; E. Gagné, 1985; Lindsay & Norman, 1977; Norman & Rumelhart, 1975; Rumelhart, Lindsay, & Norman, 1972). A propositional network is one in which propositions and their interrelationships are stored in a networklike fashion. As an illustration, let's return to a sentence we considered earlier:

Mary's uncle, whom she adores, owns a red Ferrari.

and to the four assertions it contains:

1. Mary has an uncle.
2. Mary adores the uncle.
3. The uncle owns a Ferrari.
4. The Ferrari is red.

The four assertions can be diagrammed as propositions, as shown in Figure 11–6. These diagrams, using Anderson's (1990) symbols, each show a proposition (symbolized by an oval) that encompasses one relation and one or more arguments.

Figure 11–6
Diagrams of separate
propositions

1. Mary has an uncle.

2. Mary adores the uncle.

3. The uncle owns a Ferrari.

4. The Ferrari is red.

As you should notice, the four diagrams in Figure 11–6 share several objects, or arguments; in particular, Mary, uncle, and Ferrari each appear in two or more propositions. Such commonalities allow the propositions to be linked in a network; an example is shown in Figure 11–7. A propositional network model of long-term memory is obviously more flexible than a hierarchical model. A hierarchy includes only superordinate-subordinate relationships; a network, on the other hand, can easily include a wide variety of relationships (e.g., possession, location, opposition).

Network models are often conceptualized as including not only propositions (meanings), but other memory codes (such as imagery and productions) as well

Figure 11–7
A propositional network

Mary's uncle, whom she adores, owns a red Ferrari.

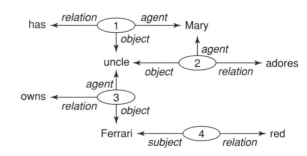

(E. Gagné, 1985; Glass et al., 1979; Paivio, 1971, 1986). For example, you might have a visual image of a Ferrari stored in association with the information about Mary's uncle and his red sportscar. Perhaps not too far away in the same network are productions related to how you drive a car.

Parallel Distributed Processing

Up to now, we have been speaking as if various items of information are each stored in a single "location" in long-term memory. However, some theorists believe that any given piece of information may actually be stored in *numerous* places, called **nodes**, throughout long-term memory. The nodes associated with each item are interconnected, so that when one is activated, the others become activated as well. At the same time, any single node may be associated with several pieces of information. Such a view of long-term memory is often called **parallel distributed processing** (PDP): Pieces of information are stored in a "distributed" fashion throughout long-term memory, with numerous nodes being processed simultaneously in a "parallel" fashion (e.g., Ackley, Hinton, & Sejnowski, 1985; Ballard, 1986; Hinton & Anderson, 1981; Hinton, McClelland, & Rumelhart, 1986; McClelland & Rumelhart, 1986; Rumelhart & McClelland, 1986). PDP is also known as **connectionism**, but should not be confused with Edward Thorndike's connectionism described in Chapter 2.

The parallel distributed processing model is still in the early stages of development, and it is not without its critics (e.g., Fodor & Pylyshyn, 1988; Holyoak, 1987; Lachter & Bever, 1988; Pinker & Prince, 1988). Nevertheless, the model provides a useful reminder that a single piece of information may in fact be stored in long-term memory in a multiple, "distributed" fashion, and that different pieces of information may overlap through the nodes they have in common.

Regardless of how long-term memory is organized, it clearly *is* organized. Furthermore, organization is a critical factor affecting how information is stored in long-term memory in the first place. Let's turn now to the topic of long-term memory storage processes.

STORAGE PROCESSES

Before we begin our discussion of long-term memory storage, try this exercise. Here is a short story entitled "The War of the Ghosts." Read it silently *one time only*, then cover the page and write down as much of the story as you can remember.

The War of the Ghosts

One night two young men from Egulac went down to the river to hunt seals, and while they were there it became foggy and calm. Then they heard war-cries, and they thought, "Maybe this is a war-party." They escaped to the shore, and hid behind a log. Now canoes came up, and they heard the noise of paddles, and saw one canoe coming up to them. There were five men in the canoe, and they said:

"What do you think? We wish to take you along. We are going up the river to make war on the people."

One of the young men said: "I have no arrows."

"Arrows are in the canoe," they said.

"I will not go along. I might be killed. My relatives do not know where I have gone. But you," he said, turning to the other, "may go with them."

So one of the young men went, but the other returned home.

And the warriors went on up the river to a town on the other side of Kalama. The people came down to the water, and they began to fight, and many were killed. But presently the young man heard one of the warriors say, "Quick, let us go home: that Indian has been hit." Now he thought: "Oh, they are ghosts." He did not feel sick, but they said he had been shot.

So the canoes went back to Egulac, and the young man went ashore to his house, and made a fire. And he told everybody and said, "Behold I accompanied the ghosts, and we went to fight. Many of our fellows were killed, and many of those who attacked us were killed. They said I was hit, and I did not feel sick."

He told it all, and then he became quiet. When the sun rose he fell down. Something black came out of his mouth. His face became contorted. The people jumped up and cried.

He was dead. (Bartlett, 1932, p. 65)

Now cover the story and write down everything you can remember of it.

Once you have finished, compare your reproduction with the original. What differences do you notice? Your reproduction is probably shorter than the original. Some details are almost certainly omitted. Perhaps you even added some things. But you probably maintained the gist of the story: You included its main ideas and events, mostly in their proper sequence.

Using this Native American ghost story, Frederic Bartlett (1932) conducted one of the earliest studies of the long-term memory of meaningful verbal information. Bartlett asked his students at Cambridge University to read the story two times, then to recall it at various times later on. Students' recalled stories differed from the actual story in a number of ways.

1. *The words themselves were changed.* In other words, recall was not verbatim.
2. *The gist of the story, including the major sequence of events, was usually retained.* Some details, especially ones that were either essential to the story or particularly striking, were retained. Unimportant details and meaningless information, however, were omitted. For example, such details as "something black came out of his mouth" and "he was dead"

were likely to be remembered; such details as "the young man . . . made a fire" and "a town on the other side of Kalama" were frequently forgotten.

3. *Parts of the story were distorted and other information was added to make the story more logical and consistent with English culture.* For example, people rarely go "to the river to hunt seals," because seals are salt water animals. Students might therefore say that the men went to the river to *fish*. Similarly, the supernatural element did not fit comfortably with the religious beliefs of most Cambridge students and was often altered. In the following recollection, written by a student six months after he had read the original story, several additions and distortions are evident:

Four men came down to the water. They were told to get into a boat and to take arms with them. They inquired, "What arms?" and were answered "Arms for battle." When they came to the battle-field they heard a great noise and shouting, and a voice said: "The black man is dead." And he was brought to the place where they were, and laid on the ground. And he foamed at the mouth. (Bartlett, 1932, pp. 71–72)

The main idea of the story—a battle—is retained. But after six months, the story has been so distorted that it is barely recognizable!

4. *There was a tendency to explain the story's events in addition to describing them.* For example, one student insisted on explaining events in parentheses:

The young man did not feel sick (i.e., wounded), but nevertheless they proceeded home (evidently the opposing forces were quite willing to stop fighting). (Bartlett, 1932, p. 86)

Bartlett's findings illustrate several general principles of long-term memory storage. First, individuals select some pieces of information to store and exclude others. Second, they are more likely to store underlying meanings (perhaps in the form of propositions) than verbatim input. Third, they use their existing knowledge about the world (i.e., things they have already stored in long-term memory) to help them understand new information. And, fourth, some of that existing knowledge may be added to the new information, such that what is learned may be more than, and perhaps different from, the information actually presented.

In this section, we will look at five processes related to long-term memory storage. We will first look at selection, the process of determining which information is stored and which is not. We will also examine rehearsal, a means of processing information in a relatively nonmeaningful, rote manner. We will then turn to three processes that involve encoding information in terms of its meanings: meaningful learning, internal organization, and elaboration.

Selection

As you learned in the previous chapter, working memory is a bottleneck in the human memory system: It can hold only a fraction of what enters the sensory register. Furthermore, information in working memory must undergo additional processing before being stored in long-term memory. Individuals must be extremely selective about the information they choose to process and must therefore have a means of determining what is important and what is not.

Long-term memory plays a critical role in selecting information for processing through the memory system. Individuals' knowledge about the world, their priorities, and their predictions about what environmental input is likely to be useful affect what they pay attention to and hence also affect what information moves from the sensory register into working memory (e.g., Schwartz & Reisberg, 1991; Voss & Schauble, 1992). A student who has learned that a teacher's lecture content will probably reappear on an upcoming exam is likely to pay attention to what the teacher is saying. A student who has learned that a teacher's exam questions solely reflect reading assignments or one who has decided that an active social life is more important than classroom achievement may instead attend to something more relevant—perhaps the flattering new hairstyle worn by the student on her right.

In some cases, once information has been attended to, it is automatically stored into long-term memory (Hasher & Zacks, 1984; Zacks, Hasher, & Hock, 1986). For example, consider this question: Which word occurs more frequently in English—*bacon* or *pastrami*? You probably had no difficulty answering correctly that *bacon* is the more frequent word. Hasher and Zacks (1984) found that people could easily answer such questions about the frequency of events even though they had never bothered to count them. Similarly, they could answer questions about the spatial and temporal locations of events without having intentionally processed such information.

However, more meaningful information apparently must be encoded as well as attended to if it is to be stored effectively in long-term memory. Such encoding takes time. For example, Simon (1974) has estimated that each new piece of information takes about 10 seconds to encode. Using this estimate and her own estimate that 30 new propositions may be presented in a minute of a typical classroom lecture, one theorist (E. Gagné, 1985) has estimated that students can only process six propositions per minute—*one fifth* of lecture content!

Given the capacity and time constraints of human memory, how can teachers help students select important information? An obvious way is simply to tell students what information is important and what is not; when students are told *not* to remember certain information, that information is less likely to go beyond working memory (Bjork, 1972). Another way is to build redundancy into lectures and instructional materials by repeating important points. For example, when I am presenting an important idea to my students, I typically present it several different times. I state the idea once and then state it again using different words. I then illustrate it with at least two examples (often as many as five), and I present the idea itself once again. Notice the redundancy in the last four sentences—it should have been very difficult not to process my meaning at least once!

Rehearsal

You should recall from the previous chapter that rehearsal provides a means of maintaining information indefinitely in working memory. Atkinson and Shiffrin (1971) proposed that rehearsal is also a method of storing information in long-term memory, and there is some evidence that they were right. Several studies have shown that individuals remember more-rehearsed items better than less-rehearsed ones (Nelson, 1977; Rundus, 1971; Rundus & Atkinson, 1971).

However, a number of theorists (e.g., Craik & Watkins, 1973; Klatzky, 1975; Watkins & Watkins, 1974), have argued that rehearsal only leads to storage in long-term memory if that rehearsal facilitates association of the new information with existing information. From their perspective, mere repetition of information—maintenance rehearsal—is sufficient to keep the information in working memory but *in*sufficient to move it into long-term memory. Rehearsal that makes the information more meaningful and easier to understand—**elaborative rehearsal**—does facilitate storage in long-term memory. For example, in a study by Craik and Watkins (1973), college students were asked to perform two tasks simultaneously: They had to keep one word in their working memories (by rehearsing it) while at the same time examining additional words to see if they met certain criteria. In this situation, the amount of rehearsal did *not* influence the extent to which the subjects were able to recall the words they had rehearsed; apparently the second task kept them busy enough that they were unable to make associations with the rehearsed words. However, when the additional words were presented at a slower rate, recall of the rehearsed words improved, presumably because the subjects could devote more working memory capacity to forming associations with those words.

Learning information primarily through repetition is sometimes called **rote learning** (e.g., Ausubel, Novak, & Hanesian, 1978; Ausubel & Robinson, 1969). In rote learning, there is little or no attempt to make the information meaningful or to understand it in terms of things one already knows. If such information is stored in long-term memory at all, it is stored unconnected to, and isolated from, other related information. As you will see in the following chapter, information stored in this unconnected fashion becomes difficult to retrieve.

So many times I have seen students engage in simple repetition as a means of trying to learn new information. This process, often referred to as "memorizing," emphasizes learning verbatim information rather than underlying meanings. Although young children (e.g., elementary school students) are especially likely to use this strategy when trying to learn new information (Cuvo, 1975), I have observed high school and college students using it as well. Teachers must help students understand that mere repetition is an inefficient means of storing information for the long run, if in fact it even works at all! The three processes we turn to now—meaningful learning, internal organization, and elaboration—are clearly more effective methods of long-term memory storage.

Meaningful Learning

Look at this list of 15 letters:

MAIGUWRSENNFLOD

And now look at this list:

MEANINGFULWORDS

Both lists are the same length, and both contain exactly the same letters. Which list is easier to learn? No doubt you will agree that the second list is easier, because you can relate it to words you already know. In the same way, my daughter Tina related a phrase from "America the Beautiful" to her existing knowledge about the world (which unfortunately included *bastard* but not *alabaster*), as did my son Alex, who heard *spaceship skies* instead of *spacious skies*. By relating new information to knowledge already stored in their long-term memories, people find a *meaning* in that information. Hence, this process is most frequently known as **meaningful learning**; it is also what we are referring to when we talk about understanding or comprehension.

We learn information meaningfully by storing it in long-term memory in association with similar, related pieces of information. Meaningful learning appears to facilitate both storage and retrieval: The information goes in more quickly and is remembered more easily (e.g., Ausubel et al., 1978). To illustrate, consider this passage from an experiment by Bransford and Johnson (1972):

> The procedure is actually quite simple. First you arrange things into different groups. Of course, one pile may be sufficient depending on how much there is to do. If you have to go somewhere else due to lack of facilities that is the next step, otherwise you are pretty well set. It is important not to overdo things. That is, it is better to do too few things at once than too many. In the short run this may not seem important, but complications can easily arise. A mistake can be expensive as well. At first the whole procedure will seem complicated. Soon, however, it will become just another facet of life. It is difficult to foresee any end to the necessity for this task in the immediate future, but then one never can tell. After the procedure is completed one arranges the materials into different groups again. Then they can be put into their appropriate places. Eventually they will be used once more and the whole cycle will then have to be repeated. However, that is part of life. (p. 722)

All the words in this passage were undoubtedly familiar to you, yet you may have had some difficulty understanding what you were reading. Because you did not know what the passage was about, you could not relate it to your existing long-term memory. But now try reading it again, this time thinking of it as a passage about washing clothes. Bransford and Johnson found that college students who knew the topic of the passage remembered twice as much as those who had no topic with which to connect things.

Individuals also store nonverbal material more easily when it has meaning to them. For example, in a study by Bower, Karlin, and Dueck (1975), students were asked to remember somewhat meaningless line drawings; examples of these "droodles" appear in Figure 11–8. Students who were given meaningful labels for such pictures, such as "a midget playing a trombone in a telephone booth" or "an early bird who caught a very strong worm" were more likely to remember them correctly a week later than students who weren't given such labels.

Relating new information to one's *self* can have a particularly dramatic effect on learning. This point was clearly illustrated in a study by Rogers, Kuiper, and Kirker (1977). College students received a list of 40 adjectives (some words were presented in large type and some in small type) and were asked to respond to one of four questions about each word. They were then unexpectedly asked to remember as many of the 40 adjectives as they could. Below are the four questions asked about different adjectives and the amount of incidental learning that resulted from answering each of them:

Question	Percent Recalled
1. Does it have big letters?	3%
2. Does it rhyme with _____?	7%
3. Does it mean the same as _____?	13%
4. Does it describe you?	30%

Figure 11–8
Droodles from Bower, Karlin, and Dueck (1975)

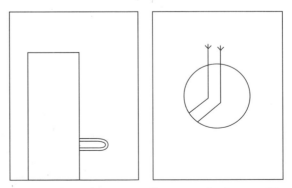

From "Comprehension and Memory for Pictures" by G. H. Bower, M. B. Karlin, and A. Dueck, 1975, *Memory and Cognition*, *3*, p. 217. Reprinted by permission of Psychonomic Society, Inc.

When subjects were required to relate the word to something they already knew (question 3), they remembered more than when they were asked to deal with superficial characteristics of the word (questions 1 and 2). But when they were asked to relate the word to themselves (question 4), incidental learning was more than *twice* what it was for meaningful but not self-related processing.

Exactly how does meaningful learning occur? Using a hierarchical model of long-term memory organization, Ausubel described the process as being one of **subsumption**, whereby people place new information under an appropriate superordinate category in their knowledge hierarchy (Ausubel, 1963, 1968; Ausubel et al., 1978; Ausubel & Robinson, 1969). For example, students are more likely to learn meaningful information about an animal known as a skink if they are told that it is "a kind of lizard that looks like a snake" than if they are told that it is "brightly colored" or "a shy, seldom-seen creature."

Using a propositional network model of long-term memory, meaningful learning can be characterized as a process of storing new propositions with related propositions in the network. For example, let's assume that you have already stored some propositions concerning Mary's uncle and his red Ferrari in a form similar to what I depicted earlier in Figure 11–7. You then read the following sentence:

> *The uncle is named Charles.*

You might connect this proposition to your existing propositions about the uncle and perhaps to propositions concerning another Charles that you know, as illustrated in Figure 11–9.

Because meaningful learning allows new information to be organized with previously learned information, it is sometimes referred to as **external organization** (e.g., E. Gagné, 1985). Another equally important process is the organiza-

Figure 11–9
Meaningful learning in a propositional network

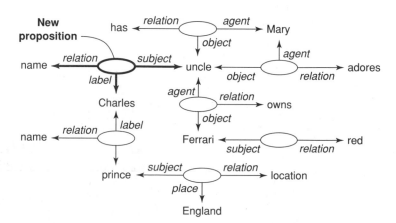

tion of a new body of information within itself—that is, **internal organization**. We turn to this process now.

Internal Organization

A body of new information to be learned is stored more effectively and remembered more completely when it is organized—in other words, when the various pieces are interconnected in some way. In fact, people seem to have a natural tendency to organize and integrate the information they receive. As an example, you may recall the Bransford and Franks (1971) study described in Chapter 8, in which you learned how "The ants in the kitchen ate the sweet jelly which was on the table."

You have undoubtedly had teachers whose lectures were unorganized, with one point following another in an unpredictable sequence. As you might expect, material that is presented in such an unorganized fashion is more difficult to learn than clearly organized material. An experiment by Bower and colleagues (Bower, Clark, Lesgold, & Winzenz, 1969) demonstrates just how significant internal organization can be. College students were given four study trials in which to learn 112 words that fell into four categories (e.g., minerals, plants, etc.). Some students had words arranged randomly, while other students had words arranged in four conceptual hierarchies (the minerals hierarchy in Figure 11–10 is an example). After one study trial, students who had studied the organized words could remember more than three times as many words as those who

Figure 11–10
Example of a conceptual hierarchy from Bower et al. (1969)

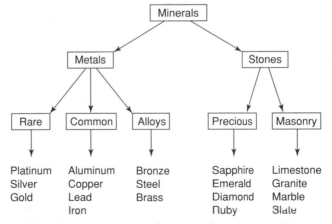

From "Hierarchical Retrieval Schemes in Recall of Categorized Word Lists" by G. H. Bower, M. C. Clark, A. M. Lesgold, & D. Winzenz, 1969, *Journal of Verbal Learning and Verbal Behavior, 8*, p. 324. Copyright 1969 by Academic Press. Reprinted by permission.

had studied the randomized words. After four study trials, the students in the organized group remembered all 112, while those in the random group remembered only 70.

Many good students organize information spontaneously as they learn it, and such student-generated organization can in fact be very effective (Buschke, 1977; Mandler & Pearlstone, 1966; McDaniel & Einstein, 1989; Tulving, 1962). Furthermore, providing students with specific organizational schemes can dramatically affect student learning and retrieval (DuBois, 1987; DuBois, Kiewra, & Fraley, 1988; Kiewra, DuBois, Christian, McShane, Meyerhoffer, & Roskelly, 1988). We will explore ways of facilitating students' organizational processes as we examine metacognition and study strategies in Chapter 15.

Elaboration

Suffering from cold symptoms? Consider this:

> Aren't you tired of sniffles and runny noses all winter? Tired of always feeling less than your best? Get through a whole winter without colds. Take Eradicold Pills as directed. (Harris, 1977, p. 605)

Do Eradicold Pills prevent colds? If you believe that they do, then you are the unwitting victim of **elaboration**: You added your own information to the passage you read and "learned" that information along with what you had actually read. In a study by Harris (1977), subjects who read the preceding passage asserted that Eradicold Pills prevented colds almost as frequently as those who read an explicit statement to that effect.

When individuals receive new information, they often use what they have already learned about the world to help them understand that information—that is, to learn it meaningfully. Sometimes the new information is incomplete: Missing pieces need to be filled in. When new information in some way reminds people of previously experienced events, then they are likely to impose and learn assumptions, interpretations, and inferences drawn from those previous events as well as the information itself. Elaboration, then, is a process of learning *more than the information actually presented.* I like to think of it as *learning between the lines.*

Numerous studies of elaboration lead to the same conclusion: People frequently elaborate on the information they receive and later have difficulty distinguishing between the actual "truth" and their elaborations of it (Bower, Black, & Turner, 1979; Graessner & Bower, 1990; Harris, 1977; Johnson, Bransford, & Solomon, 1973; Owens, Bower, & Black, 1979; Reder, 1982; Reder & Ross, 1983). To illustrate, here is a passage from an experiment by Owens et al. (1979). Read it *one time only:*

Nancy woke up feeling sick again and she wondered if she really were pregnant. How would she tell the professor she had been seeing? And the money was another problem.

Nancy went to the doctor. She arrived at the office and checked in with the receptionist. She went to see the nurse, who went through the usual procedures. Then Nancy stepped on the scale and the nurse recorded her weight. The doctor entered the room and examined the results. He smiled at Nancy and said, "Well, it seems my expectations have been confirmed." When the examination was finished, Nancy left the office. (Owens, Bower, & Black, 1979, pp. 185–186)

Did the doctor tell Nancy she was pregnant? The fact is, he did not. Yet in the study conducted by Owens and his colleagues, when students read the passage and then were asked a day later to recall information about it, they "remembered" considerably more than they had actually read. Many of their recalled elaborations were directly related to Nancy's suspected condition. Other students in the experiment read only the second paragraph of the passage, so were unaware that Nancy thought she was pregnant; these students added far fewer elaborations.

As may have been the case for you when you read about Eradicold Pills, elaboration sometimes leads to distortions and errors in what is learned. But most of the time, elaboration is a highly effective means of long-term memory storage: Elaborated information is typically learned and remembered far more easily than nonelaborated information (Anderson, 1990; Bobrow & Bower, 1969; Craik & Tulving, 1975; McDaniel & Einstein, 1989; Myers & Duffy, 1990; Pressley, 1982; Stein & Bransford, 1979; van der Broek, 1990). As Anderson (1990) has pointed out, most elaborations reflect correct assumptions and interpretations of an event, not incorrect ones.

Elaboration appears to be especially effective when it helps to tie new information together. For example, in studies by Stein, Bransford, and their colleagues (Stein & Bransford, 1979; Stein, Bransford, Franks, Owings, Vye, & McGraw, 1982), fifth graders and college students were instructed to learn a series of sentences. Each sentence involved a particular kind of man and a particular activity; here are some examples:

The fat man read the sign.
The hungry man got into the car.

The sentences were elaborated with phrases added on to them, elaborations generated either by the experimenters or by the subjects themselves. Some of the elaborative phrases (*precise* elaborations) explained the connection between a man's characteristic and his activity, like so:

The fat man read the sign warning about the thin ice.
The hungry man got into the car to go to the restaurant.

Other elaborative phrases (*imprecise* elaborations) did not tie the characteristic and activity together; here are some examples:

> *The fat man read the sign that was two feet high.*
> *The hungry man got into the car and drove away.*

Precise elaborations were much more effective than imprecise ones in helping subjects learn the sentences.

Elaboration probably facilitates long-term memory for several reasons. First, elaborated information is less likely to be confused with other, similar information stored in long-term memory (Ellis & Hunt, 1983). Second, elaboration provides additional means through which the information can later be retrieved (Anderson, 1990); in a sense, it provides more places to "look" for the information. And third, elaboration may help with inferences about what the information was *likely* to have been when the information itself cannot be accurately recalled (Anderson, 1990).

I suspect that many students try to learn information strictly at face value, without trying to understand it, organize it, or elaborate upon it. (Perhaps teachers' frequent overreliance on tests that measure verbatim knowledge encourages such an ineffective approach to learning.) Students should instead develop study strategies that use meaningful learning, internal organization, and elaboration processes. For instance, they can state ideas in their own words, generate their own examples of ideas, make connections between new concepts and their own past experiences, and draw logical inferences from the data they receive. As we will discover in Chapter 15, students don't always know how best to learn and stand to benefit from specific instruction in studying techniques.

FACTORS AFFECTING LONG-TERM MEMORY STORAGE

As we have seen, long-term memory storage is most likely to be effective when new material has numerous connections to existing knowledge. Such connections occur in working memory, the "processing" component of the memory system. And naturally, the kinds of connections and elaborations that learners are likely to make depend to some extent on the specific information—correct or incorrect—that they already possess. Let's take a closer look at three influential factors in long-term memory storage: working memory, prior knowledge, and misconceptions.

Working Memory

To make a connection between a new piece of information and a piece of information that they already possess, learners must be *aware* of the relationship between the two (Ausubel, 1963, 1968; Ausubel & Robinson, 1969). Therefore, the connection will be made only when the new information and any relevant prior knowledge are in working memory at the same time (Bellezza, 1986; Daneman, 1987; Gagné & Driscoll, 1988; Glanzer & Nolan, 1986; Kintsch & van Dijk, 1978).

An experiment by Hayes-Roth and Thorndyke (1979) illustrates this principle. In this experiment, students read one of two passages describing a fictional country; the same pieces of information appeared in both passages, but in a different order. (In one passage, related pieces of information appeared in sequential sentences, while in the other, they appeared in separate paragraphs.) Students more frequently made the connection between the two related pieces of information (and thus could draw an inference from them) when those pieces of information were presented one right after the other, presumably because they were more likely to be stored in working memory at the same time.

Certainly, though, learners don't *have* to experience two things in sequence to make connections between them. In many cases, new information reminds them of something they already know, leading them to retrieve that knowledge to working memory. In other cases, a wise teacher might point out the relationships between the new information and previously learned material, thus encouraging retrieval of relevant ideas.

Prior Knowledge

Storage processes such as meaningful learning and elaboration can occur only to the extent that learners have existing knowledge to which they can connect new material. Thus, one of the most important factors affecting long-term memory storage is what an individual *already knows* (Ausubel et al., 1978). Individuals who have a large body of information already stored in long-term memory have more ideas to which they can relate their new experiences and so can more easily learn at a meaningful level. Individuals who lack relevant knowledge must resort to inefficient rote-learning strategies. To put it bluntly, the rich (in knowledge) get richer, and the poor stay relatively poor. (This may be one reason that older children and adults usually learn most things more quickly than younger children: They have more prior knowledge from which they can draw [e.g., Kail, 1990].)

Numerous studies have illustrated the importance of previous knowledge for learning new information (Chase & Simon, 1973; Chiesi, Spilich, & Voss, 1979; Dole, Duffy, Roehler, & Pearson, 1991; Gauntt, 1991; Hall, 1989; Novak & Musonda, 1991; Ormrod, Ormrod, Wagner, & McCallin, 1988; Saxe, 1988; Schneider, 1993; Spilich, Vesonder, Chiesi, & Voss, 1979). For example, some of my colleagues and I once conducted a study of how well people from different disciplines learn and remember maps (Ormrod et al., 1988). We asked faculty members and students in three disciplines—geography, sociology, and education—to study two maps and then reproduce them from memory. The first of these maps, shown in Figure 11–11, depicts a city arranged in accordance with usual "city-like" patterns—that is, its arrangement is *logical*. Notice how the downtown business district can be easily reached from different directions (this is typical), and the mills, lumberyard, and low-income housing are situated near the railroad tracks (also typical). The second map, shown in Figure 11–12, is on a larger scale and depicts several political regions (countries, perhaps). Several things about this map make no sense—that is, its arrangement is *illogical*. Notice how a river originates in the plains and runs *up* into the mountains, transportation networks do not interconnect, and towns are not located at transportation junctions. My colleagues and I predicted that geographers would remember more of the logical city map than either sociologists or educators because they could use their knowledge of typical urban patterns to learn the map meaningfully. We also predicted that the geographers would have no advantage over the other disciplines on the illogical "countries" map because geographic principles were largely inapplicable in making sense out of the map. The results confirmed our predictions: Geographers showed better recall than the other two groups for the

Figure 11–11
The logical city map from Ormrod et al. (1988)

Reprinted from "Reconceptualizing Map Learning" by J. E. Ormrod, R. K. Ormrod, E. D. Wagner, & R. C. McCallin, 1988, *American Journal of Psychology*, *101*, p. 428. Reprinted with permission of the University of Illinois Press.

Figure 11–12
The illogical country map from Ormrod et al. (1988)

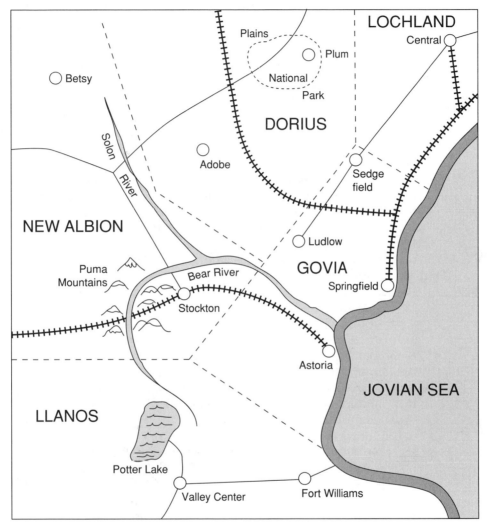

Reprinted from "Reconceptualizing Map Learning" by J. E. Ormrod, R. K. Ormrod, E. D. Wagner, & R. C. McCallin, 1988, *American Journal of Psychology*, *101*, p. 429. Reprinted with permission of the University of Illinois Press.

logical city map but not for the illogical countries map. Because we had asked our subjects to "think aloud" as they studied the maps, we were also able to examine the strategies they employed; as we expected, the geographers learned the maps more meaningfully than the other groups, and all three groups learned the city map more meaningfully than the countries map. Our nongeographers used primarily rote learning strategies, mostly in the form of simple repetition.

Other studies have yielded similar results. For example, children who know a lot about spiders remember more from a reading passage about spiders than do children who initially know very little (Pearson, Hansen, & Gordon, 1979). People who know a lot about baseball can remember more about the specific events of a baseball game than people relatively uninformed about the sport (Spilich et al., 1979). Experts at the game of chess can remember the locations of pieces on a chessboard more accurately than chess novices, but only when the placement of pieces is logical within the framework of an actual game (Chase & Simon, 1973; deGroot, 1965). Second graders in Brazil who have experience as street vendors learn basic arithmetic more easily than students without street-vending experience (Saxe, 1988).

Schemas and Scripts

The terms *schema* and *script* provide a useful way to understand how prior knowledge may affect new learning. As you should recall from Chapter 8, Jean Piaget used the concept of schema to refer to a mental unit representing a class of similar actions or thoughts. More recently, psychologists have been using the same term in a somewhat different sense. In contemporary cognitive theory, the term **schema** usually refers to an organized body of knowledge about a specific topic (Anderson, 1990; Bartlett, 1932; Bem, 1981; Martin & Halverson, 1981; Posner, 1978; Rumelhart & Ortony, 1977).

To illustrate, suppose you went to see a faculty member at your university. What objects would you expect to find in that faculty member's office? Probably at least a desk, a chair, shelves, and books. Your schema of a faculty office might then color your later memory of what the office was actually like. In a study by Brewer and Treyens (1981), 30 students were brought, one at a time, to a room they believed to be the experimenter's office. After waiting in the office for less than a minute, they were taken to another room and asked to write down everything they could remember about the room. Most students correctly remembered things that one would expect to find in an office (e.g., a desk, a chair, and shelves). Relatively few of them remembered items not likely to be part of an office schema (e.g., a skull, a clown-shaped light switch, and a tennis racket). And 9 of the 30 "remembered" books that hadn't actually been there at all!

People often form schemas about events as well as objects; such event schemas are sometimes called **scripts** (e.g., Bower et al., 1979; Schank, 1975; Schank & Abelson, 1977). For example, what things usually happen when people go to a doctor's office? In a study by Bower et al. (1979), most individuals agreed that this series of activities is typical of a visit to the doctor:

They check in with the receptionist.
They sit down.
They read a magazine.
The nurse performs tests.
The doctor examines them.
They leave the office.

An individual's mental script of an event will influence what information is "learned" from a given instance of that event. For example, in another study by Bower et al. (1979), college students read this passage:

> John was feeling bad today so he decided to go see the family doctor. He checked in with the doctor's receptionist, and then looked through several medical magazines that were on the table by his chair. Finally the nurse came and asked him to take off his clothes. The doctor was very nice to him. He eventually prescribed some pills for John. Then John left the doctor's office and headed home. (p. 190)

The students in the experiment "remembered" reading about many activities that were likely to be part of a visit to the doctor (e.g., arriving at the doctor's office) but that they had in fact *not* read.

Other research provides further support for the idea that schemas and scripts influence how learners process and store new information. To illustrate, students (especially those with stereotypical schemas about how males and females behave) more accurately remember pictures and films that portray men and women behaving in a stereotypical manner (Cordua, McGraw, & Drabman, 1979; Signorella & Liben, 1984). They also have an easier time remembering events consistent with their own culture (Lipson, 1983; Reynolds, Taylor, Steffensen, Shirey, & Anderson, 1982; Steffensen, Joag-Dev, & Anderson, 1979).

Remember, the human memory system typically encounters more information than it can possibly handle. Schemas and scripts provide a means for reducing this information overload: They help people focus their attention on information that is likely to be important and to ignore what is probably unimportant (Martin & Halverson, 1981; Posner, 1978; West, Farmer, & Wolff, 1991; Wilson & Anderson, 1986). For example, when going to see the doctor, it is more important that you check in with the receptionist than that you attend to the style of clothing worn by other people in the waiting room. Schemas also enable people to make sense out of an incomplete set of information (R. Anderson, 1984; Martin & Halverson, 1981; Mayer, 1992; Posner, 1978; Rumelhart & Ortony, 1977; Wilson & Anderson, 1986). For example, if you hear someone describe an experience at the doctor's office, you can assume that the person entered the examination room, even if that statement is not explicitly stated. In the previous passage about John visiting the doctor's office, it is highly unlikely that the nurse asked John to take off his clothes in the waiting room, although that is in fact what the passage implies!

Because everyone has somewhat different knowledge about the world, people are likely to elaborate on the same information in different ways and, as a result, learn different things. For example, how would you interpret this newspaper headline (from Leinhardt, 1992)?

VIKINGS CREAM DOLPHINS

Your interpretation might depend on whether you're more attuned to American football or to possible early Scandinavian cuisine (Leinhardt, 1992). And consider the following passage from a study conducted by Anderson, Reynolds, Schallert, and Goetz (1977):

> Rocky slowly got up from the mat, planning his escape. He hesitated a moment and thought. Things were not going well. What bothered him most was being held, especially since the charge against him had been weak. He considered his present situation. The lock that held him was strong but he thought he could break it. He knew, however, that his timing would have to be perfect. Rocky was aware that it was because of his early roughness that he had been penalized so severely—much too severely from his point of view. The situation was becoming frustrating; the pressure had been grinding on him for too long. He was being ridden unmercifully. Rocky was getting angry now. He felt he was ready to make his move. He knew that his success or failure would depend on what he did in the next few seconds. (p. 372)

Is this story about a wrestling match? Or is it about a prison escape? Read the passage again, and you should notice that it could be about either one. Anderson and his colleagues found that students' interpretations of the story depended on their background: Physical education majors more frequently viewed it as a wrestling match, while music education majors (most of whom had little or no knowledge of wrestling) were more likely to interpret it as a prison escape. Obviously, people elaborate the same information in different ways depending on their previous experience.

Misconceptions

As we noted earlier, elaboration typically facilitates people's learning and retention of new information. But what happens when people use inaccurate "knowledge" to elaborate? If new information is clearly "wrong" within the context of what people believe about the world, they may sometimes ignore the information altogether. In other situations, they may change the information to be consistent with their "knowledge"; as a result, they learn something *other* than what was actually presented to them (Alexander & Judy, 1988; Bishop & Anderson, 1990; Dole et al., 1991; Lipson, 1982, 1985; Nussbaum, 1985; Roth & Anderson, 1988; Sneider & Pulos, 1983).

We saw one instance of such *mis*learning in Bartlett's (1932) study: Many students distorted "The War of the Ghosts" to make it consistent with English culture. A study by Eaton, Anderson, and Smith (1984) provides another example. Fifth-graders spent several weeks studying a unit on light in their science curriculum. A pretest had shown that many students had a particular misconception about light: They believed that people see things because the light shines on them and makes them brighter. The unit presented the correct explanation of human sight: Light reflecting off objects and traveling to the eye allows people to see those objects. Yet despite their reading and hearing this information, most students retained their misconceptions about vision in a test given at the end of the unit. Only 24% to 30% of them correctly indicated in their answers that light must travel not only from the light source to the object but also from the object to the eye.

Similar results have been reported by Champagne, Klopfer, and Gunstone (1982) for students studying physics. Many children have misconceptions about basic principles of physics that then interfere with their learning in a physics class. To illustrate, a misconception held by many students is that objects float on water because they are light rather than heavy, when in fact an object's *relative* weight, compared to water of equal volume, determines whether the object floats or sinks. Even when students correctly recite physics principles, they may continue to apply their earlier misconceptions when asked to explain real-world situations (Champagne et al., 1982). Hence, a student may accurately use the relative weight principle in describing how objects float on water yet have difficulty using that principle to explain why a heavy metal battleship doesn't immediately sink to the bottom of the ocean.

We see cases of distortion even at the college level (Bishop & Anderson, 1990; Brown & Campione, in press; Holt-Reynolds, 1992). For example, students in teacher education programs may disregard a professor's definition of a concept, instead using their own (perhaps erroneous) understanding of what that concept means. And they are likely to ignore any recommendations for teaching practice that are inconsistent with their own beliefs about what "good teaching" is (Holt-Reynolds, 1992). Some of my own undergraduate teacher education students behave exactly as Holt-Reynolds has described. For example, they sometimes stick to their existing definitions of such words as *egocentrism*, *maturation*, and *elaboration*, even though I point out quite emphatically that a psychologist defines these words differently than a lay person does. And, despite the evidence I present on the effectiveness of meaningful learning, some of them stubbornly continue to believe that rote learning is a better approach.

While people have a fairly easy time learning information consistent with their existing schemas, they have a difficult time learning information accurately when it conflicts with those schemas. For example, when adults behave in ways that are inconsistent with traditional gender stereotypes, children frequently remember something different than what they have seen—for example, they may recall that a female doctor was actually a nurse (Cordua, McGraw, & Drabman, 1979; Martin & Halverson, 1981; Signorella & Liben, 1984). And, just as Bartlett found for college students, children are likely to distort the events they witness and read about in ways that reflect their own culture—for example, children in India may reinterpret what they read about an American wedding to be consistent with their knowledge of Indian weddings (Lipson, 1983; Reynolds et al., 1982; Steffensen et al., 1979).

Teachers often present information to students thinking that it will correct any erroneous beliefs that students may have. Unfortunately, what often happens instead is that students stubbornly stick to their preconceived notions about the

world and alter new information to fit those notions. Changing students' erroneous beliefs is therefore a difficult, although not impossible, task. I will present
some suggestions for changing students' misconceptions in Chapter 13's discussion of conceptual change.

CONSTRUCTION IN STORAGE

In Chapter 9, I described perception as a constructive process: People use the
sensations they receive to construct a perception of that event. Long-term memory storage is often constructive as well. Elaboration is a case in point: It involves
using both new information and one's existing knowledge about the world to
construct a meaningful interpretation of that new information. For example, if
you thought that Eradicold Pills prevent colds or that Nancy was pregnant, then
you constructed those conclusions yourself.

In recent years, an increasing number of learning theorists have begun to
acknowledge the role of construction in long-term memory storage (e.g., Bransford & Franks, 1971; Brophy, 1992; Chan, Burtis, Scardamalia, & Bereiter, 1992;
Di Vesta, 1987; Doyle, 1983; Hegland & Andre, 1992; Kulhavy, Peterson, &
Schwartz, 1986; Prawat, 1992; Spiro, 1980a, 1980b). For example, people construct meanings and mental images based on the things they read (Dole et al.,
1991; Tversky, 1991). And, with luck, they construct a general understanding of
mathematics from the various mathematical facts and procedures they acquire
(Resnick, 1989). This view that the learner constructs knowledge, rather than
simply acquiring it in some way from the environment, is known as **construc-
tivism**.

SOME FINAL REMARKS ABOUT
LONG-TERM MEMORY STORAGE

Before we leave our discussion of storage processes, we should note a few final
points about long-term memory storage.

•*Information tends to be stored in ways that are convenient rather than
logical.* Earlier in the chapter I mentioned a finding by Rips et al. (1973) that
people can verify that "A collie is an animal" more quickly than they can verify
that "A collie is a mammal." It is probably a more economical use of long-term
memory "space" that one remember that a collie is a mammal and that a mammal
is an animal; one can then easily infer that a collie must be an animal. Yet it
appears from these researchers' results that individuals store the fact that a collie
is an animal as well, a fact that is redundant with other knowledge in long-term
memory but probably convenient for the owner of that long-term memory.

•*Storage of new information may affect previously stored information as
well.* People do not always distort new material to fit their existing beliefs. In

some situations, a new piece of information may help them recognize that something stored earlier was inaccurate or that two other pieces of information are related in a way they have not previously recognized.

•*Long-term memory is idiosyncratic.* Any two people store different information from the same situation. First of all, they attend to different aspects of the situation, so that different information is placed in their working memories. Second, they encode that information differently; for example, some people use visual imagery more than others (Clark & Paivio, 1991; Riding & Calvey, 1981). And, third, they bring their own unique background experiences to the situation so that interpretations of what they observe are truly their own.

•*The way in which information is stored in long-term memory determines the ease with which it can be retrieved later.* Long-term memory storage and retrieval processes are closely related. In the next chapter, we will turn to the topic of long-term memory retrieval, including its relationship to storage processes.

SUMMARY

Information may be encoded in long-term memory in a number of different forms, including verbal codes, imagery, meanings (e.g., propositions), and productions. These various forms of encoding are clearly interconnected in long-term memory; theorists have proposed at least three models (a hierarchical model, a network model, and parallel distributed processing) regarding the nature of such interconnections.

Long-term memory storage entails at least five processes. *Selection* is the process of determining which information is eventually stored and which is not. *Rehearsal* is repeating something over and over again in a relatively meaningless (rote) fashion; its effectiveness in promoting long-term memory storage is questionable at best. *Meaningful learning* is connecting new material with similar ideas already stored in memory—in other words, making sense out of that material. *Internal organization* is the integration of various pieces of new information into a cohesive, interrelated whole. And *elaboration* involves imposing one's own previously acquired knowledge and beliefs on that information.

Existing knowledge usually promotes long-term memory storage when it is accurate; however, it may lead to distortions in learned information when it is incorrect. Presumably, new material is connected with existing knowledge only when both are in working memory at the same time. Many theorists now believe that long-term memory storage processes are constructive in nature.

CHAPTER 12

Long-Term Memory II: Retrieval, Forgetting, and Classroom Practice

Here are definitions of words in the English language. Can you identify the specific words to which they refer?

- The fluid part of blood
- A picture form of writing used in ancient Egypt
- A game whose object is to snap small plastic disks into a container
- A zigzag trim used to decorate clothing
- A small, hard-shelled, ocean-dwelling animal that attaches itself to rocks and ships

You probably identified some of these words almost without thinking. But there is a good chance that you could not retrieve all five instantaneously. For one or more of them, you may have found yourself looking around in your long-term memory, perhaps for a lengthy period, in "places" where a word might be located. (In case you could not retrieve all five words, they are *plasma*, *hiero-glyphics*, *tiddlywinks*, *rickrack*, and *barnacle*.)

Retrieving information from long-term memory is sometimes easy and automatic, at other times slow and strenuous, and at still other times virtually impossible. We tend to remember frequently used information without conscious effort; for instance, people usually retrieve the locations of their homes and the names of close friends with ease. Information that is seldom used, however, may be difficult to retrieve. For example, people often have trouble remembering rarely used words: They may even feel that the words are on the tip of their tongues, yet cannot recall them (Brown & McNeill, 1966). Similarly, people may experience difficulty in identifying people whom they have not seen recently or frequently (Yarmey, 1973).

In this chapter, we will look at how memory theorists believe retrieval works and at how retrieval is related to storage. We will examine the concept of retrieval cue, a type of hint that helps us locate desired information in long-term memory. We will find that retrieval sometimes involves a process of construction (just as perception and storage do) and that review and practice can facilitate retrieval over the long run. Later in the chapter, we will explore several explanations of why we are sometimes unable to retrieve the things we think we have learned—in other words, why we forget. Finally, we will apply principles of long-term memory storage and retrieval to classroom practice.

HOW RETRIEVAL WORKS

How easily something is retrieved from long-term memory depends on how well it was stored in the first place. Unlike working memory, which is apparently quite small, long-term memory is so large that an exhaustive exploration of it all is probably impossible. A search of long-term memory must therefore be selective and explore only certain sections (e.g., Hopkins & Atkinson, 1968). If the sought-after information is not stored in one of those sections, it will not be retrieved.

The organization of long-term memory affects the ease with which we retrieve information. To understand the role organization plays in retrieval, let's first look at an analogous situation—your great grandmother's attic. (I am going back three generations, because young families typically have homes without much attic space, and many grandparents seem to live in condominiums.) Granny probably kept many items in her attic, including furniture, books, old clothes, seldom used cooking utensils, and holiday decorations. Granny may have been a very organized woman, one who stored all the books in one place, all the clothes in another, and all the holiday decorations somewhere else. On the other hand, she may have been more haphazard, throwing things up there any old place, so that some cooking utensils were with books, others were with clothes, and still others were stuffed in an old dresser or on the top shelf of a dilapidated armoire. How Granny stored items in her attic undoubtedly affected her ability to find those items again. If she stored things systematically (e.g., books with books and cooking utensils with cooking utensils), she would have been able to find them easily when she needed them. But if she stored things in a helter-skelter fashion, she may have had to purchase new canning jars every summer because she couldn't locate her jars from any of the previous 13 years.

So it is with long-term memory. Retrieval is more effective when related pieces of information are stored in close association with one another, because the individual then has a good idea about where to find a certain piece of information. To illustrate, try answering this quick quiz item testing your memory of an earlier chapter:

What is a discriminative stimulus?

Organized long-term memory makes things easier to retrieve.

You may be able to answer the question quickly and easily, or you may have to search your long-term memory for a while. Your ability to retrieve the answer will depend partly on how well you have organized the information you acquired from previous chapters. The word *stimulus* should of course lead you to look among the information you have stored about behaviorist learning theories. The word *discriminative* might suggest that you look more specifically in your information about discrimination. If your knowledge about discrimination is stored with what you know about stimulus control (and it should be, because the two concepts are related), then you should find the answer to the question. A discriminative stimulus sets the occasion in which a response is reinforced.

Lindsay and Norman (1977) have characterized long-term memory retrieval as similar to looking for something in a large, dark room with just a small flashlight. Imagine that the electricity goes off in Granny's house on a dark, moonless night. Because Granny can no longer use either her electric can opener or her electric lights, she takes a flashlight up to the attic to find the manual can opener she stored there last October. She switches on her flashlight and begins her search. Unfortunately, the flashlight cannot illuminate the whole attic at once. Instead, she must aim the light first at one spot, then at another, until eventually she finds the can opener. The necessity to search the attic one spot at a time will not be a problem if Granny knows the exact location of the can opener (e.g., in a drawer with other small cooking utensils), but she may search all night without success if she has no idea where she might have put the thing. In much the same way, retrieval from long-term memory may be a process of looking in various small "locations" in memory, just one location at a time. Information that has been stored in a logical place (i.e., associated with similar ideas) will probably be found quickly. Information that has been stored haphazardly, in a rote-learning fashion, will turn up only after a great deal of searching or possibly not at all.

An experiment by Bower and Holyoak (1973) illustrates this dependence of retrieval on earlier storage. In this study, college students listened to a set of tape-recorded sounds and identified something that each sound might be (for example, chirping crickets or soldiers clumping down stairs). Two weeks later, they listened to a second set of sounds, including some of the sounds they had heard previously and some new sounds as well. Once again they were asked to identify what each sound might be and to indicate whether they had heard that exact sound during the first session. When students labeled a sound the same way in the second session as they had in the first session, they were likely to recognize the sound as being one they had heard before. When they labeled it in a different way in the two sessions (for example, once as a bouncing ball and once as a heartbeat), they were less likely to recognize it as being a familiar one. Other students, who had labels provided for them by the experimenter, showed similar results. By using a label they had used before, subjects apparently were more likely to search the part of long-term memory where the previous sound was stored.

You may recall the activation model of memory that I described in Chapter 10. According to this model, all information stored in memory is in either an active or an inactive state. Information in an active state is what we might think of as being in working memory, whereas inactive information is in long-term memory. The activation model lends itself particularly well to an understanding of how long-term memory retrieval might work. From this perspective, our starting point in long-term memory might be an idea that something in the environment triggers. Retrieval is then a process of **spreading activation**, with the activation flowing through connected propositions within the propositional network (e.g., Anderson, 1990; Collins & Loftus, 1975; E. Gagné, 1985). Only a small part of the network can be activated at once, thus accounting for the limited capacity ("flashlight" quality) of retrieval. If the activation eventually spreads to that part of the network in which the information is located—something more likely if similar ideas are closely associated in that network—the individual will retrieve the desired information.

We should note here that retrieval is typically easier when an individual is relaxed rather than anxious about retrieving information. To illustrate, think about what happens when you are looking for your car keys and are desperate to find them *immediately* because you are already late for an appointment. As you begin to panic, your search strategies become less and less efficient. You begin to look in the same places over and over again, rather than thinking creatively about the wide variety of places in which the keys might be lurking. So, too, does anxiety adversely affect retrieval: Long-term memory is not searched in an "open-minded" manner, reducing the chances of the desired information being found.

Retrieval is obviously easier when people know more or less where to look in their long-term memories—that is, when they know which part of long-term memory to activate. Therefore, hints about where to find a certain piece of information are helpful. It is to these hints—these **retrieval cues**—that we turn now.

RETRIEVAL CUES

Can you fill in the blank in this sentence from "The War of the Ghosts"?

The warriors went on up the river to a town on the other side of _____ .

See if you can remember the name of the town before you continue reading.

Any luck? If not, then perhaps you will recognize the town from among these four choices: (1) Bisantri, (2) Dormro, (3) Muckaruck, (4) Kalama. Is it any easier to fill in the blank now? It should be. I hope you have now identified (4) as the correct answer. In this question, I gave you a type of retrieval cue known as an **identity cue** (e.g., Bourne, Dominowski, Loftus, & Healy, 1986), because it was identical to the information you were trying to retrieve. Recognition tests, such as multiple choice, are often easier than recall tests (e.g., Semb, Ellis, & Araujo, 1993), presumably because of the identity cues recognition tests provide.

Now try this exercise. Read the list of 24 words below *one time only*. I will ask you to recall them as soon as you have finished.

tulip	pencil	spoon	bed	baker	ruby
hat	mountain	doctor	paper	daisy	shirt
chair	fork	diamond	canyon	knife	table
hill	soldier	rose	pen	shoe	emerald

Now that you have read all 24 words, cover the page and write as many of them as you can remember. Do not peek back at the list just yet.

If you cannot remember all 24, see if these words and phrases help you:

clothing	professions
eating utensils	writing supplies
gemstones	furniture
flowers	land forms

These category names should help you remember more of the words, because all of the 24 words fall into one of those categories. Such **associate cues** are related to the words you were searching for; as such, they should direct your search toward relevant parts of your long-term memory.

Still a third kind of retrieval cue is an organizational structure, or **frame**, that guides the retrieval process systematically through long-term memory (e.g., Calfee, 1981). For example, in the previous chapter I described an experiment by Bower and his colleagues (Bower, Clark, Lesgold, & Winzenz, 1969) in which presenting words in an organized format (e.g., the "minerals" hierarchy shown in Figure 11–10) rather than in a random order facilitated learning. The effectiveness of an organizational structure probably lies partly in the fact that it provides one or more retrieval cues (e.g., "Hmmm, now that I've remembered the rare and common metals, I need to remember the alloys").

Consider this sentence that science education students often tell me they use to remember the biological classification system:

King Philip comes over for good spaghetti.

The students use the first letter of each word in the sentence to help them remember these terms in their correct order: *kingdom*, *phylum*, *class*, *order*, *family*, *genus*, *species*. Each word in the sentence provides a retrieval cue—it limits the search of long-term memory to words that begin with a particular letter.

Retrieval cues definitely aid recall of information (e.g., Tulving & Thomson, 1973). They are likely to be most effective when they have been associated frequently with information an individual is trying to remember (Ellis & Hunt, 1983; Tulving, 1968, 1975; Tulving & Thomson, 1971; Underwood, 1983). For example, in retrieving the list of 24 words I gave you earlier, once you remembered *table*, you should have had little trouble remembering *chair* as well (or vice versa), because the two words often occur together in conversation.

The environmental context in which information was originally learned is likely to be stored in association with that information, a phenomenon that Tulving (1983) calls **encoding specificity**. Thus, being in that same environmental context can later serve as an effective retrieval cue: Retrieval is easier when conducted in the same place as the original learning (Godden & Baddeley, 1975; Smith, Glenberg, & Bjork, 1978). In an unusual demonstration of this principle, Godden and Baddeley (1975) had scuba divers learn 36 unrelated words in either of two environments: on shore or 20 feet below the water's surface. They were then asked to remember the words in either the same or a different environment. On a free recall task, the divers were able to recall more words when they were in the same environment in which they had learned the words than when they were in the other environment.

Although retrieval cues usually facilitate the recall of information, they can hinder it when they direct a person's search to a part of long-term memory *other* than that which holds the information. For example, in a study by Brown (1968), an experimental group of college students was given a list of 25 U.S. states to read, while a control group had no such list. Both groups were then asked to recall as many of the 50 states as they could. Compared to the control group, the experimental group remembered more of the states they had previously read, but *fewer* of the states they had not read. Thus, retrieval cues are helpful only to the extent that they direct an individual to that part of long-term memory containing the desired information.

CONSTRUCTION IN RETRIEVAL

Consider this passage used in an experiment by Sulin and Dooling (1974):

Carol Harris' Need for Professional Help

Carol Harris was a problem child from birth. She was wild, stubborn, and violent. By the time Carol turned eight, she was still unmanageable. Her parents were very concerned about her mental health. There was no good institution for her problem in her state. Her parents finally decided to take some action. They hired a private teacher for Carol.

Now cover the passage and answer this question: Did you read the statement, "She was deaf, dumb, and blind," anywhere in the passage?

You probably answered no to my question, just as subjects in Sulin and Dooling's study did. However, another group of subjects read the same passage, with one exception: The name Helen Keller was substituted for Carol Harris. Immediately after reading the passage, 20% of these subjects stated that the passage *had* included a statement about Helen being "deaf, dumb, and blind" (none of the subjects in the "Carol Harris" group made that mistake). One week later, the number asserting they had read such a statement rose to 50% for the "Helen Keller" group, but only to 5% for the "Carol Harris" group. In a follow-up study using the same passage, Dooling and Christiaansen (1977) found that subjects who read about Carol Harris, but who were told at recall a week later that the passage was really about Helen Keller, were also likely to "remember" the statement about her being "deaf, dumb, and blind." Apparently, the subjects in the two studies were using their prior knowledge about Helen Keller as well as their actual memory of what they had read at the time of retrieval. The longer the interval between storage and retrieval time, the greater the impact that prior knowledge had.

Results such as these indicate that long-term memory retrieval, like LTM storage, may involve constructive processes. Individuals often retrieve only a portion of the information that has previously been presented to them; on such occasions, they may fill in the holes in their memory based on what is logical or consistent with their existing schemas and knowledge about the world (Anderson, 1983a; R. Anderson, 1984; Halpern, 1985; Heit, 1993; Kolodner, 1985; Loftus, 1991; Neisser, 1981; Rumelhart & Ortony, 1977; Spiro, 1980a, 1980b; Wilson & Anderson, 1986).

Construction can occur in retrieval of nonverbal as well as verbal material. For example, in the previous chapter, I described research by Carmichael, Hogan, and Walters (1932), in which subjects' reproductions of line drawings reflected the labels (e.g., eyeglasses or dumbbells) assigned to them. The subjects probably remembered only parts of those drawings and filled in the rest based on what they knew about the objects that the labels identified. Another example of constructive retrieval of nonverbal material can be found in the recall of a crime one has witnessed. Eyewitness testimony is sometimes an inaccurate representation of what actually happened (Buckhout, 1974; Lindsay, 1993; Loftus, 1991, 1992; Wells & Loftus, 1984). People's descriptions of the crime may vary considerably, depending on prior knowledge about the individuals involved, expectations about what typically happens in such a situation, and additional information presented at a later time.

As an illustration of constructive processes in eyewitness retrieval, consider an experiment by Loftus and Palmer (1974). Subjects in five groups watched a film depicting a car accident, then individuals in each group were asked one of five questions about how fast the car was going. Subjects' estimates of the speed varied significantly, depending on how the question was worded (italics highlight the variations in wording):

Question Asked	Estimated Speed (mph)
About how fast were the cars going when they *contacted* each other?	31.8
About how fast were the cars going when they *hit* each other?	34.0
About how fast were the cars going when they *bumped* into each other?	38.1
About how fast were the cars going when they *collided* into each other?	39.3
About how fast were the cars going when they *smashed* into each other?	40.8

As you can see, the subjects' reconstructions of the accident were influenced to some extent by the severity of the crash implied by the questions that were asked.

The Loftus and Palmer study illustrates the **misinformation effect**: We see distortions in people's memory for an event when they subsequently receive inaccurate information about that event (Lindsay, 1993; Loftus, 1991, 1992; Neisser, 1981; Thelen, 1989). Apparently, people integrate the misinformation with the original knowledge of the event and may use the two in combination to reconstruct what "must" have happened.

Although constructive processes may be responsible for many errors in what people remember, construction more often facilitates long-term memory retrieval. When memory of an event is incomplete, an individual can fill in details based on what makes sense (Halpern, 1985; Kintsch, Mandel, & Kozminsky, 1977; Kolodner, 1985; Reder, 1982). A student may not immediately remember which general surrendered at Appomattox but can reason that, because the South lost the Civil War and General Robert E. Lee commanded the Southern troops, then it was probably General Lee who surrendered at Appomattox. A student trying to remember how to spell the word *ascertain* may surmise that, because the word is related in meaning to the word *certain*, it should be spelled similarly.

In some cases, retrieval is almost entirely constructive, requiring an individual to provide information that has never actually been stored. For example, consider this arithmetic problem:

$$1/2 \times 0 = ?$$

You may never have been given the answer to this specific problem, yet you no doubt learned long ago that anything times zero equals zero. Hence you are able to construct the correct answer:

$$1/2 \times 0 = 0$$

Constructive retrieval enables individuals to produce information beyond what they have specifically stored. At the same time, it must be recognized that such construction takes time (Anderson, 1985). In a study by Stazyk, Ashcraft, and Hamann (1982), students easily retrieved multiplication facts they had practiced many times over so that they quickly answered such problems as 2×3 and 4×6. On the other hand, they were slower to answer "zero" problems such as 2×0 and 0×6. Many students probably store a general rule for such problems (i.e., that anything times zero is zero) rather than specific answers to each problem and must therefore construct their answer from the rule each time such a problem is presented. When fast reaction times are essential (e.g., when numerous basic math facts are needed to solve complex problems), it is probably to a student's advantage to learn the specific information rather than a more general rule from which it can be deduced.

THE VALUE OF REPETITION AND REVIEW

In the preceding two chapters, we noted that rehearsal—repeating information over and over within the course of a few seconds or minutes—maintains it in working memory indefinitely but is a relatively ineffective way to promote long-term memory storage. On the other hand, repeating stored information at periodic intervals over the course of a few weeks, months, or years—for example, by occasionally reviewing or practicing that information—clearly promotes retrieval over the long run. This principle seems to hold true for people of all ages, even young infants (Anderson & Schooler, 1991; Bahrick, Bahrick, Bahrick, & Bahrick, 1993; Calfee, 1981; Linton, 1986; Rovee-Collier, 1993; West & Stanovich, 1991).

Things are more easily retrieved when many possible retrieval cues point in their direction—in other words, when they are connected to many other things in long-term memory. The more frequently information is used and practiced, the more pieces of information it will be associated with in long-term memory and the stronger those associations will be (e.g., Anderson, 1990; Calfee, 1981). In other words, practice makes perfect, at least in terms of retrieval.

Continued practice seems to have an additional advantage as well: it promotes automaticity in processing and retrieval, as we shall see now.

Automaticity

Walter Schneider and Richard Shiffrin (Schneider & Shiffrin, 1977; Shiffrin & Schneider, 1977) have distinguished between two types of information processing: controlled and automatic. **Controlled processing** requires much of an individual's attention and is likely to use most (possibly all) of the individual's working memory capacity. In other words, controlled processing requires conscious thought and effort. An example is the cognitive processing necessary for learning to drive a car. I still remember the summer evening in 1964 that my father tried to teach me to drive a standard shift in our 1951 Ford convertible. Trying to steer the car in the right direction while monitoring the speed and negotiating the stick shift and clutch pedal consumed all my attention and working memory capacity. In fact, my working memory must have been overflowing, because I kept forgetting to step on the clutch, thus jerking the car forward and almost catapulting my father into outer space. (Dad enrolled me in driver education the following morning.)

On the other hand, **automatic processing**, also known as **automaticity**, occurs with little or no conscious attention or effort and requires little working memory capacity; it is, in a sense, "thoughtless." For example, today, 30 years after that jerky start, I can drive with few mistakes and little thought. I do not have to remind myself to step on the clutch every time I want to shift gears or to remove my foot from the brake when I want to increase speed. Except under difficult conditions such as heavy traffic or inclement weather, I can make the hour's drive to Denver while drinking coffee, harmonizing with the radio, talking to a friend, or shouting at the kids to keep their hands to themselves. Even though I still drive with a standard transmission, driving is an automatic activity for me.

Controlled processes become increasingly automatic through repetition and practice (Anderson, 1983a, 1987; Cheng, 1985; Fisk, 1986; Norman, 1976; Piontkowski & Calfee, 1979; Schneider & Shiffrin, 1977; Shiffrin & Schneider, 1977). As I continued to drive that 1951 Ford, I not only became more proficient, I also devoted less and less mental effort to the task of driving itself. With several months of persistent practice, I was cruising Main Street with my friends, tapping my fingers to early Beatles' music on the radio, munching McDonald's fries (12 cents a bag in those days), and perusing the sidewalk for male classmates of particular interest.

As you should recall from Chapter 9, people can usually attend to only one demanding task—one task that requires conscious, controlled processing—at a time. On the other hand, they can probably attend to several tasks simultaneously when each of them involves only automatic processing. How many mental activities one can conduct at the same time, then, depends on how automatically one can perform each of them. Remember, working memory has a limited capacity; people can only perform as many activities simultaneously as that capacity will allow.

Many academic tasks, such as reading, writing, and mathematics, require performing a number of "subtasks" at more or less the same time. For successful performance of these tasks, some of the subtasks should probably be automatic (Lesgold, 1983; Perfetti, 1983; Resnick, 1989; Resnick & Johnson, 1988). Consider the case of reading as an example. Comprehending what one reads is often a difficult task involving controlled, conscious effort. If students are going to understand what they read, more basic reading processes, such as letter and word identification, must occur automatically. In fact, research is clear on this point: The more effort a student must devote to identifying the words on the page, the lower the student's comprehension of a passage is likely to be (LaBerge & Samuels, 1974; Perfetti & Hogaboam, 1975; Perfetti & Lesgold, 1979).

In research on the writing process, Birnbaum (1982) and Pianko (1979) found that good writers paid attention primarily to the communicative aspect of writing (expressing one's thoughts in a clear, logical, and organized fashion). Apparently, these individuals had already learned the mechanics of writing (e.g., spelling, grammar, punctuation) thoroughly enough to apply them automatically. Less skilled writers, on the other hand, paid more attention to mechanics and less to communicating their ideas. Poor writers may possibly become better writers through the automatization of the mechanical aspects of writing. They should be able to attend more carefully to the task of clear self-expression if they are not so bogged down in concerns about subject–verb agreement or the correct spelling of *psychology*.

Similarly, some aspects of mathematics—in particular, the basic math facts—need to become second nature (e.g., Gagné, 1983). For example, in my course on educational testing, students must be able to solve problems like this one before they can learn to interpret intelligence test (IQ) scores:

$$\frac{70 - 100}{15} = ?$$

To solve such a problem easily, my students must have certain arithmetic facts at their fingertips; in this case, they must be able to subtract 100 from 70 quickly and must automatically know that −30 divided by 15 equals −2. I have frequently observed that when my students must consciously and arduously calculate a simple arithmetic problem, they lose sight of the overall task they are trying to accomplish.

In the previous chapter, I emphasized the importance of meaningful learning: When students understand the information that they store in long-term memory, they can more easily retrieve it. At the same time, in the case of many basic skills, understanding is not enough, because these skills must be retrieved quickly and automatically. Such skills must be repeated and practiced, perhaps at a rote level, often enough that they become second nature and students can perform them essentially without thinking.

Learning information and skills to a level of automaticity is the most effective way of ensuring quick, easy retrieval of those things. We turn our attention now to explanations of why attempts at retrieval sometimes prove fruitless—in other words, to why we forget.

THEORIES OF FORGETTING

Over time, people remember less and less about the events they have experienced and the information they have learned (e.g., Wixted & Ebbesen, 1991). But forgetting is not necessarily a bad thing. Many of the things we learn on any particular occasion have little use to us later (especially *much* later), and we rarely need to remember things *exactly* as we originally experienced them (Anderson & Schooler, 1991; Schwartz & Reisberg, 1991).

As you should recall from Chapter 10, most information loss from the sensory register and working memory is believed to be due to decay and interference. Information is probably "forgotten" from long-term memory in a number of different ways. Let's look at seven possibilities: decay, obliterative subsumption, interference, failure to retrieve, repression, construction error, and failure to store.

Decay

Theorists disagree about the permanence of information stored in long-term memory (Loftus & Loftus, 1980). Some theorists believe that information, once stored in long-term memory, remains there permanently; they attribute information "loss" to such factors as interference or an inability to retrieve (Loftus & Loftus, 1980). Others, however, believe that information can fade, or **decay**, from long-term memory, particularly when that information is not used.

Some evidence indicates that information may indeed remain in long-term memory for a long time. For example, in a study by Bahrick (1984), individuals remembered a considerable amount of the Spanish they had learned in high school or college as many as 50 years before, even if they had not spoken Spanish since that time. Other evidence is found in experiments in which subjects *re*learn information they have previously learned but can no longer recall or recognize: These subjects nonetheless learn the information more quickly than subjects who have not previously learned the same material (Nelson, 1971, 1978).

The observations of neurosurgeon Wilder Penfield (e.g., Penfield, 1958, 1959; Penfield & Roberts, 1959) are widely cited as evidence for the permanence of long-term memory. Penfield sometimes operated on locally anesthetized but otherwise conscious patients. In doing so, he discovered that stimulating portions of the brain with a weak electric current could promote vivid sensations in his patients. Patients would describe hearing a song, delivering a baby, or going to a circus as if the experience were actually happening to them at that very moment. They acted almost as if they were reliving previous events in their lives.

Unfortunately, no conclusive evidence confirms the permanence of long-term memory: Research findings do not (and quite possibly *can*not) demonstrate that *all* information stored in long-term memory remains there for the life of the individual (e.g., Eysenck & Keane, 1990). Penfield's work has drawn additional criticism, because Penfield never determined whether the events his patients "remembered" had actually occurred. Ultimately, determining whether items in long-term memory are subject to decay over time may be an impossible task.

Obliterative Subsumption

A variation of the decay theory is Ausubel's notion of **obliterative subsumption** (Ausubel, 1963, 1968; Ausubel et al., 1978; Ausubel & Robinson, 1969). According to Ausubel, meaningful learning is a process of subsuming new pieces of information into long-term memory under more general, superordinate pieces of information. Over time, these specific pieces of information may be absorbed by their superordinates; in other words, they are *obliteratively subsumed*. For example, a teacher may present a general concept and then illustrate that concept with a number of examples; the student probably subsumes the examples under the concept. Over time, however, some of the examples may lose their distinctiveness from the concept itself and eventually blend in with the subsuming concept. At that point, the concept continues to be remembered, but the examples are forgotten.

As evidence for his theory, Ausubel has pointed out that general ideas are more likely to be remembered than specific details. Furthermore, details that are distinctive in some way are remembered, while less distinctive ones are forgotten or confused (e.g., Eysenck, 1979). To illustrate, when I think back to my early lessons in U.S. history, I remember the general idea behind the American Revolution: The colonists were fighting for independence from British rule. I also remember certain distinctive details: For example, the Battle of Bunker Hill is commemorated by a monument I visited frequently as a child, and the Boston Tea Party was a unique and colorful illustration of American dissatisfaction with British taxation policies. However, I have forgotten the details of many other events, because, to my young mind, they consisted of undistinctive people and places.

The notion of obliterative subsumption is certainly consistent with what we commonly observe to be true regarding the kinds of information we remember and the kinds of information we forget. However, as is true regarding decay theory, to date little evidence either supports or refutes its validity as a major, distinct factor in forgetting.

Interference

In Chapter 8, I described the phenomena of proactive and retroactive inhibition: In both situations, learning one set of verbal material interferes with the ability to recall another set. Verbal learning theorists (e.g., McGeoch, 1942; Melton & Irwin, 1940; Postman & Underwood, 1973; Underwood, 1948) proposed that such **interference** is a major cause of forgetting verbal information. In support of this idea, recall of word lists can be as high as 85% when sources of interference are removed from a serial learning task (Underwood, 1957).

Imagine that you need to learn a list of 20 words. You are then asked to learn another list of 20 more words. Now try to remember the first list. Learning the second list has probably made it more difficult to recall the first list; to some extent, you have forgotten which words are in which list! The interference theory of forgetting might best be described as a theory of confusion: An individual has learned numerous responses and gets them mixed up. Using more conventional behaviorist terminology, verbal learning theorists called this phenomenon **response competition** (e.g., Melton & Irwin, 1940).

An experiment by Anderson (1974) helps us place interference within a contemporary cognitive framework. Undergraduates learned a long list of propositions, each of which involved a person and a place; here are some examples:

A hippie is in the park.
A hippie is in the church.
A policeman is in the park.
A sailor is in the park.

The people and places appeared in varying numbers of propositions; some items (e.g., the policeman) appeared in only one proposition, whereas others (e.g., the park) appeared several times. The subjects studied the sentences until they knew them very well—more specifically, until they could respond to a long list of questions (e.g., "Who is in the park?" "Where are the hippies?") with 100% accuracy. At that point, they were given a new set of propositions and asked to indicate whether or not these had been among the previous set. The more frequently the person and the place had appeared in the previous set of propositions, the longer it took the subjects to determine whether the person and place had appeared *together* in that first set. Anderson (1974, 1976, 1983a, 1990) has explained these results as being a function of the numerous associations the subjects developed to the frequently appearing people and places. For example, the more frequently that certain places had been associated with *hippie* in the original set of propositions, the longer subjects would take to search among their associations with *hippie* to determine if a new proposition about a hippie had been among the previous set. Thus, multiple associations with a concept can slow down retrieval time for information connected with that concept, a phenomenon that Anderson calls the **fan effect**.

Interference is probably more relevant in forgetting rote-learned information than meaningfully learned information (Good & Brophy, 1986). Response competition and confusion are more likely to be a problem when associations between pieces of information are arbitrary rather than logical.

Failure to Retrieve

Inability to retrieve information clearly affects "forgetting" from long-term memory. The fact that an individual can have difficulty remembering a piece of information at one time yet remember it later indicates that the information did not disappear from memory but rather remained unfound when first sought.

Inability to retrieve is most likely to occur when an individual neglects to search that part of long-term memory storing the desired information. Given appropriate retrieval cues, the information may eventually be found (Tulving, 1975; Tulving & Psotka, 1971; Underwood, 1983).

Repression

Yet another explanation of forgetting is **repression**, a situation in which information is simply too painful or emotionally distressing to remember (a traumatic accident and an instance of child abuse are possible examples). Although repression was first proposed by Sigmund Freud (e.g., 1915/1957; 1922), several theorists have explained it within an information processing framework (Erdelyi, 1985; Erdelyi & Goldberg, 1979; Jones, 1993; Wegman, 1985). To describe repression in contemporary memory terminology, painful information begins to produce anxiety whenever the relevant part of long-term memory is approached.

Because anxiety itself is unpleasant, the memory search will tend to steer clear of the anxiety-arousing part of long-term memory. Thus, the painful memory, as well as any other information stored in close association with it, will remain forgotten.

Repression is reportedly quite common in clinical settings (Erdelyi, 1985; Erdelyi & Goldberg, 1979). Over a series of therapy sessions, a client gradually recalls bits and pieces of a traumatic incident and eventually, perhaps, remembers the entire event. Recalling the incident often relieves the symptoms for which the client has sought the therapist's assistance (Erdelyi & Goldberg, 1979). Unfortunately, however, many presumably repressed "memories" are never checked for accuracy; thus, they may or may not be based on something that actually occurred (Holmes, 1990; Loftus, 1993).

A few research studies support the existence of repression (e.g., Davis, 1987; Davis & Schwartz, 1987; Eriksen & Kuethe, 1956; Zeller, 1950), but overall the evidence is more spotty than that found in therapeutic settings. Repression is apparently difficult to create in the laboratory, leading at least one psychologist to question its existence (Holmes, 1974, 1990). It may be, however, that sufficiently traumatic events to bring about repression cannot easily or ethically be created in the laboratory, or that many adults simply do not repress painful information as a matter of course (Erdelyi, 1985; Jones, 1993). Until these various possibilities are investigated, theorists will undoubtedly have difficulty reaching consensus about the extent to which repression plays a role in human forgetting.

Construction Error

We have already seen how construction can lead to errors in recall. Construction may occur either at storage (learner-invented information is stored) or at retrieval (the learner "remembers" information that was never presented). Construction at retrieval time is particularly likely to occur when there are holes in the information retrieved—holes possibly due to decay, interference, or unsuccessful retrieval. So, as you might expect, erroneous reconstruction of an event or a body of learned information is especially likely to occur as time goes on (Anderson & Pichert, 1978; Dooling & Christiaansen, 1977; Spiro, 1977).

Failure to Store

A final explanation of "forgetting" is the fact that some information may never have been learned in the first place (e.g., Bourne et al., 1986; Ellis & Hunt, 1983). Perhaps you didn't pay attention to the information, so it never entered working memory. Or perhaps you didn't process it sufficiently to store it in long-term memory. Simply being in the right place at the right time does not mean that information will be assimilated by the memory system.

Probably all the explanations I have just described are partially responsible for the universal human problem of "forgetting." The problem is particularly evident in the classroom, where students often seem to lose information almost as soon as they have acquired it. I hope this chapter has given you some ideas on how to facilitate students' retrieval of information and how to minimize their forgetting.

To wrap up our discussion of long-term memory in this and the preceding chapter, let's look at some general principles likely to be useful in facilitating long-term memory storage and retrieval in classroom learning situations.

FACILITATING STORAGE AND RETRIEVAL IN THE CLASSROOM

As you discovered in Chapter 11, some ways of storing information in long-term memory are more productive than others. And as you have seen in this chapter, retrieval of that information, although sometimes easy and automatic, can on other occasions be slow, difficult, or even unsuccessful. Here are several general principles that teachers can use to help their students store and retrieve classroom material effectively.

•*Meaningful learning is more effective than rote learning.* As we have seen, meaningful learning—associating new information with things that have already been learned—promotes more effective storage and more successful retrieval than rote learning. Associative networks provide "routes" from one piece of information to another. The more routes to a particular piece of information, the more likely it is that the information will be discovered when it is needed.

Unfortunately, some educators seem to forget this basic principle. All too often, classroom instruction and testing methods emphasize the learning of classroom material at a verbatim level, with little or no regard for its underlying meaning (Dansereau, 1978; Doyle, 1983, 1986b; Fennema, Carpenter, & Peterson, 1989; Schoenfeld, 1985b). Many school textbooks are equally guilty, presenting lists of facts with few interrelationships between them and without regard to what students are likely to know (Beck & McKeown, 1988; Brown & Campione, in press; Calfee & Chambliss, 1988; Chambliss, Calfee, & Wong, 1990; McKeown & Beck, 1990). For example, Beck and McKeown (1988) examined a number of elementary school social studies textbooks and found them often lacking a meaningful presentation of concepts and events. Beck and McKeown illustrated their point by describing how four widely used history texts describe the events leading to the American Revolution. In these books, events are frequently described as isolated incidents (thus promoting a disorganized, rote learning of them) rather than as having any significant cause–effect relationships with one another or the revolution. Beck and McKeown argued that history texts should instead help students make sense of history; for example, the French and Indian War, the Boston Tea Party, and the Intolerable Acts all contributed to the colonists' eventual rebellion against Britain and should be learned within that context.

Perhaps as a result of instruction, assignments, and evaluation methods that downplay the importance of learning classroom subject matter in a meaningful fashion, students often engage in relatively ineffective, rote learning processes—processes that are, over the long run, unlikely to facilitate students' retrieval and use of the things they learn (Novak & Musonda, 1991; Perkins & Simmons, 1988; Prawat, 1989).

Let me list just a few of the countless possible ways in which teachers can promote meaningful learning. Among other things, teachers can show students how a new fact or procedure is similar to something students have previously learned. They can provide a series of reading assignments on a particular topic, in which each assignment builds on those that have preceded it (Beck, 1985; Wilson & Anderson, 1986). They can incorporate students' own backgrounds, both personal and cultural, into the topics being discussed in class (Garcia, 1992). They can use new material within the context of everyday activities and problems—for example, by using mapping skills to map the school or neighborhood or studying metric units as part of a cooking class (Brophy & Alleman, 1991; Reesink, 1984). And teachers should of course be sure that classroom tests and assignments emphasize the *meaning* of material rather than its word-for-word repetition.

•*Meaningful learning can occur only when the learner has relevant prior knowledge to which new material can be related.* Teaching subject matter that does not overlap with students' existing knowledge is likely to be a slow and, in the long run, futile effort. When students are observed processing material in a rote fashion (e.g., rehearsing it), they probably either lack the appropriate background knowledge for learning that material effectively (hence the need for identifying prerequisites in many cases) or are unaware that the material can in fact be understood in terms of that background knowledge. For example, history textbooks frequently refer to American distress over Britain's "taxation without representation" policy, without always providing an adequate explanation of why this policy was so upsetting to the colonists (Beck & McKeown, 1988; McKeown & Beck, 1990). Many adults can easily relate the idea of taxation without representation to their own frustrations with high taxes. Most fifth graders, however, have little if any experience upon which to draw in understanding the colonists' situation.

Whenever introducing a new topic, teachers must consider what related knowledge students already possess about the topic and begin instruction at that point. As an example, early mathematics instruction might build on the informal counting procedures children have developed on their own (Fennema et al., 1989). *Or,* when students seem to have almost no knowledge at all about a particular topic, teachers might create classroom experiences to which they can relate new concepts. For example, a teacher might introduce *taxation without representation* by conducting an activity in which students are told to give valued objects to fellow students (only temporarily) without regard for their own wishes in the matter.

•*The internal organization of a body of information facilitates its storage and retrieval.* When material is presented in an organized fashion—for example, when hierarchical structures, cause–effect relationships, and so on are clearly laid out—students are more likely to store it in a similar organizational network. And when information in long-term memory is organized, it can be more easily retrieved.

When students *don't* see the interconnections among the things they learn, they sometimes try to pull those things together in a constructive, perhaps creative—but often inaccurate—manner. Turning to U.S. history once again, here is what one fourth grader (apparently from Michigan) had to say about why the Americas were once called the New World:

> Because they used to live in England, the British, and they didn't know about . . . they wanted to get to China 'cause China had some things they wanted. They had some cups or whatever—no, they had furs. They had fur and stuff like that and they wanted to have a shorter way to get to China so they took it and they landed in Michigan, but it wasn't called Michigan. I think it was the British that landed in Michigan and they were there first and so they tried to claim that land, but it didn't work out for some reason so they took some furs and brought them back to Britain and they sold them, but they mostly wanted it for the furs. So then the English landed there and they claimed the land and they wanted to make it a state, and so they got it signed by the government or whoever, the big boss, then they were just starting to make it a state so the British just went up to the Upper Peninsula and they thought they could stay there for a little while. Then they had to fight a war, then the farmers, they were just volunteers, so the farmers went right back and tried to get their family put together back again. (VanSledright & Brophy, 1992, p. 849)

•*In most situations, elaboration facilitates storage and retrieval.* Students are more likely to remember classroom material over the long run if they expand on that material based on the things they already know. As examples, they might draw an inference that has not been explicitly stated, form a visual image of what a story character might look like, or think about how they might apply a scientific principle at home.

Many classroom activities can potentially promote student elaboration of classroom subject matter. For example, asking students to talk about academic subject matter, perhaps within the context of a class discussion or cooperative learning activity, almost forces them to do *something* (mentally) with that material (Brown & Campione, 1986; Prawat, 1989; Yager, Johnson, & Johnson, 1985). Asking students to write about what they are learning—perhaps in a research paper or on an essay question—enables them pull their thoughts together and perhaps to identify and resolve gaps and inconsistencies in their understanding (Prawat, 1989). And when students tutor their classmates on subject matter they presumably know quite well, they learn it at an even higher level of understanding (Brown & Palincsar, 1987; Semb, Ellis, & Araujo, 1993).

•*Occasionally, elaboration leads to the learning of misinformation.* When students have misconceptions about a topic, they may inappropriately elaborate on new information related to that topic. Teachers must continually monitor students' understanding of classroom material—perhaps by asking questions, assigning regular homework, or giving occasional quizzes—and then take steps to correct any misinterpretations that students' responses reveal. (We will identify strategies for changing stubborn misconceptions in our discussion of conceptual change in Chapter 13.)

•*Information that must be retrieved within a particular context should be stored within that context.* People are most likely to retrieve information relevant to a situation when they have stored it in close association with other aspects of that situation. If they have stored it elsewhere, they are much less likely to stumble on it at times when it will be useful. Thus, information should be stored with retrieval in mind.

In light of this principle, teachers should give students numerous opportunities to relate classroom material to the various situations that are later likely to require its retrieval. For example, a student is more likely to retrieve mathematical ideas relevant to accounting, surveying, or engineering if the mathematics teacher includes some simple problems in accounting, surveying, and engineering during instruction. Similarly, a student studying for a psychology test stressing application becomes better prepared by using study time to consider numerous situations in which psychological principles can be applied.

•*Repetition, while not especially effective as a means of storing information, promotes easier retrieval when used over the long run.* Repetition is most advantageous when it is spread out over a long time; thus, previously learned information should periodically be reviewed and integrated into the context of new lessons. Repetition is particularly important for facts and skills that students need every day—for example, for basic number factors, words frequently encountered in reading, and rules of punctuation. (Computers can sometimes make such drill and practice more palatable; e.g., see Lesgold, 1983, Perfetti, 1983, and Resnick & Johnson, 1988.) Basic information and skills should certainly be learned as meaningfully as possibly, but they should also be practiced until students can retrieve them quickly and automatically.

•*Students' memories will probably never be totally reliable records of information.* Long-term memory storage and retrieval are both constructive processes and therefore will always be fallible. Students' memories can undoubtedly be improved, but they can probably never be perfected.

In addition to the general principles I have just listed, contemporary memory theory yields numerous specific educational applications. We will examine several of them in the following chapter.

SUMMARY

Retrieval from long-term memory appears to be a process of searching, in one "location" at a time, until the desired information is found. Retrieval is easier when information has previously been stored in a meaningful, organized fashion and when retrieval cues are present. Retrieval is often a partially constructive process: Some pieces of information may be retrieved and others filled in so that an event is remembered completely, albeit sometimes inaccurately.

Although repetition of information within a few seconds or minutes (rehearsal) is not an effective way of storing information in the first place, occasional repetition of information *already stored* makes that information easier to remember over the long run. Knowledge and skills needed on a regular basis often must be practiced over and over until they are learned to a level of automaticity—that is, until they can be retrieved quickly and effortlessly.

Numerous explanations have been offered for why people "forget" things they have presumably learned. Possibilities include decay, obliterative subsumption, interference, failure to retrieve, repression, reconstruction error, and failure to store information in the first place.

Principles of long-term memory storage and retrieval have many applications to educational practice. For example, teachers should encourage students to learn classroom material meaningfully and in an organized fashion. They should also be encouraged to elaborate on that material, but be monitored for possible inaccurate or inappropriate elaborations. And, in general, students should store information with retrieval in mind, connecting it with the situations and contexts in which they are likely to need it later on.

CHAPTER 13

Applications of Human Information Processing Theory

As cognitive psychologists develop a better understanding of how people process and learn information, they are also beginning to investigate how to help people learn more effectively. In this chapter, we will focus on several specific applications of human information processing theory to classroom practice. We will first consider how classroom lectures and other forms of expository instruction can be presented in such a way that they promote effective long-term memory storage processes. Then, as we look at mnemonics, we will discover several techniques for helping students store information that, to them, is relatively "meaningless" and therefore difficult to learn and remember. We will see how teachers can encourage students to elaborate on classroom material by asking certain kinds of questions and giving students time to formulate their responses. Later in the chapter, we will identify strategies for promoting conceptual change—for presenting new information in such a way that students are likely to discard or modify their existing misconceptions about the world. And finally, we will consider how classroom testing practices affect the ways in which students process classroom subject matter.

EXPOSITORY INSTRUCTION

Much of your education has undoubtedly taken the form of **expository instruction**: You were *exposed* to information in essentially the same form you were expected to learn it. Lectures, explanations, textbooks, and educational films are all examples of expository instruction: Each technique lays out before you all the information you need to know.

Over the years, some psychologists and educators have criticized expository instruction—especially the lecture method—as being a relatively ineffective pedagogical technique. For example, B. F. Skinner proposed that learning can occur only when an individual makes an active response; because the typical classroom lecture does not allow much active responding, it is unlikely to promote learning. Jerome Bruner (e.g., 1961a, 1961b) has been similarly critical of lectures, proposing that students can better understand ideas when they have hands-on experiences with those ideas. Bruner has argued that a discovery approach to teaching—one in which students discover various properties of the environment through manipulation of concrete objects—should be more effective than a traditional lecture.

Nevertheless, the lecture method has some strong advocates, including many human information processing theorists. David Ausubel (e.g., Ausubel, 1963; Ausubel, Novak, & Hanesian, 1978; Ausubel & Robinson, 1969) has argued that students listening to a lecture are not necessarily the passive nonresponders that Skinner portrayed. Instead, students, although perhaps not overtly active, are nevertheless *cognitively* active; they busily attend to and meaningfully interpret the information they hear. Furthermore, although some students (those that Piaget would describe as being concrete operational) may require the concrete experiences that discovery learning provides, other students (those that Piaget would describe as formal operational) are quite capable of understanding concepts presented at an abstract, verbal level. For the latter group of students, a concise, organized lecture may be the most rapid and efficient means of presenting classroom subject matter.

Ausubel acknowledges that expository instruction is not always as effective as it might be. For example, when it is presented without regard for how students will learn material meaningfully, it may yield disappointing results in student achievement. Ausubel describes four particularly "inept" practices in expository teaching:

1. Premature use of pure verbal techniques with cognitively immature pupils [e.g., preoperational or concrete operational students].
2. Arbitrary presentation of unrelated facts without any organizing or explanatory principles.
3. Failure to integrate new learning tasks with previously presented materials.
4. The use of evaluation procedures that merely measure ability to recognize discrete facts or to reproduce ideas in the same words or in the identical context as originally encountered. (Ausubel et al., 1978, p. 124)

As you might guess, such practices are more likely to encourage rote learning than meaningful learning; thus, anything learned is unlikely to be retained over the long run.

Ausubel and his colleagues (1978) propose that, for meaningful learning to occur during expository instruction, three conditions must exist:

1. *Students must have previous knowledge to which they can relate new material.* As we noted in Chapter 11, students who have a large body of information already stored in long-term memory have more ideas to which they can connect their new experiences and so can more easily learn at a meaningful level. Those who lack such relevant knowledge are likely to resort to inefficient rote learning.
2. *Students must be aware of the relationship between the new material and their existing knowledge.* They are only likely to make connections between the new and the old when they know that such connections are possible. To use information processing terminology, students must have both things in working memory at the same time.
3. *Students must have a meaningful learning set.* Students must approach new information with the attitude that they can understand and make sense of it—something that Ausubel calls a **meaningful learning set**. Students are more likely to have this attitude when teachers emphasize meanings rather than verbatim recitation (Ausubel et al., 1978); for example, they are more apt to learn material meaningfully when they know they will be expected to explain it in their own words than when they will have to reproduce textbook definitions. A meaningful learning set is also more likely to occur when students are confident that they *can* understand new material. Students who have learned through past experience that a certain subject is confusing are more likely to resort to a rote learning approach (Ausubel, 1963, 1968; Ausubel & Robinson, 1969).

A growing body of research confirms Ausubel's belief that expository instruction, when delivered properly, is an effective pedagogical technique. Let's look at several things likely to promote student learning during expository instruction.

Advance Organizers

In Chapter 11, I distinguished between *internal organization*—how various ideas within a body of new information are interrelated—and *external organization*—how that information is related to what students already know. One means of facilitating both forms of organization is through the use of **advance organizers** (e.g., Ausubel et al., 1978). An advance organizer is a general introduction to new material that is typically designed to accomplish either or both of two purposes. An **expository organizer** provides a rough overview or outline of the material, describing the general topics (superordinate concepts) that will be presented and their relationship to one another; thus, it provides the beginnings of an internal organizational scheme. (The outlines and introductory paragraphs appearing at the beginning of each chapter in this book are examples of expository organizers.) A **comparative organizer** shows how the new material relates to students' previous experiences, to information they have previously learned in school, or possibly to their own purposes for studying the material; it also points out the similarities between the new information and the old. In this way, the organizer facilitates external organization. An additional advantage of a comparative organizer, as Ausubel has pointed out, is that it establishes a meaningful learning set: the student anticipates being able to understand the new material at a meaningful level and thus approaches the learning task with meaningful learning in mind.

Research consistently demonstrates the effectiveness of advance organizers in facilitating student learning, particularly when students have difficulty organizing on their own or when material is not clearly organized (Ausubel et al., 1978; Corkill, 1992; Mayer, 1979a, 1979b). Advance organizers also appear to promote more meaningful learning and consequently to facilitate the application of learned information to new situations (Mayer, 1987).

Although Ausubel originally conceptualized them as abstract introductions, advance organizers are typically more effective when they are fairly concrete (Corkill, 1992; Corkill, Glover, & Bruning, 1988; Mayer & Bromage, 1980; Zook, 1991). A variety of formats of advance organizers—for example, overviews, outlines, analogies, examples, and thought-provoking questions—all appear to be effective (Alexander, Frankiewicz, & Williams, 1979; Corkill, 1992; Frase, 1975; Glynn & Di Vesta, 1977; Mayer, 1984; Zook, 1991). For example, here is how a teacher might introduce a lesson on radar by means of an analogy—a comparative advance organizer:

> Radar means the detection and location of remote objects by reflection of radio waves. The phenomenon of acoustic echoes is familiar. Sound waves reflected from a building or cliff are received back at the observer after a lapse of a short interval. The effect is similar to you shouting in a canyon and, seconds later, hearing a nearly exact replication of your voice. Radar uses exactly the same principle except that the waves involved are radio waves, not sound waves. These travel very much faster than sound waves, 186,000 miles per second, and can cover much longer distances. Thus, radar involves simply measuring the time

between transmission of the waves and their subsequent return or echo, and then converting that to a distance measure. (Mayer, 1984, p. 30)

In some situations, an advance organizer might even take a graphic rather than strictly verbal form. For example, when introducing a unit on minerals, a hierarchical diagram similar to the one in Chapter 11's Figure 11–10 might provide a helpful visual overview—an expository advance organizer.

Ongoing Connections to Prior Knowledge

Instruction is clearly more effective when it begins with what students know and proceeds from there (e.g., Bobango, 1988; Wilson & Anderson, 1986). Too often, teachers assume that students know more than they really do and begin instruction at a point beyond what students can comprehend. Before any instructional unit, students' existing levels of knowledge should be ascertained through either formal pretesting or informal questioning.

Even when students do have existing knowledge to which they can relate new material, they frequently do not recognize the connections they might make (Paris & Lindauer, 1976; Spires, Donley, & Penrose, 1990; Stodolsky, Salk, & Glaessner, 1991). Hence, theorists recommend that expository instruction include some means of **prior knowledge activation**—some means of encouraging students to retrieve relevant knowledge to working memory. For example, teachers and students might discuss a topic in class *before* they begin a reading assignment about that topic (Hansen & Pearson, 1983; Wilson & Anderson, 1986). And when content learned earlier in the year (or perhaps in previous years) is important for understanding something new, teachers might provide a quick review of that content—a "refresher," if you will.

Teachers should continue to make connections between the new and the old throughout an expository lesson. Such techniques as familiar examples, in-class activities, and small group discussions about particular aspects of the instructional material may help students understand information within the context of their own experience.

When students have little "obvious" knowledge to which they can relate new subject matter, analogies to familiar concepts and situations once again provide an alternative strategy; Figure 13–1 lists some examples. Analogies help students learn information more meaningfully and retrieve it more easily, particularly when the topic is new to students or when the material is relatively abstract (Anderson & Schustack, 1979; Duit, 1990; Hayes & Henk, 1986; Newby & Stepich, 1987; Royer & Cable, 1976; Simons, 1984; Stepich & Newby, 1988; Zook, 1991). At the same time, teachers must be sure to point out ways in which the two things being compared are *different*; otherwise, students may take an analogy too far and draw some incorrect conclusions (Duit, 1990; Zook & Di Vesta, 1991).

Figure 13–1
Examples of analogies that promote connections between new ideas and existing student knowledge

- If we think of the earth's history as a *24-hour day,* then humans have been in existence only for the last minute of that day (Hartmann, Miller, & Lee, 1984).

- The growth of a glacier is like *pancake batter being poured into a frying pan.* As more and more substance is added to the middle, the edges spread farther and farther out (courtesy of R. K. Ormrod).

- The Ural Mountains in Russia are like *the Appalachian Mountains in the United States.* They are old, worn-down mountains that served as temporary barriers of migration (Andrews, 1987).

- The human circulatory system is similar to a *parcel delivery system.* "Red blood cells work like trucks, carrying needed materials from a central distribution point for delivery throughout the body. Arteries and veins are like roads, acting as access routes through which the various points of delivery are reached. The heart is like the warehouse or the central point in which vehicles are loaded and dispatched, and to which empty vehicles are returned to be reloaded" (Stepich & Newby, 1988, p.136).

- The process of heat flow is similar to *falling dominos.* In both cases, one thing affects the thing next to it, which in turn affects the thing next to *it,* and so on (Royer & Cable, 1976).

- Electricity going through a wire is like *people going through a tunnel.* Everything that enters at one end comes out at the other (Duit, 1990; Gentner & Gentner, 1983).

- Tying a bowline knot is like *a rabbit guarding the territory around its home.* You hold the rope vertically and make a loop near the middle. The loop is the rabbit hole, the upper end of the rope is the tree, and the lower end is the rabbit. The rabbit goes up and out of the hole, around the tree, and back down the hole again (Hayes & Henk, 1986).

- A dual-store model of memory is like *the information selection and storage system you use at home.* Some things (e.g., junk mail) are discarded as soon as they arrive, others (e.g., bills) are only briefly dealt with, and still others (e.g., driver's license) are used regularly and saved for a long period of time (see Chapter 10).

- Retrieval from long-term memory is like *looking for something in a large, dark room with just a small flashlight.* You can only look at one small spot at a time, and it is virtually impossible to look everywhere (see Chapter 12).

Coherent Organization

Expository instruction is often more effective when it presents new information in the basic organizational format in which students should store it in memory (e.g., Tennyson & Cocchiarella, 1986; Tennyson, Tennyson, & Rothen, 1980). For example, teachers facilitate students' learning when they present ideas in a logical sequence, identify any hierarchical relationships that exist among concepts, and make cause–effect relationships clear. Organization of information may be particularly important for low-ability students; apparently, high-ability students can sometimes organize poorly sequenced information themselves (Buckland, 1968; Mayer, 1989a).

Signals

When expository instruction provides a great deal of information, students some-times have trouble deciding which things are important and which things are not (Dole, Duffy, Roehler, & Pearson, 1991; Garner, Alexander, Gillingham, Kulikowich, & Brown, 1991; Reynolds & Shirey, 1988). For example, students may focus their attention on interesting, relatively trivial details at the expense of less interesting but more important ideas (Garner et al., 1991; Ward, 1991). Or they may look at the equations they see in a scientific proof while disregarding any verbal explanation of those equations (Dee-Lucas & Larkin, 1991).

A variety of **signals** as to what information is most important can facilitate students' learning from expository instruction (Armbruster, 1984; Lorch, Lorch, & Inman, 1993; Reynolds & Shirey, 1988). For example, writing key points on the chalkboard is a means of emphasizing those points. Underlining important phrases and sentences in a textbook passage makes them more prominent (Hart-ley, Bartlett, & Branthwaite, 1980; McAndrew, 1983). Specific objectives for a les-son let students know what is expected of them (McAshan, 1979). Questions interspersed throughout a lecture or textbook passage draw students' attention to particular ideas (McDaniel & Einstein, 1989). Even just telling students what's important probably makes a difference (Reynolds & Shirey, 1988).

Visual Aids

As we noted in Chapter 11, visual imagery provides a highly effective way of encoding information; it is particularly valuable when used in conjunction with other forms of encoding. Thus, presenting information in visual form—through physical objects, pictures, maps, diagrams, live models, and so on—is an impor-tant supplement to verbal material (Clark & Paivio, 1991; Denis, 1984; Levin & Berry, 1980; Mayer, 1989a; Prawat, 1989; Small, Lovett, & Scher, 1993; Waddill, McDaniel, & Einstein, 1988; Winn, 1991).

In most situations, visual aids should be simple and concise, and they should include major ideas without overwhelming students with detail (Mayer, 1989a). In addition to promoting visual imagery, many visual aids can also show students how major ideas relate to and affect one another; thus they provide one more way of helping students organize the information they receive (Mayer, 1989a; Winn, 1991).

Summaries

As we noted earlier in our discussion of advance organizers, students tend to learn more effectively when they receive advance notice of the things they will be learning. Students also tend to benefit from summaries presented at the end of a verbal lecture or written passage: They learn more effectively when they hear or read a synopsis of the information they have just studied (Hartley & Trueman, 1982; Lorch et al., 1993).

Summaries probably serve multiple functions for students. Among other things, they may help students to: (1) review material, (2) determine which of the many ideas they have studied are most important, and (3) pull key ideas into a more cohesive organizational structure.

When expository instruction is delivered in such a way that it promotes meaningful, organized information storage, it can serve as an efficient and effective means of presenting information to a large number of students. But what do teachers do in situations when important information is difficult to teach meaningfully and organize logically? In such situations, mnemonic devices provide a viable alternative.

MNEMONICS

Looking back upon your own educational experiences, you can no doubt recall many situations in which you had difficulty learning important information. Perhaps the troublesome material consisted of long lists of items, unfamiliar vocabulary words in a foreign language, or particular rules of grammar, spelling, or mathematics. **Mnemonics**—memory "tricks"—are devices that facilitate the learning and recall of many such forms of difficult material. In this section, we will look at four different types of mnemonics—verbal mediation, visual imagery, superimposed meaningful structures, and external retrieval cues—and will then examine some of the reasons that mnemonics are so effective.

Verbal Mediation

Imagine that you are trying to learn that the German word *Handschuh* means "glove." Playing off how the word sounds phonetically, you might remember this word by thinking of a glove as a "shoe for the hand." Such a mnemonic is an example of **verbal mediation**, in which two words or ideas are associated by a word or phrase (the verbal mediator) that connects them. Here are some examples of verbal mediators for other German vocabulary words:

German Word	English Meaning	Mediator
der Hund	dog	hound
das Schwein	pig	swine
die Gans	goose	gander
der Stier	bull	steer

Notice that in every case, the verbal mediator bridges the gap between the German word and its English equivalent. By storing the mediator, you can make a connection between the two words.

Verbal mediators clearly facilitate learning (e.g., Bugelski, 1962), and their use is not necessarily restricted to the learning of foreign vocabulary words. For example, here is a mnemonic sometimes seen in spelling instruction:

The principal is my pal.

Retrieving this sentence will enable a student to remember that the correct spelling for a school administrator is "princi*pal*" rather than "princi*ple*." As another example, my daughter remembers the chemical symbol for gold—Au— by thinking, "*Ay, you* stole my *gold* watch!"

Visual Imagery

As we noted in Chapter 11, a visual image is a powerful storage code that can be formed quickly and retained for a relatively long time (e.g., Shepard, 1967; Standing, 1973; Standing, Conezio, & Haber, 1970). Accordingly, visual imagery forms the basis for a number of effective mnemonic devices. Here we will focus on three of them: the method of loci, the pegword method, and the keyword method.

Method of Loci

In the days of the Greek and Roman empires, orators used a particular technique to help them remember the major ideas they wished to include in their hours-long harangues at the local forum (lecture notes were apparently not acceptable in those days). These orators would think about a familiar route that they walked frequently—the route from home to the forum, for example—and about the significant landmarks along the way—perhaps a bridge, a large tree, and a brothel, in that order. Then, when planning a speech, they would translate each key point into some sort of concrete, observable object and form a visual image of each successive key point located at each landmark along the familiar route. For example, let's say that an orator's first three points in his speech were the frequent traffic jams near the forum, the importance of a mass transit system in downtown Rome, and the consequent necessity for a tax increase. He might store images such as these: (1) numerous horses and pedestrians entangled in a traffic jam on the bridge (first landmark), (2) a gigantic, 30-person chariot perched among the branches of the large tree (second landmark), and (3) several toga-clad prostitutes pitching coins at a tax collector from the upstairs window of the brothel (third landmark). Later, when pontificating at the forum, the orator would take a mental walk along his familiar route; as he passed each landmark, he would readily retrieve the image of that landmark and the object symbolizing the next major point of his speech. In this manner, he could easily remember all the main ideas of the oration and their correct order.

The **method of loci** (*loci* is the Latin word for "places") is clearly an effective mnemonic technique (Christen & Bjork, 1976; Groninger, 1971; Snowman, 1986) and lends itself readily to the storage and retention of lists of items. For example, in a study by Groninger (1971), some subjects learned a list of 25 words using the method of loci while others learned the words simply by grouping them. Subjects using the method of loci learned the words faster and remembered more of them on a free recall task five weeks later. Both groups of subjects performed equally well, however, when asked to recognize the words; thus, it appears that the benefit of the method of loci may lie in the imagery-based retrieval cues it provides.

Pegword Method

The **pegword method** is another technique for effectively learning a list of items and their relative positions (Bower, 1972; Bugelski, Kidd, & Segmen, 1968; Higbee, 1976; Mastropieri & Scruggs, 1989, 1992). This method consists of using a well-known or easily learned list of items that then serves as a series of "pegs" on which another list is hung through visual imagery.

To illustrate, here is a poem that is sometimes used as a pegboard:

One is a bun.
Two is a shoe.
Three is a tree.
Four is a door.
Five is a hive.
Six is sticks.
Seven is heaven.
Eight is a gate.
Nine is a line; and
Ten is a hen.
(Miller, Galanter, & Pribram, 1960, p. 135)

This poem should be easy to remember because its lines are composed of the numbers 1 through 10 in conjunction with rhyming nouns. Now suppose you need to remember a list of items in a certain order. You take the first item on the list and form a visual image of it interacting with the noun that rhymes with *one* (in this case, *bun*), then take the second list item and imagine it interacting with the noun that rhymes with *two* (*shoe*), and so on. Images can be formed quickly and typically need not be practiced to be remembered.

Consider this food chain as an example of a list to be learned using the "One is a bun" poem:

Algae in a lake are eaten by
Water fleas, which are eaten by
Minnows, which are eaten by
Larger fish, which are eaten by
Eagles.

Using the pegword method, you form an image of algae and a bun together—perhaps a hamburger bun covered with green algae. Similarly, you visualize water fleas in conjunction with a shoe—perhaps you see a shoe filled with water and several water fleas doing the backstroke across the surface. For the last three items of the food chain, you might form images of a tree with minnows hanging down like fruit, a door with a large fish stuffed through the keyhole, and an eagle wearing a beehive for a hat. Remembering the food chain, then, is simply a matter of thinking, "One is a bun," conjuring up the image of the bun with algae, then thinking, "Two is a shoe," retrieving the shoe image, and so on.

Keyword Method

I have already described the use of verbal mediation in learning foreign language words. But as you may have noticed, the German words I chose for my illustrations of verbal mediation closely resembled English words. More often, words in a foreign language are not so obviously related to their English meanings. In such situations, the **keyword method** provides an effective alternative. This technique, which is actually a combination of verbal mediation and visual imagery, involves two steps: (1) identifying an English word or phrase (the keyword) that sounds similar to the foreign word, then (2) forming a visual image of the English sound-alike word with the English meaning. For example, consider how we might remember these German words:

German Word	English Meaning	Keyword(s)	Visual Image
das Pferd	horse	Ford	A *horse* driving a *Ford*
das Kaninchen	rabbit	can on chin	A *rabbit* with a *can on* its *chin*
der Waschbär	raccoon	wash, bar	A *raccoon wash*ing with a *bar* of soap
das Stachelschwein	porcupine	stash, swine	A *porcupine stash*ing nuts under a pig (*swine*)

The keyword method has been shown to be an effective instructional device in teaching both English and foreign language words; it is also useful in teaching such paired associates as states and their capitals and cities and their products

Using a keyword to remember that a horse is a *"pferd."*

(Atkinson, 1975; Levin, 1981; Levin, McCormick, Miller, Berry, & Pressley, 1982; Mastropieri & Scruggs, 1989; Pressley, Levin, & Delaney, 1982; Pressley, Levin, & McCormick, 1980; Raugh & Atkinson, 1975). Furthermore, older students (such as eighth graders) often spontaneously apply this mnemonic to new learning tasks once they have been trained in its use (Jones & Hall, 1982; Mastropieri & Scruggs, 1989). Although only concrete objects can actually be visualized, the technique can be used with more abstract words as well, provided that they can be adequately represented by a concrete object. For example, consider the Spanish word for "love," *el amor*: this word might be learned by picturing a heart (symbolizing "love") wearing a suit of armor (the keyword).

When presenting mnemonics based on visual imagery, teachers must keep three things in mind. First, many young children cannot generate effective images on their own, so teachers probably need to provide pictures for them (Mayer, 1987). Second, for imagery to be an effective means of remembering a connection between two items (e.g., between a bridge and mass transit, or between love and *amor*), the two items must be incorporated into the same image in an *interacting* fashion (Bower, 1972; Dempster & Rohwer, 1974). Thus, while an image of a heart wearing armor is an effective way of remembering the Spanish word for "love," an image of a heart standing beside a suit of armor probably is not. Third, as I indicated in Chapter 11, imagery does not preserve details very effectively (Anderson, 1990); therefore, it may not help one remember such specific information as the exact shape of a heart or the number of dents on a suit of armor.

Superimposed Meaningful Structure

One of my most vivid memories from my years as an undergraduate psychology major is being required to learn the 12 cranial nerves: olfactory, optic, oculomotor, trochlear, trigeminal, abducens, facial, auditory, glossopharyngeal, vagus, spinal accessory, and hypoglossal. It is not the nerves themselves that I remember, but rather how painfully difficult it was to learn them all in their correct order. I had little luck drilling the list into my thick skull (I was using the tried-and-not-so-true method of rote memorization) until a friend passed along this mnemonic:

> *On old Olympus' towering top, a Finn and German viewed some hops.*

Notice that the first letters of the words in the sentence correspond with the first letters of the 12 cranial nerves: Just like in the list of nerves, the first three words in the sentence begin with O, the next two begin with T, and so on. And the sentence, while a bit strange, is fairly easy to remember because of the structure provided by its rhythm and rhyme.

"On old Olympus" is an example of a mnemonic I call a **superimposed meaningful structure** (sometimes also known as *semantic elaboration*). The technique is simple: The learner imposes a familiar structure on the body of information to be learned. That structure can be a sentence, story, poem, acronym, or anything else already meaningful to the learner. Figure 13–2 shows some examples.

To illustrate just how effective such superimposed structures can be, let's look at an experiment by Bower and Clark (1969). Two groups of college students learned 12 lists of 10 nouns: Group 1 learned each list through repetition, while Group 2 composed narrative stories that included all 10 words of each list. Here is an example of such a Group 2 story (the nouns to be remembered are in capital letters):

> A LUMBERJACK DARTed out of a forest, SKATEd around a HEDGE past a COLONY of DUCKS. He tripped on some FURNITURE, tearing his STOCKING while hastening toward the PILLOW where his MISTRESS lay. (Bower & Clark, 1969, p. 182)

After the students had learned each of the 12 lists perfectly, they were then asked to recall all 120 words (the first word of each list was given as a retrieval cue). Students in Group 1 (repetition) recalled only 13% of the words; in contrast, students in Group 2 (stories) recalled 93%!

External Retrieval Cues

One of my own memory problems is remembering to remember. I forget to turn off my car lights after driving to work on a foggy morning. I occasionally forget important meetings. Sometimes I forget to bring crucial handouts or overheads

Figure 13–2
Examples of superimposed meaningful structures

The Mnemonic	What It Represents
ROY G. BIV	The spectrum: red, orange, yellow, green, blue, indigo, violet.
HOMES	The five Great Lakes: Huron, Ontario, Michigan, Erie, Superior.
Every good boy does fine.	The lines on the treble clef: E G B D F.
When the "mites" go up, the "tites" come down.	The distinction between stalagmites and stalactites.
A "boot."	The shape of Italy.
A "bearskin rug."	The shape of France.
George Ellen's old grandmother rode a pig home yesterday.	The correct spelling of "geography."
I before *E*, except after *C*.	The correct spelling of words like "receive."
Thirty days has September. . . .	The number of days in each month.

to class. Yes, yes, I know what you're thinking: I'm suffering from the absent-minded professor syndrome.

It's not that I lose information from my long-term memory. When I go to the parking lot at the end of the day and find that my car has a dead battery, I readily remember the fact that I turned on my car lights that morning. When I'm reminded of the important meeting I've just missed or get to the point in a lecture where I need the overhead I've forgotten to bring, I think, "Of course!" My problem is that I *forget to retrieve* important information at the appropriate time. Given the number of my students who sometimes forget homework assignments (or even that they have class!), I know my problem is not unique to me.

When you need to remember to retrieve, an **external retrieval cue**—a physical object outside of (external to) your memory system—can be helpful. The classic example is the proverbial string around the finger: the string is tied in a spot impossible to overlook and serves as a reminder that something needs to be remembered. Finger strings are terribly unfashionable, but other external retrieval cues can be equally effective. Appointment books, to-do lists, and little self-reminder notes increase the likelihood that students remember important assignments and engagements and also help them learn to be responsible for their own retrieval.

Why Mnemonics Work

It should be clear by now that mnemonics can be extremely helpful learning aids. As you may have noticed, their effectiveness lies in their conformity with a few critical principles of storage and retrieval. First, they often impose a structure or organization on the material to be learned. Second, they help the learner relate the new material to information already stored in long-term memory (e.g., the number system or a familiar poetic meter). And, third, they provide retrieval cues that help learners find the information at a later time.

Yet people rarely use mnemonics (Morris, 1977), perhaps because they are unaware of their existence or their benefits. Teachers can obviously help students learn difficult information if they identify or develop mnemonics for that information. Furthermore, they can help students become more independent learners by showing then how to develop effective mnemonics on their own.

The preceding discussions of expository instruction and mnemonics have, I hope, given you some useful ideas for promoting meaningful learning and internal organization. But how do teachers encourage students to *elaborate* on information as well? Teacher questioning is one possible strategy.

TEACHER QUESTIONS

In Chapter 5's discussion of instructional objectives, we made a distinction between lower-level skills and higher-level skills. This was essentially a distinction between simply *knowing* something versus *doing* something (mentally) with that knowledge—for example, applying, analyzing, synthesizing, or evaluating it. We can make a similar distinction between **lower-level questions** and **higher-level questions**: The former ask students to retrieve something pretty much as they have stored it in memory, while the latter ask students to elaborate on that retrieved information.

Numerous studies show the benefits of asking questions in class. We noted one such benefit in Chapter 9: Questions help to focus students' attention on classroom activities. Questions also provide a feedback mechanism through which teachers and students alike can discover how much students have learned from a current lesson or can remember from previous lessons (Connolly & Eisenberg, 1990; Fox & LeCount, 1991). But higher-level questions have the additional advantage of encouraging (forcing?) students to go beyond the information itself (e.g., Feldhusen & Treffinger, 1980; Torrance & Myers, 1970). As an example, consider these questions from a lesson on the telegraph:

> Was the need for a rapid communications system [in America] greater during the first part of the nineteenth century than it had been during the latter part of the eighteenth century? Why do you think so? (Torrance & Myers, 1970, p. 214)

To answer these questions, students must recall what they know about the eighteenth and nineteenth centuries (including the increasing movement of U.S. settlers to distant western territories) and pull that knowledge together in a way they have perhaps never done before.

All too often, teachers and instructional materials pose lower-level, fact-based questions, with few (if any) higher-level questions to facilitate student elaboration (Armbruster, 1988; Freiberg, 1987; Raudenbush, Rowan, & Cheong, 1993; Tobin, 1987). Such a state of affairs is unfortunate. Research indicates quite clearly that teachers and instructional materials (e.g., textbooks) promote greater student achievement when they ask higher-level questions in addition to lower-level ones—for example, when they call for inferences, applications, justifications, and solutions to problems as well as asking for knowledge (Brophy, 1992; Frederiksen, 1984b; Liu, 1990; Redfield & Rousseau, 1981).

We should remind ourselves that elaboration takes *time*. It is unreasonable to expect students to formulate insightful, creative responses to higher-level questions in a split second. What happens when teachers give students the time they need to process and reprocess information? Let's find out.

WAIT TIME

When teachers ask students a question, they typically wait one second or less for a response; if students don't respond in that short time interval, teachers tend to speak again—perhaps by asking different students the same question, rephrasing the question, or even answering the question themselves (Rowe, 1974, 1987). Teachers are equally reluctant to let much time elapse after students answer questions or make comments in class; once again, they typically allow one second or less of silence before responding to a statement or asking another question (Rowe, 1987).

The amount of time teachers allow to pass after their own and students' questions and comments is known as **wait time**. One second is, in many instances, probably *not* sufficient time for students to think about (process) the questions teachers ask and the comments students make in class. After all, they must retrieve the things they know and, in the case of higher-level questions, must construct a response they have not previously stored.

Research indicates that students benefit tremendously simply from being given a little time to think. For example, when teachers increase their wait time by allowing at least three seconds to elapse (instead of just one) after both their own questions and students' remarks, we see changes in student behavior such as these (Mohatt & Erickson, 1981; Rowe, 1974, 1987; Tharp, 1989; Tobin, 1987):

- *Increased student participation:*
  - Students talk more and are more likely to answer questions correctly.
  - More students participate in class; previously quiet students (including many minority students) become more active contributors.
  - Students are more likely to contribute spontaneously to a class discussion—for example, by asking questions and presenting their own perspectives.
  - Students are more likely to talk *to one another* (as well as to their teacher) within the context of a classroom discussion.
- *Better quality of student responses*:
  - Students' responses are longer and more sophisticated.
  - Students are more likely to support their responses with evidence or logic.
  - Students are more likely to give a variety of responses to the same question.
  - Students are more likely to speculate when they don't know an answer.
- *Better classroom performance:*
  - Students are less likely to feel confused by course content; they are more likely to feel confident that they can master the material.
  - Students' motivation to learn class material increases.
  - Students show higher achievement, especially for complex material.
  - Discipline problems decrease (as one fifth grade boy put it, "It's the first time in all my years in school that anybody cared what I really thought—not just what I am supposed to say" [Rowe, 1987, p. 40]).

We also see changes in teacher behavior when we increase wait time to at least three seconds. More specifically, we see changes such as these (Rowe, 1974, 1987; Tobin, 1987):

- *Different kinds of questions*:
  - Teachers ask fewer "simple" questions (e.g., questions requiring the recall of facts).
  - Teachers ask more complex questions (e.g., questions requiring students to elaborate or develop alternative explanations).
- *Increased flexibility in teaching*:
  - Teachers modify the direction of discussion to accommodate students' comments and questions.
  - Teachers allow their classes to pursue a topic in greater depth than they originally anticipated.
- *Changes in expectations*:
  - Teachers' expectations for many students, especially previously low-achieving students, begin to improve.

From an information processing perspective, increasing wait time during class discussions and question–answer sessions appears to benefit student learning in two ways (Tobin, 1987). First, it allows students more time to process information. Second, it appears to change the very nature of teacher–student discussions: For example, teachers are more likely to ask challenging, thought-provoking questions. In fact, the nature of the questions that teachers ask is probably as important as—and perhaps even more important than—the amount of wait time per se (Giaconia, 1988).

Wait time may be equally important during expository instruction, for the same reason—students need time to process (to encode and elaborate on) the things they see and hear (Johnson, 1989; Rowe, 1987). For example, when giving a lecture, Mary Budd Rowe (1987) has suggested lecturing for 8 or 10 minutes, then giving students a 2-minute interval in which to compare notes and clarify subject matter with one another. And when reading, students may want to provide wait time for *themselves*, pausing occasionally to draw inferences, generate examples, consider applications, and so on from the new ideas they encounter. Within this context, the whole notion of speed reading becomes counterintuitive, and, in fact, speed reading is probably effective only when readers already know much of the information they're reading (Carver, 1971; Crowder & Wagner, 1992).

When the objective is recall of facts—when students need to retrieve information very quickly, to "know it cold"—then wait time during a question–answer session should be short. There is a definite advantage to rapid-fire drill and practice for skills that teachers want students to learn to a level of automaticity (Tobin, 1987). But when objectives include more complex processing of ideas and issues, longer wait time provides both teachers and students the time they need to think things through.

PROMOTING CONCEPTUAL CHANGE

Information processing theorists suggest that students rarely come to class as "blank slates"; rather, they bring prior knowledge to class and build on that knowledge when learning new material. But as we noted in Chapter 11, some of this "knowledge" may be incorrect. Students are likely to have numerous misconceptions about how the world operates; Figure 13–3 provides typical examples. In some situations, then, teachers may need not only to teach students new ideas, but also to *change students' minds* about existing beliefs; in other words, they may need to promote **conceptual change** (sometimes called *restructuring*) (Brophy, 1992; Carey, 1986; Kyle & Shymansky, 1989; Pintrich, Marx, & Boyle, 1993; Prawat, 1989; Roth, 1990; Roth & Anderson, 1988; Vosniadou & Brewer, 1987).

Unfortunately, thanks to the processes of meaningful learning and elaboration—processes that usually facilitate learning—students may change or distort

Figure 13–3
Examples of common student misconceptions

Astronomy

- *Fact:* The earth revolves around the sun.

  Misconception: The sun revolves around the earth. It "rises" in the morning and "sets" in the evening, at which point it "goes" to the other side of the earth (Vosniadou & Brewer, 1987).

- *Fact:* The earth is shaped more or less like a sphere.

  Misconception: The earth is shaped like a round, flat disk (Nussbaum, 1985; Sneider & Pulos, 1983; Vosniadou & Brewer, 1987).

- *Fact:* Space has no "up" or "down."

  Misconception: Space has an absolute up and down; people standing at the South Pole will fall off the earth (Sneider & Pulos, 1983).

Biology

- *Fact:* A living thing is something that carries on such life processes as metabolism, growth, and reproduction.

  Misconception: A living thing is something that moves and/or grows. The sun, wind, clouds, and fire are living things (Kyle & Shymansky, 1989).

- *Fact:* A plant produces its own food through the process of photosynthesis.

  Misconception: Plants "eat" soil, fertilizer, and water, just as people eat meat and vegetables (Roth & Anderson, 1988).

Physics

- *Fact:* An object remains in uniform motion until a force acts on it; a force is needed only to *change* speed or direction.

  Misconception: Any moving object has a force acting on it. For example, a ball thrown into the air continues to be pushed upward by the force of the throw until it begins its descent (Carey, 1986; Kyle & Shymansky, 1989).

new information to fit their prior misconceptions. And thanks to the process of rote learning—storing material without relating it to anything else that is known—students may hold two inconsistent or contradictory ideas in long-term memory at the same time. As a result, students may leave a classroom with their erroneous ideas intact, perhaps even "confirmed," rather than corrected (Alexander & Judy, 1988; Bishop & Anderson, 1990; Carey, 1986; Chambliss, Calfee, & Wong, 1990; Perkins & Simmons, 1988; Roth, 1990; Roth & Anderson, 1988).

Research in classrooms indicates that students often hold quite stubbornly to their misconceptions, even after considerable instruction that explicitly contradicts those misconceptions (Carey, 1986; Chinn & Brewer, 1993; Eaton, Anderson, & Smith, 1984; Kyle & Shymansky, 1989; Roth & Anderson, 1988). Consider this situation as an example:

> A class of fifth graders was about to study a unit on light and vision. Based on results of a pretest, it was clear that most students believed incorrectly that vision occurs simply as the result of light shining on an object and making it bright. During the unit, the correct explanation of human vision was presented:

- *Fact:* Gravity is the force whereby any two masses are attracted together.

  Misconception: Gravity is the "glue" that holds people to the earth. There is no gravity without air (Kyle & Shymansky, 1989).

- *Fact:* When an electric current lights up a light bulb, it flows from the power source, through the bulb, and back to the power source.

  Misconception: The electric current is "used up" (consumed) by the light bulb and disappears (Kyle & Shymansky, 1989).

Geography

- *Fact:* The Great Lakes contain fresh water.

  Misconception: The Great Lakes contain salt water (courtesy of R. K. Ormrod).

- *Fact:* Rivers run from higher elevation to lower elevation.

  Misconception: Rivers run from north to south. For example, rivers can run from Canada into the United States, but not vice versa (courtesy of R. K. Ormrod).

Human Learning

- *Fact:* Negative reinforcement is the removal of a stimulus (usually an aversive one). It increases the frequency of the behavior it follows.

  Misconception: Negative reinforcement is the presentation of an aversive stimulus (for example, a scolding or a spanking). Its effect, if any, is to decrease the frequency of a behavior it follows. (I have repeatedly observed this misconception in my own students; I have even seen it in the published works of some educators.)

- *Fact:* Meaningful learning is more effective than rote learning.

  Misconception: Rote learning is more effective than meaningful learning (Lennon, Ormrod, Burger, & Warren, 1990).

light must be reflected off an object *and then travel to the eye* before the object can be seen. Even though students both read and heard the correct explanation of how people see objects, most of them "learned" what they already believed: that an object can be seen as soon as light hits it. Posttest results indicated that only 24% of the class had learned the correct explanation. (Eaton, Anderson, & Smith, 1984)

Teachers, then, face a two-fold challenge. Not only must they help their students learn new things, they must also help students *un*learn existing misconceptions about the world. Although research on promoting conceptual change is still in its infancy, learning theorists are now beginning to identify ways to promote conceptual change in the classroom. Here are several strategies to keep in mind.

•*Students should learn correct information at a meaningful rather than rote level.* Students will only notice inconsistencies between new information and their previously acquired beliefs when they try to make connections between the "new" and the "old." To use levels-of-processing terminology for a moment, students are most likely to modify their misconceptions in light of new data if they process those data in depth—in other words, if they become actively engaged in learning and truly try to understand the information being presented to them (Chinn & Brewer, 1993; Lee & Anderson, 1993; Pintrich, Marx, & Boyle, 1993).

Instruction is most likely to promote conceptual change when it focuses on a few key ideas presented meaningfully rather than covering many topics superficially (Kyle & Shymansky, 1989; Roth & Anderson, 1988). To put this idea in the words of many educators, "less is more": *less* material presented more thoroughly is learned *more* completely and with greater understanding.

•*Before instruction begins, teachers should determine what misconceptions about a topic exist.* Teachers can more easily address students' misconceptions when they know what those misconceptions *are* (Kyle & Shymansky, 1989; Roth & Anderson, 1988; Vosniadou & Brewer, 1987). Thus, a lesson might begin with informal questioning or a pretest to probe students' current understanding of the subject at hand. As teachers gain experience teaching a particular topic over the years, they can begin to anticipate what students' prior beliefs and misbeliefs about that topic are likely to be.

•*Students are most likely to revise their current way of thinking when they believe revision is in order.* Thus, students should be shown how new information contradicts things they currently believe and why their existing conceptions are inadequate. With this point in mind, teachers might consider strategies such as these to promote conceptual change (Anderson, 1977; Brophy, 1992; Chinn & Brewer, 1993; McKeown & Beck, 1990; Posner, Strike, Hewson, & Gertzog, 1982; Prawat, 1989; Roth, 1990; Roth & Anderson, 1988; Vosniadou & Brewer, 1987):

- Asking questions that challenge students' current beliefs
- Describing an event or phenomenon that students cannot adequately explain within their existing perspective

- Engaging students in discussions of the pros and cons of various explanations
- Pointing out, explicitly, what the differences between students' beliefs and "reality" are
- Showing how the correct explanation of an event or phenomenon is more plausible (i.e., it makes more sense) than anything students themselves can offer

•*Students must **want** to learn the correct explanation.* Students are most likely to engage in deep processing and meaningful learning when they are motivated to do so (Lee & Anderson, 1993; Pintrich et al., 1993). For example, they must be interested in the subject matter, set their sights on mastering it, and have sufficient self-efficacy to believe that they *can* master it (Pintrich et al., 1993). (In the final two chapters of the book, we will identify more specific strategies teachers can use to promote such student motivation.)

•*Students' understanding should be monitored throughout a lesson for particularly tenacious misconceptions.* Because of students' natural tendency to reinterpret new information in light of what they already "know," some misconceptions may persist in spite of a teacher's best efforts. These misconceptions are sometimes blatantly incorrect; at other times, they may be "sort of, but not quite" correct. To illustrate the latter situation, let's consider an example offered by Roth and Anderson (1988), once again dealing with the topic of vision. Students sometimes define *transparent* as "something you can see through." Although such a definition is consistent with how we speak about transparency on a day-to-day basis, it may nevertheless reflect the erroneous belief that sight originates with the eye and goes outward to and through the transparent object. *Transparent* is more accurately defined as "something light passes through."

Throughout a lesson, a prudent teacher will continue to check students' beliefs about the topic at hand, looking for subtle signs that students' understanding is not quite accurate and giving corrective feedback when necessary. As an example, consider this classroom discussion described by Roth and Anderson (1988):

Ms. Ramsey:	(Puts up transparency) Why can't the girl see around the wall?
Annie:	The girl can't see around the wall because the wall is opaque.
Ms. Ramsey:	What do you mean when you say the wall is opaque?
Annie:	*You can't see through it. It is solid.*
Brian:	(calling out) The rays are what can't go through the wall.
Ms. Ramsey:	I like that answer better. Why is it better?
Brian:	The rays of light bounce off the car and go to the wall. They can't go through the wall.
Ms. Ramsey:	Where are the light rays coming from originally?
Students:	The sun.
Annie:	*The girl can't see the car because she is not far enough out.*

Ms. Ramsey:	So you think her position is what is keeping her from seeing it. (She flips down the overlay with the answer.) Who was better?
Students:	Brian.
Ms. Ramsey:	(to Annie) Would she be able to see if she moved out beyond the wall?
Annie:	Yes.
Ms. Ramsey:	Why?
Annie:	*The wall is blocking her view.*
Ms. Ramsey:	Is it blocking her view? What is it blocking?
Student:	Light rays.
Ms. Ramsey:	Light rays that are doing what?
Annie:	If the girl moves out beyond the wall, then the light rays that bounce off the car are not being blocked. (pp. 129–130)

Notice how Ms. Ramsey is not satisfied with Annie's original answer that the wall is opaque. With further questioning, it becomes clear that Annie's understanding of opaqueness is off target: She talks about the girl being unable to "see through" the wall rather than light's inability to pass through the wall. With Ms. Ramsey's continuing insistence on precise language, Annie eventually begins to bring light rays into her explanation (Roth & Anderson, 1988).

Assessment of students' comprehension is important *after* a lesson as well. Teachers are more likely to detect misconceptions when they ask students to *use* and *apply* the things they have learned (as Ms. Ramsey does in the conversation just described) rather than only to spit back facts, definitions, and formulas memorized at a rote level (Roth, 1990; Roth & Anderson, 1988). In fact, not only are tests a means of assessing students' comprehension of classroom subject matter, they can actually promote better comprehension, as we shall see now.

PROMOTING LONG-TERM MEMORY THROUGH CLASSROOM TESTING PRACTICES

As a college professor, I typically give my students a test every three to five weeks (undergraduate students get them more frequently than graduate students do). I use my tests not only as a means of assessing what my students have learned, but also as a means of helping them learn and remember course material more effectively. Corny as it may sound, I think of my classroom tests as learning experiences in and of themselves.

From the perspective of information processing theory, tests can, *when designed appropriately*, potentially enhance students' long-term memory storage and retrieval in at least four ways:

1. *By encouraging review before the test.* As we discovered in Chapter 12, students have a better chance of remembering things over the long run

when they review them periodically. Studying for tests is one way of reviewing classroom material. Most students study class material more and learn it better when they are told they will be tested on it rather than when they are simply told to learn it (Frederiksen, 1984b; Halpin & Halpin, 1982). We should note here, however, that students typically spend more time studying information they think will be on a test than the things they think a test won't cover (Corbett & Wilson, 1988; Frederiksen, 1984b; Frederiksen & Collins, 1989).

2. *By promoting effective storage processes.* Students tend to study differently, depending on the kind of test they expect to take. For example, students are likely to focus on memorizing isolated facts at a rote level if they believe the test will require verbatim recall. They are more likely to try to make sense of what they are studying—that is, to engage in meaningful learning—when they know they will have to put things in their own words. And they are more likely to elaborate on class material if such elaboration will be required at test time—for example, if their test questions will ask them to apply, analyze, or synthesize the material.

3. *By requiring review during the test itself.* Taking a test is, in and of itself, an occasion for retrieving and reviewing previously learned information. Generally speaking, the very process of taking a test on classroom material helps students learn that material better (Frederiksen, 1984b; Foos & Fisher, 1988). But once again, the nature of the test probably makes a difference here: A test that requires students to go beyond the material itself (for example, to draw inferences) is likely to be more effective than one that asks only for recall of facts presented in class (Foos & Fisher, 1988). And test questions that require a broad search of long-term memory (as essay questions are likely to do) promote more comprehensive review than do relatively specific, recognition-type items (as true–false questions are likely to be) (Frederiksen & Ward, 1978; Murnane & Raizen, 1988).

4. *By providing feedback.* Tests provide a concrete mechanism for letting students know what things they have learned correctly and what things they have learned either *in*correctly or not at all. For example, when students get constructive comments on their essay tests—comments that point out the strengths and weaknesses of each response, indicate where answers are ambiguous or imprecise, suggest how an essay might be more complete or better organized, and so on—their understanding of class material and their writing skills are both likely to improve (e.g., Baron, 1987).

It is relatively easy to write test items that measure simple knowledge of facts. As a result, these fact-based questions turn up most frequently on both standardized and teacher-made achievement tests (Bloom, 1984b; Frederiksen & Collins, 1989; Murnane & Raizen, 1988; Nickerson, 1989). But if a teacher wants students to do *more* than memorize facts, that teacher must construct a test that encourages students to process information in certain ways—perhaps to rephrase ideas in their own words, generate their own examples of concepts, relate principles and procedures to real world situations, use course material to solve problems, or examine ideas with a critical eye.

SUMMARY

Human information processing theory is now being translated into a variety of educational applications. Expository instruction (presenting information in the form that students are to learn it) promotes effective learning *if* it facilitates effective storage processes—for example, if it promotes meaningful rather than rote learning, emphasizes the structure and interrelationships within the material, and focuses student attention on important ideas. Mnemonics provide a mechanism whereby learners can store what is otherwise relatively meaningless material through the use of verbal mediation, visual imagery, and internal organization.

Teacher questions asked in a rapid-fire fashion are useful for developing automaticity of basic facts and skills. But in other situations, higher-level questions—those that ask students to infer, apply, justify, problem-solve, and so on—facilitate more effective long-term memory storage and retrieval. Students are more likely to respond appropriately to teacher questions, and to achieve at higher levels in general, when teachers allow sufficient wait time for students to process the information they receive and the questions they are asked.

When students have erroneous beliefs about a particular topic, they may impose those beliefs as they elaborate on new information; thus, they are likely to misinterpret the new information, learning something other than what their teacher actually presented. Several strategies are useful in promoting conceptual change; as examples, teachers should encourage meaningful learning of a few key ideas rather than learning a great deal of material at a rote level, and they should show students how new explanations are better than the misconceptions students currently possess. Classroom tests provide a means of detecting students' misconceptions and, particularly when they include higher-level questions, encourage effective long-term memory storage and retrieval in general.

PART FIVE

COMPLEX LEARNING AND COGNITION

CHAPTER 14

Learning Concepts

ne night in late May, my son Jeff and I had a discussion about the seasons. It went something like this:

Jeff:	When are spring and summer coming?
Mom:	Spring is already here. Haven't you noticed how warm it is, and how the leaves are back on the trees, and how the birds are singing again?
Jeff:	Oh. Then when is summer coming?
Mom:	Well, you only have one more week of school, and then a couple weeks after that, summer will be here.
Jeff:	Summer is when we go swimming, right?
Mom:	(I pause and think about how to answer.) Right.

As a 4-year-old, Jeff had not precisely defined the concepts of spring and summer yet. When I myself was a child, summer was a season of heat, humidity, and no school. As an adult, I now define it more formally as the three-month period between the summer solstice and the autumn equinox. To Jeff, however, summer was simply the time when he could swim.

Much of our cognitive growth involves the learning and refinement of concepts. Some concepts are defined by readily observable characteristics and thus are fairly easy to learn. For example, the word *milk* refers to a white liquid with a particular taste. Similarly, the word *red* refers to a certain range of light wavelengths (although people disagree about exactly where "red" ends and "orange" begins). Other concepts are defined by less salient attributes, so are more slowly learned and more easily misconstrued. For instance, the four seasons of the year are "officially" designated by the occurrences of solstices and equinoxes that most individuals are unaware of, so many people erroneously define them in terms of different weather conditions. Still other concepts may be even harder to grasp, because they are based on abstract and sometimes elusive criteria. For example, psychologists have wrestled with the concept of *intelligence* for many years and still cannot agree on what the term means.

This chapter will examine the multifaceted process of learning concepts. We will define the term *concept* and examine how concepts affect learning and information processing. We will look at different kinds of concepts and at advantages (and a possible disadvantage) of using concepts in thinking about and interpreting experiences. We will then define terms related to concept learning and use those terms to explore several theories of concept learning. Later in the chapter, as we consider Robert Gagné's perspective, we will see how concept learning may be related to other forms of learning. Finally, we will apply current views of concept learning to classroom practice.

THE NATURE OF CONCEPTS

Before we explore theories of concept learning, we must first address three basic issues: the meaning of the term *concept*, the benefits of concepts for human learning and information processing, and a possible difficulty that concepts may create.

Defining a Concept

Ironically, psychologists have not agreed on how to define the concept of **concept**. Behaviorists (e.g., Hunt, 1962; Kendler, 1961) have frequently defined a concept as the same response to different stimuli, as illustrated here:

Cognitivists, on the other hand, are more likely to define a concept as a mental phenomenon—as a category of objects or events that share one or more common properties (e.g., Klausmeier, 1990; Schwartz & Reisberg, 1991). Many *schemas*—organized bodies of knowledge about a particular topic—are probably related to specific concepts.

Theorists of both persuasions find it useful to distinguish between two general kinds of concepts (Cohen, 1983; R. Gagné, 1985; Hull, 1943; Newby & Stepich, 1987; Wasserman, DeVolder, & Coppage, 1992). **Concrete concepts** can be easily identified by their physical appearance; *cow*, *red*, and *round* are examples. Concrete concepts may develop, at least in part, as a result of stimulus generalization: Once an organism has learned to respond in a certain way to one stimulus, it tends to respond in the same way to similar stimuli. In contrast, **abstract concepts** are difficult to conceptualize in terms of specific, observable characteristics; examples include *intelligence*, *charisma*, and *work*. Such concepts are probably best described in terms of a formal definition (R. Gagné, 1985); for example, biologists define *mammal* as a particular form of vertebrate that gives birth to and suckles live offspring. Because stimulus generalization is unlikely to occur when objects or events don't *look* similar, abstract concepts are most likely to develop as a result of specific training or instruction (Hull, 1943; Wasserman et al., 1992).

In many cases, people first learn a concept in a concrete form, then later acquire a more abstract definition of it (R. Gagné, 1985). When I was a child, *summer* was a concrete concept for me: Heat, humidity, and no school were easily observable characteristics. I later acquired an abstract concept of summer as I learned how the seasons are determined by the tilt of the earth in relation to the sun. In a similar way, children first learn about a *circle* as a concrete concept (i.e., a "roundish" thing); later, perhaps in high school geometry class, they may develop an abstract concept of a circle (i.e., all points on a plane equidistant from another single point). As you will learn from our discussion of Gagné's work later in the chapter, the processes by which we learn concrete and abstract concepts may be somewhat different.

Most concepts are identified by a label—a word that symbolizes the concept and represents it in both thought and communication. For example, you have probably formed a concept that encompasses the many items you have seen with the following characteristics:

- Shorter and wider than most adult humans
- Covered with a short, bristly substance
- Appended at one end by an object similar in appearance to a paintbrush
- Appended at the other end by a lumpy thing with four pointy objects sticking upward (two soft and floppy, two hard and curved around)
- Held up from the ground by four spindly sticks, two at each end
- Usually observed in pastures or barns
- Almost always eating

You have no doubt attached a particular label to these similar looking objects: *cow*.

Advantages of Concepts

As people develop and learn, they acquire an ever increasing number of concepts. Concepts have several advantages.

•*Concepts reduce the world's complexity* (Bruner, 1957; Bruner, Goodnow, & Austin, 1956; Sokal, 1977). Classifying similar objects and events makes life simpler and easier to understand. For example, when you drive along a country road, it is easier to think to yourself, "There are some cows," than to think, "There is a brown object, covered with bristly stuff, appended by a paintbrush and a lumpy thing, and held up by four sticks. Ah, yes, and I also see a black-and-white spotted object, covered with bristly stuff, appended by a paintbrush and a lumpy thing, and held up by four sticks. And over there is a brown-and-white spotted object. . . ." In other words, concepts condense and summarize information.

•*Concepts facilitate generalization to new situations* (Bruner, 1957; Bruner et al., 1956; Johnson-Laird & Wason, 1977). When people learn a concept, they associate certain characteristics with it. Then, when they encounter a new instance of the concept, they can draw on their knowledge of associated characteristics to form assumptions and inferences about the new instance. For example, if you see a herd of cattle as you drive through the countryside, you can assume that you are passing through either dairy or beef country, depending on whether you see large udders hanging down between two of the spindly sticks. If you purchase a potted flower, you know that you must water it regularly because of something you have learned about the concept *flower*: It needs water to live. Thanks to concepts, people don't have to learn from scratch in each new situation.

•*Concepts allow abstraction of the environment* (Bruner, 1966). An object covered with bristly stuff, appended by a paintbrush and a lumpy thing, and held up by four sticks is a very concrete thing. The concept of *cow*, however, can be more abstract: it incorporates such characteristics as "female," "supplier of milk," and, to the dairy farmer, "economic asset." Concepts and their labels allow individuals to think about their experiences without necessarily having to consider all their concrete, perceptual aspects; to put it in information processing terms, concepts provide a means of *encoding* environmental events. In fact, as we noted earlier, many abstract concepts do not have easily identifiable real-world referents at all.

•*Concepts enhance the power of thought* (Bruner, 1966). When you are thinking about an object covered with bristly stuff, appended by a paintbrush and a lumpy thing, held up by four sticks, and so on, you can think of little else; to express this point in terms of contemporary memory theory, your working memory capacity is exhausted. On the other hand, when you simply think *cow*, you can also think about *horse*, *dog*, *goat*, and *pig* at the same time.

•*Interrelationships among concepts can be established* (Bruner, 1957; Bruner et al., 1956). Once information has been condensed and abstracted into concepts, those concepts can be associated and interrelated in long-term memory. For instance, the concept *cow* is related to the concepts *bull* and *calf* in a familial way and to *mammal*, *animal*, and *living thing* in a hierarchical fashion.

A Potential Disadvantage of Concepts

By identifying a new stimulus as being an instance of a certain concept, people are likely to react to that stimulus as they would to any other instance of the concept. In the process, they may lose sight of the unique qualities of that particular stimulus. Furthermore, if they have identified the stimulus incorrectly, their response to it may be inappropriate. I remember as a young child trying to make a vehicle using square pieces of wood for wheels. Calling those pieces of wood *wheels* was an inaccurate identification, and, as you can imagine, my car didn't move very far.

BASIC CONCEPTS IN CONCEPT LEARNING

Before we examine theories of concept learning, we must first define some concepts related to it. In particular, we need to distinguish between positive and negative instances and to specify what features and rules are.

Positive and Negative Instances

A **positive instance** is a particular example of a concept. To illustrate, you and I are positive instances of the concept *person*, and this thing you are reading is a positive instance of the concept *book*. A **negative instance** is a nonexample of the concept. You and I are negative instances of the concept *cow*, and this book is a negative instance of the concept *pencil*.

One sign that individuals have truly learned a concept is that they correctly identify all positive and negative instances of that concept. A child who vehemently denies that a Chihuahua is a dog has not completely learned the concept of *dog*; neither has the child who calls the neighbor's cow "doggie." Denying that a Chihuahua is a dog—**undergeneralization**—reflects an inability to recognize all positive instances. Identifying a cow as a dog—**overgeneralization**—reflects an inability to reject all negative instances.

Features

Features (some theorists instead use the term **attributes**) are the characteristics of a concept's positive instances. For example, consider my dog Anna. She has numerous features worthy of note, including these:

- Hairy
- At one time physiologically equipped to give birth to live young
- Likely to bark loudly at any negative instance of an Ormrod
- Wearing a chain collar
- At present located on my office floor

Some features are important for identifying positive instances of a concept; others are not. **Defining features** (also known as *critical* or *criterial* features) are characteristics that must be present in all positive instances. For example, to be a dog, Anna must have hair and, as a female, must have (or once have had) the capability of giving birth to live young. **Correlational features** are frequently found in positive instances but are not essential for concept membership. For example, most dogs bark and many dogs wear collars, but neither of these features is a characteristic of *all* dogs. **Irrelevant features** are characteristics that are unrelated to membership in the concept. Anna's location on my office floor is totally irrelevant to her dogness.

Let's pause here for a brief exercise. Figure 14–1 presents eight positive instances and eight negative instances of the concept *gudge*. Can you identify one or more defining features of a gudge?

As you may have surmised, the two defining features of a gudge are that it be gray and square. A large black dot is a correlational feature: Black dots are found on six of the eight gudges, but on only one nongudge. White dots and topside

Figure 14–1
Positive and negative
instances of a *gudge*

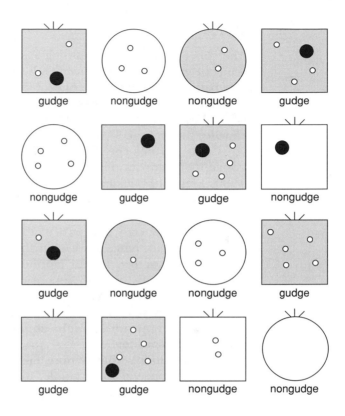

"whiskers" are irrelevant features, because they are found equally often on gudges and nongudges.

Concept learning is a process of learning what features are important for identifying positive instances of that concept. In essence, one must learn that certain features are an essential component of the concept and that other features are frequently present but unessential. Learning to differentiate between a concept's defining and correlational features takes time and experience, often many years' worth. For example, consider this question that Saltz (1971) posed to children:

> A father goes to work. On the way home from work in the evening he stops at a bar to have a drink. His friends there are drunkards and he becomes a drunkard too. Is he still a father? (p. 28)

Saltz found that, even at the age of eight, most children denied that a drunkard could still be a father. Apparently, many young children believe that "goodness" defines fatherhood rather than correlating with it, a belief that they are likely to discard only when they encounter enough "bad" positive instances of a father.

Rules

The concept *red* has one defining feature: a particular range of wavelengths. The concept *gudge* has two that must both be present: square and gray. An *out* in baseball is an example of a concept for which no single defining feature is always present: For example, it can be three strikes while a player is at bat, the tagging of a player who is running from base to base, or a fly ball caught before it touches the ground.

Concept **rules** specify how defining features are combined to define those concepts. Theorists (e.g., Bourne, 1967; Bruner et al., 1956; Dodd & White, 1980; Klein, 1987; Saltz, 1971) have identified a number of different concept rules. Four rules are most commonly described:

1. **Simple.** Only one particular feature must be present; for example, *red* is a specific range of wavelengths.
2. **Conjunctive.** Two or more features must all be present; for example, a *circle* must be two-dimensional and must have all points equidistant from a center point.
3. **Disjunctive.** Two or more defining features are not all present at the same time; for example, an *out* in baseball occurs in any one of several different situations.
4. **Relational.** The relationship between two or more features determines the concept; for example, the concept *between* requires three objects, two located on opposite sides of a third.

As you might guess, the nature of a concept's features and rules influences how easily the concept is learned. Let's now look at these and other factors affecting concept learning.

FACTORS AFFECTING CONCEPT LEARNING

Numerous factors affect the ease and rapidity of concept learning: the salience, redundancy, and number of features; the complexity of rules; the frequency and nature of positive and negative instances; and the timing with which these instances are presented.

Salience of Defining Features

The more salient, or obvious, the defining features are, the easier a concept is to learn. For example, my son Jeff easily learned the correct meanings of *milk*, *hot*, and *television*, presumably because the features that define these concepts are readily observable. However, he struggled with such words as *spring*, *summer*, *work*, and *university*—concepts whose defining features are not so obvious.

Because young children typically pay attention to obvious features, their early concepts are likely to be based (sometimes erroneously) on such features. For example, in a study by DeVries (1969), children ranging in age from 3 to 6 played for a short time with a good-natured cat named Maynard. Then, as they looked on, the experimenter placed a ferocious-looking dog mask on Maynard and asked them, "What is this animal now?" Many of the 3-year-olds asserted that Maynard was now a dog and refused to pet him. The 6-year-olds, on the other hand, could overlook the dog mask, recognizing that it did not change Maynard's "catness." As children grow older, they begin to attend less to perceptually salient features and focus more on abstract qualities (Anglin, 1977; Ausubel, Novak, & Hanesian, 1978).

Redundancy of Defining and Correlational Features

As defining and correlational features become increasingly redundant with one another, positive instances of a concept become easier to identify (Good & Brophy, 1986). For example, the concept *bird* is relatively easy to learn, because many characteristics—feathers, wings, beak, small size, scrawny legs and feet—are either defining or correlational features. On the other hand, the concept *weed* is more difficult, because it has only two defining features, and one of them is fairly abstract: It is a plant, and it is in the wrong place at the wrong time.

Number of Irrelevant Features

The more irrelevant features are present, the more difficult a concept is to learn (Good & Brophy, 1986). For instance, the concept *animal* is a difficult one for many children, because most of the salient features—body covering, nature and number of limbs, facial features, shape, and size—are irrelevant. Although my son Jeff quite accurately identifies positive instances of birds, he continues to have trouble identifying some positive instances of animals: He adamantly rejects any suggestion that people, fish, or insects fall into this category.

Complexity of Rules

The rules that specify how defining features are combined influence the ease with which concepts are learned (Bourne, 1967; Haygood & Bourne, 1965; Neisser & Weene, 1962). Simple rules are typically the easiest to learn, conjunctive and disjunctive are moderately difficult, and relational are most difficult. Young children often have trouble understanding such common relational concepts as *under*, *over*, *more*, and *less*; for example, children as old as 7 years often do not fully understand what the concept *less* means (Palermo, 1973).

Positive Instances Versus Negative Instances

Generally speaking, the presentation of positive instances leads to faster concept learning than the presentation of negative instances, although exceptions to this rule have been observed (Ausubel et al., 1978; Barringer & Gholson, 1979). In other words, it is generally more helpful to see what a concept is than what it is not.

However, for accurate concept learning, both positive and negative instances are desirable if they are carefully chosen. Positive instances should illustrate the full range of the concept, so that it will not be undergeneralized. For example, to learn an accurate concept of *dog*, one should see Chihuahuas and Great Danes as well as cocker spaniels and Irish setters. Negative instances can illustrate "near misses," so that the concept will not be overgeneralized (Winston, 1973). For example, one must be informed that such creatures as cats, goats, and cows are nondogs to learn just where to draw the line on dogness.

Sequential Versus Simultaneous Presentation of Instances

In their everyday lives, individuals typically learn concepts through **sequential presentation**: They encounter a series of positive and negative instances one at a time over a period of weeks, months, or years, and receive feedback about what is and is not an example of the concept. A faster way to learn concepts is **simultaneous presentation**, in which people observe a number of positive and negative instances all at once (Bourne, Ekstrand, & Dominowski, 1971). One likely

Concepts are best learned through a simultaneous presentation of both positive and negative instances.

Each of these is a dog.

None of these is a dog.

reason for the difference in effectiveness of the two presentation methods is that, in sequential presentation, one must store in memory what is learned from each instance, and that information can be forgotten from one instance to the next. In simultaneous presentation, on the other hand, the information to be gleaned from positive and negative instances is available all at once, so demands on memory are not as great.

What exactly *is* learned in concept learning? We turn to this topic—theories of concept learning—next.

THEORIES OF CONCEPT LEARNING

A number of theorists have tried to explain concept learning; we will examine five theories here. First, we will explore a strictly behaviorist perspective based on the notion of habit strength. We will begin to see signs of cognitivism in the second theory, a neo-behaviorist model incorporating mediation. We will then examine three cognitive theories of concept learning based on the notions of hypothesis testing, prototypes, and feature lists.

Buildup of Habit Strength

Clark Hull (1920) proposed an early theory of concept learning. To use contemporary terminology, Hull suggested that any instance of a concept has both defining and irrelevant features, and that an organism that correctly identifies a stimulus as being a positive instance is reinforced for responding to both its defining and irrelevant features. When correctly identifying a second positive instance, it is again reinforced for responding to the defining and irrelevant features. In repeated trials with the same concept, the defining features are always the same; however, the irrelevant features differ from one occasion to the next. Thus, the individual is *always* reinforced for responding to the defining features but only *occasionally* reinforced for responding to various irrelevant features. Thus, the habit strength of a response to defining features is greater than that of a response to irrelevant features, and the organism learns to respond in the same way to the same (defining) features of different positive instances.

A demonstration exercise, in which you will learn the concept *mudge,* illustrates Hull's theory. Take a piece of paper and cover Figure 14–2, exposing only the top section above the first horizontal line. In the top section of the left column, you should see two objects, one of which is a mudge. Take a wild guess and see if you can pick the mudge. Once you have made your selection, move your paper down the left column to the next horizontal line, revealing the correct answer. In this section you will also see two more objects; pick the one you think is the mudge. Keep moving your paper down the page, one section at a time, on each occasion getting your feedback and then selecting a likely mudge

Figure 14–2
Pick the *mudge* in each section.

1.				5.		
Previous Pair:	mudge	nonmudge		Previous Pair:	nonmudge	mudge
2.				6.		
Previous Pair:	nonmudge	mudge		Previous Pair:	mudge	nonmudge
3.				7.		
Previous Pair:	nonmudge	mudge		Previous Pair:	mudge	nonmudge
4.				8.		
Previous Pair:	mudge	nonmudge		Previous Pair:	nonmudge	mudge

from the next pair of objects. Continue the process with the pairs in the right hand column.

You have presumably learned that *mudge* is "large." Let's analyze this concept learning task from a Hullian perspective. You were reinforced every time you chose a large square, you were never reinforced for choosing a small square, and you were reinforced for choosing black, white, left, or right squares about half of the time. Thus, the occurrence of reinforcement for choosing boxes with different characteristics was as follows:

Characteristic	Amount of Reinforcement
large	100%
small	0%
black	50%
white	50%
left	50%
right	50%

Because it has been reinforced every time, the response of selecting "large" should be the strongest habit for you, and you should therefore be most likely to choose a large square again, regardless of its color and position.

Mediation

A problem with viewing concept learning simply as a buildup of habit strength was identified by Kendler and Kendler (1959, 1961, 1962). Their series of experiments were very similar to my "mudge" example: Subjects were shown numerous pairs of different-sized black and white boxes and asked to choose the "correct" one in each pair; they were reinforced for choosing the large square each time, regardless of its color or position. Once subjects were consistently choosing the large square in each pair, without warning or explanation the characteristic that was reinforced changed. Some subjects were now reinforced for choosing the small square in each pair; the Kendlers called this a **reversal shift** (the opposite, or reverse, characteristic was being reinforced). Other subjects were instead reinforced for choosing the black square of each pair—the Kendlers called this a **nonreversal shift**.

Which group of subjects learned the new concept more quickly? Let's look at this situation from the perspective of habit strength buildup. Just as when you were learning *mudge*, subjects who were reinforced for choosing a large square were also reinforced for choosing a black square 50% of the time, but they were *never* reinforced for choosing a small square. Because the habit strength of a "black" response was greater than the habit strength of a "small" response, a nonreversal shift should have been an easier shift for subjects to make than a reversal shift.

In fact, the Kendlers found the opposite result, at least for children over 5 years old. Reversal shifts—learning to choose small boxes after previously being reinforced for choosing large ones—were easier than nonreversal shifts. They proposed that subjects **mediated** their overt responses (i.e., their choices) by first making internal, mental responses. The following figure illustrates the process that the Kendlers proposed, with uppercase letters indicating observable stimuli and responses and lowercase letters indicating mental stimuli and responses:

Subjects may have thought something along the line of "It's the size that matters," then chosen the large one in response to that mental stimulus. In the case of a reversal shift, the mediating response and stimulus ("size") would be the same, and only the overt response would need to change. However, for a nonreversal shift, the mediating response would have to change as well as the overt response, a learning task that should take more time. Curiously, however, the Kendlers found that children below the age of 5 (and animals as well) learned the nonreversal shift more easily; hence the learning of these subjects may have been more a process of forming various S-R habits.

Hypothesis Testing

In their discussion of mediation, Kendler and Kendler proposed that mental responses were involved in how people learn concepts. A few years earlier, Jerome Bruner and his colleagues (Bruner, Goodnow, & Austin, 1956) had proposed a theory of concept learning that was even more clearly cognitive in nature. But before I describe their theory, take a minute to learn the concept *studge*. Figure 14–3 provides numerous positive and negative instances of a studge. As you did in learning about mudges, use a piece of paper to reveal one section at a time and try to guess whether each object is a studge or nonstudge.

I hope you have learned that the concept *studge* is "two or three circles." Shape and number are defining features for the concept; color is irrelevant to studgeness. In learning about studges, you may have found yourself forming different hypotheses about what is a studge and what is not. For instance, the first example was a studge. You may have used that positive instance to generate one or more hypotheses such as these:

- A studge is anything gray

Figure 14–3
Positive and negative instances of a *studge*

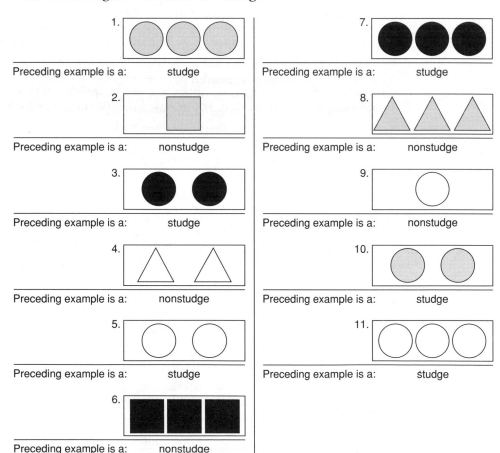

- A studge is round
- A studge is three of something
- A studge is three gray circles

The second example in Figure 14–3 was a nonstudge, so, had you held the hypothesis that a studge is gray, you would have eliminated that particular hypothesis at that point. A hypothesis such as "three of something," however, would have been confirmed with the second example, but disconfirmed with the third. Eventually you may have ended up with the correct hypothesis: A studge is two or three circles.

Bruner et al. (1956) proposed that concept learning is a process of forming various hypotheses about the features and rules that define a concept and then using positive and negative instances to confirm or reject those hypotheses. To illustrate their theory, they used stimuli similar to my positive and negative instances of studges to study concept learning in adults. They gave their subjects one positive instance of the concept and then asked them to try to select other positive instances from among an array of stimuli varying on four dimensions (shape, color, number of objects, and number of borders around the objects). By noting the selections that subjects made, Bruner and his colleagues observed several different approaches that subjects used in formulating and testing their hypotheses. Some subjects appeared to test one hypothesis at a time, choosing stimuli that varied on only one feature from a previous positive instance. If they received feedback that confirmed their hypothesis, they continued to test it; if they received contradictory feedback, they would form a different hypothesis and begin to test that one. Other subjects appeared to hold several hypotheses in mind at the same time and eliminate them simultaneously with their selection of different stimuli. This latter strategy would of course be faster, but it would also place greater demands on memory, hence leading to more errors. This tendency to test several hypotheses simultaneously has also been observed by Levine (1966).

Although some hypothesis testing may very well occur when people learn concepts, it is probably not the only process involved in concept learning. Experiments in which hypothesis testing has been observed, such as those of Bruner et al. (1956) and Levine (1966), have been criticized as being artificial and not resembling real-world concept learning conditions (e.g., Glass, Holyoak, & Santa, 1979; Rosch, 1973a). People rarely encounter a situation in which they can pick possible examples of a concept in any systematic fashion; more typically, they find a positive instance here, a negative instance there, and so on, in a somewhat haphazard fashion over time. Furthermore, in several experiments (Brooks, 1978; Reber & Allen, 1978; Reber, Kassin, Lewis, & Cantor, 1980), subjects who were instructed to identify the rules underlying certain classification schemes (i.e., to form hypotheses) actually performed more poorly than subjects who were not so instructed. In these cases, the more successful subjects were the less analytic ones: They simply remembered early positive instances and compared new examples to them. A different theory of concept learning—one involving the formation of prototypes—better explains such findings.

Prototypes

Eleanor Rosch (1973a, 1973b, 1977a; Rosch, Mervis, Gray, Johnson, & Boyes-Braem, 1976) and other theorists (e.g., Eysenck & Keane, 1990; Wittgenstein, 1958) have argued that many real-world concepts are difficult to delineate in terms of defining features and precise rules. Objects can lack important features, yet still be recognized as positive instances of a particular concept. For example, a salient feature of human beings is that they have two legs, yet you can still recognize a person with no legs as a human. Similarly, although birds typically fly, most people correctly identify nonflying penguins and ostriches as birds. Thus, it appears that people often use correlational features rather than defining features to identify positive instances of a concept.

Furthermore, concepts often have fuzzy boundaries, so that in certain borderline cases correct identification of positive and negative instances is difficult (Labov, 1973; Rosch, 1973a, 1978; Zazdeh, Fu, Tanak, & Shimura, 1975). For example, is a stroke a disease? In a study by McCloskey and Glucksberg (1978), some people believed that it was and others did not. Is turquoise a shade of blue or a shade of green? My husband insists that turquoise is green, but I know better—it's blue.

Instead, Rosch (1973a, 1973b, 1975, 1977a, 1977b, 1978; Rosch et al., 1976) and others (Attneave, 1957; Tennyson & Cocchiarella, 1986; Walton & Bower, 1993) have proposed that people form concepts by developing a **prototype**, or representative example, of a typical member of that category. To illustrate, form an image in your mind of a *bird*. What probably comes to mind is a small creature, perhaps about the shape and size of a robin or sparrow. It is unlikely that you would instead imagine a penguin or an ostrich because these animals, while birds, are not as typically birdlike in appearance as robins and sparrows. Similarly, imagine a *vehicle*. Your image probably resembles a car or a truck rather than a canoe or hot-air balloon, because cars and trucks are more commonly observed instances of vehicles. Now imagine *red*. You probably picture a color similar to that red crayon you had when you were 5 rather than pink or maroon.

A prototype is likely to incorporate features of the most typical, commonly observed positive instances of the concept. For instance, your prototype of a human being probably has two arms and two legs, stands upright, and is slightly less than two meters tall. Your prototype of a table is likely to be a rectangular flat surface held up by four legs, one of them at each of the four corners. New objects are identified as positive instances of a particular concept when they are compared to the concept prototype and found to be sufficiently similar. A positive identification does not require that all features be present, however; a legless man can still be recognized as a human being, and a three-legged object can still be recognized as a table.

At least two sources of evidence support the idea that concepts are represented in memory in the form of prototypes. First of all, people easily identify positive instances of a concept that closely resemble the prototype but have difficulty identifying positive instances that are less similar (e.g., Glass, Holyoak, & O'Dell, 1974; Posner & Keele, 1968, 1970; Rips, Shoben, & Smith, 1973; Rosch, 1973b, 1978; Rosch & Mervis, 1975; Rosch, Simpson, & Miller, 1976; Wilkins, 1971). In one experiment by Rosch (1973b), elementary school and undergraduate students identified as birds those creatures that looked particularly birdlike (e.g., robins and sparrows) more quickly than they identified creatures less similar to the prototype (e.g., chickens and ducks).

A second source of evidence for prototypes is the fact that people sometimes recognize positive instances they have never encountered before when those instances closely resemble the prototype. In fact, subjects recognize them more easily than positive instances they *have* encountered that do not closely match the prototype (Franks & Bransford, 1971; Posner, Goldsmith, & Welton, 1967; Posner & Keele, 1968). For example, in an experiment by Franks and Bransford (1971), college students viewed a series of geometric patterns that involved one or more variations from a particular "base" pattern; the base pattern itself was not presented. Subjects were then shown another series of patterns and asked to identify which ones they had previously seen (they had actually seen none of them before). Subjects were most likely to "recognize" patterns that closely resembled the base pattern; subjects were most confident that they had seen the base pattern itself. Presumably, the base pattern represented the single best example of the various stimuli that had originally been viewed and thus most closely approximated the pattern prototype that subjects had formed.

Rosch and her colleagues (1976) have suggested that conceptual prototypes may be organized in a three-level, hierarchical arrangement similar to what I described in Chapter 11. **Basic-level concepts** are the ones we use most frequently—for example, the ones we use when we name objects (this is a *chair*, this is a *hat*, this is a *car*, etc.). **Superordinate concepts** are more general categories that encompass a number of basic-level concepts (e.g., chairs and tables are both *furniture*, hats and shoes are two kinds of *clothing*, and cars and trucks are *vehicles*). **Subordinate concepts** are more specific subdivisions of basic-level concepts (e.g., *rocking chairs* and *lawn chairs* are types of chairs, *berets* and *bowlers* are types of hats, and *Volkswagen Beetles* and *Plymouth Voyagers* are types of cars). You can think of the three levels as reflecting varying degrees of abstraction: The superordinate concepts are most abstract, and the subordinate concepts are most concrete.

We can probably not explain all human concept learning strictly in terms of prototype development. For one thing, how we categorize an object depends on the context in which we find it. For example, if a cup-like object contains flowers, we might identify it as a *vase* rather than a *cup*; if it contains mashed potatoes, we might instead identify it as a *bowl* (Labov, 1973; Schwartz & Reisberg, 1991). Furthermore, not all concepts lend themselves readily to a prototypical representation (Hampton, 1981; Eysenck & Keane, 1990). To illustrate, such abstract concepts as *rule*, *belief*, and *instinct* are difficult to conceptualize in terms of a typical example.

It is possible that prototypes are used to identify positive instances in clear-cut situations and more formal definitions are used in other, more ambiguous ones (Andre, 1986; Glass & Holyoak, 1975; Glass et al., 1979). For example, I mentioned earlier that my son Jeff denies that *animals* include people, fish, and insects. His belief that these groups are nonanimals is a common phenomenon among young children, who often restrict their conception of animals to four-legged mammals (Kyle & Shymansky, 1989; Saltz, 1971). I suspect that Jeff's animal prototype may resemble the family dog or the cows he sees in the surrounding countryside. When he begins studying the animal kingdom in school, he will probably learn a biology-based definition of an animal that incorporates some of its major features: a form of life that derives its food from other organisms, responds immediately to its environment, and can move its body. At that point he will presumably acknowledge that people, fish, and creepy-crawlies are legitimate animals. (If he takes college biology at a later date, however, he may learn that biologists do not really agree on a definition of *animal*, and that true defining features of the concept are difficult to identify.)

Feature Lists

Feature list theory (e.g., Bourne, 1982; Bourne, Dominowski, Loftus, & Healey, 1986; Neumann, 1974, 1977; Rips, Shoben, & Smith, 1973; Smith, Shoben, & Rips, 1974) is in some ways similar to prototype theory but focuses more on a concept's defining and correlational features. From this perspective, learning a concept involves the following:

- Its relevant features, both defining and correlational
- The probability that each of these features is likely to be present in any specific instance—that is, the frequency with which each feature occurs
- The relationships among the features—that is, the rules for their combination

Recognizing an object as a positive instance of a concept, then, is a matter of determining whether the object possesses enough relevant features. Prototypes are recognized more quickly than other positive instances only because they encompass most or all of the concept's relevant features.

A prediction from feature list theory is that negative instances will be erroneously identified as positive instances if a sufficient number of relevant features are present. Bourne (1982) confirmed this prediction in an experiment involving an **exclusive disjunctive** concept. Earlier in the chapter, I described a disjunctive concept as being one with two or more defining features that did not all need to be present at once (the example I gave you was an *out* in baseball). An exclusive disjunctive concept is a subform of this kind of concept: An item possessing any of the defining features is a positive instance, but an item possessing all of them is not. (For example, a *pludge* is anything that is red or square, but things that are both red and square are nonpludges.) In an experiment involving undergraduate students, Bourne presented numerous positive and negative instances of an exclusive disjunctive concept that had two relevant features; an item that had one, but not both, of the features was a positive instance. Despite their training, when subjects were later asked to identify examples of the concept, they were more likely to "recognize" those stimuli possessing both relevant features than those possessing only one of the two features. But feature list theory is probably not the perfect explanation of concept learning, either. Like prototype theory, it does not account for the effects of context on concept identification. And, as we noted earlier, we cannot always identify the specific features on which concepts are based.

Regardless of which theory of concept learning may eventually be found to model human behavior most closely, two factors emerge as essential for the learning of concepts. First, individuals must learn the characteristics that determine concept membership (and discover which of those characteristics, if any, are truly definitive). Second, individuals must develop a realization of the degree of acceptable variation from best examples of the concept. For example, an ostrich is a bird even though it is much larger than the prototypic bird; however, a certain other creature that is the same size and also walks on two legs—a human being—falls outside the bird category. In other words, to learn a concept completely, one must eventually learn the boundaries of that concept.

Now that we have looked at behaviorist and cognitive explanations of how concept learning occurs, it is time to turn to a related topic: how concept learning relates to other forms of learning. Robert Gagné has offered a theory of human learning in which concept learning depends on some forms of learning and is a prerequisite to other forms.

RELATING CONCEPTS TO OTHER FORMS OF LEARNING: ROBERT GAGNÉ'S ANALYSIS

Robert Gagné (e.g., 1985; Gagné, Briggs, & Wager, 1988; Gagné & Driscoll, 1988) has incorporated concept learning into a sequence of eight types of learning of increasing complexity. He has proposed that four basic forms of learning—classical conditioning, operant learning, chaining, and verbal association—can be explained in terms of simple S-R **associations**. Four more complex forms—learning discriminations, concepts, rules, and higher-order rules—involve the use of **symbols** (i.e., mental representations of various objects, events, and ideas) to interact with the environment; Gagné refers to these four as **intellectual skills**.

Gagné theorized that simple forms of learning are necessary before other, more complex forms can occur. For example, concept learning can occur only after basic associations and discriminations have been learned. At the same time, concept formation is a prerequisite to learning rules and higher-order rules, things necessary for problem solving. Let's look at each of Gagné's eight forms of learning and at how they are interrelated.

Learning Associations

Gagné has identified four forms of learning that can be understood in terms of simple stimulus-response associations: classical conditioning, operant learning, chaining, and verbal association.

Classical Conditioning

As you should recall from Chapter 3, classical conditioning is a process whereby one learns an involuntary response to a particular stimulus. Classical conditioning occurs when one stimulus that already elicits a response (i.e., an unconditioned stimulus eliciting an unconditioned response) is paired with a stimulus that does not initially elicit a response. This second, "neutral" stimulus begins to elicit a response as well, hence becoming a conditioned stimulus that elicits a conditioned (learned) response.

Operant Learning

Gagné's description of operant learning is similar to B. F. Skinner's model of operant conditioning in that a voluntary response is learned. But, while Skinner focused more on the response-reinforcement ($R \rightarrow S_{Rf}$) connection, Gagné emphasizes the formation of a single stimulus-response (S-R) association. Nevertheless, Gagné does point out that immediate reinforcement of a response is a necessary condition for operant learning to occur.

Chaining

Chaining is the formation of a series of nonverbal stimulus-response (S-R) associations, such that a sequence of behaviors is learned. For example, using a pair of scissors involves a number of responses that typically occur in the same order: putting the forefinger through one hole, putting the thumb through the other hole, spreading the forefinger and thumb apart (thus opening the scissors), placing the open scissors against the edge of the paper to be cut, squeezing the thumb and forefinger together (thus cutting the paper), and so on. Similarly, swinging a tennis racket involves a chain of responses: watching the ball approaching, running to the ball's probable landing spot, standing with feet apart, holding the racket out with an almost straight arm, swinging to meet and return the ball, and then positioning oneself for the next return.

Depicted graphically, chaining looks like this:

$$S \rightarrow R \longrightarrow S \rightarrow R \longrightarrow S \rightarrow R \longrightarrow S \rightarrow R \longrightarrow \text{(etc.)}$$

Each response provides a new stimulus situation to which a new response is made. For example, when a child using scissors has made one cut, the cut serves as a stimulus for the next response of opening the scissors. The open scissors in turn provide a stimulus for the response of moving the scissors to the spot where additional cutting must occur. In a similar manner, each movement in a tennis swing provides a slightly altered situation (a new stimulus) that calls for a new response.

Verbal Association

Verbal association involves the chaining of verbal S-R connections. An example of verbal association is uttering a typically invariant sequence of words, such as "How are you?" or "I pledge allegiance to the flag. . . ." In such cases, each word is considered a response, and responses are performed in a particular order.

Verbal association differs from chaining in that not all stimuli and responses are necessarily observable; some of them may be mental events within the individual. For example, a French teacher might teach students how to remember that *le chien* means "dog" in this way:

> When I say le chien, *that can remind you of the word* chain, *because* chien *sounds very much like* chain. *A chain can remind you of a leash, and a leash should make you think of* dog.

The teacher is asking students to form a verbal association like this one:

$$LE\ CHIEN \rightarrow chain \rightarrow leash \rightarrow DOG$$
$$S \longrightarrow r \rightarrow s \rightarrow r \rightarrow s \longrightarrow R$$

Notice that some of the words and some of the S's and R's are capitalized, while others are lowercase. Capitalized words and letters indicate *observed* stimuli and responses; lowercase words and letters indicate internal, and therefore unobservable, stimuli and responses. The teacher presents the word *le chien* (an observable stimulus), and the students learn the mental response of *chain*. *Chain* in turn serves as a stimulus for the mental response *leash,* which in turn becomes the internal stimulus for the observable response of saying *dog*.

According to Gagné, the learning of chains and verbal associations can only occur after individual S-R connections have already been mastered; hence, classical conditioning and/or operant learning are prerequisites.

Learning Intellectual Skills

Gagné has identified four intellectual skills that cannot be easily reduced to simple S-R associations: discrimination learning, concept learning, rule learning, and the learning of higher-order rules.

Discrimination Learning

In Chapter 4, I described stimulus discrimination, something learned when a response is reinforced in the presence of one stimulus (S+) but not in the presence of another stimulus (S–). Gagné's discrimination learning is similar: An individual learns to respond to one stimulus but not to another, perhaps very similar, stimulus. We can depict discrimination learning graphically like this:

$$S_1 \longrightarrow R_1$$

$$S_2 \longrightarrow \quad \text{(no response)}$$

Discrimination learning is essentially a process of learning to distinguish among objects on the basis of their physical appearance. For example, a child might learn to say "bee" when seeing the letter b, but not when seeing such similar-looking letters as d, p, or q. Similarly, a child might begin to hear the difference between two musical notes or to feel the difference in texture of two different types of fabric.

Concept Learning

As I mentioned earlier in the chapter, Gagné and other theorists distinguish between two kinds of concepts, concrete concepts (those identified by their physical appearance) and abstract concepts (those identified by a definition); Gagné refers to the latter as *defined concepts*. Gagné restricts his view of concept learning to concrete concepts, arguing that defined concepts actually reflect a form of rule learning.

Gagné describes the learning of concrete concepts as a process of putting different stimuli into the same *class* (a mental entity) and then responding to any member of that class in the same way. For example, a child who is learning the letter A must learn that many different stimuli, such as:

A   *A*   **A**   A   A

must all be responded to in the same way:

"*ay*"

When an individual makes the same response to all members of a class, then the individual has formed a concept.

A prerequisite condition for the successful learning of concrete concepts is that discriminations among stimuli belonging to different concept classifications must already have been learned. For example, before students can form a concept of the letter A, they must be able to discriminate between such letters as these:

A vs. B   **A vs. D**   A vs. X

Because concept learning involves learning which stimuli are examples of the concept and which stimuli are not, an individual must first be able to discriminate between examples and nonexamples.

Rule Learning

Gagné defines a **rule** this way:

> A rule . . . is an inferred capability that enables the individual to respond to any instance of a class of stimulus situations with an appropriate instance of a class of performances. (R. Gagné, 1985, p. 118)

Gagné argues that rules organize human behavior and allow people to respond effectively to a wide variety of stimulus situations. Rules can be thought of as chains of two or more concepts. For example, consider this common, everyday rule:

Balls roll.

This rule includes two concepts, *ball* and *roll*, as well as the relationship between them: one (ball) accomplishes the other (roll). Here is another example of a rule, in this case from physics:

$$v = a \times t$$

This rule includes the interrelationships among five concepts: velocity (v), equality ($=$), acceleration (a), multiplication ($\times$), and time (t).

According to Gagné, defined (abstract) concepts fit in this category of learning. Defined concepts are learned through definitions—statements expressing rules for classification. Consider the concept *cousin* as an example. There is no way to learn what a cousin is simply by looking at examples of cousins and noncousins; all will have one head, two arms, two legs, and so on. Instead, a person probably learns a rule (definition) for identifying cousins: A *cousin* is an off-

One cannot learn (abstract) defined concepts such as *cousin* through physical examination alone.

Cousin Fred   Cousin Malcolm   Joe (no relation)   Tim (no relation)

spring of a parent's sibling. To learn this rule, the individual must previously have learned the concepts contained within it: *offspring*, *parent*, and *sibling*.

Rules form the basis for many intellectual skills. People cannot write, read, compute, create, or even speak without applying numerous rules. For instance, rules used in writing include the following:

1. Each sentence should have a subject and a predicate.
2. Each sentence should begin with a capital letter.
3. Each sentence should end with a period, question mark, or exclamation point.
4. Words should be spelled correctly.

Because rules include concepts, they obviously cannot be learned until those concepts have already been learned. For example, a young child can learn that *balls roll* only after learning about balls and rolling. And a physics student must master the concepts of velocity, equality, acceleration, multiplication, and time before learning that "velocity equals acceleration times time."

Learning Higher-order Rules

Sometimes two or more rules can be combined to form higher-order rules. Gagné theorizes that problem solving typically occurs through the formation of such higher-order rules. For example, consider this problem (R. Gagné, 1985):

$$24\tfrac{1}{8} - 22\tfrac{3}{16} = \ ?$$

Students who have not yet learned to solve this kind of problem may be able to do so if they have learned simpler rules—for example, how to form equivalent fractions and how to subtract one fraction from another—that they can combine to solve the problem.

We will address the topic of problem solving more thoroughly in Chapter 16. But here I want to emphasize an important point. Because higher-order rules include rules that in turn include concepts, they cannot be effectively learned until all the concepts and rules contained within them have already been mastered. In fact, all of Gagné's more complex forms of learning depend heavily on lower forms of learning. Basic associations are necessary for discrimination learning, discriminations are necessary for concept learning, concepts are necessary for rule learning, and rules are necessary for forming higher-order rules. Gagné's theory, then, can provide guidance to teachers and instructional designers regarding the order in which different intellectual skills should be taught.

Now that we have explored theories of how people learn concepts and of how concept learning might relate to other forms of learning, it is time to look at how our knowledge of concept learning relates to teaching practice.

FACILITATING CONCEPT LEARNING IN THE CLASSROOM

Theories and research related to concept learning yield a number of implications for educational practice. Here are several points to keep in mind when teaching concepts in the classroom.

•*A definition of a concept facilitates concept learning* (R. Gagné, 1985; Merrill & Tennyson, 1977; Owen, Blount, & Moscow, 1978; Tennyson & Cocchiarella, 1986). A good definition includes defining features plus any rules related to them (e.g., "all defining features must be present"). Furthermore, it describes the concept in terms of other concepts that are already familiar to students (R. Gagné, 1985).

•*Numerous and varied positive instances help to illustrate a concept* (Clark, 1971; R. Gagné, 1985; Merrill & Tennyson, 1977, 1978; Owen et al., 1978; Tennyson & Cocchiarella, 1986). Through encountering many instances of concepts, people may form prototypes of those concepts. In fact, in some situations providing a "best example" is more helpful than a definition. To illustrate, Park (1984) used two instructional methods to teach basic psychology concepts (e.g., positive and negative reinforcement) to high school students. For some students, instruction focused on the defining features of the concepts; for others, it focused on illustrative examples of the concepts. Students for whom defining features were emphasized were better able to classify new examples during instruction. However, students who had been given examples of the concepts remembered more of what they had learned after instruction was completed. Ideally, of course, definitions and examples should be presented hand in hand, and in fact this combination of methods leads to more effective concept learning than either method alone (Dunn, 1983; Tennyson, Youngers, & Suebsonthi, 1983).

Concepts are better learned with many examples than with only one or two (Kinnick, 1990; Tennyson & Park, 1980; Tennyson & Tennyson, 1975). First examples should be simple and straightforward, with as few irrelevant features as possible (Clark, 1971; Merrill & Tennyson, 1977, 1978). Line drawings of concepts are often helpful because they can emphasize defining features and deemphasize or omit irrelevant features. Later examples should be more difficult, with more irrelevant features present (Clark, 1971; Kinnick, 1990; Merrill & Tennyson, 1977). Ultimately, examples should illustrate the full range of the concept so that students do not undergeneralize (Merrill & Tennyson, 1978; Tennyson & Cocchiarella, 1986); for example, the concept *mammal* should be illustrated by whales and platypuses as well as by cats and dogs.

•*Negative instances are useful in demonstrating what a concept is **not*** (Clark, 1971; Freiburgs & Tulving, 1961; R. Gagné, 1985; Merrill & Tennyson, 1977; Owen et al., 1978; Tennyson & Cocchiarella, 1986; Winston, 1973). Although negative instances were viewed as relatively unimportant by early theorists (Hovland & Weiss, 1953; Smoke, 1932), their importance has more recently been recognized. Negative instances, particularly when they are "near misses" to the concept, are helpful in defining the concept's limits and in preventing overgeneralization (Merrill & Tennyson, 1977; Winston, 1973). For example, in learning about mammals, students can be shown such similar-looking nonmammals as lizards and frogs.

• *Positive and negative instances are more effective when presented simultaneously* (Ellis & Hunt, 1983; R. Gagné, 1985). Research consistently indicates that people learn concepts more easily when they see examples and nonexamples simultaneously rather than sequentially (Bourne et al., 1971).

• *Students' understanding of a concept should be assessed by asking them to classify new examples* (Kinnick, 1990; Merrill & Tennyson, 1977; Owen et al., 1978; Tennyson & Cocchiarella, 1986). Do students truly understand what a concept is, or have they simply memorized a definition in a rote, meaning*less* fashion? To find out, teachers can ask students to select positive instances of the concept from among numerous possibilities—a strategy that Tiagarajan (1989) calls an *eg hunt* (a tongue-in-cheek variation on "e.g."). Students who have not mastered a concept will be unable to identify all positive and negative instances accurately, particularly in borderline cases. For example, my son Jeff shows his limited understanding of the concept *animal* when he denies that people and fish are positive instances. As another example, consider a study by Patricia Wilson (1988). Sixth and eighth graders were asked to define the concept of *rectangle*: many of them defined a rectangle in such a way that squares were (appropriately) included. Yet, when shown a variety of shapes and asked to identify the rectangles, the great majority of students who had correctly defined the concept of rectangle nevertheless did *not* identify any squares as being positive instances.

• *Students should be asked to generate their own examples and applications of a concept* (Ellis & Hunt, 1983; Watts & Anderson, 1971). Such a practice helps students test and refine their own understanding of that concept. The benefits of self-generated examples and applications are illustrated in an experiment in which high school students received instruction in basic psychological concepts (Watts & Anderson, 1971). Students who were asked to *apply* those concepts to new situations remembered more of the material than students who were asked merely to recall certain facts.

• *In addition to learning individual concepts, students should be shown how various concepts are related to one another.* A single lesson may include several different concepts, as well as numerous interrelationships among those concepts. To illustrate, this chapter contains a number of concepts related to the topic of concept learning—*undergeneralization*, *overgeneralization*, *positive instances*, *negative instances*, *defining features*, and *correlational features* are just a few examples. The chapter also talks about how these concepts are related to one another and to other concepts you already know—for example, *overgeneralization* is a case of incorrectly identifying *negative instances* as examples of a concept, and *defining features* are found in all *positive instances*. How can a student remember all these interrelationships?

One method of organizing information is **concept mapping** (e.g., Novak & Gowin, 1984). A concept map is a diagram of the concepts of a unit (usually identified by circles) and the interrelationships among them (usually designated

Figure 14-4
Concept maps constructed by two fifth-grade students after watching a slide lecture on Australia

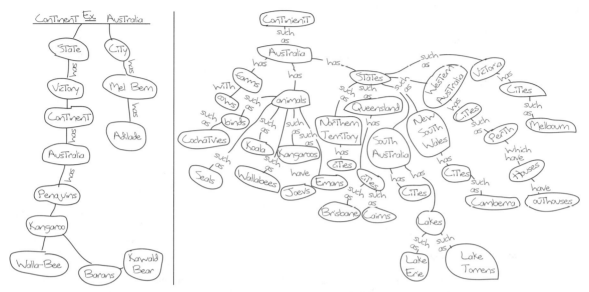

From *Learning How to Learn* (pp. 100–101) by J. D. Novak and D. B. Gowin, 1984, Cambridge, England: Cambridge University Press. Copyright 1984 by Cambridge University Press. Reprinted by permission.

by lines and by words or phrases that link two concepts together). Figure 14–4 shows concept maps constructed by two fifth-grade students after they watched a slide lecture on Australia. Notice how very different the knowledge of the two children appears to be, even though both children received the same information.

Concept maps, constructed either by a teacher or by students themselves, often facilitate students' classroom performance (Alvermann, 1981; Hawk, 1986; Holley & Dansereau, 1984). Students benefit in numerous ways from constructing their own concept maps for classroom material. By focusing on how concepts relate to one another, students organize material better. They are also more likely to notice how new concepts are related to things they already know—thus, they are more likely to learn the material meaningfully. Furthermore, when students construct a concept map from printed material, they can encode that material in long-term memory visually as well as verbally (Novak & Gowin, 1984).

Concept maps have advantages for teachers as well. By developing a concept map for a lesson, a teacher clarifies the organizational scheme of that lesson and so has a better idea about how to sequence the presentation of ideas. And by examining concept maps that students themselves have constructed, any misconceptions and "holes" in students' understanding become readily apparent (Novak & Gowin, 1984; Novak & Musonda, 1991). If you look carefully at the concept map on the left side of Figure 14–4, you should detect several misconceptions the student has about Australia. For example, Adelaide is *not* part of Melbourne, it is a different city altogether! If geographic knowledge about Australia is an instructional objective, then this student clearly needs further instruction to correct such misinformation.

•*Skills and associations that are prerequisites to understanding a concept should be identified and instruction sequenced accordingly.* Robert Gagné's theory of the interrelationships among associations and intellectual skills points out the necessity for learning relevant associations and discriminations prior to concept learning. Furthermore, the learning of concrete concepts must precede the learning of concept definitions (rules) that incorporate those concrete concepts. Finally, the formation of higher-order rules that can be used to solve problems can occur only when concrete and abstract concepts contained within them have already been mastered. We will examine the process of problem solving, as well as the related phenomenon of transfer, in Chapter 16.

SUMMARY

A concept can be defined either as the same response to different stimuli (a behaviorist perspective) or as a category of objects or events that share one or more common properties (a cognitive perspective). Concepts facilitate thought and behavior in a number of ways, for example by reducing the complexity of the environment and by facilitating generalization to new situations.

Learning a concept involves learning the features and rules that determine which objects and events are members of that concept (i.e., positive instances) and which are nonmembers (i.e., negative instances). Numerous factors affect the ease with which concepts are learned, including the salience and redundancy of defining and correlational features, the number of irrelevant features, the complexity of the rules determining the combination of features, and the frequency and timing with which positive and negative instances are presented.

Several theories of concept learning have been proposed, including habit strength build-up, mediation, hypothesis testing, prototypes, and feature lists. Robert Gagné has also proposed a theory that incorporates concept learning into a list of eight interrelated forms of learning.

Students' concept learning in the classroom can be facilitated in a number of ways—for example, by providing a definition, numerous and varied positive instances to illustrate the concept, and several negative instances to show what the concept is *not*. Students' understanding of concepts can be assessed by asking them to identify additional positive and negative instances, generate their own examples of a concept, and construct maps that portray interrelationships among several concepts. And, in light of Gagné's analysis, skills and associations that are prerequisite to understanding concepts should be identified and instruction sequenced accordingly.

CHAPTER 15

Metacognition and Study Strategies

When I look back on my days as a high school student, I think about how I used to learn, or at least *tried* to learn, and I shudder. Although I was a reasonably good student, my ideas about how I could best study for my classes were incredibly naive. For example, I remember sitting on my bed "reading" my history textbook at night: My eyes dutifully went down each page, focusing briefly on every line, but my mind was a million miles away. After completing the reading assignment, I couldn't remember a thing I had read, yet I had the crazy notion that my supposed "knowledge" of history would miraculously come to mind at test time (it didn't). I remember, too, studying vocabulary words for my class in Mandarin Chinese: I truly believed that simply repeating those words over and over again would get them through my thick skull. In retrospect, the only subject I learned well was mathematics, because the various mathematical concepts and principles I studied seemed logical based on what I already knew.

When I went to college, I continued to bumble along, spending too much time in mindless "reading" and taking notes in class that I can now make very little sense of (I have to wonder how much those notes helped me even then). It was only after a great deal of studying experience and considerable trial and error that I began to realize how important it was that I pay attention to course material with my mind as well as my eyes, and that I try to understand the things I was studying.

As you have been reading this book, I hope you have been learning a great deal about how you yourself learn and remember; perhaps you have also been modifying your approach to your learning tasks. For example, you may now be trying to pay closer attention to what you read in textbooks and what you hear in class. You may also be focusing more on understanding, organizing, and elaborating on your course material. In any case, I hope you are not reading this book the way I used to read my history text.

People's knowledge of their own learning and cognitive processes and their consequent regulation of those processes to enhance learning and memory are collectively known as **metacognition**. As you may have guessed, the concept of metacognition initially emerged within the context of information processing theory. Yet it is also consistent with social learning theorists' notion of *self-regulation*: It provides the mechanism through which children begin to regulate one aspect of their lives—their own learning (e.g., Zimmerman, 1989).

The more metacognitively sophisticated students are, the higher their school learning and achievement is likely to be (e.g., P. Peterson, 1988). Unfortunately, many students are sadly unaware of, and sometimes even misinformed about, their own learning and memory processes. You might think of metacognition as the "manager" or "coach" of a person's learning (Schoenfeld, 1985b): It guides information processing and monitors the effectiveness of various strategies being applied to a particular learning task. But just as the coach of a basketball team might be either quite knowledgeable about playing basketball or instead harbor some very counterproductive misconceptions about how best to play the game, so, too, can a learner's metacognitive knowledge be either a help or a hindrance in the learning process.

In this chapter we will look at the many things that a person's metacognitive knowledge and skills may include. We will examine several learning and study strategies that appear to promote effective learning and retention of classroom material. We will see how some of these strategies develop and improve as students grow older, yet find that students don't always use effective strategies even when they may be capable of doing so. Finally, we will identify a number of teaching practices that can help students become metacognitively more sophisticated, and thus better able to learn and achieve in the classroom, over the long run.

METACOGNITIVE KNOWLEDGE AND SKILLS

Metacognition includes such knowledge and skills as:

- *Being aware of one's own learning and memory capabilities and of what learning tasks can realistically be accomplished* (e.g., recognizing that it is probably not possible to learn everything in a 200-page reading assignment in a single evening)
- *Knowing which learning strategies are effective and which are not* (e.g., realizing that meaningful learning is more effective for long-term retention than rote learning)
- *Planning an approach to a learning task that is likely to be successful* (e.g., finding a quiet place to study where there will be few distractions)
- *Using effective learning strategies* (e.g., taking detailed notes when lecture material is likely to be difficult to remember otherwise)
- *Monitoring one's present knowledge state* (e.g., knowing when information has been successfully learned and when it has not)
- *Knowing effective strategies for retrieval of previously stored information* (e.g. thinking about the context in which a certain piece of information was probably learned)

As you can see, metacognition involves some fairly complex, and often abstract, ideas and processes. Many of these ideas and processes are not specifically taught in the classroom. As a result, it is not surprising that students typically develop metacognitive knowledge and skills only slowly and after many challenging learning experiences, and that some students develop few if any effective study strategies.

As an example of metacognition, let's consider what happens when students study their school textbooks. Their reading in this situation is clearly not just identifying the words on the page, nor is it just making sense of the sentences and paragraphs within which those words appear. The students are also trying to store the information they read in long-term memory so that they can retrieve the information later on. In other words, they are *reading for learning*.

What specifically do students do when they read for learning? Good readers—those who learn effectively from the things they read—do many of the following:

- Clarify their purpose for reading something.
- Read differently depending on whether they want to ascertain the general gist of a passage, learn the passage's content thoroughly and in great detail, or merely read for pleasure.
- Determine what is most important to learn and remember, and focus their attention and efforts on that material.
- Try to make sense of and elaborate on (e.g., draw inferences from and identify logical relationships within) what they read.

- Bring their prior knowledge into play in understanding and elaborating on what they read.
- Make predictions about what they are likely to read next in a passage.
- Ask themselves questions that they try to answer as they read.
- Periodically check themselves to make sure they understand and remember what they have read.
- Attempt to clarify any ambiguous points they encounter.
- Persist in their efforts to understand when they have initial difficulty doing so.
- Envision possible examples and applications of the ideas presented.
- Read for possible conceptual change—in other words, read with the understanding that the ideas they encounter may be inconsistent with things they now believe.
- Critically evaluate what they read.
- Summarize what they have read. (Baker, 1989; Brown & Palincsar, 1987; Brown, Palincsar, & Armbruster, 1984; Brown & Campione, in press; Dole, Duffy, Roehler, & Pearson, 1991; Myers & Duffy, 1990; Palincsar & Brown, 1989; Roth & Anderson, 1988; van der Broek, 1990)

In contrast, poor readers—those who have trouble learning and remembering the things they read—use few of the strategies I've just listed. For example, they have little focus and sense of purpose as they read a passage (Brown & Palincsar, 1987). They have difficulty drawing inferences from the ideas they encounter (Oakhill, 1993). They rarely ask themselves questions about the material, predict what's coming next, clarify ambiguous statements, or summarize what they have read (Palincsar & Brown, 1984). They overlook inconsistencies among

How, as a metacognitively naive high school student, the author read her history textbook.

How the author *should* have read her history textbook.

A critical turning point of World War II was the Japanese attack on Pearl Harbor on December 7, 1941. . . why would the attack on Pearl Harbor have been so important for the outcome of the war?. . . probably because it forced the United States to enter the war, greatly increasing the number of ships, guns, and troops available to the Allies.

ideas within the text, as well as inconsistencies between those ideas and their prior beliefs about the world (Brown & Palincsar, 1987; Roth & Anderson, 1988). And in general, poor readers seem to have little metacognitive awareness of the things they should do mentally as they read (Baker, 1989). As examples, consider three high school students' descriptions of how they studied:

- I stare real hard at the page, blink my eyes and then open them—and cross my fingers that it will be right here (points at head).
- It's easy. If [the teacher] says study, I read it twice. If she says read, it's just once through.
- I just read the first line in each paragraph—it's usually all there. (Brown & Palincsar, 1987, p. 83)

As you might guess, these students were *not* learning very effectively from the things they were reading (Brown & Palincsar, 1987).

Obviously, many students stand to benefit from developing more effective learning and study strategies. But before we talk about ways to help students with their academic learning, we must first determine which strategies are in fact effective.

EFFECTIVE LEARNING AND STUDY STRATEGIES

In the next few pages, we will consider research findings regarding several learning and study strategies: meaningful learning and elaboration, organizing, note taking, identifying important information, comprehension monitoring, and summarizing.

Meaningful Learning and Elaboration

In Chapter 11, I described *meaningful learning* as a process of relating new material to knowledge already stored in long-term memory and *elaboration* as a process of using prior knowledge to interpret and expand on that new material. Both processes involve making connections between new information and the things you already know, and both processes clearly facilitate learning as you study (e.g., Dole et al., 1991; Pressley, 1982; Waters, 1982; Weinstein, 1978; Wittrock & Alesandrini, 1990).

A study by Van Rossum and Schenk (1984) illustrates this point well. College students studied and took notes on a historical passage, then took a test on the contents of the passage and answered questions about how they had studied. Approximately half the students described rote-learning approaches to studying; they interpreted the objective of the assignment as one of memorizing facts (as one student described it, "learning everything by heart"). The other half described meaningful learning approaches to the study process: They attempted to understand, interpret, abstract meaning, and apply what they read. One student's self-report illustrates this meaningful learning approach:

> First I read the text roughly through and try to form a picture of the content. The second time I read more accurately and try through the structure of the text to make the small connections in and between the paragraphs. The third or fourth time I try to repeat to myself, without looking at the text, the main lines of the argument, emphasizing reasonings. This is my usual way to study texts. (Van Rossum & Schenk, 1984, p. 77)

There were no differences between the two groups of students in their performance on multiple choice questions that tested their knowledge of the passage. However, students who used meaningful learning strategies performed better on multiple choice questions that required drawing inferences and produced better integrated and qualitatively superior responses to an essay test over the same material.

Students appear to interpret information differently depending on whether they are trying to remember facts or generate applications. In a dissertation by one of my doctoral students (McCallin, 1988), undergraduate education majors enrolled in two educational psychology classes completed a questionnaire that assessed their approach to learning the course material. Some students described themselves as preferring to be given specific procedures for classroom teachers—that is, they wanted to be told what to do. Other students described themselves as preferring to understand psychological principles of human learning and behavior so that they could develop their *own* procedures. Following the course's unit on educational testing and measurement, McCallin used concept mapping (described in Chapter 14); more specifically, she gave the students a list of basic concepts in educational testing and asked them to write the concepts and their interrelationships on a blank piece of paper. Students with a tell-me-what-to-do attitude tended to describe relationships among concepts that were simplistically factual or procedural (e.g., "Raw scores are used to compute a *mean*"). On the other hand, students with a let-me-apply-it-myself attitude described conceptual interrelationships that reflected more sophisticated processing, including hierarchical structures, cause–effect relationships, and deductive reasoning (e.g., "*Reliability* affects the *standard error of measurement*").

Organizing

In Chapter 11, we found evidence for the importance of *internal organization*—finding connections and interrelationships within a body of new information—for long-term memory storage. Making oneself aware of the inherent organizational structure of new material facilitates learning; so, too, does imposing an organizational structure on material when that structure doesn't initially exist (Gauntt, 1991; Kail, 1990; Wade, 1992).

Nevertheless, students often fail to develop appropriate organizational structures for information presented in lectures and written materials. Rather than recognizing and taking advantage of the interrelationships inherent in a body of information, students frequently "organize" various ideas simply as a list of unrelated facts (Meyer, Brandt, & Bluth, 1980). Furthermore, students are less likely to organize information as material becomes more difficult for them (Kletzien, 1988).

One way to enhance the internal organization of new material is to create an outline of it. When students learn how to outline the things they hear in lectures and read in textbooks, their classroom learning improves (McDaniel & Einstein, 1989; Wade, 1992). Curiously, though, good students are *less* likely to outline the things they read than their more "average" classmates (Baker, 1989). It may be that better students organize material easily enough in their heads that paper–pencil outlines aren't necessary.

Note Taking

In general, taking notes on information presented in lectures and textbooks is positively correlated with student learning (Benton, Kiewra, Whitfill, & Dennison, 1993; Cohn, Hult, & Engle, 1990; Hale, 1983; Kiewra, 1989; Shrager & Mayer, 1989). Note taking probably serves two functions for students (Di Vesta & Gray, 1972; Kiewra, 1989). For one thing, it facilitates *encoding* of material: By writing information down and looking at it, students are likely to encode it both

The effectiveness of note taking depends on the type of notes taken.

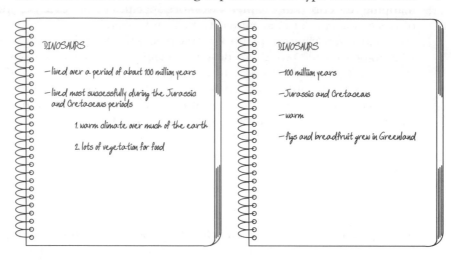

verbally and visually. As evidence for the encoding function of note taking, students remember more when they take notes even if they have no opportunity to review those notes (e.g., Howe, 1970; Weinstein & Mayer, 1986). Secondly, notes serve as a form of concrete *external storage* for information presented in class: Given the notorious fallibility of long-term memory (see Chapter 12), pen and paper often provide a dependable alternative (e.g., Benton et al., 1993). Once lecture content is recorded on paper, it can be reviewed at regular intervals later on.

In my own classes, I have often observed how very different the notes of different students can be, even though all the students have sat through the same lectures. Some students write extensively; others write very little. Some students try to capture all the main ideas of a lecture, whether I have written them down or not, whereas others only copy the specific words I write on the board—mostly terms and their definitions. Some students include details and examples in their notes; others do not.

Not surprisingly, just how effective note taking is depends on the type of notes taken. For example, notes are more useful to students when they are relatively complete representations of the presented material (Benton et al., 1993; Cohn et al., 1990; Kiewra, 1989). They are more likely to promote learning when they represent an encoding of the information that is consistent with the objectives of the instructional unit; hence, those objectives should be clear to students (Barnett, Di Vesta, & Rogozinski, 1981; Snowman, 1986). Notes are also more likely to be effective when they summarize main ideas and include details that support those main ideas (Brown, Campione, & Day, 1981; Doctorow, Wittrock, & Marks, 1978; Kiewra, 1985; Taylor, 1982). And notes that go beyond the material—those that include students' own elaborations of it—may be especially beneficial (Barnett et al., 1981; Kiewra, 1989; King, 1992).

Another effective technique is reorganizing and elaborating on notes after a lecture has been attended or a reading assignment has been completed (DuBois, Kiewra, & Fraley, 1988; Kiewra, 1985; Kiewra, DuBois, Christian, McShane, Meyerhoffer, & Roskelly, 1988; Shimmerlick & Nolan, 1976). Particularly in a lecture situation, students have no control over how fast information is presented and may not have time to process everything meaningfully. In such a case, students may need to focus merely on writing information during class and then organizing and encoding it appropriately afterward.

Kiewra (1989) has offered a number of suggestions to teachers for improving the quality and completeness of their students' notes. For example, writing important ideas on the chalkboard may be helpful, since students are far more likely to write down those things that their teacher also writes. Repeating important ideas also increases the likelihood that students will record those ideas on paper. And providing some kind of general organizational framework—a skeletal outline, a compare-and-contrast matrix, or the like—facilitates students' ability to organize information as the teacher envisions it (also see Benton et al., 1993).

Identifying Important Information

Students often encounter more information than they can possibly store in their long-term memories, at least within a reasonable time. As a result, they must determine which things are most important for them to learn and study—for example, they must separate main ideas from trivial details (e.g., Dole et al., 1991; Reynolds & Shirey, 1988). The task is often a challenging one, partly because the relative "importance" of different ideas is ultimately determined by the teacher, who may have a different perspective on the material than students do.

The various *signals* present in a lecture or textbook (specified objectives of a lesson, underlined or italicized words, ideas written on the chalkboard, etc.) can help students discriminate between important and unimportant information (see Chapter 13's discussion of expository instruction). In some instances, however, students may overlook or misinterpret such signals; in other instances, signals may be few and far between. Thus, students often have trouble identifying the main points of a lecture or reading assignment; this is particularly true when they have little background knowledge about the subject matter they are studying (Dole et al., 1991; Garner, Alexander, Gillingham, & Kulikowich, 1991). Many students use relatively inadequate methods of selecting information—for example, focusing on first sentences of paragraphs and on distinctive pieces of information (such as definitions and formulas)—and often miss critical ideas as a result (Mayer, 1984). Even graduate students are fallible in this respect, because they are often distracted away from central information by relatively unimportant but interesting (and perhaps more concrete) details (Garner et al., 1991; Garner, Brown, Sanders, & Menke, 1992; Sadoski, Goetz, & Fritz, 1993).

Once students become proficient at identifying important information, then underlining or highlighting the information, at least in purchased textbooks and students' lecture notes, is likely to be beneficial. I encourage my own students to underline or highlight the important points their textbooks present—doing so is less time-consuming than taking notes on a book's content and keeps specific information within its larger context. But underlining and highlighting are probably only effective when used sparingly to emphasize main ideas and essential details (Snowman, 1986). Highlighting an entire page, as if with a paint roller, is essentially useless.

Comprehension Monitoring

Good students—those who learn most effectively—periodically check themselves to be sure they are actually absorbing what they are hearing in class or reading in a textbook. They also take steps to remediate any comprehension difficulties they have—for example, by asking questions or rereading a passage. In other words, good students engage in **comprehension monitoring** (Baker, 1989; Dansereau, 1978; Dole et al., 1991; Haller, Child, & Walberg, 1988; Pressley, Borkowski, & Schneider, 1987).

Unfortunately, many students of all ages *don't* monitor their comprehension as they sit in class or read a textbook (Baker & Brown, 1984; Flavell, 1979; Markman, 1979; Mayer, 1992; Otero & Kintsch, 1992). As a result, they are often ignorant about what they know and what they don't know, and they may think they

Students are not always accurate judges of what they know and what they do not.

understand something they actually *mis*understand; such phenomena are sometimes referred to as the **illusion of knowing** or **secondary ignorance** (Baker, 1989; Horgan, 1990; Sieber, 1968, cited in Brown, 1978; Voss & Schauble, 1992). For example, students often think they know how to spell words that they actually do not (Adams & Adams, 1960; Johnson, Langford, & Quorn, 1981; Ormrod & Wagner, 1987).

When students think they know classroom material, they are likely to stop studying it. Thus, students who only have the *illusion* of knowing it will stop studying prematurely (Horgan, 1990; Voss & Schauble, 1992). And they are likely to be quite puzzled when, as a result, they perform poorly on an exam or assignment (Horgan, 1990). For example, I frequently have students appear at my office confused about why they did so poorly on an exam when they "knew" the information so well. When I ask these students specific questions about the material, I usually find that they don't really have a good grasp of it at all!

One strategy for facilitating students' comprehension monitoring is to have them formulate questions before a lesson or reading assignment that they then answer as they go along (Bragstad & Stumpf, 1982; Robinson, 1961; Thomas & Robinson, 1972). As an example, Robinson (1961) has suggested that, when reading a textbook, a student should turn each heading and subheading into a question to be answered and then read sections of text with the intention of finding answers to those questions. Such **self-questioning** is probably even more effective when students do it *throughout* a lesson or reading assignment (Brozo, Stahl, & Gordon, 1985; Dole et al., 1991; Haller et al., 1988; Wong, 1985). For example, undergraduate students who ask themselves questions as they take notes in a lecture class take better notes, understand the material better, and remember it longer (King, 1992; Spires, 1990).

By asking themselves questions periodically, students are more likely to know when they know something and when they do not. After reviewing research on the effectiveness of self-questioning, however, Snowman (1986) concluded that positive effects are limited to the acquisition of facts, without any noticeable impact on more sophisticated behaviors such as application or evaluation of those facts. I suspect that students may be asking themselves fact-based questions (e.g., "When did Columbus reach the New World?") rather than higher-level questions (e.g., "Why did Columbus risk his life to find a new route to India?") partly because they have learned to expect mostly fact-based questions on their classroom examinations. To promote meaningful learning, elaboration, and, in general, higher-level processing of information, teachers might encourage students to continually ask themselves questions such as these:

Explain why (how) . . .?
What is the main idea of . , .?
How would you use . . . to . . .?
What is a new example of . . .?
What do you think would happen if . . .?
What is the difference between . . . and . . .?
How are . . . and . . . similar?

What conclusions can you draw about . . .?
How does . . . affect . . .?
What are the strengths and weaknesses of . . .?
What is the best . . . and why?
How is . . . related to . . . that we studied earlier? (King, 1992, p. 309)

Ideally, students should assess their understanding of class material at some later time as well. People are often inaccurate and overly optimistic judges of how much they will remember about something they have just read (Nelson & Dunlosky, 1991; Pressley, Borkowski, & Schneider, 1987). In a simple illustration of this principle (Nelson & Dunlosky, 1991), undergraduate students studied a series of 60 paired associates (e.g., *ocean—tree*) for eight seconds apiece. Students were asked how confident they were that in 10 minutes' time they would be able to remember the second word in each pair when cued with the first; this question was sometimes asked immediately after a word pair had been presented (the immediate condition) and sometimes after several minutes had elapsed (the delayed condition). After studying all 60 pairs, students were tested for their actual ability to recall the second word in every pair. Their estimates of how much they would remember were far more accurate for word pairs in the delayed condition than for pairs in the immediate condition; for the latter word pairs, students believed they would remember many more than they actually did. The problem with judging one's knowledge of something immediately after studying it, Nelson and Dunlosky reasoned, is that the information is still in working memory and therefore can be easily retrieved. Ideally, students need to judge the likelihood that they can retrieve information from long-term memory as well—something they can do only when they monitor their comprehension after several minutes, hours, or days have elapsed.

Summarizing

Students are often encouraged to summarize the material they read and hear—for example, by condensing and integrating it, deriving abstract representations of it, or identifying suitable headings to label it. Doing so seems to facilitate learning and retention of that material (Dole et al., 1991; Jonassen, Hartley, & Trueman, 1986; King, 1992; Wittrock & Alesandrini, 1990).

Unfortunately, many students have difficulty adequately summarizing the things they read and hear (Brown & Palincsar, 1987; Jonassen et al., 1986). After reviewing research on the effectiveness of summarizing for learning and remembering information, Snowman (1986) concluded that summaries are only effective when students have some idea of how they are going to be evaluated and can therefore tailor their summaries toward the evaluation criteria. Concerns about selecting important information apply here as well: Students who have difficulty identifying main ideas will certainly have difficulty combining those main ideas into a summary.

In the last few pages, we have identified a number of effective learning and study strategies. Some of these—such as outlining, taking notes, and writing summaries—are **overt strategies**; in other words, they are behaviors we can actually see. Others—such as elaborating, identifying important information, and monitoring comprehension—are **covert strategies**; they are internal mental processes we often can*not* see. Ultimately, it is probably the ways in which students process the information they receive—the covert strategies—that determine how effectively they learn and remember that information (Kardash & Amlund, 1991).

What kinds of learning and study strategies are we likely to see in students of different ages? Let's take a peek at the development of metacognitive knowledge and skills.

THE DEVELOPMENT OF METACOGNITIVE KNOWLEDGE AND SKILLS

Preschoolers know that *thinking* is different from such activities as *seeing, talking*, and *knowing* (Flavell, 1993). And they have a few simple strategies—for example, looking, pointing, and touching—for learning the things they want to remember (Kail, 1990). But more sophisticated metacognitive knowledge and skills emerge after children enter school (perhaps as a result of children's school learning experiences) and continue to improve throughout the school years (Duell, 1986; Flavell, 1979, 1985; Kail, 1990; Siegler, 1986). Let's look at three developmental trends in metacognition in school-age children.

•*Children become increasingly realistic about their memory capabilities and limitations* (Cavanaugh & Perlmutter, 1982; Duell, 1986; Flavell, Friedrichs, & Hoyt, 1970; Markman, 1979). Young children typically overestimate how much they can remember of the things they are about to learn. For example, in a study by Flavell et al. (1970), four age groups of children (ranging from nursery school to fourth grade) were shown strips of paper picturing from 1 to 10 objects and asked to predict how many objects they thought they could remember at a time (a working memory task). The children were then tested to determine how many objects they actually could remember. All four groups of children tended to overestimate their working memory capacities, but the estimates of the older children were more realistic. For example, kindergarten children predicted that they could remember an average of 8.0 objects, but in fact remembered only 3.6. The fourth graders, on the other hand, estimated that they could remember 6.1 objects and actually recalled 5.5 (a much closer guess).

•*Children develop an increasing ability to use effective learning and memory strategies.* Young children have little metacognitive awareness of effective strategies; older children are more likely to have a variety of strategies and know when to use each one (Brown, Bransford, Ferrera, & Campione, 1983; Kail, 1990; Siegler, 1986). Consider these research findings as illustrations:

- When asked to study and remember 36 common objects (e.g., a bell, a flag, a wagon) over a series of learning trials, and when given the opportunity to review half of the items after each trial, third graders chose to study those items they have failed to remember on the previous trial. In contrast, first graders chose their study items randomly, without consideration of past memory failures (Masur, McIntyre, & Flavell, 1973).
- Adolescents use rehearsal (rote repetition of information) as a way of trying to learn information, emphasizing important material as they do so. Seven-year-olds use rehearsal as well, but they do so indiscriminately, without regard for the relative importance of various items (Kail, 1990).
- The use of elaboration continues to increase throughout the school years (Kail, 1990; Pressley, 1982; Siegler, 1986). For example, tenth graders are more likely to use elaboration when trying to remember paired associates (e.g., *doctor—machine*, *acorn—bathtub*) than eighth graders are (Waters, 1982). Sixth graders often draw inferences from the things they read, whereas first graders rarely do (Chan, Burtis, Scardamalia, & Bereiter, 1992).

Even when young children can verbally describe which learning and memory strategies are effective and which are not, when left to their own devices they will often use relatively ineffective strategies (Strage, Christopoulos, Rohwer, Thomas, Delucchi, & Curley, 1988).

•*Children engage in more comprehension monitoring as they get older; hence, they become increasingly able to determine when they actually know something.* In the previously described study by Flavell et al. (1970), children of different ages were also asked to study a series of pictures until they were certain they could recall all of them in the correct order. Older children (second and fourth graders) were relatively accurate in ascertaining their own knowledge levels and were able to recall most of the pictures after their self-terminated study periods. On the other hand, younger children (those in nursery school and kindergarten) terminated their study sessions before they were able to recall the pictures accurately.

Despite such developmental improvements in metacognitive knowledge and skills over the years, many students continue *not* to use effective learning and study strategies, even in high school, college, and beyond. Why not? Let's find out.

WHY STUDENTS DON'T ALWAYS USE EFFECTIVE STRATEGIES

As theorists and researchers have focused greater attention on metacognition in recent years, they have identified several reasons that students continue to use relatively ineffective learning and study strategies throughout much of their academic career.

•*Students are uninformed or misinformed about effective strategies.* Many students, even those at the high school and undergraduate levels, are metacognitively naive about how they can best learn (Alexander & Judy, 1988; Flavell & Wellman, 1977; Knight, 1988; Ormrod & Jenkins, 1988; Palmer & Goetz, 1988). For example, some students believe that all they need to do to learn information better is to exert more effort—that is, to *try harder*—with little regard for how they should mentally process information (O'Sullivan & Joy, 1990; Pressley, Borkowski, & Schneider, 1987). Some think that learning is an all-or-nothing thing; for example, an undergraduate student in one research study naively claimed that "almost all the information you can learn from a textbook you will get during the first reading" (Schommer, 1990). And many students believe (incorrectly) that trying to learn information meaningfully—that is, trying to understand and make sense out of the things they study—interferes with their ability to do well on classroom tests that emphasize rote memorization and knowledge of isolated facts (Crooks, 1988).

When I present a unit on cognitive psychology to my junior-level educational psychology class, my description of such basic strategies as organizing information and relating it to familiar concepts and experiences appears to be a major revelation to about half of my students. Sadly, too many of these students have viewed learning as being best approached through rote memorization throughout their many years in school.

•*Students have little relevant prior knowledge on which they can draw.* Students who use ineffective learning and study strategies tend to know less about the subject matter they are studying, and less about the world in general, than students who use effective strategies (Alexander & Judy, 1988; Carpenter & Just, 1986; Chi, 1981; Hasselhorn & Körkel, 1986; Pressley, Borkowski, & Schneider, 1987; Schneider, 1993; Woloshyn, Pressley, & Schneider, 1992). For example, students may know too little about a topic to determine what's important and what isn't (Carpenter & Just, 1986; McDaniel & Einstein, 1989). They may have few concepts or experiences to which they relate new material in a meaningful fashion; thus, they have greater difficulty comprehending the things they read (Dole et al., 1991; Gauntt, 1991; Hall, 1989; Schneider, 1993; Voss, 1987; Wilson & Anderson, 1986; Woloshyn et al., 1992). And they are likely to have fewer organizational frameworks and schemas that they can impose on what might otherwise appear to be an unrelated set of ideas (Carpenter & Just, 1986).

•*Students have low self-efficacy about their ability to learn in an academic setting.* Some students, especially those with a history of failure in the classroom, develop the belief that they are incapable of learning, regardless of what they do. Such students may believe (erroneously) that *no* strategy is likely to make any appreciable difference in their school achievement (Palmer & Goetz, 1988; Pressley, Borkowski, & Schneider, 1987).

•*Students think that sophisticated learning strategies require too much effort to make them worthwhile.* If students believe that certain strategies require too much time and effort, they are unlikely to use them, no matter how effective those strategies might be (Palmer & Goetz, 1988; Pressley et al., 1990).

To convince students otherwise, teachers may need to help students discover—perhaps in some concrete fashion, such as an unexpected (and probably ungraded) quiz—how little they are actually learning and remembering using their current, ineffective strategies.

Many teachers assume that students will use the same relatively sophisticated study strategies that they themselves use—an assumption that is probably unwarranted in many cases. But can metacognitive knowledge and skills be taught? Most psychologists believe that they can, and furthermore that they *should*, be taught. Instruction about how to study and learn can make a difference—sometimes a dramatic one—in student achievement, as we shall see now.

PROMOTING EFFECTIVE LEARNING AND STUDY STRATEGIES

As students move through the grade levels—from elementary school to middle or junior high school, then to high school, and perhaps eventually on to college—their learning tasks become increasingly more complex and challenging (e.g., Eccles & Midgley, 1989; J. Wilson, 1988). For example, students must remember more information, do more with it (in terms of application, problem solving, critical analysis, and so on), and understand it at a more abstract level. Thus, there is a greater need for sophisticated learning and study strategies as the years go by (Baker, 1989).

Unfortunately, when teaching complex subject matter, teachers rarely teach effective strategies for learning that material (Pressley et al., 1990; J. Wilson, 1988). Yet when left to their own devices, students typically acquire effective strategies slowly (if at all), and some students develop counterproductive misconceptions about how best to learn (e.g., Alexander & Judy, 1988; Kail, 1990).

Many theorists suggest that schools should provide explicit instruction in how to study and learn (e.g., Brown & Campione, in press; Kail, 1990; Pressley et al., 1990; Schoenfeld, 1985b; West, Farmer, & Wolff, 1991). This instruction may be especially valuable for "at-risk" students—those with a history of academic difficulties and a high probability of dropping out of school prematurely (Alderman, 1990; Brown & Palincsar, 1987; Weinstein, Hagen, & Meyer, 1991). In the next few pages we will examine research regarding the effectiveness of study skills training; we will then consider some specific classroom strategies for promoting and enhancing students' metacognitive capabilities.

The Effectiveness of Study Skills Training

Initially, most programs designed to enhance metacognitive knowledge and skills were at the college level (J. Wilson, 1988). But in recent years we have also seen these programs at the high school, junior high, and even upper elementary levels. The collective results of these programs indicate that students *can* be taught more effective learning and study strategies, with consequent improvements in their classroom performance and academic achievement; such training appears to be especially beneficial for low-ability students (Baker, 1989; Cook, 1983; Dansereau, 1978; Dansereau et al., 1979; Haller et al, 1988; Hansen & Pearson, 1983; Holley & Dansereau, 1984; Kulik, Kulik, & Shwalb, 1983; Linden and Wittrock, 1981; Mastropieri & Scruggs, 1989; Palincsar & Brown, 1984, 1989; Paris, 1988; Paris, Cross, & Lipson, 1984; Pressley, 1982; Pressley, Borkowski, & Schneider, 1987; Shrager & Mayer, 1989; Wade, 1983; Weinstein, Goetz, & Alexander, 1988; Weinstein, Hagen, & Meyer, 1991; J. Wilson, 1988).

Effective programs tend to be multifaceted, teaching a wide variety of learning and study strategies. For example, successful reading-for-learning instruction is likely to teach students to: (a) determine their purpose in reading a particular passage and modify their reading behavior accordingly, (b) retrieve background information and experiences relevant to the topic, (c) identify and attend to main ideas, (d) draw inferences from the things they read, and (e) monitor their reading comprehension as they go along. And general learning and study strategies programs typically include instruction about meaningful learning, organizational strategies, elaboration, mnemonics, note taking, and summarizing. Aside from such commonalities, training programs often differ markedly from one another; I invite you to explore some of the possibilities by consulting the references listed in the preceding paragraph.

As an example of how a training program might take shape, let's consider an approach that shows particular promise for teaching students how to read for learning—an approach known as reciprocal teaching.

An Example: Reciprocal Teaching

Annemarie Palincsar and Ann Brown (1984) identified four key strategies that good readers typically use:

Summarizing: they identify the gist and main ideas of what they read
Questioning: they ask themselves questions to make sure they understand what they are reading, thereby monitoring their comprehension as they proceed through reading material
Clarifying: they take steps to clarify confusing or ambiguous parts of the text, perhaps by rereading or imposing their own knowledge on those things
Predicting: they anticipate what they are likely to read next based on cues in the text (e.g., headings) and ideas that have already been presented

Palincsar and Brown noted that poor readers—students who learn little from textbooks and other things they read—rarely summarize, question, clarify, or predict. For example, many students cannot adequately summarize a typical *fifth*-grade textbook until high school or even junior college (Brown & Palincsar, 1987; Palincsar & Brown, 1984).

Yet summarizing, questioning, clarifying, and predicting are activities that typically occur internally rather than externally; they are cognitive processes rather than observable behaviors. Palincsar and Brown reasoned that students might acquire these strategies more easily if they first practiced them out loud and in cooperation with their classmates. In **reciprocal teaching** (Brown & Palincsar, 1987; Palincsar, 1986; Palincsar & Brown, 1984, 1989), a classroom teacher and several students meet in a group to read a section of text, stopping to discuss that text as they proceed. Initially, the teacher leads the discussion, asking questions about the text to promote summarizing, questioning, clarifying, and predicting. But gradually, he or she turns the role of "teacher" over to different students, who then take charge of the discussion and ask one another the same kinds of questions their teacher has modeled. Eventually, students can read and discuss a text almost independently of the teacher, working together to construct its meaning and checking one another for comprehension and possible misunderstandings.

Reciprocal teaching sessions often begin with students making predictions about what they will read based on the title of a passage and their prior knowledge of a topic. Then, as they proceed through the text, they periodically stop to check their comprehension (e.g., by asking one another fact-based and inferential questions), clarify any potentially ambiguous statements or unfamiliar vocabulary, summarize what they have read, and predict what may be coming next. After finishing the passage, the "teacher" summarizes it, with other students possibly adding to and elaborating on that summary.

As an illustration, here is a reciprocal teaching session for a group of six first graders reading a passage about snowshoe rabbits. In this particular case, the classroom teacher reads the text in small segments (at higher grade levels, the students themselves take turns reading). After each segment, the teacher pauses while students discuss and process that segment. As you read the dialogue, look for examples of summarizing, questioning, clarifying, and predicting (there is at least one instance of each):

The children were reading about the snowshoe rabbit and it was the sixteenth day of dialogue. The teacher had just read a segment of text describing the season in which baby rabbits are born and the ways in which the mother rabbit cares for her babies. A student named Kam is the dialogue leader.

Kam:	When was the babies born?
Teacher:	That's a good question to ask. Call on someone to answer that question.
Kam:	Robby? Milly?
Milly:	Summer.
Teacher:	What would happen if the babies were born in the winter? Let's think.

Several children make a number of responses including: "The baby would be very cold." "They would need food." "They don't have no fur when they are just born."

Kam:	I have another question. How does she get the babies safe?
Kris:	She hides them.
Kam:	That's right but something else. . . .

Teacher:	There is something very unusual about how she hides them that surprised me. I didn't know this.
Travis:	They are all in a different place.
Teacher:	Why do you think she does this?
Milly:	Probably because I heard another story and when they're babies they usually eat each other or fight with each other.
Teacher:	That could be! And what about when that lynx comes?

Several children comment that that would be the end of all the babies.

Travis:	If I was the mother, I would hide mine, I would keep them all together.
Kris:	If the babies are hidden and the mom wants to go and look at them how can she remember where they are?
Teacher:	Good question. Because she does have to find them again. Why? What does she bring them?
Milly:	She needs to bring food. She probably leaves a twig or something.
Teacher:	Do you think she puts out a twig like we mark a trail?

Several children disagree and suggest that she uses her sense of smell. One child, recalling that the snowshoe rabbit is not all white in the winter suggests that the mother might be able to tell her babies apart by their coloring.

Teacher:	So we agree that the mother rabbit uses her senses to find her babies after she hides them. Kam, can you summarize for us now?
Kam:	The babies are born in the summer. . . .
Teacher:	The mother. . . .
Kam:	The mother hides the babies in different places.
Teacher:	And she visits them. . . .
Kam:	To bring them food.
Travis:	She keeps them safe.
Teacher:	Any predictions?
Milly:	What she teaches her babies . . . like how to hop.
Kris:	They know how to hop already.
Teacher:	Well, let's read and see.

(Dialogue courtesy of A. Palincsar.)

Studies of reciprocal teaching have yielded significant and often dramatic improvements in students' reading and listening comprehension (Brown & Palincsar, 1987; Palincsar, 1986; Palincsar & Brown, 1984, 1989). Furthermore, students continue to show the benefits of this approach for at least six months after instruction (Brown & Palincsar, 1987). For example, in an early study of reciprocal teaching (Palincsar & Brown, 1984), six seventh-grade students with a history of reading difficulty participated in 20 reciprocal teaching sessions, each lasting about 30 minutes. Despite the relatively short intervention, the students showed changes such as these:

- They became increasingly able to process reading material in an effective manner—for example, by summarizing and questioning—and to do so independently of their classroom teacher.
- They demonstrated increasingly better comprehension of the passages they were reading. Average scores on daily comprehension tests increased from 30% before instruction to 70%–80% (a level similar to that for average readers) after instruction.
- Three months after the reciprocal teaching intervention, their scores on a standardized reading comprehension test reflected an improvement in reading comprehension typically observed after 15 months of traditional schooling—more than a year's worth!
- They generalized their new reading strategies to other classes; for example, they showed improved performance in their science and social studies classes, sometimes even surpassing the level of their classmates (Palincsar & Brown, 1984; Brown & Palincsar, 1987).

A reciprocal teaching approach to reading instruction has been used successfully with a wide variety of students, ranging from third graders to learning disabled college students. Furthermore, it can be used to foster more effective listening comprehension beginning in first grade (the earlier dialogue is an example). And it can be employed with an entire classroom of students almost as easily as a small group. Although teachers are often very skeptical of such a radically different approach to teaching and learning, their enthusiasm grows once they've tried it themselves (Brown & Palincsar, 1987; Palincsar & Brown, 1989).

Clearly, then, learning and study skills can be taught, with resulting improvement in students' school achievement. And reciprocal teaching is by no means the only effective approach. Let's turn to some general guidelines for helping students develop and use appropriate learning and study strategies.

Guidelines for Promoting Effective Strategies

Theorists and researchers have identified a number of practices that appear to promote the development of more sophisticated metacognitive knowledge and skills. Here are some guidelines to keep in mind.

•*Students learn strategies more effectively when those strategies are taught within the context of specific subject domains and actual academic learning tasks* (Brown & Palincsar, 1987; Pressley, El-Dinary, Marks, Brown, & Stein, 1992; Pressley, Harris, & Marks, 1992). As students encounter specific academic content, they should simultaneously learn ways to study that content. For example, when presenting new information in class, a teacher might: (a) suggest how students can organize their notes, (b) describe mnemonics for things that are difficult to remember, and (c) ask various students to summarize the ideas presented. When assigning textbook pages to be read over the weekend, a teacher might: (d) suggest that students consider what they know about a topic *before* they begin reading about it, (e) ask students to use headings and subheadings to make predictions about upcoming content, and (f) provide questions for students to ask themselves as they read.

• *Students can only use sophisticated learning strategies when they have a knowledge base to which they can relate new material* (Brown, Campione, & Day, 1981; Weinstein & Mayer, 1986). The knowledge and skills that students bring to the classroom affect their ability to learn new information meaningfully, identify main ideas, and engage in such elaborative activities as drawing inferences and clarifying ambiguities. Teachers must be careful not to present difficult material until students have mastered the prerequisite knowledge and skills essential for a genuine understanding of that material.

• *Students should learn a wide variety of strategies, as well as the situations in which each one is appropriate* (Nist, Simpson, Olejnik, & Mealey, 1991; Paris, 1988; Pressley, El-Dinary, Marks, Brown, & Stein, 1992; Pressley, Harris, & Marks, 1992). Different strategies are useful in different situations; for example, meaningful learning may be more effective for learning general principles within a discipline, while mnemonics may be more effective for learning hard-to-remember pairs and lists. Organizing ideas in a hierarchical fashion may be appropriate for one unit; organizing them in a two-by-two matrix may be appropriate for another.

• *Effective strategies should be practiced with a variety of tasks and on an ongoing basis* (Brown & Palincsar, 1987; Pressley, El-Dinary, Marks, Brown, & Stein, 1992; Pressley, Harris, & Marks, 1992). When students learn a strategy only within the context of one particular task, they are unlikely to use that strategy in other contexts (Pressley et al., 1990). But when they learn to apply the same strategy to many different tasks over a long period, they are likely to recognize the strategy's value and to generalize its use to new situations. Effective strategy instruction is clearly not a one-shot deal.

• *Strategy instruction should include covert as well as overt strategies* (Kardash & Amlund, 1991). Certainly students stand to benefit from guidance about how to take notes from a lecture, underline the material they read in their textbooks, and write summaries of the material they study. But the sophisticated cognitive processes that underlie these behaviors—learning meaningfully, organizing, elaborating, comprehension monitorings and so on—are ultimately the most important strategies for students to acquire.

• *Teachers can model effective strategies by thinking out loud about new material* (Brown & Palincsar, 1987; Pressley, El-Dinary, Marks, Brown, & Stein, 1992; Pressley, Harris, & Marks, 1992). Early strategy instruction programs provided suggestions such as "review" and "generate questions," but gave students little guidance about how to carry out those activities (Dansereau, 1978). When teachers think aloud about the content their class is studying (e.g., "There is something very unusual about how [the mother rabbit] hides [her babies] that surprised me" or "I remember that *Au* is the symbol for gold by remembering,

'*Ay, you* stole my gold watch!'"), they provide their students with specific, concrete examples of how to process information.

• *Teachers should scaffold students' initial attempts at using new strategies, gradually phasing out that scaffolding as students become more proficient.* As you may recall from Chapter 8, Lev Vygotsky proposed that children's early efforts on difficult tasks (those within the zone of proximal development) are more likely to be successful when they are *scaffolded*—that is, when those efforts are guided and supported by a more competent individual. Vygotsky argued that complex cognitive processes, including metacognitive activities, can and should be scaffolded just as observable behaviors are, and that such scaffolding should be slowly removed as students become capable of using those processes independently (Vygotsky, 1978). Many contemporary theorists now believe that Vygotsky was right (Brophy, 1992; Brown & Campione, in press; Brown & Palincsar, 1987; Dole et al., 1991; Paris, 1988; Pontecorvo, 1993; Pressley, El-Dinary, Marks, Brown, & Stein, 1992; Pressley, Harris, & Marks, 1992; Rogoff, 1990; Rosenshine & Meister, 1992; Spires, Donley, & Penrose, 1990; Tobin, 1987).

We saw an example of such scaffolding in the reciprocal teaching dialogue I presented earlier. If you look back at that dialogue for a moment, you may notice how the teacher models elaborative questions and connections to prior knowledge ("What would happen if the babies were born in the winter?"; "Do you think she puts out a twig like we mark a trail?") and provides general guidance and occasional hints about how students should process the passage about snowshoe rabbits ("Kam, can you summarize for us now?"; "And she visits them. . . . "). Notice in the dialogue, too, how students support one another in their efforts to process what they are reading; consider this exchange as an example:

Kam:	I have another question. How does she get the babies safe?
Kris:	She hides them.
Kam:	That's right but something else. . . .

Many theorists believe that such group discussion and processing of classroom material facilitate metacognitive growth by allowing students to model effective processes for one another and to otherwise scaffold one another's efforts (e.g., Brown & Campione, in press; Brown & Reeve, 1987; Palincsar & Brown, 1989; Paris & Winograd, 1990). In this way, the very nature of learning itself becomes concrete and visible to everyone.

Scaffolding is most likely to be beneficial when students are studying subject matter they find difficult to comprehend, yet *can* comprehend when they apply appropriate metacognitive strategies (Pressley, El-Dinary, Marks, Brown, & Stein, 1992). As students become more proficient in the use of these strategies, instruction should gradually proceed through increasingly more challenging material (Rosenshine & Meister, 1992).

• *Students must understand why the skills they are taught are helpful.* Research indicates that strategy instruction is more successful when students not only learn effective strategies, but also learn *how* and *why* these strategies are effective (Paris, 1988; Paris, Newman, & McVey, 1982; Pressley, Borkowski, & Schneider, 1987; Pressley, Harris, & Marks, 1992). For example, in my own classes I sometimes do little "experiments," presenting information that is difficult to learn and remember, then giving some students a mnemonic for learning the information while giving other students no guidance at all. As a class, we then find out how much students in each group can recall (e.g., by writing on the board the specific number of items each student remembers). The amount of information that the two groups can remember is usually so dramatically different that students readily acknowledge the mnemonic's usefulness.

•*Students must believe that, with sufficient effort and appropriate strategies, they* **can** *learn and understand challenging material.* Strategy instruction must give students a general sense of self-efficacy about their ability to learn classroom material (McCombs, 1988; Palmer & Goetz, 1988; Paris, 1988). And it must show them that their success in learning *is* in fact related to the specific strategies they use (Pressley, Borkowski, & Schneider, 1987; Pressley, El-Dinary, Marks, Brown, & Stein, 1992).

By teaching students the metacognitive knowledge and skills they need to learn challenging classroom material, teachers not only help students learn that material more successfully, they also help students become more effective learners over the long run. And it is the long run for which schools must ultimately prepare their students.

SUMMARY

People's knowledge of their own learning and cognitive processes and their regulation of these processes to enhance learning are collectively known as metacognition. Students' metacognitive knowledge and skills are significantly related to their classroom performance and academic achievement.

Effective learning and study strategies include meaningful learning, elaboration, organizing, note taking, identifying important information, comprehension monitoring, and summarizing. Most important are the internal mental processes (covert strategies) that students use; any observable study behaviors (overt strategies) are likely to be effective only when the covert strategies that underlie them are appropriate. Children show increasing metacognitive sophistication as they grow older and gain more experience with academic learning tasks; nevertheless, many students at the high school and college levels are surprisingly uninformed about how best to learn.

Research indicates that training in effective learning and study strategies can significantly enhance students' classroom achievement. Theorists and researchers have offered a number of suggestions for promoting more effective strategy use. For example, strategy instruction is more successful when taught within the context of specific academic content rather than as a group of isolated skills. It is also more successful when students have numerous opportunities to practice specific strategies and when their teacher and classmates scaffold their initial efforts. And teachers must help students discover that, with sufficient effort and appropriate strategies, challenging classroom material *can* be learned and understood.

Transfer and Problem Solving

T hree days a week, I teach a course in educational psychology to under-graduate education majors. In various class sessions, I introduce such top-ics as operant conditioning, information processing theory, motivation, classroom management, and educational testing. Many of my students seem to learn the material well: They carry on informed discussions in class and demon-strate comprehension and application on assignments and examinations. But I always wonder about what happens to these students when they finish my course. Does the information they have learned in educational psychology make a difference in the way they eventually teach their own students? Do they really apply the things I have taught them? Does educational psychology help them solve classroom problems?

When something you learn in one situation affects how you learn or perform in another situation, **transfer** has occurred. Sometimes you transfer knowledge and skills you've previously learned to solve a problem; hence, **problem solving** is a form of transfer.

Ideally, transfer and problem solving should be two of our educational system's top priorities (e.g., Brown & Campione, in press; Prawat, 1989). Schools at all levels, from preschools to doctoral programs, teach knowledge and skills with the implicit assumption that students will then apply what they have learned to the "real world." Yet the things people learn in school do not always seem to transfer to new situations and new problems. Many adults cannot use basic addition and subtraction procedures to balance their own checkbooks. Many teachers reinforce inappropriate behaviors in their classrooms, ignoring the basic operant conditioning principles they learned in their undergraduate education classes. People of all ages may know right from wrong without relating that knowledge to their own behaviors.

In this chapter we will examine concepts, principles, theories, and research related to both transfer and problem solving. We will also consider a variety of factors that either facilitate or interfere with successful application of acquired knowledge and skills to new situations and problems. At the end of the chapter, we will look at implications for educational practice.

TRANSFER

Transfer is a part of everyday life. Individuals continually encounter new situations and draw on their previously acquired knowledge and skills to deal with them. In fact, transfer is an essential component of human functioning. Without it, people would have to learn from scratch about how to behave in every new circumstance and would spend most of their time in trial-and-error learning.

We should note here that, in a sense, we have already talked about transfer. When we discussed classical and operant conditioning earlier in the book, we considered the phenomenon of *generalization*: After an organism learns a response to one stimulus, it often makes the same response to similar stimuli. Generalization is clearly an instance of transfer, because learning in one stimulus situation influences behavior in a slightly different situation. However, as we discuss transfer in the pages that follow, we will not always limit ourselves to a stimulus-response perspective.

In the next few pages, we will explore various aspects of transfer. We will consider several different types of transfer, then examine theories of transfer, looking first at early theories and subsequently moving to more contemporary views. We will also look at what affects the likelihood that transfer will occur.

Types of Transfer

The concept of transfer refers to many different, although related, phenomena. Theorists distinguish among types of transfer in terms of at least three dimensions: positive versus negative, vertical versus lateral, and specific versus general.

Positive Versus Negative Transfer

When learning in one situation facilitates learning or performance in another situation, we say that **positive transfer** has occurred. Learning basic mathematics procedures should facilitate a person's ability to balance a checkbook. Learning principles of reinforcement should improve a teacher's ability to modify student behavior. Knowing the difference between right and wrong should have a positive impact on moral and ethical behavior.

In a sense, meaningful learning involves positive transfer, because previously learned information is used in understanding and remembering new information (Ausubel, Novak, & Hanesian, 1978; Brooks & Dansereau, 1987; Voss, 1987). "Old" information can help new learning in a variety of ways; for instance, it can serve as a conceptual framework to which new material is attached, facilitate elaboration of new ideas, or provide an analogy that helps make those ideas better understood (Brooks & Dansereau, 1987). Many of the examples of meaningful learning and mnemonics that I describe in Chapters 11 and 13 are forms of positive transfer because old information is being applied to facilitate the storage of new information.

On the other hand, when something learned in one situation hinders a person's ability to learn or perform in a second situation, then **negative transfer** has occurred. For example, when I play tennis after having played racquetball the day before, I find myself missing the ball a lot: I keep positioning myself too close to the ball because I am accustomed to a short racquetball racquet rather than to the much longer tennis racket. Individuals accustomed to driving a standard transmission who then find themselves behind the wheel of a car with an automatic transmission often step on a clutch that isn't there. People who learn a second language typically apply patterns of speech production characteristic of their native tongue, thus giving them a foreign accent (Schmidt & Young, 1987). Students accustomed to memorizing facts in other college courses often don't perform well on my own application-oriented examinations.

An example of a situation in which negative transfer frequently rears its ugly head is in work with decimals: Students often erroneously apply mathematical rules they have learned for whole numbers. For example, when asked to compare two decimals such as these:

2.34 versus 2.8

students sometimes apply the rule that "more digits mean a larger number," thus concluding that 2.34 is the larger of the two decimal numbers (Behr & Harel, 1988). Another rule that is inappropriately transferred to decimals is this whole-number rule: "When a number is divided, the result is a smaller number." Even college students show negative transfer of this rule; for instance, many assert that the answer to this problem:

$$5 \div 0.65$$

is a number smaller than five (Tirosh & Graeber, 1988). The answer is actually 7.69, a *larger* number.

As you can see, transfer may or may not be beneficial. At the end of the chapter, we will look at ways to maximize positive transfer while minimizing negative transfer.

Vertical Versus Lateral Transfer

In some subject areas, topics build on one another in a hierarchical fashion, so that an individual must almost certainly know one topic before moving to the next. For example, a student should probably master principles of addition before moving on to multiplication, because multiplication is an extension of addition. Similarly, a medical student must have expertise in human anatomy before studying surgical techniques: It's difficult to perform an appendectomy when you can't find the appendix. **Vertical transfer** refers to such situations—an individual acquires new knowledge or skills by building on more basic information and procedures.

In other situations, knowledge of one topic may affect learning a second topic even though the first is not a prerequisite to the second. Knowledge of French is not essential for learning Spanish, yet knowing French should facilitate one's learning of Spanish because many words are similar in the two languages. When knowledge of the first topic is not essential to learning the second one, but it nevertheless has an impact, we say that **lateral transfer** has occurred.

Specific Versus General Transfer

In **specific transfer**, the original learning task and the transfer task overlap in content. For example, having knowledge about the anatomy of a human should help a veterinary student learn the anatomy of a dog, because the two species have many parallel anatomical features. A student who knows Spanish should easily learn Portuguese, because the two languages have similar vocabulary and syntax.

In **general transfer**, the original task and the transfer task are different in content. For example, if knowledge of Latin helps a student learn physics, or if the study habits a student develops in a physics course facilitate the learning of sociology, then general transfer is occurring.

Research clearly shows that specific transfer is more common than general transfer (Gray & Orasanu, 1987; Perkins & Salomon, 1989). In fact, the question of whether general transfer can occur at all has been the subject of much debate over the years. We turn now to both early and contemporary theories of transfer, which vary considerably in their perspectives of what things transfer, and when.

Theories of Transfer

How does transfer occur? Let's look first at an early view of transfer—one that predates twentieth-century learning theories—and then examine both behaviorist and cognitive views.

A Historical Perspective: Formal Discipline

In days of yore, serious scholars studied many difficult topics—for instance, Latin, Greek, calculus, and formal logic—that are not as frequently studied today. Although these subject areas may have had no specific applicability to an individual's day-to-day functioning, scholars believed that learning such subjects would nevertheless improve their learning and performance in many other aspects of their lives. As recently as the middle of the twentieth century, students were given frequent practice in memorizing poems, apparently as a method of improving their general learning capabilities. Such practices reflect the notion of **formal discipline**: Just as you exercise muscles to develop strength, you exercise your mind to learn more quickly and deal with new situations more effectively.

The theory of formal discipline, a predominant view in educational circles until the turn of the century, emphasized the importance and likelihood of general transfer, the idea being that learning in one situation improves learning and performance in another situation regardless of how different the two situations might be. However, as human learning began to be studied empirically, this notion of "mind as muscle" was soon discarded. For example, William James (1890) memorized a new poem each day over the course of several weeks, assuming that he would begin to learn poems more quickly with practice. However, he soon found that his poem-learning did not improve; if anything, he learned his later poems more *slowly* than his early ones. And more recently, researchers have found that learning computer programming—a skill requiring precise, detailed thinking about a logical sequence of events—does not facilitate people's performance in areas unrelated to computer use (Perkins & Salomon, 1989). The consensus of contemporary learning theorists is that general transfer, in the extreme sense portrayed by the formal discipline perspective, probably does not occur.

An Early Behaviorist Theory: Thorndike's Identical Elements

Edward Thorndike (1903, 1924; Thorndike & Woodworth, 1901) proposed a theory of transfer that emphasized specific transfer: Transfer occurs only to the extent that the original and transfer tasks have *identical elements*. In an early study supporting Thorndike's theory (Thorndike & Woodworth, 1901), subjects received extensive training in estimating the areas of rectangles. This training improved their subsequent ability to estimate the areas of rectangles and other two-dimensional forms (e.g., triangles and circles) as well. However, training had less of an impact on the judgment of nonrectangular shapes, presumably because nonrectangles had elements both similar and dissimilar to the elements of rectangles. In a later study, Thorndike (1924) examined the interrelationships of high school students' academic achievement in different curricular areas.

Achievement in one subject area appeared to facilitate students' achievement in another only when the two subjects were similar. For example, arithmetic achievement was related to performance in a bookkeeping course, but Latin proficiency was not. Thorndike concluded that the value of studying specific topics was due not to the benefits of mental exercise, but to "the special information, habits, interests, attitudes, and ideals which they demonstrably produce" (Thorndike, 1924, p. 98).

A Later Behaviorist Perspective: Similarity of Stimuli and Responses

Since Thorndike's work, behaviorist views of transfer have focused on how transfer is affected by stimulus and response characteristics in both the original and transfer situations. As an illustration, consider these four lists of paired associates:

List 1	List 2	List 3	List 4
lamp-shoe	lamp-sock	rain-shoe	lamp-goat
boat-fork	boat-spoon	bear-fork	boat-shop
wall-lawn	wall-yard	sofa-lawn	wall-rice
corn-road	corn-lane	book-road	corn-fish

Imagine that you first learn List 1, then are asked to learn List 2. Will your knowledge of the pairs in List 1 help you learn the pairs in List 2? Based on the results of verbal learning studies (Hall, 1966, 1971), the answer is yes: The stimulus words are identical in the two situations and the responses are similar, so positive transfer from one list to the other is likely to occur.

Now, however, imagine that you have to learn List 1 and then List 3. Will prior learning of List 1 help with List 3? The answer again is yes (Hall, 1966, 1971). Even though the stimulus words are very different, the responses in List 3 are identical to those of List 1—hence they have already been learned—and merely need to be attached to the new stimuli.

On the other hand, let's now suppose that, after learning List 1, you need to learn List 4. Here is a case in which very different responses from those of List 1 must be learned to the very same stimuli. Learning List 1 is likely to make learning List 4 more difficult because you will sometimes remember the List 1 response instead of the List 4 response (Hall, 1966, 1971), and negative transfer will result.

In general, principles of transfer that have emerged from behaviorist literature (e.g., Osgood, 1949; Thyne, 1963) include the following:

1. When stimuli and responses are similar in the two situations, maximal positive transfer will occur.
2. When stimuli are different and responses are similar, some positive transfer will occur.
3. When stimuli are similar and responses are different, negative transfer will occur.

As an example of this last point, I remember one year as a high school student when my class schedule included second-period Latin and third-period French.

The word for "and" (*et*) is spelled the same in both languages but pronounced very differently ("et" in Latin and "ay" in French), hence meeting the conditions for negative transfer (similar stimuli, different responses). On several occasions I blurted out an "et" in my French class—a response that inevitably evoked a disgusted scowl from my French teacher.

As learning theorists move away from behaviorist perspectives to more molar, cognitive explanations of how human beings learn, they speak less and less of specific stimulus-response connections. Nevertheless, we see hints of behaviorist notions even in today's conceptions of transfer. For example, similarity between something already learned and the demands of a new situation clearly *is* an important factor affecting the extent to which transfer occurs. And John Anderson (1987) has proposed that transfer occurs to the extent that procedures (productions) used in one situation apply to a second situation—a cognitive variation on Thorndike's theory of identical elements.

Human Information Processing Theory

Cognitive psychologists have become increasingly interested in transfer in recent years (Fleishman, 1987) and are beginning to develop their own views of how and when transfer occurs. A currently prominent view of transfer is as follows: Relevant information and skills are transferred to a new situation only when they are retrieved to working memory within the context of that new situation (Brooks & Dansereau, 1987; Cormier, 1987; Gick & Holyoak, 1987; Prawat, 1989). Given the low probability that any particular piece of information will be retrieved, as well as the limited capacity of working memory, many potentially relevant pieces of information may very well *not* be transferred in situations in which they would be helpful.

The presence or absence of retrieval cues in the transfer situation determines what relevant information, if any, is retrieved to working memory. A new situation is more likely to call to mind previously learned information when aspects of the situation are closely associated with the relevant information in long-term memory. This will happen, for instance, if a learner anticipated the situation when storing the new information, so that the situation and information relevant to it were stored in a connected fashion.

Current Views on General Transfer

We have already seen two extreme perspectives regarding general transfer. Advocates of formal discipline argued that learning rigorous and demanding subject matter facilitates later learning tasks because it strengthens and "disciplines" the mind. Thorndike, on the other hand, argued that one task will transfer to another only to the extent that the two tasks have identical elements. Current views concerning general transfer are somewhere in between: General transfer is not as common as specific transfer, but learning occurring at one time *can* facilitate learning at another time if, in the process, the individual *learns how to learn*.

In several early studies of learning to learn, Harry Harlow (1949, 1950, 1959) found that monkeys and young children became progressively faster at discrimination-learning tasks. More recently, a number of studies have examined the transfer value of metacognitive knowledge and skills; as we noted in Chapter 15, effective study methods and habits often do generalize from one subject matter to another (see also Brooks & Dansereau, 1987; Brown, 1978; Pressley, Snyder, & Cariglia-Bull, 1987).

As long as two tasks have something in common, the possibility of transfer from one to the other exists (Gray & Orasanu, 1987). But commonalities among tasks do not guantee transfer. In fact, transfer does not occur nearly as often as it could or should (Perkins & Salomon, 1989). When is transfer most likely to take place? We turn to this topic now.

Factors Affecting Transfer

A number of factors influence the probability that information or skills learned in one situation will transfer to another situation. Let's look at several principles that can help us predict when transfer is most likely to take place.

•*Meaningful learning promotes better transfer than rote learning.* In Chapters 11 and 12, I explained that meaningfully learned information is more easily stored and retrieved than information learned at a rote level. Now we see an additional advantage of meaningful learning: It promotes positive transfer (Ausubel et al., 1978; Brooks & Dansereau, 1987; Mayer, 1987; Prawat, 1989). For example, in a study by Brownell and Moser (1949, cited in Mayer, 1977), third-grade students were taught the idea of borrowing in subtraction in a presumably meaningful manner: Two-digit numbers were represented by individual sticks and groups of 10 sticks bundled together, with borrowing represented by the untying of one group of 10. These students solved a variety of subtraction problems more successfully than students taught the same information simply through verbally presented rules. Along a similar vein, in an experiment by Mayer and Greeno (1972), two groups of undergraduate students received one of two methods of instruction on a formula related to basic probability theory. Group 1 received instruction that focused on the formula itself, whereas Group 2 received instruction that emphasized the relationship of the formula to subjects' general knowledge. Group 1 subjects were better able to apply the formula to problems similar to those they had studied during instruction, but Group 2 subjects were better able to use the formula in ways that had not specifically been covered in instruction—that is, they could transfer the formula to a wider variety of situations. Apparently, Group 2 subjects had made more connections between the new material and existing information in their long-term memories, and those connections enabled the subjects to transfer probability theory in ways that Group 1 subjects could not.

•*The more thoroughly something is learned, the more likely it is to be transferred to a new situation.* Research is clear on this point: the probability of transfer increases when students know something *well* (Brophy, 1992; Cormier & Hagman, 1987; Gick & Holyoak, 1987; Voss, 1987).

Acquiring knowledge and skills thoroughly takes time. In fact, some conditions that make initial learning slower and more difficult may actually be beneficial for both retention and transfer over the long run. For example, increasing the variability of the tasks learners are asked to practice during instruction—having them perform several different tasks or several variations on the same task within a single instructional unit—lowers their performance initially but enhances their ability to transfer what they have learned to new situations later on (Schmidt & Bjork, 1992). Furthermore, although a certain amount of feedback is essential for learning to take place, limited rather than continual feedback about one's performance appears to promote performance over the long run, even though it may result in slower improvement initially (Schmidt & Bjork, 1992). It may be that learners need practice not only in performing certain tasks, but also in retrieving relevant knowledge in a multitask context and in providing their *own* feedback about their performance (Schmidt & Bjork, 1992).

Clearly, then, there is a trade-off between transfer and expediency. Teachers who teach a few things in-depth are more likely to promote transfer than those who teach many things quickly—the "less is more" principle we encountered in our discussion of conceptual change in Chapter 13. Students should demonstrate thorough mastery of material if they will be expected to apply that material in future situations.

•*Principles are more easily transferred than knowledge.* General principles and rules are more applicable than specific facts and information (Cheng, Holyoak, Nisbett, & Oliver, 1986; Fong, Krantz, & Nisbett, 1986; Gick & Holyoak, 1983, 1987; Judd, 1932; Perkins & Salomon, 1987). For example, if you have read Chapter 4's discussion of operant conditioning, then you probably remember the general principle of reinforcement: A reinforcer is a stimulus that increases the later frequency of a response it follows. This principle is easily transferable to a wide variety of situations, whereas specific facts that I mentioned in the same chapter (e.g., who wrote what, and when) are not. Similarly, when students are trying to understand such current events as revolutions and international wars, general principles from history—for example, the principle that two groups of people will engage in battle when other attempts at reaching a mutually satisfying state of affairs have failed—are probably more applicable than precise knowledge of World War II battles. And when students study geography, general map interpretation skills—for example, determining why various features are located where they are—are probably more useful than the names and locations of specific rivers, mountain ranges, and state capitals (Bochenhauer, 1990).

•*The more similar two situations are, the more likely it is that what is learned in one situation will be applied to the other situation.* Behaviorists have argued that similarity of either stimuli or responses is necessary for transfer to occur. Cognitivists have proposed instead that because transfer depends on retrieval of relevant information at the appropriate time, the *perceived* similarity rather than actual similarity of the two situations is important (Bassok, 1990; Bassok & Holyoak, 1993; Blake & Clark, 1990; Di Vesta & Peverly, 1984; Gick &

Holyoak, 1987; Voss, 1987). Either way, one thing is clear: Similarity between two situations affects transfer.

•*Numerous and varied examples and opportunities for practice increase the extent to which information and skills will be applied in new situations.* You may recall the concept of encoding specificity from Chapter 12: Knowledge is often stored in association with the context in which it has been encountered. A learner who stores a particular skill or piece of information in connection with one situation is likely to retrieve that knowledge—and perhaps to use it—when encountering the same situation once again; however, the learner is *un*likely to retrieve it when in a different situation (Di Vesta & Peverly, 1984; Stein, 1989; Sternberg & Frensch, 1993).

People who learn things only within a single content domain often don't see the relevance of those things for another content domain. For example, carpenters may learn such mathematical concepts as *parallel* and *perpendicular* within the context of carpentry, yet not realize that their knowledge is applicable in other situations requiring the same concepts (Millroy, 1991). High school students may have difficulty transferring things they have learned in a physics class to their later use of algebra (Bassok & Holyoak, 1990, 1993). Elementary students don't recognize that the things they learn in science are useful in solving world problems (Rakow, 1984). And in general, students don't see the connections between the things they learn in school and the situations they encounter in the outside world (Alexander & Judy, 1988; diSessa, 1982; Sternberg & Frensch, 1993).

Students are most likely to transfer something when they have encountered it in a wide variety of examples and practice situations (Cheng et al., 1986; Cormier, 1987; Fong et al., 1986; Gick & Holyoak, 1987; Perkins & Salomon, 1987; Schmidt & Bjork, 1992; Schmidt & Young, 1987; see Bassok & Holyoak, 1993, for an exception). Individuals trained in this fashion store what they have learned in association with multiple contexts and are therefore more likely to retrieve the information when they again find themselves in one of those contexts. As an illustration, when students are learning basic arithmetic principles, they might be asked to apply those principles in determining best buys at a grocery store, dividing items fairly among friends, running a lemonade stand, and so on. Arithmetic will then be associated in long-term memory with all of these situations, and when the need arises to determine which of two grocery products yields the most for the money, relevant arithmetic procedures should be readily retrieved.

•*The probability of transfer decreases as the time interval between the original task and the transfer task increases.* Most research on transfer has focused on very short delays between the original task and the transfer task (Gick & Holyoak, 1987). Yet transfer decreases as the time interval between the original and transfer situations increases (Gick & Holyoak, 1987). Here is another principle that is probably due to retrieval: Information that has been learned recently is more likely, and more able, to be retrieved than information acquired farther back in time.

How and when do people transfer information they have learned to find solutions to problems? It is to this topic—problem solving—that we turn next.

PROBLEM SOLVING

Can you solve these three problems?

1. What number is obtained when 3354 is divided by 43?
2. How can a 45-year-old educational psychologist be helped to control her junk food habit?
3. How can two groups of people of differing political persuasions and a mutual lack of trust be convinced to reduce their military defense spending and instead work toward cooperation and peaceful coexistence?

The world presents us with many different kinds of problems. Some, such as Problem 1, are straightforward: all the information necessary for a solution is presented, and the solution is definitely right or wrong. Others, such as Problem 2, may necessitate seeking out additional information (e.g., does the educational psychologist keep physically active, or does she sit around the house all day watching television game shows?), and there may be two or more solutions to the problem (self-reinforcement for altered eating habits, six months on a deserted island, etc.). Still others, such as Problem 3, may be so complicated that, even after considerable research and creative thought, no easy solution emerges (as I write this, events in Eastern Europe and the Mideast come to mind). Different kinds of problems require different procedures and different solutions; this multifaceted nature of problem solving has made the theoretical study of problem solving a very challenging endeavor indeed.

In the following pages, we will explore a number of topics related to the complex activity of human problem solving. We will first define some basic concepts that appear in problem solving literature, then examine both behaviorist and cognitive theories of problem solving. Because cognitive views are predominant at the present time, we will then look in-depth at memory factors and cognitive strategies involved in problem solving.

Basic Concepts in Problem Solving

Among the more basic concepts appearing in problem solving literature are problem components, algorithms, heuristics, and well-defined problems versus ill-defined problems.

Components of a Problem
Any problem has at least three components (Glass, Holyoak, & Santa, 1979; Wickelgren, 1974):

- **Givens**—pieces of information that are provided when the problem is presented

- **Goal**—the desired end state—what a problem solution will hopefully accomplish
- **Operations**—actions that can be performed to approach or reach the goal

Operations are frequently described in terms of *productions*, the "if-then" conditional actions described in Chapter 11 (e.g., see Anderson, 1983a, 1987). When one or more operations can be applied to reach the goal state, the problem is successfully solved.

Algorithms and Heuristics

Some problems can be approached using a set of specified operations that always lead to a correct solution. For example, the problem of dividing 3354 by 43 can be solved using either of two procedures: (1) applying prescribed methods of long division, or (2) pushing the appropriate series of buttons on a calculator. Either approach produces the correct answer—78. Similarly, a cherry pie recipe, if followed to the letter in terms of ingredients, measurements, and oven temperatures, provides a series of steps that guarantees a delicious dessert. Such specific, step-by-step procedures for solving problems are called **algorithms**.

Unfortunately, not all problems can be solved with algorithms. No algorithm can eliminate a junk food addiction or establish world peace. In such situations, people use other approaches to problem solving—approaches that may or may not work. These approaches, known collectively as **heuristics**, comprise general problem solving strategies, rules of thumb, and "best guesses" based on past experience with similar problems. For example, in helping an educational psychologist reduce her junk food intake, one heuristic is to think of as many different solutions as possible (a technique known as **brainstorming**), in hopes that one of them will be acceptable. The problem of disarmament of two warring factions can perhaps be solved by analogy: If two coworkers can resolve their differences when they sit down and talk about them, maybe the same strategy will be effective with political groups (hence the frequent summit conferences among world leaders).

Heuristics are also used when algorithms are impractical or time-consuming. For example, I once coordinated a chili supper for the Parent-Teacher Association of the local elementary school and needed numerous volunteers to assist me. The PTA board suggested an algorithm for me to use: Contact the more than 200 individuals who had indicated on a questionnaire several months earlier that they would help at PTA functions. Being pressed for time, I instead chose a heuristic: I contacted people I knew personally, aware that I could shame many of them into helping out. Similarly, although an algorithm exists for determining the best move in a game of checkers, people tend not to use it because of its impracticality. This algorithm, as Samuel (1963) has described it, is as follows: Consider every possible move, and then consider every possible next move that the opponent could make in response to each of those moves, then consider every follow-up move that could be made in response to each of *those* moves, and so on, until the winner is projected for every conceivable series of moves.

Such an algorithm would take either a sophisticated computer programmer or several lifetimes of complete dedication to a single game of checkers.

Well-defined Versus Ill-defined Problems

Problems vary greatly in terms of how well they are structured or defined. Many theorists have found it helpful to distinguish between well-defined and ill-defined problems (e.g., Eysenck & Keane, 1990; Frederiksen, 1984a; Reitman, 1964, 1965; Simon, 1973, 1978), a distinction that actually reflects a continuum of problem structure rather than a rigid dichotomy (Frederiksen, 1984a). At one extreme is the **well-defined problem**, one for which goals and givens are clearly stated, all the necessary information for solving the problem is presented, and an algorithm exists that will lead to a correct solution. At the other extreme is the **ill-defined problem**, one in which the desired goal is ambiguous, some information necessary for problem solution is lacking, and no relevant algorithm for problem solution exists. Well-defined problems often have only one right solution, whereas ill-defined problems often have several possible solutions that vary in terms of their relative "rightness" or acceptability. The problem of dividing 3354 by 43 is well-defined, while that of military disarmament is ill-defined (for example, the goal of "cooperation and peaceful coexistence" is ambiguous). As you might guess, ill-defined problems are typically more difficult to solve and require more complex problem solving strategies than well-defined ones.

Unfortunately, researchers have focused on well-defined problems (often somewhat artificial ones) rather than on the ill-defined problems that life more typically presents (Eysenck & Keane, 1990; Ohlsson, 1983). You will undoubtedly notice this bias as we proceed with our discussion of problem solving. Nevertheless, most of the theories and principles I will present presumably apply to both kinds of problems. And in fact, later in the chapter we will find that one strategy for solving ill-defined problems is to define them more specifically and concretely—in other words, to make them well-defined.

Theories of Problem Solving

Since Edward Thorndike's early work with the cat in the puzzle box, several theories of problem solving have emerged from both the behaviorist and cognitive perspectives. We will first look at two behaviorist views: trial-and-error and response hierarchy. We will then examine three more cognitive approaches: Gestalt psychology, stages of problem solving, and human information processing.

Trial-and-error Learning

In Chapter 2, you read about Thorndike's (1898) classic work with a cat in a puzzle box. The cat needed to solve a problem: how to get out of a confining situation. It explored the box, manipulating its various parts, and eventually triggered the mechanism that opened the door. Once again it was put back in the box, and once again it tried different behaviors until it triggered the release mechanism. In each succeeding trial, escape from the box took less time than in the previous trial. The cat's approach to the problem situation appeared to be one of trial and error, with the correct solution being followed by a positive consequence (escape from the box).

A trial-and-error approach is often observed in the problem solving behavior of children. For example, consider the way many young children assemble jigsaw puzzles: They try to fit different pieces into the same spot, often without considering each piece's shape and appearance, until eventually they find a piece that fits.

Response Hierarchy

Another concept that you encountered in Chapter 2 was Clark Hull's notion of a habit family hierarchy, now more generally known as a **response hierarchy**: An organism learns several different responses to the same stimulus, each of which is associated with that stimulus with a different degree of habit strength. When a stimulus is presented, an organism will, if possible, make the response for which the habit strength is the strongest. If that response fails or is prevented from occurring, the organism will make the second response, and so on down the hierarchy (e.g., Hull, 1934, 1937, 1938).

A response hierarchy can be graphically depicted like this:

In this case, three responses have been learned to the same stimulus, with stronger stimulus-response associations being indicated by thicker arrows. The organism first emits the response with the strongest association to the stimulus (R_1). If that response fails to achieve its goal, the response with the second strongest association (R_2) is emitted, then the third strongest response (R_3), and so on, until eventually the goal is attained.

A number of behaviorists (e.g., Davis, 1966; Mayzner & Tresselt, 1958, 1966; Skinner, 1966a) have applied the notion of response hierarchy to a problem solving situation. Stimuli in the problem situation may evoke a number of different responses, and those responses will be produced, one at a time and in order of their strength, until either the problem is solved or the organism exhausts its repertoire of responses. To illustrate, my daughter Tina is often confronted with the same problem: getting permission from her parents to do something we may not want her to do. Given this problem, she tries three different responses, usually in the same order. First she smiles sweetly and describes how much she would like to engage in that forbidden activity (such a response, apparently, is associated most strongly with this particular problem situation). If that tactic is unproductive, she speaks indignantly about how her parents never let her do anything. As a last resort, she runs off to her room, slamming her door and shouting that her parents hate her. Unfortunately, Tina has not yet learned that some problems, such as engaging in forbidden activities, will be solved over her parents' dead bodies.

In their emphasis on trial-and-error learning and habit strength, behaviorists have obviously focused on the role that stimulus-response connections play in problem solving. Although such an approach can often be used to explain problem solving behavior, contemporary theorists have largely abandoned it to focus more on the mental processes involved in problem solving. Consistent with this trend, we too will abandon behaviorism at this point and embrace a more cognitively oriented perspective for the rest of our discussion.

An Early Cognitive View: Gestalt Psychology

In Chapter 8, I described Wolfgang Köhler's (1925) observations of chimpanzee behavior in problem solving situations. Köhler observed little trial-and-error behavior of the form that Thorndike had described. Rather, it appeared to him that the chimpanzees carefully examined the components of a problem situation (sizing things up, so to speak), and mentally combined and recombined those components until they eventually found a winning combination. At this point of **insight**, the chimps would immediately move into action, performing the required responses in a deliberate manner until the problem was solved. From such observations, Köhler (1925, 1929) concluded that problem solving was a process of mentally **restructuring** a problem situation until insight into the problem's solution was reached.

Stages of Problem Solving

Another early cognitive approach to problem solving was to identify the mental stages through which problem solving proceeded (e.g., Polya, 1957; Wallas, 1926). For example, Wallas (1926) identified four steps in problem solving:

1. **Preparation.** Defining the problem and gathering information relevant to its solution.
2. **Incubation.** Thinking about the problem at a subconscious level while engaging in other activities.
3. **Inspiration.** Having a sudden insight into the solution of the problem.
4. **Verification.** Checking to be certain that the solution is correct.

Similarly, Polya (1957) listed these four steps:

1. **Understanding the problem.** Identifying the problem's knowns (givens) and unknowns and, if appropriate, using suitable notation, such as mathematical symbols, to represent the problem.

2. **Devising a plan.** Determining appropriate actions to take to solve the problem.
3. **Carrying out the plan.** Executing the actions that have been determined to solve the problem and checking their effectiveness.
4. **Looking backward.** Evaluating the overall effectiveness of the approach to the problem, with the intention of learning something about how similar problems may be solved on future occasions.

Unfortunately, Wallas and Polya derived their conceptualizations of problem solving more from introspection and informal observation than from controlled experimentation, and they were somewhat vague about how each of their four steps could be accomplished (e.g., Lester, 1985; Mayer, 1992). For example, Wallas' notion of incubation revealed little about how to behave to facilitate the occurrence of inspiration. Similarly, Polya recommended devising a plan with little consideration of just how one would go about doing that. For reasons such as these, early theories of problem solving were of limited value in helping psychologists determine what specific cognitive processes are involved in solving problems successfully.

Human Information Processing Theory

Most contemporary theories focus less on the steps people follow in solving problems and more on the specific mental processes they use to reach problem solutions (e.g., Andre, 1986). These information processing theories emphasize the role of such factors as working memory capacity, meaningful learning, organization of long-term memory, retrieval of relevant information, and specific cognitive strategies. The bulk of current research in problem solving reflects inquiry into the nature of these cognitive processes; in the following pages we will look at them in detail.

Cognitive Factors in Problem Solving

The ability to solve problems successfully depends on a number of factors related to the human information processing system. Here we will focus on five such factors: working memory capacity, encoding and storage in long-term memory, long-term memory retrieval, the specific knowledge base related to the problem, and metacognition. As we go along, we will identify several differences between problem solving "experts" and "novices" within a particular content domain, discovering reasons why some individuals solve problems quickly, easily, and effectively while others solve them either with great difficulty or not at all.

Working Memory Capacity

As you should recall, working memory is the component of memory in which active, conscious processing of information occurs. Yet this component has a limited capacity: It can hold and process only a small amount of information at a time. If the information and processes necessary to solve a problem exceed working memory capacity, the problem cannot be solved (Anderson, 1987; Johnstone & El-Banna, 1986; Pulos, 1980; Salthouse, 1991; Tourniaire & Pulos, 1985). For example, you may remember from Chapter 11 how difficult it can be to solve long division problems in your head.

The working memory limitation can be overcome in problem solving situations in at least two ways. First of all, some of the information necessary to solve the problem can be written down (i.e., stored externally). This is the method typically used in solving complicated arithmetic problems. Second, as I indicated in Chapter 12, some skills involved in problem solving should be learned well enough that they become automatic, thus requiring only minimal working memory capacity.

Encoding and Storage of the Problem

Consider this classic children's riddle:

> *As I was going to St. Ives,*
> *I met a man with seven wives.*
> *Every wife had seven sacks.*
> *Every sack had seven cats.*
> *Every cat had seven kits.*
> *Kits, cats, sacks, wives.*
> *How many were going to St. Ives?*

Many people take this logical approach to the problem: 1 traveler plus 1 man plus 7 wives plus 7^2 sacks (49) plus 7^3 cats (343) plus 7^4 kits (2401) equal a total of 2802 going to St. Ives. People who solve the problem in this manner have encoded the problem incorrectly. In particular, they have overlooked the first line of the riddle: "As *I* was going to St. Ives." The problem statement doesn't tell us where the polygamist was taking his harem and menagerie—perhaps to St. Ives, perhaps not.

Here is a passage containing some information you will need to solve a mathematical problem. Read the information, then, after you have finished, turn the page to read the problem:

I went to the store and made the following purchases:

A roasting chicken for $4
A dozen eggs for $1 per dozen
Three avocados for 50¢ each
Two cans of tomato sauce for 25¢ each
Five apples for 20¢ each

Now for the problem: How many items did I buy?

Did you find that you stored the wrong information? You may have been expecting the problem "How much did I spend?" If so, then you probably determined the total amount spent in each line of the problem and added the amounts together for a grand total. Using this approach, however, you would not have stored the information actually necessary for solving the problem—the number of items mentioned in each line.

One critical factor in problem solving is *what* specific information is stored in memory (Chi, Glaser, & Farr, 1988; Glaser, 1987; Sternberg, 1985; Sternberg & Davidson, 1982, 1983). A difficulty you may have had with the grocery shopping problem is that some irrelevant information was presented (i.e., the prices of items), and you may have stored that information instead of more essential data. Irrelevant information can be distracting, thus interfering with successful problem solving. For example, when I give examinations to my own students, I often present more information than is necessary to answer questions, and some students have difficulty sorting through it all. Similarly, I have noticed that my daughter has trouble with mathematics problems that include superfluous information. My students and my daughter behave almost as if they have learned that they need to use *all* the information they are given. This attitude may be the result of their own prior school experiences: Most problems presented in the classroom (especially mathematics problems) present only the information needed to solve the problem—no more, no less.

A second critical factor related to long-term storage is *how* a problem is encoded in memory (Mayer, 1982, 1986, 1992; Ormrod, 1979; Prawat, 1989; Resnick, 1989; Reusser, 1990; Schwartz, 1971; Sternberg & Davidson, 1982, 1983). For example, Mayer (1982) examined undergraduate students' ability to recall problems such as this one:

> *A truck leaves Los Angeles en route to San Francisco at 1 PM. A second truck leaves San Francisco at 2 PM en route to Los Angeles going along the same route. Assume the two cities are 465 miles apart and that the trucks meet at 6 PM. If the second truck travels at 15 mph faster than the first truck, how fast does each truck go? (Mayer, 1982, p. 202)*

Mayer's subjects had considerable difficulty encoding and storing relational information (e.g., one truck traveling *15 mph faster* than another). They made three times as many errors in recalling relational aspects of problems as they did in recalling basic assertions (e.g., two cities being 465 miles apart).

Wertheimer (1945) has provided another example of the importance of encoding in problem solving: calculating the area of a parallelogram. As you probably know, the area of a rectangle is determined by multiplying its height by its width. But how is the area of a parallelogram determined? Problem solution is easier once you realize that the extra "triangle" at one end of the parallelogram is identical to the missing triangle at the other end, as illustrated in Figure 16–1.

How people encode a problem—and therefore how they solve it—is partly a function of how they classify the problem to begin with (Hinsley, Hayes, &

Figure 16–1
Finding the area of a parallelogram

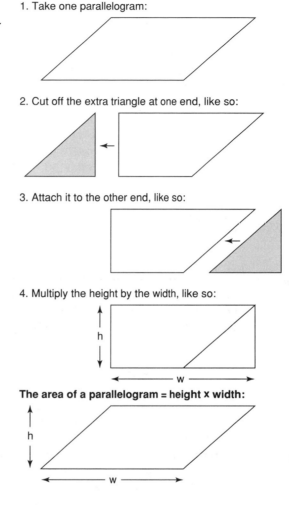

1. Take one parallelogram:

2. Cut off the extra triangle at one end, like so:

3. Attach it to the other end, like so:

4. Multiply the height by the width, like so:

The area of a parallelogram = height × width:

Simon, 1977; Resnick, 1989; Sternberg & Davidson, 1982, 1983). To illustrate, consider this problem:

> *Ana went shopping. She spent $3.50 and then counted her money when she got home. She had $2.35 left. How much did Ana have when she started out? (Resnick, 1989, p. 165)*

If you recognize this as an addition problem, you will probably get the correct answer of $5.85. However, if the word *left* in the problem leads you to classify the problem as one requiring subtraction (because many subtraction problems ask such questions as "How many are *left*?"), you may very well get an incorrect answer such as $1.15 (Resnick, 1989).

Expert and novice problem solvers within a particular content domain seem to classify problems differently (Alexander & Judy, 1988; Anderson, 1990; Blake

& Clark, 1990; Chi, Feltovich, & Glaser, 1981; Chi et al., 1988; Di Vesta & Peverly, 1984; Larkin, 1980, 1983; Schoenfeld & Herrmann, 1982; Silver, 1981). Experts generally classify a problem on the basis of abstract concepts, principles, patterns, and schemas that can be applied to its solution. Novices, on the other hand, tend to focus on specific, concrete aspects of a problem and to retrieve information related only to those aspects. As an illustration, Schoenfeld and Herrmann (1982) compared the ways that mathematics professors and students classified a variety of mathematical problems. Professors classified them on the basis of abstract principles related to problem solution: For example, those solved by analogy were grouped together, as were those solved by contradiction, and so on. Students, on the other hand, classified the problems on the basis of more superficial characteristics, such as whether they contained polynomial expressions or whether they included figures from plane geometry. After a course in mathematics, the students were asked to repeat the classification task; at this point, they began to classify the problems as their professors did.

Mental sets in encoding. Individuals are often predisposed to approach and encode problems in particular ways, a phenomenon known as **mental set** (Gestalt psychologists called it *Einstellung*). Here is a problem in which people are often the victims of a mental set:

> *How can you throw a tennis ball so that it goes a short distance, comes to a complete stop, then reverses its direction? You may not bounce the ball against a surface, nor may you attach any other object (such as a string) to it. (Adapted from Gardner, 1978)*

I once gave this problem to a masters level learning class, and only a handful of my 35 students were able to solve it. Most of them worked on the assumption that the ball had to be thrown horizontally (some may even have encoded the problem as a visual image of a pitcher). Once you break this mental set, the answer is quite simple: You throw the ball *up*.

As another example of mental set, consider this "candle" problem adapted from a similar one used by Duncker (1945):

> *You are in a room with a bulletin board firmly affixed to the wall. Your task is to stand a candle upright beside the bulletin board about 4 feet above the floor. You do not want the candle touching the bulletin board, because the candle's flame must not singe the bulletin board. Instead, you need to place the candle about a centimeter away. How can you accomplish the task, given the following materials:*
> *A small candle (birthday cake size)*
> *A match*
> *A box of thumbtacks*
> *A twelve-inch wooden ruler*
> *A metal knitting needle*

Develop a solution for the problem before you continue reading.

When I have brought these materials into my graduate classes, students typically identify three different solutions. One solution is to stab the knitting needle through the candle and into the bulletin board; this action inevitably splits the candle and gouges the bulletin board. A second solution is to form a flat surface for the candle with the ruler, propping it against the bulletin board with thumbtacks; however, the precariously placed ruler usually falls to the floor once the candle is placed on it. Only a third solution works: Take the thumbtacks out of the box, use the tacks to attach the box to the bulletin board, then affix the candle to the top side of the box (with either melted wax or a tack). The solution is obvious once you think about it, but many people have difficulty with the problem because they encode the box as a container and fail to consider its other possible functions.

The tendency to think of objects as having only one function, thereby overlooking other possible uses, is a form of mental set known as **functional fixedness** (e.g., Birch & Rabinowitz, 1951; Duncker, 1945; Maier & Janzen, 1968). The degree to which individuals experience functional fixedness depends at least in part on situational conditions. For instance, subjects more easily solve the candle problem if the tacks are presented *outside* the box, presumably because they are less likely to think of the box only as a container for the tacks (Duncker, 1945). The problem is also easier to solve if the box itself is labeled "box" (Glucksberg & Weisberg, 1966), possibly because the label draws attention to the box as something that can be used in solving the problem.

Mental set and functional fixedness are at least partly the result of past experience: If a particular approach to a problem has worked in the past, an individual is likely to continue using that same approach even in situations where it is inappropriate or unnecessarily cumbersome. The Luchins' experiments with water jar problems (Luchins, 1942; Luchins & Luchins, 1950) illustrate just how strongly one's past experiences can influence problem solving. Imagine, if you will, that you have three jars of three different sizes, like so:

Jar A holds 20 ounces of water.
Jar B holds 59 ounces of water.
Jar C holds 4 ounces of water.

You need exactly 31 ounces of water. Assuming that you have an unlimited amount of water, how can you get the exact amount of water using only the three jars that you have? Try to find a solution before you read further.

The solution to the water jar problem is as follows:

1. Fill Jar B. This gives you 59 ounces of water.
2. Pour water from Jar B into Jar A until A is full. This leaves 39 ounces in Jar B.
3. Pour water from Jar B into Jar C until C is full. This leaves 35 ounces in Jar B.
4. Pour the water out of Jar C.

5. Once again pour water from B into C. At this point you have 31 ounces in Jar B, the exact amount that you need.

Mathematically speaking, the solution to the problem is

B – A – 2C

Luchins (1942) gave his subjects a series of such problems, with the answer always being the same: B – A – 2C. He then presented these three problems:

Jar A holds:	Jar B holds:	Jar C holds:	Obtain this amount:
23	49	3	20
15	39	3	18
28	76	3	25

Almost everyone solved the first two of these using the same formula as before: B – A – 2C. They had difficulty solving the third problem because the standard formula did not apply. But notice that all three can be solved quite easily: The solution for the first and third problems is A – C, and that for the second problem is A + C. Luchins' subjects (who in fact were professors and graduate students!) were victims of a problem solving mental set established through prior experience.

In most situations, one's predisposition to approach similar problems in similar ways facilitates successful problem solving (Maier, 1945). A mental set does influence the way in which a problem is encoded in memory, however, and this encoding in turn influences the parts of long-term memory that are searched for information potentially relevant to the problem. If a problem's encoding steers an individual in the wrong "direction" in long-term memory, it hinders problem solving performance (Alexander & Judy, 1988; Glass et al., 1979; Mayer, 1992; Stein, 1989). Let's now consider retrieval from long-term memory as yet another cognitive factor affecting problem solving success.

Retrieval from Long-term Memory

To use previously learned information to solve a problem, the information must be retrieved at the time the problem is being considered. Thus, the factors that facilitate long-term memory retrieval—for example, meaningful learning and organized storage—facilitate problem solving success as well (e.g., Ausubel et al., 1978).

In searching long-term memory for information relevant to a problem, individuals begin by looking in logical "places." People tend to retrieve familiar ideas first, identifying original or unusual problem solutions later or not at all (Bourne, Dominowski, Loftus, & Healy, 1986). People also tend to retrieve information closely associated with aspects of the problem situation; for example, subjects more easily solve the candle problem when they have previously learned a paired-associate list that includes the pair "candle-box" (Weisberg, DiCamillo, & Phillips, 1979). Hints that provide important retrieval cues can be helpful, at least if individuals perceive their relevance (Bassok & Holyoak, 1993; Bourne et al.,

1986; Gick & Holyoak, 1987). For example, the solution of anagrams such as this one:

Unscramble these letters to form a real word: NEEPLATH

is easier when subjects know that the solution belongs to a particular category such as *animals* (Safren, 1962). (The solution, by the way, is elephant.)

As I mentioned in Chapter 12, anxiety interferes with retrieval by restricting the part of long-term memory that is searched. Anxious individuals are therefore likely to have difficulty solving problems whose solutions are not readily apparent. For example, Glucksberg (1962) asked four groups of subjects to solve the candle problem. For two groups of subjects, the tacks were out of the box (the easy version of the problem), and for the other two groups, the tacks were in the box (the difficult version). Two groups were given no reason to be anxious about solving the problem; their success or failure in finding a solution had no consequences. The other two groups had an incentive to make them more eager and anxious about finding a solution: The fastest 25% of the problem solvers would receive $5, and the fastest individual would receive $25 (a tidy sum back in 1962). Here are the mean reaction times (in minutes) for the four groups of problem solvers; larger numbers indicate greater difficulty in solving the problem:

	Easy Version	**Difficult Version**
Low anxiety	4.99	7.41
High anxiety	3.67	11.08

When the box was empty, its use as a platform for the candle was obvious, and anxiety facilitated problem solving. But when the box was already being used as a container, anxiety made the problem even more difficult to solve than it already was!

The effects of anxiety on problem solving seem to be reduced or eliminated when individuals know where to search in long-term memory. Although high-anxiety individuals typically perform more poorly on problem solving tasks than low-anxiety individuals, performance of the two groups is similar when memory aids that promote appropriate retrieval are provided (Gross & Mastenbrook, 1980; Leherissey, O'Neil, & Hansen, 1971).

If information relevant to a problem is to be retrieved from long-term memory, it must obviously be *in* long-term memory to begin with. So another factor affecting problem solving success is an individual's knowledge base in a particular content domain, as we shall see now.

Knowledge Base

Successful (expert) problem solvers have a more complete and better organized knowledge base for the problems they solve (Alexander & Judy, 1988; Bédard & Chi, 1992; Chi, Glaser, & Rees, 1982; Cochran, 1988; Heller & Hungate, 1985; Mayer, 1992; Smith, 1991; Voss, Greene, Post, & Penner, 1983). For example, using the concept mapping technique described in Chapter 14, Cochran (1988) examined the achievement (much of which involved problem solving) of high school physics students studying a unit on electricity. The higher achievers were students who had better organized information about concepts related to electricity in long-term memory; not only did they know better which concepts should be associated with which, but they also knew the particular relationships that different concepts had with one another. Low achievers were often uncertain about just how the different aspects of electricity fit together and were more often wrong about how the concepts interrelated. By having more information relative to a specific content domain, as well as more interconnections among various bits of information, expert problem solvers can more quickly and easily retrieve the things they need to solve a problem; they can also make inferences about the problem that may facilitate its solution (Bédard & Chi, 1992; Chi et.al., 1982; Mayer, 1992; Stein, 1989).

Successful problem solvers also appear to have more knowledge of specific strategies they can use to solve problems within their area of expertise. For example, once they have categorized a problem as falling into a particular category or being consistent with a certain schema, they readily apply certain procedures to solve that problem (Gick, 1986; Mayer, 1986, 1992; Prawat, 1989; Reed, 1993). And they have often learned some of the more basic problem solving procedures to a level of automaticity (Chi et al., 1988; Glaser, 1987). Novice problem solvers, lacking the rich knowledge base of experts, are more likely to engage in ineffective problem solving strategies—for example, resorting to trial and error, persevering with unproductive procedures, making unwarranted assumptions, and applying procedures and equations in a rote, meaningless fashion (Perkins & Simmons, 1988).

Metacognition
Metacognition obviously plays a role in problem solving: An individual must know which strategies to employ, plan a course of action, and monitor progress toward a problem solution (Kilpatrick, 1985; Lester, 1985; Schoenfeld, 1983, 1985a; Silver, 1982). As an illustration, consider this train of thought regarding a particular problem:

> I'm sloppy at doing [algorithm]; I'd better go slow. This is complicated. I should go through the steps carefully. This method isn't working. I'll try something else. I need to vocalize what I'm doing to help me keep on track. I need to write these steps out. (Lester, 1985, p. 63)

This individual, while obviously not an expert at solving the problem in question, is bringing several beneficial metacognitive skills to bear on the problem—for example, acknowledging the need to go slowly and carefully, recognizing when a strategy is unproductive, and identifying specific behaviors that may facilitate problem solving success.

We have spoken of the need to have appropriate strategies for solving particular problems and to regulate (metacognitively) the effectiveness of those strategies in achieving a problem solution. But what specific strategies do people use? We turn to this topic now.

Problem Solving Strategies

Some types of problems—long division problems, for example—have specific algorithms associated with them that always yield a correct solution. Such algorithms are typically domain-specific: They are useful with particular problems in a particular content area but are, for the most part, inapplicable to problems in other areas.

What do people do when they haven't learned an algorithm for solving a problem, or perhaps when no algorithm for a problem exists? In such cases, they typically resort to more general heuristic strategies (e.g., Gick, 1986; Perkins & Salomon, 1989; Prawat, 1989). Among such strategies are combining algorithms, hill climbing, means-ends analysis, working backward, drawing analogies, and "shortcut" heuristics.

Combining Algorithms

Sometimes, when a single algorithm is insufficient to solve a problem, several algorithms in combination may lead to a correct solution; Robert Gagné's (1985) notion of a higher-order rule, in which two or more simple rules are incorporated, reflects this idea. Mathematics problems (e.g., algebraic equations, geometric proofs) are frequently solved through a combination of algorithms.

In some cases, individuals may have to learn, through either formal classroom instruction or informal experiences, the process of combining algorithms. A study by Scandura (1974) illustrates this point. Elementary school children were taught trading rules such as these:

n caramels $= n + 1$ toy soldiers
n toy soldiers $= n + 2$ pencils

They were then asked to make trades that involved combining two of these rules (e.g., trading caramels for pencils). Children who were unable to combine rules successfully were identified, and half of them were given specific instruction on how to combine the rules. Subsequently, all of these instructed children effectively combined the trading rules (one of them first required additional instruction), while none of the children in an untrained control group were able to do so.

Hill Climbing

Hill climbing (Andre, 1986; Mayer, 1983b; Wickelgren, 1974) is a problem solving strategy in which individuals make any move that brings them closer to the problem goal. For example, consider this problem:

You have a pile of 24 coins. Twenty-three of these coins have the same weight, and one is heavier. Your task is to determine which coin is heavier and to do so in the minimum number of weighings. You are given a beam balance (scale), which will compare the weight of any two sets of coins out of the total set of 24 coins. (Wickelgren, 1974, p. 34)

Stop to figure out a solution before you continue.

You undoubtedly used hill climbing to solve the problem, weighing different groups of coins against one another and gradually eliminating some of them, until eventually only the single heavier coin remained. How many weighings did you use? In fact, as Wickelgren (1974) has pointed out, the heavy coin can be identified with only *three* weighings, like so:

1. Divide the 24 coins into three groups of 8 coins each. Whichever of the three groups is heavier than the other two must contain the heavy coin. Weigh one group against a second; if one group tips the scale, it must contain the heavy coin. If the two groups balance each other, the third group must contain the heavy coin.
2. Divide the eight-coin group containing the heavy coin into three smaller groups, with two groups of three coins and one group of two coins. Weigh the two three-coin groups against each other. As before, the scale will tell you if one group is heavier (in which case it contains the heavy coin). If the two groups balance each other, the group of two coins must contain the heavy coin.
3. Using the same reasoning as in the previous two steps, the heavy coin can be identified from the group of two or three coins with only one additional weighing.

Hill climbing often leads to correct problem solution. It will be ineffective, however, in situations in which the problem solution requires one or more temporary steps *backward*. To illustrate, consider this problem:

A zookeeper must transport three lions and three giraffes across a river. She has a barge that can hold only herself and two other animals, so she will have to make several trips and leave some of her animals unattended some of the time. However, whenever she leaves a group of animals, the giraffes must outnumber the lions; otherwise, the lions will gang up on one of the giraffes and kill it. How can the zookeeper transport all six animals safely across the river?

Try to solve the zookeeper's problem before you read further.

The zookeeper can transport her animals across the river in this manner:

1. She takes two lions to the other side, leaving three giraffes and one lion behind (since the giraffes outnumber the lion, they will be safe).
2. She comes back alone.

3. She takes one giraffe to the other side, leaving two giraffes and one lion behind.
4. She *brings back* the two lions, leaving one giraffe alone on the other side.
5. She takes the two giraffes to the other side, leaving the three lions behind.
6. She comes back alone, leaving the three giraffes behind.
7. She takes two lions to the other side, leaving one lion behind.
8. She comes back alone, leaving three giraffes and two lions behind.
9. She takes the last lion across the river.

Problem solution, then, requires a step backward: the zookeeper must bring two of the lions back to the first side of the river (Step 4). A person using a hill-climbing strategy would not consider such a step and would be unable to solve the problem.

Means-ends Analysis

Means-ends analysis (Anderson, 1990, 1993; Newell & Simon, 1972; Restle & Davis, 1962; Resnick & Glaser, 1976) is a process whereby an individual breaks a problem down into two or more subgoals and then works successively on each of those subgoals. To illustrate, consider this situation:

I have just had a brick barbecue built in my backyard. I have had it built with metric dimensions: The grill is 1 meter wide and 1.5 meters long. Rich and Marcy Jones look over from their yard next door and say, "Oooo, nice barbecue, almost as big as ours."

"Mine is bigger," I reply.

"Can't be," they say. "Our grill is 3.5 feet by 5 feet."

The question: Have I kept up with the Jones family by buying a bigger barbecue grill? I can solve this problem by breaking it into four subgoals and solving each one in turn:

1. Convert the dimensions of the Jones' grill into metric units. One foot equals approximately 0.30 meters; multiplying the "feet" dimensions by 0.30 yields dimensions of 1.05 by 1.5 meters.
2. Compute the area of the Jones' grill. Multiplying 1.05 by 1.5 equals 1.575 square meters.
3. Compute the area of my grill. Multiplying 1 by 1.5 equals 1.5 square meters.
4. Compare the areas of the two grills. Rich and Marcy's grill is still larger than mine. I have not kept up with the Joneses.

Means-ends analysis appears to be a relatively common method of solving problems (Greeno, 1973; Newell & Simon, 1972) and is most likely to be used when the goal is clearly specified (Sweller & Levine, 1982). However, a potential disadvantage of this approach is that, by attending to only one subgoal at a time, one may lose sight of the problem as a whole (Sweller & Levine, 1982).

Working Backward

Consider this game, similar to one described by Wickelgren (1974):

> *There are 21 pennies on a table. Two players, Mary and Susan, take turns removing pennies from the table; in any given turn, a player must take one, two, or three pennies. The player who removes the last penny from the table wins the game and keeps all 21 pennies. Mary begins by taking two pennies. What strategy can Susan use to be sure that she wins the game?*

See if you can solve the problem before reading further.

The problem is solved by beginning at the *end* of the game, at the point where Susan removes the last penny, and then going backward to the first move. In what situation will Mary be in the position of allowing Susan to win? Remember, each player can remove one, two, or three pennies on a turn. Let's look at the solution as a series of steps:

1. Mary must be forced into a situation in which she has to leave one, two, or three pennies on the table. Susan can then take them all, and victory is hers.
2. If, on the preceding turn, Susan leaves four pennies, then Mary's options are such that she must leave one to three pennies on her turn.
3. For Susan to leave four pennies, Mary must, on the previous turn, leave five, six, or seven pennies.
4. For Mary to leave five to seven pennies, Susan must leave eight pennies for Mary to choose from.

Continuing the steps in this manner, we see a pattern: Susan must always leave a number divisible by four. Therefore, when Mary removes 2 pennies, leaving 19 on the table, Susan should take 3 pennies.

The method I used to help Susan figure out how to win the game every time illustrates the process of **working backward** (e.g., Matlin, 1983; Newell, Shaw, & Simon, 1958; Wickelgren, 1974). This strategy is to begin at the problem goal and then work backward, one step at a time, toward the initial problem state. In each step backward, the individual identifies one or more conditions that would produce the present condition. In a sense, working backward is the opposite approach to that of means-ends analysis.

Working backward is frequently used in solving algebra and geometry proofs. Students are given an initial situation—a formula or a geometric configuration with certain characteristics—then are asked to prove how another formula or another characteristic (the goal) must also be true through a series of mathematically logical steps. Sometimes it is easier to move logically from the goal backward to the initial state; mathematically speaking, this approach is just as valid.

Drawing Analogies

See if you can solve this problem originally used by Duncker (1945) and adapted by Gick and Holyoak (1980):

Suppose you are a doctor faced with a patient who has a malignant tumor in his stomach. It is impossible to operate on the patient, but unless the tumor is destroyed the patient will die. There is a kind of ray that can be used to destroy the tumor. If the rays reach the tumor all at once at a sufficiently high intensity, the tumor will be destroyed. Unfortunately, at this intensity the healthy tissue that the rays pass through on the way to the tumor will also be destroyed. At lower intensities the rays are harmless to healthy tissue, but they will not affect the tumor either. What type of procedure might be used to destroy the tumor with the rays, and at the same time avoid destroying the healthy tissue? (pp. 307–308)

If you are having difficulty with the problem, then consider this situation:

A general wishes to capture a fortress located in the center of a country. There are many roads radiating outward from the fortress. All have been mined so that, while small groups of men can pass over the roads safely, any large force will detonate the mines. A full-scale direct attack is therefore impossible. The general's solution is to divide his army into small groups, send each group to the head of a different road, and have the groups converge simultaneously on the fortress. (Gick & Holyoak, 1980, p. 309)

Now go back to the tumor problem. Perhaps the general's strategy in capturing the fortress has given you an idea about how to destroy the tumor. It can be destroyed by shooting a number of low-intensity rays from different directions, such that they all converge on the tumor simultaneously. Gick and Holyoak found that subjects were much more likely to solve the tumor problem when they had first read the solution to the fortress problem, because the two problems can be solved in analogous ways.

Drawing an analogy between a problem situation and another situation sometimes provides insights into how a problem can be solved (Clement, 1987; Holyoak, 1985; Mayer, 1992; Schultz & Lochhead, 1991). For example, a student might solve a mathematics problem by finding a similar problem that has already been solved correctly using a particular procedure (Mayer, 1985, 1992). As another example, consider a problem that the Greek scientist Archimedes confronted sometime around 250 B.C.:

King Hiero had ordered a crown of pure gold from the local goldsmith. He suspected that the goldsmith had cheated him by replacing some of the gold with silver, a cheaper metal. The only way to determine the goldsmith's honesty was to compare the crown's weight against its volume. Any metal has a particular volume for any given weight, and that ratio is different for each metal. The crown could be weighed easily enough. But how could its volume be measured?

Archimedes was pondering the problem one day as he stepped into his bathtub. He watched the bath water rise and, through analogy, immediately identified a solution to the king's problem: The crown's volume could be determined by placing it in a container of water and measuring the amount of water that was displaced.

The major drawback to using analogies as a problem solving strategy is that individuals seldom retrieve analogous situations when they face a particular problem situation. The fact is, people rarely use analogies in solving problems (Gick & Holyoak, 1980; Reed, Ernst, & Banerji, 1974). When they do, it is often because they serendipitously encounter both the problem and the analogous situation at the same time. In other words, it may often be a matter of luck—of just happening to think of the right thing at the right time.

Shortcut Heuristics: Representativeness and Availability

Some problem solving strategies can be executed quickly and simply. Two commonly described examples are representativeness and availability (Kahneman & Tversky, 1972, 1973; Klein, 1987; Mayer, 1992; Tversky & Kahneman, 1973, 1974). But as you will discover, such shortcuts may lead to inaccurate problem solutions.

Representativeness involves jumping to conclusions about a solution based on obvious characteristics of the problem. Let me illustrate by adapting a problem used by Kahneman and Tversky (1973). Imagine that I have a stack of 100 personality profiles of 30 engineers and 70 lawyers, all of whom are successful in their careers. I pull this description randomly from the pile:

> *Jack is a 45-year-old man. He is married and has four children. He is generally conservative, careful, and ambitious. He shows no interest in political and social issues and spends most of his free time on his many hobbies, which include home carpentry, sailing, and mathematical puzzles (Kahneman & Tversky, 1973, p. 241).*

Now for the problem: What is the probability that this man is one of the 30 engineers?

The probability that the man is an engineer is 30%, because the stack of 100 individuals contained 30 engineers. Yet many subjects in Kahneman and Tversky's study gave a higher figure; they jumped to a conclusion based on obvious characteristics about Jack that many people associate stereotypically with engineers (e.g., conservatism and enjoyment of mathematical puzzles).

A second shortcut heuristic, **availability**, is a strategy wherein a problem is solved based only on information that comes immediately to mind (i.e., is retrieved from long-term memory) when the problem is encountered. Typically, the problem will be solved using recently acquired information rather than information acquired in the distant past, because recent experiences are more likely to be retrieved than those from long ago. For example, imagine that you are trying to decide whether to go to California or Florida for a sunny March vacation at the beach. You learned many years ago that Florida has more rainfall than California. In February, just as you are about to make your choice, you hear on the news that California has just been drenched in a heavy rainstorm. You may easily book a flight to Florida, retrieving the available information about the California rainstorm rather than the overall frequency of rainfall in the two states.

At this point, we have surveyed a variety of different problem solving strategies. Because many problems have no right or wrong solutions, no single "best" strategy may exist for solving them. Obviously, different strategies are appropriate in different situations. But sometimes people use strategies at the wrong times, often because they have learned such strategies at a rote, meaningless level. Let's look at what happens when individuals use problem solving strategies either meaninglessly or meaningfully.

Meaningless Versus Meaningful Problem Solving

See if you can solve this problem before you read further:

The number of quarters a man has is seven times the number of dimes he has. The value of the dimes exceeds the value of the quarters by two dollars and fifty cents. How many has he of each coin? (Paige & Simon, 1966, p. 79).

If you found an answer to the problem—any answer at all—then you overlooked an important point: Quarters are worth more than dimes. If there are more quarters than dimes, the value of the dimes cannot possibly be greater than the value of the quarters. The fact is, the problem makes no sense, and so it cannot be solved.

When people learn algorithms at a rote level, without understanding their underlying logic, they may sometimes apply those algorithms "unthinkingly" and inappropriately (Perkins & Simmons, 1988; Prawat, 1989; Resnick, 1989; Resnick & Glaser, 1976; Schoenfeld, 1982, 1985a; Silver, Shapiro, & Deutsch, 1991). As a result, they may obtain illogical or physically impossible results. Consider these instances of meaningless mathematical problem solving as examples:

- A student is asked to figure out how many chickens and how many pigs a farmer has if the farmer has 21 animals with 60 legs in all. The student adds 21 and 60, reasoning that, since the problem says "how many in all," addition is the logical operation (Lester, 1985).
- A student uses subtraction whenever a word problem contains the word *left*—even when a problem actually requiring addition includes the phrase "John left the room to get more apples" (Schoenfeld, 1982).
- Middle school students are asked to calculate how many 40-person buses are needed to transport 540 people to a baseball game. The majority give

an answer that includes a fraction, without acknowledging that in the case of buses, only whole numbers are possible (Silver et al., 1991).

All too often, when schools teach problem solving, they focus on teaching algorithms for well-defined problems while omitting explanations of why the algorithms work (Cooney, 1991; Perkins & Salomon, 1989; Perkins & Simmons, 1988; Porter, 1989; Resnick, 1986, 1989). For example, perhaps you can remember learning how to solve a long division problem, but you probably don't remember learning *why* you multiply the divisor by each digit in your answer and write the product in a particular location below the dividend. Or perhaps you were taught a "key word" method for solving word problems: Words such as "altogether" indicate addition, and words such as "left" mean subtraction. This approach is a meaningless one indeed and, as we noted for both the "Ana" and "John" problems presented earlier, often leads to an erroneous solution.

How can teachers help students engage in more meaningful problem solving? And, in general, how can they help students become more expert at problem solving and other forms of transfer? We turn now to the topic of facilitating transfer and problem solving in educational settings.

FACILITATING TRANSFER AND PROBLEM SOLVING IN THE CLASSROOM

Unfortunately, students often do not see the relevance of what they have learned in school to new school tasks or to out-of-school problems (Gick & Holyoak, 1987; Perkins & Simmons, 1988; Schoenfeld, 1985a; Tobin, Treagust, & Fraser, 1988). Thus, a major objective of our educational system—positive transfer—is probably not being achieved. At the same time, students sometimes erroneously apply what they have learned to situations in which it is not appropriate—a case of negative transfer.

Learning theorists are only beginning to understand the complex processes of transfer and problem solving. Nevertheless, theories and research in both areas provide numerous suggestions for educational practice.

•*Students need to learn information meaningfully and thoroughly.* Theorists agree that a solid knowledge base is a prerequisite for successful transfer and problem solving (Ausubel et al., 1978; Frederiksen, 1984a; Greeno, 1973; Mayer, 1975; Norman, 1980; Reif & Heller, 1982; Simon, 1980; Simon & Hayes, 1976). In the process of acquiring this knowledge base, students should develop a multitude of interconnections and relationships among the concepts and ideas they learn; they should also discover the potential relevance of such concepts and ideas for the various situations they may encounter later on (Brophy & Alleman, 1991; Brown & Campione, in press; Perkins & Salomon, 1987; Prawat, 1989; Sternberg & Frensch, 1993).

Unfortunately, many school curricula include long lists of topics that must be taught, the result being that no single topic is taught very thoroughly (e.g., see

Porter, 1989). Breadth of coverage occurs at the expense of depth of coverage—and at the expense of successful transfer and problem solving as well.

•*Students should also learn problem solving strategies at a meaningful level.* All too often, students learn problem solving algorithms as procedures separate from anything they have previously learned about the world. For example, they may learn mathematics—its symbols, principles, and algorithms—in total isolation from the concrete physical world they deal with on a daily basis (Carpenter, 1985; Hiebert & Wearne, 1993; Resnick, 1989). When students learn an algorithm at a rote, meaningless level, they are likely to use it mechanically, thoughtlessly, and often incorrectly, and they are *un*likely to recognize many of the situations in which it might legitimately be applied (Greeno, 1991; Hiebert & Wearne, 1993; Perkins & Simmons, 1988; Kilpatrick, 1985).

Rather than simply learning algorithms at a rote level, students should understand *why* they do the things they do to solve problems; in other words, they should connect abstract, symbol-based procedures to things they already know and to concrete reality (Carpenter, 1985; Greeno, 1991; Heller & Hungate, 1985; Prawat, 1989; Resnick, 1983, 1989). As one simple example, a teacher might demonstrate the rationale behind "borrowing" in subtraction by using toothpicks, some of which have been bundled into groups of 10 or 100, then untying and borrowing from the bundles when necessary. By demonstrating the logic behind problem solving procedures, a teacher increases the likelihood that students will apply those procedures at appropriate times and obtain plausible results.

•*Students must have a mental set for transfer.* Earlier we noted that mental sets in problem solving—predispositions to solve problems in particular ways—sometimes interfere with successful problem solving. On the other hand, a general mental set to transfer school learning—a predisposition to use and apply the things learned in the classroom—is clearly beneficial (Stein, 1989; Sternberg & Frensch, 1993). To promote such a mental set, teachers can point out how academic content can be applied to a variety of situations both in and out of school (Brophy, 1992; Fennema, Carpenter, & Peterson, 1989; Perkins & Salomon, 1989; Prawat, 1989; Resnick, 1989; Sternberg & Frensch, 1993; Voss, 1987). And they can encourage their students to be constantly thinking "How might I use this information?" as they listen, read, and study (Perkins & Salomon, 1987; Stein, 1989; Sternberg & Frensch, 1993).

•*Some prerequisite skills should be practiced until they are learned to the point of automaticity* (Anderson, 1987; Frederiksen, 1984a; Gagné, 1982; Heller & Hungate, 1985; Mayer, 1985; Perkins & Salomon, 1987; Resnick, 1989). Remember that problem solving occurs in working memory—a component of the memory system that has a limited capacity for holding and processing information at any single moment. To the extent that students can process the simple and familiar aspects of a problem automatically, thereby using only a minimal amount of working memory capacity, they can devote more working memory "space" to the problem's difficult and novel aspects.

•*Numerous and varied examples and opportunities for practicing transfer and problem solving should be provided* (Chase & Chi, 1980; Cormier, 1987;

Frederiksen, 1984a; Gagné & Driscoll, 1988; Kilpatrick, 1985; Perkins & Salomon, 1987). Experience with many practice examples promotes associations in long-term memory between newly learned information and a variety of relevant situations; hence, the new information is more likely to be retrieved when it is needed later on. For example, in an experiment by Pepper (1981), students studied computer programming techniques from one of three instructional booklets. Two booklets were taken from actual programming textbooks. The third was a modified text in which simple examples were inserted to illustrate all major points and most minor ones; it was therefore longer and wordier than either of the other booklets. Despite its length, the example-filled booklet was liked most by students and led to the highest performance on an examination (83% for the example-filled booklet versus 58%–67% for the other two booklets).

•*Students should have experience identifying problems for themselves.* Teachers usually provide the problems they want their students to solve. But beyond the classroom—for example, at home and in the world of employment—people must often identify and define for themselves the problems that stand in their way. Some theorists suggest that students may benefit from getting a head start on such problem-finding (Brown & Walter, 1990; Perkins & Simmons, 1988; Porter, 1989). For example, in a mathematics lesson, students might be given data describing the quantities and prices of items in a grocery store and asked to generate a number of questions that could be answered by that data. Or, in a history lesson, they might be given a scenario of an American Civil War battle in progress, instructed to identify the problems facing either the North or the South, and asked to propose possible solutions to those problems.

•*To minimize negative transfer, differences between two ideas should be emphasized.* Insects and spiders are similar stimuli—they are both small arthropods with exoskeletons and a generally creepy-crawly nature—and so students may inappropriately transfer what they know about one group of creepy-crawlies to the other. For similar stimuli, negative transfer can be reduced if differences rather than similarities are emphasized (e.g., Sternberg & Frensch, 1993). For instance, insects and spiders are different in a number of ways (e.g., six legs vs. eight legs, three body parts vs. two, antennae vs. no antennae); if emphasized, those differences could reduce negative transfer from one group to the other. Additionally, if negative transfer between two ideas is anticipated, it can be reduced by teaching each in a different environment (Bilodeau & Schlosberg, 1951; Greenspoon & Ranyard, 1957)—for example, by teaching students about insects while sitting in the classroom and teaching them about spiders while on a field trip to the natural history museum.

•*Problem solving skills are sometimes better learned through a discovery approach.* Although expository teaching is in many cases the most efficient means of transmitting information to students in an organized fashion, instructional approaches that emphasize guided discovery learning may facilitate better transfer of problem solving skills to new situations (Gagné & Brown, 1961; Mayer, 1974, 1987; Roughead & Scandura, 1968; Shymansky, Hedges, & Woodworth, 1990). Discovery is probably most appropriate when problems are ill-structured and students have a solid knowledge base (Doyle, 1983; Frederiksen, 1984a). However, for well-structured problems that can be solved by a specific algorithm (e.g., long division problems), and for students relatively unsophisticated about a particular topic, direct instruction of the algorithm may be preferable (Frederiksen, 1984a; R. Gagné, 1985).

•*Teaching general learning and problem solving skills may be helpful.* As I indicated in Chapter 15, training in study skills can be effective and appears to improve classroom learning and achievement. At the same time, remember that not everything will apply to everything else: Latin will help a student learn physics only to the extent that, while studying Latin, the student develops better learning strategies that are also applicable to the study of physics.

Many theorists believe that teaching general problem solving strategies can enhance students' ability to solve problems successfully (e.g., E. Gagné, 1985; Glaser, 1979; Mayer, 1987; Resnick, 1976; Schoenfeld, 1979; Simon, 1980). A study by Herrnstein and his colleagues (Herrnstein, Nickerson, de Sánchez, & Swets, 1986) provides some optimism about the effectiveness of training problem solving skills: Seventh-grade Venezuelan students who took a year-long course in reasoning, problem solving, and decision-making skills showed greater improvement in both the specific skills taught and general intellectual ability than did students in an untrained control group. However, we should note here that, just as study strategies may be better learned when taught within the context of specific academic content areas (see Chapter 15), so, too, may general problem solving strategies be more effectively learned when connected to content domains to which they are applicable (Mayer, 1992; Resnick, 1987; Schoenfeld & Herrmann, 1982).

Several problem solving strategies may work in a wide variety of problem situations. One helpful strategy is talking aloud about the problem; this may facilitate students' ability to guide and monitor their own progress (in a metacognitive sense) toward a problem solution (Gagné & Smith, 1962; Heller & Hungate, 1985; Stinessen, 1975; Vygotsky, 1962). A second is using paper and pencil to diagram a problem or list its components; this may help students encode a problem more concretely and see the interrelationships among various elements more clearly (Lindvall, Tamburino, & Robinson, 1982; Mayer, 1985, 1986, 1989a 1989b, 1992; Prawat, 1989; Schultz & Lochhead, 1991; Wickelgren, 1974). Still a third is brainstorming—thinking of as many hypothetical problem solutions as possible without initially evaluating any of them (e.g., Osborn, 1963). The absence of evaluation when brainstorming ideas can potentially facilitate a broader search of long-term memory for unusual and creative possibilities. After generating a long and seemingly exhaustive list of problem solutions, an individual can critically examine the various solutions for workable and unworkable ones.

Some theorists (e.g., Anderson, 1990; Ellis & Hunt, 1983; Wallas, 1926) have suggested that the incubation of a problem—letting it remain unsolved in memory for a period—can be a helpful strategy, although there are mixed reviews on its effectiveness (Anderson, 1990; Bourne et al., 1986; Dominowski & Jenrick, 1972). The benefits of an incubation period are more likely to be evident for difficult problems than for easy ones. For one thing, some of the factors that interfere with problem solving, such as fatigue and anxiety, may diminish during the incubation period (Ellis & Hunt, 1983). In addition, the individual may find more appropriate mental sets or more relevant information in long-term memory after leaving the problem alone for a while (Anderson, 1990; Ellis & Hunt, 1983).

• *Students should learn strategies for defining ill-defined problems.* As Frederiksen (1984a) has pointed out, most problems presented in the classroom are well-defined. Students are asked to identify the protagonist and antagonist in a story, use a dictionary to find two different pronunciations of the word *wind*, or calculate how many candy bars six boys can each have if there are 18 bars altogether. On the other hand, most real-world problems are ill-defined. People need to find viable means of home financing, decide what life insurance policy to purchase (if any), and maintain friendly and productive relationships with obnoxious work associates.

Ill-defined problems often require an individual to search outside sources to find relevant and potentially helpful information (Simon, 1978). Students should therefore be well versed in techniques for finding information through such resources as libraries, computer databases, and government agencies. Students should also learn techniques for more precisely defining ill-defined problems; for example, one helpful technique is to break a larger problem into a number of subproblems and to define and impose constraints on each of those subproblems (Reitman, 1965; Simon, 1973). Finally, to the extent that students possess a solid knowledge base, they will be better able to define the problems they encounter (Bédard & Chi, 1992; Frederiksen, 1984a).

• *Students' early attempts to solve difficult problems should be scaffolded.* While considering Vygotsky's ideas in Chapter 8, we encountered the concept of *scaffolding*—providing a structure that supports students in their efforts on difficult tasks. Then, in Chapter 15, we noted the importance of scaffolding students' early attempts to use sophisticated metacognitive strategies. Some theorists suggest that scaffolding may facilitate problem solving performance as well (e.g., Heller & Hungate, 1985; Wood, Bruner, & Ross, 1976). Teachers can help students in their initial attempts at challenging problems in a number of ways; for example, teachers can simplify early problems, model problem solutions, show students that they are in fact making progress in their problem solving attempts, point out errors along the way, and in general keep students' frustration at a reasonable level. As students become more adept at solving problems on their own, such scaffolding can be gradually phased out.

• *The development of effective problem solving strategies can often be facilitated through cooperative group problem solving.* The notion of **cooperative learning**—of students working together in small groups to help one another learn—is gaining popularity among today's educators (e.g., see Johnson & Johnson, 1987; Slavin, 1983a, 1990). Several theorists have suggested that a cooperative learning environment may be ideal for promoting successful problem solving (Kilpatrick, 1985; Mayer, 1985; Noddings, 1985; Palincsar & Brown, 1989; Schoenfeld, 1985b). By discussing concepts and principles relevant to the problem solution, students may identify more interrelationships among the things they know and clarify the things about which they are confused (Kilpatrick, 1985; Noddings, 1985). By thinking aloud about how to solve a problem, they may gain a better understanding of what they are mentally doing (Schoenfeld, 1985b; Whimbey & Lochhead, 1986). And, by observing the more effective strategies that their classmates sometimes use, they may begin to adopt those strategies themselves, leaving their inefficient strategies behind (Mayer, 1985; Noddings, 1985; Schoenfeld, 1985b). As an illustration of my last point, consider this incident in a cooperative problem solving setting:

> . . . a youngster suggested that the group should "add, subtract, and multiply these two numbers" and then see which answer "looked" best. Other members of the group were shocked and said, "Donna! We can't do that. We have to figure it out." Donna tried that strategy only once more and then it disappeared from her public repertoire. (Noddings, 1985, pp. 350–351)

•*Classroom evaluation practices should include measures of transfer and problem solving.* As we noted in Chapter 13, classroom tests too often emphasize the learning of specific facts. Certainly basic knowledge and skills are important; among other things, they form the foundation for more sophisticated academic behaviors. However, when teachers' instructional objectives also include transfer and problem solving, they should ask students to demonstrate the ability to apply classroom subject matter to a variety of situations (Foos & Fisher, 1988; Massialas & Zevin, 1983; Sternberg & Frensch, 1993). This practice can help successful transfer and problem solving become common phenomena rather than rare occurrences.

Teaching for effective transfer and problem solving takes time. Too often, schools seem to rush through a curriculum at the expense of providing sufficient practice at any single point along the way. Educators should probably slow down and give children time to use and apply the information and skills they learn. Students are likely to accomplish more over the long run.

SUMMARY

Transfer is the process of applying information and skills learned in one situation to one's learning or performance in another situation. Several theories of transfer have been proposed; current views incorporate basic notions of information processing theory. The consensus among contemporary theorists is that transfer from one situation to another occurs only to the extent that the two situations are similar in some way. Among the factors that facilitate transfer are meaningful learning, thoroughness of learning, number and variety of examples and opportunities for practice, and retrieval of relevant information in the transfer situation.

Problem solving is a form of transfer, in that previously learned information is applied to resolve a problem situation. Both behaviorist and cognitive theories of problem solving have been proposed, with information processing theory predominating today; such cognitive factors as working memory capacity, encoding, retrieval, one's knowledge base, and metacognition influence problem solving success. Many problems can be solved through specific algorithms, procedures that guarantee correct solutions. Others may be solved through more general heuristics, shortcuts without guaranteed outcomes; examples of such heuristics include means-ends analysis, working backward, hill climbing, and drawing analogies. People often apply problem solving procedures more effectively and appropriately when they understand the logic behind those procedures.

Theory and research yield numerous suggestions for promoting transfer and problem solving in classroom settings. For example, a school's prescribed curriculum should make it possible for teachers to teach a few things thoroughly and meaningfully rather many things superficially and at a rote level (i.e., "less is more"). Students should have a mental set for transfer; that is, they should approach school subject matter with the idea that they may be able to use it on future occasions. And such techniques as discovery learning, scaffolding, and cooperative learning may facilitate the development of effective problem solving skills.

MOTIVATION

CHAPTER 17

Motivation and Affect

O ver the years, I have learned how to do a great many things. For example, I have learned how to teach and write about psychology. I have learned how to find my favorite junk food in the supermarket and my favorite television game show in *TV Guide*. I have learned how to control my tongue and temper in a university committee meeting. I have learned how to mow the lawn, file a tax return, cook lima beans, clean the garage, and pick up after slovenly children.

Yet you don't see me doing all these things on a regular basis. I engage in some activities (e.g., writing about psychology, eating junk food, and watching television game shows) because I like doing them. I engage in others (e.g., behaving myself at committee meetings, filing tax returns, and mowing the lawn) not because I enjoy them, but because they bring me things I *do* enjoy, such as productive relationships with my university colleagues, IRS refunds, or a well-kept backyard. But there are some things that I never do because they aren't fun and they reap me few if any rewards. For example, you won't find me cooking lima beans (yuck), cleaning the garage (who cares if it's clean?), or picking up children's messy bedrooms (a never-ending battle).

Once we have learned how to do something, the extent to which we continue to do it is a function of **motivation**—an internal state that arouses us to action, pushes us in particular directions, and keeps us engaged in certain activities. Learning and motivation are equally essential for performance: The former enables us to acquire new knowledge and skills, and the latter provides the impetus for demonstrating the things we have learned.

People are almost always motivated in one way or another. For example, Lee and Anderson (1991) found students in a sixth grade classroom to have a variety of motives. Some students clearly wanted to learn the subject matter being presented in class. Others were more interested in getting good grades, outperforming their classmates, pleasing their teacher and parents, or simply completing assignments as quickly and painlessly as possible.

We have touched on human motivation in previous chapters—for example, within the context of reinforcement in Chapter 4 and in our discussion of modeling in Chapter 7. In this chapter, we begin to look at the topic in greater depth. We will identify the specific ways in which motivation influences behavior, cognition, and learning. We will make a distinction between extrinsic and intrinsic motivation, finding that each influences learning and performance differently. We will examine several theoretical perspectives of motivation, including drive and incentive theories, Maslow's hierarchy of needs, individual differences in motives, and the contemporary cognitive viewpoint. We will consider the role of *affect* (emotional state) in learning and behavior, with particular attention to anxiety. Finally, we will identify several things teachers can do to motivate their students in appropriate and productive directions. In the following chapter, we will return to the cognitive perspective once again as we see how motivation and cognition are very much intertwined.

GENERAL EFFECTS OF MOTIVATION

In general, more motivated people achieve at higher levels (e.g., Walberg & Uguroglu, 1980). Motivation appears to affect learning and performance in at least four ways.

• *It increases an individual's energy and activity level* (Maehr, 1984; Pintrich, Marx, & Boyle, 1993; Vernon, 1969). It influences the extent to which an individual is likely to engage in a certain activity intensively and vigorously, or half-heartedly and lackadaisically.

• *It directs an individual toward certain goals* (Dweck & Elliott, 1983; Eccles & Wigfield, 1985; Maehr, 1984; Pintrich et al., 1993). Motivation affects the choices people make and the consequences they find reinforcing.

We should note here that, when people exert effort toward some goals, they often must direct it away from others. For example, as I write this, my son Alex (now in junior high school) would like to enroll in both "Industrial Arts" and "Yearbook" classes next semester, but his schedule allows him to enroll in only one of them. In a similar way, a student may sometimes have to choose between pleasing a parent who values academic success versus pleasing a friend who thinks schoolwork is for nerds (Dodge, Asher, & Parkhurst, 1989).

•*It promotes initiation of certain activities and persistence in those activities* (Eccles & Wigfield, 1985; Maehr, 1984; Pintrich et al., 1993; Stipek, 1988). Motivation increases the likelihood that people will begin something on their own initiative, persist in the face of difficulty, and resume a task after a temporary interruption.

Educators have long recognized that *time on task* is an important factor affecting school learning and achievement (e.g., Davis & Thomas, 1989). The more time students spend engaged in a particular learning activity, the more academically successful they will be. Although time on task is partly determined by how teachers plan and schedule the classroom curriculum—that is, by how much time they devote to different topics—it also depends to some extent on students' motivation to study and persist with those topics, both in and out of school.

•*It affects the learning strategies and cognitive processes an individual employs* (e.g., Dweck & Elliott, 1983; Eccles & Wigfield, 1985). Motivation increases the likelihood that people will pay attention to something, study and practice it, and try to learn it in a meaningful fashion. It also increases the likelihood that they will seek help when they encounter difficulty.

Here we should note that time on task is, in and of itself, insufficient for successful learning. Certain cognitive processes—paying attention, learning meaningfully, elaborating, monitoring comprehension, identifying inconsistencies between new information and prior knowledge, and so on—must occur as people engage in a particular learning activity. In other words, learners must be *thinking about* what they are seeing, hearing, and doing (Carroll, 1989; Lee, 1991; Lee & Anderson, 1993; Pintrich et al., 1993; Tobin, 1986; Wittrock, 1986). Such **cognitive engagement** is one of the benefits of a high level of motivation.

Yet not all forms of motivation have exactly the same effect on human learning and performance. In fact, extrinsic motivation and intrinsic motivation yield somewhat different results, as we shall see now.

EXTRINSIC VERSUS INTRINSIC MOTIVATION

At the beginning of the chapter, I mentioned that I engage in some activities because they bring about desirable consequences (i.e., they are extrinsically reinforced), while I engage in others simply because they are intrinsically enjoyable. Just as operant conditioning theorists distinguish between extrinsic and intrinsic reinforcement, motivation theorists distinguish between extrinsic and intrinsic motivation.

Extrinsic motivation exists when the source of motivation lies outside the individual and the task being performed. For example, I file an income tax return every year partly because I always get a refund when I do so and partly because I will be fined if I *don't* file. I go to university committee meetings because university service is part of my job description and I am quite dependent on my monthly paycheck. I give my house a thorough cleaning when planning a party, because I'd hate for my friends to discover I'm a slob. In contrast, **intrinsic motivation** exists when the source of motivation lies within the individual and task: The individual finds the task enjoyable or worthwhile in and of itself. For example, I frequently read books and articles about human learning because they continue to shed new light on a topic that is, to me, utterly fascinating. I watch television game shows because I enjoy playing along as a home viewer. I eat junk food because it tastes good.

Extrinsic motivation can certainly promote successful learning and productive behavior, as evidenced by the effectiveness of behavior modification programs (see Chapter 5). Extrinsic reinforcement for engaging in a particular activity increases an individual's time on task, and performance is likely to improve as a result (Emmer & Evertson, 1981). However, extrinsic motivation in the classroom has its drawbacks: extrinsically motivated students are likely to exert only the minimal behavioral and cognitive effort they need to execute a task successfully (occasionally this may mean copying someone else's work), and they may stop an activity as soon as reinforcement disappears (e.g., Lee, 1991).

Intrinsic motivation has numerous advantages over extrinsic motivation. For any particular task, intrinsically motivated learners are more likely to:

- Pursue the task on their own initiative, without having to be prodded or cajoled
- Be cognitively engaged in the task (e.g., by keeping attention focused on it)
- Learn information in a meaningful rather than rote fashion
- Undertake more challenging aspects of the task
- Show creativity in their performance
- Persist in the face of failure
- Seek out additional opportunities to pursue the task
- Experience pleasure in what they are doing
  (Brophy, 1986; Hennessey & Amabile, 1987; Lee, 1991; Lee & Anderson, 1991; Maehr, 1984; Spaulding, 1992; Stipek, 1988).

Obviously, intrinsic motivation is the optimal state of affairs in the classroom. At the end of the chapter, we will identify several ways in which teachers can help their students become intrinsically motivated to learn classroom material. And in Chapter 18, we will discover the cognitive factors likely to influence students' intrinsic motivation to achieve academic success.

THEORETICAL PERSPECTIVES OF MOTIVATION

Over the years, varying perspectives of motivation have been proposed. In the next few pages, we will consider drives and incentives, Maslow's hierarchy of needs, individual differences, and the contemporary cognitive viewpoint.

Drives and Incentives

Drive theory (e.g., Freud, 1949; Hull, 1943, 1951, 1952; Woodworth, 1918) is based on the notion that organisms try to maintain physiological homeostasis; in other words, they try to keep their bodies at an optimal state of functioning. A **drive** is an internal state of need within an organism: Something necessary for optimal functioning (e.g., food, water, warmth, or rest) is missing. When a drive exists, the organism behaves in ways that reduce the need and bring the body back into balance. For example, a hungry person eats, a thirsty person drinks, a cold person seeks out a source of heat, and a tired person goes to bed. If a response that reduces the need is not immediately possible, the organism shows a general increase in activity—activity that may eventually lead to an encounter with a need-reducing stimulus.

From the perspective of drive theory, a reinforcer is effective to the extent that it reduces a need state, thus simultaneously reducing drive. For example, a drink of water is only reinforcing if an organism is thirsty, and a source of heat is only reinforcing if an organism is cold. Behaviors that reduce a need state— behaviors that are reinforced—are likely to be repeated when the same need emerges at some later point in time.

Probably the most widely cited version of drive theory is that of Clark Hull (1943, 1951, 1952), a perspective we encountered briefly in Chapter 2. In 1943, Hull proposed that drive was due to physiological needs such as hunger and thirst. All these needs contributed to the general drive state of the organism; drive was not specific to a particular need. Hull further proposed that the strength and intensity of a behavior is a function of both *habit strength* (i.e., the degree to which associations between a particular stimulus and response have been learned) and drive, like this:

$$\text{Strength of behavior} = \text{Habit} \times \text{Drive}$$

In such a multiplicative relationship, both habit (prior learning) and drive must be present; if either is zero, the strength of the behavior—the likelihood that it will occur—is also zero.

Hull based his notion of *habit times drive* on experiments conducted by two of his students (Perin, 1942; Williams, 1938). In these experiments, rats were placed in Skinner boxes and trained to press a bar for a food reinforcer. Different groups of rats received varying amounts of training, with a greater number of reinforced responses presumably leading to greater habit strength. Later, after going without food for either 3 hours (low drive) or 22 hours (high drive), the rats were once again placed in Skinner boxes, and their frequency of bar pressing was recorded under nonreinforcement (extinction) conditions. The hungrier rats pressed the bar many more times than the less hungry rats; similarly, rats who had received more training pressed the bar more often than those who had undergone little training. Rats with little drive (three hours of food deprivation) and low habit strength (five training trials) pressed the bar, on the average, only once.

In 1951, Hull revised his thinking in two significant ways. First of all, he observed that some behaviors serve no apparent biological purpose. He therefore proposed that some drives are **acquired drives**: They develop when previously neutral stimuli are associating with drive-reducing stimuli such as food. (To repeat the example I presented in Chapter 2, an individual might become "driven" by a need for approval if approval has previously been associated with candy.) Reinforcement therefore became strictly a function of drive reduction rather than being due to the reduction of specific physiological needs.

At the same time, Hull also took into account research by Crespi (1942) and others indicating that reinforcers may affect performance rather than learning. (We encountered Crespi's experiment in our discussion of reinforcement in Chapter 4. To refresh your memory, rats running down a runway for food began to run faster when the amount of reinforcement was increased; they ran more slowly when the amount of reinforcement was decreased.) Accordingly, Hull introduced the concept of *incentive* into his theory, acknowledging that behaviors are influenced by the characteristics of a goal object—for example, by the amount of food at the end of a runway. Incentive became a third essential ingredient for a behavior to occur, as follows:

Strength of behavior = Habit × Drive × Incentive

The absence of any of the three factors—habit strength, drive, or incentive—meant that the behavior was not emitted.

Other theorists expanded on Hull's notion that the characteristics of goal objects (incentives) are motivating forces in behavior (Mowrer, 1960; Overmier & Lawry, 1979; Spence, 1956). From their perspective, **incentive motivation** serves as a mediator (M) between stimuli and responses, affecting which stimuli are responded to and which are not. Symbolically, we could describe the relationship this way:

$$S \rightarrow M_{\text{incentive}} \rightarrow R$$

For example, I find a bag of Cheetos quite enticing after several hours of food-free book writing (thus leading to a reach-in-and-grab-a-handful response); however, the same bag provokes no response whatsoever right after a Thanksgiving dinner, when I have stuffed myself with turkey, mashed potatoes, and pumpkin pie.

Incentives undoubtedly play a role in human motivation. Just as Crespi's rats ran faster when they knew that mass quantities of food lay waiting at the end of the runway, so, too, do we humans apparently work harder when incentives are more attractive (Klinger, 1975, 1977). When our progress toward particular goals is temporarily stymied, we often intensify our efforts (Klinger, 1975). And when our progress is permanently blocked, we are likely to respond with regression (i.e., immature behavior) or aggression (Barker, Dembo, & Lewin, 1941; Dollard, Doob, Miller, Mowrer, & Sears, 1939; Hinton, 1968; Johnson, 1972).

While incentives remain in vogue as a probable source of motivation, theorists have largely left drive reduction theory by the wayside (e.g., Bolles, 1967, 1975). For one thing, learning sometimes occurs in the absence of any apparent drive reduction (Sheffield, Wulff, & Backer, 1951; Sheffield & Roby, 1950; Sheffield, Roby, & Campbell, 1954). For example, male rats will make responses that allow them to mount receptive female rats, even though they are pulled away from the females before they can consummate their affectionate relationship and thus reduce their sexual drive (Sheffield et al., 1951). Furthermore, organisms sometimes behave in ways that actually *increase* their drive states (e.g., Olds & Milner, 1954). For example, when rats have electrodes implanted in particular areas of their brains (called "pleasure centers"), they eagerly press a bar to obtain electrical stimulation of those areas, and they continue in their bar pressing until they're completely exhausted (Olds & Milner, 1954). In much the same way, we humans voluntarily increase our drive states by going to scary movies, reading suspense novels, and riding roller coasters.

As a result of such findings, drive theory plays little part in contemporary views of motivation. However, physiological needs figure prominently in Maslow's theory of motivation, as we shall see now.

Maslow's Hierarchy of Needs

Another early perspective of motivation was that of Abraham Maslow (1959, 1973a, 1973b, 1987). Maslow's theory is a critical aspect of **humanism**, a movement in psychology that gained prominence in the 1960s and 1970s. Humanism has its roots in counseling psychology and focuses its attention on how individuals acquire emotions, attitudes, values, and interpersonal skills. Humanist perspectives tend to be grounded more in philosophy than in research, but they provide useful insights into human motivation nevertheless.

In an attempt to pull together his informal observations of human behavior, Maslow proposed that people have five different sets of needs:

1. **Physiological needs:** People are motivated to satisfy needs related to their immediate physical survival—needs for food, water, oxygen, warmth, exercise, rest, sex, and so on. For example, if you've been sitting still in class for a long time, you may find yourself getting restless and fid-

gety, and if you're hungry, you may think more about your growling stomach than about a professor's lecture. Maslow's physiological needs are essentially the same as those of drive theory.

2. **Safety needs:** People have a need to feel safe and secure in their environment. Although they may enjoy an occasional surprise, generally speaking, they prefer structure and order in their lives. For example, most students like to know what things are expected of them and prefer classroom routines that are somewhat predictable.

3. **Love and belongingness needs:** People seek affectionate relationships with others and like to feel that they "belong" and are accepted as part of a group. For example, a fourth grader may place great importance on having a best friend. And many adolescents take great pains to fit in with the cool crowd—for example, by wearing a certain hairstyle or buying clothes with a certain brand name placed conspicuously upon them.

4. **Esteem needs:** People need to feel good about themselves (**need for self-esteem**) and to believe that others also feel positively about them (**need for esteem from others**). To develop positive self-esteem, individuals will strive for achievement and mastery of their environment. To attain the esteem and respect of others, they will behave in ways that gain them recognition, appreciation, and prestige. For example, a second grader can partially satisfy the need for self-esteem by reading a book "all by myself" or by achieving a special merit badge in Cub Scouts or Campfire Girls. A high school student may try to satisfy the need for esteem from others by running for student council treasurer or becoming a star athlete. When their esteem needs are satisfied, people are self-confident and have a sense of self-worth; when these needs go unmet, people feel weak and inferior.

5. **Need for self-actualization:** People have a need to **self-actualize**—to develop and become all they are capable of becoming (also see Rogers, 1951, 1961). Individuals striving toward self-actualization seek out new activities as a way of expanding their horizons and want to learn simply for the sake of learning. For example, people seeking self-actualization might be driven by their own curiosity to learn everything they can about a particular topic, or they might pursue an active interest in ballet both as a means of developing muscle tone and as an outlet for creative self-expression.

Maslow proposed that the five sets of needs form a hierarchy, as illustrated in Figure 17–1. When two or more of these needs are unmet, people tend to satisfy them in a particular sequence. They begin with the lowest needs in the hierarchy, satisfying physiological needs first, safety needs next, and so on. They attempt to fulfill higher needs only when lower needs have been at least partially met.

To illustrate Maslow's hierarchy, a boy with a need for exercise (a physiological need) may become excessively restless in class even though he is scolded by his teacher for his hyperactivity (thereby *not* satisfying his need for esteem from others). A girl with an unfulfilled need for love and belonging may choose not to

Figure 17–1
Maslow's hierarchy of
needs

Growth need

Deficiency needs

5. Need for Self-Actualization

4. Esteem Needs

3. Love and Belonging Needs

2. Safety Needs

1. Physiological Needs

enroll in intermediate algebra—a class that would satisfy her desire to learn more math—if the peers whose friendships she most values tell her the class is only for nerds and various other uncool individuals. I once knew a boy living in a Philadelphia ghetto who had a strong interest in learning yet often stayed home from school to avoid the violent gangs that hung out on the local street corner. This boy's need for safety took precedence over any need for self-actualization that he might have had.

According to Maslow, the first four needs on the hierarchy—physiological, safety, love and belonging, and esteem needs—result from things that a person *lacks*; hence, Maslow called them **deficiency needs**. Deficiency needs can be met only by external sources—by people and events in one's environment. Furthermore, once these needs are fulfilled, there is no reason to satisfy them further. Self-actualization, on the other hand, is a **growth need**: Rather than addressing a deficiency in a person's life, it serves to enhance the person's growth and development and thus is rarely satisfied completely. Self-actualizing activities tend to be intrinsically motivated: People engage in them because doing so gives them pleasure and satisfies their desire to know and grow.

Needs that are satisfied most of the time have little effect on behavior. For example, many people in our society routinely satisfy their physiological and safety needs. The needs for love and esteem are more likely to go unfulfilled; hence, people may direct much of their effort toward gaining the acceptance and respect of others and toward developing their own sense of competence and self-worth. But people are likely to strive for self-actualization—a need that is almost never completely satisfied—only when all four deficiency needs are at least partially met.

Self-actualized individuals have a number of noteworthy characteristics. For example, they are independent, spontaneous, creative, and sympathetic to the plights of others. They perceive themselves, other people, and the world in general in an objective, realistic light, and they are quite comfortable with who they are. They typically have an mission in life—an important problem that they are concerned about solving. Maslow suggested that few people—probably less than

1% of the population—become fully self-actualized, and then only in the later years of life.

Despite its intuitive appeal, Maslow's hierarchy has been criticized on several counts. For one thing, little hard evidence exists to substantiate the hierarchical nature of human motivation. Maslow derived his theory from his informal, subjective observations of presumably "self-actualized" personal friends and published descriptions of such historical figures as Thomas Jefferson and Abraham Lincoln; it would be almost impossible for other investigators to confirm that these individuals had the characteristics Maslow identified. Furthermore, self-actualization is so rare that the hierarchy may not provide an accurate description of people in general (Petri, 1991).

An alternative perspective is that some people simply have stronger needs than others in particular areas. For example, some individuals may have a greater need for love and belongingness—what many theorists call a *need for affiliation*. Let's look at several individual differences in motivation that may exist.

Individual Differences in Motivation

Some theorists have proposed a number of needs that might be stronger for some people than for others. Here we will talk about three in particular: the need for affiliation, the need for approval, and the need for achievement.

Need for Affiliation

The **need for affiliation** is the degree to which a person wants and needs friendly relationships with others (e.g., Boyatzis, 1973; McClelland, 1984). For example, my daughter Tina can't stand the thought of being home "alone" (i.e., with her parents and brothers) on a Friday or Saturday night and so always finds something to do with her friends. When she *is* home on a weeknight, she talks to her boyfriend on the telephone for at least an hour and touches base with her best friend several times throughout the evening. In a similar way, my son Alex has a good friend that he seemingly cannot live without. Jeff, on the other hand, can play alone quite happily for hours at a time.

People with a high need for affiliation have a number of characteristics in common. For example, they tend to become nervous when other individuals observe their performance (Boyatzis, 1973). They spend considerable time communicating with others, and their attitudes and opinions are easily influenced by those around them (Boyatzis, 1973). They are more interested in interpersonal relationships than in task accomplishment; hence, when choosing a work partner, they are apt to select an incompetent friend over a competent person they don't particularly care for (Boyatzis, 1973; French, 1956; Vernon, 1969). Children with a high need for affiliation tend to have lower grade point averages than their equal-ability peers (Ringness, 1967); they earn better classroom grades when they have warm, nurturing teachers (McKeachie, 1961; McKeachie, Lin, Milholland, & Isaacson, 1966).

Many children and adolescents appear to have high affiliation needs. A high priority during the school day is on socializing with friends, and they may spend only the minimum energy and effort necessary to get their classwork done (Doyle, 1986a). Unfortunately, they may find that it is impossible to please everyone simultaneously; for example, as we noted earlier, maintaining friendships with classmates who place little value on academics may occur at the expense of not pleasing parents and teachers who look for high classroom performance.

Need for Approval

In addition to having a high need for affiliation, some people have a strong desire to "look good" to others; in other words, they have a high **need for approval** (e.g., Boyatzis, 1973; Crowne & Marlowe, 1964). For example, one student may continually seek teacher recognition for even the smallest accomplishments in the classroom. Another may do everything possible to appear cool in front of peers.

People with a high need for approval are often those with low self-esteem (Crowne & Marlowe, 1964). They go out of their way to behave in ways they think will please others, often compromising any standards that they themselves may have regarding appropriate behavior (Crowne & Marlowe, 1964). But such efforts are often counterproductive: perhaps because they are trying *too* hard to be liked, they tend to be relatively unpopular with their peers (Boyatzis, 1973; Crowne & Marlowe, 1964).

Need for Achievement

The **need for achievement**, sometimes called **achievement motivation**, is the need for excellence for its own sake, without regard for any external rewards that one's accomplishments might bring (Atkinson, 1957, 1964; Atkinson & Feather, 1966; McClelland, Atkinson, Clark, & Lowell, 1953; Veroff, McClelland, & Ruhland, 1975; Vernon, 1969). For example, a person with a high need for achievement might work diligently to maintain a 4.0 GPA, practice long hours to become a professional basketball player, or simply play Monopoly with a vengeance.

People with a high need for achievement are realistic about the tasks they can accomplish, and they persist at tasks that are challenging yet achievable (Vernon, 1969; Veroff et al., 1975). They rarely rest on their laurels; instead, they set increasingly higher standards for excellence as their current standards are met (Veroff et al., 1975). And they are willing and able to delay gratification: They put off small, immediate rewards for the larger rewards that their long-term efforts are likely to bring (French, 1955; Vernon, 1969; Veroff et al., 1975).

An early and widely cited theory of achievement motivation is that of John Atkinson and his associates (e.g., Atkinson, 1957, 1964; Atkinson & Birch, 1978; Atkinson & Feather, 1966; Atkinson & Raynor, 1978). These theorists proposed that the tendency to strive for achievement is a function of two related needs: the **motive for success**, or M_s (the desire to do well and accomplish goals) and the **motive to avoid failure**, or M_{af} (anxiety about failing to accomplish goals and the resulting inhibition of activities likely to result in failure). For many people, one of these needs is stronger than the other, and achievement behavior depends on which need is predominant.

Individuals with a stronger motive for success tend to seek and tackle moderately difficult tasks—those that are challenging yet can feasibly be accomplished. Because these individuals have a relatively low motive to avoid failure, they don't worry about the mistakes they may make or the stumbling blocks they may encounter. Furthermore, they recognize that success on difficult tasks is more noteworthy than success on easy tasks.

In contrast, individuals with a stronger motive to avoid failure typically forego such risks in favor of a sure thing. They steer clear of the moderately difficult tasks that their high M_s counterparts select. Instead, they often choose tasks they can almost certainly accomplish. Even though their success on such tasks may be meaningless, they are nevertheless able to avoid the failure they fear. Curiously, though, high M_{af} individuals sometimes choose extremely difficult tasks—those at which they can't possibly succeed. When they fail at such tasks, they have a built-in explanation—after all, the task was impossible—and so the failure is easily rationalized.

Atkinson and Litwin (1960) demonstrated the hypothesized effects of M_s and M_{af} in a concrete fashion. Their experiment involved a ring toss game—throwing rings to land around an upright peg. Male undergraduate students, some of whom had been identified as having a higher M_s and others as having a higher M_{af}, were told that they could stand wherever they wished, within a 15-foot range, as they attempted to throw 10 rings, 1 at a time, around the peg. The great majority of the high M_s students opted to stand about 8 to 12 feet away from the peg (thus taking on a moderate challenge). Of the high M_{af} students, only half stood in the 8- to 12-foot range; the other half stood either within 7 feet of the peg (thus making the task an easy one) or at least 13 feet away from it (thus making it extremely difficult). Isaacson (1964) found the same pattern in the course selections of college students: Those with a higher M_s tended to choose classes of moderate difficulty, while those with a higher M_{af} chose either very easy or very difficult classes.

Researchers have noted that achievement motivation does not necessarily remain constant throughout a person's lifetime. For example, it may decrease as children progress through the school grades and may be especially low when they make the often anxiety-arousing transition from elementary school to junior high (Eccles & Midgley, 1989; Harter, 1981). And children's very conception of what achievement *is* changes as they develop: As they progress through the elementary school years, they increasingly define success as doing better than their peers rather than as achieving a particular goal per se (Feld, Ruhland, & Gold, 1979; Ruble, 1980).

In its earliest conceptualization, the need for achievement was thought to be a general characteristic that people exhibit consistently in a variety of tasks across many domains. More recently, however, theorists have proposed that this need may instead be somewhat specific to particular tasks and occasions (Dweck & Elliott, 1983; Eccles & Wigfield, 1985; Jackson, Ahmed, & Heapy, 1976; Ruble, 1980; Stipek, 1988; Veroff et al., 1975; Weinstein, 1969). As one simple example, research indicates that most males and females have greater achievement motivation in arenas that are stereotypically appropriate for their gender (Berk, 1989; Lueptow, 1984; Shaffer, 1988; Stein, 1971; Tobin & Fox, 1980). Theorists are also beginning to explain people's need for achievement in terms of specific cognitive factors that influence the choices they make and the tasks they pursue. We turn briefly to the contemporary cognitive perspective of motivation now.

The Contemporary Cognitive Perspective

Within the past three decades, theorists have radically changed their approach to studying human motivation (e.g., Dweck, 1986). Talk of physiological needs and drives has largely gone by the wayside. Concrete, external reinforcers play less of a role in conceptions of human learning (note the declining popularity of the operant conditioning perspective in recent years). And interest in global needs that may vary from one individual to another—needs for achievement, affiliation, and the like—is diminishing.

Most contemporary theorists describe human motivation as being a function of human cognition (e.g., see Dweck, 1986; Dweck & Elliott, 1983; Voss & Schauble, 1992). For example, people set specific *goals* toward which they strive. They form *expectations* regarding the likelihood of success in different activities. They construct *interpretations* of why certain consequences happen and make *predictions* about the future consequences of their behavior.

As we noted earlier in the chapter, motivation affects cognition as well—for example, by increasing attention and cognitive engagement and by promoting effective learning strategies. Ultimately, motivation and cognition are probably inextricably intertwined (e.g., Nenniger, 1992).

The cognitive perspective of motivation has gone in a variety of directions in recent years. We will explore the many aspects of this current perspective in greater depth in Chapter 18.

THE ROLE OF AFFECT

When we talk about motivation, it is difficult not to talk about **affect**—the feelings and emotions that an individual brings to bear on a task—at the same time. For example, earlier in the chapter we noted that intrinsically motivated individuals typically find pleasure in what they are doing. On the other hand, too much motivation—perhaps wanting something too much—may lead to an intense sense of anxiety. Pleasure, anxiety, excitement, pride, depression, anger, guilt—all of these are forms of affect.

Affect is clearly a factor in learning and cognition. For example, while learning how to perform a task, we simultaneously learn whether we like doing it (Zajonc, 1980). Problem solving is easier when we enjoy what we're doing, and successful problem solutions often bring on feelings of excitement, pleasure, and pride (Bloom & Broder, 1950; Cobb, Yackel, & Wood, 1989; McLeod & Adams, 1989; Smith, 1991; Thompson & Thompson, 1989). Our failed attempts at a task are likely to make us feel frustrated or anxious, especially if the task is an easy one, and we are apt to develop a dislike for that task (Eccles & Wigfield, 1985; Stodolsky, Salk, & Glaessner, 1991). We can retrieve information from long-term memory more successfully when our mood at the time of retrieval is the same as our mood when we initially stored the information (Gilligan & Bower, 1984). And, although we may repress extremely painful memories (see Chapter 12), in general, we can more easily retrieve information with high emotional content than we can recall relatively nonemotional information (Baddeley, 1982; Kleinsmith & Kaplan, 1963; Heuer & Reisberg, 1990).

As an example of the last principle, let's consider an experiment by Heuer and Reisberg (1990). Undergraduate students looked at a series of slides that depicted one of two stories. Both stories involved a boy and his mother visiting the boy's father at his workplace. For some students (the emotional-content group), the father was a surgeon operating on an accident victim; among other things, these students saw slides of surgery in progress (with a person's internal organs in full view) and the badly scarred legs of a child. For other students (the neutral-content group), the father was an auto mechanic repairing a broken-

People often remember more when information packs an emotional wallop.

down car; these students saw the internal workings of the car, including a piece that was clearly broken. Two weeks later, all the students were given an unexpected quiz about the things they had observed. Students who had seen the emotion-laden sequence remembered both the general gist of the story and many of the tiny details depicted in the slides far more accurately than did students who had seen the neutral sequence. In fact, although they did not expect to be tested on what they had seen, subjects in the emotional-content group remembered more than subjects who had watched the neutral sequence and specifically been told to remember its plot and details.

Probably the most widely studied form of affect, at least within the context of human learning, is anxiety. For example, in Chapter 3, we discovered that anxiety may be acquired through classical conditioning, becoming a conditioned response to previously neutral stimuli. In Chapter 6, we noted that fear or anxiety may play a prominent role in avoidance learning. In Chapters 12 and 16, we found that anxiety often interferes with both long-term memory retrieval and problem solving performance. Anxiety has numerous other effects as well; some are beneficial while others are not. Let's look more closely at how anxiety influences learning and performance.

Anxiety

Anxiety is a feeling of uneasiness and apprehension concerning a situation, typically one with an uncertain outcome. Fear and anxiety are related concepts, but with a distinct difference: Fear is a response to a specific threat, whereas anxiety is vague and relatively unfocused. For example, people are *afraid* of certain things, but they don't always know exactly what they're *anxious* about. Associated with anxiety are such physiological responses as muscular tension (e.g., stomach "butterflies"), increased heartbeat, and perspiration, and such behavioral responses as restlessness and pacing.

Psychologists have found it useful to distinguish between two types of anxiety: state versus trait. **State anxiety** is a temporary condition elicited by a particular stimulus. For example, you might experience state anxiety when working on an especially challenging mathematics problem or when thinking about an upcoming exam in a notoriously difficult class. **Trait anxiety** is a relatively stable state of affairs, such that an individual is chronically anxious in certain situations. For example, you might have general mathematics anxiety or test anxiety, becoming anxious whenever you encounter numbers or think about exams.

Effects of Anxiety
Early studies focused on the effects of anxiety on learning and performance. More recently, with the advent of cognitivism, studies have investigated the effects anxiety is likely to have on cognitive processes. Let's consider the evidence in each of these areas.

Effects on Learning and Performance

Psychologists use the term **arousal** to refer to the level of internal energy an organism is currently experiencing. Organisms experiencing low levels of arousal are relaxed, perhaps even asleep. Organisms experiencing high levels of arousal are highly energized, perhaps to the point of being excessively anxious.

Early researchers found that arousal affects learning and performance in a curvilinear ("inverted U") fashion (Broadhurst, 1959; Fiske & Maddi, 1961; Hebb, 1955; Yerkes & Dodson, 1908). More specifically, a small degree of arousal (e.g., a low level of anxiety) facilitates learning and performance. A high degree of arousal (e.g., high anxiety) may facilitate learning and performance when the task is easy, but is likely to interfere when a task is more difficult. For any task, there is probably some **optimal level of arousal** (reflected by the top point of the inverted U) at which learning and performance are maximized (see Figure 17–2).

A classic experiment with mice by Yerkes and Dodson (1908) provides a concrete illustration of how arousal level and task difficulty interact. Each mouse was placed in a chamber from which it could escape by either of two doors. The wall opposite the doors was slowly moved to make the chamber smaller and smaller, until the mouse was eventually forced to escape through one door or the other. One door led to a safe, comfortable "nest box"; the other led to electric shock. The experimenters provided a clue to help the mouse determine which door was which: The doorway leading to the nest box was consistently brighter than the doorway leading to shock.

For different groups of mice, the experimenters varied arousal level by the amount of shock they administered—mild, intense, or somewhere in between—when the "wrong" door was entered. They varied task difficulty by the relative similarity or difference between the two doorways: some mice had to choose between white and black (an easy task), others chose between light and dark gray (a moderately difficult task), and still others chose between similar shades of gray (a very difficult, although not impossible, task).

Figure 17–2
The inverted "U" curve, depicting the curvilinear relationship between arousal and performance

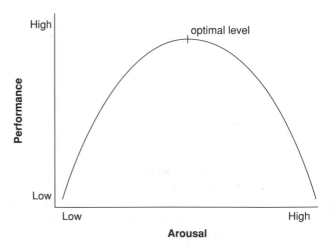

Figure 17–3
Arousal level interacts with
task difficulty, resulting in
different optimal levels for
different tasks.

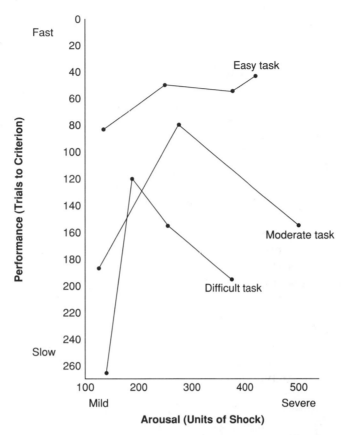

Source: From data reported in "The relation of strength of stimulus to rapidity of habit-formation" by R. M. Yerkes and J. D. Dodson, 1908, *Journal of Comparative Neurology and Psychology, 18*, pp. 459–482.

The experimenters established a criterion of 30 correct door choices in a row as an indication that a mouse had successfully learned the brightness discrimination. Figure 17–3 shows the average number of learning trials for mice in each condition; because the Y-axis reflects quality of performance (speed of learning), groups needing fewer trials to criterion appear higher in the figure than groups with more trials. Notice how the mice with an easy choice performed best under high arousal (intense shock) conditions. Those with a moderately difficult task performed better with moderate arousal (moderate shock). Those with an extremely difficult discrimination performed best when shock and arousal were relatively low.

This principle—that easy tasks are best accomplished with a relatively high level of arousal while more difficult tasks are better accomplished with a low or moderate level—is often known as the **Yerkes-Dodson law**. The principle holds true not only for mice, but for human beings as well. A high level of anxiety enhances our performance on easy and automatic tasks, such as running a mile or reciting the alphabet; here we have a case of **facilitating anxiety**. But the same high level interferes with our performance on a difficult task, such as writing a psychology textbook or speaking before a large audience; in this situation, we have **debilitating anxiety**.

We find the Yerkes-Dodson law at work in the classroom as well. For example, students who experience a small amount of muscular tension during mathematical problem solving are more successful problem solvers than students who experience no tension at all (Bloom & Broder, 1950). Highly anxious students sometimes perform better than low-anxious students on tasks requiring verbatim recall of simple information; however, they perform comparatively poorly on tasks requiring flexible, creative thought (Kirkland, 1971). Low levels of anxiety throughout the course of instruction may facilitate students' learning; a high degree of anxiety at the tail end of the same course (e.g., at final exam time) is likely to be counterproductive (Kirkland, 1971). And the same degree of anxiety about a test may enhance the performance of high-ability students, for whom the test is easy, while lowering the performance of low-ability students, for whom the test is more difficult (Spielberger, 1966).

A useful distinction in this context is the difference between threat and challenge (Combs, Richards, & Richards, 1976). A **threat** is a situation in which individuals believe they have little chance of success—they see failure as an almost inevitable outcome. In contrast, a **challenge** is a situation in which individuals believe they can probably succeed if they try hard enough. Students are likely to have debilitating anxiety when they perceive a situation to be threatening. They respond to challenges more favorably; for example, they are likely to be highly motivated to do their best, and they express considerable excitement and satisfaction when they succeed (Cobb et. al., 1989; Natriello & Dornbusch, 1984; Thompson & Thompson, 1989).

For most students, school tasks are more often challenging than easy. Accordingly, we should expect students with lower levels of anxiety to perform more effectively in the classroom. This in fact is the case: Students with relatively low trait anxiety achieve greater academic success (e.g., higher grade point averages) than their peers of equal ability who have high trait anxiety (Gaudry & Spielberger, 1971; Stipek, 1988; Tobias, 1980).

Effects on Cognition

Imagine yourself sitting in class taking a test. Here are some possible thoughts running through your mind as you do so:

- Oh, yes, my professor introduced this concept last week. It refers to. . . .
- Here is a situation we didn't specifically talk about in class. Let me see if I can relate it to something we *did* talk about. . . .
- The best way to solve this problem might be to. . . .
- These questions are getting harder and harder. . . .
- Oh, no, I only have 10 minutes left. I can't possibly finish. . . .
- What if I fail this test? It's required for my program. . . .

The first three thoughts are clearly relevant to the task at hand and should help you do your best on the test. In contrast, the last three are irrelevant to your task: You are spending your time worrying rather than thinking about how to answer the test questions. As you should recall from our discussions of attention (Chapter 9) and working memory (Chapter 10), we can attend to and process only a small amount of information at any one time. The more time and attention we devote to worrying about the test we are taking, the less capacity we have for dealing with and responding to the test itself.

Anxiety interferes with an individual's attention to a task (Eysenck, 1992; Green, 1980; Tobias, 1977, 1980; Wine, 1980). And because "worrying" thoughts take up a certain amount of working memory capacity, anxiety also interferes with effective cognitive processing (Eccles & Wigfield, 1985; Eysenck, 1992; Mueller, 1980; Naveh-Benjamin, 1991; Tobias, 1977, 1980). Such effects are particularly likely when a learning or memory task is difficult and when it involves considerable retrieval of information from long-term memory (Tobias, 1980).

In general, anxiety's debilitative effect is a distractive one: When performing a difficult task, highly anxious people are more likely to think irrelevant thoughts, be diverted by irrelevant stimuli, and exhibit irrelevant responses (Dusek, 1980; Eccles & Wigfield, 1985; Eysenck & Keane, 1990; Wine, 1980).

Common Sources of Anxiety

People become anxious about a variety of things. For example, they may be anxious about physically hurting themselves (King & Ollendick, 1989). They may be concerned about their personal appearance (King & Ollendick, 1989). They may worry about how they perform in comparison with their peers, and about what their peers might think of them as a result (King & Ollendick, 1989; Vernon, 1969). They are likely to feel insecure when entering a new, unknown, and perhaps unsettling situation—for example, when, as budding adolescents, they make the transition from elementary school to junior high school (Eccles & Midgley, 1989). And, in general, they are likely to become anxious whenever their self-esteem is threatened—when they receive some form of feedback that portrays them in an unflattering light (Stipek, 1988).

Two forms of trait anxiety—test anxiety and mathematics anxiety—have been the focus of considerable study. Let's look at what research tells us about each of these.

Test anxiety.

Most of us get a little bit anxious about tests, and, as we have already seen, a small amount of anxiety may actually help us do better on tests. But some students become extremely anxious in test-taking situations, and these students typically get lower test scores than their less-anxious classmates (e.g., Sarason, 1972; Spielberger, 1966). Such students appear to be concerned primarily about the evaluative aspect of tests: They fear that someone else (such as their teacher) will make negative judgments about them (Harter, Whitesell, & Kowalski, 1992; Phillips, Pitcher, Worsham, & Miller, 1980; Wine, 1980).

Test anxiety is rare in the early grades, but increases throughout the elementary school years (Kirkland, 1971; Sarason, 1972). Many secondary and upper elementary students have test anxiety that interferes with their test performance; we are especially likely to see such debilitative test anxiety in minority students, students with special needs, and students with a history of academic failure (Kirkland, 1971; Phillips et al., 1980).

Mathematics anxiety.   Of all the subjects taught in schools, none seems to elicit as much anxiety for as many students as mathematics. Mathematics anxiety has two components. First, math-anxious people have negative emotional reactions to math: They fear and dislike it, often intensely so. Second, they firmly believe that they are incapable of succeeding at mathematical tasks (Wigfield & Meece, 1988).

One possible reason why students become anxious about math is that, as we noted in our discussion of classical conditioning (Chapter 3), school curricula frequently introduce mathematical concepts and procedures before students are cognitively ready to handle them. For example, developmentalists such as Jean Piaget have proposed that the abilities to understand proportions and to deal with abstract ideas don't usually emerge until early adolescence and then continue to develop for several years after that. Yet we often expose students to such proportions as fractions and ratios, and to such abstract ideas as negative numbers and *pi* (π), in the upper elementary and early junior high school years. If students are asked to deal with mathematical tasks they can't understand, many of them will undoubtedly encounter frustration and failure. And when students associate frequent failure with math, we can expect them to develop a dislike for the subject and a belief that they are incapable of doing well in it.

As you might expect, students with high math anxiety do less well in mathematics classes than students with low math anxiety; furthermore, highly math-anxious students are less likely to enroll in additional mathematics classes of their own volition (Eccles & Jacobs, 1986; McCoy, 1990; Meece, Wigfield, & Eccles, 1990). Such differences between high math-anxious and low math-anxious students appear even when the two groups of students have done equally well in previous math classes. In fact, math anxiety may have a greater influence on students' future plans for taking (or not taking) mathematics than does their previous achievement level and degree of success in math (Eccles & Jacobs, 1986). Math anxiety, which is more common in girls than in boys even when achievement levels are the same, may be a key reason why so few girls pursue advanced study or careers in mathematics (Eccles & Jacobs, 1986; Fennema, 1980). And for students of both genders, math anxiety may inhibit the desire to pursue a career in science (Chipman, Krantz, & Silver, 1992).

To perform most effectively in the classroom, students should be motivated to do their best, yet not be overly anxious about their performance. In the final section of the chapter, we will consider some general strategies for promoting students' motivation to achieve academic success and for keeping their anxiety at productive levels.

PROMOTING STUDENT MOTIVATION

The principles and theories we've examined in this chapter have numerous implications for classroom practice. Here are several things for teachers to keep in mind in their efforts to promote student motivation.

• *Students learn more effectively and demonstrate more productive classroom behaviors when they are intrinsically motivated to learn and achieve.* Historically, parents, teachers, and society in general have emphasized the extrinsic advantages of classroom success (Spaulding, 1992). For example, parents give their children money and privileges for good report cards. Schools award athletic letters for sports participation. Teachers and guidance counselors point out that students will gain admission to college, find more employment opportunities, and earn higher salaries if they obtain their high school diplomas. Yet as we have seen, *intrinsically* motivated students are more likely to exhibit initiative, independence, ambition, meaningful learning, and enjoyment regarding academic activities than is true for their extrinsically motivated counterparts.

Researchers have identified several strategies that appear to promote intrinsic motivation. Talking about intrinsic rather than extrinsic motives for pursuing classroom activities is one effective approach (Hennessey & Amabile, 1987). For example, a teacher might say, "It's always nice to get good grades, but it's more important that you understand what you are studying and enjoy what you are doing," or, "You must be very proud of yourself for passing the district writing test." Models who express intrinsic enjoyment of something they are doing (e.g., saying "I feel wonderful" after giving something generously to someone else) promote observers' intrinsic motivation for the same activity (Bryan, 1971). And relating classroom topics to students' own lives, experiences, needs, and feelings (e.g., in geography, identifying students with roots in the regions being studied, or, in history, having students imagine how they might have felt leaving home at the age of twelve to work as an apprentice during the Middle Ages) increases the likelihood that students will genuinely want to study those topics (Brophy, 1986).

Intrinsic motivation is also more likely to emerge when certain cognitive factors are present—for example, when people believe they are capable of accomplishing tasks successfully and when they consider themselves to be in control of their lives. As we study such cognitive factors in the following chapter, we will identify additional strategies for helping students genuinely *want* to learn and achieve.

• *Students are more likely to focus on their schoolwork when their nonacademic needs have been met.* As we examined drive theory, Maslow's hierarchy, and individual differences, we identified a number of nonacademic needs that students may have. They are likely to have physiological needs on some occasions; for example, they may be hungry, thirsty, tired, or restless. They may feel uncertain or insecure about what will happen to them in class, in the schoolyard, or on the way home. And many students will have a strong desire to socialize with others (classmates and teachers alike), gaining the acceptance, approval, and respect of those around them.

Teachers can do a number of simple things to make sure students' physiological needs are met. For example, they can help students from low-income families apply for free lunch programs. They can alternate quiet, in-seat tasks with opportunities for physical activity. They can refer students with apparently untreated illnesses to the school nurse. And they should certainly include bathroom breaks and trips to the drinking fountain in the daily schedule.

To meet students' need for safety and security in the classroom, and to keep their anxiety about academic tasks and activities at a reasonable, facilitative level, teachers must create an environment that is somewhat orderly and predictable (Brophy, 1987; Dowaliby & Schumer, 1973; Grimes & Allinsmith, 1970; Klein, 1975; Stipek, 1988; Wlodkowski, 1978). For example, they might have regular procedures for handing out and sharing materials, meeting with cooperative learning groups, doing homework, and turning in assignments. They should clearly describe expectations for academic performance and classroom behavior. They should deal with misbehaviors in a fair and consistent fashion. And they should provide opportunities for students to air any questions and concerns that may arise.

Students' needs for love, belonging, affiliation, and approval can be met in a variety of ways. Teacher–student relationships are, by their very nature, somewhat business-like; after all, teachers and students both have a job to do. At the same time, teachers can express their interest and affection for students through the many "little things" they do throughout the day—for example, by acknowledging birthdays and other special occasions, taking students' ideas and opinions seriously, and offering a supportive and nonjudgmental ear when a particular student seems angry or depressed. And they can provide opportunities for students to interact frequently with their classmates—for example, through such group-oriented instructional techniques as discussions, cooperative learning, reciprocal teaching, and role playing.

To make sure students' need for esteem from others is met, teachers can acknowledge students' accomplishments both in and out of class. They can schedule activities in such a way that all students are able to demonstrate their particular strengths at some point during the school day. They can "brag" about their students' accomplishments in many subtle ways—for example, by posting students' art projects on the wall, describing noteworthy achievements at parent–teacher conferences, displaying students' best work at open houses, and sending occasional "good news" reports home to parents. And to ensure that students have adequate self-esteem as well, teachers must do everything they can to help students achieve classroom success.

• *Teachers can capitalize on the role that affect plays in learning.* There is no reason for academic subjects to be dry and emotionless. On the contrary, students will probably remember more if they have feelings about the things they study. For example, a scientific discovery might be exciting. A look at social injustices might make students angry. A poem might convey peace and serenity. One simple way that teachers can promote positive affect is to model their own enthusiasm and excitement about classroom subject matter—perhaps by bringing in newspaper articles and other outside materials they have run across, presenting material in an animated or even impassioned fashion, and sharing the particular questions and issues about which they themselves are concerned (Brophy, 1986, 1987; Wlodkowski, 1978).

We must remember, too, that students should associate pleasure and other forms of positive affect with classroom activities. For example, although teachers don't necessarily want to give the impression that schoolwork is all fun and games, they can occasionally incorporate a few game-like features into classroom tasks and activities (Brophy, 1986)—perhaps by using simple crossword puzzles to introduce new spelling words or by using a television game show format for a class history review. And, in general, teachers must make sure that most of students' experiences with any task or subject matter, and especially *early* experiences, are positive and nonthreatening ones (e.g., Wlodkowski, 1978).

•*Evaluations of students' performance should be portrayed as a means of enhancing future achievement rather than as judgments of ability and worth.* Under the best of circumstances, tests and other forms of classroom evaluation *can* serve as effective motivators for student learning. For example, most students study class material more and learn it better when they are told they will be tested on it rather than when they are simply told to learn it (Frederiksen, 1984b; Halpin & Halpin, 1982). Tests are especially effective as motivators when they challenge students to perform at their very best (Natriello & Dornbusch, 1984). However, we should note several situations in which a test will definitely *not* motivate students to do well or—even worse—may motivate them to do *poorly*:

- When they believe they will be penalized for doing too well on the test—for example, when they think they will receive more challenging work (extra readings, more difficult test questions, etc.) if they attain a high test score (Sax, 1989)
- When they think they will lose the esteem of their peers for doing too well—for example, when they are afraid of becoming nerds or "school girls" (Sax, 1989)
- When they think their teacher's high standards for test performance are impossible to attain (Natriello & Dornbusch, 1984)
- When they consistently perform at lower levels than most of their classmates (Natriello, 1987)
- When they believe a test is a poor reflection of what they know (Paris, Lawton, Turner, & Roth, 1991)

Thus, a classroom test is most likely to serve as a motivator for learning when students perceive it to be a valid measure of course objectives, when they believe that successful performance on the test is possible, and when they are confident that successful performance will be rewarded rather than punished.

But as we have seen, many students are so concerned about performing well on tests that they become overly anxious about taking them. There are probably several reasons that high school and upper elementary students experience debilitative anxiety in testing situations. Perhaps, when teachers talk about an upcoming test, they too often imply that it is an event to be feared or revered. Perhaps they too often stress the dire consequences of failing. Perhaps teachers and other school personnel make too many major decisions—about grades, scholarships, admission to special programs, and so on—on the basis of a single test score.

Researchers and theorists offer several suggestions for keeping students' test anxiety at a facilitative level. First of all, teachers can base students' classroom grades on many sources of data (perhaps including scores on numerous small tests) instead of on only one or two test scores (Gaudry & Bradshaw, 1971; Gaynor & Millham, 1976; Sax, 1989). Second, they can encourage students to do their best without creating unnecessary anxiety about the consequences of doing poorly (I. Sarason, 1980; S. Sarason, 1972,; Sax, 1989; Sinclair, 1971). Third, a classroom test should be short enough that students can easily complete it within the allotted time; this strategy is especially beneficial for high-anxiety students (Brophy, 1986; Hill, 1984; Hill & Eaton, 1977). And fourth, students should be given whatever support (scaffolding) is appropriate to help them perform successfully. For example, students can be given pretests for practice and feedback, instructed on effective test-taking strategies, and allowed to use notes or other resources when there is no inherent value in committing certain information (formulas, trivial facts, etc.) to memory (Brophy, 1986; Kirkland, 1971; Leherissey, O'Neil, & Hansen, 1971; Sax, 1989; Sieber, Kameya, & Paulson, 1970; Stipek, 1988; Wine, 1980).

Above all, though, teachers and students alike must keep tests and other forms of evaluation in the proper context—as means of promoting learning and achievement, especially over the long run, rather than as means of making judgments about students' ability and worth. For example, evaluation procedures should provide frequent and informative feedback to students about what they have mastered and how they can improve (Brophy, 1986; Spaulding, 1992; Wine, 1980). And they should allow for the mistakes that are an inevitable part of the learning process. When students know they will have the chance to correct their errors, they are more likely to take on challenging, risky tasks (Brophy, 1986; Wlodkowski, 1978).

Students are most likely to exhibit high motivation to achieve, and therefore to gain the maximum benefits of classroom instruction, when they find the subject matter they are studying to be interesting, when they are more concerned about learning than about looking "good" for their teacher and classmates, when they know they are capable of achieving instructional objectives, and when they believe they have some control over the things that happen in the classroom. We will consider these points further when we examine cognitive factors in motivation in the next chapter.

SUMMARY

Motivation is an internal state that arouses us to action, pushes us in particular directions, and keeps us engaged in certain activities. Motivation determines the extent to which we exhibit the particular responses we have learned. It also affects the ways in which we process the information we receive. Intrinsic motivation is ultimately more beneficial than extrinsic motivation; for example, intrinsically motivated individuals do things on their own initiative, maintain their attention on tasks, and process information in a meaningful fashion.

Numerous theories of motivation have been proposed. Drive theorists postulate that human beings and other organisms behave in ways that reduce their physiological needs and thus maintain homeostasis. Incentive theorists propose that characteristics of goal objects mediate a stimulus-response relationship, affecting which stimuli are responded to and which are not. From the perspective of Maslow's hierarchy, people have five different sets of needs (ranging from physiological needs to self-actualization) that they strive to meet in a particular order. Other theories focus on the individual differences that may exist in such motives as the need for affiliation, the need for approval, and the need for achievement. Most contemporary theories emphasize the cognitive aspects of motivation; these theories are described in the following chapter.

Related to motivation is the concept of **affect**—the feelings and emotions that an individual brings to bear on a task. Affect influences learning; for example, we can typically retrieve information with high emotional content more easily than we can recall relatively nonemotional information. Anxiety is the form of affect most thoroughly studied by researchers. It facilitates performance on easy tasks, but high levels interfere with performance on difficult tasks, presumably by interfering with effective cognitive processing and otherwise distracting people from what they are doing.

Theorists and researchers offer numerous suggestions for promoting students' motivation to achieve and succeed in the classroom. For example, teachers should emphasize the intrinsically motivating aspects of school learning rather than the external rewards. Evaluation of students' performance should be portrayed as a means of enhancing future achievement rather than as a judgment of ability and worth. And students are more likely to focus on their schoolwork when their nonacademic needs have been met.

CHAPTER 18

Cognitive Factors in Motivation

Many of the people I meet marvel at how anyone could have the fortitude and persistence to get a doctoral degree. And to be honest, when I was growing up in the 1950s and 1960s, I myself expected only to become a housewife and mother, certainly not a college professor with "Ph.D." attached to my name. So how did I get here? It's really quite simple.

For one thing, I've always been concerned about children, and in particular about their education. While attending a small liberal arts college during the late 1960s—the era of the Vietnam War, the civil rights movement and sit-ins on the home front, and heightened soul-searching on many campuses across the country—I realized that I wanted my life to have an impact on society far beyond that of my own family and friends. By the end of my senior year, I had identified what I wanted to do when I grew up: I wanted to make education better for my children's generation than it had been for mine.

I began applying to graduate schools and ultimately chose Penn State's educational psychology program, partly because of the reputation of its faculty, partly because of the financial package it offered, and partly because of central Pennsylvania's incredible pastoral charm and serenity. I had been a psychology major as an undergraduate and knew that psychology was something I was "good at." I had also done well in the required statistics courses that led half of my fellow psychology majors to find another major by their junior year. So I worked hard during my years at Penn State, knowing I would certainly be successful if I was conscientious about my studies. Besides, I found educational psychology to be absolutely fascinating; the many books and articles I read were hard to put down because they gave me innumerable insights into how human beings learn and many intriguing ideas about how to help people learn better. My doctoral dissertation took longer than I had anticipated (a year and a half from start to finish), but with each passing month I came noticeably closer to completing it, and I *did* complete it in time to graduate in June of 1975.

So why did I initiate and persist in my efforts to earn a doctoral degree? Because, among other things, I valued a better world, had a goal for myself, and discovered an interest in human learning theory. Furthermore, I believed I was capable of graduate work in educational psychology. All these things—values, goals, interests, and beliefs—are among the cognitive factors that kept me motivated throughout my doctoral program.

In the preceding chapter, we found that motivation affects cognition: Motivated individuals are more likely to pay attention to and process information in ways that promote effective learning and memory. But cognition affects motivation as well: The things we think and believe have a significant influence on the tasks we pursue and the activities in which we engage.

In this chapter, we will explore the cognitive aspects of human motivation. We will talk first about the various goals that people set for themselves and the effects that different kinds of goals are likely to have on behavior. We will examine two factors that influence people's decisions to pursue particular goals: their values regarding what's important and their expectations for success. We will consider, too, the role that interest plays in human behavior, looking at personal characteristics and situational variables that determine whether a particular topic or task is interesting. Later in the chapter, we will explore attribution theory—the view that people's behaviors after reinforcing and punishing consequences are a function of their beliefs about the causes of those consequences. We will also identify two probable prerequisites for intrinsic motivation—control and competence—and find out why extrinsic reinforcement for academic achievement may sometimes *not* be such a good idea. Finally, we will look at how challenging situations often promote motivation and at how competition often undermines it, and we will consider additional strategies for promoting student motivation in the classroom.

GOALS

As we discovered in our discussion of social learning theory in Chapter 7, setting goals is a critical part of self-regulated behavior. Social learning theorists propose that people's internal goals and standards for success motivate them to move in particular directions. Goal attainment results in considerable self-satisfaction; it also leads to greater self-efficacy and higher standards for future performance (Bandura, 1986, 1989). Furthermore, people are more likely to be motivated to work toward goals, and thus more likely to accomplish them, when they have set those goals for themselves rather than when others have imposed goals upon them (Schunk, 1985, 1991). We must note, however, that goals are beneficial only to the extent that they are accomplishable; if they are unrealistically high, the continual failure to achieve them may result in excessive stress or depression (Bandura, 1986).

Goals figure prominently in motivation theory as well. In the next few pages, we will look at two types of goals that individuals may set for themselves—learning goals and performance goals. We will find that each type results in somewhat different behaviors and cognitions.

Learning Goals Versus Performance Goals

Contemporary theorists have proposed that achievement motivation takes one of several forms, depending on the specific goal an individual has in mind (e.g., Ames & Archer, 1988; Dweck & Elliott, 1983; Stipek, 1988). To illustrate, let's consider what three different girls might be thinking during the first day of a basketball unit in a physical education class:

Jane: This is my chance to show all the girls what a great basketball player I am. If I stay near the basket, Joan and

	June will keep passing to me, and I'll score a lot of points. I can really impress Coach and my friends.
Joan:	Boy, I hope I don't screw this up. If I shoot at the basket and miss, I'll look like a real jerk. Maybe I should just stay outside the three-point line and keep passing to Jane and June.
June:	I'd really like to become a better basketball player. I can't figure out why I don't get more of my shots into the basket. I'll ask Coach to give me feedback about how I can improve my game. Maybe some of my friends will have suggestions, too.

All three girls want to play basketball well, but for different reasons. Jane is concerned mostly about her performance—that is, about looking good in front of her coach and classmates—and so she wants to maximize opportunities to demonstrate her skill on the court. Joan is also concerned about the impression she will make, but she just wants to make sure she *doesn't* look *bad*. Unlike Jane and Joan, June isn't even thinking about how her performance will appear to others. Instead, she is interested mainly in developing her skill—in mastering the game of basketball—and doesn't expect herself to be an expert on the first day. For June, making mistakes is an inevitable part of learning a new skill, not a source of embarrassment or humiliation.

June's approach to basketball illustrates a **learning goal**—a desire to achieve competence by acquiring additional knowledge or mastering new skills. In contrast, Jane and Joan are each setting a **performance goal**—a desire either to look good and receive favorable judgments from others or *not* look bad and *not* receive unfavorable judgments.

Before they reach school age, children seem to focus primarily on learning goals. For example, even infants seek out experiences that are likely to increase their competence and mastery of the environment, and they derive genuine pleasure from new accomplishments (Dweck & Elliott, 1983). But when they enter school at five or six years of age, two things happen that orient them more toward performance goals (Dweck & Elliott, 1983). First of all, they suddenly have many peers around them to whom they can compare their own behavior; as a result, they may begin to define success more in terms of doing better than their classmates than in terms of task mastery. Second, whereas they have previously dealt primarily with physical tasks (e.g., learning to walk, fasten buttons, and ride a tricycle), they are now being asked to deal with tasks of an intellectual and somewhat abstract nature (e.g., learning to read, write, and add). The value of these school tasks may not be readily apparent to them, and their efforts in accomplishing them might therefore seem unnecessarily laborious. Furthermore, they may have greater difficulty assessing their progress on such tasks, to the point where they must rely on others (e.g., their teachers) to make judgments about their competence.

Effects of Different Goals

When we compare individuals who set learning goals with those who set performance goals, we often find different behaviors, beliefs, attitudes, learning strategies, and affect. Table 18–1 describes some of the differences we are likely to see.

Let's look at learning and performance goals in the context of schools and classrooms. As Table 18–1 indicates, students with learning goals tend to engage in the very activities that will help them learn; for example, they pay attention in class, process information in ways that promote effective long-term memory storage, and approach class assignments with the intention of getting the maximum benefit from them. Furthermore, students with learning goals have a healthy perspective about learning, effort, and failure: They realize that learning is a process of trying hard and continuing to persevere even in the face of temporary setbacks. Consequently, it is usually these students who benefit the most from their classroom experiences. In contrast, students with performance goals—those concerned primarily about how they appear to others—may stay away from some of the very tasks that, because of their challenging nature, would do the most to promote mastery of new skills (Dweck, 1986). Furthermore, because these students may exert only the minimal effort necessary to achieve desired performance outcomes, they may learn only a fraction of what their teachers have to offer them (Brophy, 1986, 1987).

Motivation to Learn

Some people seem to choose learning goals over performance goals fairly consistently. These people can be thought of as having a strong **motivation to learn**—a tendency to find learning activities meaningful and worthwhile and therefore to attempt to get the maximum benefit from them (Brophy, 1986, 1987; McCombs, 1988). The motivation to learn puts a new twist on the concept of achievement motivation: People want to engage in the cognitive processes that lead to successful learning as well as the behaviors that lead to achievement.

At least two additional variables influence people's choices to engage in some tasks but not others. We turn now to these variables—to expectancies and values.

EXPECTANCIES AND VALUES

Some theorists (e.g., Atkinson, 1964; Dweck & Elliott, 1983; Eccles [Parsons], 1983; Feather, 1982; Wigfield, 1994) have proposed that motivation for performing a particular task is a function of two variables. First of all, people must believe they can succeed; in other words, they must have a high **expectancy** about their task performance (a notion similar to social learning theorists' con-

Table 18–1

Characteristics of people with learning goals versus performance goals

People with Learning Goals	People with Performance Goals
Believe that competence develops over time through practice and effort	Believe that competence is a stable characteristic (people either have talent or they don't), and think that competent people shouldn't have to try very hard
Choose tasks that maximize opportunities for learning	Choose tasks that maximize opportunities for demonstrating competence, and avoid tasks that might make them look incompetent
React to easy tasks with feelings of boredom or disappointment	React to success on easy tasks with feelings of pride or relief
Are more likely to be intrinsically motivated to learn course material	Are more likely to be extrinsically motivated—that is, by expectations of external reinforcement and punishment
Invest considerable effort in tasks	Invest the minimal effort needed to succeed
Use learning strategies that promote true comprehension of course material (e.g., meaningful learning, elaboration, comprehension monitoring)	Use learning strategies that promote only rote learning of course material (e.g., repetition, copying, word-for-word memorization)
Seek feedback that accurately describes their ability and helps them improve	Seek feedback that flatters them
Evaluate their own performance in terms of the progress they make	Evaluate their own performance in terms of how they compare to others
View errors as a normal and useful part of the learning process, and use them to help improve performance	View errors as a sign of failure and incompetence
Are satisfied with their performance if they try hard and make progress, even if their efforts result in failure	Are satisfied with their performance only if they succeed
Interpret failure as a sign that they need to exert more effort	Interpret failure as a sign of low ability and therefore predictive of continuing failure in the future
Persist in the face of failure	Give up easily when they fail, and avoid tasks that have previously led to failure
View a teacher as a resource and guide to help them learn	View a teacher as a judge, and as a rewarder or punisher
As students, are more likely to be enthusiastic about, and become actively involved in, school activities	As students, are more likely to distance themselves from the school environment

Sources: Ames & Archer, 1988; Brophy, 1986; Dweck, 1986; Dweck & Elliott, 1983; Garcia, 1992; Jagacinski & Nicholls, 1984, 1987; Nolen, 1988; Powell, 1990; Stipek, 1988.

cept of self-efficacy). Second, people must believe that there are direct or indirect benefits in performing a task; in other words, they must place **value** on the task itself or on the outcomes that are likely to result.

From this perspective, motivated behavior occurs only when both expectancy and value are present. For example, as a doctoral student in educational psychology, I found value in human learning theory and had a high expectancy that I could master it; thus, I was motivated to learn as much as I could about how human beings learn. I value good music, too, but have a low expectancy for becoming an accomplished musician (I have an uninspired singing voice and am all butterfingers on the piano), so I don't work very hard or very often at my music. I'm much better at cooking lima beans than I am at singing, but I never cook them because I place absolutely no value on cooking the abominable things. And there are some things that, for me, are associated with both low expectancy and low value; playing my sons' video games and walking barefoot on hot coals are two activities that spring to mind.

People's expectancies are probably the result of several factors. Prior successes and failures at a particular task will of course make a difference; for example, people will form increasingly lower expectations after experiencing a series of failures (e.g., Dweck, Goetz, & Strauss, 1980). Other factors affect expectancy level as well: self-efficacy, an individual's general work habits, perceived difficulty of a task, environmental resources, the quality of instruction, and the anticipated effort necessary to succeed are all likely to make a difference (Dweck & Elliott, 1983; Eccles [Parsons], 1983; Zimmerman, Bandura, & Martinez-Pons, 1992). From factors such as these, an individual comes to a conclusion—perhaps correct, perhaps not—about the likelihood of success.

Value is equally subjective in nature. Eccles and Wigfield (1985; Eccles [Parsons], 1983) have suggested several possible reasons why it might be high or low. Some activities are valued because they are associated with certain personal qualities; for example, a boy who wants to be smart and thinks that smart people do well in school will place a premium on academic success. Other activities have high value because they are seen as means to a desired goal; for example, much as she detests mathematics, my daughter Tina is struggling through four years of high school math classes because so many colleges require that much math. Still other activities are valued simply because they bring pleasure and enjoyment; for example, junk food doesn't help me achieve any of my long-range goals (it may even interfere with my goal of losing 15 pounds this year), but it sure does taste good.

We can also anticipate the circumstances in which an activity will probably *not* be valued very much (Eccles & Wigfield, 1985; Eccles [Parsons], 1983, 1984). Some activities may require so much effort that they are simply not worth it. For example, I could undoubtedly improve my piano-playing skills with lessons and practice, but right now I have more important things to which I need to devote my time and energy. Other activities may be associated with too many bad feelings. For example, I can't imagine hang gliding or bungee jumping because I am deathly afraid of heights. And anything likely to threaten one's self-esteem is a "must" to avoid. For example, you may know individuals who rarely make the first move with people of the opposite sex for fear that they might be rejected.

While examining operant conditioning in Chapter 4, we discovered that people may sometimes not exhibit certain behaviors, despite potential reinforcement, because they have too much to lose or too little to gain by doing so. We can explain such a cost-benefit analysis quite easily within an expectancies/values framework (Eccles [Parsons], 1984; Eccles & Wigfield, 1985; Feather, 1982; Paris & Byrnes, 1989). We will see people exhibit a particular behavior when they believe that: (a) they can accomplish the task successfully with a reasonable amount of effort (high expectancy), and (b) the activity or its outcome is worthwhile (high value). We will probably *not* see them exhibit that behavior if they think they will have to exert an inordinate amount of effort to achieve success (if they achieve it at all), nor will we see them do so when they place little value on the activity and its consequence.

One common reason we value something is that we find it interesting. Let's find out what theorists have said about the role of interest in human motivation.

INTEREST

When we say that people have **interest** in a particular topic or activity, we mean that they find the topic or activity intriguing and enticing. Interest, then, is one source of intrinsic motivation. Positive affect accompanies interest; for example, people pursuing a task in which they are interested experience such feelings as pleasure, excitement, and liking (Hidi & Anderson, 1992).

Theorists distinguish between two general types of interest (Hidi, 1990; Krapp, Hidi, & Renninger, 1992). Some interests reside within the individual; people tend to have personal preferences regarding the topics they pursue and the activities in which they engage. Because such **personal interests** are relatively stable over time, we see a consistent pattern in the choices people make. For example, my husband has a strong interest in football, so is often found in front of the television set on Saturdays, Sundays, and Monday nights from September to January. (Fortunately, these are not the times when my favorite television game shows are broadcast.) And each of my children has shown unique individual interests from an early age. Jeff spends many happy hours playing with his plastic "little people." Tina spends just as many hours either talking to or talking about boys. Alex reads voraciously about lizards and usually has one or two live ones residing involuntarily in his bedroom.

In contrast to personal interest, **situational interest** is evoked by something in the environment—something that is perhaps new, unusual, or surprising. For example, as I was driving to Boulder one day a number of years ago, I saw what looked like a llama out of the corner of my eye. Well, I knew very well that Colorado's eastern plains are cattle and horse country, not llama country, so I slowed down to take a closer look, eventually confirming the unlikely llama hypothesis. For the time being, I was more interested in identifying the strange creature I saw than in getting to Boulder. In much the same way, you might have your interest temporarily piqued by a traffic accident at the side of the road, a "strange but true" tidbit in the newspaper, or a large, brightly wrapped gift with your name on it.

Effects of Interest

When people are interested in a particular activity, they are likely to set learning goals (rather than performance goals) related to that activity (Schiefele, 1992). For example, Alex's interest in lizards has led him to subscribe to a herpetologists' magazine and to read every issue from cover to cover. Similarly, people interested in antique automobiles might tinker with an old Model T engine until they know that engine inside and out. And people interested in gymnastics might spend a good portion of their free time at the gym practicing, practicing, practicing.

In addition, interest promotes more effective information processing. People who are interested in a particular topic show greater cognitive engagement in that topic (Pintrich, Marx, & Boyle, 1993). They are also more likely to process information in a meaningful and elaborative fashion—for example, by relating it to things they already know, drawing inferences, and generating their own examples (Hidi, 1990; Hidi & Anderson, 1992; Schiefele, 1992). As an illustration, ninth graders in an experiment by Bernstein (1955) read two prose passages that, in terms of objective measures, were equally readable. "The Get-Away Boy" was an action-packed, suspenseful story with a teenage hero and colorful images. "The House on Smith Street," adapted from Nathaniel Hawthorne's *The House of the Seven Gables*, contained dull, descriptive passages and included no human action whatsoever. After reading both stories, students rated them for their interest level and took a test that measured meaningful learning and elaboration of each one (items assessed such elaborative processes as drawing inferences, recognizing literary devices, and determining the writer's purpose). Students' ratings of the two stories confirmed the experimenters' belief that "The Get-Away Boy" was considerably more interesting than "The House on Smith Street." Furthermore, the students' test results revealed significantly more meaningful learning and elaboration for "The Get-Away Boy."

As you might guess, then, students who are interested in the things they study are more likely to remember them over the long run and thus able to build on them in future learning (Garner, Brown, Sanders, & Menke, 1992; Garner, Alexander, Gillingham, Kulikowich, & Brown, 1991; Hidi, 1990; Renninger, 1992). As a result, interested students show higher academic achievement (Krapp, Hidi, & Renninger, 1992; Schiefele, Krapp, & Winteler, 1992).

Factors Promoting Interest

Researchers have identified several sources of situational interest. Some topics—for example, death, destruction, danger, money, romance, and sex—appear to be inherently interesting for human beings (Schank, 1979). Things that are new, different, or unexpected often generate interest, as do things with a high activity level or intense emotions (Deci, 1992; Hidi, 1990; Hidi & Anderson, 1992; Schank, 1979; Wade, 1992). Works of fiction—novels, short stories, movies, and so on—are more engaging when they include themes and characters with which people can personally identify (Hidi, 1990; Hidi & Anderson, 1992; Schank, 1979; Wade, 1992). Nonfiction is more interesting when it is easy to understand and relationships among ideas are clear (Wade, 1992). And, for children at least, challenging tasks are often more interesting than easy ones (Danner & Lonky, 1981; Harter, 1978), a fortunate state of affairs if, as Lev Vygotsky proposed, challenges promote cognitive growth.

Interesting information sometimes appears within the context of larger, less interesting content. Consider this passage as an example:

> Some insects live alone, and some live in large families. Wasps that live alone are called solitary wasps. A Mud Dauber Wasp is a solitary wasp. Click Beetles live alone. When a click beetle is on its back, it flips itself into the air and lands right side up while it makes a clicking noise. Ants live in large families. There are many kinds of ants. Some ants live in trees. Black Ants live in the ground. (Garner, Gillingham, & White, 1989, p. 46)

If you're like me, you may have found the sentence about an upside-down beetle making a clicking noise as it rights itself to be the one interesting detail in an otherwise ho-hum passage. Yet notice that this sentence does *not* contribute to the paragraph's general theme, the social or nonsocial nature of various species of insects. Such "seductive details"—interesting but irrelevant tidbits—do not necessarily enhance learning and retention of the overall content in which they appear; in fact, they may in many cases steal readers' attention from more important, and perhaps more abstract, ideas (Garner et al., 1989, 1991, 1992). This is particular likely to be so when readers have only limited background knowledge about a topic and therefore have little basis for determining what's important and what's not (Garner et al., 1991).

The origins of personal interest have not been investigated to the extent that sources of situational interest have. Many personal interests probably come from people's prior experiences with various topics and activities. For example, people may have previously associated a certain activity with enjoyment and pleasure, perhaps in a classically conditioned fashion, and thus be eager to engage in it further. Or they may have found that acquiring more knowledge and skill in a particular area enhanced their self-esteem and self-efficacy, thereby providing intrinsic reinforcement.

People are more likely to be interested in pursuing an activity when they think their behaviors will lead to desired outcomes. But some individuals fail to recognize existing contingencies between the behaviors they exhibit and the consequences that result. To what sources do people attribute the events that occur in their lives? What things do they blame when they fail? To what things do they give credit when they succeed? We'll find out as we explore attribution theory in the next section.

ATTRIBUTIONS

You have undoubtedly gotten A's on some of the classroom exams you have taken. On those occasions, why do you think you did so well? Did you study hard? Were the exams easy? Did you luck out and guess right on questions you knew little about? Or is it simply that you are a highly intelligent human being?

And now let's consider those exams you haven't done so well on. To what did you attribute your failures? Did you spend too little time studying or perhaps study the wrong things? Were the exams too difficult? Were the questions poorly worded, so that you misinterpreted many that you should have answered correctly? Were you too tired or sick to think clearly? Or do you just not have what it takes?

People's various explanations for success and failure—their beliefs about what causes what—are **attributions**. Many theorists contend that attributions play a major role in the choices people make and the behaviors they ultimately exhibit (e.g., Dweck, 1986; Weiner, 1979, 1980, 1984, 1986). From an attribution theory perspective, how people interpret the reinforcements and punishments they experience—for example, whether they think an event is the result of something that they themselves have done or instead the result of something that has been done *to* them—influences the long-term effects that reinforcement and punishment are likely to have.

Attribution theory has been a major focus of scientific investigation in recent years. In the pages that follow, we'll look at the kinds of attributions we are likely to see and at their various effects on behavior and cognition. We'll identify reasons why different people form different attributions. We'll discover that many individuals are consistent in their interpretations of events and consequences, with some exhibiting a mastery orientation and others demonstrating learned helplessness. And we'll find that, given certain environmental conditions, people can acquire more productive attributions than they currently possess.

Dimensions Underlying People's Attributions

People are apt to explain events in a variety of ways. For example, school children may attribute their successes and failures in the classroom to such things as effort, ability, luck, task difficulty, health, mood, physical appearance, or teachers' or peers' behaviors (Schunk, 1990). It is important to note that attributions are as much a function of people's *perceptions* as of reality; thus, they are often distorted in line with one's self-concept and existing schemas about how the world operates (Dweck, 1978; Dweck & Elliott, 1983; Paris & Byrnes, 1989). For example, your poor performance on exams in years past may very well have been due to ineffective study strategies; like many students, you may have tried to learn class material in a rote, meaningless fashion (you obviously hadn't read my book yet). But because you thought of yourself as a smart person and believed you *had* studied adequately, you instead attributed your low score to the exam's exceptional difficulty or your teacher's capriciousness.

Bernard Weiner (1984, 1986) has proposed that attributions differ from one another in five ways—locus, temporal stability, cross-situational generality, controllability, and intentionality:

- **Locus ("place"): internal vs. external.** We sometimes attribute the causes of events to *internal* things—that is, to factors within ourselves. Thinking that a good grade is due to your own hard work and believing that a poor grade is due to your lack of ability are examples of internal attributions. At other times, we attribute events to *external* things—to factors outside of ourselves. Concluding that you received a scholarship because you were lucky and interpreting a classmate's scowl as being due to her bad mood (rather than anything you yourself have done to deserve it) are examples of external attributions. Theorists sometimes refer to this "locus" dimension as **locus of control**.

- **Temporal stability: stable vs. unstable.** Sometimes we believe that events are due to *stable* factors—to things that probably won't change much in the near future. For example, if you believe that you do well in school because of inherited ability or that you have trouble making friends because you're too fat, then you may be attributing events to stable, relatively unchangeable causes. But sometimes we instead believe that events are the result of *unstable* factors—to things that can change from one time to the next. Thinking that winning a tennis game was all a matter of luck and believing that you got a bad test grade because you were tired when you took the test are examples of attributions involving unstable factors.

- **Cross-situational generality: global vs. specific.** We sometimes attribute events to *global* factors that influence many aspects of our lives. For example, you may believe that you did poorly on an exam because you are a complete ignoramus about anything academic. At other times, we attribute events to causes that are *specific* to a particular situation. For example, you may think you landed an especially lucrative job simply because you were in the right place at the right time.

- **Controllability: controllable vs. uncontrollable.** On some occasions, we attribute events to *controllable* factors—to things we ourselves can influence and change. For example, if you believe that a classmate invited you to coffee because you always smile and say nice things to her, and if you think you probably failed a test simply because you didn't study the right things, then you are attributing these events to controllable factors. On other occasions, we attribute events to *uncontrollable* factors—to things over which we have no control. For example, if you think you were chosen for a title role in *Romeo and Juliet* because the director likes you, or that you played a lousy game of basketball because you had a mild case of the flu, then you are attributing these events to uncontrollable factors.

- **Intentionality: intentional vs. unintentional.** Our attributions may be due to either *intentional* or *unintentional* factors—to things we either did or didn't mean to do. Believing you failed an exam because you didn't study hard enough is an intentional factor: you consciously chose to do things other than study. On the other hand, using ineffective learning strategies is *un*intentional: You approached your class material in a rote, meaningless fashion only because you didn't know any better.

We can analyze virtually any attribution in terms of these five dimensions. For example, viewing success on a task as being due to inherited ability is an internal, stable, global, uncontrollable, and unintentional attribution. Believing failure on a task was a case of bad luck is an external, unstable, specific, uncontrollable, and unintentional attribution. As a further illustration, Table 18–2 analyzes eight common attributions that students are likely to make along three of the five dimensions—locus, stability, and controllability.

As you look at Table 18–2, you might think to yourself that "ability can change with practice, so is unstable and controllable," or that "teachers' attitudes toward students often depend on how students behave in the classroom, so are really due to internal, unstable, and controllable factors." Perhaps you are right, but keep in mind that people's *beliefs* about the locus, stability, and controllability of their attributions are what affect their future behavior, not the reality of the situation.

Generally speaking, we tend to attribute our successes to internal causes (e.g., high ability or hard work) and our failures to external causes (e.g., bad luck or the inconsiderate behavior of others) (Igoe & Sullivan, 1991; Marsh, 1986, 1990). By patting ourselves on the back for the things we do well and putting the blame elsewhere for poor performance, we are able to maintain a positive self-concept (Katkovsky, Crandall, & Good, 1967; Paris & Byrnes, 1989). When we attribute our behaviors inaccurately to factors outside of ourselves, however, we are unlikely to change our behavior in ways that will lead to greater success. Let's

Table 18–2
Analyzing various student attributions in terms of the three dimensions

Success or Failure Attributed to:	Locus	Stability	Controllability
Inherited "ability"	Internal	Stable	Uncontrollable
Personality	Internal	Stable	Uncontrollable
Effort	Internal	Unstable	Controllable
Health	Internal	Unstable	Uncontrollable
Energy level	Internal	Unstable	Uncontrollable
Task difficulty	External	Stable	Uncontrollable
Teacher's attitudes	External	Stable	Uncontrollable
Luck	External	Unstable	Uncontrollable

look more closely at the various effects that attributions, accurate or otherwise, are likely to have on how we think, feel, and behave.

Effects of Attributions

Attributions influence numerous aspects of behavior and cognition. Among other things, they affect an individual's: (a) emotional reactions to success and failure, (b) expectations for future success or failure, (c) effort and persistence, (d) learning strategies, (e) future choices, (f) self-efficacy, and (g) responses to failure situations.

Emotional Reactions to Success and Failure

People are of course happy when they succeed. But do they also feel *proud* of their accomplishments? When they believe that their successes are due to the actions of another person or to some other outside force, they are apt to feel grateful rather than proud. Individuals feel pride and satisfaction about their successes only when they attribute those successes to internal causes—that is, to something they themselves have done (Weiner, Russell, & Lerman, 1978, 1979).

Along a similar vein, people usually feel a certain amount of sadness after a failure. When they believe that failure is due to external causes—to events and people outside of themselves—they are apt to feel angry and resentful. When they instead believe that their failure is due to their own lack of ability or effort—they are likely to feel guilty or ashamed (Eccles & Wigfield, 1985; Weiner et al., 1978, 1979). People who attribute failure to internal causes, and especially to their lack of ability, often have lower self-esteem as a result (Covington, Spratt, & Omelich, 1980).

Expectations for Future Success or Failure

When people attribute their successes and failures to stable factors, they will expect their future performance to be similar to their current performance. In this situation, success leads to an anticipation of future success, and failure breeds an expectation of more failure to come. In contrast, when people attribute their successes and failures to *un*stable factors—for example, to effort or luck—then their current success rate will have less influence on their expectation for future success (Dweck, 1978; Fennema, 1987; Schunk, 1990; Weiner, 1986). The most optimistic individuals—those who have the highest expectations for future success—are the ones who attribute their successes to stable factors (such as innate ability) and their failures to unstable yet controllable factors (such as lack of effort) (Eccles [Parsons], 1983; Fennema, 1987; Murray & Jackson, 1982/83; Schunk, 1990; Weiner, 1984).

We should note here that, as children grow older, they change their beliefs about the stability of intelligence and ability. When they first enter school, they typically believe that ability is a function of effort, and therefore is an unstable and controllable entity. However, as they progress through the elementary grades, they begin to view ability as an inherited characteristic that they either do or do not possess—thus, as something that is stable and uncontrollable (Dweck, 1986; Paris & Byrnes, 1989; Ruble, 1980; Schunk, 1990). As you might predict, then, younger children who experience a temporary failure are far more optimistic about their chances for future success than are older children and adolescents (Dweck & Elliott, 1983; Eccles & Wigfield, 1985; Paris & Byrnes, 1989; Stipek & Gralinski, 1990).

We should also note a difference between males and females that appears consistently in research studies (Deaux, 1984; Durkin, 1987; Dweck, 1978; Fennema, 1987; Huston, 1983; Stipek & Gralinski, 1990). Males are more likely to attribute their successes to ability and their failures to lack of effort, thus having the attitude that *I know I can do this because I have the ability*. Females show the reverse pattern: They attribute their successes to effort and their failures to lack of ability, believing that *I don't know if I can keep on doing it, because I'm not very good at this type of thing*. This gender difference is evident even when males' and females' previous levels of achievement are the same; we are especially likely to see it for stereotypically "male" activities such as mathematics and sports (Eccles & Jacobs, 1986; Eccles, Jacobs, Harold-Goldsmith, Jayaratne, & Yee, 1989; Stipek, 1984). As a result, males set higher expectations for themselves than females do, particularly in traditionally masculine arenas.

Effort and Persistence

When people believe that their failures are due to their own lack of effort—that they do have the ability to succeed if they try hard enough—they are likely to exert more effort in future situations and to persist in the face of difficulty. When they instead attribute failure to a lack of innate ability (they couldn't do it even if they tried), they give up easily and sometimes can't even perform tasks they have previously accomplished successfully (Brophy, 1986; Dweck, 1978; Eccles [Parsons], 1983; Feather, 1982; Rowe, 1983; Weiner, 1984). Students with a history of academic failure are especially likely to attribute their classroom difficulties to low ability, and they often stop trying as a result (Pressley, Borkowski, & Schneider, 1987).

Learning Strategies

People's attributions and resulting expectations for future performance clearly affect the cognitive strategies they apply to learning tasks. Students who expect to succeed in the classroom and believe that academic success is a result of their own doing are more likely to apply effective study strategies when trained in their use (Palmer & Goetz, 1988; Pressley, Borkowski, & Schneider, 1987). These students are also more likely to seek their teacher's assistance when they don't understand course material, and to attend extra help sessions when they need them (Ames, 1983; Ames & Lau, 1982). And students with high expectations for success are more likely to approach problem solving tasks in a logical, systematic, and meaningful fashion (Tyler, 1958). In contrast, students who expect failure and believe that their academic performance is largely out of their hands often reject effective learning and problem-solving strategies in favor of rote learning approaches.

Future Choices

As you might expect, individuals whose attributions lead them to expect success in a particular subject area are more likely to pursue that area—for example, by enrolling in more courses in the same discipline (Dweck, 1986; Eccles [Parsons], 1984; Stipek & Gralinski, 1990; Weiner, 1986). Individuals who believe their chances for future success in an activity are slim will avoid that activity whenever they can. And when people don't continue to pursue an activity, they can't possibly get better at it.

Self-efficacy

In our culture, young children, particularly those in kindergarten and first grade, tend to believe they have the ability to do well in school if they expend a reasonable amount of effort (Dweck & Elliott, 1983; Stipek & Gralinski, 1990). As students get older, many of them increasingly begin to attribute their successes and failures to inherited intelligence or natural talent—things they believe are stable and beyond their control. If these students are usually successful at school activities, they come to believe that they have high ability; in other words, they develop a high sense of self-efficacy for academic tasks. On the other hand, if students experience frequent failure in their schoolwork, and especially if they attribute this failure to low ability rather than to lack of effort or poor study strategies, they may develop low self-efficacy concerning their competence in academic subjects (Dweck, 1986; Dweck & Elliott, 1983; Eccles [Parsons], 1983; Schunk, 1990).

This state of affairs is likely to lead to a self-fulfilling prophecy. As we discovered in Chapter 7, people with low self-efficacy choose less challenging tasks, give up more easily, and ultimately learn and achieve at lower levels than their more self-confident peers. As a result, they experience few of the successes they need to feel more efficacious. Furthermore, children with low self-efficacy tend to attribute the successes they do achieve to external factors while attributing failures to internal factors, thereby giving themselves little credit for the things they do well and blaming themselves for the things they do poorly (Ickes & Layden, 1978).

Responses to Failure Situations

As we have seen, many people believe that ability is an uncontrollable, stable characteristic—a built-in, "natural" talent. Many also believe that there is an inverse relationship between ability and effort: Success with little effort reflects high ability, and success that comes only with a great deal of effort is a sign of low ability (Barker & Graham, 1987; Covington & Omelich, 1979; Dweck & Elliott, 1983; Eccles [Parsons], 1983; Graham, 1990). These beliefs are especially prevalent when people have performance goals rather than learning goals (see Table 18–1).

For such individuals, effort is probably a "double-edged sword" (Covington & Omelich, 1979; Covington, Spratt, & Omelich, 1980; Eccles & Wigfield, 1985). Those who perceive themselves to have low ability are in a no-win situation. If they don't try hard, failure is inevitable. If they *do* try hard and fail anyway, they look "stupid," at least in their own eyes. Many of them will therefore not try very hard, perhaps as a way of saving face and hiding the low ability they believe they have (Covington & Beery, 1976; Covington et al., 1980; Dweck, 1986; Eccles & Wigfield, 1985; Jagacinski & Nicholls, 1990; Murray & Jackson, 1982/83; Schunk, 1990). They may also decide that the activity isn't worth doing—in other words, they will attach little value to it (Covington & Beery, 1976; Eccles & Wigfield, 1985).

Attribution theorists propose that people respond most favorably to failure situations when they attribute these failures to internal, unstable, and controllable variables such as effort and strategies (Clifford, 1984; Curtis & Graham, 1991; Pressley, Borkowski, & Schneider, 1987). But blaming lack of effort alone can backfire. Individuals who try hard and still fail are likely to reach the conclusion that they have low ability—that they simply don't have what it takes. Therefore, it is more beneficial to attribute failure to strategies as well—to believe that they could succeed if they did things *differently* (Curtis & Graham, 1991; Pressley, Borkowski, & Schneider, 1987). Such attributions often characterize good students, who know that they need not only work hard, but also work strategically (Brophy, 1987; Pressley, Borkowski, & Schneider, 1987; Weinstein, Hagen, & Meyer, 1991).

Why do different people attribute the same events to different causes? For example, why does one individual believe that a failure is merely a temporary setback due to an inappropriate strategy, while another attributes the same failure to low ability, and still another believes it to be the result of someone else's capricious and unpredictable actions? Let's look at variables affecting the development of different attributions.

Factors Influencing the Development of Attributions

Researchers have identified at least five variables that influence the development of different attributions for success and failure: past successes and failures, the degree to which successes and failures have been followed by reinforcement or punishment, situational cues, the expectations that others communicate, and the attributions that others assign to one's performance.

Past Successes and Failures

As you might expect, the attributions people develop result partially from their previous success and failure experiences (Klein, 1990; Paris & Byrnes, 1989; Pressley, Borkowski, & Schneider, 1987; Schunk, 1990; Stipek, 1988). Those who have tried and succeeded in the past are more likely to believe that success is due to internal factors such as effort or high ability. Those who have tried and failed, or who have had an inconsistent pattern of successes and failures, are likely to believe that success is due to something beyond their control—perhaps to an ability they don't possess, or to such external factors as a tough break or poor instruction.

When we consider students in the classroom, metacognition plays a role here as well. In Chapter 15, we discovered that students often think they have learned something they in fact have *not* learned; in other words, they have an *illusion of knowing*. When these students do poorly on an exam, they cannot attribute their performance to internal factors—after all, they studied hard and so "know" the material. Instead, they are likely to attribute it to such external factors as bad luck, exam difficulty, or teacher capriciousness (Horgan, 1990).

Reinforcement and Punishment

Generally speaking, children are more likely to attribute events to internal, controllable causes when adults reinforce their successes but don't punish their failures. Conversely, children are more likely to make external attributions when adults punish failures and ignore successes (Katkovsky et al., 1967). It appears that people are more likely to accept responsibility for their failures if others don't made a big deal of them.

Situational Cues

Characteristics specific to a particular situation may influence the attributions that people make. Features of the task being performed are one influential characteristic; for example, complex math problems (e.g., those that include more numbers) are perceived as being more difficult, and so failure to solve those problems can readily be attributed to task difficulty rather than internal causes (Schunk, 1990). The performance of others provides another cue; for example, a failure is apt to be attributed to task difficulty if everyone else is failing, whereas it is more likely to be attributed to an internal source—such as lack of ability—if others are succeeding (Schunk, 1990; Weiner, 1984).

Others' Expectations

Other people communicate their beliefs about an individual's ability, and thus their expectations for the individual's performance, in a variety of subtle ways. For example, teachers who hold high expectations for students' performance are likely to teach more material and more difficult material, insist on high student performance, give students more opportunities to respond to questions, rephrase questions when students are having trouble answering them, and provide specific feedback about the strengths and weaknesses of various responses (Brophy & Good, 1970; Cooper, 1979; Harris & Rosenthal, 1985). In contrast, teachers who hold low expectations for their students often present easy rather than challenging tasks, give students more assistance than necessary, accept low levels of performance, criticize incorrect answers to questions, and overlook good performance when it occurs (Brophy & Good, 1970; Cooper, 1979; Graham, 1991; Graham & Barker, 1990; Schunk, 1989b). Minority students with a history of academic failure are especially likely to be the recipients of such low-ability signals (Graham, 1990).

To some extent, teachers' expectations reflect the performance students have previously demonstrated. Yet even when several students all have the same history of success and failure, teachers and other adults may hold different expectations for each of these students, and their expectations in turn lead to different student attributions and varying levels of performance (Brophy & Good, 1970; Eccles & Wigfield, 1985; Eccles [Parsons] et al., 1983; Miller, Brickman, & Bolen, 1975; Murray & Jackson, 1982/83; Palardy, 1969; Yee & Eccles, 1988). As an illustration, a study by Miller and his colleagues (1975) demonstrates the effect of teacher expectations on students' littering behavior. One group of fifth graders was repeatedly labeled neat and clean; for example, a poster of a Peanuts character on the wall proclaimed that "We are Andersen's litter-conscious class," and, after noticing a piece of litter on the floor, the teacher stated that "Our class is clean and would not do that." For a second group of students, persuasion was used in various forms to alter littering behavior; for example, a poster of a Peanuts character advocated, "Don't be a litterbug," and the teacher explained why garbage should always be thrown away (e.g., it draws flies and endangers health). To test the relative effects of the two treatments, the experimenters provided opportunities for the students to litter (by distributing candy wrapped in cellophane and, two weeks later, by handing out toy puzzles in disposable plastic containers); they also scattered several candy wrappers and plastic puzzle containers on the floor while the students were at recess. A short time later, the experimenters counted the number of candy wrappers and plastic containers that remained on the floor: Students who had consistently been labeled neat and clean left significantly fewer pieces of litter than those who had specifically been persuaded not to litter.

With the effects of teacher expectations in mind, we should note that teacher assistance, while often a valuable source of scaffolding on difficult tasks, may be counterproductive if students don't really need it. When students struggle temporarily with a task, the unsolicited help of their teacher may communicate the message that they have low ability and little control regarding their own successes and failures. In contrast, allowing students to struggle on their own for a reasonable time conveys the belief that students do have the ability to succeed on their own (Graham, 1990; Graham & Barker, 1990; Weiner, 1984).

Others' Attributions

Just as we ourselves form attributions regarding the causes of our performance, those around us may form their own opinions regarding why we have succeeded or failed (Eccles & Wigfield, 1985; Graham, 1990; Seligman, 1991; Weiner, 1984). Research indicates that children's attributions for their own successes and failures are often similar to the attributions that parents and teachers assign to those successes and failures (Dweck, Davidson, Nelson, & Enna, 1978; Lueptow, 1984; Parsons, Adler, & Kaczala, 1982; Schunk, 1982; Yee & Eccles, 1988).

In some cases, other people communicate their attributions verbally and explicitly. For example, consider the things a teacher might say about a student's success:

- You did it! You're so smart!
- That's wonderful. Your hard work has really paid off, hasn't it?
- You've done very well. It's clear that you really know how to study.
- Terrific! This is really your lucky day!

Consider, also, the statements a teacher might make about a student's failure:

- Hmmm, maybe this just isn't something you're good at. Perhaps we should try something different.
- Why don't you practice a little more and then try again?
- Let's see if we can come up with some study strategies that might work better for you.
- Maybe you're just having a bad day.

All of these are well-intended comments, presumably designed to make a student feel good, but notice the different attributions they imply. In some cases, success or failure is attributed to controllable (and therefore changeable) student behaviors—that is, to hard work or lack of practice, or to the use of effective or ineffective study strategies. But in other cases, the student's success or failure is attributed to uncontrollable ability—that is, to being smart or not "good at" something. And in still other cases the student's success is attributed to external, uncontrollable causes—that is, to a lucky break or a bad day.

Other individuals may also communicate their attributions indirectly through the things they say and do. For example, when teachers express anger about students' poor performance, they convey the message that students have sufficient ability to master the task and simply aren't trying hard enough. But when teachers express pity for the same performance, they communicate their belief that students' low ability is the reason for their failure (Graham, 1984, 1990, 1991; Weiner, 1984). Frequent praise is often a message that students' successes are due to their efforts; however, by praising students for *easy* tasks, teachers may simultaneously convey the message that success wasn't expected—in other words, that students have low ability (Graham, 1990, 1991; Schunk, 1989b; Stipek, 1988).

As an illustration, Barker and Graham (1987) asked 4- to 12-year-old children to watch a videotape depicting two boys either solving single digit math problems at the chalkboard or throwing balls through a large hoop in the gymnasium; the two tasks appeared to be easy ones for the boys to accomplish. Some of the subjects saw a videotape in which both boys succeeded; the teacher praised one boy (e.g., "Great job!"), while giving the other only neutral feedback (e.g., "Correct"). Other subjects saw a videotape in which the two boys failed at their task; one was criticized for this failure (e.g., "What's the matter with you? That's not the right answer!") or, again, given neutral feedback (e.g., "No, not quite"). The subjects were subsequently asked to rate the two boys for either intelligence (for the math problem videos) or throwing ability (for the ball throwing videos) on a five-point scale. Younger subjects (4- and 5-year-olds) concluded that the boy praised for his success had higher ability than the other boy; in contrast, older subjects (11- and 12-year-olds) concluded that the praised boy had *lower* ability. At the same time, younger subjects deduced that the boy criticized for his failure had lower ability, while older subjects came to the opposite conclusion. Eight- and 9-year-old subjects assigned similar ratings to both boys in both success and failure situations. Thus, we see a developmental change as children grow older: They become increasingly likely to interpret praise for an easy success as a sign of low ability and blame for failure on an easy task as an indication of high ability.

Operant conditioning theorists propose that praise is a form of reinforcement; hence, it should increase the behavior it follows. Here we see an opposing viewpoint: Praise may sometimes be counterproductive, at least for easy tasks. When it communicates low ability, students may be unwilling to exert much effort on later tasks. Praise for students' effort is only likely to be effective when students *have* exerted that effort.

For reasons we have just identified, different people may interpret the same events in very different ways. Over time, students gradually develop predictable patterns of attributions and expectations for their future performance. Some remain optimistic, confident that they can master new tasks and succeed in a variety of endeavors. But others, either unsure of their own chances for success or else convinced that they *can't* succeed, display a growing sense of futility. Theorists have characterized this difference among students as being one of a mastery orientation versus learned helplessness.

Explanatory Style: Mastery Orientation Versus Learned Helplessness

As we discussed the effects of aversive stimuli in Chapter 6, we examined the phenomenon of learned helplessness: When organisms repeatedly encounter aversive stimuli they cannot avoid, escape, or terminate, they eventually give up and passively accept those stimuli. Although much of the early research on learned helplessness involved animals, this concept has been incorporated into cognitive theorists' notion of explanatory style.

A person's **explanatory style** is the general way in which the individual interprets daily events and consequences. Some people typically attribute their accomplishments to their own abilities and efforts; they have an *I can do it* attitude known as a **mastery orientation**. Others attribute successes to outside and uncontrollable factors and believe that their failures reflect a lack of ability; they have an *I can't do it* attitude known as **learned helplessness** (Dweck, 1986; Dweck & Licht, 1980; Dweck & Reppucci, 1973; Eccles & Wigfield, 1985; Wood, Schau, & Fiedler, 1990). You should think of this distinction as a continuum of individual differences rather than a complete dichotomy. You might also look at it as a difference between *optimists* and *pessimists* (Peterson, 1990; Seligman, 1991).

To illustrate, consider these two boys, keeping in mind that both have the same ability level:

- Jerry is an enthusiastic, energetic learner. He enjoys working hard at school activities and takes obvious pleasure in doing well. He is always looking for a challenge and especially likes to solve the "brain teaser" problems that his teacher assigns as extra credit work each day. He can't always solve the problems, but he takes failure in stride and is eager for more problems the following day.
- Jason is an anxious, fidgety student. He doesn't seem to have much confidence in his ability to accomplish school tasks successfully. In fact, he is always underestimating what he can do; even when he has succeeded, he doubts that he can do it again. He seems to prefer filling out drill-and-practice worksheets that help him practice skills he's already mastered rather than attempting new tasks and problems. As for those daily brain teasers, he sometimes takes a stab at them, but he gives up quickly if the answer isn't readily apparent.

Jerry exhibits a mastery orientation: He clearly has his life (and his attributions) under control, and he is optimistic about his future performance. In contrast, Jason displays learned helplessness: He believes that challenging tasks are out of his reach and beyond his control, and he expects failure rather than success.

Researchers have identified a number of ways in which people with a mastery orientation differ from those with learned helplessness. For example, in an academic context, those with a mastery orientation tend to perform better in the classroom than we would predict from their aptitude test scores and previous grade point averages (Seligman, 1991). In an athletic context, optimists bounce back from a lost game more readily, and overcome injuries more quickly, than do equally capable but more pessimistic athletes (Peterson, 1990).

Table 18–3 lists additional differences between a mastery orientation and learned helplessness. As you can see from this table, people with a mastery orientation behave in ways that lead to higher achievement over the long run: They set high goals, seek challenging situations, and persist in the face of failure. Students feeling learned helplessness behave very differently: Because they underestimate their own ability, they set goals they can easily accomplish, avoid situations likely to maximize their learning and growth, and respond to failure in counterproductive ways.

In a nutshell, people with a mastery orientation attribute their successes to internal, global, and somewhat stable factors, and they believe that the reasons for their failures are temporary and often within their control. In contrast, those with learned helplessness attribute their successes to external and uncontrollable factors, and they interpret their failures as reflecting a relatively pervasive and permanent lack of ability.

Table 18–3
Characteristics of a mastery orientation versus learned helplessness

People with a Mastery Orientation	People with Learned Helplessness
Have higher self-esteem and greater self-efficacy about their chances for success	Have low self-esteem and poor self-efficacy
Set high goals for themselves	Set low, easy goals for themselves
Prefer new and challenging tasks	Prefer easy tasks and tasks they have already completed successfully
Strive for success	Try to avoid failure
Believe that prior successes are an indication of high ability and future success	Don't see prior successes as indicative of high ability and future success; *do* see prior failures as an indication of low ability and future failure
Accurately estimate their number of prior successes	Underestimate their prior successes; may even forget about them
View failure as a challenge to be met	Define themselves as a "failure" when they fail
Persist when facing difficulty; try to determine the source of difficulty; seek assistance if needed	Become anxious and discouraged when facing difficulty; use ineffective strategies
Increase effort and concentration after failure	Decrease effort and concentration after failure; give up quickly
Take pride in their accomplishments	Don't take pride in their accomplishments because they don't believe they *caused* them
Perform and achieve at higher levels	Perform and achieve at lower levels

Sources: Abramson, Seligman, & Teasdale, 1978; Diener & Dweck, 1978; Dweck, 1975, 1986; Dweck & Licht, 1980; Dweck & Reppucci, 1973; Peterson, 1990; Peterson & Barrett, 1987; Seligman, 1991; Wood, Schau, & Fiedler, 1990.

Can people's attributions and explanatory styles be changed? Let's look at what research tells us about this question.

Changing Attributions

A number of studies have shown that, for school-age children at least, attributions can be altered, with more persistence in the face of failure as a result (Andrews & Debus, 1978; Chapin & Dyck, 1976; Dweck, 1975; Fowler & Peterson, 1981). In these **attribution retraining** studies, children are asked to engage in a particular task (e.g., reading difficult sentences, solving arithmetic problems, or constructing geometric puzzles), with occasional failures interspersed among more frequent successes. Within this context, one viable approach for changing attributions is for an experimenter to interpret each success in terms of the effort a child has exerted and each failure in terms of insufficient effort (Chapin & Dyck, 1976; Dweck, 1975; Fowler & Peterson, 1981). Another effective approach is to reinforce children for attributing their *own* successes and failures to effort or a lack thereof (Andrews & Debus, 1978; Fowler & Peterson, 1981).

Early studies focused on effort attributions, but later studies indicated that effort attributions are not always the most beneficial attributions for children to acquire. For example, greater self-efficacy may result when an experimenter attributes a child's successes (but not failures) to ability rather than effort (e.g., "You're good at this") (Schunk, 1983a). And attributions to effective and ineffective learning strategies (for success and failure, respectively) are often more productive than effort attributions, particularly when such attribution retraining accompanies a study strategies training program (Pressley, Borkowski, & Schneider, 1987; Weinstein et al., 1991).

Despite the apparent success of attribution retraining programs, we should take heed of Paris' (1990) cautionary note: people's views of themselves and their abilities don't easily change overnight. For those with a history of learned helplessness, attribution training probably needs to be an ongoing endeavor rather than a one shot deal.

Ultimately, people are most likely to be optimistic about their futures when they believe they can control their destinies and have the confidence that they can succeed in their endeavors. In the next few pages, we look more closely at the role that feelings of self-determination and competence play in human motivation.

SELF-DETERMINATION AND COMPETENCE

As you should recall from the preceding chapter, intrinsic motivation has several advantages over extrinsic motivation. For instance, when people are intrinsically motivated, they are more likely to pursue a task on their own initiative, keep their attention focused on it, learn meaningfully, and persist in the face of failure. Edward Deci and Richard Ryan (1985, 1987; also see McCombs, 1988, and Spaulding, 1992) have proposed that intrinsic motivation is most likely to be present when two conditions exist. First of all, individuals must believe that they can to some extent choose and regulate the course of their lives; in other words, they must have a sense of **self-determination**. Second, individuals must believe they are capable of successfully executing the tasks before them; that is, they must have a sense of **competence** (we have previously called this *self-efficacy*). When both conditions are present, people experience greater pleasure and satisfaction in performing a task.

Let's look more closely at the concepts of self-determination and competence. As we do so, we'll identify a number of variables likely to promote intrinsic motivation.

Self-Determination

I should first point out that Deci's and Ryan's concept of self-determination over-laps with, yet is also somewhat different from, attribution theory's notion of controllability (Deci & Ryan, 1987). Attribution to controllable factors relates to our beliefs that environmental events and circumstances are within our purview to influence and alter. In contrast, self-determination refers to our beliefs that we can autonomously choose our behaviors and, ultimately, our fate (also see deCharms, 1968). For example, when we think "I *want* to do this" or "I'd *find it valuable* to do that," we have a high sense of self-determination. In contrast, when we think "I *have to*" or "I *should*," we are telling ourselves that someone or something else is making our choices for us.

Deci and Ryan (1987) have identified several variables that influence people's sense of self-determination one way or the other. Here we will look at six of them: choices, threats and deadlines, controlling statements, surveillance and evaluation, feedback, and extrinsic rewards.

Choices

People have a greater sense of self-determination, and are therefore more intrinsically motivated, when they are able to make choices, within reasonable limits, about the things they do (Deci & Ryan, 1987; Morgan, 1984; Stipek, 1988). For example, in an early study by Lewin, Lippitt, and White (1939), 10-year-old boys participating in after-school recreational programs were in one of three experimental conditions. In the *autocratic* group, adults made all the decisions about what the boys would do. In the *laissez-faire* group, the boys did as they pleased, with little if any adult input. In the *democratic* group, the adults and boys engaged in group decision making about daily activities. The boys were most productive in the democratic setting: They showed greater initiative and on-task behavior related to group projects, and they were less likely to be aggressive toward other group members. Other researchers have found similar results in classroom settings. Thus, when students have choices (again, within appropriate limits) about the activities in which they engage, they show greater interest and involvement in their classwork (Morgan, 1984; Stipek, 1988).

Threats and Deadlines

Threats (e.g., "Do this or else!") and deadlines (e.g., "This is due by January 15—no exceptions!") are typically experienced as controlling people's behaviors. As a result, they lessen self-determination and intrinsic motivation (Clifford, 1990; Deci & Ryan, 1987).

Controlling Statements

While not necessarily threatening in nature, some things that people say to us nevertheless convey the message that others control our fate. As an example, in an experiment by Koestner, Ryan, Bernieri, and Holt (1984), first and second graders were asked to paint a picture of a house they would like to live in. The children were given the materials they needed—a paintbrush, a set of watercolor paints, two sheets of paper, and several paper towels—then told some rules about how to proceed. For some children (the controlling-limits condition), restrictions described things they could and couldn't do, as follows:

> Before you begin, I want to tell you some things that you will have to do. They are rules that we have about painting. You have to keep the paints clean. You can paint only on this small sheet of paper, so don't spill any paint on the big sheet. And you must wash out your brush and wipe it with a paper towel before you switch to a new color of paint, so that you don't get the colors all mixed up. In general, I want you to be a good boy (girl) and don't make a mess with the paints. (Koestner et al., 1984, p. 239)

For other children (the informational-limits condition), restrictions were presented only as information, like this:

> Before you begin, I want to tell you some things about the way painting is done here. I know that sometimes it's really fun to just slop the paint around, but here the materials and room need to be kept nice for the other children who will use them. The smaller sheet is for you to paint on, the larger sheet is a border to be kept clean. Also, the paints need to be kept clean, so the brush is to be washed and wiped in the paper towel before switching colors. I know that some kids don't like to be neat all the time, but now is a time for being neat. (Koestner et al., 1984, p. 239)

Each child was allowed 10 minutes of painting time. The experimenter then took the child's painting to another room, saying he would return in a few minutes. As he departed, he placed two more sheets of paper on the child's table, saying, "You can paint some more on this piece of paper if you like, or, if you want, you can play with the puzzles over on that table." In the experimenter's absence, the child was surreptitiously observed and painting time was measured. Children in the informational-limits condition spent more time painting (so were apparently more intrinsically motivated to paint), and their paintings were judged to be more creative, than was true for their counterparts in the controlling-limits condition.

Surveillance and Evaluation

People who know they are going to be evaluated on their performance have a lower sense of self-determination and, as a result, are less intrinsically motivated (Clifford, 1990; Deci & Ryan, 1987; Harter, Whitesell, & Kowalski, 1992). In fact, the mere presence of a potential evaluator undermines intrinsic motivation (Clifford, 1990; Deci & Ryan, 1987). For example, even though I have a mediocre singing voice, I like to sing and will often do so when no one else is around to hear me (e.g., when I'm mowing the lawn or driving alone on business). But my intrinsic motivation to sing vanishes when anyone else is in earshot (fortunately for the "anyone else").

In Chapter 13, we discovered that classroom tests often promote long-term memory storage. Among other things, tests encourage students to review classroom material more regularly and process information more thoroughly. But here we see the down side of tests: They may undermine students' intrinsic motivation to learn (Benware & Deci, 1984; Grolnick & Ryan, 1987; Spaulding, 1992; Stipek, 1988). A study by Benware and Deci (1984) illustrates this point well. College students studied an article about brain functioning under either of two conditions: Some studied it with the expectation of being tested on it, while others studied it with the expectation that they would have to teach the material to someone else (a presumably nonevaluative situation). Compared with those in the first group, students in the second group enjoyed their learning experience more, found the material more interesting, and learned it more meaningfully.

Feedback

In Chapter 4, I talked about positive feedback as a form of reinforcement; from an operant conditioning perspective, then, the behavior it follows should increase in frequency. But Deci and Ryan tell us the effects of feedback are not so simple. Positive feedback is most likely to enhance performance when it affirms an individual's feelings of competence; it is *un*likely to enhance performance when it is communicated in a controlling fashion (also see Ryan, Mims, & Koestner, 1983). For example, I respond to my children more favorably when they tell me:

> *Boy, Mom, these brownies you made are really good.*

than when they say:

> *It's a good thing you finally baked something around here, Ma. All my friends' mothers do it all the time.*

Compliments about things I do well are always welcome. But statements about what "good" parents are supposed to do make me feel as if I'm not really in charge in my own home. Furthermore, I have no intention of letting my children tell *me* how to behave.

Just as is true for positive feedback, Deci and Ryan propose that negative feedback can either enhance or inhibit behavior. If it provides information about how to improve in the future, thereby presuming an individual's ability to be successful eventually, it is likely to facilitate performance. If it instead imposes a feeling of outside control or conveys the message that an individual is incompetent, it is apt to undermine any intrinsic motivation to continue engaging in a task.

Extrinsic Rewards

In Chapter 5, one of the concerns I expressed about using extrinsic reinforcement is that it may undermine the intrinsic reinforcement that an activity provides. Deci and Ryan propose that extrinsic reinforcers are most likely to have this adverse influence when people perceive the reinforcers as controlling or manipulating their behavior rather than as providing information about their progress (also see Spaulding, 1992). Rewards are unlikely to be beneficial, at least over the long run, when people interpret them as bribes or as limits on their freedom (Deci & Ryan, 1985, 1987; Lepper & Hodell, 1989; Ryan et al., 1983).[1]

On the other hand, we must remind ourselves that reinforcement may be useful when desirable behaviors will apparently not occur any other way. People may initially find a new activity difficult or frustrating and therefore need external encouragement to continue. However, with continuing practice, their competence and skill are likely to improve, and they may eventually find the activity intrinsically rewarding.

When environmental circumstances and events lead us to conclude that we have little involvement in determining the course of our lives, we may comply with external demands but are unlikely to have much intrinsic motivation (Deci & Ryan, 1987). As an example, I think back to 1989 when the Berlin Wall came down: East German workers reportedly showed little initiative or stick-to-it-iveness on the job, quite possibly because they had for so long been told exactly what to do and what not to do under the Communist regime. Furthermore, when our reasons for doing something lie outside of ourselves, we are likely to undertake the easy things we know we can do rather than challenges at which we might fail (Stipek, 1988).

In contrast, when circumstances and events confirm our feelings of self-determination, we are likely to engage in tasks for long periods; to think meaningfully, creatively, and flexibly about those tasks; and to experience pleasure in our activities (Deci, 1992; Deci & Ryan, 1987). Furthermore, we are likely to undertake the challenges that will maximize our long-term learning and development (Deci & Ryan, 1985).

Competence

In Chapter 7, we learned that we are more inclined to engage in an activity when we believe we are or can become competent at that activity—in other words, when we have high self-efficacy. Here we see an additional benefit of self-perceived competence: It promotes interest and intrinsic motivation. Conversely, as you might guess, feelings of incompetence lead to decreased interest and motivation (Deci, 1992; Deci & Ryan, 1985, 1987; Harter et al., 1992).

---

[1]Deci and Ryan don't specifically talk about the informational or controlling messages that punishment might communicate, but we can logically deduce a similar pattern here as well. Certainly punishment can be presented in either of two ways—as a means of control or as a source of information about appropriate behavior. As we discovered in Chapter 6, punishment is more effective when it is accompanied by reasons (information) about why the punished behavior is unacceptable.

As we discussed self-efficacy in Chapter 7, we identified three variables that help us believe we can succeed at a task. One such variable is persuasion—someone else encouraging us and convincing us that we can do it. A second is the successful performance of our peers; after all, if they can do it, so can we. But ultimately the most important variable affecting feelings of competence and self-efficacy is our own success, success, and more success.

When we feel incompetent, no amount of self-determination is going to make us feel intrinsically motivated to do something. To show you what I mean, let's consider a study by Spaulding (1992, pp. 54–55). Seventh grade students, including some who believed themselves to be competent writers and others who did not, were asked to write an essay concerning what they had learned in English class that year. Some students were asked to write it for their teacher, someone they believed would evaluate their work; hence, this group experienced low self-determination. Other students were asked to write the essay for the researcher so that she could tell future teachers what students study in English; without the threat of evaluation looming over them, these students presumably experienced relatively high self-determination. As the students wrote the essay, Spaulding measured their task engagement (and, indirectly, their intrinsic motivation) in several different ways. Students who believed themselves to be competent writers showed greater intrinsic motivation in the high self-determination condition—that is, when writing for the researcher. In contrast, students who believed they were poor writers were more engaged in the task when writing for the teacher; apparently self-determination in the absence of perceived competence did not promote intrinsic motivation.

As you can see, self-determination and competence go hand in hand. We are most likely to be intrinsically motivated when we believe we have some choice about what we do and simultaneously have the confidence that we can successfully accomplish the tasks we undertake. Learning and intrinsic motivation are parts of a "vicious" cycle: Learning enhances our competence, which in turn enhances our intrinsic motivation, which (as we have seen) enables us to process information and learn more effectively (Deci & Ryan, 1985; Harter & Connell, 1984). We couldn't ask for a better situation.

EFFECTS OF CHALLENGE AND COMPETITION

In various places throughout the book I have alluded to the positive effects of challenging tasks. For example, as we discovered in Chapter 8, challenges promote cognitive development. From Piaget's perspective, accommodation occurs and new schemas emerge only when events cannot be readily assimilated into existing schemas. From Vygotsky's perspective, tasks within a child's zone of proximal development are optimal for long-term cognitive growth. Furthermore, as we learned in Chapter 15, students are most likely to develop maximally effective metacognitive strategies when the learning tasks they face are not easily accomplished using such simplistic strategies as repetition and rote memorization.

Competition and other forms of social comparison also play a role in learning. For example, when we examined the "good behavior game" in Chapter 5, we discovered that, when two groups of students compete for privileges based on good behavior, students in both groups show marked improvements in classroom behavior. Furthermore, as we learned in Chapter 7, students develop high or low self-efficacy partially as a function of what they see their peers able to do.

Challenge and competition have implications for human motivation as well as learning. Let's look at both of these within the context of the cognitive motivational factors we've explored in this chapter.

Challenge

As I defined it in the preceding chapter, a challenge is a situation in which individuals believe that, although they risk possible failure, they are likely to succeed if they exert sufficient effort. From a motivational standpoint, the advantages of challenges are three-fold.

• *Challenges heighten interest and minimize boredom* (Brophy, 1987; Spaulding, 1992). We typically become bored with easy tasks, yet we are frustrated by tasks at which we always seem to fail. Challenges provide a happy medium: They have those unexpected little twists and turns that maintain our interest, but we know that, with persistence, we can achieve success.

• *It is difficult to attribute success on challenging tasks to external factors such as task ease or luck* (Clifford, 1990; C. Peterson, 1988, 1990). When we succeed at a very easy task—one on which we have exerted very little effort—we are likely to attribute our success to the fact that, hey, anybody can do it. When we succeed at an extremely difficult task—something we thought ourselves incapable of doing—we might attribute our success to good luck or somebody else's assistance. However, when we succeed on a challenging task—one that we know we can do if we try long and hard enough—we can't dismiss it as being due to task ease, and we have little reason to attribute our performance to luck or assistance. Our best alternative is to attribute our hard-won success to our own efforts and clever strategies.

• *Success at challenging tasks promotes a greater sense of competence and self-efficacy* (Clifford, 1990; Deci & Ryan, 1985). Take a minute to do this little exercise:

> *Write the numbers 1 to 10 on a piece of paper. See if you can do it in less than 10 seconds.*

Were you successful? If so, how good does your success make you feel? I myself just did the task in about four seconds' time, and I had little reason to feel particularly proud. After all, I'm 45 years old; if I can't write these numbers quickly and accurately by now, something must be terribly wrong.

Success on easy tasks, while virtually guaranteed, does little to enhance our sense of competence and self-efficacy. Sure, we can do it, but so can anyone else. On the other hand, challenges are not so easily accomplished: Perhaps we have failed to accomplish them in the past, or perhaps we know others who have failed. When we successfully meet a challenge, we must obviously be pretty competent folks. Success on a challenging task, then, gives us feelings of satisfaction that are not possible with an easier one. Furthermore, because it enhances our feelings of competency, it also increases our intrinsic motivation (Clifford, 1990; Deci & Ryan, 1985).

When are people most likely to take on new risks and challenges? Theorists suggest that conditions such as these are optimal:

- There are few, if any, penalties for errors.
- The same rewards cannot be obtained by engaging in easier tasks, or rewards are greater for challenging tasks than for easy ones.
- Standards for success are realistic for each individual.
- People attribute their successes to their own ability, efforts, and strategies.
- People have a sense of self-determination and a sense of competence (Clifford, 1990; Deci & Ryan, 1985; Dweck & Elliott, 1983; Stipek, 1988).

A moment ago, I stated that success on challenging tasks promotes feelings of competence. But the last of the conditions I just listed indicates that the reverse is also true; that is, competence increases the challenges that people undertake. Here we see a cyclical effect similar to what we saw for learning and intrinsic motivation: Challenge promotes competence, and competence promotes challenge.

Competition

In a competitive situation, success doesn't depend on absolute mastery of a task; instead, it results from performing better than others. Competition is a pervasive element of our society. In the business world, the people who have the best ideas, make the most money, or work the longest hours are (usually) the ones who get ahead. We often see competition in recreation, too—for example, in the games we play and the athletic events we watch on television. And our democratic political system is based on competition in the most basic sense: Those who get more votes than anybody else are the ones who end up in office.

Competition is prevalent in our schools as well (Ames, 1984). We find school personnel comparing students in virtually every arena. For example, when teachers grade on the curve, their grades reflect how students stack up against one another, and only those at the top of the stack are defined as successes. When students take college aptitude tests, their test scores reflect not what they know and can do, but how their performance compares with that of their peers. Participation in sports is competitive, especially at the high school level: Even before students compete against other teams, they compete among themselves to make the team and achieve first string status. And many of the concepts we use when we talk about students' abilities—intelligence, giftedness, special needs, and so on—are defined by psychologists only in a normative sense.

What conditions promote a competitive atmosphere? One likely condition is uncertainty regarding others' expectations for our performance: In the absence of definitive criteria about what "good" performance is, we compare ourselves with our peers as a general indication of how well we are doing (Ames, 1984). A second condition, certainly, is a competitive reward structure, one that reinforces us for outperforming everyone else.

Many people are motivated by competition *if* they believe they have a reasonable chance of winning (Brophy, 1986). But competition has several negative side effects, both behavioral and cognitive, of which you should be aware.

•*Competition sometimes leads to undesirable or counterproductive behaviors* (Ames, 1984). In a competitive situation, people often behave in ways that interfere with their own learning and achievement or with the learning and achievement of others. For example, they may cheat if cheating puts them ahead of the pack. They may deny others' access to the resources necessary for success. They may have little regard for equity and fairness. And because they are accustomed to working against one another, they may have a difficult time working *with* one another cooperatively.

•*Competition promotes performance goals rather than learning goals* (Ames, 1984; Nicholls, 1984; Spaulding, 1992). When the key to success is doing better than everyone else, people will inevitably focus their attention on how good they appear to others rather than on how much they are learning. And they will define success as being better than everyone else rather than as improving their abilities and skills over time.

•*For the losers, competition promotes a low sense of competence and poor self-efficacy* (Ames, 1984; Ames & Ames, 1981). When people define success as mastery of a task or improvement in an activity over time, success is likely to come frequently and so to enhance self-efficacy. But when people instead define success as coming out on top, most will inevitably be losers. In the face of such "failure," they may understandably begin to believe themselves incompetent.

•*Competition promotes attributions to ability rather than to effort* (Ames, 1984; Stipek, 1988). Many people lose in competitive situations even when they exert a great deal of effort. They quite logically reach the conclusion that effort is not enough—that some sort of natural ability is the critical ingredient for success. Their failures, then, are due to their lack of that elusive ability, and they become pessimistic about their future prognosis for success.

As you can see, competition is not productive in situations where we want and expect *all* individuals to learn and achieve at the highest possible level. Thus, it is generally not a recommended strategy in school settings, where individual student achievement is the number one goal.

What other educational implications can we draw from what we have learned about cognitive factors in motivation? Let's take a look.

PROMOTING COGNITIONS THAT MOTIVATE

We have considered several cognitive factors that influence motivation, including goals, expectancies, values, interests, attributions, and perceptions of self-determination and competence. Teachers can help students think about and interpret classroom events in productive ways—in ways that ultimately lead students to direct their efforts and behaviors toward effective learning and classroom achievement. Here are some guidelines we can derive from cognitive views of motivation.

• *Teachers should encourage students to focus more on learning goals than on performance goals.* Performance goals—for example, completing classroom assignments, obtaining high scores on college admissions tests, and graduating from high school—are often important for students to attain. But learning goals are the ones most likely to promote effective learning and performance over the long run. Learning goals are especially motivating when they are specific ("I want to learn how to ride a bicycle"), challenging ("Writing a limerick looks difficult, but I'm sure I can do it"), and short-term ("I'm going to learn to count to 100 in French by the end of the month") (Alderman, 1990; Brophy, 1987).

Through their own classroom behaviors, teachers can demonstrate that improving and mastering skills and subject matter are the objectives most important for students to accomplish. For example, teachers can present tasks that students find valuable in and of themselves (Ames, 1992; Dweck & Elliott, 1983; Pintrich et al., 1993). They can provide mechanisms through which students may easily record and assess academic progress (Spaulding, 1992). They can communicate that mistakes are a normal part of learning and therefore to be expected (Clifford, 1990; Dweck, 1975; Dweck & Elliott, 1983). They can give specific feedback about how students can improve rather than simply assigning relatively uninformative grades (Brophy, 1986; Butler, 1987; Spaulding, 1992). And they should *not* repeatedly remind students that classwork will be evaluated and graded (Stipek, 1988).

• *Instruction should help students see value in learning subject matter.* Teachers can do many things to enable students to find value in school activities. For example, they can identify the specific knowledge and skills that students will acquire from an instructional unit (Keller, 1987). They can show how things learned in the classroom will help fulfill students' present needs and long-term goals (Brophy, 1986, 1987; Keller, 1987; Parsons, Kaczala, & Meece, 1982). They can show how they themselves value academic activities—for example, by sharing their fascination with certain topics and describing how they use the things they've learned in school (Brophy, 1987; Brophy & Alleman, 1991). And they should refrain from asking students to engage in activities with little long-term benefit: memorizing trivial facts for no good reason, reading material that is clearly beyond students' comprehension level, and so on (Brophy, 1987).

• *Students should find classroom material interesting as well as informative.* Almost all students learn more when subject matter is interesting; students with little background knowledge in the topic are especially likely to benefit (Garner et al., 1991).

Certainly teachers should capitalize on students' personal interests whenever possible (Brophy, 1986, 1987; Wlodkowski, 1978). But situational interest factors can also be incorporated into classroom subject matter and activities. For example, students typically enjoy opportunities to respond actively during a learning activity—perhaps by manipulating and experimenting with physical objects, creating new products, or discussing controversial issues with classmates (Brophy, 1987; Sadker & Sadker, 1985). They are often curious about things that are new and different and about events that are surprising and puzzling (Brophy, 1986, 1987; Lepper & Hodell, 1989; Spaulding, 1992; Stipek, 1988; Wlodkowski, 1978). They like to engage in fantasy and make-believe—for example, playing out the roles of key figures in historical events, or imagining what it must be like to be weightless in space (Brophy, 1986, 1987; Lepper & Hodell, 1989). Keep in mind, however, that adding interesting—but *non*important—information may be counterproductive, distracting students' attention from more important material (Wade, 1992).

• *Teachers should attribute students' successes to both stable and unstable internal factors, and their failures only to unstable and controllable internal factors.* To be most optimistic about their future performance, students should attribute their successes partly to stable internal factors such as natural talent (thus, they will know that success wasn't a fluke) and partly to unstable but controllable factors such as effort and strategies (thus, they will continue to work hard). At the same time, they should attribute their failures primarily to factors they can control and change.

Teachers can help promote such attributions in their students through the causes they themselves attribute to student performance (Alderman, 1990; Brophy, 1987; Schunk, 1990; Spaulding, 1992; Stipek, 1988). Consider these teacher statements as examples:

- "You've done very well. Obviously you're good at this, and you've been trying very hard to get better."
- "Your project shows a lot of talent and a lot of hard work."
- "The more you practice, the better you will get."
- "Perhaps you need to study a little bit more next time. And let me give you some suggestions on how you might study a little differently, too."

Teachers should attribute student failures solely to a lack of effort only when students clearly haven't given classroom tasks their best shot. When students fail at a task at which they have expended a great deal of effort and are then told that they didn't try hard enough, they are likely to conclude that they simply don't have the ability to perform the task successfully (Alderman, 1990; Curtis & Graham, 1991; Schunk, 1990). In many cases, it may be more productive, and probably more accurate, to attribute failures to ineffective strategies and subsequently to help students acquire more effective ones (Clifford, 1984; Curtis & Graham, 1991; Pressley, Borkowski, & Schneider, 1987; Weinstein et al., 1991).

• *Students should feel they have some self-determination with respect to classroom events.* For both pedagogical and logistical reasons, students often have little control over the things that happen in school. For example, societal needs and district curricula often dictate the objectives that students must achieve. The use of the same facilities and resources by many different students requires adhering to certain schedules. And to keep students' attention focused on school tasks, teachers must maintain some semblance of order in the classroom.

Yet there are numerous little things teachers can do to give students some sense of self-determination about classroom activities. For example, they can establish general routines and procedures that students should typically follow, thus minimizing the need to give explicit instructions for each and every assignment (Spaulding, 1992). They can inform students well ahead of time about upcoming deadlines, so that students can budget their time accordingly (Spaulding, 1992). They can ask for regular feedback about how classroom activities might be improved (Keller, 1987). They can provide opportunities to learn independently—through computer-assisted instruction, for example (Swan, Mitrani, Guerrero, Cheung, & Schoener, 1990). When the same objective can be accomplished in two or more different ways, they can give students a choice about how best to proceed (Brophy, 1987; Hennessey & Amabile, 1987; Keller, 1987; Spaulding, 1992). And when evaluation is useful in promoting academic progress, teachers can provide mechanisms (checklists, feedback sheets, etc.) through which students can evaluate *themselves* (Spaulding, 1992; Wlodkowski, 1978).

•*Feedback and other forms of extrinsic reinforcement should communicate information rather than decreasing students' sense of control.* In an ideal world, all students would be intrinsically motivated to learn in the classroom and succeed at classroom activities. But in reality, external stimuli—feedback, praise, privileges, and so on—are sometimes necessary to keep students on task.

As we discovered earlier in the chapter, reinforcement may undermine students' intrinsic motivation, particularly if it conveys the idea that adults are trying to control their behavior. Yet feedback and other forms of reinforcement can be beneficial when, instead, they communicate information about students' current performance and offer suggestions for improvement (Bangert-Drowns, Kulik, Kulik, & Morgan, 1991; Clifford, 1990; Deci & Ryan, 1985, 1987; Harris & Rosenthal, 1985). Whenever possible, teachers should provide such information immediately, so that students can store it in working memory simultaneously with their recollection of what they have just done; in this way, the two are easily integrated (Anderson, 1987).

•*Most classroom activities should be noncompetitive in nature.* In any public situation, including the classroom, people will invariably compare themselves with one another. Yet teachers can take steps to minimize the extent to which comparison and competition among students occur. For example, they can keep students' performance on classroom tasks private and confidential, minimizing the degree to which students are even aware of classmates' performance levels (Schunk, 1990; Spaulding, 1992). At any one time, they can have different students doing different things (Stipek, 1988). They can assess students' performance independently of how well classmates are doing and encourage students to assess their own performance in a similar manner (Spaulding, 1992; Wlodkowski, 1978). When little competitions among students (debates, team math games, etc.) do seem appropriate, teachers can make sure that all students or teams have a reasonable (perhaps equal) chance of winning (Brophy, 1986, 1987) and make no big deal about whoever the ultimate winners are.

• *Students must feel competent about classroom activities and have high expectations for academic success.* Throughout the book, we have encountered strategies for promoting students' academic success. For example, we have found that students learn new material more effectively when they have sufficient knowledge and skills to which they can relate that material. We have found that expository instruction is more successful when it provides advance organizers, visual aids, mnemonics, and so on, to help students process information in a meaningful, organized, and elaborative fashion. We have found that some learning and study strategies promote more effective learning and memory than others, and that students can learn to use such strategies.

In addition to promoting success itself, several strategies may also enhance students' sense of competence and expectations for academic success. For one thing, teachers can communicate their own high expectations for student performance. They can help students develop a realistic perspective as to what success *is* (monthly improvement qualifies, consistent perfection does not). They can cast students' errors in an appropriate light—as inevitable minor stumbling blocks on the road to success—and make sure that, despite such errors, students eventually do succeed with effort, persistence, and appropriate strategies.

• *Teachers should encourage students to take on challenges and risks.* Success on difficult and challenging tasks promotes feelings of competence and self-efficacy in ways that easier tasks never can. Teachers should help students recognize that a hard-won success is far more significant than the "easy A." And they shouldn't penalize students for trying new approaches that don't pan out.

On the other hand, the school day shouldn't necessarily be one challenge after another. Such a state of affairs would be absolutely exhausting, and probably quite discouraging as well. Instead, teachers should probably strike a balance between easy tasks—those that will boost their self-confidence over the short run—and the challenging tasks so critical for a long-term sense of competence and self-efficacy (Keller, 1987; Spaulding, 1992; Stipek, 1988).

We must recognize that school activities will not always be intrinsically enjoyable. But when students see the value of those activities, believe themselves capable of school success, and ultimately achieve that success, they are likely to be motivated and productive learners.

SUMMARY

Numerous cognitions influence the amount and type of motivation we see. As one example, people set goals toward which they direct their behaviors. Learning goals tend to promote more effective learning and performance than performance goals: Among other things, people with learning goals seek challenging tasks and are persistent until they succeed at those tasks, with little concern for the errors they make along the way. People are also likely to pursue certain activities when they place value on those activities, find them interesting, and expect to succeed at them.

People's attributions for the things that happen to them—their interpretations regarding the causes of their successes and failures—are equally important variables affecting behavior. People are most likely to take pride in a success when they believe they themselves were responsible for that success. And they are most likely to modify their behavior after a failure when they see that failure as being due to internal factors they can control, such as effort and strategies.

Some theorists believe that intrinsic motivation is the result of two conditions. First, people must have a sense of self-determination—they must believe they can make choices and regulate the course of their lives. Second, they must have a sense of competence—they must believe they are capable of successfully executing the tasks before them.

Such cognitive motivational factors have numerous implications for classroom practice. For example, challenging tasks are likely to enhance students' sense of competence and expectations for future success. Competitive situations are usually counterproductive, in that most students are the inevitable losers. Students are more intrinsically motivated when they have choices and an appropriate degree of control over their classroom activities. And ultimately, students must experience academic success on a regular basis.

REFERENCES

Abramson, L. Y., Seligman, M. E. P., & Teasdale, J. (1978). Learned helplessness in humans: Critique and reformulation. *Journal of Abnormal Psychology*, 87, 49–74.

Ackley, D. H., Hinton, G. E., & Sejnowski, T. J. (1985). A learning algorithm for Boltzmann machines. *Cognitive Science*, 9, 147–169.

Adams, J. A. (1980). *Learning and memory* (rev. ed.). Homewood, IL: Dorsey.

Adams, P. A., & Adams, J. K. (1960). Confidence in the recognition and reproduction of words difficult to spell. *American Journal of Psychology*, 73, 544–552.

Alderman, K. (1990). Motivation for at-risk students. *Educational Leadership*, 48(1), 27–30.

Alexander, L., Frankiewicz, R., & Williams, R. (1979). Facilitation of learning and retention of oral instruction using advance and post organizers. *Journal of Educational Psychology*, 71, 701–707.

Alexander, P. A., & Judy, J. E. (1988). The interaction of domain-specific and strategic knowledge in academic performance. *Review of Educational Research*, 58, 375–404.

Alford, G. S., & Rosenthal, T. L. (1973). Process and products of modeling in observational concept attainment. *Child Development*, 44, 714–720.

Alvermann, D. E. (1981). The compensatory effect of graphic organizers on descriptive text. *Journal of Educational Research*, 75, 44–48.

Ames, C. (1984). Competitive, cooperative, and individualistic goal structures: A cognitive-motivational analysis. In R. Ames & C. Ames (Eds.), *Research on motivation in education: Vol. 1. Student motivation*. Orlando: Academic Press.

Ames, C. (1992). Classrooms: Goals, structures, and student motivation. *Journal of Educational Psychology*, 84, 261–271.

Ames, C., & Ames, R. (1981). Competitive versus individualistic goal structures: The salience of past performance information for causal attributions and affect. *Journal of Educational Psychology*, 73, 411–418.

Ames, C., & Archer, J. (1988). Achievement goals in the classroom: Students' learning strategies and motivation processes. *Journal of Educational Psychology*, 80, 260–267.

Ames, R. (1983). Help-seeking and achievement orientation: Perspectives from attribution theory. In A. Nadler, J. Fisher, & B. DePaulo (Eds.), *New directions in helping*, Vol. 2. New York: Academic Press.

Ames, R., & Lau, S. (1982). An attributional analysis of student help-seeking in academic settings. *Journal of Educational Psychology*, 74, 414–423.

Anderson, J. R. (1974). Retrieval of propositional information from long-term memory. *Cognitive Psychology*, 6, 451–474.

Anderson, J. R. (1976). *Language, memory, and thought*. Hillsdale, NJ: Erlbaum.

Anderson, J. R. (1983a). *The architecture of cognition*. Cambridge, MA: Harvard University Press.

Anderson, J. R. (1983b). A spreading activation theory of memory. *Journal of Verbal Learning and Verbal Behavior*, 22, 261–295.

Anderson, J. R. (1984). Spreading activation. In J. R. Anderson & S. M. Kosslyn (Eds.), *Tutorials in learning and memory*. San Francisco: W. H. Freeman.

Anderson, J. R. (1985). *Cognitive psychology and its implications* (2nd ed.). New York: W. H. Freeman.

Anderson, J. R. (1987). Skill acquisition: Compilation of weak-method problem solutions. *Psychological Review*, 94, 192–210.

Anderson, J. R. (1990). *Cognitive psychology and its implications* (3rd ed.). New York: W. H. Freeman.

Anderson, J. R. (1993). Problem solving and learning. *American Psychologist*, 48, 35–44.

Anderson, J. R., & Bower, G. H. (1973). *Human associative memory*. Washington, DC: Winston.

Anderson, J. R., & Schooler, L. J. (1991). Reflections of the environment in memory. *Psychological Science*, 2, 396–408.

Anderson, J. R., & Schustack, M. W. (1979). Effects of analogy to prior knowledge on memory for new information. *Journal of Verbal*

Learning and Verbal Behavior, 18, 565–583.

Anderson, R. C. (1977). The notion of schemata and the educational enterprise. In R. C. Anderson, R. J. Spiro, & W. E. Montague (Eds.), *Schooling and the acquisition of knowledge.* Hillsdale, NJ: Erlbaum.

Anderson, R. C. (1984). Role of reader's schema in comprehension, learning, and memory. In R. C. Anderson, J. Osborn, & R. J. Tierney (Eds.), *Learning to read in American schools: Basal readers and content texts.* Hillsdale, NJ: Erlbaum.

Anderson, R. C., & Biddle, B. (1975). On asking people questions about what they are reading. In G. H. Bower (Ed.), *Psychology of learning and motivation* (Vol. 9). New York: Academic Press.

Anderson, R. C., & Pichert, J. (1978). Recall of previously unrecallable information following a shift in perspective. *Journal of Verbal Learning and Verbal Behavior, 17,* 1–12.

Anderson, R. C., Reynolds, R. E., Schallert, D. L., & Goetz, E. T. (1977). Frameworks for comprehending discourse. *American Educational Research Journal, 14,* 367–381.

Andre, T. (1979). Does answering higher-level questions while reading facilitate productive learning? *Review of Educational Research, 49,* 280–318.

Andre, T. (1986). Problem solving and education. In G. D. Phye & T. Andre (Eds.), *Cognitive classroom learning: Understanding, thinking, and problem solving.* Orlando, FL: Academic Press.

Andrews, A. C. (1987). The analogy theme in geography. *Journal of Geography, 86,* 194–197.

Andrews, G. R., & Debus, R. L. (1978). Persistence and the causal perception of failure: Modifying cognitive attributions. *Journal of Educational Psychology, 70,* 154–166.

Anglin, J. M. (1977). *Word, object, and conceptual development.* New York: W. W. Norton.

Anker, A. L., & Crowley, T. J. (1982). Use of contingency contracts in specialty clinics for cocaine abuse. *National Institute on Drug Abuse: Research Monograph Series, 4,* 452–459.

Appel, J. B., & Peterson, N. J. (1965). Punishment: Effects of shock intensity on response suppression. *Psychological Reports, 16,* 721–730.

Arlin, M. (1984). Time, equality, and mastery learning. *Review of Educational Research, 54,* 65–86.

Armbruster, B. B. (1984). The problem of "inconsiderate text." In G. G. Duffy, L. R. Roehler, & J. Mason (Eds.), *Comprehension instruction: Perspectives and suggestions.* New York: Longman.

Armbruster, B. B. (1988, April). Questions in content area textbooks: Do they function?. In R. Peterson (Chair), *What do we know about learning from textbooks? Part I.* Symposium conducted at the American Educational Research Assn., New Orleans.

Aronfreed, J. (1968). Aversive control of socialization. In W. J. Arnold (Ed.), *Nebraska Symposium on Motivation.* Lincoln, NE: University of Nebraska Press.

Aronfreed, J., & Reber, A. (1965). Internalized behavioral suppression and the timing of social punishment. *Journal of Personality and Social Psychology, 1,* 3–16.

Atkinson, J. W. (1957). Motivational determinants of risk-taking behavior. *Psychological Review, 64,* 359–372.

Atkinson, J. W. (1958). *Motives in fantasy, action, and sobriety.* Princeton, NJ: Van Nostrand.

Atkinson, J. W. (1964). *Introduction to motivation.* Princeton, NJ: Van Nostrand.

Atkinson, J. W., & Birch, D. (1978). *Introduction to motivation* (2nd ed.). New York: Van Nostrand.

Atkinson, J. W., & Feather, N. T. (Eds.). (1966). *A theory of achievement motivation.* New York: Wiley.

Atkinson, J. W., & Litwin, G. H. (1960). Achievement motive and test anxiety conceived as motive to approach success and motive to avoid failure. *Journal of Abnormal and Social Psychology, 60,* 52–63.

Atkinson, J. W., & Raynor, J. O. (1978). *Personality, motivation, and achievement.* Washington, DC: Hemisphere.

Atkinson, R. C. (1975). Mnemotechnics in second-language learning. *American Psychologist, 30,* 821–828.

Atkinson, R. C., & Shiffrin, R. M. (1968). Human memory: A proposed system and its control processes. In K. W. Spence & J. T. Spence (Eds.), *The psychology of learning and motivation: Advances in research and theory* (Vol. 2). New York: Academic Press.

Atkinson, R. C., & Shiffrin, R. M. (1971). The control of short-term memory. *Scientific American, 225*(2), 82–90.

Attneave, A. (1957). Transfer of experience with a class schema to identification learning of patterns and shapes. *Journal of Experimental Psychology, 54,* 81–88.

Ausubel, D. P. (1963). *The psychology of meaningful verbal learning.* New York: Grune & Stratton.

Ausubel, D. P. (1968). *Educational psychology: A cognitive view.* New York: Holt, Rinehart & Winston.

Ausubel, D. P., Novak, J. D., & Hanesian, H. (1978). *Educational psychology: A cognitive view* (2nd ed.). New York: Holt, Rinehart & Winston.

Ausubel, D. P., & Robinson, F. G. (1969). *School learning: An introduction to educational psychology.* New York: Holt, Rinehart & Winston.

Ayllon, T., Layman, D., & Kandel, H. J. (1975). A behavioral-educational alternative to drug control of hyperactive children. *Journal of Applied Behavior Analysis, 8,* 137–146.

Azrin, N. H. (1960). Effects of punishment intensity during variable-interval reinforcement. *Journal of the Experimental Analysis of Behavior, 3,* 123–142.

Azrin, N. H. (1967, May). Pain and aggression. *Psychology Today, 1,* 27–33.

Azrin, N. H., & Holz, W. C. (1966). Punishment. In W. K. Honig (Ed.), *Operant behavior: Areas of research and application.* New York: Appleton-Century-Crofts.

Baddeley, A. D. (1978). The trouble with levels: A reexamination of Craik and Lockhart's framework for memory research. *Psychological Review, 85,* 139–152.

Baddeley, A. D. (1982). *Your memory: A user's guide.* New York: Macmillan.

Baddeley, A. D. (1986). *Working memory.* Oxford, England: Clarendon Press.

Baddeley, A. D., & Hitch, G. (1974). Working memory. In G. H. Bower (Ed.), *The psychology of learning and motivation* (Vol. 8). New York: Academic Press.

Bahrick, H. P. (1984). Semantic memory content in permastore: Fifty years of memory for Spanish learned in school. *Journal of Experimental Psychology: General, 113,* 1–29.

Bahrick, H. P., Bahrick, L. E., Bahrick, A. S., & Bahrick, P. E. (1993). Maintenance of foreign language vocabulary and the spacing effect. *Psychological Science, 4,* 316–321.

Baker, L. (1989). Metacognition, comprehension monitoring, and the adult reader. *Educational Psychology Review, 1,* 3–38.

Baker, L., & Brown, A. L. (1984). Metacognitive skills of reading. In D. Pearson (Ed.), *Handbook of reading research*. New York: Longman.

Ballard, D. H. (1986). Cortical connections and parallel processing. *Behavioural and Brain Sciences, 9*(1), 67–120.

Bandura, A. (1965a). Behavioral modification through modeling practices. In L. Krasner & L. Ullman (Eds.), *Research in behavior modification*. New York: Holt, Rinehart & Winston.

Bandura, A. (1965b). Influence of models' reinforcement contingencies on the acquisition of imitative responses. *Journal of Personality and Social Psychology, 1*, 589–595.

Bandura, A. (1969). *Principles of behavior modification*. New York: Holt, Rinehart, & Winston.

Bandura, A. (1973). *Aggression: A social learning analysis*. Englewood Cliffs, NJ: Prentice-Hall.

Bandura, A. (1977a). Self-efficacy: Toward a unifying theory of behavioral change. *Psychological Review, 84*, 191–215.

Bandura, A. (1977b). *Social learning theory*. Englewood Cliffs, NJ: Prentice-Hall.

Bandura, A. (1982). Self-efficacy mechanism in human agency. *American Psychologist, 37*, 122–147.

Bandura, A. (1986). *Social foundations of thought and action: A social cognitive theory*. Englewood Cliffs, NJ: Prentice-Hall.

Bandura, A. (1989). Human agency in social cognitive theory. *American Psychologist, 44*, 1175–1184.

Bandura, A., Grusec, E., & Menlove, F. L. (1967). Vicarious extinction of avoidance behavior. *Journal of Personality and Social Psychology, 5*, 16–23.

Bandura, A., & Jeffery, R. W. (1973). Role of symbolic coding and rehearsal processes in observational learning. *Journal of Personality & Social Psychology, 26*, 122–130.

Bandura, A., Jeffery, R. W., & Bachicha, D. L. (1974). Analysis of memory codes and cumulative rehearsal in observational learning. *Journal of Research in Personality, 7*, 295–305.

Bandura, A., & Kupers, C. J. (1964). Transmission of patterns of self-reinforcement through modeling. *Journal of Abnormal & Social Psychology, 69*, 1–9.

Bandura, A., & McDonald, F. J. (1963). Influences of social reinforcement and the behavior of models in shaping children's moral judgments. *Journal of Abnormal and Social Psychology, 67*, 274–281.

Bandura, A., & Menlove, F. L. (1968). Factors determining vicarious extinction of avoidance behavior through symbolic modeling. *Journal of Personality and Social Psychology, 5*, 16–23.

Bandura, A., & Perloff, B. (1967). Relative efficacy of self-monitored and externally imposed reinforcement systems. *Journal of Personality and Social Psychology, 7*, 111–116.

Bandura, A., Ross, D., & Ross, S. A. (1961) Transmission of aggression through imitation of aggressive models. *Journal of Abnormal & Social Psychology, 63*, 575–582.

Bandura, A., Ross, D., & Ross, S. A. (1963). Imitation of film-mediated aggressive models. *Journal of Abnormal & Social Psychology, 66*, 3–11.

Bandura, A., & Walters, R. H. (1963). *Social learning and personality development*. New York: Holt, Rinehart & Winston.

Bandura, A., & Whalen, C. K. (1966). The influence of antecedent reinforcement and divergent modeling cues on patterns of self-reward. *Journal of Personality & Social Psychology, 3*, 373–382.

Bangert-Drowns, R. L., Kulik, C. C., Kulik, J. A., & Morgan, M. (1991). The instructional effect of feedback in test-like events. *Review of Educational Research, 61*, 213–238.

Barker, G. P., & Graham, S. (1987). Developmental study of praise and blame as attributional cues. *Journal of Educational Psychology, 79*, 62–66.

Barker, R. H., Dembo, T., & Lewin, K. (1941). Frustration and regression: An experiment with young children. *University of Iowa Studies in Child Welfare, 18*, 1–314.

Barnett, J. E., Di Vesta, F. J., & Rogozinski, J. T. (1981). What is learned in note taking? *Journal of Educational Psychology, 73*, 181–192.

Baron, A., Kaufman, A., & Stauber, K. A. (1969). Effects of instructions and reinforcement feedback on human operant behavior maintained by fixed-interval reinforcement. *Journal of the Experimental Analysis of Behavior, 12*, 701–712.

Baron, J. B. (1987). Evaluating thinking skills in the classroom. In J. B. Baron & R. J. Sternberg (Eds.), *Teaching thinking skills: Theory and practice*. New York: W. H. Freeman.

Barringer, C., & Gholson, B. (1979). Effects of type and combination of feedback upon conceptual learning by children: Implications for research in academic learning. *Review of Educational Research, 49*, 459–478.

Barrish, H. H., Saunders, M., & Wolf, M. M. (1969). Good behavior game: Effects of individual contingencies for group consequences on disruptive behavior in a classroom. *Journal of Applied Behavior Analysis, 2*, 119–124.

Barth, R. (1979). Home-based reinforcement of school behavior: A review and analysis. *Review of Educational Research, 49*, 436–458.

Bartlett, F. C. (1932). *Remembering: A study in experimental and social psychology*. Cambridge: University Press.

Bassok, M. (1990). Transfer of domain-specific problem-solving procedures. *Journal of Experimental Psychology: Learning, Memory, and Cognition, 16*, 522–533.

Bassok, M., & Holyoak, K. (1990, April). Transfer of solution procedures between quantitative domains. Paper presented at the annual meeting of the American Educational Research Association, Boston.

Bassok, M., & Holyoak, K. J. (1993). Pragmatic knowledge and conceptual structure: Determinants of transfer between quantitative domains. In D. K. Detterman & R. J. Sternberg (Eds.), *Transfer on trial: Intelligence, cognition, and instruction*. Norwood, NJ: Ablex.

Bates, J. A. (1979). Extrinsic reward and intrinsic motivation: A review with implications for the classroom. *Review of Educational Research, 49*, 557–576.

Baumrind, D. (1983). Rejoinder to Lewis's reinterpretation of parental firm control effects: Are authoritative families really harmonious? *Psychological Bulletin, 94*, 132–142.

Bechterev, V. M. (1913). *The psychologie objective*. Paris: Alcan.

Beck, I. L. (1985). Comprehension instruction in the primary grades. In J. Osborn, P. Wilson, & R. C. Anderson (Eds.), *Reading education: Foundations for a literate America*. Lexington, MA: Lexington Books.

Beck, I. L., & McKeown, M. G. (1988). Toward meaningful accounts in history texts for young learners. *Educational Researcher, 47*(6), 31–39.

Becker, W. C. (1971). *Parents are teachers*. Champaign, IL: Research Press.

Becker, W. C., Madsen, C. H., Arnold, C. R., & Thomas, D. R. (1967). The contingent use of teacher attention and praise in reducing classroom behavior problems. *Journal of Special Education, 1*, 287–307.

Bédard, J., & Chi, M. T. H. (1992). Expertise. *Current Directions in Psychological Science, 1*, 135–139.

Bee, H. (1985). *The developing child* (4th ed.). New York: Harper & Row.

Behr, M., & Harel, G. (1988, April). Cognitive conflict in procedure applications. In D. Tirosh (Chair), *The role of inconsistent ideas in learning mathematics*. Symposium conducted at the annual meeting of American Educational Research Assn., New Orleans.

Bell-Gredler, M. E. (1986). *Learning and instruction: Theory into practice*. New York: Macmillan.

Bellezza, F. S. (1986). Mental cues and verbal reports in learning. In G. H. Bower (Ed.), *The psychology of learning and motivation: Advances in research and theory* (Vol. 20). Orlando: Academic Press.

Bem, S. L. (1981). Gender schema theory: A cognitive account of sex typing. *Psychological Review, 88*, 354–364.

Beneke, W. N., & Harris, M. B. (1972). Teaching self-control of study behavior. *Behaviour Research and Therapy, 10*, 35–41.

Benton, S. L., Kiewra, K. A., Whitfill, J. M., & Dennison, R. (1993). Encoding and external-storage effects on writing processes. *Journal of Educational Psychology, 85*, 267–280.

Benware, C., & Deci, E. L. (1984). Quality of learning with an active versus passive motivational set. *American Educational Research Journal, 21*, 755-765.

Berk, L. E. (1989). *Child development*. Boston: Allyn & Bacon.

Berkowitz, L., & LePage, A. (1967). Weapons as aggression-eliciting stimuli. *Journal of Personality and Social Psychology, 7*, 202–207.

Berlyne, D. E. (1960). *Conflict, arousal, and curiosity*. New York: McGraw-Hill.

Bernstein, M. R. (1955). Relationship between interest and reading comprehension. *Journal of Educational Research, 49*, 283–288.

Bersh, P. J. (1951). The influence of two variables upon the establishment of a secondary reinforcer for operant responses. *Journal of Experimental Psychology, 41*, 62–73.

Bilodeau, I. M., & Schlosberg, H. (1951). Similarity in stimulating conditions as a variable in retroactive inhibition. *Journal of Experimental Psychology, 41*, 199–204.

Birch, H. G., & Rabinowitz, H. S. (1951). The negative effect of previous experience on productive thinking. *Journal of Experimental Psychology, 41*, 121–125.

Birnbaum, J. C. (1982). The reading and composing behaviors of selected fourth- and seventh-grade students. *Research in the Teaching of English, 16*, 241–260.

Bishop, B. A., & Anderson, C. W. (1990). Student conceptions of natural selection and its role in evolution. *Journal of Research in Science Teaching, 27*, 415–427.

Bjork, R. A. (1972). Theoretical implications of directed forgetting. In A. W. Melton & E. Martin (Eds.), *Coding processes in human memory*. Washington, DC: V. H. Winston.

Blake, S. B., & Clark, R. E. (1990, April). The effects of metacognitive selection on far transfer in analogical problem solving tasks. Paper presented at the annual meeting of the American Educational Research Association, Boston.

Blanchard, F. A., Lilly, T., & Vaughn, L. A. (1991). Reducing the expression of racial prejudice. *Psychological Science, 2*, 101–105.

Block, J. H. (1980). Promoting excellence through mastery learning. *Theory Into Practice, 19*(1), 66–74.

Block, J. H., & Burns, R. B. (1976). Mastery learning. In L. Shulman (Ed.), *Review of research in education* (Vol. 4). Itasca, IL: Peacock.

Bloom, B. S. (1968). Mastery learning. In *Evaluation comment*, (Vol. 1, No. 2). Los Angeles: University of California at Los Angeles, Center for the Study of Evaluation of Instructional Programs.

Bloom, B. S. (1974). An introduction to mastery learning theory. In J. H. Block (Ed.), *Schools, society, and mastery learning*. New York: Holt, Rinehart & Winston.

Bloom, B. S. (1976). *Human characteristics and school learning*. New York: McGraw-Hill.

Bloom, B. S. (1981). *All our children learning*. New York: McGraw-Hill.

Bloom, B. S. (1984a). The search for methods of group instruction as effective as one-to-one tutoring. *Educational Leadership, 41*(8), 4–17.

Bloom, B. S. (1984b). The 2 sigma problem: The search for methods of group instruction as effective as one-to-one tutoring. *Educational Researcher, 13*(6), 4–16.

Bloom, B. S., & Broder, L. J. (1950). *Problem-solving processes of college students*. Chicago: University of Chicago Press.

Bloom, B. S., Englehart, M. B., Furst, E. J., Hill, W. H., & Krathwohl, D. R. (1956). *Taxonomy of educational objectives. The classification of educational goals. Handbook I: Cognitive domain*. New York: Longmans Green.

Bobango, J. C. (1988, April). The effect of phase-based instruction on high school geometry students' van Hiele levels and achievement. Paper presented at the American Educational Research Assn., New Orleans.

Bobrow, S., & Bower, G. H. (1969). Comprehension and recall of sentences. *Journal of Experimental Psychology, 80*, 455–461.

Bochenhauer, M. H. (1990, April). Connections: Geographic education and the National Geographic Society. Paper presented at the annual meeting of the American Educational Research Association, Boston.

Boe, E. E., & Church, R. M. (1967). Permanent effects of punishment during extinction. *Journal of Comparative & Physiological Psychology, 63*, 486–492.

Bolles, R. C. (1967). *Theory of motivation*. New York: Harper & Row.

Bolles, R. C. (1975). *Theory of motivation* (2nd ed.). New York: Harper & Row.

Bolstad, O., & Johnson, S. (1972). Self-regulation in the modification of disruptive classroom behavior. *Journal of Applied Behavior Analysis, 5*, 443–454.

Born, D. G., & Davis, M. L. (1974). Amount and distribution of study in a personalized instruction course and in a lecture course. *Journal of Applied Behavior Analysis, 7*, 365–375.

Bourne, L. E., Jr. (1967). Learning and utilization of conceptual rules. In B. Kleinmuntz (Ed.), *Concepts and the structure of memory*. New York: Wiley.

Bourne, L. E., Jr. (1982). Typicality effects in logically defined concepts. *Memory and Cognition, 10*, 3–9.

Bourne, L. E., Jr., Dominowski, R. L., Loftus, E. F., & Healy, A. F. (1986). *Cognitive processes* (2nd ed.). Englewood Cliffs, NJ: Prentice-Hall.

Bourne, L. E., Jr., Ekstrand, D. R., & Dominowski, R. L. (1971). *The psychology of thinking*. Englewood Cliffs, NJ: Prentice-Hall.

Bousfield, W. A. (1953). The occurrence of clustering in the recall of randomly arranged associates. *Journal of General Psychology, 49*, 229–240.

Bower, G. H. (1972). Mental imagery and associative learning. In L. W. Gregg (Ed.), *Cognition in learning and memory*. New York: Wiley.

Bower, G. H., Black, J. B., & Turner, T. J. (1979). Scripts in memory for text. *Cognitive Psychology, 11*, 177–220.

Bower, G. H., & Clark, M. C. (1969). Narrative stories as mediators for serial learning. *Psychonomic Science, 14*, 181–182.

Bower, G. H., Clark, M. C., Lesgold, A. M., & Winzenz, D. (1969). Hierarchical retrieval schemes in recall of categorized word lists. *Journal of Verbal Learning and Verbal Behavior, 8*, 323–343.

Bower, G. H., & Hilgard, E. R. (1981). *Theories of learning* (5th ed.). Englewood Cliffs, NJ: Prentice-Hall.

Bower, G. H., & Holyoak, K. J. (1973). Encoding and recognition memory for naturalistic sounds. *Journal of Experimental Psychology, 101*, 360–366.

Bower, G. H., Karlin, M. B., & Dueck, A. (1975). Comprehension and memory for pictures. *Memory and Cognition, 3*, 216–220.

Bower, G. H., McLean, J., & Meachem, J. (1966). Value of knowing when reinforcement is due. *Journal of Comparative and Physiological Psychology, 62*, 184–192.

Bower, G. H., & Springston, F. (1970). Pauses as recoding points in letter series. *Journal of Experimental Psychology, 83*, 421–430.

Boyatzis, R. E. (1973). Affiliation motivation. In D. C. McClelland & R. S. Steele (Eds.), *Human motivation: A book of readings*. Morristown, NJ: General Learning Press.

Bragstad, B. J., & Stumpf, S. M. (1982). *A guidebook for teaching study skills and motivation*. Boston: Allyn & Bacon.

Brainerd, C. J., & Reyna, V. F. (1992). Explaining "memory free" reasoning. *Psychological Science, 3*, 332–339.

Bramel, D., Taub, B., & Blum, B. (1968). An observer's reaction to the suffering of his enemy. *Journal of Personality and Social Psychology, 8*, 384–392.

Bransford, J. D., & Franks, J. J. (1971). The abstraction of linguistic ideas. *Cognitive Psychology, 2*, 331–350.

Bransford, J. D., & Johnson, M. K. (1972). Contextual prerequisites for understanding: Some investigations of comprehension and recall. *Journal of Verbal Learning and Verbal Behavior, 11*, 717–726.

Braukmann, C. J., Ramp, K. K., & Wolf, M. M. (1981). Behavioral treatment of juvenile delinquency. In S. W. Bijou & R. Ruiz (Eds.), *Behavior modification: Contributions to education*. Hillsdale, NJ: Erlbaum.

Breitmeyer, B. B., & Ganz, L. (1976). Implications of sustained and transient channels for theories of visual pattern masking, saccadic suppression, and information processing. *Psychological Review, 83*, 1–36.

Brewer, W. F., & Treyens, J. C. (1981). Role of schemata in memory for places. *Cognitive Psychology, 13*, 207–230.

Briggs, L. J., & Reed, H. B. (1943). The curve of retention for substance material. *Journal of Experimental Psychology, 32*, 513–517.

Broadbent, D. E. (1958). *Perception and communication*. London: Pergamon Press.

Broadhurst, P. L. (1959). The interaction of task difficulty and motivation: The Yerkes-Dodson law revived. *Acta Psychologia, 16*, 321–338.

Broden, M., Hall, R. V., & Mitts, B. (1971). The effect of self-recording on the classroom behavior of two eighth grade students. *Journal of Applied Behavior Analysis, 4*, 191–199.

Bronfenbrenner, U. (1970). *Two worlds of childhood: U.S. and U.S.S.R.* New York: Russell Sage Foundation.

Brooke, R. R., & Ruthren, A. J. (1984). The effects of contingency contracting on student performance in a PSI class. *Teaching of Psychology, 11*, 87–89.

Brooks, L. R. (1978). Nonanalytic concept formation and memory for instances. In E. Rosch & B. B. Lloyd (Eds.), *Cognition and categorization*. Hillsdale, NJ: Erlbaum.

Brooks, L. W., & Dansereau, D. F. (1987). Transfer of information: An instructional perspective. In S. M. Cormier & J. D. Hagman (Eds.), *Transfer of learning: Contemporary research and applications*. San Diego: Academic Press.

Brophy, J. E. (1981). Teacher praise: A functional analysis. *Review of Educational Research, 51*, 5–32.

Brophy, J. E. (1986). *On motivating students*. Occasional Paper No. 101, Institute for Research on Teaching, Michigan State University, East Lansing, MI.

Brophy, J. E. (1987). Synthesis of research on strategies for motivating students to learn. *Educational Leadership, 45*(2), 40–48.

Brophy, J. (1992). Probing the subtleties of subject-matter teaching. *Educational Leadership, 49*(7), 4–8.

Brophy, J. E., & Alleman, J. (1991). Activities as instructional tools: A framework for analysis and evaluation. *Educational Researcher, 20*(4), 9–23.

Brophy, J. E., & Good, T. L. (1970). Teachers' communication of differential expectations for children's classroom performance: Some behavioral data. *Journal of Educational Psychology, 61*, 365–374.

Brown, A. L. (1978). Knowing when, where, and how to remember: A problem of metacognition. In R. Glaser (Ed.), *Advances in instructional psychology*, Hillsdale, NJ: Erlbaum.

Brown, A. L., Bransford, J. D., Ferrera, R. A., & Campione, J. C. (1983). Learning, remembering, and understanding. In J. Flavell & E. Mankman (Eds.), *Carmichael's manual of children psychology* (Vol. 1). New York: Wiley.

Brown, A. L., & Campione, J. C. (1986). Psychological theory and the study of learning disabilities. *American Psychologist, 41*, 1059–1068.

Brown, A. L., & Campione, J. C. (in press). Communities of learning and thinking, or a context by any other name. *Human Development*.

Brown, A. L., Campione, J., & Day, J. (1981). Learning to learn: On training students to learn from texts. *Educational Researcher, 10*(2), 14–21.

Brown, A. L., & Palincsar, A. S. (1987). Reciprocal teaching of comprehension strategies: A natural history of one program for enhancing learning. In J. Borkowski & J. D. Day (Eds.), *Cognition in special education: Comparative approaches to retardation, learning disabilities, and giftedness*. Norwood, NJ: Ablex.

Brown, A. L., Palincsar, A. S., & Armbruster, B. B. (1984). Instructing comprehension fostering activities in interactive learning situations. In H. Mandl, N. Stein, & T. Trabasso (Eds.), *Learning and comprehension of text*. Hillsdale, NJ: Erlbaum.

Brown, A. L., & Reeve, R. A. (1987). Bandwidths of competence: The role of supportive contexts in learning and development. In L. S. Liben (Ed.), *Development and learning: Conflict or congruence?* Hillsdale, NJ: Erlbaum.

Brown, J. (1968). Reciprocal facilitation and impairment of free recall. *Psychonomic Science, 10,* 41–42.

Brown, R., & Herrnstein, R. J. (1975). *Psychology.* Boston: Little, Brown.

Brown, R., & McNeill, D. (1966). The "tip of the tongue" phenomenon. *Journal of Verbal Learning and Verbal Behavior, 5,* 325–337.

Brown, S. I., & Walter, M. I. (1990). *The art of problem posing* (2nd ed.). Hillsdale, NJ: Erlbaum.

Brown, W. H., Bryson-Brockmann, W., & Fox, J. J. (1986). The usefulness of J. R. Kantor's setting event concept for research on children's social behavior. *Child and Family Behavior Therapy, 8*(2), 15–25.

Brown, W. H., Fox, J. J., & Brady, M. P. (1987). Effects of spatial density on 3- and 4-year-old children's socially directed behavior during freeplay: An investigation of a setting factor. *Education and Treatment of Children, 10,* 247–258.

Brozo, W. G., Stahl, N. A., & Gordon, B. (1985). Training effects of summarizing, item writing, and knowledge of information sources on reading test performance. In J. A. Niles & R. V. Lalik (Eds.), *Issues in literacy.* Rochester, NY: National Reading Conference.

Bruner, J. S. (1957). On going beyond the information given. In *Contemporary approaches to cognition.* Cambridge, MA: Harvard University Press.

Bruner, J. S. (1961a). The act of discovery. *Harvard Educational Review, 31,* 21–32.

Bruner, J. S. (1961b). *The process of education.* Cambridge, MA: Harvard University Press.

Bruner, J. S. (1966). *Toward a theory of instruction.* New York: Norton.

Bruner, J. S., Goodnow, J., & Austin, G. (1956). *A study of thinking.* New York: Wiley.

Bryan, J. H. (1971). Model affect and children's imitative altruism. *Child Development, 42,* 2061–2065.

Bryan, J. H. (1975). Children's cooperation and helping behaviors. In E. M. Hetherington (Ed.), *Review of child development research* (Vol. 5). Chicago: University of Chicago Press.

Buckhout, R. (1974). Eyewitness testimony. *Scientific American, 231*(6), 23–31.

Buckland, P. R. (1968). The ordering of frames in a linear program. *Programmed Learning and Educational Technology, 5,* 197–205.

Bufford, R. K. (1976). Evaluation of a reinforcement procedure for accelerating work rate in a self-paced course. *Journal of Applied Behavior Analysis, 9,* 208.

Bugelski, B. R. (1962). Presentation time, total time, and mediation in paired-associate learning. *Journal of Experimental Psychology, 63,* 409–412.

Bugelski, B. R., & Alampay, D. A. (1961). The role of frequency in developing perceptual sets. *Canadian Journal of Psychology, 15,* 205–211.

Bugelski, B. R., Kidd, E., & Segmen, J. (1968). Image as a mediator in one-trial paired-associate learning. *Journal of Experimental Psychology, 76,* 69–73.

Burron, A., & Claybaugh, A. (1992). *Basic concepts in reading instruction: A programmed approach.* Longmont, CO: Sopris.

Buschke, H. (1977). Two-dimensional recall: Immediate identification of clusters in episodic and semantic memory. *Journal of Verbal Learning and Verbal Behavior, 16,* 201–215.

Bushell, D., Wrobel, P. A., & Michaelis, M. L. (1968). Applying "group" contingencies to the classroom study behavior of preschool children. *Journal of Applied Behavior Analysis, 1,* 55–61.

Butler, R. (1987). Task-involving and ego-involving properties of evaluation: Effects of different feedback conditions on motivational perceptions, interest, and performance. *Journal of Educational Psychology, 79,* 474–482.

Calfee, R. (1981). Cognitive psychology and educational practice. In D. C. Berliner (Ed.), *Review of Research in Education* (Vol. 9). Washington, DC: American Educational Research Association.

Calfee, R. C., & Chambliss, M. J. (1988, April). The structure of social studies textbooks: Where is the design? Paper presented at the annual meeting of the American Educational Research Association, New Orleans.

Carey, S. (1985). Are children fundamentally different kinds of thinkers and learners than adults? In S. F. Chipman, J. W. Segal, & R. Glaser (Eds.), *Learning and thinking skills: Vol. 2. Research and open questions.* Hillsdale, NJ: Erlbaum.

Carey, S. (1986). Cognitive science and science education. *American Psychologist, 41,* 1123–1130.

Carlson, B. E. (1984). The father's contribution to child care: Effects on children's perceptions of parental roles. *American Journal of Orthopsychiatry, 54,* 123–136.

Carmichael, L., Hogan, H. P., & Walters, A. A. (1932). An experimental study of the effect of language on the reproduction of visually perceived form. *Journal of Experimental Psychology, 15,* 73–86.

Carpenter, P. A., & Just, M. A. (1986). Cognitive processes in reading. In J. Orasanu (Ed.), *Reading comprehension: From research to practice.* Hillsdale, NJ: Erlbaum.

Carpenter, T. P. (1985). Learning to add and subtract: An exercise in problem solving. In E. A. Silver (Ed.), *Teaching and learning mathematical problem solving: Multiple research perspectives.* Hillsdale, NJ: Erlbaum.

Carroll, J. B. (1963). A model of school learning. *Teachers College Record, 64,* 723–733.

Carroll, J. B. (1989). The Carroll model: A 25-year retrospective and prospective view. *Educational Researcher, 18*(1), 26–31.

Carver, R. P. (1971). *Sense and nonsense in speed reading.* Silver Springs, MD: Revrac.

Case, R. (1985). *Intellectual development: Birth to adulthood.* Orlando, FL: Academic Press.

Catania, A. C. (1985). The two psychologies of learning: Blind alleys and nonsense syllables. In S. Koch & D. E. Leary (Eds.), *A century of psychology as science.* New York: McGraw-Hill.

Catania, A. C., & Reynolds, G. S. (1968). A quantitative analysis of the responding maintained by interval schedules of reinforcement. *Journal of the Experimental Analysis of Behavior, 11,* 327–383.

Cavanaugh, J. C., & Perlmutter, M. (1982). Metamemory: A critical examination. *Child Development, 53,* 11–28.

Cermak, L. S., & Craik, F. I. M. (Eds.). (1979) *Levels of processing in human memory.* Hillsdale, NJ: Erlbaum.

Chambliss, M. J., Calfee, R. C., & Wong, I. (1990, April). Structure and content in science textbooks: Where is the design? Paper presented at the annual meeting of the American Educational Research Association, Boston, MA.

Champagne, A. B., Klopfer, L. E., & Gunstone, R. F. (1982). Cognitive research and the design of science instruction. *Educational Psychologist*, *17*, 31–53.

Chan, C. K. K., Burtis, P. J., Scardamalia, M., & Bereiter, C. (1992). Constructive activity in learning from text. *American Educational Research Journal*, *29*, 97–118.

Chapin, M., & Dyck, D. G. (1976). Persistence in children's reading behavior as a function of N length and attribution retraining. *Journal of Abnormal Psychology*, *85*, 511–515.

Chase, W. G., & Chi, M. T. H. (1980). Cognitive skill: Implications for spatial skill in large-scale environments. In J. Harvey (Ed.), *Cognition, social behavior, and the environment*. Potomac, MD: Erlbaum.

Chase, W. G., & Simon, H. A. (1973). Perception in chess. *Cognitive Psychology*, *4*, 55–81.

Cheng, P. W. (1985). Restructuring versus automaticity: Alternative accounts of skill acquisition. *Psychological Review*, *92*, 414–423.

Cheng, P. W., Holyoak, K. J., Nisbett, R. E., & Oliver, L. M. (1986). Pragmatic versus syntactic approaches to training deductive reasoning. *Cognitive Psychology*, *18*, 293–328.

Cherry, E. C. (1953). Some experiments on the recognition of speech, with one and with two ears. *Journal of the Acoustical Society of America*, *25*, 975–979.

Cheyne, J. A., & Walters, R. H. (1970). Punishment and prohibition: Some origins of self-control. In T. M. Newcomb (Ed.), *New directions in psychology*. New York: Holt, Rinehart & Winston.

Chi, M. T. H. (1981). Knowledge development and memory performance. In M. P. Friedman, J. P. Das, & N. O'Connor (Eds.), *Intelligence and learning*. New York: Plenum Press.

Chi, M. T. H., Feltovich, P., & Glaser, R. (1981). Categorization and representation of physics problems by experts and novices. *Cognitive Science*, *5*, 121–152.

Chi, M. T. H., Glaser, R., & Farr, M. J. (Eds.). (1988). *The nature of expertise*. Hillsdale, NJ: Erlbaum.

Chi, M. T. H., Glaser, R., & Rees, E. (1982). Expertise in problem solving. In R. J. Sternberg (Ed.),

Advances in the psychology of human intelligence. Hillsdale, NJ: Erlbaum.

Chiesi, H. L., Spilich, G. J., & Voss, J. F. (1979). Acquisition of domain-related information in relation to high and low domain knowledge. *Journal of Verbal Learning and Verbal Behavior*, *18*, 257–273.

Chinn, C. A., & Brewer, W. F. (1993). The role of anomalous data in knowledge acquisition: A theoretical framework and implications for science instruction. *Review of Educational Research*, *63*, 1–49.

Chipman, S. F., Krantz, D. H., & Silver, R. (1992). Mathematics anxiety and science careers among able college women. *Psychological Science*, *3*, 292–295.

Chomsky, N. (1957). *Syntactic structures*. The Hague: Mouton.

Christen, F., & Bjork, R. A. (1976). On updating the loci in the method of loci. Paper presented at the annual meeting of the Psychonomic Society, St. Louis.

Church, R. M. (1993). Human models of animal behavior. *Psychological Science*, *4*, 170–173.

Clark, D. C. (1971). Teaching concepts in the classroom: A set of teaching prescriptions derived from experimental research. *Journal of Educational Psychology*, *62*, 253–278.

Clark, J. M., & Paivio, A. (1991). Dual coding theory and education. *Educational Psychology Review*, *3*, 149–210.

Clement, J. (1987). Overcoming students' misconceptions in physics: The role of anchoring intuitions and analogical validity. In *Proceedings of the Second International Seminar on Misconceptions and Educational Strategies in Science and Mathematics* (Vol. 3). Ithaca, NY: Cornell University.

Clifford, M. M. (1984). Thoughts on a theory of constructive failure. *Educational Psychologist*, *19*, 108–120.

Clifford, M. M. (1990). Students need challenge, not easy success. *Educational Leadership*, *48*(1), 22–26.

Coates, B., & Hartup, W. W. (1969). Age and verbalization in observational learning. *Developmental Psychology*, *1*, 556–562.

Cobb, P., Yackel, E., & Wood, T. (1989). Young children's emotional acts while engaged in mathematical problem solving. In D. B. McLeod & V. M. Adams (Eds.), *Affect and mathematical problem solving: A new perspective*. New York: Springer-Verlag.

Cochran, K. F. (1988, April). Cognitive structure representation in physics. Paper presented at the annual meeting of American Educational Research Assn., New Orleans.

Cofer, C. (1971). Properties of verbal materials and verbal learning. In J. Kling & L. Riggs (Eds.), *Woodworth and Schlosberg's experimental psychology*. New York: Holt, Rinehart & Winston.

Cohen, G. (1983). *The psychology of cognition* (2nd ed.). London: Academic Press.

Cohen, R. L. (1989). Memory for action events: The power of enactment. *Educational Psychology Review*, *1*, 57–80.

Cohn, S., Hult, R. E., & Engle, R. W. (1990, April). Working memory, notetaking, and learning from a lecture. Paper presented at the annual meeting of the American Educational Research Association, Boston.

Cole, N. S. (1990). Conceptions of educational achievement. *Educational Researcher*, *19*(3), 2–7.

Collier, G., Hirsh, E., & Hamlin, P. H. (1972). The ecological determinants of reinforcement in the rat. *Physiology and Behavior*, *9*, 705–716.

Collins, A. M., & Loftus, E. F. (1975). A spreading-activation theory of semantic processing. *Psychological Review*, *82*, 407–428.

Collins, A. M., & Quillian, M. R. (1969). Retrieval time from semantic memory. *Journal of Verbal Learning and Verbal Behavior*, *8*, 240–247.

Collins, A. M., & Quillian, M. R. (1972). How to make a language user. In E. Tulving & W. Donaldson (Eds.), *Organization of memory*. New York: Academic Press.

Collins, J. L. (1982, March). Self-efficacy and ability in achievement behavior. Paper presented at the annual meeting of the American Educational Research Association, New York.

Coltheart, M., Lea, C. D., & Thompson, K. (1974). In defense of iconic memory. *Quarterly Journal of Experimental Psychology*, *26*, 633–641.

Colwill, R. M. (1993). An associative analysis of instrumental learning. *Current Directions in Psychological Science*, *2*, 111–116.

Colwill, R. M., & Rescorla, R. A. (1986). Associative structures in instrumental learning. In G. H. Bower (Ed.), *The psychology of learning and motivation* (Vol. 20). Orlando: Academic Press.

Combs, A. W., Richards, A. C., & Richards, F. (1976). *Perceptual psy-*

chology: A humanistic approach to the study of persons. New York: Harper & Row.

Connolly, F. W., & Eisenberg, T. E. (1990). The feedback classroom: Teaching's silent friend. *T.H.E. Journal*, *17*(5), 75–77.

Conrad, R. (1962). An association between memory errors and errors due to acoustic masking of speech. *Nature, 193*, 1314–1315.

Conrad, R. (1964). Acoustic confusions in immediate memory. *British Journal of Psychology, 55*, 75–84.

Conrad, R. (1971). The chronology of the development of covert speech in children. *Developmental Psychology, 5*, 398–405.

Conrad, R. (1972). Short-term memory in the deaf: A test for speech coding. *British Journal of Psychology, 63*, 173–180.

Conrad, R., & Hull, A. J. (1964). Information, acoustic confusion, and memory span. *British Journal of Psychology, 55*, 429–432.

Cook, L. K. (1983). Instructional effects of text structure-based reading strategies on the comprehension of scientific prose. (Doctoral dissertation, University of California, Santa Barbara.) *Dissertation Abstracts International, 44*, 2411A.

Cooney, J. B. (1991). Reflections on the origin of mathematical intuition and some implications for instruction. *Learning and Individual Differences, 3*, 83–107.

Cooper, H. M. (1979). Pygmalion grows up: A model for teacher expectation communication and performance influence. *Review of Educational Research, 49*, 389–410.

Cooper, L. A., & Shepard, R. N. (1973). The time required to prepare for a rotated stimulus. *Memory and Cognition, 1*, 246–250.

Copeland, J. T. (1993). Motivational approaches to expectancy confirmation. *Current Directions in Psychological Science, 2*, 117–121.

Corbett, H. D., & Wilson, B. (1988). Raising the stakes in statewide mandatory minimum competency testing. *Politics of Education Association Yearbook*, 27–39.

Cordua, G. D., McGraw, K. O., & Drabman, R. S. (1979). Doctor or nurse: Children's perception of sex typed occupations. *Child Development, 50*, 590–593.

Corkill, A. J. (1992). Advance organizers: Facilitators of recall. *Educational Psychology Review, 4*, 33–67.

Corkill, A. J., Glover, J. A., & Bruning, R. H. (1988). Advance organizers: Concrete versus abstract. *Journal of Educational Research, 82*, 76–81.

Cormier, S. M. (1987). The structural processes underlying transfer of training. In S. M. Cormier & J. D. Hagman (Eds.), *Transfer of learning: Contemporary research and applications*. San Diego: Academic Press.

Cormier, S. M., & Hagman, J. D. (1987). Introduction. In S. M. Cormier & J. D. Hagman (Eds.), *Transfer of learning: Contemporary research and applications*. San Diego: Academic Press.

Corte, H. E., Wolf, M. M., & Locke, B. J. (1971). A comparison of procedures for eliminating self-injurious behavior of retarded adolescents. *Journal of Applied Behavior Analysis, 4*, 201–214.

Covington, M. V., & Beery, R. M. (1976). *Self-worth and school learning*. New York: Holt, Rinehart & Winston.

Covington, M. V., & Omelich, C. (1979). Effort: The double-edged sword in school achievement. *Journal of Educational Psychology, 71*, 169–182.

Covington, M. V., Spratt, M., & Omelich, C. (1980). Is effort enough or does diligence count too? Student and teacher reactions to effort stability in failure. *Journal of Educational Psychology, 72*, 717–729.

Craik, F. I. M., & Lockhart, R. S. (1972). Levels of processing: A framework for memory research. *Journal of Verbal Learning and Verbal Behavior, 11*, 671–684.

Craik, F. I. M., & Tulving, E. (1975). Depth of processing and the retention of words in episodic memory. *Journal of Experimental Psychology: General, 104*, 268–294.

Craik, F. I. M., & Watkins, M. J. (1973). The role of rehearsal in short-term memory. *Journal of Verbal Learning and Verbal Behavior, 12*, 598–607.

Crespi, L. P. (1942). Quantitative variation of incentive and performance in the white rat. *American Journal of Psychology, 55*, 467–517.

Crooks, T. J. (1988). The impact of classroom evaluation practices on students. *Review of Educational Research, 58*, 438–481.

Crowder, N. A., & Martin, G. (1961). *Trigonometry*. Garden City, NY: Doubleday.

Crowder, R. G., & Wagner, R. K. (1992). *The psychology of reading: An introduction* (2nd ed.). New York: Oxford University Press.

Crowley, T. J. (1984). Contingency contracting treatment of drug-abusing physicians, nurses, and dentists. *National Institute on Drug Abuse: Research Monograph Series, 46*, 68–83.

Crowne, D. P., & Marlowe, D. (1964). *The approval motive: Studies in evaluative dependence*. New York: Wiley.

Curtis, K. A., & Graham, S. (1991, April). Altering beliefs about the importance of strategy: An attributional intervention. Paper presented at the annual meeting of the American Educational Research Association, Chicago.

Cuvo, A. J. (1975). Developmental differences in rehearsal and free recall. *Journal of Experimental Child Psychology, 19*, 65–78.

Dallett, K. M. (1964). Implicit mediators in paired-associate learning. *Journal of Verbal Learning and Verbal Behavior, 3*, 209–214.

D'Amato, M. R. (1955). Secondary reinforcement and magnitude of primary reinforcement. *Journal of Comparative and Physiological Psychology, 48*, 378–380.

D'Amato, M. R. (1970). *Experimental psychology: Methodology, psychophysics, and learning*. New York: McGraw-Hill.

Daneman, M. (1987). Reading and working memory. In J. R. Beech & A. M. Colley (Eds.), *Cognitive approaches to reading*. Chichester, England: Wiley.

Daneman, M., & Carpenter, P. A. (1980). Individual differences in working memory and reading. *Journal of Verbal Learning and Verbal Behavior, 19*, 450–466.

Danner, F. W., & Lonky, E. (1981). A cognitive-developmental approach to the effects of rewards on intrinsic motivation. *Child Development, 52*, 1043–1052.

Dansereau, D. F. (1978). The development of a learning strategies curriculum. In H. F. O'Neil, Jr. (Ed.), *Learning strategies*. New York: Academic Press.

Dansereau, D. F., Collins, K. W., McDonald, B. A., Holley, C. D., Garland, J. C., Diekhoff, G., & Evans, S. H. (1979). Development and evaluation of a learning strategy training program. *Journal of Educational Psychology, 71*, 64–73.

Darley, J. M., & Gross, P. H. (1983). A hypothesis-confirming bias in labeling effects. *Journal of Personality and Social Psychology, 44*, 20–33.

Darwin, C. J., Turvey, M. T., & Crowder, R. G. (1972). An auditory analogue of the Sperling partial report procedure: Evidence for brief auditory storage. *Cognitive Psychology, 3,* 255–267.

Davis, G. A. (1966). Current status of research and theory in human problem solving. *Psychological Bulletin, 66,* 36–54.

Davis, G. A., & Thomas, M. A. (1989). *Effective schools and effective teachers.* Boston, MA: Allyn & Bacon.

Davis, P. J. (1987). Repression and the inaccessibility of affective memories. *Journal of Personality and Social Psychology, 53,* 585–593.

Davis, P. J., & Schwartz, G. E. (1987). Repression and the inaccessibility of affective memories. *Journal of Personality and Social Psychology, 52,* 155–162.

de Villiers, P. A. (1977). Choice in concurrent schedules and a quantitative formulation of the law of effect. In W. K. Honig & J. E. R. Staddon (Eds.), *Handbook of operant behavior.* Englewood Cliffs, NJ: Prentice-Hall.

Deaux, K. (1984). From individual differences to social categories: Analysis of a decade's research on gender. *American Psychologist, 39,* 105–116.

deCharms, R. (1968). *Personal causation: The internal affective determinants of behavior.* New York: Academic Press.

Deci, E. L. (1971). Effects of externally mediated rewards on intrinsic motivation. *Journal of Personality and Social Psychology, 18,* 105–115.

Deci, E. L. (1992). The relation of interest to the motivation of behavior: A self-determination theory perspective. In K. A. Renninger, S. Hidi, & A. Krapp (Eds.), *The role of interest in learning and development.* Hillsdale, NJ: Erlbaum.

Deci, E. L., & Porac, J. (1978). Cognitive evaluation theory and the study of human motivation. In M. R. Lepper & D. Greene (Eds.), *The hidden costs of reward.* Hillsdale, NJ: Erlbaum.

Deci, E. L., & Ryan, R. M. (1985). *Intrinsic motivation and self-determination in human behavior.* New York: Plenum Press.

Deci, E. L., & Ryan, R. M. (1987). The support of autonomy and the control of behavior. *Journal of Personality and Social Psychology, 53,* 1024–1037.

Dee-Lucas, D., & Larkin, J. H. (1991). Equations in scientific proofs: Effects on comprehension. *American Educational Research Journal, 28,* 661–682.

deGroot, A. D. (1965). *Thought and choice in chess.* The Hague: Mouton.

Dempster, F. N., & Rohwer, W. D. (1974). Component analysis of the elaborative encoding effect in paired-associate learning. *Journal of Experimental Psychology, 103,* 400–408.

Denis, M. (1984). Imagery and prose: A critical review of research on adults and children. *Text, 4,* 381–401.

Denny, M. R., & Weisman, R. G. (1964). Avoidance behavior as a function of the length of nonshock confinement. *Journal of Comparative and Physiological Psychology, 58,* 252–257.

Deregowski, J. B. (1972). Pictorial perception and culture. *Scientific American, 227*(5), 82–88.

DeVries, R. (1969). Constancy of generic identity in the years three to six. *Monographs of the Society for Research in Child Development, 34* (Whole No. 127).

Di Vesta, F. J. (1987). The cognitive movement and education. In J. A. Glover & R. R. Ronning (Eds.), *Historical foundations of educational psychology.* New York: Plenum Press.

Di Vesta, F. J., & Gray, S. G. (1972). Listening and notetaking. *Journal of Educational Psychology, 63,* 8–14.

Di Vesta, F. J., & Ingersoll, G. M. (1969). Influence of pronounceability, articulation, and test mode on paired-associate learning by the study-recall procedure. *Journal of Experimental Psychology, 79,* 104–108.

Di Vesta, F. J., & Peverly, S. T. (1984). The effects of encoding variability, processing activity and rule example sequences on the transfer of conceptual rules. *Journal of Educational Psychology, 76,* 108–119.

Diaz, R. M. (1990, April). The social origins of self-regulation: A Vygotskian perspective. In B. McCombs (Chair), *Theoretical perspectives on socialization and children's development of self-regulated learning.* Symposium conducted at the meeting of the American Educational Research Association, Boston.

Diener, C. I., & Dweck, C. S. (1978). An analysis of learned helplessness: Continuous changes in performance, strategy, and achievement cognitions following failure. *Journal of Personality and Social Psychology, 36,* 451–462.

Dinsmoor, J. A. (1954). Punishment: I. The avoidance hypothesis. *Psychological Review, 61,* 34–46.

Dinsmoor, J. A. (1955). Punishment: II. An interpretation of empirical findings. *Psychological Review, 62,* 96–105.

DiSciullo, M. (1984). In-school suspension: An alternative to unsupervised out-of-school. *Clearing House, 57,* 328–330.

diSessa, A. A. (1982). Unlearning Aristotelian physics: A study of knowledge-based learning. *Cognitive Science, 6,* 37–75.

Doctorow, M., Wittrock, M. C., & Marks, C. (1978). Generative processes in reading comprehension. *Journal of Educational Psychology, 70,* 109–118.

Dodd, D. H., & White, R. M. (1980). *Cognition: Mental structures and processes.* Boston: Allyn & Bacon.

Dodge, K. A., Asher, S. R., & Parkhurst, J. T. (1989). Social life as a goal-coordination task. In C. Ames & R. Ames (Eds.), *Research on motivation in education: Vol. 3. Goals and cognitions.* San Diego: Academic Press.

Dole, J. A., Duffy, G. G., Roehler, L. R., & Pearson, P. D. (1991). Moving from the old to the new: Research on reading comprehension instruction. *Review of Educational Research, 61,* 239–264.

Dollard, J. C., Doob, L., Miller, N., Mowrer, O., & Sears, R. (1939). *Frustration and aggression.* New Haven, CT: Yale University Press.

Dominowski, R. L., & Jenrick, R. (1972). Effects of hints and interpolated activity on solution of an insight problem. *Psychonomic Science, 26,* 335–338.

Donaldson, M. (1978). *Children's minds.* New York: W. W. Norton.

Dooling, D. J., & Christiaansen, R. E. (1977). Episodic and semantic aspects of memory for prose. *Journal of Experimental Psychology: Human Learning and Memory, 3,* 428–436.

Dowaliby, F. J., & Schumer, H. (1973). Teacher-centered versus student-centered mode of college classroom instruction as related to manifest anxiety. *Journal of Educational Psychology, 64,* 125–132.

Downs, R. M., & Stea, D. (1977). *Maps in minds.* New York: Harper & Row.

Doyle, W. (1983). Academic work. *Review of Educational Research, 53,* 159–199.

Doyle, W. (1986a). Classroom organization and management. In M. C. Wittrock (Ed.), *Handbook of research on teaching* (3rd ed.). New York: Macmillan.

Doyle, W. (1986b). Content representation in teachers' definitions of academic work. *Journal of Curriculum Studies, 18*, 365–379.

Doyle, W. (1990). Classroom management techniques. In O. C. Moles (Ed.), *Student discipline strategies: Research and practice*. Albany, NY: State University of New York Press.

Drabman, R. S. (1976). Behavior modification in the classroom. In W. E. Craighead & M. J. Mahoney (Eds.), *Behavior modification principles, issues, and applications*. Boston: Houghton Mifflin.

Drabman, R. S., & Spitalnik, R. (1973). Social isolation as a punishment procedure: A controlled study. *Journal of Experimental Child Psychology, 16*, 236–249.

Dressel, P. L. (1977). The nature and role of objectives in instruction. *Educational Technology, 17*(5), 7–15.

DuBois, N. F. (1987, April). Training students to become autonomous learners. Paper presented at American Educational Research Assn., Washington, DC.

DuBois, N. F., Kiewra, K. A., & Fraley, J. (1988, April). Differential effects of a learning strategy course. Paper presented at American Educational Research Assn., New Orleans.

Duell, O. K. (1986). Metacognitive skills. In G. D. Phye & T. Andre (Eds.), *Cognitive classroom learning: Understanding, thinking, and problem solving*. Orlando: Academic Press.

Duit, R. (1990, April). On the role of analogies, similes and metaphors in learning science. Paper presented at the annual meeting of the American Educational Research Association, Boston.

DuNann, D. G., & Weber, S. J. (1976). Short- and long-term effects of contingency managed instruction on low, medium, and high GPA students. *Journal of Applied Behavior Analysis, 9*, 375–376.

Duncker, K. (1945). On problem solving. *Psychological Monographs, 58* (Whole No. 270).

Dunn, C. S. (1983). The influence of instructional methods on concept learning. *Science Education, 67*, 647–656.

Durkin, K. (1987). Social cognition and social context in the construction of sex differences. In M. A. Baker (Ed.), *Sex differences in human performance*. Chichester, England: Wiley.

Dusek, J. B. (1980). The development of test anxiety in children. In I. G. Sarason (Ed.), *Test anxiety: Theory, research, and applications*. Hillsdale, NJ: Erlbaum.

Dweck, C. S. (1975). The role of expectations and attributions in the alleviation of learned helplessness. *Journal of Personality and Social Psychology, 31*, 674–685.

Dweck, C. S. (1978). Achievement. In M. E. Lamb (Ed.), *Social and personality development*. New York: Holt, Rinehart & Winston.

Dweck, C. S. (1986). Motivational processes affecting learning. *American Psychologist, 41*, 1040–1048.

Dweck, C. S., Davidson, W., Nelson, S., & Enna, B. (1978). Sex differences in learned helplessness: II. The contingencies of evaluative feedback in the classroom; III. An experimental analysis. *Developmental Psychology, 14*, 268–276.

Dweck, C. S., & Elliott, E. S. (1983). Achievement motivation. In E. M. Hetherington (Ed.), *Handbook of child psychology: Vol. 4. Socialization, personality, and social development* (4th ed.). New York: Wiley.

Dweck, C. S., Goetz, T. E., & Strauss, N. L. (1980). Sex differences in learned helplessness: IV. An experimental and naturalistic study of failure generalization and its mediators. *Journal of Personality and Social Psychology, 38*, 441–452.

Dweck, C. S., & Licht, B. (1980). Learned helplessness and intellectual achievement. In J. Garber & M. E. P. Seligman (Eds.), *Human helplessness: Theory and applications*. New York: Academic Press.

Dweck, C. S., & Reppucci, N. D. (1973). Learned helplessness and reinforcement responsibility in children. *Journal of Personality and Social Psychology, 25*, 109–116.

Dyer, H. S. (1967). The discovery and development of educational goals. *Proceedings of the 1966 Invitational Conference on Testing Problems*. Princeton, NJ: Educational Testing Service.

Eaton, J. F., Anderson, C. W., & Smith, E. L. (1984). Students' misconceptions interfere with science learning: Case studies of fifth-grade students. *Elementary School Journal, 84*, 365–379.

Ebbinghaus, H. (1913). *Memory: A contribution to experimental psychology* (H. A. Ruger & C. E. Bussenius, trans.). New York: Teachers College. (Original work published 1885).

Eccles, J. S., & Jacobs, J. E. (1986). Social forces shape math attitudes and performance. *Signs: Journal of Women in Culture and Society, 11*, 367–380.

Eccles, J. S., Jacobs, J., Harold-Goldsmith, R., Jayaratne, T., & Yee, D. (1989, April). The relations between parents' category-based and target-based beliefs: Gender roles and biological influences. Paper presented at the Society for Research in Child Development, Kansas City.

Eccles, J. S., & Midgley, C. (1989). Stage-environment fit: Developmentally appropriate classrooms for young adolescents. In C. Ames & R. Ames (Eds.), *Research on motivation in education: Vol. 3. Goals and cognition*. New York: Academic Press.

Eccles, J., & Wigfield, A. (1985). Teacher expectations and student motivation. In J. B. Dusek (Ed.), *Teacher expectancies*. Hillsdale, NJ: Erlbaum.

Eccles (Parsons), J. (1983). Expectancies, values, and academic behaviors. In J. T. Spence (Ed.), *Achievement and achievement motivation*. San Francisco: Freeman.

Eccles (Parsons), J. (1984). Sex differences in mathematics participation. In M. Steinkamp & M. Maehr (Eds.), *Women in science*. Greenwich, CT: JAI Press.

Eccles (Parsons), J. S., Adler, T. F., Futterman, R., Goff, S. B., Kaczala, C. M., Meece, J. L., & Midgley, C. (1983). Expectations, values, and academic behaviors. In J. T. Spence (Ed.), *Achievement and achievement motivation*. San Francisco: Freeman.

Elliott, R., & Vasta, R. (1970). The modeling of sharing: Effects associated with vicarious reinforcement, symbolization, age, and generalization. *Journal of Experimental Child Psychology, 10*, 8–15.

Ellis, H. C., & Hunt, R. R. (1983). *Fundamentals of human memory and cognition* (3rd ed.). Dubuque, IA: Wm C. Brown.

Emmer, E. T., & Evertson, C. M. (1981). Synthesis of research on classroom management. *Educational Leadership, 38*, 342–347.

English, H. B., Welborn, E. L., & Killian, C. D. (1934). Studies in substance memorization. *Journal of General Psychology, 11,* 233–260.

Epstein, H. (1978). Growth spurts during brain development: Implications for educational policy and practice. In J. Chall & A. Mirsky (Eds.), *Education and the brain: The 77th yearbook of the National Society for the Study of Education, Part II.* Chicago: University of Chicago Press.

Epstein, R. (1991). Skinner, creativity, and the problem of spontaneous behavior. *Psychological Science, 2,* 362–370.

Erdelyi, M. H. (1985). *Psychoanalysis: Freud's cognitive psychology.* New York: Freeman.

Erdelyi, M. H., & Goldberg, B. (1979). Let's not sweep repression under the rug: Toward a cognitive psychology of repression. In J. F. Kihlstrom & F. J. Evans (Eds.), *Functional disorders of memory.* Hillsdale, NJ: Erlbaum.

Eriksen, C. W., & Kuethe, J. L. (1956). Avoidance conditioning of verbal behavior without awareness: A paradigm of repression. *Journal of Abnormal and Social Psychology, 53,* 203–209.

Estes, W. K. (1969a). New perspectives on some old issues in association theory. In N. J. Mackintosh & W. K. Honig (Eds.), *Fundamental issues in associative learning.* Halifax, Canada: Dalhousie University Press.

Estes, W. K. (1969b). Outline of a theory of punishment. In B. A. Campbell & R. M. Church (Eds.), *Punishment and aversive behavior.* New York: Appleton-Century-Crofts, 1969.

Evans, G. W., & Oswalt, G. L. (1968). Acceleration of academic progress through the manipulation of peer influence. *Behaviour Research and Therapy, 6,* 189–195.

Eysenck, M. W. (1979). Depth, elaboration, and distinctiveness. In L. S. Cermak & F. I. M. Craik (Eds.), *Levels of processing in human memory.* Hillsdale, NJ: Erlbaum.

Eysenck, M. W. (1992). *Anxiety: The cognitive perspective.* Hove, England: Erlbaum.

Eysenck, M. W., & Keane, M. T. (1990). *Cognitive psychology: A student's handbook.* Hove, United Kingdom: Erlbaum.

Fagen, J. W., & Rovee, C. K. (1976). Effects of qualitative shifts in a visual reinforcer in the instrumental response of infants. *Journal of Experimental Child Psychology, 21,* 349–360.

Fantino, E. (1973). Aversive control. In J. A. Nevin & G. S. Reynolds (Eds.), *The study of behavior.* Glenview, IL: Scott, Foresman.

Farah, M. J., Hammond, K. M., Levine, D. N., & Calvanio, R. (1988). Visual and spatial mental imagery: Dissociable systems of representation. *Cognitive Psychology, 20,* 439–462.

Farnham-Diggory, S. (1972). The development of equivalence systems. In S. Farnham-Diggory (Ed.), *Information processing in children.* New York: Academic Press.

Faust, G. W., & Anderson, R. C. (1967). Effects of incidental material in a programmed Russian vocabulary lesson. *Journal of Educational Psychology, 58,* 3–10.

Feather, N. T. (1982). *Expectations and actions: Expectancy-value models in psychology.* Hillsdale, NJ: Erlbaum.

Feld, S., Ruhland, D., & Gold, M. (1979). Developmental changes in achievement motivation. *Merrill-Palmer Quarterly, 25,* 43–60.

Feldhusen, J. F. (1963). Taps for teaching machines. *Phi Delta Kappan, 44,* 265–267.

Feldhusen, J. F., & Treffinger, D. J. (1980). *Creative thinking and problem solving in gifted education.* Dubuque, IA: Kendall/Hunt.

Fennema, E. (1980). Sex-related differences in mathematics achievement: Where and why. In L. H. Fox, L. Brody, & D. Tobin (Eds.), *Women and the mathematical mystique.* Baltimore: Johns Hopkins University Press.

Fennema, E. (1987). Sex-related differences in education: Myths, realities, and interventions. In V. Richardson-Koehler (Ed.), *Educators' handbook: A research perspective.* New York: Longman.

Fennema, E., Carpenter, T. P., & Peterson, P. L. (1989). Learning mathematics with understanding: Cognitively guided instruction. In J. Brophy (Ed.), *Advances in research on teaching* (Vol. 1). Greenwich, CT: JAI Press.

Ferster, C. B., & Skinner, B. F. (1957). *Schedules of reinforcement.* Englewood Cliffs, NJ: Prentice-Hall.

Field, D. (1987). A review of preschool conservation training: An analysis of analyses. *Developmental Review, 7,* 210–251.

Fisk, A. D. (1986). Frequency encoding is not inevitable and is not automatic: A reply to Hasher & Zacks. *American Psychologist, 41,* 215–216.

Fiske, D. W., & Maddi, S. R. (1961). *Functions of varied experience.* Homewood, IL: Dorsey.

Flaherty, C. F. (1985). *Animal learning and cognition.* New York: Alfred Knopf.

Flavell, J. H. (1963). *The developmental psychology of Jean Piaget.* New York: Van Nostrand Reinhold.

Flavell, J. H. (1976). Metacognitive aspects of problem solving. In L. B. Resnick (Ed.), *The nature of intelligence.* Hillsdale, NJ: Erlbaum.

Flavell, J. H. (1979). Metacognition and cognitive monitoring: A new area of cognitive-developmental inquiry. *American Psychologist, 34,* 906–911.

Flavell, J. H. (1985). *Cognitive development* (2nd ed.). Englewood Cliffs, NJ: Prentice-Hall.

Flavell, J. H. (1993). Young children's understanding of thinking and consciousness. *Current Directions in Psychological Science, 2,* 40–43.

Flavell, J. H., Friedrichs, A. G., & Hoyt, J. D. (1970). Developmental changes in memorization processes. *Cognitive Psychology, 1,* 324–340.

Flavell, J. H., & Wellman, H. M. (1977). Metamemory. In R. V. Kail, Jr., & J. W. Hagen (Eds.), *Perspectives on the development of memory and cognition.* Hillsdale, NJ: Erlbaum.

Fleishman, E. A. (1987). Foreword. In S. M. Cormier & J. D. Hagman (Eds.), *Transfer of learning: Contemporary research and applications.* San Diego: Academic Press.

Fodor, J. A., & Pylyshyn, Z. W. (1988). Connectionism and cognitive architecture: A critical analysis. *Cognition, 28,* 3–71.

Fong, G. T., Krantz, D. H., & Nisbett, R. E. (1986). The effects of statistical training on thinking about everyday problems. *Cognitive Psychology, 18,* 253–292.

Foos, P. W., & Fisher, R. P. (1988). Using tests as learning opportunities. *Journal of Educational Psychology, 80,* 179–183.

Fowler, J. W., & Peterson, P. L. (1981). Increasing reading persistence and altering attributional style of learned helpless children. *Journal of Educational Psychology, 73,* 251–260.

Fowler, S. A., & Baer, D. M. (1981). "Do I have to be good all day?" The timing of delayed reinforcement as a factor in generalization. *Journal of Applied Behavior Analysis, 14,* 13–24.

Fox, P. W., & LeCount, J. (1991, April). When more is less: Faculty misestimation of student learning. Paper presented at the annual meeting of the American Educational Research Association, Chicago.

Foxx, R. M., & Shapiro, S. T. (1978). The timeout ribbon: A nonexclusionary timeout procedure. *Journal of Applied Behavior Analysis*, *11*, 125–136.

Franks, J. J., & Bransford, J. D. (1971). Abstraction of visual patterns. *Journal of Experimental Psychology*, *90*, 65–74.

Frase, L. T. (1975). Prose processing. In G. H. Bower (Ed.), *The psychology of learning and motivation* (Vol. 9). New York: Academic Press.

Frederiksen, J. R., & Collins, A. (1989). A systems approach to educational testing. *Educational Researcher*, *18*(9), 27–32.

Frederiksen, N. (1984a). Implications of cognitive theory for instruction in problem-solving. *Review of Educational Research*, *54*, 363–407.

Frederiksen, N. (1984b). The real test bias: Influences of testing on teaching and learning. *American Psychologist*, *39*, 193–202.

Frederiksen, N., & Ward, W. C. (1978). Measures for the study of creativity in scientific problem solving. *Applied Psychological Measurement*, *2*, 1–24.

Freiberg, H. J. (1987). Teacher self-evaluation and principal supervision. *NASSP Bulletin* (National Association of Secondary School Principals), *71*, 85–92.

Freiburgs, V., & Tulving, E. (1961). The effect of practice on utilization of information from positive and negative instances in concept identification. *Canadian Journal of Psychology*, *15*, 101–106.

French, E. G. (1955). Some characteristics of achievement motivation. *Journal of Experimental Psychology*, *50*, 232–236.

French, E. G. (1956). Motivation as a variable in work partner selection. *Journal of Abnormal and Social Psychology*, *53*, 96–99.

Freud, S. (1922). *Beyond the pleasure principle*. London: International Psychoanalytic Press.

Freud, S. (1949). Instincts and their vicissitudes. In *Collected papers of Sigmund Freud* (Vol. IV). (trans. J. Riviere). London: Hogarth. (Original work published 1915.)

Freud, S. (1957). Repression. In J. Strachey (Ed.), *The standard edition of the complete psychological works of Sigmund Freud*, (Vol. 14). London: Hogarth Press. (Original work published 1915)

Friedrich, L. K., & Stein, A. H. (1973). Aggressive and pro-social television programs and the natural behavior of preschool children. *Society for Research in Child Development Monographs*, *38* (Whole No. 151).

Frith, U. (1978). From print to meaning and from print to sound, or how to read without knowing how to spell. *Visible Language*, *12*, 43–54.

Frith, U. (1980). Unexpected spelling problems. In U. Frith (Ed.), *Cognitive processes in spelling*. London: Academic Press.

Furedy, J. J., & Riley, D. M. (1987). Human Pavlovian autonomic conditioning and the cognitive paradigm. In G. Davey (Ed.), *Cognitive processes and Pavlovian conditioning in humans*. Chichester, England: Wiley.

Furst, E. J. (1981). Bloom's taxonomy of educational objectives for the cognitive domain: Philosophical and educational issues. *Review of Educational Research*, *51*, 441–453.

Gage, N. L., & Berliner, D. C. (1984). *Educational psychology* (3rd ed.). Boston: Houghton Mifflin.

Gagné, E. D. (1985). *The cognitive psychology of school learning*. Boston: Little, Brown.

Gagné, R. M. (1982). Developments in learning psychology: Implications for instructional design; and effects of computer technology on instructional design and development. *Educational Technology*, *22*(6), 11–15.

Gagné, R. M. (1983). Some issues in the psychology of mathematics instruction. *Journal of Research in Mathematics Education*, *14* (1), 7–18.

Gagné, R. M. (1985). *The conditions of learning and theory of instruction* (4th ed.). New York: Holt, Rinehart & Winston.

Gagné, R. M., Briggs, L. J., & Wager, W. W. (1988). *Principles of instructional design* (3rd ed.). New York: Holt, Rinehart & Winston.

Gagné, R. M., & Brown, L. T. (1961). Some factors in the programming of conceptual learning. *Journal of Experimental Psychology*, *62*, 313–321.

Gagné, R. M., & Driscoll, M. P. (1988). *Essentials of learning for instruction* (2nd ed.). Englewood Cliffs, NJ: Prentice-Hall.

Gagné, R. M., & Smith, E. C. (1962). A study of the effects of verbalization on problem solving. *Journal of Experimental Psychology*, *63*, 12–18.

Garb, J. L., & Stunkard, A. J. (1974). Taste aversions in man. *American Journal of Psychiatry*, *131*, 1204–1207.

Garcia, E. E. (1992). "Hispanic" children: Theoretical, empirical, and related policy issues. *Educational Psychology Review*, *4*, 69–93.

Garcia, J., & Koelling, R. A. (1966). The relation of cue to consequence in avoidance learning. *Psychonomic Science*, *4*, 123–124.

Gardner, M. (1978). *Aha! Insight*. New York: Scientific American.

Garner, R., Alexander, P. A., Gillingham, M. G., Kulikowich, J. M., & Brown, R. (1991). Interest and learning from text. *American Educational Research Journal*, *28*, 643–659.

Garner, R., Brown, R., Sanders, S., & Menke, D. J. (1992). "Seductive details" and learning from text. In K. A. Renninger, S. Hidi, & A. Krapp (Eds.), *The role of interest in learning and development*. Hillsdale, NJ: Erlbaum.

Garner, R., Gillingham, M. G., & White, C. S. (1989). Effects of "seductive details" on macroprocessing and microprocessing in adults and children. *Cognition and Instruction*, *6*, 41–57.

Gasper, K. L. (1980). The student perspective. *Teaching Political Science*, *7*, 470–471.

Gaudry, E., & Bradshaw, G. D. (1971). The differential effect of anxiety on performance in progressive and terminal school examinations. In E. Gaudry & C. D. Spielberger (Eds.), *Anxiety and educational achievement*. Sydney, Australia: Wiley.

Gaudry, E., & Spielberger, C. D. (Eds.) (1971). *Anxiety and educational achievement*. Sydney, Australia: Wiley.

Gauntt, H. L. (1991, April). The roles of prior knowledge of text structure and prior knowledge of content in the comprehension and recall of expository text. Paper presented at the annual meeting of the American Educational Research Association, Chicago.

Gaynor, J., & Millham, J. (1976). Student performance and evaluation under variant teaching and testing methods in a large college course. *Journal of Educational Psychology, 68*, 312–317.

Gentner, D., & Gentner, D. R. (1983). Flowing waters or teeming crowds: Mental models of electricity. In D. Gentner & A. L. Stevens (Eds.), *Mental models*. Hillsdale, NJ: Erlbaum.

Gerst, M. S. (1971). Symbolic coding processes in observational learning. *Journal of Personality & Social Psychology, 19*, 7–17.

Giaconia, R. M. (1988). Teacher questioning and wait-time (Doctoral dissertation, Stanford University, 1988). *Dissertation Abstracts International, 49*, 462A.

Gibson, E., & Rader, N. (1979). Attention: The perceiver as performer. In G. A. Hale & M. Lewis (Eds.), *Attention and cognitive development*. New York: Plenum Press.

Gick, M. L. (1986). Problem-solving strategies. *Educational Psychologist, 21*, 99–120.

Gick, M. L., & Holyoak, K. J. (1980). Analogical problem solving. *Cognitive Psychology, 12*, 306–355.

Gick, M. L., & Holyoak, K. J. (1983). Schema induction and analogical transfer. *Cognitive Psychology, 15*, 1–38.

Gick, M. L., & Holyoak, K. J. (1987). The cognitive basis of knowledge transfer. In S. M. Cormier & J. D. Hagman (Eds.), *Transfer of learning: Contemporary research and applications*. San Diego: Academic Press.

Gilligan, S. G., & Bower, G. H. (1984). Cognitive consequences of emotional arousal. In C. Izard, J. Kagen, & R. Zajonc (Eds.), *Emotions, cognition, and behaviour*. New York: Cambridge University Press.

Glanzer, M., & Cunitz, A. R. (1966). Two storage mechanisms in free recall. *Journal of Verbal Learning and Verbal Behavior, 5*, 351–360.

Glanzer, M., & Nolan, S. D. (1986). Memory mechanisms in text comprehension. In G. H. Bower (Ed.), *The psychology of learning and motivation: Advances in research and theory* (Vol. 20). Orlando, FL: Academic Press.

Glaser, R. (1979). Trends and research questions in psychological research on learning and schooling. *Educational Researcher, 8*, 6–13.

Glaser, R. (1987). Thoughts on expertise. In C. Schooler & W. Schaie (Eds.), *Cognitive functioning and*

social structure over the life course. Norwood, NJ: Ablex.

Glass, A. L., & Holyoak, K. J. (1975). Alternative conceptions of semantic memory. *Cognition, 3*, 313–339.

Glass, A. L., Holyoak, K. J., & O'Dell, C. (1974). Production frequency and the verification of quantified statements. *Journal of Verbal Learning and Verbal Behavior, 13*, 237–254.

Glass, A. L., Holyoak, K. J., & Santa, J. L. (1979). *Cognition*. Reading, MA: Addison-Wesley.

Gleitman, H. (1985). Some trends in the study of cognition. In S. Koch & D. E. Leary (Eds.), *A century of psychology as science*. New York: McGraw-Hill.

Glenberg, A. (1976). Monotonic and nonmonotonic lag effects in paired-associated and recognition memory paradigms. *Journal of Verbal Learning and Verbal Behavior, 15*, 1–16.

Glover, J., & Gary, A. L. (1976). Procedures to increase some aspects of creativity. *Journal of Applied Behavior Analysis, 9*, 79–84.

Glucksberg, S. (1962). The influence of strength of drive on functional fixedness and perceptual recognition. *Journal of Experimental Psychology, 63*, 36–41.

Glucksberg, S., & Weisberg, R. W. (1966). Verbal behavior and problem solving: Some effects of labeling in a functional fixedness problem. *Journal of Experimental Psychology, 71*, 659–664.

Glueck, S., & Glueck, E. (1950). *Unraveling juvenile delinquency*. Cambridge, MA: Harvard University Press.

Glynn, S. M., & Di Vesta, F. J. (1977). Outline and hierarchical organization as aids for study and retrieval. *Journal of Educational Psychology, 69*, 89–95.

Godden, D. R., & Baddeley, A. D. (1975). Context-dependent memory in two natural environments: On land and underwater. *British Journal of Psychology, 66*, 325–332.

Good, T. L. (1987). Two decades of research on teacher expectations: Findings and future directions. *Journal of Teacher Education, 38*(4), 32–47.

Good, T. L., & Brophy, J. E. (1984). *Looking in classrooms*. New York: Harper & Row.

Good, T. L., & Brophy, J. E. (1986). *Educational psychology: A realistic approach*. New York: Longman.

Gorman, A. M. (1961). Recognition memory for nouns as a function of abstractness and frequency. *Journal of Experimental Psychology, 61*, 23–29.

Grabe, M. (1986). Attentional processes in education. In G. D. Phye & T. Andre (Eds.), *Cognitive classroom learning: Understanding, thinking, and problem solving*. Orlando: Academic Press.

Graessner, A. C., & Bower, G. H. (Eds.) (1990). *Inferences and text comprehension. The psychology of learning and motivation: Advances in research and theory* (Vol. 25). Orlando: Academic Press.

Graf, P., & Schachter, D. L. (1985). Implicit and explicit memory for new associations in normal and amnesic subjects. *Journal of Experimental Psychology: Learning, Memory, and Cognition, 10*, 164–178.

Graham, S. (1984). Communicating sympathy and anger to black and white students: The cognitive (attributional) consequences of affective cues. *Journal of Personality and Social Psychology, 47*, 40–54.

Graham, S. (1990). Communicating low ability in the classroom: Bad things good teachers sometimes do. In S. Graham & V. S. Folkes (Eds.), *Attribution theory: Applications to achievement, mental health, and interpersonal conflict*. Hillsdale, NJ: Erlbaum.

Graham, S. (1991). A review of attribution theory in achievement contexts. *Educational Psychology Review, 3*, 5–39.

Graham, S., & Barker, G. (1990). The downside of help: An attributional-developmental analysis of helping behavior as a low ability cue. *Journal of Educational Psychology, 82*, 7–14.

Granger, R. H., Jr., & Schlimmer, J. C. (1986). The computation of contingency in classical conditioning. In G. H. Bower (Ed.), *The psychology of learning and motivation: Advances in research and theory* (Vol. 20). Orlando, FL: Academic Press.

Gray, J. A., & Wedderburn, A. A. I. (1960). Grouping strategies with simultaneous stimuli. *Quarterly Journal of Experimental Psychology, 12*, 180–184.

Gray, W. D., & Orasanu, J. M. (1987). Transfer of cognitive skills. In S. M. Cormier & J. D. Hagman (Eds.), *Transfer of learning: Contemporary research and applications*. San Diego: Academic Press.

Green, L., & Rachlin, H. (1977). Pigeon's preferences for stimulus information: Effects of amount of information. *Journal of the Experimental Analysis of Behavior, 27*, 255–263.

Green, R. G. (1980). Test anxiety and cue utilization. In I. G. Sarason (Ed.), *Test anxiety: Theory, research, and applications*. Hillsdale, NJ: Erlbaum.

Greeno, J. G. (1973). The structure of memory and the process of solving problems. In R. L. Solso (Ed.), *Contemporary issues in cognitive psychology: The Loyola Symposium*. Washington, DC: Winston.

Greeno, J. G. (1991). A view of mathematical problem solving in school. In M. U. Smith (Ed.), *Toward a unified theory of problem solving: Views from the content domains*. Hillsdale, NJ: Erlbaum.

Greenspoon, J., & Ranyard, R. (1957). Stimulus conditions and retroactive inhibition. *Journal of Experimental Psychology, 53*, 55–59.

Greer, R. D. (1983). Contingencies of the science and technology of teaching and pre-behavioristic research practices in education. *Educational Researcher, 12*(1), 3–9.

Greiner, J. M., & Karoly, P. (1976). Effects of self-control training on study activity and academic performance: An analysis of self-monitoring, self-reward, and systematic planning components. *Journal of Counseling Psychology, 23*, 495–502.

Griffore, R. J. (1981). *Child development: An educational perspective*. Springfield, IL: Charles C. Thomas.

Grimes, J. W., & Allinsmith, W. (1961). Compulsivity, anxiety and school achievement. *Merrill-Palmer Quarterly, 7*, 247–271.

Grimes, J. W., & Allinsmith, W. (1970). Compulsivity, anxiety, and school achievement. In P. H. Mussen, J. J. Conger, & J. Kagan (Eds.), *Readings in child development and personality*. New York: Harper & Row.

Grolnick, W. S., & Ryan, R. M. (1987). Autonomy in children's learning: An experimental and individual difference investigation. *Journal of Personality and Social Psychology, 52*, 890–898.

Groninger, L. D. (1971). Mnemonic imagery and forgetting. *Psychonomic Science, 23*, 161–163.

Gronlund, N. E. (1978). *Stating objectives for classroom instruction* (2nd ed.). New York: Macmillan.

Gross, T. F., & Mastenbrook, M. (1980). Examination of the effects of state anxiety on problem-solving efficiency under high and low memory conditions. *Journal of Educational Psychology, 72*, 605–609.

Guevremont, D. C., Osnes, P. G., & Stokes, T. F. (1988). The functional role of preschoolers' verbalization in the generalization of self-instructional training. *Journal of Applied Behavior Analysis, 21*, 45–55.

Guskey, T. R. (1985). *Implementing mastery learning*. Belmont, CA: Wadsworth.

Guthrie, E. R. (1935). *The psychology of learning*. New York: Harper & Row.

Guthrie, E. R. (1942). Conditioning: A theory of learning in terms of stimulus, response, and association. In *The psychology of learning*, 41st Yearbook of the National Society for the Study of Education, Part II. Chicago: University of Chicago Press.

Hale, G. A. (1983). Students' predictions of prose forgetting and the effects of study strategies. *Journal of Educational Psychology, 75*, 708–715.

Hall, J. F. (1966). *The psychology of learning*. Philadelphia: J. B. Lippincott.

Hall, J. F. (1971). *Verbal learning and retention*. Philadelphia: J. B. Lippincott.

Hall, R. V., Axelrod, S., Foundopoulos, M., Shellman, J., Campbell, R. A., & Cranston, S. S. (1971). The effective use of punishment to modify behavior in the classroom. *Educational Technology, 11*(4), 24–26. Reprinted in K. D. O'Leary & S. O'Leary (Eds.) (1972), *Classroom management: The successful use of behavior modification*. New York: Pergamon.

Hall, W. S. (1989). Reading comprehension. *American Psychologist, 44*, 157–161.

Hallahan, D. P., Marshall, K. J., & Lloyd, J. W. (1981). Self-recording during group instruction: Effects of attention to task. *Learning Disabilities Quarterly, 4*, 407–413.

Haller, E. P., Child, D. A., & Walberg, H. J. (1988). Can comprehension be taught? A quantitative synthesis of "metacognitive" studies. *Educational Researcher, 17*(9), 5–8.

Halpern, D. F. (1985). The influence of sex-role stereotypes on prose recall. *Sex Roles, 12*, 363–375.

Halpin, G., & Halpin, G. (1982). Experimental investigations of the effects of study and testing on student learning, retention, and ratings of instruction. *Journal of Educational Psychology, 74*, 32–38.

Hampton, J. A. (1981). An investigation of the nature of abstract concepts. *Memory and Cognition, 9*, 149–156.

Hansen, J., & Pearson, P. D. (1983). An instructional study: Improving the inferential comprehension of good and poor fourth-grade readers. *Journal of Educational Psychology, 75*, 821–829.

Harari, H., & McDavid, J. W. (1973). Name stereotypes and teachers' expectations. *Journal of Educational Psychology, 65*, 222–225.

Haring, T. G., Roger, B., Lee, M., Breen, C., & Gaylord-Ross, R. (1986). Teaching social language to moderately handicapped students. *Journal of Applied Behavior Analysis, 19*, 159–171.

Harlow, H. F. (1949). The formation of learning sets. *Psychological Review, 56*, 51–65.

Harlow, H. F. (1950). Analysis of discrimination learning by monkeys. *Journal of Experimental Psychology, 40*, 26–39.

Harlow, H. F. (1959). Learning set and error factor theory. In S. Koch (Ed.), *Psychology: A study of science*. New York: McGraw-Hill.

Harlow, H. F., & Zimmerman, R. R. (1959). Affectional responses in the infant monkey. *Science, 130*, 421–432.

Harris, K. R. (1986). Self-monitoring of attentional behavior versus self-monitoring of productivity: Effects of on-task behavior and academic response rate among learning disabled children. *Journal of Applied Behavior Analysis, 19*, 417–423.

Harris, M. (1985). Visualization and spelling competence. *Journal of Developmental Education, 9*(2), 2–5; 31.

Harris, M. J., & Rosenthal, R. (1985). Mediation of interpersonal expectancy effects: 31 meta-analyses. *Psychological Bulletin, 97*, 363–386.

Harris, R. J. (1977). Comprehension of pragmatic implications in advertising. *Journal of Applied Psychology, 62*, 603–608.

Harris, V. W., & Sherman, J. A. (1973). Use and analysis of the "Good Behavior Game" to reduce disruptive classroom behavior. *Journal of Applied Behavior Analysis, 6*, 405–417.

Harrow, A. J. (1972). *A taxonomy of the psychomotor domain: A guide for developing behavioral objectives.* New York: David McKay.

Harter, S. (1978). Pleasure derived from optimal challenge and the effects of extrinsic rewards on children's difficulty level choices. *Child Development, 49*, 788–799.

Harter, S. (1981). A new self-report scale of intrinsic versus extrinsic orientation in the classroom: Motivational and informational components. *Developmental Psychology, 17*, 300–312.

Harter, S. (1983). Developmental perspectives on the self-system. In E. M. Hetherington (Ed.), *Handbook of child psychology: Vol. 4. Socialization, personality, and social development*. New York: John Wiley.

Harter, S., & Connell, J. P. (1984). A comparison of alternative models of the relationships between academic achievement and children's perceptions of competence, control, and motivational orientation. In J. Nicholls (Ed.), *The development of achievement-related cognitions and behaviors*. Greenwich, CT: JAI Press.

Harter, S., Whitesell, N. R., & Kowalski, P. (1992). Individual differences in the effects of educational transitions on young adolescents' perceptions of competence and motivational orientation. *American Educational Research Journal, 29*, 777–807.

Hartley, J., Bartlett, S., & Branthwaite, A. (1980). Underlining can make a difference—sometimes. *Journal of Educational Research, 73*, 218–224.

Hartley, J., & Trueman, M. (1982). The effects of summaries on the recall of information from prose: Five experimental studies. *Human Learning, 1*, 63–82.

Hartmann, W. K., Miller, R., & Lee, P. (1984). *Out of the cradle: Exploring the frontiers beyond earth*. New York: Workman.

Hasher, L., & Zacks, R. T. (1984). Automatic processing of fundamental information. *American Psychologist, 39*, 1372–1388.

Hasselhorn, M., & Körkel, J. (1986). Metacognitive versus traditional reading instructions: The mediating role of domain-specific knowledge on children's text-processing. *Human Learning, 5*, 75–90.

Hastings, W. M. (1977). In praise of regurgitation. *Intellect, 105*, 349–350.

Hativa, N., & Shorer, D. (1989). Socioeconomic status, aptitude, and gender differences in CAI gains of arithmetic. *Journal of Educational Research, 83*(1), 11–21.

Hawk, P. P. (1986). Using graphic organizers to increase achievement in middle school life science. *Science Education, 70*, 81–87.

Hayes, D. A., & Henk, W. A. (1986). Understanding and remembering complex prose augmented by analogic and pictorial illustration. *Journal of Reading Behavior, 18*, 63–78.

Hayes, K. J., & Hayes, C. (1952). Imitation in a home-raised chimpanzee. *Journal of Comparative & Physiological Psychology, 45*, 450–459.

Hayes, S. C., Rosenfarb, I., Wulfert, E., Munt, E. D., Korn, Z., & Zettle, R. D. (1985). Self-reinforcement effects: An artifact of social standard setting? *Journal of Applied Behavior Analysis, 18*, 201–214.

Hayes–Roth, B., & Thorndyke, P. W. (1979). Integration of knowledge from text. *Journal of Verbal Learning and Verbal Behavior, 18*, 91–108.

Haygood, R. C., & Bourne, L. E., Jr. (1965). Attribute- and rule-learning aspects of conceptual behavior. *Psychological Review, 72*, 175–195.

Hebb, D. O. (1955). Drives and the c. n. s. (conceptual nervous system). *Psychological Review, 62*, 243–254.

Hegland, S., & Andre, T. (1992). Helping learners construct knowledge. *Educational Psychology Review, 4*, 223–240.

Heit, E. (1993). Modeling the effects of expectations on recognition memory. *Psychological Science, 4*, 244–251.

Heller, J. I., & Hungate, H. N. (1985). Implications for mathematics instruction of research on scientific problem solving. In E. A. Silver (Ed.), *Teaching and learning mathematical problem solving: Multiple research perspectives*. Hillsdale, NJ: Erlbaum.

Henle, M. (1985). Rediscovering gestalt psychology. In S. Koch & D. E. Leary (Eds.), *A century of psychology as science*. New York: McGraw-Hill.

Hennessey, B. A., & Amabile, T. M. (1987). *Creativity and learning*. Washington, DC: National Education Association.

Herbert, J. J., & Harsh, C. M. (1944). Observational learning by cats. *Journal of Comparative Psychology, 37*, 81–95.

Hergenhahn, B. R. (1988). *An introduction to theories of learning* (3rd ed.). Englewood Cliffs, NJ: Prentice-Hall.

Herrnstein, R. J. (1969). Method and theory in the study of avoidance. *Psychological Review, 76*, 49–69.

Herrnstein, R. J. (1977). The evolution of behaviorism. *American Psychologist, 32*, 593–603.

Herrnstein, R. J. (1990). Behavior, reinforcement and utility. *Psychological Science, 1*, 217–223.

Herrnstein, R. J., Nickerson, R. S., de Sánchez, M., & Swets, J. A. (1986). Teaching thinking skills. *American Psychologist, 41*, 1279–1289.

Hess, R. D., & McDevitt, T. M. (1984). Some cognitive consequences of maternal intervention techniques: A longitudinal study. *Child Development, 55*, 2017–2030.

Hess, R. D., & McDevitt, T. M. (1989). Family. In E. Barnouw (Ed.), *International encyclopedia of communications*. New York and Oxford: Oxford University Press.

Heuer, F., & Reisberg, D. (1990). Vivid memories of emotional events: The accuracy of remembered minutiae. *Memory and Cognition, 18*, 496–506.

Hidi, S. (1990). Interest and its contribution as a mental resource for learning. *Review of Educational Research, 60*, 549–571.

Hidi, S., & Anderson, V. (1992). Situational interest and its impact on reading and expository writing. In K. A. Renninger, S. Hidi, & A. Krapp (Eds.), *The role of interest in learning and development*. Hillsdale, NJ: Erlbaum.

Hiebert, J., & Wearne, D. (1993). Instructional tasks, classroom discourse, and students' learning in second-grade arithmetic. *American Educational Research Journal, 30*, 393–425.

Higbee, K. L. (1976). Can young children use mnemonics? *Psychological Reports, 38*, 18.

Hill, K. T. (1984). Debilitating motivation and testing: A major educational problem, possible solutions, and policy applications. In R. Ames & C. Ames (Eds.), *Research on motivation in education: Vol. 1. Student motivation*. New York: Academic Press.

Hill, K. T., & Eaton, W. O. (1977). The interaction of test anxiety and success/failure experiences in determining children's arithmetic performance. *Developmental Psychology, 13*, 205–211.

Hillerich, R. L. (1976). *Spelling: An element in written expression*. Columbus, OH: Merrill.

Hinsley, D., Hayes, J. R., & Simon, H. A. (1977). From words to equations. In P. Carpenter & M. Just (Eds.), *Cognitive processes in comprehension.* Hillsdale, NJ: Erlbaum.

Hinton, B. L. (1968). Environmental frustration and creative problem solving. *Journal of Applied Psychology, 52,* 211–217.

Hinton, G. E., & Anderson, J. A. (1981). *Parallel models of associative memory.* Hillsdale, NJ: Erlbaum.

Hinton, G. E., McClelland, J. L., & Rumelhart, D. E. (1986). Distributed representations. In D. E. Rumelhart, J. L. McClelland, & the PDP Research Group (Eds.), *Parallel distributed processing: Vol. 1. Foundations.* Cambridge, MA: M.I.T. Press.

Hintzman, D. L. (1978). *The psychology of learning and memory.* San Francisco: W. H. Freeman.

Hiroto, D. S. (1974). Locus of control and learned helplessness. *Journal of Experimental Psychology, 102,* 187–193.

Hiroto, D. S., & Seligman, M. E. P. (1975). Generality of learned helplessness in man. *Journal of Personality and Social Psychology, 31,* 311–327.

Hobbs, T. R., & Holt, M. M. (1976). The effects of token reinforcement on the behavior of delinquents in cottage settings. *Journal of Applied Behavior Analysis, 9,* 189–198.

Hockman, C. H., & Lipsitt, L. P. (1961). Delay-of-reward gradients in discrimination learning with children for two levels of difficulty. *Journal of Comparative and Physiological Psychology, 54,* 24–27.

Hoffman, M. L. (1984). Interaction of affect and cognition in empathy. In C. E. Izard, J. Kagan, & R. B. Zajonc (Eds.), *Emotions, cognition, and behavior.* Cambridge, England: Cambridge University Press.

Hokanson, J. E., & Burgess, M. (1962). The effects of three types of aggression on vascular processes. *Journal of Abnormal and Social Psychology, 64,* 446–449.

Holley, C. D., & Dansereau, D. F. (1984). *Spatial learning strategies: Techniques, applications, and related issues.* Orlando: Academic Press.

Holmes, D. S. (1974). Investigation of repression: Differential recall of material experimentally or naturally associated with ego threat. *Psychological Bulletin, 81,* 632–653.

Holmes, D. S. (1990). The evidence for suppression: An examination of sixty years of research. In J. Singer (Ed.), *Repression and dissociation: Implications for personality theory, psychopathology, and health.* Chicago: University of Chicago Press.

Holt-Reynolds, D. (1992). Personal history-based beliefs as relevant prior knowledge in course work. *American Educational Research Journal, 29,* 325–349.

Holyoak, K. J. (1985). The pragmatics of analogical transfer. In G. H. Bower (Ed.), *The psychology of learning and motivation: Advances in research and theory* (Vol. 19). Orlando: Academic Press.

Holyoak, K. J. (1987). Review of parallel distributed processing. *Science, 236,* 992.

Holz, W. C., & Azrin, N. H. (1962). Recovery during punishment by intense noise. *Psychological Reports, 11,* 655–657.

Homme, L. E., Csanyi, A. P., Gonzales, M. A., & Rechs, J. R. (1970). *How to use contingency contracting in the classroom.* Champaign, IL: Research Press.

Homme, L. E., deBaca, P. C., Devine, J. V., Steinhorst, R., & Rickert, E. J. (1963). Use of the Premack principle in controlling the behavior of nursery school children. *Journal of the Experimental Analysis of Behavior, 6,* 544.

Hopkins, R. H., & Atkinson, R. C. (1968). Priming and the retrieval of names from long-term memory. *Psychonomic Science, 11,* 219–220.

Horgan, D. (1990, April). Students' predictions of test grades: Calibration and metacognition. Paper presented at the annual meeting of the American Educational Research Association, Boston, MA.

Hovland, C. I., & Weiss, W. (1953). Transmission of information concerning concepts through positive and negative instances. *Journal of Experimental Psychology, 43,* 175–182.

Howard, D. V. (1983). *Cognitive psychology: Memory, language, and thought.* New York: Macmillan.

Howe, M. J. A. (1970). Using students' notes to examine the role of the individual learner in acquiring meaningful subject matter. *Journal of Educational Research, 64,* 61–63.

Hudspeth, W. J. (1985). Developmental neuropsychology: Functional implications of quantitative EEG maturation. [Abstract] *Journal of Clinical and Experimental Neuropsychology, 7,* 606.

Huff, J. A. (1988). Personalized behavior modification: An in-school suspension program that teaches students how to change. *School Counselor, 35,* 210–214.

Hughes, J. N. (1988). *Cognitive behavior therapy with children in schools.* New York: Pergamon.

Hull, C. L. (1920). Quantitative aspects of the evolution of concepts: An experimental study. *Psychological Monographs, 28* (Whole No. 123).

Hull, C. L. (1934). The concept of the habit-family hierarchy and maze learning. *Psychological Review, 41,* 33–54.

Hull, C. L. (1937). Mind, mechanism, and adaptive behavior. *Psychological Review, 44,* 1–32.

Hull, C. L. (1938). The goal-gradient hypothesis applied to some "field-force" problems in the behavior of young children. *Psychological Review, 45,* 271–299.

Hull, C. L. (1943). *Principles of behavior: An introduction to behavior theory.* New York: Appleton-Century-Crofts.

Hull, C. L. (1951). *Essentials of behavior.* New Haven, CT: Yale University Press.

Hull, C. L. (1952). *A behavior system: An introduction to behavior theory concerning the individual organism.* New Haven, CT: Yale University Press.

Hulse, S. H. (1993). The present status of animal cognition: An introduction. *Psychological Science, 4,* 154–155.

Humphreys, L. G. (1939). Acquisition and extinction of verbal expectations in a situation analogous to conditioning. *Journal of Experimental Psychology, 25,* 294–301.

Hundert, J. (1976). The effectiveness of reinforcement, response cost, and mixed programs on classroom behaviors. *Journal of Applied Behavior Analysis, 9,* 107.

Hunt, E. B. (1962). *Concept learning: An information processing problem.* New York: Wiley.

Hunter, M. (1982). *Mastery teaching.* El Segundo, CA: TIP Publications.

Huston, A. C. (1983). Sex-typing. In E. M. Hetherington (Ed.), *Handbook of child psychology: Vol. 4. Socialization, personality, and social development* (4th ed.). New York: Wiley.

Huston, A. C., Watkins, B. A., & Kunkel, D. (1989). Public policy and children's television. *American Psychologist, 44,* 424–433.

Hyde, T. S., & Jenkins, J. J. (1969). Differential effects of incidental tasks on the organization of recall of a list of highly associated words. *Journal of Experimental Psychology*, *82*, 472–481.

Ickes, W. J., & Layden, M. A. (1978). Attributional styles. In J. Harvey, W. Ickes, & R. Kidd (Eds.), *New directions in attributional research* (Vol. 2). Hillsdale, NJ: Erlbaum.

Igoe, A. R., & Sullivan, H. (1991, April). Gender and grade–level differences in student attributes related to school learning and motivation. Paper presented at the annual meeting of the American Educational Research Association, Chicago.

Inhelder, B., & Piaget, J. (1958). *The growth of logical thinking from childhood to adolescence*. (A. Parsons & S. Milgram, Trans.) New York: Basic Books.

Isaacson, R. L. (1964). Relation between achievement, test anxiety, and curricular choices. *Journal of Abnormal and Social Psychology*, *68*, 447–452.

Iwata, B. A. (1987). Negative reinforcement in applied behavior analysis: An emerging technology. *Journal of Applied Behavior Analysis*, *20*, 361–378.

Iwata, B. A., & Bailey, J. S. (1974). Reward versus cost token systems: An analysis of the effects on students and teacher. *Journal of Applied Behavior Analysis*, 7, 567–576.

Jackson, D. N., Ahmed, S. A., & Heapy, N. A. (1976). Is achievement motivation a unitary construct? *Journal of Research in Personality*, *10*, 1121.

Jacoby, L. L., & Hayman, C. A. G. (1987). Specific visual transfer in word identification. *Journal of Experimental Psychology: Learning, Memory, and Cognition*, *13*, 456–463.

Jacoby, L. L., & Witherspoon, D. (1982). Remembering without awareness. *Canadian Journal of Psychology*, *36*, 300–324.

Jagacinski, C., & Nicholls, J. (1984). Conceptions of ability and related affects in task involvement and ego involvement. *Journal of Educational Psychology*, *76*, 909–919.

Jagacinski, C., & Nicholls, J. (1987). Competence and affect in task involvement and ego involvement: The impact of social comparison information. *Journal of Educational Psychology*, *79*, 107–114.

Jagacinski, C. M., & Nicholls, J. G. (1990). Reducing effort to protect perceived ability: "They'd do it but I wouldn't." *Journal of Educational Psychology*, *82*, 15–21.

James, W. (1890). *Principles of psychology*. New York: Holt.

Jenkins, J. J., & Russell, W. A. (1952). Associative clustering during recall. *Journal of Abnormal and Social Psychology*, *47*, 818–821.

Johnson, D. W., & Johnson, R. T. (1987). *Learning together and alone: Cooperative, competitive, and individualistic learning* (2nd ed.). Englewood Cliffs, NJ: Prentice-Hall.

Johnson, M. K., Bransford, J. D., & Solomon, S. K. (1973). Memory for tacit implications of sentences. *Journal of Experimental Psychology*, *98*, 203–205.

Johnson, R. N. (1972). *Aggression in man and animals*. Philadelphia: Saunders.

Johnson, R. T. (1989, October). Ways to change the way we teach. Workshop presented at the University of Northern Colorado, Greeley, CO.

Johnson, T. D., Langford, K. G., & Quorn, K. C. (1981). Characteristics of an effective spelling program. *Language Arts*, *58*, 581–588.

Johnson-Laird, P. N., & Wason, P. C. (1977). Introduction to conceptual thinking. In P. N. Johnson-Laird & P. C. Wason (Eds.), *Thinking: Readings in cognitive science*. Cambridge: Cambridge University Press.

Johnstone, A. H., & El-Banna, H. (1986). Capacities, demands and processes—a predictive model for science education. *Education in Chemistry*, *23*, 80–84.

Jonassen, D., Hartley, J., & Trueman, M. (1986). The effects of learner-generated versus text-provided headings on immediate and delayed recall and comprehension: An exploratory study. *Human Learning*, *5*, 139–150.

Jones, B. F., & Hall, J. W. (1982). School applications of the mnemonic keyword method as a study strategy by eighth graders. *Journal of Educational Psychology*, *74*, 230–237.

Jones, B. P. (1993). Repression: The evolution of a psychoanalytic concept from the 1890's to the 1990's. *Journal of the American Psychoanalytic Association*, *41*(1), 63–93.

Jones, H. E., & English, H. B. (1926). Notional vs. rote memory. *American Journal of Psychology.*, *37*, 602–603.

Jones, M. C. (1924). The elimination of children's fears. *Journal of Experimental Psychology*, *7*, 382–390.

Judd, C. H. (1932). Autobiography. In C. Murchison (Ed.), *History of psychology in autobiography* (Vol. 2). Worcester, MA: Clark Univ. Press.

Juvonen, J. (1991, April). The effect of attributions and interpersonal attitudes on social emotions and behavior. Paper presented at the annual meeting of the American Educational Research Association, Chicago.

Kahneman, D. (1973). *Attention and effort*. Englewood Cliffs, NJ: Prentice-Hall.

Kahneman, D., & Tversky, A. (1972). Subjective probability: A judgment of representativeness. *Cognitive Psychology*, *3*, 430–454.

Kahneman, D., & Tversky, A. (1973). On the psychology of prediction. *Psychological Review*, *80*, 237–251.

Kail, R. (1990). *The development of memory in children* (3rd ed.). New York: Freeman.

Kamin, L. J. (1956). The effects of termination of the CS and avoidance of the US on avoidance learning. *Journal of Comparative and Physiological Psychology*, *49*, 420–424.

Kamin, L. J., Brimer, C. J., & Black, A. H. (1963). Conditioned suppression as a monitor of fear of the CS in the course of avoidance training. *Journal of Comparative and Physiological Psychology*, *56*, 497–501.

Kantor, J. R. (1959). *Interbehavioral psychology*. Granville, OH: Principia Press.

Kardash, C. M., & Amlund, J. T. (1991). Self-reported learning strategies and learning from expository text. *Contemporary Educational Psychology*, *16*, 117-138.

Katkovsky, W., Crandall, V. C., & Good, S. (1967). Parental antecedents of children's beliefs in internal-external control of reinforcements in intellectual achievement situations. *Child Development*, *38*, 765–776.

Kaufman, A., Baron, A., & Kopp, R. E. (1966). Some effects of instructions on human operant behavior. *Psychonomic Monograph Supplements*, *1*, 243–250.

Kazdin, A. E. (1972). Response cost: The removal of conditional reinforcers for therapeutic change. *Behavior Therapy*, *3*, 533–546.

Keele, S. W. (1973). *Attention and human performance*. Pacific Palisades, CA: Goodyear.

Keller, F. S. (1968). Goodbye teacher. *Journal of Applied Behavior Analysis*, *1*, 79–89.

Keller, F. S. (1974). An international venture in behavior modification. In F.

S. Keller & E. Ribes-Inesta (Eds.), *Behavior modification: Applications to education*. New York: Academic Press.

Keller, J. M. (1987). Development and use of the ARCS model of instructional design. *Journal of Instructional Development, 10*(3), 2–10.

Kelley, M. L., & Carper, L. B. (1988). Home-based reinforcement procedures. In J. C. Witt, S. N. Elliott, & F. M. Gresham (Eds.), *Handbook of behavior therapy in education*. New York: Plenum Press.

Kendler, H. H. (1985). Behaviorism and psychology: An uneasy alliance. In S. Koch & D. E. Leary (Eds.), *A century of psychology as science*. New York: McGraw-Hill.

Kendler, H. H., & Kendler, T. S. (1961). Effect of verbalization on reversal shifts in children. *Science, 134*, 1619-1620.

Kendler, H. H., & Kendler, T. S. (1962). Vertical and horizontal processes in problem solving. *Psychological Review, 69*, 1–16.

Kendler, T. S. (1961). Concept formation. *Annual Review of Psychology, 13*, 447–472.

Kendler, T. S., & Kendler, H. H. (1959). Reversal and nonreversal shifts in kindergarten children. *Journal of Experimental Psychology, 58*, 56–60.

Keppel, G., & Underwood, B. J. (1962). Proactive inhibition in short-term retention of single items. *Journal of Verbal Learning and Verbal Behavior, 1*, 153–161.

Kiewra, K. A. (1985). Investigating notetaking and review: A depth of processing alternative. *Educational Psychologist, 20*, 23–32.

Kiewra, K. A. (1989). A review of notetaking: The encoding-storage paradigm and beyond. *Educational Psychology Review, 1*, 147–172.

Kiewra, K. A., DuBois, N. F., Christian, D., McShane, A., Meyerhoffer, M., & Roskelly, D. (1988, April). Theoretical and practical aspects of taking, reviewing and borrowing conventional, skeletal or matrix lecture notes. Paper presented at American Educational Research Assn., New Orleans.

Killeen, P. R. (1991). Behavior's time. In G. H. Bower (Ed.), *The psychology of learning and motivation: Advances in research and theory* (Vol. 27). San Diego: Academic Press.

Kilpatrick, J. (1985). A retrospective account of the past 25 years of research on teaching mathematical problem solving. In E. A. Silver (Ed.), *Teaching and learning mathematical problem solving: Multiple research perspectives*. Hillsdale, NJ: Erlbaum.

King, A. (1992). Comparison of self-questioning, summarizing, and note-taking-review as strategies for learning from lectures. *American Educational Research Journal, 29*, 303–323.

King, N. J., & Ollendick, T. H. (1989). Children's anxiety and phobic disorders in school settings: Classification, assessment, and intervention issues. *Review of Educational Research, 59*, 431–470.

Kinnick, V. (1990). The effect of concept teaching in preparing nursing students for clinical practice. *Journal of Nursing Education, 29*, 362–366.

Kintsch, W. (1977). Reading comprehension as a function of text structure. In A. S. Reber & D. L. Scarborough (Eds.), *Toward a psychology of reading*. New York: Wiley.

Kintsch, W., Mandel, T. S., & Kozminsky, E. (1977). Summarizing scrambled stories. *Memory and Cognition, 5*, 547–552.

Kintsch, W., & van Dijk, T. A. (1978). Toward a model of text comprehension and production. *Psychological Review, 85*, 363–394.

Kirkland, M. C. (1971). The effect of tests on students and schools. *Review of Educational Research, 41*, 303–350.

Klatzky, R. L. (1975). *Human memory*. San Francisco: Freeman.

Klausmeier, H. J. (1990). Conceptualizing. In B. F. Jones & L. Idol (Eds.), *Dimensions of thinking and cognitive instruction*. Hillsdale, NJ: Erlbaum.

Klein, J. D. (1990, April). The effect of interest, task performance, and reward contingencies on self-efficacy. Paper presented at the annual meeting of the American Educational Research Association, Boston.

Klein, P. S. (1975). Effects of open vs. structured teacher-student interaction on creativity of children with different levels of anxiety. *Psychology in the Schools, 12*, 286–288.

Klein, S. B. (1987). *Learning: Principles and applications*. New York: McGraw-Hill.

Kleinsmith, L. J., & Kaplan, S. (1963). Paired associate learning as a function of arousal and interpolated interval. *Journal of Experimental Psychology, 65*, 190–193.

Kletzien, S. B. (1988, April). Achieving and non-achieving high school readers' use of comprehension strategies for reading expository text. Paper presented at the American Educational Research Assn., New Orleans.

Klinger, E. (1975). Consequences of commitment to and disengagement from incentives. *Psychological Review, 82*, 1–25.

Klinger, E. (1977). *Meaning and void: Inner experience and the incentives in people's lives*. Minneapolis: University of Minnesota Press.

Knight, S. L. (1988, April). Examining the relationship between teacher behaviors and students' cognitive reading strategies. Paper presented at the American Educational Research Assn., New Orleans.

Koestner, R., Ryan, R. M., Bernieri, F., & Holt, K. (1984). Setting limits on children's behavior: The differential effects of controlling vs. informational styles on intrinsic motivation and creativity. *Journal of Personality, 52*, 233–248.

Koffka, K. (1935). *Principles of Gestalt psychology*. New York: Harcourt, Brace.

Kohler, I. (1962) Experiments with goggles. *Scientific American, 206*(5), 62–72.

Köhler, W. (1925). *The mentality of apes*. London: Routledge & Kegan Paul.

Köhler, W. (1929). *Gestalt psychology*. New York: Liveright.

Köhler, W. (1938). *The place of value in a world of facts*. New York: Liveright.

Köhler, W. (1940). *Dynamics in psychology*. New York: Liveright.

Köhler, W. (1947). *Gestalt psychology: An introduction to new concepts in modern psychology*. New York: Liveright.

Köhler, W. (1959). Gestalt psychology today. *American Psychologist, 14*, 727–734.

Köhler, W. (1969). *The task of Gestalt psychology*. Princeton, NJ: Princeton University Press.

Kolodner, J. (1985). Memory for experience. In G. H. Bower (Ed.), *The psychology of learning and motivation: Advances in research and theory* (Vol. 19). Orlando: Academic Press.

Kosslyn, S. M. (1980). *Image and mind*. Cambridge, MA: Harvard University Press.

Kosslyn, S. M. (1981). The medium and the message in mental imagery: A theory. *Psychological Review, 88,* 44–66.

Kosslyn, S. M. (1983). *Ghosts in the mind's machine: Creating and using images in the brain.* New York: Norton.

Krapp, A., Hidi, S., & Renninger, K. A. (1992). Interest, learning, and development. In K. A. Renninger, S. Hidi, & A. Krapp (Eds.), *The role of interest in learning and development.* Hillsdale, NJ: Erlbaum.

Krathwohl, D. R., Bloom, B. S., & Masia, B. B. (1964). *Taxonomy of educational objectives. Handbook II: Affective domain.* New York: David McKay.

Krueger, W. C. F. (1929). The effect of overlearning on retention. *Journal of Experimental Psychology, 12,* 71–78.

Krumboltz, J. D., & Krumboltz, H. B. (1972). *Changing children's behavior.* Englewood Cliffs, NJ: Prentice-Hall.

Kulhavy, R. W., Lee, J. B., & Caterino, L. C. (1985). Conjoint retention of maps and related discourse. *Contemporary Educational Psychology, 10,* 28–37.

Kulhavy, R. W., Peterson, S., & Schwartz, N. H. (1986). Working memory: The encoding process. In G. D. Phye & T. Andre (Eds.), *Cognitive classroom learning: Understanding, thinking, and problem solving.* Orlando: Academic Press.

Kulhavy, R. W., Schwartz, N. H., & Shaha, S. H. (1983). Spatial representation of maps. *American Journal of Psychology, 96,* 337–351.

Kulik, C. C., Kulik, J. A., & Bangert–Drowns, R. L. (1990). Effectiveness of mastery learning programs: A meta–analysis. *Review of Educational Research, 60,* 265–299.

Kulik, C. C., Kulik, J. A., & Shwalb, B. J. (1983). College programs for high–risk and disadvantaged students: A meta–analysis of findings. *Review of Educational Research, 53,* 397–414.

Kulik, J. A., & Kulik, C. C. (1988). Timing of feedback and verbal learning. *Review of Educational Research, 58,* 79–97.

Kulik, J. A., Kulik, C. C., & Cohen, P. A. (1979). A meta–analysis of outcome studies of Keller's Personalized System of Instruction. *American Psychologist, 34,* 307–318.

Kulik, J. A., Kulik, C. C., & Cohen, P. A. (1980). Effectiveness of computer-based college teaching: A meta–

analysis of findings. *Review of Educational Research, 50,* 525–544.

Kyle, W. C., & Shymansky, J. A. (1989, April). Enhancing learning through conceptual change teaching. *NARST News, 31,* 7–8.

LaBerge, D., & Samuels, S. J. (1974). Toward a theory of automatic information processing in reading. *Cognitive Psychology, 6,* 293–323.

Labov, W. (1973). The boundaries of words and their meanings. In C.-J. N. Bailey & R. W. Shuy (Eds.), *New ways of analyzing variations in English.* Washington, DC: Georgetown University Press.

Lachter, J., & Bever, T. G. (1988). The relation between linguistic structure and associative theories of language learning—a critique of some connectionist learning models. *Cognition, 28,* 195–247.

Landauer, T. K. (1962). Rate of implicit speech. *Perceptual and Motor Skills, 15,* 646.

Lange, P. C. (1972). What's the score on programmed instruction? *Today's Education, 61,* 59.

Larkin, J. H. (1980). Teaching problem solving in physics: The psychological lab and the practical classroom. In D. T. Tuma & F. Reif (Eds.), *Problem solving and education: Issues in teaching and research.* Hillsdale, NJ: Erlbaum.

Larkin, J. H. (1983). The role of problem representation in physics. In D. Gentner & A. L. Stevens (Eds.), *Mental models.* Hillsdale, NJ: Erlbaum.

Lee, J. F., Jr., & Pruitt, K. W. (1984). *Providing for individual differences in student learning: A mastery learning approach.* Springfield, IL: Charles C. Thomas.

Lee, O. (1991, April). Motivation to learn subject matter content: The case of science. Paper presented at the annual meeting of the American Educational Research Association, Chicago.

Lee, O., & Anderson, C. W. (1991, April). Student motivation in middle school science classrooms. Paper presented at the annual meeting of the American Educational Research Association, Chicago.

Lee, O., & Anderson, C. W. (1993). Task engagement and conceptual change in middle school science classrooms. *American Educational Research Journal, 30,* 585–610.

Leff, R. (1969). Effects of punishment intensity and consistency on the internalization of behavioral sup-

pression in children. *Developmental Psychology, 1,* 345–356.

Leherissey, B. L., O'Neil, H. F., Jr., & Hansen, D. N. (1971). Effects of memory support on state anxiety and performance in computer–assisted learning. *Journal of Educational Psychology, 62,* 413–420.

Leinhardt, G. (1992). What research on learning tells us about teaching. *Educational Leadership, 49*(7), 20–25.

Lennon, R., Ormrod, J. E., Burger, S. F., & Warren, E. (1990, October). Belief systems of teacher education majors and their possible influences on future classroom performance. Paper presented at the Northern Rocky Mountain Educational Research Association, Greeley, CO.

Lentz, F. E. (1988). Reductive procedures. In J. C. Witt, S. N. Elliott, & F. M. Gresham (Eds.), *Handbook of behavior therapy in education.* New York: Plenum Press.

Lepper, M. R., & Greene, D. (Eds.) (1978). *The hidden costs of reward.* Hillsdale, NJ: Erlbaum.

Lepper, M. R., Greene, D., & Nisbett, R. E. (1973). Understanding children's intrinsic interest with extrinsic rewards: A test of the "overjustification" hypothesis. *Journal of Personality and Social Psychology, 28,* 129–137.

Lepper, M. R., & Gurtner, J. (1989). Children and computers: Approaching the twenty-first century. *American Psychologist, 44,* 170–178.

Lepper, M. R., & Hodell, M. (1989). Intrinsic motivation in the classroom. In C. Ames and R. Ames (Eds.), *Research on motivation in education: Vol. 3. Goals and cognitions.* San Diego: Academic Press.

Lesgold, A. M. (1983). A rationale for computer–based reading instruction. In A. C. Wilkinson (Ed.), *Classroom computers and cognitive science.* New York: Academic Press.

Lester, F. K., Jr. (1985). Methodological considerations in research on mathematical problem–solving instruction. In E. A. Silver (Ed.), *Teaching and learning mathematical problem solving: Multiple research perspectives.* Hillsdale, NJ: Erlbaum.

Lett, B. T. (1973). Delayed reward learning: Disproof of the traditional theory. *Learning and Motivation, 4,* 237–246.

Lett, B. T. (1975). Long delay learning in the T–maze. *Learning and Motivation, 6,* 80–90.

Levin, G. R. (1983). *Child psychology*. Monterey, CA: Brooks/Cole.

Levin, J. R., & Berry, J. K. (1980). Children's learning of all the news that's fit to picture. *Educational Communications and Technology*, 28, 177–185.

Levin, J. R. (1981). The mnemonic '80s: Keywords in the classroom. *Educational Psychologist*, 16, 65–82.

Levin, J. R., McCormick, C. B., Miller, G. E., Berry, J. K., & Pressley, M. (1982). Mnemonic versus nonmnemonic vocabulary learning strategies for children. *American Educational Research Journal*, 19, 121–136.

Levine, M. (1966). Hypothesis behavior by humans during discrimination learning. *Journal of Experimental Psychology*, 71, 331–338.

Lewin, K., Lippitt, R., & White, R. (1939). Pattern of aggressive behavior in experimentally created "social climates." *Journal of Social Psychology*, 10, 271–299.

Lewis, D. J., & Maher, B. A. (1965). Neural consolidation and electroconvulsive shock. *Psychological Review*, 72, 225–239.

Lima, S. D. (1993). Word–initial letter sequences and reading. *Current Directions in Psychological Science*, 2, 139–142.

Lindsay, D. S. (1993). Eyewitness suggestibility. *Current Directions in Psychological Science*, 2, 86–89.

Lindsay, P. H., & Norman, D. A. (1977). *Human information processing*. New York: Academic Press.

Lindvall, C. M., Tamburino, J. L., & Robinson, L. (1982, March). An exploratory investigation of the effect of teaching primary grade children to use specific problem–solving strategies in solving simple story problems. Paper presented at the annual meeting of the American Educational Research Association, New York.

Linton, M. (1986). Ways of searching and the contents of memory. In D. C. Rubin (Ed.), *Autobiographical memory*. Cambridge, England: Cambridge University Press.

Lipsitt, L. P., & Kaye, H. (1964). Conditioned sucking in the human newborn. *Psychonomic Science*, 1, 29–30.

Lipsitt, L. P., & Kaye, H. (1965). Change in neonatal response to optimizing and non–optimizing sucking stimulation. *Psychonomic Science*, 2, 221–222.

Lipson, M. Y. (1982). Learning new information from text: The role of prior knowledge and reading ability. *Journal of Reading Behavior*, 14, 243–261.

Lipson, M. Y. (1983). The influence of religious affiliation on children's memory for text information. *Reading Research Quarterly*, 18, 448–457.

Lipson, M. Y. (1985). The influence of religious affiliation on children's memory for text comprehension. *Reading Research Quarterly*, 18, 448–457.

Liu, L. G. (1990, April). The use of causal questioning to promote narrative comprehension and memory. Paper presented at the annual meeting of the American Educational Research Association, Boston.

Loftus, E. F. (1991). Made in memory: Distortions in recollection after misleading information. In G. H. Bower (Ed.), *The psychology of learning and motivation: Advances in research and theory* (Vol. 27). San Diego: Academic Press.

Loftus, E. F. (1992). When a lie becomes memory's truth: Memory distortion after exposure to misinformation. *Current Directions in Psychological Science*, 1, 121–123.

Loftus, E. F. (1993). The reality of repressed memories. *American Psychologist*, 48, 518–537.

Loftus, E. F., & Loftus, G. R. (1980). On the permanence of stored information in the human brain. *American Psychologist*, 35, 409–420.

Loftus, E. F., & Palmer, J. C. (1974). Reconstruction of automobile destruction: An example of the interaction between language and memory. *Journal of Verbal Learning and Verbal Behavior*, 13, 585–589.

Loftus, G. R., & Loftus, E. F. (1976). *Human memory: The processing of information*. New York: Wiley.

Logue, A. W. (1979). Taste aversion and the generality of the laws of learning. *Psychological Bulletin*, 86, 276–296.

Lorch, R. F., Jr., Lorch, E. P., & Inman, W. E. (1993). Effects of signaling topic structure on text recall. *Journal of Educational Psychology*, 85, 281–290.

Lovitt, T. C., Guppy, T. E., & Blattner, J. E. (1969). The use of free–time contingency with fourth graders to increase spelling accuracy. *Behaviour Research and Therapy*, 7, 151–156.

Luchins, A. S. (1942). Mechanization in problem solving: The effect of Einstellung. *Psychological Monographs*, 54 (Whole No. 248).

Luchins, A. S., & Luchins, E. H. (1950). New experimental attempts at preventing mechanization in problem solving. *Journal of General Psychology*, 42, 279–297.

Lueptow, L. B. (1984). *Adolescent sex roles and social change*. New York: Columbia University Press.

Mace, F. C., Belfiore, P. J., & Shea, M. C. (1989). Operant theory and research on self-regulation. In B. J. Zimmerman & D. H. Schunk (Eds.), *Self-regulated learning and academic achievement: Theory, research, and practice*. New York: Springer–Verlag.

Mace, F. C., Hock, M. L., Lalli, J. S., West, B. J., Belfiore, P., Pinter, E., & Brown, D. K. (1988). Behavioral momentum in the treatment of noncompliance. *Journal of Applied Behavior Analysis*, 21, 123–141.

Mace, F. C., & Kratochwill, T. R. (1988). Self-monitoring. In J. C. Witt, S. N. Elliott, & F. M. Gresham (Eds.), *Handbook of behavior therapy in education*. New York: Plenum Press.

Mace, F. C., Page, T. J., Ivancic, M. T., & O'Brien, S. (1986). Effectiveness of brief time–out with and without contingent delay: A comparative analysis. *Journal of Applied Behavior Analysis*, 19, 79–86.

Macfarlane, A. (1978). What a baby knows. *Human Nature*, 1, 74–81.

MacPherson, E. M., Candee, B. L., & Hohman, R. J. (1974). A comparison of three methods for eliminating disruptive lunchroom behavior. *Journal of Applied Behavior Analysis*, 7, 287–297.

Madsen, C. H., Becker, W. C., & Thomas, D. R. (1968). Rules, praise, and ignoring: Elements of elementary classroom control. *Journal of Applied Behavior Analysis*, 1, 139–150.

Maehr, M. L. (1984). Meaning and motivation: Toward a theory of personal investment. In R. Ames & C. Ames (Eds.), *Research on motivation in education. Vol. 1: Student motivation*. Orlando: Academic Press.

Mager, R. F. (1962). *Preparing instructional objectives*. Belmont, CA: Fearon.

Mager, R. F. (1972). *Goal analysis*. Belmont, CA: Fearon.

Mager, R. F. (1984). *Preparing instructional objectives* (2nd ed.). Belmont, CA: David S. Lake.

Mahoney, M. J., & Thoresen, C. E. (1974). *Self-control: Power to the person*. Monterey, CA: Brooks–Cole.

Maier, N. R. F. (1945). Reasoning in humans III: The mechanisms of equivalent stimuli and of reasoning. *Journal of Experimental Psychology, 35*, 349–360.

Maier, N. R. F., & Janzen, J. C. (1968). Functional values as aids and distractors in problem solving. *Psychological Reports, 22*, 1021–1034.

Maier, S. F., & Seligman, M. E. P. (1976). Learned helplessness: Theory and evidence. *Journal of Experimental Psychology: General, 105*, 3–46.

Mandler, G., & Pearlstone, Z. (1966). Free and constrained concept learning and subsequent recall. *Journal of Verbal Learning and Verbal Behavior, 5*, 126–131.

Mandler, J. M., & Johnson, N. S. (1976). Some of the thousand words a picture is worth. *Journal of Experimental Psychology: Human Learning and Memory, 2*, 529–540.

Mandler, J. M., & Parker, R. E. (1976). Memory for descriptive and spatial information in complex pictures. *Journal of Experimental Psychology: Human Learning and Memory, 2*, 38–48.

Mandler, J. M., & Ritchey, G. H. (1977). Long–term memory for pictures. *Journal of Experimental Psychology: Human Learning and Memory, 3*, 386–396.

Markman, E. (1979). Realizing that you don't understand: Elementary school children's awareness of inconsistencies. *Child Development, 50*, 643–655.

Marsh, H. W. (1986). Verbal and math self-concepts: An internal external frame of reference model. *American Educational Research Journal, 23*, 129–149.

Marsh, H. W. (1990). A multidimensional, hierarchical model of self-concept: Theoretical and empirical justification. *Educational Psychology Review, 2*, 77–172.

Martin, C. L., & Halverson, C. F. (1981). A schematic processing model of sex typing and stereotyping in children. *Child Development, 52*, 1119–1134.

Martin, I., & Levey, A. B. (1987). Learning what will happen next: Conditioning, evaluation, and cognitive processes. In G. Davey (Ed.), *Cognitive processes and Pavlovian conditioning in humans*. Chichester, England: Wiley.

Martin, S. S., Brady, M. P., & Williams, R. E. (1991). Effects of toys on the social behavior of preschool children in integrated and noninte-grated groups: Investigation of a setting event. *Journal of Early Intervention, 15*, 153–161.

Maslow, A. H. (1959). *New knowledge in human values*. New York: Harper & Row.

Maslow, A. H. (1973a). Self-actualizing people: A study of psychological health. In R. J. Lowry (Ed.), *Dominance, self-esteem, self-actualization: Germinal papers of A. H. Maslow*. Monterey, CA: Brooks–Cole.

Maslow, A. H. (1973b). Theory of human motivation. In R. J. Lowry (Ed.), *Dominance, self-esteem, self-actualization: Germinal papers of A. H. Maslow*. Monterey, CA: Brooks–Cole.

Maslow, A. H. (1987). *Motivation and personality* (3rd ed.). New York: Harper & Row.

Massialas, B. G., & Zevin, J. (1983). *Teaching creatively: Learning through discovery*. Malabar, FL: Robert E. Krieger.

Mastropieri, M. A., & Scruggs, T. E. (1989). Constructing more meaningful relationships: Mnemonic instruction for special populations. *Educational Psychology Review, 1*, 83–111.

Mastropieri, M. A., & Scruggs, T. E. (1992). Science for students with disabilities. *Review of Educational Research, 62*, 377–411.

Mastropieri, M. A., Scruggs, T. E., McLoone, B., & Levin, J. R. (1985). Facilitating learning disabled students' acquisition of science classifications. *Learning Disability Quarterly, 8*, 299–309.

Masur, E. F., McIntyre, C. W., & Flavell, J. H. (1973). Developmental changes in apportionment of study time among items in a multitrial free recall task. *Journal of Experimental Child Psychology, 15*, 237–246.

Mathews, J. R., Friman, P. C., Barone, V. J., Ross, L. V., & Christophersen, E. R. (1987). Decreasing dangerous infant behaviors through parent instruction. *Journal of Applied Behavior Analysis, 20*, 165–169.

Matlin, M. W. (1983). *Cognition*. New York: Holt, Rinehart & Winston.

Maurer, A. (1974). Corporal punishment. *American Psychologist, 29*, 614–626.

Mayer, G. R., & Butterworth, T. N. (1979). A preventive approach to school violence and vandalism: An experimental study. *Personnel Guidance Journal, 57*, 436–441.

Mayer, R. E. (1974). Acquisition processes and resilience under vary-ing testing conditions for structurally different problem solving procedures. *Journal of Educational Psychology, 66*, 644–656.

Mayer, R. E. (1975). Information processing variables in learning to solve problems. *Review of Educational Research, 45*, 525–541.

Mayer, R. E. (1977). *Thinking and problem solving: An introduction to human cognition and learning*. Glenview, IL: Scott, Foresman.

Mayer, R. E. (1979a). Can advance organizers influence meaningful learning? *Review of Educational Research, 49*, 371–383.

Mayer, R. E. (1979b). Twenty years of research on advance organizers: Assimilation theory is still the best predictor of results. *Instructional Science, 8*, 133–167.

Mayer, R. E. (1982). Memory for algebra story problems. *Journal of Educational Psychology, 74*, 199–216.

Mayer, R. E. (1983a). Can you repeat that? Qualitative effects of repetition and advance organizers on learning from science prose. *Journal of Educational Psychology, 75*, 40–49.

Mayer, R. E. (1983b). *Thinking, problem solving, and cognition*. New York: Freeman.

Mayer, R. E. (1984). Aids to text comprehension. *Educational Psychologist, 19*, 30–42.

Mayer, R. E. (1985). Implications of cognitive psychology for instruction in mathematical problem solving. In E. A. Silver (Ed.), *Teaching and learning mathematical problem solving: Multiple research perspectives*. Hillsdale, NJ: Erlbaum.

Mayer, R. E. (1986). Mathematics. In R. F. Dillon & R. J. Sternberg (Eds.), *Cognition and instruction*. San Diego: Academic Press.

Mayer, R. E. (1987). *Educational psychology: A cognitive approach*. Boston: Little, Brown.

Mayer, R. E. (1989a). Models for understanding. *Review of Educational Research, 59*, 43–64.

Mayer, R. E. (1989b). Teaching for thinking: Research on the teachability of thinking skills. In I. S. Cohen (Ed.), *The G. Stanley Hall Lecture Series* (Vol. 9). Washington, DC: American Psychological Association.

Mayer, R. E. (1992). *Thinking, problem solving, cognition* (2nd ed.). New York: Freeman.

Mayer, R. E., & Bromage, B. (1980). Different recall protocols for technical texts due to advance organizers.

Journal of Educational Psychology, *72*, 209–225.

Mayer, R. E., & Greeno, J. G. (1972). Structural differences between learning outcomes produced by different instructional methods. *Journal of Educational Psychology*, *63*, 165–173.

Mayzner, M. S., & Tresselt, M. E. (1958). Anagram solution times: A function of letter–order and word frequency. *Journal of Experimental Psychology*, *56*, 350–376.

Mayzner, M. S., & Tresselt, M. E. (1966). Anagram solution times: A function of multiple–solution anagrams. *Journal of Experimental Psychology*, *71*, 66–73.

Mazur, J. E. (1993). Predicting the strength of a conditioned reinforcer: Effects of delay and uncertainty. *Current Directions in Psychological Science*, *2*, 70–74.

McAllister, W. R., & McAllister, D. E. (1965). Variables influencing the conditioning and the measurement of acquired fear. In W. F. Prokasy (Ed.), *Classical conditioning*. New York: Appleton-Century-Crofts.

McAndrew, D. A. (1983). Underlining and notetaking: Some suggestions from research. *Journal of Reading*, *27*, 103–108.

McAshan, H. H. (1979). *Competency-based education and behavioral objectives*. Englewood Cliffs, NJ: Educational Technology.

McCallin, R. C. (1988). *Knowledge application orientation, cognitive structure, and achievement*. Unpublished doctoral dissertation, University of Northern Colorado, Greeley, CO.

McClelland, D. C. (1984). *Motives, personality, and society: Selected papers*. New York: Praeger.

McClelland, D. C., Atkinson, J. W., Clark, R. A., & Lowell, E. L. (1953). *The achievement motive*. New York: Appleton-Century-Crofts.

McClelland, J. L., & Rumelhart, D. E. (1986). *Parallel distributed processing* (Vol. 2). Cambridge, MA: M.I.T. Press.

McCloskey, M. E., & Glucksberg, S. (1978). Natural categories: Well-defined or fuzzy sets? *Memory and Cognition*, *6*, 462–472.

McCombs, B. L. (1988). Motivational skills training: Combining metacognitive, cognitive, and affective learning strategies. In C. E. Weinstein, E. T. Goetz, & P. A. Alexander (Eds.), *Learning and study strategies: Issues in assessment, instruction, and evaluation*. San Diego: Harcourt Brace Jovanovich.

McCord, W., McCord, J., & Zola, I. K. (1959). *Origins of crime: A new evaluation of the Cambridge-Somerville Youth Study*. New York: Columbia University Press.

McCoy, L. P. (1990, April). Correlates of mathematics anxiety. Paper presented at the annual meeting of the American Educational Research Association, Boston.

McCrary, J. W., & Hunter, W. S. (1953). Serial position curves in verbal learning. *Science*, *117*, 131–134.

McDaniel, M. A., & Einstein, G. O. (1989). Material-appropriate processing: A contextualist approach to reading and studying strategies. *Educational Psychology Review*, *1*, 113–145.

McGeoch, J. A. (1942). *The psychology of human learning*. New York: David McKay.

McHale, M. A., Brooks, Z., & Wolach, A. H. (1982). Incentive shifts with different massed and spaced trial cues. *Psychological Record*, *32*, 85–92.

McKeachie, W. J. (1961). Motivation, teaching methods, and college learning. In M. R. Jones (Ed.), *Nebraska symposium on motivation*. Lincoln, NE: University of Nebraska Press.

McKeachie, W. J., Lin, Y., Milholland, J., & Isaacson, R. (1966). Student affiliation motives, teacher warmth, and academic achievement. *Journal of Personality and Social Psychology*, *4*, 457–461.

McKenzie, H. S., Clark, M., Wolf, M. M., Kothera, R., & Benson, C. (1968). Behavior modification of children with learning disabilities using grades as tokens and allowances as back up reinforcers. *Exceptional Children*, *34*, 745–752.

McKeown, M. G., & Beck, I. L. (1990). The assessment and characterization of young learners' knowledge of a topic in history. *American Educational Research Journal*, *27*, 688–726.

McLaughlin, T. F., & Malaby, J. (1972). Intrinsic reinforcers in a classroom token economy. *Journal of Applied Behavior Analysis*, *5*, 263–270.

McLaughlin, T. F., & Williams, R. L. (1988). The token economy. In J. C. Witt, S. N. Elliott, & F. M. Gresham (Eds.), *Handbook of behavior therapy in education*. New York: Plenum Press.

McLeod, D. B., & Adams, V. M. (Eds.) (1989). *Affect and mathematical problem solving: A new perspective*. New York: Springer–Verlag.

McNamara, E. (1987). Behavioural approaches in the secondary school. In K. Wheldall (Ed.), *The behaviourist in the classroom*. London: Allen & Unwin.

Meece, J. L., Wigfield, A., & Eccles, J. S. (1990). Predictors of math anxiety and its influence on young adolescents' course enrollment intentions and performance in mathematics. *Journal of Educational Psychology*, *82*, 60–70.

Meehl, P. E. (1950). On the circularity of the law of effect. *Psychological Bulletin*, *47*, 52–75.

Meichenbaum, D. (1985). Teaching thinking: A cognitive-behavioral perspective. In S. F. Chipman, J. W. Segal, & R. Glaser (Eds.), *Thinking and learning skills: Vol. 2. Research and open questions*. Hillsdale, NJ: Erlbaum.

Meichenbaum, D., & Goodman, J. (1971). Training impulsive children to talk to themselves: A means of developing self-control. *Journal of Abnormal Psychology*, *77*, 115–126.

Melton, A. W. (1963). Implications of short-term memory for a general theory of memory. *Journal of Verbal Learning and Verbal Behavior*, *2*, 1–21.

Melton, A. W., & Irwin, J. M. (1940). The influence of degree of interpolated learning on retroactive inhibition and the overt transfer of specific responses. *American Journal of Psychology*, *53*, 173–203.

Melton, R. F. (1978). Resolution of conflicting claims concerning the effect of behavioral objectives on student learning. *Review of Educational Research*, *48*, 291–302.

Merrill, M. D., & Tennyson, R. D. (1977). *Concept teaching: An instructional design guide*. Englewood Cliffs, NJ: Educational Technology.

Merrill, M. D., & Tennyson, R. D. (1978). Concept classification and classification errors as a function of relationships between examples and nonexamples. *Improving Human Performance*, *7*, 351–364.

Meyer, B. J. F., Brandt, D. H., & Bluth, G. J. (1980). Use of top-level structure in text: Key for reading comprehension of ninth-grade students. *Reading Research Quarterly*, *16*, 72–103.

Michael, J. L. (1974). The essential components of effective instruction and why most college teaching is not. In F. S. Keller & E. Ribes–Inesta (Eds.),

Behavior modification: Applications to education. New York: Academic Press.

Miller, G. A. (1956). The magical number seven, plus or minus two: Some limits on our capacity for processing information. *Psychological Review*, 63, 81–97.

Miller, G. A., Galanter, E., & Pribram, K. H. (1960). *Plans and the structure of behavior.* New York: Holt, Rinehart & Winston.

Miller, N. E. (1948). Studies of fear as an acquirable drive: I. Fear as motivation and fear–reduction as reinforcement in the learning of new responses. *Journal of Experimental Psychology*, 38, 89–101.

Miller, N. E., & Dollard, J. C. (1941). *Social learning and imitation.* New Haven, CN: Yale University Press.

Miller, R. L., Brickman, P., & Bolen, D. (1975). Attribution versus persuasion as a means for modifying behavior. *Journal of Personality and Social Psychology*, 31, 430–441.

Miller, R. R., & Barnet, R. C. (1993). The role of time in elementary associations. *Current Directions in Psychological Science*, 2, 106–111.

Millroy, W. L. (1991). An ethnographic study of the mathematical ideas of a group of carpenters. *Learning and Individual Differences*, 3, 1–25.

Mischel, W., & Grusec, J. E. (1966). Determinants of the rehearsal and transmission of neutral and aversive behaviors. *Journal of Personality and Social Psychology*, 3, 197–205.

Mohatt, G., & Erickson, F. (1981). Cultural differences in teaching styles in an Odawa school: A sociolinguistic approach. In H. T. Trueba, G. P. Guthrie, & K. H. Au (Eds.), *Culture and the bilingual classroom: Studies in classroom ethnography.* Rowley, MA: Newbury House.

Moles, O. C. (Ed.) (1990). *Student discipline strategies: Research and practice.* Albany, NY: State University of New York Press.

Moletzsky, B. (1974). Behavior recording as treatment: A brief note. *Behavior Therapy*, 5, 107–111.

Mooney, C. M. (1957). Age in the development of closure ability in children. *Canadian Journal of Psychology*, 11, 219–226.

Moray, N., Bates, A., & Barnett, R. (1965). Experiments on the four-eared man. *Journal of the Acoustical Society of America*, 38, 196–201.

Morgan, M. (1984). Reward-induced decrements and increments in intrinsic motivation. *Review of Educational Research*, 54, 5–30.

Morris, C. D., Bransford, J. D., & Franks, J. J. (1977). Levels of processing versus transfer appropriate processing. *Journal of Verbal Learning and Verbal Behavior*, 16, 519–533.

Morris, E. K. (1982). Some relationships between interbehavioral psychology and radical behaviorism. *Behaviorism*, 10, 187–216.

Morris, P. (1977). Practical strategies for human learning and remembering. In M. J. A. Howe (Ed.), *Adult learning: Psychological research and applications.* London: Wiley.

Morris, R. J. (1985). *Behavior modification with exceptional children: Principles and practices.* Glenview, IL: Scott, Foresman.

Morris, R. J., Kratochwill, T. R., & Aldridge, K. (1988). Fears and phobias. In J. C. Witt, S. N. Elliott, & F. M. Gresham (Eds.), *Handbook of behavior therapy in education.* New York: Plenum Press.

Mowrer, O. H. (1938). Preparatory set (expectancy): A determinant in motivation and learning. *Psychological Review*, 45, 62–91.

Mowrer, O. H. (1939). A stimulus-response analysis and its role as a reinforcing agent. *Psychological Review*, 46, 553–565.

Mowrer, O. H. (1956). Two-factor learning theory reconsidered, with special reference to secondary reinforcement and the concept of habit. *Psychological Review*, 63, 114–128.

Mowrer, O. H. (1960). *Learning theory and behavior.* New York: John Wiley.

Mowrer, O. H., & Lamoreaux, R. R. (1942). Avoidance conditioning and signal duration: A study of secondary motivation and reward. *Psychological Monographs*, 54 (Whole No. 247).

Mueller, J. H. (1980). Test anxiety and the encoding and retrieval of information. In I. G. Sarason (Ed.), *Test anxiety: Theory, research, and applications.* Hillsdale, NJ: Erlbaum.

Murnane, R. J., & Raizen, S. A. (Eds.) (1988). *Improving indicators of the quality of science and mathematics education in grades K–12.* Washington, DC: National Academy Press.

Murray, C. B., & Jackson, J. S. (1982/83). The conditioned failure model of black educational underachievement. *Humboldt Journal of Social Relations*, 10, 276–300.

Murray, F. B. (1978). Teaching strategies and conservation training. In A. M.

Lesgold, J. W. Pellegrino, S. D. Fokkema, & R. Glaser (Eds.), *Cognitive psychology and instruction.* New York: Plenum Press.

Myers, J. L., & Duffy, S. A. (1990). Causal inferences and text memory. In A. C. Graessner & G. H. Bower (Eds.), *Inferences and text comprehension. The psychology of learning and motivation: Advances in research and theory* (Vol. 25). Orlando: Academic Press.

Natriello, G. (1987). The impact of evaluation processes on students. *Educational Psychologist*, 22, 155–175.

Natriello, G., & Dornbusch, S. M. (1984). *Teacher evaluative standards and student effort.* New York: Longman.

Naveh-Benjamin, M. (1991). A comparison of training programs intended for different types of text-anxious students: Further support for an information-processing model. *Journal of Educational Psychology*, 83, 134–139.

Neisser, U. (1967). *Cognitive psychology.* New York: Appleton-Century-Crofts.

Neisser, U. (1981). John Dean's memory: A case study. *Cognition*, 9, 1–22.

Neisser, U., & Weene, P. (1962). Hierarchies in concept formation. *Journal of Experimental Psychology*, 64, 644–645.

Nelson, T. O. (1971). Savings and forgetting from long–term memory. *Journal of Verbal Learning and Verbal Behavior*, 10, 568–576.

Nelson, T. O. (1977). Repetition and depth of processing. *Journal of Verbal Learning and Verbal Behavior*, 16, 151–171.

Nelson, T. O. (1978). Detecting small amounts of information in memory: Savings for nonrecognized items. *Journal of Experimental Psychology: Human Learning and Memory*, 4, 453–468.

Nelson, T. O., & Dunlosky, J. (1991). When people's judgments of learning (JOLs) are extremely accurate at predicting subsequent recall: The "delayed-JOL effect." *Psychological Science*, 2, 267–270.

Nelson, T. O., & Rothbart, R. (1972). Acoustic savings for items forgotten from long-term memory. *Journal of Experimental Psychology*, 93, 357–360.

Nenniger, P. (1992). Task motivation: An interaction between the cognitive and content-oriented dimensions in learning. In K. A. Renninger, S. Hidi, & A. Krapp (Eds.), *The role of inter-*

est in learning and development. Hillsdale, NJ: Erlbaum.

Neumann, P. G. (1974). An attribute frequency model for the abstraction of prototypes. *Memory and Cognition*, *2*, 241–248.

Neumann, P. G. (1977). Visual prototype formation with discontinuous representation of dimensions of variability. *Memory and Cognition*, *5*, 187–197.

Nevin, J. A., Mandell, C., & Atak, J. R. (1983). The analysis of behavioral momentum. *Journal of the Experimental Analysis of Behavior*, *39*, 49–59.

Newby, T. J., & Stepich, D. A. (1987). Learning abstract concepts: The use of analogies as a mediational strategy. *Journal of Instructional Development*, *10*(2), 20–26.

Newell, A., Shaw, J. C., & Simon, H. A. (1958). Elements of a theory of human problem solving. *Psychological Review*, *65*, 151–166.

Newell, A., & Simon, H. (1972). *Human problem solving*. Englewood Cliffs, NJ: Prentice-Hall.

Nicholls, J. G. (1984). Conceptions of ability and achievement motivation. In R. Ames & C. Ames (Eds.), *Research on motivation in education: Vol. 1. Student motivation*. Orlando: Academic Press.

Nickerson, R. S. (1989). New directions in educational assessment. *Educational Researcher*, *18*(9), 3–7.

Nisbett, R. E., & Bellows, N. (1977). Verbal reports about causal influences on social judgments: Private access versus public theories. *Journal of Personality and Social Psychology*, *35*, 613–624.

Nisbett, R. E., & Wilson, T. D. (1977). Telling more than we can know: Verbal reports on mental processes. *Psychological Review*, *84*, 231–259.

Nist, S. L., Simpson, M. L., Olejnik, S., & Mealey, D. L. (1991). The relation between self-selected study processes and test performance. *American Educational Research Journal*, *28*, 849–874.

Noddings, N. (1985). Small groups as a setting for research on mathematical problem solving. In E. A. Silver (Ed.), *Teaching and learning mathematical problem solving: Multiple research perspectives*. Hillsdale, NJ: Erlbaum.

Nolen, S. B. (1988). Reasons for studying: Motivational orientations and study strategies. *Cognition and Instruction*, *5*, 269–287.

Norman, D. A. (1969). *Memory and attention: An introduction to human information processing*. New York: Wiley.

Norman, D. A. (1976). *Memory and attention: An introduction to human information processing* (2nd ed.). New York: Wiley.

Norman, D. A. (1980). Cognitive engineering and education. In D. T. Tuma & F. Reif (Eds.), *Problem solving and education: Issues in teaching and research*. Hillsdale, NJ: Erlbaum.

Norman, D. A., & Bobrow, D. G. (1975). On data-limited and resource-limited processes. *Cognitive Psychology*, *7*, 44–64.

Norman, D. A., & Rumelhart, D. E. (1975). *Explorations in cognition*. San Francisco: W. H. Freeman.

Novak, J. D., & Gowin, D. B. (1984). *Learning how to learn*. Cambridge, England: Cambridge University Press.

Novak, J. D., & Musonda, D. (1991). A twelve-year longitudinal study of science concept learning. *American Educational Research Journal*, *28*, 117–153.

Nussbaum, J. (1985). The earth as a cosmic body. In R. Driver (Ed.), *Children's ideas of science*. Philadelphia: Open University Press.

Oakhill, J. (1993). Children's difficulties in reading comprehension. *Educational Psychology Review*, *5*, 223–237.

Ohlsson, S. (1983). On natural and technical knowledge domains. *Scandinavian Journal of Psychology*, *25*, 89–91.

Olds, J., & Milner, P. (1954). Positive reinforcement produced by electrical stimulation of septal area and other regions of rat brain. *Journal of Comparative and Physiological Psychology*, *47*, 419–427.

O'Leary, K. D., & Becker, W. C. (1967). Behavior modification of an adjustment class: A token reinforcement program. *Exceptional Children*, *33*, 637–642.

O'Leary, K. D., Kaufman, K. F., Kass, R. E., & Drabman, R. S. (1970). The effects of loud and soft reprimands on the behavior of disruptive students. *Exceptional Children*, *37*, 145–155.

O'Leary, K. D., & O'Leary, S. G. (Eds.) (1972). *Classroom management: The successful use of behavior modification*. New York: Pergamon Press.

Ormrod, J. E. (1979). Cognitive processes in the solution of three-term series problems. *American Journal of Psychology*, *92*, 235–255.

Ormrod, J. E. (1985). Proofreading *The Cat in the Hat*: Evidence for different reading styles of good and poor spellers. *Psychological Reports*, *57*, 863–867.

Ormrod, J. E. (1986a). Differences between good and poor spellers in reading style and short-term memory. *Visible Language*, *20*, 437–447.

Ormrod, J. E. (1986b). Learning to spell: Three studies at the university level. *Research in the Teaching of English*, *20*, 160–173.

Ormrod, J. E. (1986c). Learning to spell while reading: A follow-up study. *Perceptual and Motor Skills*, *63*, 652–654.

Ormrod, J. E. (1995). *Educational psychology*. Columbus, OH: Merrill.

Ormrod, J. E., & Jenkins, L. (1988, April). Study strategies for learning spelling: What works and what does not. Paper presented at the annual meeting of the American Educational Research Assn., New Orleans.

Ormrod, J. E., Ormrod, R. K., Wagner, E. D., & McCallin, R. C. (1988). Reconceptualizing map learning. *American Journal of Psychology*, *101*, 425–433.

Ormrod, J. E., & Wagner, E. D. (1987, October). Spelling conscience in undergraduate students: Ratings of spelling accuracy and dictionary use. Paper presented at Northern Rocky Mountain Educational Research Assn., Park City, UT.

Ornstein, R. E. (1972). *The psychology of consciousness*. San Francisco: W. H. Freeman.

Osborn, A. F. (1963). *Applied imagination* (3rd ed.). New York: Scribner.

Osborne, J. G. (1969). Free-time as a reinforcer in the management of classroom behavior. *Journal of Applied Behavior Analysis*, *2*, 113–118.

Osgood, C. E. (1949). The similarity paradox in human learning: A resolution. *Psychological Review*, *56*, 132–143.

O'Sullivan, J. T., & Joy, R. M. (1990, April). Children's theories about reading difficulty: A developmental study. Paper presented at the annual meeting of the American Educational Research Association, Boston.

Otero, J., & Kintsch, W. (1992). Failures to detect contradictions in a text:

What readers believe versus what they read. *Psychological Science, 3,* 229–235.

Overmier, J. B., & Lawry, J. A. (1979). Pavlovian conditioning and the mediation of behavior. In G. H. Bower (Ed.), *The psychology of learning and motivation* (Vol. 13). New York: Academic Press.

Owen, S., Blount, H., & Moscow, H. (1978). *Educational psychology: An introduction.* Boston: Little, Brown.

Owens, J., Bower, G. H., & Black, J. B. (1979). The "soap opera" effect in story recall. *Memory and Cognition, 7,* 185–191.

Packard, R. G. (1970). The control of "classroom attention": A group contingency for complex behavior. *Journal of Applied Behavior Analysis, 3,* 13–28.

Paige, J. M., & Simon, H. A. (1966). Cognitive processes in solving algebra word problems. In B. Kleinmuntz (Ed.), *Problem solving.* New York: Wiley.

Paivio, A. (1963). Learning of adjective-noun paired associates as a function of adjective-noun word order and noun abstractness. *Canadian Journal of Psychology, 17,* 370–379.

Paivio, A. (1971). *Imagery and verbal processes.* New York: Holt, Rinehart & Winston.

Paivio, A. (1975). Coding distinctions and repetition effects in memory. In G. H. Bower (Ed.), *The psychology of learning and motivation* (Vol. 9). New York: Academic Press.

Paivio, A. (1986). *Mental representations: A dual-coding approach.* New York: Oxford University Press.

Palardy, J. M. (1969). What teachers believe—what children achieve. *Elementary School Journal, 69,* 370–374.

Palermo, D. S. (1973). More about less: A study of language comprehension. *Journal of Verbal Learning and Verbal Behavior, 12,* 211–221.

Palincsar, A. S. (1986, April). Interactive cognition to promote listening comprehension. Paper presented at the American Educational Research Association, San Francisco.

Palincsar, A. S., & Brown, A. L. (1984). Reciprocal teaching of comprehension-fostering and comprehension-monitoring activities. *Cognition and Instruction, 1,* 117–175.

Palincsar, A. S., & Brown, A. L. (1989). Classroom dialogues to promote self-regulated comprehension. In J. Brophy (Ed.), *Advances in research on teaching* (Vol. 1). Greenwich, CT: JAI Press.

Palmer, D. J., & Goetz, E. T. (1988). Selection and use of study strategies: The role of the studier's beliefs about self and strategies. In C. E. Weinstein, E. T. Goetz, & P. A. Alexander (Eds.), *Learning and study strategies: Issues in assessment, instruction, and evaluation.* San Diego: Academic Press.

Paris, S. G. (1988). Models and metaphors of learning strategies. In C. E. Weinstein, E. T. Goetz, & P. A. Alexander (Eds.), *Learning and study strategies: Issues in assessment, instruction, and evaluation.* San Diego: Academic Press.

Paris, S. G. (1990, April). Discussant's comments. In B. McCombs (Chair), *Theoretical perspectives on socialization and children's development of self-regulated learning.* Symposium presented at the annual meeting of the American Educational Research Association, Boston.

Paris, S. G., & Byrnes, J. P. (1989). The constructivist approach to self-regulation and learning in the classroom. In B. J. Zimmerman & D. H. Schunk (Eds.), *Self-regulated learning and academic achievement: Theory, research, and practice.* New York: Springer-Verlag.

Paris, S. G., Cross, D. R., & Lipson, M. Y. (1984). Informed strategies for learning: A program to improve children's reading awareness and comprehension. *Journal of Educational Psychology, 76,* 1239–1252.

Paris, S. G., Lawton, T. A., Turner, J. C., & Roth, J. L. (1991). A developmental perspective on standardized achievement testing. *Educational Researcher, 20*(5), 12–20, 40.

Paris, S. G., & Lindauer, B. K. (1976). The role of inference in children's comprehension and memory. *Cognitive Psychology, 8,* 217–227.

Paris, S. G., Newman, R. S., & McVey, K. A. (1982). Learning the functional significance of mnemonic actions: A microgenetic study of strategy acquisition. *Journal of Experimental Child Psychology, 34,* 490–509.

Paris, S. G., & Winograd, P. (1990). How metacognition can promote academic learning and instruction. In B. F. Jones & L. Idol (Eds.), *Dimensions of thinking and cognitive instruction.* Hillsdale, NJ: Erlbaum.

Park, O. (1984). Example comparison strategy versus attribute identification strategy in concept learning. *American Educational Research Journal, 21,* 145–162.

Parke, R. D. (1972). Some effects of punishment on children's behavior. In W. W. Hartup (Ed.), *The young child* (Vol. 2). Washington, DC: National Association for the Education of Young Children.

Parke, R. D. (1974). Rules, roles, and resistance to deviation: Explorations in punishment, discipline, and self-control. In A. Pick (Ed.), *Minnesota Symposia on Child Psychology* (Vol. 8). Minneapolis: University of Minnesota Press.

Parke, R. D. (1977). Some effects of punishment on children's behavior—revisited. In E. M. Hetherington & R. D. Parke (Eds.), *Contemporary readings in child psychology.* New York: McGraw-Hill.

Parke, R. D., & Deur, J. L. (1972). Schedule of punishment and inhibition of aggression in children. *Developmental Psychology, 7,* 266–269.

Parke, R. D., & Walters, R. H. (1967). Some factors determining the efficacy of punishment for inducing response inhibition. *Monograph for the Society for Research in Child Development, 32* (Whole No. 109).

Parrish, J. M., Cataldo, M. F., Kolko, D. J., Neef, N. A., & Egel, A. L. (1986). Experimental analysis of response covariations among compliant and inappropriate behaviors. *Journal of Applied Behavior Analysis, 19,* 241–254.

Parsons, J. E., Adler, T. F., & Kaczala, C. M. (1982). Socialization of achievement attitudes and beliefs: Parental influences. *Child Development, 53,* 310–321.

Parsons, J. E., Kaczala, C. M., & Meece, J. L. (1982). Socialization of achievement attitudes and beliefs: Classroom influences. *Child Development, 53,* 322–339.

Pashler, H. (1992). Attentional limitations in doing two tasks at the same time. *Current Directions in Psychological Science, 1,* 44–48.

Pavlov, I. P. (1927). *Conditioned reflexes.* (G. V. Anrep, Trans.). London: Oxford University Press.

Pearson, P. D., Hansen, J., & Gordon, C. (1979). The effect of background knowledge on young children's comprehension of explicit and implicit information. *Journal of Reading Behavior, 11*(3), 201–209.

Penfield, W. (1958). Some mechanisms of consciousness discovered during electrical stimulation of the brain.

Proceedings of the National Academy of Sciences, 44, 51–66.

Penfield, W. (1959). Consciousness, memory, and man's conditioned reflexes. In K. Pribram (Ed.), *On the biology of learning*. New York: Harcourt, Brace, & World.

Penfield, W., & Roberts, L. (1959). *Speech and brain-mechanisms*. Princeton, NJ: Princeton University Press.

Pepper, J. (1981). Following students' suggestions for rewriting a computer programming textbook. *American Educational Research Journal, 18*, 259–270.

Perfetti, C. A. (1983). Reading, vocabulary, and writing: Implications for computer-based instruction. In A. C. Wilkinson (Ed.), *Classroom computers and cognitive science*. New York: Academic Press.

Perfetti, C. A., & Hogaboam, T. (1975). The relationship between single word coding and reading comprehension skill. *Journal of Educational Psychology, 67*, 461–469.

Perfetti, C. A., & Lesgold, A. M. (1979). Coding and comprehension in skilled reading and implications for reading instruction. In L. B. Resnick & P. Weaver (Eds.), *Theory and practice of early reading* (Vol. 1). Hillsdale, NJ: Erlbaum.

Perin, C. T. (1942). Behavior potentiality as a joint function of the amount of training and the degree of hunger at the time of extinction. *Journal of Experimental Psychology, 30*, 93–113.

Perin, C. T. (1943). A quantitative investigation of the delay-of-reinforcement gradient. *Journal of Experimental Psychology, 32*, 37–51.

Perkins, D. N., & Salomon, G. (1987). Transfer and teaching thinking. In D. N. Perkins, J. Lochhead, & J. Bishop (Eds.), *Thinking: The second international conference*. Hillsdale, NJ: Erlbaum.

Perkins, D. N., & Salomon, G. (1989). Are cognitive skills context-bound? *Educational Researcher, 18*(1), 16–25.

Perkins, D. N., & Simmons, R. (1988). Patterns of misunderstanding: An integrative model for science, math, and programming. *Review of Educational Research, 58*, 303–326.

Perone, M., & Baron, A. (1980). Reinforcement of human observing behavior by a stimulus correlated with extinction or increased effort. *Journal of the Experimental Analysis of Behavior, 34*, 239–261.

Perry, D. G., & Perry, L. C. (1983). Social learning, causal attribution, and moral internalization. In J. Bisanz, G. L. Bisanz, & R. Kail (Eds.), *Learning in children: Progress in cognitive development research*. New York: Springer-Verlag.

Peterson, C. (1988, August). Explanatory style and academic performance. Paper presented at the annual meeting of the American Psychological Association, Atlanta.

Peterson, C. (1990). Explanatory style in the classroom and on the playing field. In S. Graham & V. S. Folkes (Eds.), *Attribution theory: Applications to achievement, mental health, and interpersonal conflict*. Hillsdale, NJ: Erlbaum.

Peterson, C., & Barrett, L. C. (1987). Explanatory style and academic performance among university freshmen. *Journal of Personality and Social Psychology, 53*, 603–607.

Peterson, L. R., & Peterson, M. J. (1959). Short–term retention of individual items. *Journal of Experimental Psychology, 58*, 193–198.

Peterson, L. R., & Peterson, M. J. (1962). Minimal paired–associate learning. *Journal of Experimental Psychology, 63*, 521–527.

Peterson, P. L. (1988). Teachers' and students' cognitional knowledge for classroom teaching and learning. *Educational Researcher, 17*(5), 5–14.

Petri, H. L. (1991). *Motivation: Theory, research, and applications* (3rd ed.). Belmont, CA: Wadsworth.

Pezdek, K. (1977). Cross-modality semantic integration of sentence and picture memory. *Journal of Experimental Psychology: Human Learning and Memory, 3*, 515–524.

Pfiffner, L. J., & O'Leary, S. G. (1987). The efficacy of all–positive management as a function of the prior use of negative consequences. *Journal of Applied Behavior Analysis, 20*, 265–271.

Pfiffner, L. J., Rosén, L. A., & O'Leary, S. G. (1985). The efficacy of an all-positive approach to classroom management. *Journal of Applied Behavior Analysis, 18*, 257–261.

Phillips, B. N., Pitcher, G. D., Worsham, M. E., & Miller, S. C. (1980). Test anxiety and the school environment. In I. G. Sarason (Ed.), *Test anxiety: Theory, research, and applications*. Hillsdale, NJ: Erlbaum.

Phillips, E. L., Phillips, E. A., Fixsen, D. L., & Wolf, M. M. (1971). Achievement place: Modification of the behaviors of predelinquent boys within a token economy. *Journal of Applied Behavior Analysis, 4*, 45–59.

Piaget, J. (1928). *Judgment and reasoning in the child*. (M. Warden, Trans.) New York: Harcourt, Brace.

Piaget, J. (1952). *The origins of intelligence in children*. (M. Cook, Trans.) New York: W. W. Norton.

Piaget, J. (1959). *The language and thought of the child* (3rd ed.). (M. Gabain, Trans.) New York: Humanities Press.

Piaget, J. (1970). Piaget's theory. In P. H. Mussen (Ed.), *Carmichael's manual of psychology*. New York: Wiley.

Piaget, J. (1971). *Psychology and epistemology: Towards a theory of knowledge*. (A. Rosin, Trans.). New York: Viking.

Piaget, J. (1972). *The principles of genetic epistemology*. (W. Mays, Trans.) New York: Basic Books.

Piaget, J. (1980). *Adaptation and intelligence: Organic selection and phenocopy* (S. Eames, Trans.). Chicago: University of Chicago Press.

Piaget, J., & Inhelder, B. (1969). *The psychology of the child*. (H. Weaver, Trans.) New York: Basic Books.

Pianko, S. (1979). A description of the composing processes of college freshmen writers. *Research in the Teaching of English, 13*, 5–22.

Piersel, W. C. (1987). Basic skills education. In C. A. Maher & S. G. Forman (Eds.), *A behavioral approach to education of children and youth*. Hillsdale, NJ: Erlbaum.

Pigott, H. E., Fantuzzo, J. W., & Clement, P. W. (1986). The effects of reciprocal peer tutoring and group contingencies on the academic performance of elementary school children. *Journal of Applied Behavior Analysis, 19*, 93–98.

Piliavin, I. M., Piliavin, J. A., & Rodin, J. (1975). Costs, diffusion, and the stigmatized victim. *Journal of Personality and Social Psychology, 32*, 429–438.

Piliavin, J. A., Dovidio, J. F., Gaertner, S. L., & Clark, R. D., III (1981). Responsive bystanders: The process of intervention. In J. Grzelak & V. Derlega (Eds.), *Living with other people: Theory and research on cooperation and helping*. New York: Academic Press.

Pinker, S., & Prince, A. (1988). On language and connectionism: Analysis of a parallel distributed processing model of language acquisition. *Cognition, 28*, 73–193.

Pintrich, P. R., Marx, R. W., & Boyle, R. A. (1993). Beyond cold conceptual change: The role of motivational beliefs and classroom contextual factors in the process of conceptual change. *Review of Educational Research, 63,* 167–199.

Piontkowski, D., & Calfee, R. (1979). Attention in the classroom. In G. A. Hale & M. Lewis (Eds.), *Attention and cognitive development.* New York: Plenum Press.

Plummer, S., Baer, D. M., and LeBlanc, J. M. (1977). Functional considerations in the use of procedural time out and an effective alternative. *Journal of Applied Behavior Analysis, 10,* 689–706.

Poche, C., Yoder, P., & Miltenberger, R. (1988). Teaching self-protection to children using television techniques. *Journal of Applied Behavior Analysis, 21,* 253–261.

Polya, G. (1957). *How to solve it.* Garden City, NY: Doubleday.

Pontecorvo, C. (1993). Social interaction in the acquisition of knowledge. *Educational Psychology Review, 5,* 293–310.

Popham, W. J. (1988). *Educational evaluation* (2nd ed.). Englewood Cliffs, NJ: Prentice-Hall.

Porter, A. (1989). A curriculum out of balance: The case of elementary school mathematics. *Educational Researcher, 18*(5), 9–15.

Posner, G. J. (1978, April). Cognitive science: Implications for curricular research and development. Paper presented at the annual meeting of the American Educational Research Assn., Toronto.

Posner, G. J., & Rudnitsky, A. N. (1986). *Course design: A guide to curriculum development for teachers* (3rd ed.). New York: Longman.

Posner, G. J., Strike, K. A., Hewson, P. W., & Gertzog, W. A. (1982). Accommodation of a scientific conception: Toward a theory of conceptual change. *Science Education, 66,* 211–227.

Posner, M. I., Goldsmith, R., & Welton, K. E., Jr. (1967). Perceived distance and the classification of distorted patterns. *Journal of Experimental Psychology, 73,* 28–38.

Posner, M. I., & Keele, S. W. (1968). On the genesis of abstract ideas. *Journal of Experimental Psychology, 77,* 353–363.

Posner, M. I., & Keele, S. W. (1970). Retention of abstract ideas. *Journal of Experimental Psychology, 83,* 304–308.

Postman, L. (1964). Short–term memory and incidental learning. In A. W. Melton (Ed.), *Categories of human learning.* New York: Academic Press.

Postman, L., & Phillips, L. (1965). Short–term temporal changes in free recall. *Quarterly Journal of Experimental Psychology, 17,* 132–138.

Postman, L., & Underwood, B. J. (1973). Critical issues in interference theory. *Memory and Cognition, 1,* 19–40.

Powell, B. M. (1990, April). Children's perceptions of classroom goal orientation: Relationship to learning strategies and intrinsic motivation. Paper presented at the annual meeting of the American Educational Research Association, Boston.

Prawat, R. S. (1989). Promoting access to knowledge, strategy, and disposition in students: A research synthesis. *Review of Educational Research, 59,* 1–41.

Prawat, R. S. (1992). From individual differences to learning communities—our changing focus. *Educational Leadership, 49*(7), 9–13.

Premack, D. (1959). Toward empirical behavior laws: I. Positive reinforcement. *Psychological Review, 66,* 219–233.

Premack, D. (1963). Rate differential reinforcement in monkey manipulation. *Journal of Experimental Analysis of Behavior, 6,* 81–89.

Prentice, N. M. (1972). The influence of live and symbolic modeling on prompting moral judgments of adolescent delinquents. *Journal of Abnormal Psychology, 80,* 157–161.

Pressey, S. L. (1926). A simple apparatus which gives tests and scores—and teaches. *School and Society, 23,* 373–376.

Pressey, S. L. (1927). A machine for automatic teaching of drill material. *School and Society, 24,* 549–552.

Pressley, M. (1982). Elaboration and memory development. *Child Development, 53,* 296–309.

Pressley, M., Borkowski, J. G., & Schneider, W. (1987). Cognitive strategies: Good strategy users coordinate metacognition and knowledge. In R. Vasta & G. Whitehurst (Eds.), *Annals of child development* (Vol. 5). New York: JAI Press.

Pressley, M., El–Dinary, P. B., Marks, M. B., Brown, R., & Stein, S. (1992). Good strategy instruction is motivating and interesting. In K. A. Renninger, S. Hidi, & A. Krapp (Eds.), *The role of interest in learning and development.* Hillsdale, NJ: Erlbaum.

Pressley, M., Harris, K. R., & Marks, M. B. (1992). But good strategy instructors are constructivists! *Educational Psychology Review, 4,* 3–31.

Pressley, M., Levin, J. R., & Delaney, H. D. (1982). The mnemonic keyword method. *Review of Educational Research, 52,* 61–91.

Pressley, M., Levin, J. R., & McCormick, C. B. (1980). Young children's learning of foreign language vocabulary: A sentence variation of the keyword method. *Contemporary Educational Psychology, 5,* 22–29.

Pressley, M., Snyder, B. L., & Cariglia-Bull, T. (1987). How can good strategy use be taught to children? Evaluation of six alternative approaches. In S. M. Cormier & J. D. Hagman (Eds.), *Transfer of learning: Contemporary research and applications.* San Diego: Academic Press.

Pressley, M., Woloshyn, V., Lysynchuk, L. M., Martin, V., Wood, E., & Willoughby, T. (1990). A primer of research on cognitive strategy instruction: The important issues and how to address them. *Educational Psychology Review, 2,* 1–58.

Pulos, S. (1980, August). *M* capacity as a developmental constraint on structural learning. Paper presented at the annual meeting of the American Psychological Association, Montreal, Canada.

Pulos, S., & Linn, M. C. (1981). Generality of the controlling variables scheme in early adolescence. *Journal of Early Adolescence, 1,* 26–37.

Pylyshyn, Z. W. (1973). What the mind's eye tells the mind's brain: A critique of mental imagery. *Psychological Bulletin, 80,* 1–24.

Pylyshyn, Z. W. (1979). Imagery theory: Not mysterious—just wrong. *Behavioural and Brain Sciences, 2,* 561–563.

Pylyshyn, Z. W. (1981). The imagery debate: Analogue media versus tacit knowledge. *Psychological Review, 88,* 16–45.

Pylyshyn, Z. W. (1984). *Computation and cognition.* Cambridge, MA: M.I.T. Press.

Rachlin, H. (1990). Why do people gamble and keep gambling despite heavy losses? *Psychological Science, 1,* 294–297.

Rachlin, H. (1991). *Introduction to modern behaviorism* (3rd ed.). New York: Freeman.

Rachlin, H., & Herrnstein, R. J. (1969). Hedonism revisited: On the negative law of effect. In B. A. Campbell & R.

M. Church (Eds.), *Punishment and aversive behavior*. New York: Appleton-Century-Crofts.

Radebaugh, M. R. (1985). Children's perceptions of their spelling strategies. *The Reading Teacher, 38*, 532–536.

Radke–Yarrow, M., Zahn–Waxler, C., & Chapman, M. (1983). Children's prosocial dispositions and behavior. In E. M. Hetherington (Ed.), *Handbook of child psychology: Vol. 4. Socialization, personality, and social development*. New York: Wiley.

Rakow, S. J. (1984). What's happening in elementary science: A national assessment. *Science and children, 21*(4), 39–40.

Rapport, M. D., & Bostow, D. E. (1976). The effects of access to special activities on performance in four categories of academic tasks with third–grade students. *Journal of Applied Behavior Analysis, 9*, 372.

Rapport, M. D., Murphy, H. A., & Bailey, J. S. (1982). Ritalin vs. response cost in the control of hyperactive children: A within-subject comparison. *Journal of Applied Behavior Analysis, 15*, 205–216.

Raudenbush, S. W., Rowan, B., & Cheong, Y. F. (1993). Higher order instructional goals in secondary schools: Class, teacher, and school influences. *American Educational Research Journal, 30*, 523–553.

Raugh, M. R., & Atkinson, R. C. (1975). A mnemonic method for learning a second language vocabulary. *Journal of Educational Psychology, 67*, 1–16.

Rayner, K. (1993). Eye movements in reading. *Current Directions in Psychological Science, 2*, 81–85.

Reber, A. S., & Allen, R. (1978). Analogical and abstraction strategies in synthetic grammar learning: A functionalist interpretation. *Cognition, 6*, 189–221.

Reber, A. S., Kassin, S. M., Lewis, S., & Cantor, B. (1980). On the relationship between implicit and explicit modes in the learning of a complex rule structure. *Journal of Experimental Psychology: Human Learning and Memory, 6*, 492–502.

Redd, W. H., Morris, E. K., & Martin, J. A. (1975). Effects of positive and negative adult-child interactions on children's social preference. *Journal of Experimental Child Psychology, 19*, 153–164.

Reder, L. M. (1982). Plausibility judgment versus fact retrieval: Alternative strategies for sentence verification. *Psychological Review, 89*, 250–280.

Reder, L. M., & Ross, B. H. (1983). Integrated knowledge in different tasks: Positive and negative fan effects. *Journal of Experimental Psychology: Human Learning and Memory, 8*, 55–72.

Redfield, D. L., & Rousseau, E. W. (1981). A meta-analysis of experimental research on teacher questioning behavior. *Review of Educational Research, 51*, 237–245.

Reed, S. K. (1993). A schema-based theory of transfer. In D. K. Detterman & R. J. Sternberg (Eds.), *Transfer on trial: Intelligence, cognition, and instruction*. Norwood, NJ: Ablex.

Reed, S. K., Ernst, G. W., & Banerji, R. (1974). The role of analogy in transfer between similar problem states. *Cognitive Psychology, 6*, 436–450.

Reese, H. W., & Lipsitt, L. P. (1970). *Experimental child psychology*. New York: Academic Press.

Reese, H. W., & Parnes, S. J. (1970). Programming creative behavior. *Child Development, 41*, 413–423.

Reesink, C. J. (1984). Metric munchies. *Science and Children, 21*(7), 16–17.

Reif, F., & Heller, J. I. (1982). Knowledge structure and problem solving in physics. *Educational Psychologist, 17*, 102–127.

Reiser, R. A., & Sullivan, H. J. (1977). Effects of self-pacing and instructor-pacing in a PSI course. *Journal of Educational Research, 71*, 8–12.

Reitman, J. S. (1974). Without surreptitious rehearsal, information in short-term memory decays. *Journal of Verbal Learning and Verbal Behavior, 13*, 365–377.

Reitman, W. R. (1964). Heuristic decision procedures, open constraints, and the structure of ill-defined problems. In M. W. Shelley & G. L. Bryan (Eds.), *Human judgments and optimality*. New York: Wiley.

Reitman, W. R. (1965). *Cognition and thought: An information processing approach*. New York: Wiley.

Renninger, K. A. (1992). Individual interest and development: Implications for theory and practice. In K. A. Renninger, S. Hidi, & A. Krapp (Eds.), *The role of interest in learning and development*. Hillsdale, NJ: Erlbaum.

Repp, A. C., & Deitz, S. M. (1974). Reducing aggressive and self-injurious behavior of institutionalized retarded children through reinforcement of other behaviors. *Journal of Applied Behavior Analysis, 7*, 313–325.

Rescorla, R. A. (1967). Pavlovian conditioning and its proper control procedures. *Psychological Review, 74*, 71–80.

Rescorla, R. A. (1987). A Pavlovian analysis of goal-directed behavior. *American Psychologist, 42*, 119–129.

Rescorla, R. A. (1988). Pavlovian conditioning: It's not what you think it is. *American Psychologist, 43*, 151–160.

Rescorla, R. A., & Wagner, A. R. (1972). A theory of Pavlovian conditioning: Variations in the effectiveness of reinforcement and non-reinforcement. In A. H. Black & W. F. Prokasy (Eds.), *The psychology of learning and motivation* (Vol. 4). New York: Academic Press.

Resnick, L. B. (1976). Task analysis in instructional design: Some cases from mathematics. In D. Klahr (Ed.), *Cognition and instruction*. Hillsdale, NJ: Erlbaum.

Resnick, L. B. (1983). Mathematics and science learning: A new conception. *Science, 220*, 477–478.

Resnick, L. B. (1986). The development of mathematical intuition. In M. Perlmutter (Ed.), *Minnesota Symposia on Child Psychology: Vol. 19. Perspectives on intellectual development*. Hillsdale, NJ: Erlbaum.

Resnick, L. B. (1987). *Education and learning to think*. Washington, DC: National Academy Press.

Resnick, L. B. (1989). Developing mathematical knowledge. *American Psychologist, 44*, 162–169.

Resnick, L. B., & Glaser, R. (1976). Problem solving and intelligence. In L. B. Resnick (Ed.), *The nature of intelligence*. Hillsdale, NJ: Erlbaum.

Resnick, L. B., & Johnson, A. (1988). Intelligent machines for intelligent people: Cognitive theory and the future of computer–assisted learning. In R. S. Nickerson & P. P. Zodhiates (Eds.), *Technology in education: Looking toward 2020*. Hillsdale, NJ: Erlbaum.

Restle, F., & Davis, J. H. (1962). Success and speed of problem solving by individuals and groups. *Psychological Review, 69*, 520–536.

Reusser, K. (1990, April). Understanding word arithmetic problems: Linguistic and situational factors. Paper presented at the annual meeting of the American Educational Research Association, Boston.

Reynolds, G. S. (1975). *A primer of operant conditioning* (rev. ed.). Glenview, IL: Scott, Foresman.

Reynolds, R. E., & Shirey, L. L. (1988). The role of attention in studying and learning. In C. E. Weinstein, E. T. Goetz, & P. A. Alexander (Eds.), *Learning and study strategies: Issues in assessment, instruction, and evaluation*. San Diego: Academic Press.

Reynolds, R. E., Taylor, M. A., Steffensen, M. S., Shirey, L. L., & Anderson, R. C. (1982). Cultural schemata and reading comprehension. *Reading Research Quarterly*, 17, 353–366.

Riding, R. J., & Calvey, I. (1981). The assessment of verbal-imagery learning styles and their effect on the recall of concrete and abstract prose passages by 11-year-old children. *British Journal of Psychology*, 72, 59–64.

Rimm, D. C., & Masters, J. C. (1974). *Behavior therapy: Techniques and empirical findings*. New York: Academic Press.

Ringness, T. A. (1967). Identification patterns, motivation, and school achievement of bright junior high school boys. *Journal of Educational Psychology*, 58, 93–102.

Rips, L. J., Shoben, E. J., & Smith, E. E. (1973). Semantic distance and the verification of semantic relations. *Journal of Verbal Learning and Verbal Behavior*, 12, 1–20.

Ritts, V., Patterson, M. L., & Tubbs, M. E. (1992). Expectations, impressions, and judgments of physically attractive students: A review. *Review of Educational Research*, 62, 413–426.

Roberts, K. T., & Ehri, L. C. (1983). Effects of two types of letter rehearsal on word memory in skilled and less skilled beginning readers. *Contemporary Educational Psychology*, 8, 375–390.

Robinson, F. P. (1961). *Effective study*. New York: Harper & Row.

Robinson, N. M., & Robinson, H. B. (1961). A method for the study of instrumental avoidance conditioning with children. *Journal of Comparative and Physiological Psychology*, 54, 20–23.

Roediger, H. L. (1980). Memory metaphors in cognitive psychology. *Memory and Cognition*, 8, 231–246.

Roediger, H. L., & Crowder, R. G. (1976). A serial position effect in recall of United States presidents. *Bulletin of the Psychonomic Society*, 8, 275–278.

Rogers, C. R. (1951). *Client-centered therapy: Its current practice, implication, and theory*. Boston: Houghton Mifflin.

Rogers, C. R. (1961). *On becoming a person: A therapist's view of psychotherapy*. Boston: Houghton Mifflin.

Rogers, T. B., Kuiper, N. A., & Kirker, W. S. (1977). Self-reference and the encoding of personal information. *Journal of Personality and Social Psychology*, 35, 677–688.

Rogoff, B. (1990). *Apprenticeship in thinking: Cognitive development in social context*. New York: Oxford University Press.

Rolider, A., & Van Houten, R. (1985). Movement suppression time-out for undesirable behavior in psychotic and severely developmentally delayed children. *Journal of Applied Behavior Analysis*, 18, 275–288.

Rosch, E. H. (1973a). Natural categories. *Cognitive Psychology*, 4, 328–350.

Rosch, E. H. (1973b). On the internal structure of perceptual and semantic categories. In T. E. Moore (Ed.), *Cognitive development and the acquisition of language*. New York: Academic Press.

Rosch, E. H. (1975). Cognitive representations of semantic categories. *Journal of Experimental Psychology: General*, 104, 192–253.

Rosch, E. H. (1977a). Classification of real-world objects: Origins and representations in cognition. In P. N. Johnson-Laird & P. C. Wason (Eds.), *Thinking: Readings in cognitive science*. Cambridge, MA: Cambridge University Press.

Rosch, E. H. (1977b). Human categorization. In N. Warren (Ed.), *Advances in cross-cultural psychology* (Vol. 1). London: Academic Press.

Rosch, E. H. (1978). Principles of categorization. In E. Rosch & B. Lloyd (Eds.), *Cognition and categorization*. Hillsdale, NJ: Erlbaum.

Rosch, E. H., & Mervis, C. B. (1975). Family resemblances: Studies in the internal structure of categories. *Cognitive Psychology*, 7, 573–605.

Rosch, E. H., Mervis, C. B., Gray, W. D., Johnson, D. M., & Boyes-Braem, P. (1976). Basic objects in natural categories. *Cognitive Psychology*, 8, 382–439.

Rosch, E. H., Simpson, C., & Miller, R. S. (1976). Structural bases of typicality effects. *Journal of Experimental Psychology: Human Perception and Performance*, 2, 491–502.

Rosenshine, B., & Meister, C. (1992). The use of scaffolds for teaching higher-level cognitive strategies. *Educational Leadership*, 49(7), 26–33.

Rosenthal, R., & Jacobson, L. (1968). *Pygmalion in the classroom: Teacher expectation and pupils' intellectual development*. New York: Holt, Rinehart & Winston.

Rosenthal, T. L., Alford, G. S., & Rasp, L. M. (1972). Concept attainment, generalization, and retention through observation and verbal coding. *Journal of Experimental Child Psychology*, 13, 183–194.

Rosenthal, T. L., & Bandura, A. (1978). Psychological modeling: Theory and practice. In S. L. Garfield & A. E. Begia (Eds.), *Handbook of psychotherapy and behavior change: An empirical analysis* (2nd ed.). New York: John Wiley.

Rosenthal, T. L., & Zimmerman, B. J. (1978). *Social learning and cognition*. New York: Academic Press.

Roth, K. J. (1990). Developing meaningful conceptual understanding in science. In B. F. Jones & L. Idol (Eds.), *Dimensions of thinking and cognitive instruction*. Hillsdale, NJ: Erlbaum.

Roth, K., & Anderson, C. (1988). Promoting conceptual change learning from science textbooks. In P. Ramsden (Ed.), *Improving learning: New perspectives*. London: Kogan Page.

Roughead, W. G., & Scandura, J. M. (1968). What is learned in mathematical discovery. *Journal of Educational Psychology*, 59, 283–289.

Rovee–Collier, C. (1993). The capacity for long-term memory in infancy. *Current Directions in Psychological Science*, 2, 130–135.

Rowe, M. B. (1974). Wait-time and rewards as instructional variables, their influence on language, logic, and fate control: Part one—wait time. *Journal of Research in Science Teaching*, 11, 81–94.

Rowe, M. B. (1983). Science education: A framework for decision-makers. *Daedalus*, 112(2), 123–142.

Rowe, M. B. (1987). Wait time: Slowing down may be a way of speeding up. *American Educator*, 11(1), 38–43, 47.

Royer, J., M., & Cable, G. W. (1976). Illustrations, analogies, and facilitation of transfer in prose learning. *Journal of Educational Psychology*, 68, 205–209.

Rubin, D. C. (1977). Very long-term memory for prose and verse. *Journal of Verbal Learning and Verbal Behavior*, 16, 611–621.

Ruble, D. N. (1980). A developmental perspective on theories of achievement motivation. In L. J. Fyans, Jr.

(Ed.), *Achievement motivation: Recent trends in theory and research*. New York: Plenum Press.

Ruble, D. N., & Ruble, T. L. (1982). Sex stereotypes. In A. G. Miller (Ed.), *In the eye of the beholder*. New York: Praeger.

Rueger, D. B., & Liberman, R. P. (1984). Behavioral family therapy for delinquent substance-abusing adolescents. *Journal of Drug Abuse, 14*, 403–418.

Rumelhart, D. E., Lindsay, P. H., & Norman, D. A. (1972). A process model for long-term memory. In E. Tulving & W. Donaldson (Eds.), *Organization of memory*. New York: Academic Press.

Rumelhart, D. E., & McClelland, J. L. (1986). *Parallel distributed processing* (Vol. 1). Cambridge, MA: M.I.T. Press.

Rumelhart, D. E., & Ortony, A. (1977). The representation of knowledge in memory. In R. C. Anderson, R. J. Spiro, & W. E. Montague (Eds.), *Schooling and the acquisition of knowledge*. Hillsdale, NJ: Erlbaum.

Rundus, D. (1971). Analysis of rehearsal processes in free recall. *Journal of Experimental Psychology, 89*, 63–77.

Rundus, D., & Atkinson, R. C. (1971). Rehearsal processes in free recall: A procedure for direct observation. *Journal of Verbal Learning and Verbal Behavior, 9*, 99–105.

Rushton, J. P. (1975). Generosity in children: Immediate and long-term effects of modeling, preaching, and moral judgment. *Journal of Personality and Social Psychology, 31*, 459–466.

Rushton, J. P. (1980). *Altruism, socialization, and society*. Englewood Cliffs, NJ: Prentice-Hall.

Rushton, J. P. (1982). Social learning theory and the development of prosocial behavior. In N. Eisenberg (Ed.), *The development of prosocial behavior*. New York: Academic Press.

Ryan, R. M., Mims, V., & Koestner, R. (1983). Relation of reward contingency and interpersonal context to intrinsic motivation: A review and test using cognitive evaluation theory. *Journal of Personality and Social Psychology, 45*, 736–750.

Sachs, J. S. (1967). Recognition memory for syntactic and semantic aspects of connected discourse. *Perception and Psychophysics, 2*, 437–442.

Sadker, M., & Sadker, D. (1985). Sexism in the schoolroom of the '80s. *Psychology Today, 19*, 54–57.

Sadoski, M., Goetz, E. T., & Fritz, J. B. (1993). Impact of concreteness on comprehensibility, interest, and memory for text: Implications for dual coding theory and text design. *Journal of Educational Psychology, 85*, 291–304.

Safren, M. A. (1962). Associations, sets, and the solution of word problems. *Journal of Experimental Psychology, 64*, 40–45.

Salthouse, T. A. (1991). Mediation of adult age differences in cognition by reductions in working memory and speed of processing. *Psychological Science, 2*, 179–183.

Saltz, E. (1971). *The cognitive bases of human learning*. Homewood, IL: Dorsey.

Samuel, A. L. (1963). Some studies in machine learning using the game of checkers. In E. A. Feigenbaum & J. Feldman (Eds.), *Computers and thought*. New York: McGraw-Hill.

Samuels, S. J. (1967). Attentional processes in reading: The effect of pictures in the acquisition of reading responses. *Journal of Educational Psychology, 58*, 337–342.

Samuels, S. J., & Turnure, J. E. (1974). Attention and reading achievement in first-grade boys and girls. *Journal of Educational Psychology, 66*, 29–32.

Sarason, I. G. (1980). Introduction to the study of test anxiety. In I. G. Sarason (Ed.), *Test anxiety: Theory, research, and applications*. Hillsdale, NJ: Erlbaum.

Sarason, S. B. (1972). What research says about test anxiety in elementary school children. In A. R. Binter & S. H. Frey (Eds.), *The psychology of the elementary school child*. Chicago: Rand McNally.

Sasso, G. M., & Rude, H. A. (1987). Unprogrammed effects of training high-status peers to interact with severely handicapped children. *Journal of Applied Behavior Analysis, 20*, 35–44.

Sax, G. (1989). *Principles of educational and psychological measurement and evaluation* (3rd ed.). Belmont, CA: Wadsworth.

Saxe, G. B. (1988). Candy selling and math learning. *Educational Researcher, 17*(6), 14–21.

Scandura, J. M. (1974). Role of higher order rules in problem solving. *Journal of Experimental Psychology, 102*, 984–991.

Schachter, D. L. (1987). Implicit memory: History and current status. *Journal of Experimental Psychology: Learning, Memory, and Cognition, 13*, 501–518.

Schank, R. C. (1975). *Conceptual information processing*. New York: Elsevier.

Schank, R. C. (1979). Interestingness: Controlling inferences. *Artificial Intelligence, 12*, 273–297.

Schank, R. C., & Abelson, R. P. (1977). *Scripts, plans, goals, and understanding: An inquiry into human knowledge structures*. Hillsdale, NJ: Erlbaum.

Schepis, M. M., Reid, D. H., & Fitzgerald, J. R. (1987). Group instruction with profoundly retarded persons: Acquisition, generalization, and maintenance of a remunerative work skill. *Journal of Applied Behavior Analysis, 20*, 97–105.

Schiefele, U. (1992). Topic interest and levels of text comprehension. In K. A. Renninger, S. Hidi, & A. Krapp (Eds.), *The role of interest in learning and development*. Hillsdale, NJ: Erlbaum.

Schiefele, U., Krapp, A., & Winteler, A. (1992). Interest as a predictor of academic achievement: A meta-analysis of research. In K. A. Renninger, S. Hidi, & A. Krapp (Eds.), *The role of interest in learning and development*. Hillsdale, NJ: Erlbaum.

Schliefer, M., & Douglas, V. I. (1973). Effects of training on the moral judgment of young children. *Journal of Personality and Social Psychology, 28*, 62–67.

Schmidt, R. A., & Bjork, R. A. (1992). New conceptualizations of practice: Common principles in three paradigms suggest new concepts for training. *Psychological Science, 3*, 207–217.

Schmidt, R. A., & Young, D. E. (1987). Transfer of movement control in motor skill learning. In S. M. Cormier & J. D. Hagman (Eds.), *Transfer of learning: Contemporary research and applications*. San Diego: Academic Press.

Schneider, W. (1993). Domain-specific knowledge and memory performance in children. *Educational Psychology Review, 5*, 257–273.

Schneider, W., & Detweiler, M. (1987). A connectionist/control architecture for working memory. In G. H. Bower (Ed.), *The psychology of learning and motivation: Advances in research and theory* (Vol. 21). Orlando: Academic Press.

Schneider, W., & Shiffrin, R. M. (1977). Controlled and automatic human information processing: I. Detection, search, and attention. *Psychological Review*, 84, 1–66.

Schoenfeld, A. H. (1979). Explicit heuristic training as a variable in problem solving performance. *Journal for Research in Mathematics Education*, 10, 173–187.

Schoenfeld, A. H. (1982). Measures of problem-solving performance and problem-solving instruction. *Journal for Research in Mathematics Education*, 13, 31–49.

Schoenfeld, A. H. (1983). Episodes and executive decisions in mathematical problem solving. In R. Lesh & M. Landau (Eds.), *Acquisition of mathematics concepts and processes*. New York: Academic Press.

Schoenfeld, A. H. (1985a). *Mathematical problem solving*. San Diego: Academic Press.

Schoenfeld, A. H. (1985b). Metacognitive and epistemological issues in mathematical understanding. In E. A. Silver (Ed.), *Teaching and learning mathematical problem solving: Multiple research perspectives*. Hillsdale, NJ: Erlbaum.

Schoenfeld, A. H., & Herrmann, D. J. (1982). Problem perception and knowledge structure in expert and novice mathematical problem solvers. *Journal of Experimental Psychology: Learning, Memory, and Cognition*, 8, 484–494.

Schommer, M. (1990). Effects of beliefs about the nature of knowledge on comprehension. *Journal of Educational Psychology*, 82, 498–504.

Schramm, W. (1964). *The research on programed instruction: An annotated bibliography*. Washington, DC: U.S. Government Printing Office.

Schultz, K., & Lochhead, J. (1991). A view from physics. In M. U. Smith (Ed.), *Toward a unified theory of problem solving: Views from the content domains*. Hillsdale, NJ: Erlbaum.

Schunk, D. H. (1981). Modeling and attributional effects on children's achievement: A self-efficacy analysis. *Journal of Educational Psychology*, 73, 93–105.

Schunk, D. H. (1982). Effects of effort attributional feedback on children's perceived self-efficacy and achievement. *Journal of Educational Psychology*, 74, 548–556.

Schunk, D. H. (1983a). Ability versus effort attributional feedback: Differential effects on self-efficacy and achievement. *Journal of Educational Psychology*, 75, 848–856.

Schunk, D. H. (1983b). Developing children's self-efficacy and skills: The roles of social comparative information and goal setting. *Contemporary Educational Psychology*, 8, 76–86.

Schunk, D. H. (1985). Participation in goal setting: Effects on self-efficacy and skills of learning disabled children. *Journal of Special Education*, 19, 307–317.

Schunk, D. H. (1989a). Self-efficacy and achievement behaviors. *Educational Psychology Review*, 1, 173–208.

Schunk, D. H. (1989b). Self-efficacy and cognitive skill learning. In C. Ames and R. Ames (Eds.), *Research on motivation in education: Vol. 3. Goals and cognitions*. San Diego: Academic Press.

Schunk, D. H. (1989c). Social cognitive theory and self-regulated learning. In B. J. Zimmerman & D. H. Schunk (Eds.), *Self-regulated learning and academic achievement: Theory, research, and practice*. New York: Springer-Verlag.

Schunk, D. H. (1990, April). Socialization and the development of self-regulated learning: The role of attributions. Paper presented at the annual meeting of the American Educational Research Association, Boston.

Schunk, D. H. (1991). *Learning theories: An educational perspective*. New York: Merrill/Macmillan.

Schunk, D. H., & Hanson, A. R. (1985). Peer models: Influence on children's self-efficacy and achievement. *Journal of Educational Psychology*, 77, 313–322.

Schunk, D. H., Hanson, A. R., & Cox, P. D. (1987). Peer-model attributes and children's achievement behaviors. *Journal of Educational Psychology*, 79, 54–61.

Schwartz, B., & Reisberg, D. (1991). *Learning and memory*. New York: W. W. Norton.

Schwartz, S. H. (1971). Modes of representation and problem solving: Well evolved is half solved. *Journal of Experimental Psychology*, 91, 347–350.

Schwebel, A. I., & Cherlin, D. L. (1972). Physical and social distancing in teacher-pupil relationships. *Journal of Educational Psychology*, 63, 543–550.

Scoville, W. B., & Milner, B. (1957). Loss of recent memory after bilateral hippocampal lesions. *Journal of Neu-*

rology, Neurosurgery, and Psychiatry, 20, 11–19.

Sears, R. R., Maccoby, E. E., & Levin, H. (1957). *Patterns of child rearing*. Evanston, IL: Row Peterson.

Seddon, G. M. (1978). The properties of Bloom's taxonomy of educational objectives for the cognitive domain. *Review of Educational Research*, 48, 303–323.

Selfridge, O. G. (1955), Pattern recognition and modern computers, *Proceedings of the Western Joint Computer Conference*, New York: Institute of Electrical and Electronics Engineers.

Seligman, M. E. P. (1975). *Helplessness*. San Francisco: Freeman.

Seligman, M. E. P. (1991). *Learned optimism*. New York: Alfred A. Knopf.

Seligman, M. E. P., & Campbell, B. A. (1965). Effects of intensity and duration of punishment on extinction of an avoidance response. *Journal of Comparative and Physiological Psychology*, 59, 295–297.

Seligman, M. E. P., & Johnston, J. C. (1973). A cognitive theory of avoidance learning. In F. J. McGuigan & D. B. Lumsden (Eds.), *Contemporary approaches to conditioning and learning*. Washington, DC: V. H. Winston & Sons.

Seligman, M. E. P., & Maier, S. F. (1967). Failure to escape traumatic shock. *Journal of Experimental Psychology*, 74, 1–9.

Selkow, P. (1984). Effects of maternal employment on kindergarten and first-grade children's vocational aspirations. *Sex Roles*, 11, 677–690.

Semb, G. B., Ellis, J. A., & Araujo, J. (1993). Long-term memory for knowledge learned in school. *Journal of Educational Psychology*, 85, 305–316.

Shaffer, D. R. (1988). *Social and personality development* (2nd ed.). Pacific Grove, CA: Brooks/Cole.

Shafto, F., & Sulzbacher, S. (1977). Comparing treatment tactics with a hyperactive preschool child: Stimulant medication and programmed teacher intervention. *Journal of Applied Behavior Analysis*, 10, 13–20.

Sheffield, F. D., & Roby, T. B. (1950). Reward value of a non-nutritive sweet taste. *Journal of Comparative and Physiological Psychology*, 43, 471–481.

Sheffield, F. D., Roby, T. B., & Campbell, B. A. (1954). Drive reduction versus consummatory behavior as determi-

505

nants of reinforcement. *Journal of Comparative and Physiological Psychology, 47*, 349–354.

Sheffield, F. D., Wulff, J. J., & Backer, R. (1951). Reward value of copulation without sex drive reduction. *Journal of Comparative and Physiological Psychology, 44*, 3–8.

Shepard, R. N. (1967). Recognition memory for words, sentences, and pictures. *Journal of Verbal Learning and Verbal Behavior, 6*, 156–163.

Shepard, R. N., & Metzler, J. (1971). Mental rotation of three-dimensional objects. *Science, 171*, 701–703.

Shiffrin, R. M., & Cook, J. R. (1978). Short-term forgetting of item and order information. *Journal of Verbal Learning and Verbal Behavior, 17*, 189–218.

Shiffrin, R. M., & Schneider, W. (1977). Controlled and automatic human information processing: II. Perceptual learning, automatic attending, and a general theory. *Psychological Review, 84*, 127–190.

Shimmerlick, S. M., & Nolan, J. D. (1976). Reorganization and the recall of prose. *Journal of Educational Psychology, 68*, 779–786.

Shimoff, E., Catania, A. C., & Matthews, B. A. (1981). Uninstructed human responding: Sensitivity of low-rate performance to schedule contingencies. *Journal of the Experimental Analysis of Behavior, 36*, 207–220.

Short, P. M., & Noblit, G. W. (1985). Missing the mark in in-school suspension: An explanation and proposal. *NASSP Bulletin, 69* (484), 112–116.

Shrager, L., & Mayer, R. E. (1989). Note-taking fosters generative learning strategies in novices. *Journal of Educational Psychology, 81*, 263–264.

Shulman, H. G. (1971). Similarity effects in short-term memory. *Psychological Bulletin, 75*, 399–415.

Shulman, H. G. (1972). Semantic confusion errors in short-term memory. *Journal of Verbal Learning and Verbal Behavior, 11*, 221–227.

Shymansky, J. A., Hedges, L. V., & Woodworth, G. (1990). A reassessment of the effects of inquiry-based science curricula of the 60's on student performance. *Journal of Research in Science Teaching, 27*, 127–144.

Sieber, J. E., Kameya, L. I., & Paulson, F. L. (1970). Effect of memory support on the problem-solving ability of test-anxious children. *Journal of Educational Psychology, 61*, 159–168.

Siegel, S., & Andrews, J. M. (1962). Magnitude of reinforcement and choice behavior in children. *Journal of Experimental Psychology, 63*, 337–341.

Siegler, R. S. (1978). The origins of scientific reasoning. In R. S. Siegler (Ed.), *Children's thinking: What develops?* Hillsdale, NJ: Erlbaum.

Siegler, R. S. (1986). *Children's thinking*. Englewood Cliffs, NJ: Prentice-Hall.

Signorella, M. L., & Liben, L. S. (1984). Recall and reconstruction of gender-related pictures: Effects of attitude, task difficulty, and age. *Child Development, 55*, 393–405.

Silver, E. (1981). Recall of mathematic problem information: Solving related problems. *Journal for Research in Mathematics Education, 12*, 54–64.

Silver, E. A. (1982). Knowledge organization and mathematical problem solving. In F. K. Lester & J. Garofalo (Eds.), *Mathematical problem solving: Issues in research*. Philadelphia: The Franklin Institute Press.

Silver, E. A., Shapiro, L. J., & Deutsch, A. (1991, April). Sense-making and the solution of division problems involving remainders: An examination of students' solution processes and their interpretations of solutions. Paper presented at the annual meeting of the American Educational Research Association, Chicago.

Silverman, W. K., & Kearney, C. A. (1991). *Educational Psychology Review, 3*, 335–361.

Simon, H. A. (1973). The structure of ill-structured problems. *Artificial Intelligence, 4*, 181–201.

Simon, H. A. (1974). How big is a chunk? *Science, 183*, 482–488.

Simon, H. A. (1978). Information-processing theory of human problem solving. In W. K. Estes (Ed.), *Handbook of learning and cognitive processes: Vol. 5. Human information processing*. Hillsdale, NJ: Erlbaum.

Simon, H. A. (1980). Problem solving and education. In D. T. Tuma & F. Reif (Eds.), *Problem-solving and education: Issues in teaching and research*. Hillsdale, NJ: Erlbaum.

Simon, H. A., & Hayes, J. R. (1976). Understanding complex task instructions. In D. Klahr (Ed.), *Cognition and instruction*. Hillsdale, NJ: Erlbaum.

Simons, P. R. J. (1984). Instructing with analogies. *Journal of Educational Psychology, 76*, 513–527.

Sinclair, K. E. (1971). The influence of anxiety on several measures of classroom performance. In E. Gaudry & C. D. Spielberger (Eds.), *Anxiety and educational achievement*. Sydney, Australia: Wiley.

Skinner, B. F. (1938). *The behavior of organisms: An experimental analysis*. Englewood Cliffs, NJ: Prentice-Hall.

Skinner, B. F. (1948a). Superstition in the pigeon. *Journal of Experimental Psychology, 38*, 168–172.

Skinner, B. F. (1948b). *Walden Two*. New York: Macmillan.

Skinner, B. F. (1953). *Science and human behavior*. New York: Macmillan.

Skinner, B. F. (1954). The science of learning and the art of teaching. *Harvard Educational Review, 24*, 86–97.

Skinner, B. F. (1957). *Verbal behavior*. New York: Appleton-Century-Crofts.

Skinner, B. F. (1958). Reinforcement today. *American Psychologist, 13*, 94–99.

Skinner, B. F. (1963). Behaviorism at fifty. *Science, 140*(3570), 951–958.

Skinner, B. F. (1966a). An operant analysis of problem solving. In B. Kleinmuntz (Ed.), *Problem solving: Research, method and theory*. New York: Wiley.

Skinner, B. F. (1966b). What is the experimental analysis of behavior? *Journal of the Experimental Analysis of Behavior, 9*, 213–218.

Skinner, B. F. (1967). B. F. Skinner. . . An autobiography. In E. G. Boring & G. Lindzey (Eds.), *A history of psychology in autobiography* (Vol. 5). New York: Irvington.

Skinner, B. F. (1968). *The technology of teaching*. New York: Appleton-Century-Crofts.

Skinner, B. F. (1971). *Beyond freedom and dignity*. New York: Alfred Knopf.

Skinner, B. F. (1973). The free and happy student. *Phi Delta Kappan, 55*, 13–16.

Skinner, B. F. (1989). The origins of cognitive thought. *American Psychologist, 44*, 13–18.

Skinner, B. F., & Epstein, R. (1982). *Skinner for the classroom*. Champaign, IL: Research Press.

Slavin, R. E. (1983a). *Cooperative learning*. New York: Longman.

Slavin, R. E. (1983b). When does cooperative learning increase student achievement? *Psychological Bulletin, 94,* 429–445.

Slavin, R. E. (1987). Mastery learning reconsidered. *Review of Educational Research, 57,* 175–213.

Slavin, R. E. (1990). Mastery learning re-reconsidered. *Review of Educational Research, 60,* 300–302.

Small, M. Y., Lovett, S. B., & Scher, M. S. (1993). Pictures facilitate children's recall of unillustrated expository prose. *Journal of Educational Psychology, 85,* 520–528.

Smith, E. E., Shoben, E. J., & Rips, L. J. (1974). Structure and process in semantic memory: A feature model of semantic decisions. *Psychological Review, 81,* 214–241.

Smith, F. (1988). *Understanding reading* (4th ed.). Hillsdale, NJ: Erlbaum.

Smith, M. U. (1991). A view from biology. In M. U. Smith (Ed.), *Toward a unified theory of problem solving: Views from the content domains.* Hillsdale, NJ: Erlbaum.

Smith, S. M., Glenberg, A., & Bjork, R. A. (1978). Environmental context and human memory. *Memory and Cognition, 6,* 342–353.

Smoke, K. L. (1932). An objective study of concept formation. *Psychological Monographs, 42* (Whole No. 191).

Sneider, C., & Pulos, S. (1983). Children's cosmographies: Understanding the earth's shape and gravity. *Science Education, 67,* 205–221.

Snowman, J. (1986). Learning tactics and strategies. In G. D. Phye & T. Andre (Eds.), *Cognitive classroom learning: Understanding, thinking, and problem solving.* Orlando, FL: Academic Press.

Snyder, M., & Swann, W. B. (1978). Behavioral confirmation in social interaction: From social perception to social reality. *Journal of Experimental Social Psychology, 14,* 148–162.

Sokal, R. R. (1977). Classification: Purposes, principles, progress, prospects. In P. N. Johnson–Laird & P. C. Wason (Eds.), *Thinking: Readings in cognitive science.* Cambridge: Cambridge University Press.

Solnick, J. V., Rincover, A., & Peterson, C. R. (1977). Some determinants of the reinforcing and punishing effects of timeout. *Journal of Applied Behavior Analysis, 10,* 415–424.

Solomon, R. L., & Wynne, L. C. (1954). Traumatic avoidance learning: Acquisition in normal dogs. *Psychological Monographs, 67* (Whole No. 354).

Spaulding, C. L. (1992). *Motivation in the classroom.* New York: McGraw-Hill.

Spence, K. W. (1956). *Behavior theory and conditioning.* New Haven, CT: Yale University Press.

Sperling, G. (1960). The information available in brief visual presentations. *Psychological Monographs, 74* (Whole No. 498).

Sperling, G. (1967). Successive approximations to a model for short-term memory. *Acta Psychologia, 27,* 285–292.

Spielberger, C. D. (1966). The effects of anxiety on complex learning in academic achievement. In C. D. Spielberger (Ed.), *Anxiety and behavior.* New York: Academic Press.

Spielberger, C. D., & DeNike, L. D. (1966). Descriptive behaviorism versus cognitive theory in verbal operant conditioning. *Psychological Review, 73,* 306–326.

Spilich, G. J., Vesonder, G. T., Chiesi, H. L., & Voss, J. F. (1979). Text processing of domain-related information for individuals with high and low domain knowledge. *Journal of Verbal Learning and Verbal Behavior, 18,* 275–290.

Spires, H. A. (1990, April). Learning from a lecture: Effects of comprehension monitoring. Paper presented at the annual meeting of the American Educational Research Association, Boston.

Spires, H. A., Donley, J., & Penrose, A. M. (1990, April). Prior knowledge activation: Inducing text engagement in reading to learn. Paper presented at the annual meeting of the American Educational Research Association, Boston.

Spiro, R. J. (1977). Remembering information from text: The "state of schema" approach. In R. C. Anderson, R. J. Spiro, & W. E. Montague (Eds.), *Schooling and the acquisition of knowledge.* Hillsdale, NJ: Erlbaum.

Spiro, R. J. (1980a). Accommodative reconstruction in prose recall. *Journal of Verbal Learning and Verbal Behavior, 19,* 84–95.

Spiro, R. J. (1980b). Constructive processes in prose comprehension and recall. In R. J. Spiro, B. C. Bruce, & W. F. Brewer (Eds.), *Theoretical issues in reading comprehension.* Hillsdale, NJ: Erlbaum.

Staddon, J. E. R., & Higa, J. J. (1991). Temporal learning. In G. H. Bower (Ed.), *The psychology of learning and motivation: Advances in research and theory* (Vol. 27). San Diego: Academic Press.

Standing, L. (1973). Learning 10,000 pictures. *Quarterly Journal of Experimental Psychology, 25,* 207–222.

Standing, L., Conezio, J., & Haber, R. N. (1970). Perception and memory for pictures: Single-trial learning of 2560 visual stimuli. *Psychonomic Science, 19,* 73–74.

Stazyk, E. H., Ashcraft, M. H., & Hamann, M. S. (1982). A network approach to mental multiplication. *Journal of Experimental Psychology: Learning, Memory, and Cognition, 8,* 320–335.

Steele, B. G., & Pollack, C. B. (1968). A psychiatric study of parents who abuse infants and small children. In R. E. Helfer & C. H. Kempe (Eds.), *The battered child.* Chicago: University of Chicago Press.

Steffensen, M. S., Joag-Dev, C., & Anderson, R. C. (1979). A cross-cultural perspective on reading comprehension. *Reading Research Quarterly, 15,* 10–29.

Stein, A. H. (1971). The effects of sex-role standards for achievement and sex-role preference on three determinants of achievement motivation. *Developmental Psychology, 4,* 219–231.

Stein, B. S. (1978). Depth of processing reexamined: The effects of the precision of encoding and test appropriateness. *Journal of Verbal Learning and Verbal Behavior, 17,* 165–174.

Stein, B. S. (1989). Memory and creativity. In Glover, J. A., Ronning, R. R., & Reynolds, C. R. (Eds.), *Handbook of creativity.* New York: Plenum Press.

Stein, B. S., & Bransford, J. D. (1979). Constraints on effective elaboration: Effects of precision and subject generation. *Journal of Verbal Learning and Verbal Behavior, 18,* 769–777.

Stein, B. S., Bransford, J. D., Franks, J. J., Owings, R. A., Vye, N. J., & McGraw, W. (1982). Differences in the precision of self-generated elaborations. *Journal of Experimental Psychology: General, 111,* 399–405.

Steinmetz, S. K. (1977). *The cycle of violence.* New York: Praeger.

Stephens, C. E., Pear, J. J., Wray, L. D., & Jackson, G. C. (1975). Some effects of reinforcement schedules in teaching picture names to retarded children. *Journal of Applied Behavior Analysis, 8,* 435–447.

Stepich, D. A., & Newby, T. J. (1988). Analogical instruction within the information processing paradigm: Effective means to facilitate learning. *Instructional Science, 17,* 129–144.

Sternberg, R. J. (1985). *Beyond IQ: A triarchic theory of human intelligence.* Cambridge, England: Cambridge University Press.

Sternberg, R. J., & Davidson, J. E. (1982). Componential analysis and componential theory. *Behavioural and Brain Sciences, 53,* 352–353.

Sternberg, R. J., & Davidson, J. E. (1983). Insight in the gifted. *Educational Psychologist, 18,* 51–57.

Sternberg, R. J., & Frensch, P. A. (1993). Mechanisms of transfer. In D. K. Detterman & R. J. Sternberg (Eds.), *Transfer on trial: Intelligence, cognition, and instruction.* Norwood, NJ: Ablex.

Sternberg, S. (1966). High-speed scanning in human memory. *Science, 153,* 652–654.

Steuer, F. B., Applefield, J. M., & Smith, R. (1971). Televised aggression and the interpersonal aggression of preschool children. *Journal of Experimental Child Psychology, 11,* 442–447.

Stevenson, H. C., & Fantuzzo, J. W. (1986). The generality and social validity of a competency-based self-control training intervention for underachieving students. *Journal of Applied Behavior Analysis, 19,* 269–276.

Stinessen, L. (1975). Conditions which influence acquisition and application of verbal representations in problem solving. *Psychological Reports, 36,* 35–42.

Stipek, D. J. (1984). Sex differences in children's attributions for success and failure on math and spelling tests. *Sex Roles, 11,* 969–981.

Stipek, D. J. (1988). *Motivation to learn: From theory to practice.* Englewood Cliffs, NJ: Prentice-Hall.

Stipek, D. J., & Gralinski, H. (1990, April). Gender differences in children's achievement-related beliefs and emotional responses to success and failure in math. Paper presented at the annual meeting of the American Educational Research Association, Boston.

Stipek, D. J., & Kowalski, P. S. (1989). Learned helplessness in task-orienting versus performance-orienting

testing conditions. *Journal of Educational Psychology, 81,* 384–391.

Stodolsky, S. S., Salk, S., & Glaessner, B. (1991). Student views about learning math and social studies. *American Educational Research Journal, 28,* 89–116.

Strage, A., Christopoulos, J., Rohwer, W. D., Thomas, J. W., Delucchi, J. J., & Curley, R. G. (1988, April). Grade-level differences in study activities as a function of perceived and observed course characteristics. Paper presented at the American Educational Research Association, New Orleans.

Strauss, M. A., Gelles, R. J., & Steinmetz, S. K. (1980). *Behind closed doors: Violence in the American family.* Garden City, NY: Doubleday.

Sulin, R. A., & Dooling, D. J. (1974). Intrusions of a thematic idea in retention of prose. *Journal of Experimental Psychology, 103,* 255–262.

Sullivan, J. S. (1989). Planning, implementing, and maintaining an effective in-school suspension program. *Clearing House, 62,* 409–410.

Sulzer–Azaroff, B. (1981). Issues and trends in behavior modification in the classroom. In S. W. Bijou & R. Ruiz (Eds.), *Behavior modification: Contributions to education.* Hillsdale, NJ: Erlbaum.

Sund, R. B. (1976). *Piaget for educators.* Columbus, OH: Merrill.

Sussman, D. M. (1981). PSI: Variations on a theme. In S. W. Bijou & R. Ruiz (Eds.), *Behavior modification: Contributions to education.* Hillsdale, NJ: Erlbaum.

Swan, K., Mitrani, M., Guerrero, F., Cheung, M., & Schoener, J. (1990, April). Perceived locus of control and computer-based instruction. Paper presented at the annual meeting of the American Educational Research Association, Boston.

Swanson, H. L. (1987). Information processing theory and learning disabilities: An overview. *Journal of Learning Disabilities, 20,* 3–7.

Sweller, J., & Levine, M. (1982). Effects of goal specificity on means-end analysis and learning. *Journal of Experimental Psychology: Learning, Memory, and Cognition, 8,* 463–474.

Swenson, L. C. (1980). *Theories of learning: Traditional perspectives/contemporary developments.* Belmont, CA: Wadsworth.

Tanner, B. A., & Zeiler, M. (1975). Punishment of self-injurious behavior using aromatic ammonia as the aver-

sive stimulus. *Journal of Applied Behavior Analysis, 8,* 53–57.

Taylor, B. M. (1982). Text structure and children's comprehension and memory for expository material. *Journal of Educational Psychology, 74,* 323–340.

Taylor, M. J., & Kratochwill, T. R. (1978). Modification of preschool children's bathroom behaviors by contingent teacher attention. *Journal of School Psychology, 16,* 64–71.

Tennyson, C. L., Tennyson, R. D., & Rothen, W. (1980). Content structure and instructional control strategies as design variables in concept acquisition. *Journal of Educational Psychology, 72,* 499–505.

Tennyson, R. D., & Cocchiarella, M. J. (1986). An empirically based instructional design theory for teaching concepts. *Review of Educational Research, 56,* 40–71.

Tennyson, R. D., & Park, O. (1980). The teaching of concepts: A review of instructional design literature. *Review of Educational Research, 50,* 55–70.

Tennyson, R. D., & Tennyson, C. L. (1975). Rule acquisition design strategy variables: Degree of instance divergence, sequence, and instance analysis. *Journal of Educational Psychology, 67,* 852–859.

Tennyson, R. D., Youngers, J., & Suebsonthi, P. (1983). Concept learning by children using instructional presentation forms for prototype formation and classification-skill development. *Journal of Educational Psychology, 75,* 280–291.

Terrell, G., & Ware, R. (1961). Role of delay of reward in speed of size and form discrimination learning in childhood. *Child Development, 32,* 409–415.

Tharp, R. G. (1989). Psychocultural variables and constants: Effects on teaching and learning in schools. *American Psychologist, 44,* 349–359.

Thelen, D. (1989). Memory and American history. *Journal of American History, 75,* 1117–1129.

Thomas, E. L., & Robinson, H. A. (1972). *Improving reading in every class: A sourcebook for teachers.* Boston: Allyn & Bacon.

Thompson, A. G., & Thompson, P. W. (1989). Affect and problem solving in an elementary school mathematics classroom. In D. B. McLeod & V. M. Adams (Eds.), *Affect and mathematical problem solving: A new perspective.* New York: Springer-Verlag.

Thompson, R., & McConnell, J. (1955). Classical conditioning in the planarian, *Dugesia dorotocephala*. *Journal of Comparative and Physiological Psychology*, 48, 65–68.

Thorndike, E. L. (1898). Animal intelligence: An experimental study of the associative processes in animals. *Psychological Review Monograph Supplement*, 2(8).

Thorndike, E. L. (1903). *Educational psychology*. New York: Lemcke & Buechner.

Thorndike, E. L. (1911). *Animal intelligence*. New York: Macmillan.

Thorndike, E. L. (1913). *Educational psychology: The psychology of learning* (Vol. 2). New York: Teachers College Press.

Thorndike, E. L. (1924). Mental discipline in high school studies. *Journal of Educational Psychology*, 15, 1–22; 83–98.

Thorndike, E. L. (1932a). *The fundamentals of learning*. New York: Teachers College Press.

Thorndike, E. L. (1932b). Reward and punishment in animal learning. *Comparative Psychology Monograph*, 8(39).

Thorndike, E. L. (1935). *The psychology of wants, interests, and attitudes*. New York: Appleton-Century-Crofts.

Thorndike, E. L., & Woodworth, R. S. (1901). The influence of improvement in one mental function upon the efficiency of other functions. *Psychological Review*, 8, 247–261; 384–395; 553–564.

Thrailkill, N. J., & Ormrod, J. E. (1994, April). Facilitating lecture recall: Effects of embedded imagery-evoking phrases on memory for proximal and non-proximal material. Paper presented at the annual meeting of the American Educational Research Association, New Orleans.

Thyne, J. M. (1963). *The psychology of learning and techniques of teaching*. London: Univ. of London Press.

Tiagarajan, S. (1989). Interactive lectures: Seven more strategies. *Performance and Instruction*, 28(2), 35–37.

Timberlake, W., & Allison, J. (1974). Response deprivation: An empirical approach to instrumental performance. *Psychological Review*, 81, 146–164.

Tirosh, D., & Graeber, A. O. (1988, April). Inconsistencies in preservice elementary teachers' beliefs about multiplication and division. In D. Tirosh (Chair), *The role of inconsistent ideas in learning mathematics*. Symposium conducted at the annual meeting of American Educational Research Assn., New Orleans.

Tobias, S. (1977). A model for research on the effect of anxiety on instruction. In J. E. Sieber, H. F. O'Neil, Jr., & S. Tobias (Eds.), *Anxiety, learning, and instruction*. Hillsdale, NJ: Erlbaum.

Tobias, S. (1980). Anxiety and instruction. In I. G. Sarason (Ed.), *Test anxiety: Theory, research, and applications*. Hillsdale, NJ: Erlbaum.

Tobin, D., & Fox, L. H. (1980). Career interests and career education: A key to change. In L. H. Fox, L. Brody, & D. Tobin (Eds.), *Women and the mathematical mystique*. Baltimore: Johns Hopkins University Press.

Tobin, K. (1986). Student task involvement and achievement in process–oriented science activities. *Science Education*, 70(1), 61–72.

Tobin, K. (1987). The role of wait time in higher cognitive level learning. *Review of Educational Research*, 57, 69–95.

Tobin, K., Treagust, D. F., & Fraser, B. J. (1988). An investigation of exemplary biology teaching. *The American Biology Teacher*, 50(3), 142–147.

Tolman, E. C. (1932). *Purposive behavior in animals and men*. New York: Century.

Tolman, E. C. (1938). The determiners of behavior at a choice point. *Psychological Review*, 45, 1–41.

Tolman, E. C. (1942). *Drives toward war*. New York: Appleton-Century.

Tolman, E. C. (1959). Principles of purposive behavior. In S. Koch (Ed.), *Psychology: A study of a science* (Vol. 2). New York: McGraw-Hill.

Tolman, E. C., & Honzik, C. H. (1930). Introduction and removal of reward, and maze performance in rats. *University of California Publications in Psychology*, 4, 257–275.

Tolman, E. C., Ritchie, B. F., & Kalish, D. (1946). Studies in spatial learning. I. Orientation and the short-cut. *Journal of Experimental Psychology*, 36, 13–24.

Torrance, E. P., & Myers, R. E. (1970). *Creative learning and teaching*. New York: Dodd, Mead.

Tourniaire, F., & Pulos, S. (1985). Proportional reasoning: A review of the literature. *Educational Studies in Mathematics*, 16, 181–204.

Trachtenberg, D. (1974). Student tasks in text material. What cognitive skills do they tap? *Peabody Journal of Education*, 52, 54–57.

Travers, R. M. W. (1982). *Essentials of learning* (5th ed.). New York: Macmillan.

Treisman, A. M. (1964). Verbal cues, language and meaning in selective attention. *American Journal of Psychology*, 77, 215–216.

Trenholme, I. A., & Baron, A. (1975). Intermediate and delayed punishment of human behavior by loss of reinforcement. *Learning and Motivation*, 6, 62–79.

Trowbridge, M. H., & Cason, H. (1932). An experimental study of Thorndike's theory of learning. *Journal of General Psychology*, 7, 245–252.

Tryon, G. S. (1980). The measurement and treatment of test anxiety. *Review of Educational Research*, 50, 343–372.

Tulving, E. (1962). Subjective organization in free recall of "unrelated" words. *Psychological Review*, 69, 344–354.

Tulving, E. (1968). Theoretical issues in free recall. In T. R. Dixon & D. L. Horton (Eds.), *Verbal behavior and general behavior theory*. Englewood Cliffs, NJ: Prentice-Hall.

Tulving, E. (1975). Ecphoric processes in recall and recognition. In J. Brown (Ed.), *Recall and recognition*. London: Wiley.

Tulving, E. (1983). *Elements of episodic memory*. Oxford, England: Oxford University Press.

Tulving, E. (1991). Concepts of human memory. In L. R. Squire, N. M. Weinberger, G. Lynch, & J. L. McGaugh (Eds.), *Organization and locus of change*. New York: Oxford University Press.

Tulving, E. (1993). What is episodic memory? *Current Directions in Psychological Science*, 2, 67–70.

Tulving, E., & Psotka, J. (1971). Retroactive inhibition in free recall: Inaccessibility of information available in the memory store. *Journal of Experimental Psychology*, 87, 1–8.

Tulving, E., & Thomson, D. M. (1971). Retrieval processes in recognition memory: Effects of associative context. *Journal of Experimental Psychology*, 87, 116–124.

Tulving, E., & Thomson, D. M. (1973). Encoding specificity and retrieval processes in episodic memory. *Psychological Review*, 80, 352–373.

Turnbull, C. M. (1961). *The forest people*. New York: Simon & Schuster.

Turnure, J., Buium, N., & Thurlow, M. (1976). The effectiveness of interrogatives for promoting verbal elaboration productivity in young children. *Child Development*, *47*, 851–855.

Turvey, M .T., & Kravetz, S. (1970). Retrieval from iconic memory with shape as the selection criterion. *Perception and Psychophysics*, *8*, 171–172.

Tversky, A., & Kahneman, D. (1973). Availability: A heuristic for judging frequency and probability. *Cognitive Psychology*, *5*, 207–232.

Tversky, A., & Kahneman, D. (1974). Judgment under uncertainty: Heuristics and biases. *Science*, *185*, 1124–1131.

Tversky, B. (1981). Distortions in memory for maps. *Cognitive Psychology*, *13*, 407–433.

Tversky, B. (1991). Spatial mental models. In G. H. Bower (Ed.), *The psychology of learning and motivation: Advances in research and theory* (Vol. 27). San Diego: Academic Press.

Tyler, B. (1958). Expectancy for eventual success as a factor in problem solving behavior. *Journal of Educational Psychology*, *49*, 166–172.

Uhl, C. N. (1973). Eliminating behavior with omission and extinction after varying amounts of training. *Animal Learning and Behavior*, *1*, 237–240.

Uhl, C. N., & Garcia, E. E. (1969). Comparison of omission with extinction in response elimination in rats. *Journal of Comparative and Physiological Psychology*, *69*, 554–562.

Ullmann, L. P., & Krasner, L. A. (1969). *A psychological approach to abnormal behavior*. Englewood Cliffs, NJ: Prentice-Hall.

Underwood, B. J. (1948). "Spontaneous recovery" of verbal associations. *Journal of Experimental Psychology*, *38*, 429–439.

Underwood, B. J. (1954). Studies of distributed practice: XII. Retention following varying degrees of original learning. *Journal of Experimental Psychology*, *47*, 294–300.

Underwood, B. J. (1957). Interference and forgetting. *Psychological Review*, *64*, 49–60.

Underwood, B. J. (1961). Ten years of massed practice on distributed practice. *Psychological Review*, *68*, 229–247.

Underwood, B. J. (1983). *Attributes of memory*. Glenview, IL: Scott, Foresman.

Underwood, B. J., & Erlebacher, A. H. (1965). Studies of coding in verbal behavior. *Psychological Monographs*, *79*.

Underwood, B. J., Kapelak, S., & Malmi, R. (1976). The spacing effect: Additions to the theoretical and empirical puzzles. *Memory and Cognition*, *4*, 391–400.

Underwood, B. J., & Schulz, R. W. (1960). *Meaningfulness and verbal learning*. Philadelphia: J. B. Lippincott.

van der Broek, P. (1990). Causal inferences and the comprehension of narrative text. In A. C. Graessner & G. H. Bower (Eds.), *Inferences and text comprehension. The psychology of learning and motivation: Advances in research and theory* (Vol. 25). Orlando: Academic Press.

van Dijk, T. A., & Kintsch, W. (1983). *Strategies of discourse comprehension*. New York: Academic Press.

Van Rossum, E. J., & Schenk, S. M. (1984). The relationship between learning conception, study strategy and learning outcome. *British Journal of Educational Psychology*, *54*, 73–83.

VanSledright, B., & Brophy, J. (1992). Storytelling, imagination, and fanciful elaboration in children's historical reconstructions. *American Educational Research Journal*, *29*, 837–859.

Vaughan, W. (1988). Formation of equivalence sets in pigeons. *Journal of Experimental Psychology: Animal Behavior Processes*, *14*, 36–42.

Vernon, M. D. (1969). *Human motivation*. Cambridge, England: Cambridge University Press.

Veroff, J., McClelland, L., & Ruhland, D. (1975). Varieties of achievement motivation. In M. T. S. Mednick, S. S. Tangri, & L. W. Hoffman (Eds.), *Women and achievement: Social and motivational analyses*. New York: Halsted.

Vosniadou, S., & Brewer, W. F. (1987). Theories of knowledge restructuring in development. *Review of Educational Research*, *57*, 51–67.

Voss, J. F. (1987). Learning and transfer in subject-matter learning: A problem-solving model. *International Journal of Educational Research*, *11*, 607–622.

Voss, J. F., Greene, T. R., Post, T. A., & Penner, B. D. (1983). Problem-solving skill in the social sciences. In G. H. Bower (Ed.), *The psychology of learning and motivation* (Vol. 17). New York: Academic Press.

Voss, J. F., & Schauble, L. (1992). Is interest educationally interesting? An interest-related model of learning. In K. A. Renninger, S. Hidi, & A. Krapp (Eds.), *The role of interest in learning and development*. Hillsdale, NJ: Erlbaum.

Vurpillot, E., & Ball, W. A. (1979). The concept of identity and children's selective attention. In G. A. Hale & M. Lewis (Eds.), *Attention and cognitive development*. New York: Plenum Press.

Vygotsky, L. S. (1962). *Thought and language* (E. Haufmann & G. Vakar, Eds. and Trans.). Cambridge, MA: M.I.T. Press.

Vygotsky, L. S. (1978). *Mind in society: The development of higher psychological processes*. Cambridge, MA: Harvard University Press.

Vygotsky, L. S. (1981). The genesis of higher mental functions. In J. V. Wertsch (Ed.), *The concept of activity in Soviet psychology*. Armonk, NY: Sharpe.

Waddill, P. J., McDaniel, M. A., & Einstein, G. O. (1988). Illustrations as adjuncts to prose: A text-appropriate processing approach. *Journal of Educational Psychology*, *80*, 457–464.

Wade, S. E. (1983). A synthesis of the research for improving reading in the social studies. *Review of Educational Research*, *53*, 461–497.

Wade, S. E. (1992). How interest affects learning from text. In K. A. Renninger, S. Hidi, & A. Krapp (Eds.), *The role of interest in learning and development*. Hillsdale, NJ: Erlbaum.

Wadsworth, B. J. (1989). *Piaget's theory of cognitive and affective development* (4th ed.). New York: Longman.

Wagner, A. R. (1976). Priming in STM: An information processing mechanism for self-generated or retrieval-generated depression in performance. In T. J. Tighe & R. N. Leaton (Eds.), *Habituation: Perspectives from child development and animal behavior*. Hillsdale, NJ: Erlbaum.

Wagner, A. R. (1978). Expectancies and the priming of STM. In S. H. Hulse, H. Fowler, & W. K. Honig (Eds.), *Cognitive processes in animal behavior*. Hillsdale, NJ: Erlbaum.

Wagner, A. R. (1979). Habituation and memory. In A. Dickenson & R. A. Boakes (Eds.), *Mechanisms of learning and motivation*. Hillsdale, NJ: Erlbaum.

Wagner, A. R. (1981). SOP: A model of automatic memory processing in animal behavior. In N. E. Spear & R. R. Miller (Eds.), *Information processing in animals: Memory mechanisms.* Hillsdale, NJ: Erlbaum.

Wagner, A. R., & Rescorla, R. A. (1972). Inhibition in Pavlovian conditioning: Applications of a theory. In R. A. Boakes & M. S. Halliday (Eds.), *Inhibition and learning.* New York: Academic Press.

Wagner, E. D. (1989, February). Graphic facilitation effects: Instructional strategies to improve intentional learning outcomes. Paper presented at Assn. for Educational Communications and Technology, Dallas.

Wahler, R. G., & Fox, J. J. (1981). Setting events in applied behavior analysis: Toward a conceptual and methodological expansion. *Journal of Applied Behavior Analysis, 14,* 327–338.

Walberg, H. J., & Uguroglu, M. (1980). Motivation and educational productivity: Theories, results, and implications. In L. J. Fyans, Jr. (Ed.), *Achievement motivation: Recent trends in theory and research.* New York: Plenum Press.

Walker, B. S. (1974). Vividness of imagery and spelling errors. *Perceptual and Motor Skills, 39,* 823–825.

Walker, J. E., & Shea, T. M. (1984). *Behavior management: A practice approach for educators* (3rd ed.). St. Louis: Times Mirror/Mosby.

Wallas, G. (1926). *The art of thought.* New York: Harcourt Brace Jovanovich.

Walters, G. C., & Grusec, J. E. (1977). *Punishment.* San Francisco: Freeman.

Walters, R. H. (1964). Delay of reinforcement gradients in children's learning. *Psychonomic Science, 1,* 307–308.

Walters, R. H., & Parke, R. D. (1964). Influence of response consequences to a social model on resistance to deviation. *Journal of Experimental Child Psychology, 1,* 269–280.

Walters, R. H., Parke, R. D., & Cane, V. A. (1965). Timing of punishment and the observation of consequences to others as determinants of response inhibition. *Journal of Experimental Child Psychology, 2,* 10–30.

Walters, R. H., & Thomas, E. L. (1963). Enhancement of punitiveness by visual and audiovisual displays. *Canadian Journal of Psychology, 17,* 244–255.

Walters, R. H., Thomas, E. L., & Acker, W. (1962). Enhancement of punitive behavior by audio-visual displays. *Science, 136,* 872–873.

Walton, G. E., & Bower, T. G. R. (1993). Newborns form "prototypes" in less than 1 minute. *Psychological Science, 4,* 203–205.

Ward, M. H., & Baker, B. L. (1968). Reinforcement therapy in the classroom. *Journal of Applied Behavior Analysis, 1,* 323–328.

Ward, T. J., Jr. (1991, April). The effects of field articulation and interestingness on text processing. In G. Schraw (Chair), *Cognitive processing and text comprehension in specific knowledge domains.* Symposium presented at the annual meeting of the American Educational Research Association, Chicago.

Wasserman, E. A. (1993). Comparative cognition: Toward a general understanding of cognition in behavior. *Psychological Science, 4,* 156–161.

Wasserman, E. A., DeVolder, C. L., & Coppage, D. J. (1992). Non-similarity-based conceptualization in pigeons via secondary or mediated generalization. *Psychological Science, 3,* 374–379.

Waters, H. S. (1982). Memory development in adolescence: Relationships between metamemory, strategy use, and performance. *Journal of Experimental Child Psychology, 33,* 183–195.

Watkins, M. J., & Watkins, O. C. (1974). Processing of recency items for free-recall. *Journal of Experimental Psychology, 102,* 488–493.

Watson, J. B. (1913). Psychology as the behaviorist views it. *Psychological Review, 20,* 158–177.

Watson, J. B. (1914). *Behavior: An introduction to comparative psychology.* New York: Holt, Rinehart & Winston.

Watson, J. B. (1916). The place of a conditioned reflex in psychology. *Psychological Review, 23,* 89–116.

Watson, J. B. (1919). *Psychology from the standpoint of a behaviorist.* Philadelphia: J. B. Lippincott.

Watson, J. B. (1925). *Behaviorism.* New York: W. W. Norton.

Watson, J. B., & Rayner, R. (1920). Conditioned emotional reactions. *Journal of Experimental Psychology, 3,* 1–14.

Watts, G. H., & Anderson, R. C. (1971). Effects of three types of inserted questions on learning from prose. *Journal of Educational Psychology, 62,* 387–394.

Wegman, C. (1985). *Psychoanalysis and cognitive psychology.* London: Academic Press.

Weiner, B. (1979). A theory of motivation for some classroom experiences. *Journal of Educational Psychology, 71,* 3–25.

Weiner, B. (1980). *Human motivation.* New York: Holt, Rinehart & Winston.

Weiner, B. (1984). Principles for a theory of student motivation and their application within an attributional framework. In R. Ames & C. Ames (Eds.), *Research on motivation in education: Vol. 1. Student motivation.* Orlando: Academic Press.

Weiner, B. (1986). *An attributional theory of motivation and emotion.* New York: Springer-Verlag.

Weiner, B. (1992). *Human motivation: Metaphors, theories, and research.* Newbury Park, CA: Sage.

Weiner, B., Russell, D., & Lerman, D. (1978). Affective consequences of causal ascriptions. In J. Harvey, W. Ickes, & R. Kidd (Eds.), *New directions in attribution research* (Vol. 2). Hillsdale, NJ: Erlbaum.

Weiner, B., Russell, D., & Lerman, D. (1979). The cognition-emotion process in achievement-related contexts. *Journal of Personality and Social Psychology, 37,* 1211–1220.

Weinraub, M., Clemens, L. P., Sockloff, A., Ethridge, T., Gracely, E., & Myers, B. (1984). The development of sex role stereotypes in the third year: Relationships to gender labeling, gender identity, sex-typed toy preference, and family characteristics. *Child Development, 55,* 1493–1503.

Weinstein, C. E. (1978). Elaboration skills as a learning strategy. In H. F. O'Neil, Jr. (Ed.), *Learning strategies.* New York: Academic Press.

Weinstein, C. E., Goetz, E. T., & Alexander, P. A. (Eds.) (1988). *Learning and study strategies: Issues in assessment, instruction, and evaluation.* San Diego: Academic Press.

Weinstein, C. E., Hagen, A. S., & Meyer, D. K. (1991, April). Work smart ... not hard: The effects of combining instruction in using strategies, goal using, and executive control on attributions and academic performance. Paper presented at the annual meeting of the American Educational Research Association, Chicago.

Weinstein, C. E., & Mayer, R. E. (1986). The teaching of learning strategies. In M. C. Wittrock (Ed.), *Handbook of research on teaching* (3rd ed.). New York: Macmillan.

Weinstein, M. (1969). Achievement motivation and risk preference. *Journal of Personality and Social Psychology*, *13*, 153–173.

Weisberg, R. W., DiCamillo, M., & Phillips, D. (1979). Transferring old associations to new situations: A nonautomatic process. *Journal of Verbal Learning and Verbal Behavior*, *17*, 219–228.

Weiss, K. (1983). In-school suspension—Time to work, not socialize. *NASSP Bulletin*, 67(464), 132–133.

Welch, G. J. (1985). Contingency contracting with a delinquent and his family. *Journal of Behavior Therapy and Experimental Psychiatry*, *16*, 253–259.

Welford, A. T. (1977). Serial reaction-times, continuity of task, single-channel effects and age. In S. Dornic (Ed.), *Attention and performance VI*. Hillsdale, NJ: Erlbaum

Wells, G. L., & Loftus, E. F. (Eds.) (1984). *Eyewitness testimony*. Cambridge, England: Cambridge University Press.

Welsh, R. S. (1976). Severe parental punishment and delinquency: A developmental theory. *Journal of Clinical Child Psychology*, *5*, 17–23.

Wertheimer, M. (1912). Experimentelle Studien über das Sehen von Bewegung. *Zeitschrift für Psychologie*, *61*, 161–265.

Wertheimer, M. (1945). *Productive thinking*. New York: Harper.

Wertheimer, M. (1959). *Productive thinking* (enl. ed., edited by Michael Wertheimer). New York: Harper.

Wertsch, J. V. (1985). Adult–child interaction as a source of self-regulation in children. In S. R. Yussen (Ed.), *The growth of reflection in children*. Orlando: Academic Press.

West, C. K., Farmer, J. A., & Wolff, P. M. (1991). *Instructional design: Implications from cognitive science*. Englewood Cliffs, NJ: Prentice-Hall.

West, R. F., & Stanovich, K. E. (1991). The incidental acquisition of information from reading. *Psychological Science*, *2*, 325–329.

Whimbey, A., & Lochhead, J. (1986). *Problem solving and comprehension* (4th ed.). Hillsdale, NJ: Erlbaum.

Whitlock, C. (1966). Note on reading acquisition: An extension of laboratory principles. *Journal of Experimental Child Psychology*, *3*, 83–85.

Wickelgren, W. A. (1973). The long and the short of memory. *Psychological Bulletin*, *80*, 425–438.

Wickelgren, W. A. (1974). *How to solve problems: Elements of a theory of problems and problem solving*. San Francisco: Freeman.

Wielkiewicz, R. M. (1986). *Behavior management in the schools: Principles and procedures*. New York: Pergamon Press.

Wigfield, A. (1994). Expectancy-value theory of achievement motivation: A developmental perspective. *Educational Psychology Review*, *6*, 49–78.

Wigfield, A., & Meece, J. L. (1988). Math anxiety in elementary and secondary school students. *Journal of Educational Psychology*, *80*, 210–216.

Wilkins, A. T. (1971). Conjoint frequency, category size, and categorization time. *Journal of Verbal Learning and Verbal Behavior*, *10*, 382–385.

Williams, D. C. (1959). The elimination of tantrum behavior by extinction procedures. *Journal of Abnormal and Social Psychology*, *59*, 269.

Williams, S. B. (1938). Resistance to extinction as a function of the number of reinforcements. *Journal of Experimental Psychology*, *23*, 506–522.

Wilson, J. E. (1988). Implications of learning strategy research and training: What it has to say to the practitioner. In C. E. Weinstein, E. T. Goetz, & P. A. Alexander, (Eds.), *Learning and study strategies: Issues in assessment, instruction, and evaluation*. San Diego: Academic Press.

Wilson, P. S. (1988, April). The relationship of students' definitions and example choices in geometry. In D. Tirosh (Chair), *The role of inconsistent ideas in learning mathematics*. Symposium conducted at the annual meeting of the American Educational Research Assn., New Orleans.

Wilson, P. T., & Anderson, R. C. (1986). What they don't know will hurt them: The role of prior knowledge in comprehension. In J. Orasanu (Ed.), *Reading comprehension: From research to practice*. Hillsdale, NJ: Erlbaum.

Wine, J. D. (1980). Cognitive-attentional theory of test anxiety. In I. G. Sarason (Ed.), *Test anxiety: Theory, research, and applications*. Hillsdale, NJ: Erlbaum.

Wingfield, A., & Byrnes, D. L. (1981). *The psychology of human memory*. New York: Academic Press.

Winn, W. (1991). Learning from maps and diagrams. *Educational Psychology Review*, *3*, 211–247.

Winston, P. (1973). Learning to identify toy block structures. In R. L. Solso (Ed.), *Contemporary issues in cognitive psychology: The Loyola Symposium*. Washington, DC: V. H. Winston.

Witt, J. C., Elliott, S. N., & Gresham, F. M. (Eds.) (1988). *Handbook of behavior therapy in education*. New York: Plenum Press.

Wittgenstein, L. (1958). *Philosophical investigations* (2nd ed.). Oxford: Blackwell.

Wittrock, M. C. (1986). Learning science by generating new conceptions from old ideas. In L. H. T. West & A. L. Pines (Eds.), *Cognitive structure and conceptual change*. Orlando: Academic Press.

Wittrock, M. C., & Alesandrini, K. (1990). Generation of summaries and analogies and analytic and holistic abilities. *American Educational Research Journal*, *27*, 489–502.

Wixted, J. T., & Ebbesen, E. B. (1991). On the form of forgetting. *Psychological Science*, *2*, 409–415.

Wlodkowski, R. J. (1978). *Motivation and teaching: A practical guide*. Washington, DC: National Education Association.

Wolf, M. M., Braukmann, C. J., & Ramp, K. A. (1987). Serious delinquent behavior as part of a significantly handicapping condition: Cures and supportive environments. *Journal of Applied Behavior Analysis*, *20*, 347–359.

Wolf, T. M., & Cheyne, J. A. (1972). Persistence of effects of live behavioral, televised behavioral, and live verbal models on resistance to temptation. *Child Development*, *43*, 1429–1436.

Wolfe, J. B. (1936). Effectiveness of token-rewards for chimps. *Comparative Psychology Monographs*, *12* (No. 60).

Woloshyn, V. E., Pressley, M., & Schneider, W. (1992). Elaborative-interrogation and prior-knowledge effects on learning of facts. *Journal of Educational Psychology*, *84*, 115–124.

Wolpe, J. (1958). *Psychotherapy by reciprocal inhibition*. Stanford CA: Stanford University Press.

Wolpe, J. (1969). *The practice of behavior therapy*. Oxford: Pergamon.

Wong, B. Y. L. (1985). Self-questioning instructional research: A review. *Review of Educational Research*, *55*, 227–268.

Wood, C. J., Schau, C., & Fiedler, M. L. (1990, April). Attribution, motivation, and self-perception: A comparative study—elementary, middle, and high school students. Paper presented at the annual meeting of the American Educational Research Association, Boston.

Wood, D. Bruner, J. S., & Ross, G. (1976). The role of tutoring in problem-solving. *Journal of Child Psychology and Psychiatry, 17,* 89–100.

Woodworth, R. S. (1918). *Dynamic psychology.* New York: Columbia University Press.

Wozniak, R. H. (1987). Developmental method, zones of development, and theories of the environment. In L. S. Liben (Ed.), *Development and learning: Conflict or congruence?* Hillsdale, NJ: Erlbaum.

Wulbert, M., & Dries, R. (1977). The relative efficacy of methylphenidate (ritalin) and behavior-modification techniques in the treatment of a hyperactive child. *Journal of Applied Behavior Analysis, 10,* 21–31.

Yager, S., Johnson, D. W., & Johnson, R. T. (1985). Oral discussion, group to individual transfer, and achievement in cooperative learning groups. *Journal of Educational Psychology, 77,* 60–66.

Yarmey, A. D. (1973). I recognize your face but I can't remember your name: Further evidence on the tip-of-the-tongue phenomenon. *Memory and Cognition, 1,* 287–290.

Yee, D. K., & Eccles, J. S. (1988). Parent perceptions and attributions for children's math achievement. *Sex Roles, 19,* 317–333.

Yerkes, R. M., & Dodson, J. D. (1908). The relation of strength of stimulus to rapidity of habit-formation. *Journal of Comparative Neurology and Psychology, 18,* 459–482.

Zacks, R. T., Hasher, L., & Hock, H. S. (1986). Inevitability and automaticity: A response to Fisk. *American Psychologist, 41,* 216–218.

Zahorik, J. A. (1976) The virtue of vagueness in instructional objectives. *Elementary School Journal, 76,* 411–419.

Zajonc, R. B. (1980). Feeling and thinking: Preferences need no inferences. *American Psychologist, 35,* 151–175.

Zazdeh, L. A., Fu, K. S., Tanak, K., & Shimura, M. (Eds.) (1975). *Fuzzy sets and their applications to cognitive and decision processes.* New York: Academic Press.

Zechmeister, E. B., & Nyberg, S. E. (1982). *Human memory: An introduction to research and theory.* Monterey, CA: Brooks/Cole.

Zeiler, M. D. (1971). Eliminating behavior with reinforcement. *Journal of the Experimental Analysis of Behavior, 16,* 401–405.

Zeller, A. F. (1950). An experimental analogue of repression. II. The effect of individual failure and success on memory measured by relearning. *Journal of Experimental Psychology, 40,* 411–422.

Zelniker, T., & Jeffrey, W. E. (1979). Attention and cognitive style in children. In G. A. Hale & M. Lewis (Eds.), *Attention and cognitive development.* New York: Plenum Press.

Ziegler, S. G. (1987). Effects of stimulus cueing on the acquisition of groundstrokes by beginning tennis players. *Journal of Applied Behavior Analysis, 20,* 405–411.

Zimmerman, B. J. (1989). Models of self-regulated learning and academic achievement. In B. J. Zimmerman & D. H. Schunk (Eds.), *Self-regulated learning and academic achievement: Theory, research, and practice.* New York: Springer-Verlag.

Zimmerman, B. J., Bandura, A., & Martinez-Pons, M. (1992). Self-motivation for academic attainment: The role of self-efficacy beliefs and personal goal setting. *American Educational Research Journal, 29,* 663–676.

Zirin, G. (1974). How to make a boring thing more boring. *Child Development, 45,* 232–236.

Zola–Morgan, S. M., & Squire, L. R. (1990). The primate hippocampal formation: Evidence for a time-limited role in memory storage. *Science, 250,* 288–290.

Zook, K. B. (1991). Effects of analogical processes on learning and misrepresentation. *Educational Psychology Review, 3,* 41–72.

Zook, K. B., & Di Vesta, F. J. (1991). Instructional analogies and conceptual misrepresentations. *Journal of Educational Psychology, 83,* 246–252.

Zuriff, G. E. (1985). *Behaviorism: A conceptual reconstruction.* New York: Columbia Univ. Press.

Author Index

Subject Index